Percy Blandford's Favorite Woodworking Projects

Percy Blandford's Favorite Woodworking Projects

Percy W. Blandford

TAB BOOKS
Blue Ridge Summit, PA

FIRST EDITION
SECOND PRINTING

© 1992 by **TAB Books**.
TAB Books is a division of McGraw-Hill, Inc.

Library of Congress Cataloging-in-Publication Data

Blandford, Percy W.
    Percy Blandford's favorite woodworking projects / by Percy W.
  Blandford.
      p.   cm.
    Includes index.
    ISBN 0-8306-2148-2
    1. Woodwork.   I. Title.
  TT185.B6186   1991
  684'.08—dc20   91-19846
                                                    CIP

TAB Books offers software for sale. For information and a catalog, please contact
TAB Software Department, Blue Ridge Summit, PA 17294-0850.

Acquisitions Editor: Kimberly Tabor
Book Editor: April D. Nolan
Director of Production: Katherine G. Brown
Book Design: Jaclyn J. Boone
Cover by Sandra Blair Design and Brent Blair Photography, Harrisburg, PA
                                                                            HT3

The 199 projects in this book have been selected from over 1000 described and illustrated by Percy Blandford in the following books published by TAB Books.

Backyard Builder's Bonanza
Country Furniture
Designing and Building Children's Furniture
Designing and Building Colonial and Early American Furniture
Designing and Building Outdoor Furniture
Designing and Building Space-Saving Furniture
Garden Tools and Gadgets You Can Make
A Home Full of Furniture
Kitchen and Bathroom Cabinets
Small Buildings
The Woodworker's Shop
24 Table Saw Projects
24 Woodturning Projects
49 Easy-to-Build Plywood Projects
77 One-Weekend Woodworking Projects
79 Furniture Projects for Every Room
101 One-Weekend Toy Projects

Contents

Preface

I have been making things—mostly from wood—and writing about them for nearly sixty years. I have been writing books about making things for TAB Books since 1974, with about forty woodworking titles published by them. When they asked me to bring together a selection of projects from 17 of my recent woodworking books, I welcomed the opportunity to pick out some of my favorites.

In those books were over 1,000 projects. Out of those I have picked 199 to make this fairly thick book, which I hope will find a welcome place in the libraries of many woodworking enthusiasts. It can be used as a reference for its detailed drawings and instructions and as an ideas source for individual and unique personal designs.

It is in the modern amateur's workshop that much of the tradition of good craftsmanship is continued today. Professional production woodworkers often have to consider commercial factors. While many of their results are generally accepted and of good value, most of their products could not be described as *craftsmanship* in the traditional sense. The projects I describe and illustrate are intended to be made in a craftsmanlike way. I appreciate and use modern materials, together with power tools, but I do not let these things tempt me into short-cut, simplified methods that can only produce less-than-satisfying results. I hope readers go along with me and use their tools and facilities to only make things to be proud of.

In this selection of projects, there should be something for everyone, whether you have an improvised bench and a few hand tools or a separate shop with elaborate equipment—whether you are just acquiring a little skill or have mastered advanced techniques. Do not underestimate your ability. If you proceed step by step, you might surprise yourself with what you achieve. Helping you along the way is my main purpose in writing this book.

Percy W. Blandford

Introduction

Reducing a total of over 1,000 projects to only 199 has resulted in layout problems. Coupled with that are the varying purposes of the 17 original books. Most are concerned with individual new designs of furniture, utility pieces, and structures. Some deal with making tools. Others are concerned with reproductions.

For convenience, I have grouped the projects into sections. Many projects might be regarded as suitable for more than one section, but they have been put where they seemed most appropriate. For this reason, you should get to know the whole book and make good use of the Index, as well as look in the section that seems most appropriate to your needs.

It was impossible to grade projects according to difficulty, but I hope you can select projects best suited to your available materials and equipment, as well as your ability.

This is a project book. It is a collection of designs for things to make. It is assumed that you know how to use tools; there are no instructions on techniques. What you have here is a book full of ideas for things to make. You might need to look elsewhere for instructions on tool handling, but you might find it surprising how much you can learn by actually making something.

Those of you who are familiar with some of my other books will have no difficulty in recognizing the treatment of projects. Others will quickly understand the normal layout. For each project, I have provided a drawing that shows a finished example. Sizes and constructional details are shown in working drawings and all sizes quoted are in inches, unless indicated otherwise. Some projects might have an exploded drawing that shows how parts relate to each other.

The instructions provided are given step by step. Try to visualize progress along the way. Keep to the steps in turn, but also try to think ahead, so you know what has to be done. The materials lists show finished thicknesses and widths, but lengths are full to allow for cutting. It will help to show the list to your suppliers, so they can cut wood for you economically.

1

One-Weekend Projects

For many of us, the time we most enjoy making things is on the weekends. Some work may be spread over many weekends, but it is convenient and satisfying if a project can be completed in one weekend. What is possible in one weekend depends on several factors, such as the time you can allow, your degree of skill, and the extent of your tool kit and shop facilities.

If you are well equipped with tools—both hand and power—have the skill to use them, and are able to plan your work to make the maximum use of your time, it is surprising how much you can accomplish in a weekend. In fact, you might be able to complete many of the projects described elsewhere in this book in one weekend. But even for those of you with more modest facilities and skills, most projects in this section should be within your weekend capabilities.

If you want to make the most of what you have, you need to plan ahead. Have everything needed ready. Know several moves ahead all the time. You might then surprise yourself with the results of one weekend in your shop or on just an improvised bench.

Mirror Key

If keys are hung on a row of hooks, they are not very beautiful and they are obvious to people who might not have authority to use them. If the keys are hung in a shallow cabinet they are protected, but a plain door might look a little better than the exposed rack. However, if instead of a door the key cabinet has a framed picture or a mirror, the rack then acquires a new use, and the fact that it holds keys as well is much less obvious. Anyone looking in the mirror to tidy his or her hair will probably not realize what is behind the reflection, particularly if there are no handles or fasteners.

Sizes will depend on how many keys you wish to hang, but the front should also be a reasonable size. If you want to use a certain picture, that will determine size. A mirror will probably have to be cut to suit your frame, but it should still be a suitable size to use (FIG. 1-1). The sizes shown are provided as a guide to construction (FIG. 1-2).

Materials List for Mirror Key Ring

4 frames	$3/4 \times 3/4 \times 13$
4 frames	$3/4 \times 3/4 \times 10$
2 fillets	$3/8 \times 3/8 \times 12$
2 fillets	$3/8 \times 3/8 \times 9$
1 key panel	$9 \times 12 \times 1/4$ plywood

Fig. 1-1. This key rack has a mirror front to hide the keys.

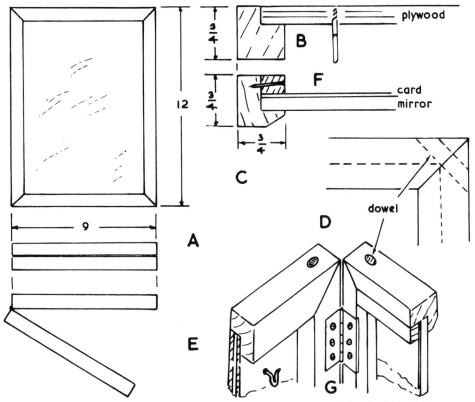

Fig. 1-2. Hooks for keys are in the back panel and the mirror is in the hinged door.

You can choose almost any wood, but a close-grained hardwood will look most attractive. If you will fit a mirror, get it first because its thickness controls the depth of the rabbet and it is easier to fit a frame to the glass than to trim glass to fit a frame. If you want to display a picture or photograph, get thin glass to match and cut a piece of hardboard to go behind it.

Cut the rabbets in the frame material. It might be easier to start with wider wood and cut it to size after working the rabbets and the chamfer on the front. Make the rabbet in the back to suit the plywood (FIG. 1-2B). For the front, you must allow for the thickness of the mirror and a piece of card behind it, or for the picture and its glass and backing. In both cases, there will be fillets nailed (FIG. 1-2C).

Make the two frames with mitered corners. You could strengthen the miters with thin nails each way, but 1/4-inch dowels are suggested (FIG. 1-2D). Make them overlength and plane them off when the glue has set. Check that the two frames are the same size.

Glue and pin the plywood into the back (FIG. 1-2E). Drill for the key hooks, but do not fit them yet. Also drill for two screws into the wall.

Cut a piece of cardboard to go behind the mirror and make fillets thick enough to come level with the inner surfaces of the frame. The fillets can either overlap at the corners or be mitered (FIG. 1-2F).

Cut recesses for hinges. For the size rack shown here, two 1¹/₂-inch hinges should be satisfactory. Let them in to give only a slight clearance when the rack is closed (FIG. 1-2G).

At the other side, fit a spring or magnetic catch inside. If you want to keep the rack as secret as possible, do not fit a handle. You can still open the door easily with a finger grip at the side.

Remove the mirror, hinges, and catch, then finish the wood. You could use a different finish for the key panel—green is appropriate. Even if you plan to give the wood a light finish, it is worthwhile to paint the inside of the mirror recess black to reduce unwanted reflections around the edges.

Reassemble the rack with the mirror or picture, the hinges, catch and key hooks, then mount it in position.

Bootjack

Removing boots can be a tricky performance, while balancing on one leg. The process can be even more complicated if the boots are muddy and you want to avoid spreading dirt around. A bootjack (FIGS. 1-3 and 1-4) is a simple device

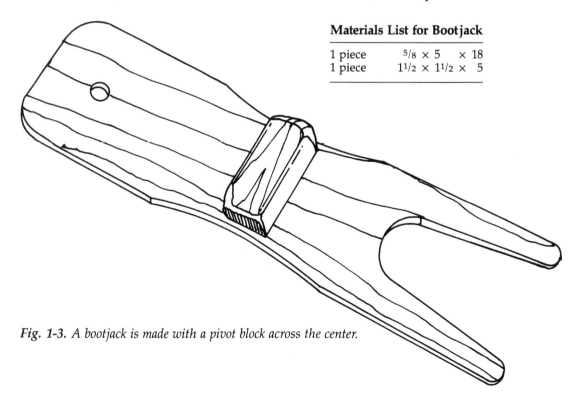

Materials List for Bootjack

| 1 piece | ⁵/₈ × 5 × 18 |
| 1 piece | 1¹/₂ × 1¹/₂ × 5 |

Fig. 1-3. A bootjack is made with a pivot block across the center.

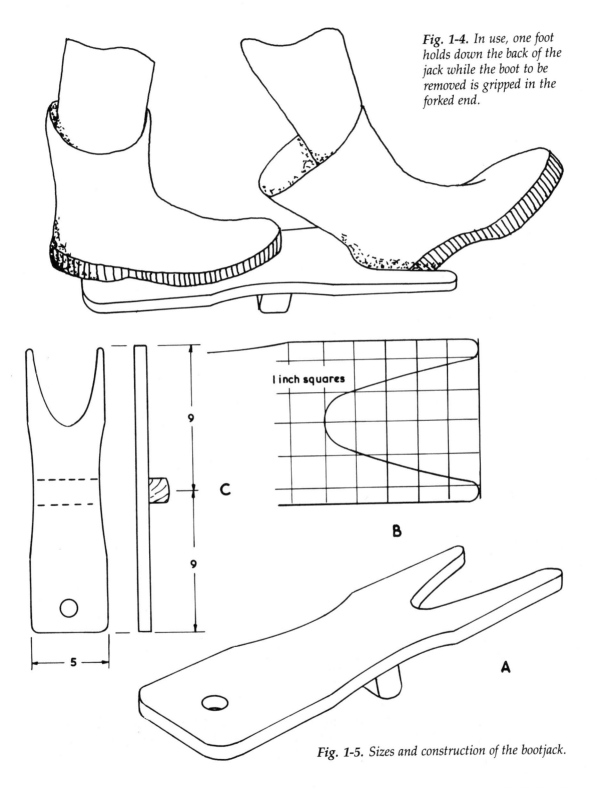

Fig. 1-4. *In use, one foot holds down the back of the jack while the boot to be removed is gripped in the forked end.*

1 inch squares

9

9

C

B

5

A

Fig. 1-5. *Sizes and construction of the bootjack.*

which takes all the bending and other contortions out of removing boots, however stubborn they are, and it limits the spread of mud. One foot holds down the rear end while the forked end grips the heel of the boot being removed.

This boot jack (FIG. 1-5A) is made of hardwood. It can be stained and varnished so that it has an acceptable appearance when hanging on a hook inside the door.

First cut the wood to size and shape the fork (FIG. 1-5B). Take sharpness off the ends, but do not round the edges of the V excessively.

At the other end, round the corners and edges, and drill a hole for hanging. You can hollow out the sides for the sake of appearance, but this is not essential.

Screw on a piece of $1\frac{1}{2}$-inch-square wood under the center (FIG. 1-5). Round the underside, including its ends, so it does not harm floor coverings.

Wastebasket

A wooden wastebasket can be attractive as well as sturdy. This wastebasket (FIG. 1-6) can be painted to match other furniture in a bathroom, or it can be stained and polished to stand beside a desk or sewing table. It is substantial enough to take the waste from a hobby in your den or shop.

Plywood $\frac{1}{4}$ inch thick and framed with strips $\frac{3}{4}$ inch square is ideal. You can substitute hardboard $\frac{1}{8}$ inch thick or thicker plywood for tougher conditions. If the contents of the wastebasket are likely to be damp, marine- or exterior-grade plywood and waterproof glue will make a watertight wooden bucket.

The slight taper shown (FIG. 1-7) allows the contents to be tipped out easily, but is not enough to make the fitting of corner angles difficult. If the sizes are altered, do not give the sides too much flare.

Fig. 1-6. A wastebasket particularly suitable for a bathroom.

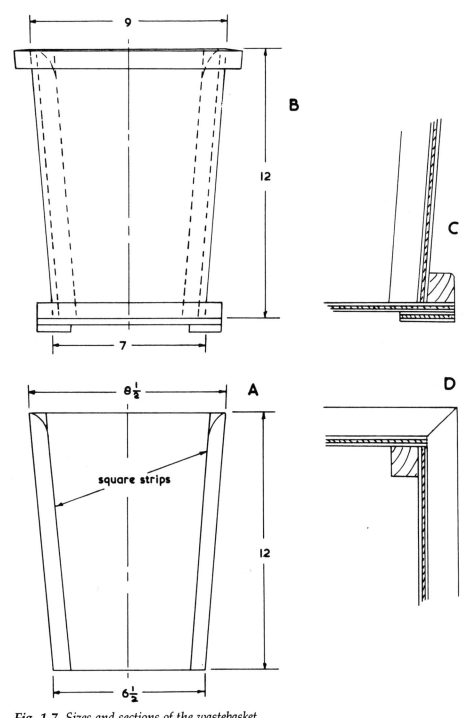

Fig. 1-7. *Sizes and sections of the wastebasket.*

Materials List for Wastebasket

4 sides	9	× 12	× 1/4 plywood
1 bottom	9	× 9	× 1/4 plywood
4 feet	1 1/2	× 1 1/2	× 1/4 plywood
4 outside strips	3/4	× 3/4 × 12	
4 outside strips	3/4	× 3/4 × 10	
4 corner strips	3/4	× 3/4 × 13	

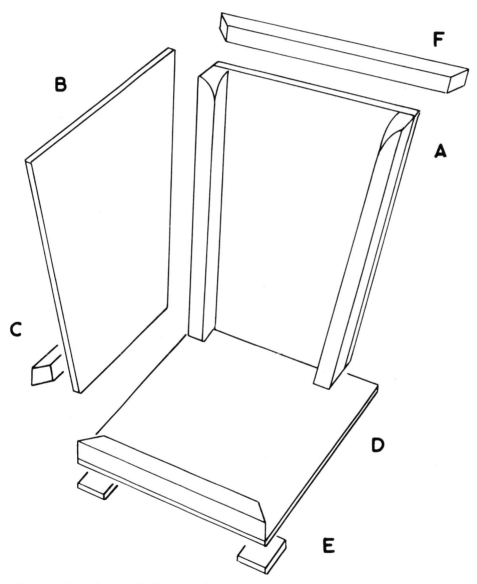

Fig. 1-8. How the wastebasket parts fit together.

Make two opposite sides, symmetrical about centerlines, with strips pinned and glued at the edges (FIG. 1-7A). Round the tops of these strips (FIG. 1-8A). Make the other two sides 1/2 inch wider (FIGS. 1-7B and 1-8B). Join the four sides with pins and glue.

Prepare the wood that will make the strips around the base by planing it to the same angle as the sides (FIG. 1-7C). Fit the strips around the bottom edge (FIG. 1-8C). They are shown mitered (FIG. 1-7D). For a painted finish that will hide constructional details, you could overlap them.

Add the bottom (FIG. 1-8D) and 4 square feet at the corners (FIG. 1-8E). Put strips around the top (FIG. 1-8F), and round all exposed edges. Finish with several coats of paint.

Laundry Basket

A container for clothing and other items ready to be washed can be plain and utilitarian, or it can be decorative. This laundry basket is a compromise (FIG. 1-9). It has a shaped top edge and a lifting lid. If carefully made and painted, it would look smart enough for a bedroom, bathroom, or laundry room. It is given a slight taper and a lift-off lid, so the contents could be tipped out easily.

The main parts are plywood (preferably exterior grade) with 3/4-inch-square strip framing. The four sides are identical, with their framing arranged to fit into the next part. Join most parts with glue and fine nails.

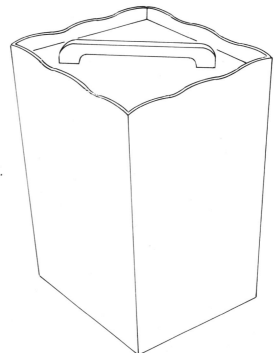

Fig. 1-9. This laundry basket is tapered and has a lift-off lid.

Set out and cut the four sides (FIG. 1-10A), and shape the top edges if you wish. The strips across meet the upright on one edge. At the other edge, they are cut short to clear the thickness of plywood and strips on the adjoining piece (FIG. 1-10B). Bring the parts together and join them (FIG. 1-11); check that the assembly is square and stands level.

Cut the bottom (FIG. 1-11A) to fit closely inside on top of the bottom strips. Glue and nail it there.

Cut the lid plywood to fit easily inside (FIG. 1-11B). It should be loose enough to put in, even if there are slight variations in the box sizes.

Make the handle to fit diagonally across the lid (FIG. 1-11C). Cut away to about half thickness, and thoroughly round all parts that will be gripped. Fix it with screws upwards through the lid.

Finish with paint. The inside could be a lighter color than the outside. If the box is to spend most of its time in the steamy atmosphere of a laundry room, use exterior-grade paint.

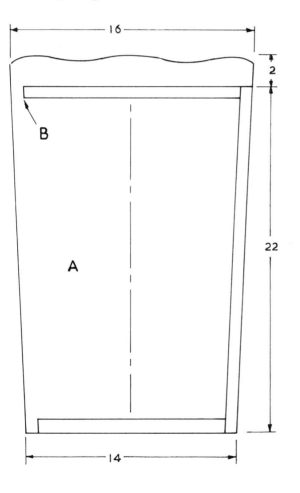

Fig. 1-10. *Sizes of a panel of the laundry basket.*

Materials List for Laundry Basket

4 sides	$25 \times 16 \times 1/2$ plywood
1 bottom	$14 \times 14 \times 1/2$ plywood
1 lid	$16 \times 16 \times 1/2$ plywood
4 frames	$14 \times 3/4 \times 3/4$
4 frames	$14 \times 3/4 \times 3/4$
4 frames	$16 \times 3/4 \times 3/4$
1 handle	$22 \times 2 \times 1$

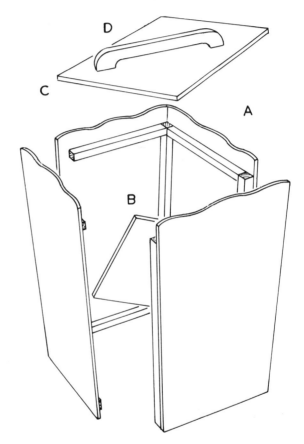

Fig. 1-11. Parts of the laundry basket.

Tie Rack

This rack is intended to be attached to a wall or inside a clothes-closet door and will hold up to eight ties, belts, ribbons, or other long, narrow items. It can be made from oddments and sizes adjusted to suit your available materials. Light-colored dowel rods look good against dark wood or the whole rack can be the same color. It would be possible to use plywood, but solid wood looks better (FIG. 1-12).

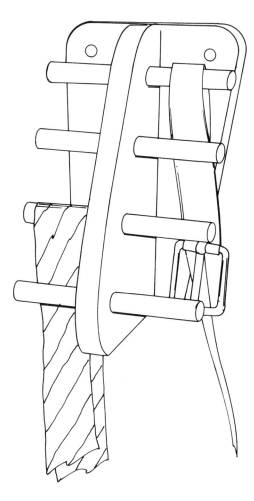

Fig. 1-12. This rack will hold ties or belts and can be mounted on a wall or inside a clothes closet.

Both parts are 4 inches wide, so you can prepare a piece long enough for both. Mark the back piece with a centerline and the position of the other part (FIG. 1-13A). Shape the corners with a $5/8$-inch radius, and drill for screws to the wall at these centers. Drill for two screws to hold the front—8 gauge by 1 inch are suitable for $1/2$-inch wood.

On the front (FIG. 1-13B), mark the centers of the top and bottom holes in the positions shown. Join these points, and space the other hole positions equally. Drill squarely for the dowel rods. Round the exposed edges of both parts.

Cut the dowel rods to the same length (FIG. 1-13C), although the lengths could be graduated, if you wish—particularly if you plan to hang wider belts. Round the ends.

Glue the dowel rods in place, then glue and screw the back to the front. Finish with stain and polish.

Materials List for Tie Rack

Back and front from 1 piece	1/2 × 4 × 16
Rods from 1 piece	18 × 1/2 diameter

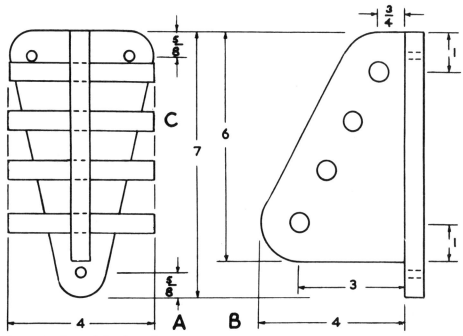

Fig. 1-13. Sizes of the tie rack.

Bath Clothes Airer

If wet things have to be hung to drip, a bathtub is the obvious place to catch the water. Even if all you want to do is hang near-dry clothes to air them indoors, over the tub is a convenient place. This airer (FIG. 1-14) can be adjusted to suit various widths of baths, and its length can be made to suit your needs. As shown here, the airer will suit a tub about 24 inches wide inside the top, but it is equally suitable for tubs several inches wider or narrower.

The two frames are made to pivot on the top rod, so the airer can be folded almost flat when out of use. Any wood can be used, but the plywood ends should be exterior- or marine-grade, if possible, to withstand damp conditions. However, ordinary plywood protected with paint should have a long life. Use waterproof glue for assembly.

The four arms are the same (FIG. 1-15A). Mark them together, and drill to suit the dowel rods. Notch the arm ends to suit the plywood (FIG. 1-16B). Round the tops and take sharpness off the edges.

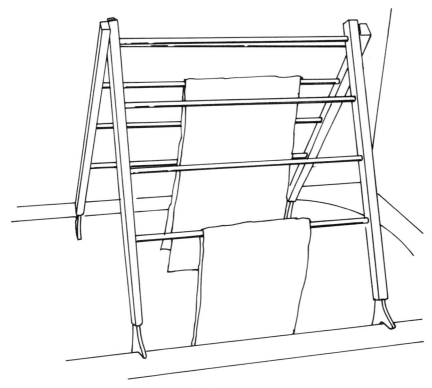

Fig. 1-14. A bath clothes airer can be fitted on a tub bath to dry or air clothes.

Materials List for
Bath Clothes Airer

4 arms	$1 \times 1 \times 24$
4 forks	$5 \times 5 \times 1/4$ plywood
7 rods	$25 \times 3/8$ or $1/2$ dowel rods

Mark and cut one fork (FIG. 1-16B) then use it as a template for the other three. Round and sand all projecting edges. Glue the forks into the arms.

Cut the dowel rods to length, using an outer frame width of 24 inches (FIG. 1-15B). Leave the top hole empty, but fit the other three rods to make the outer frame. Check that the assembly is square.

Make the inner frame so the tops of the arms fit easily inside the tops of the arms of the outer frame (FIG. 1-15C). Check for squareness to be sure the frames match when opened or closed.

Remove any surplus glue and do any sanding necessary, then pass the top rod through its holes. Glue it to the outer frame holes so the inner frame can swing on it (FIG. 1-15D).

You can leave the wood untreated, but it might be better painted white or to match the bathroom.

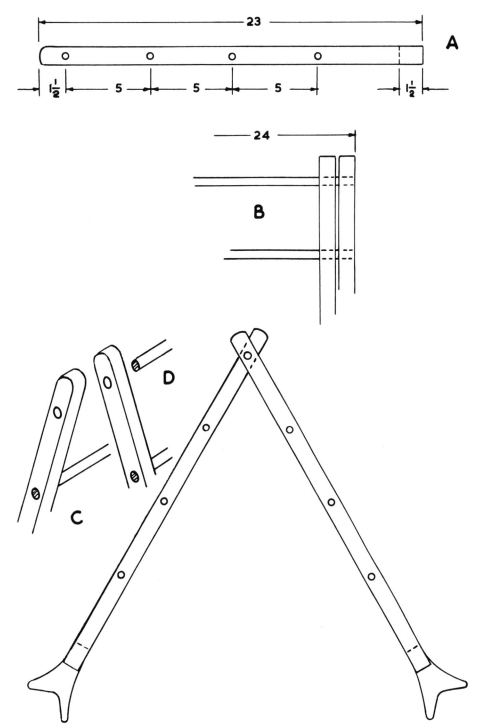

Fig. 1-15. Sizes and assembly details of the bath clothes airer.

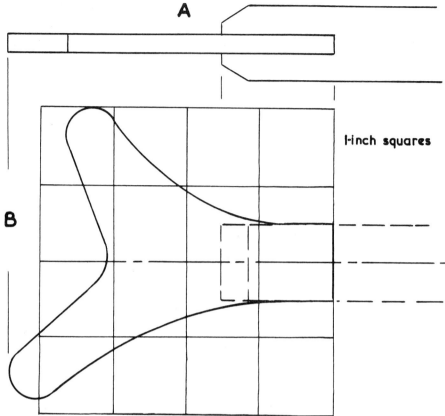

Fig. 1-16. Feet for the bath clothes airer.

Towel Holder

This holder allows four kitchen towels or other cloths to hang and dry (FIG. 1-17A). It screws to the wall and has four arms that fold against the wall when not in use. Because the arms have to be fairly slender for the best look, the wood should be a strong hardwood. A light color looks better than a dark for kitchen use. The suggested sizes suit most towels (FIG. 1-17B).

Make the four arms first (FIG. 1-17C). Start with wood 1/2 inch thick and 11/2 inches wide. The arms taper from a 5/8-inch diameter at the pivot end to a 1/2-inch diameter at the tip (FIG. 1-18A). Cut to the outline, then plane the taper first to an octagonal section. Take off the angles of the octagon with a small plane, then round the wood by pulling a strip of abrasive paper around the arm (FIG. 1-19) before finishing by sanding lengthwise. Round the tips of the arms and try to make them all the same.

At the inner end, mark the center of each dowel pivot hole. Use that point as the center for a compass to draw the curve of the end (FIG. 1-18B). Cut the shape, and drill the holes to fit the dowel.

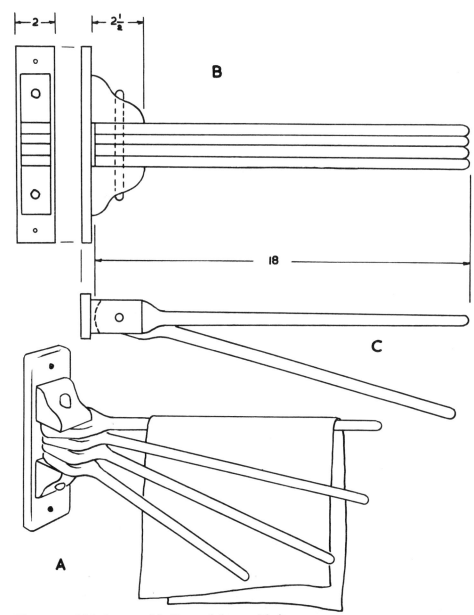

Fig. 1-17. A kitchen towel holder and dryer with four arms.

Materials List for Towel Holder

4 arms	$1/2 \times 1^1/2 \times 18$	
1 back	$1/2 \times 2 \ \ \times \ 9$	
2 blocks	$1 \times 2 \ \ \times \ 3$	
1 pivot	$8 \times \ \ 1/2$ diameter dowel rod	

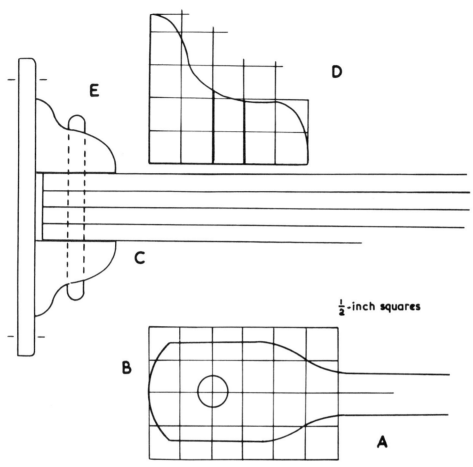

Fig. 1-18. Shapes and sizes of the kitchen towel holder.

Mark out the wood for the back. Put the four arms together to measure the thickness between the pivot blocks (FIG. 1-18C). The arms should fit tightly so they will stay in any position you might set them and will not sag after long use.

Mark out the pivot blocks (FIG. 1-18D). They could be tenoned into the back or glued and screwed from behind. Drill for the dowel pivot before shaping (FIG. 1-18E). Drill through the block, then cut their curved outlines. Round the exposed parts. Using the arms as spacers, glue and screw the blocks to the back. Drill holes at top and bottom for the fixing screws.

Before assembly, seal the wood pores to keep dirt out. A high gloss is not needed—one coat of varnish or lacquer will do.

The dowel rod pivot could be left slightly too long during assembly, then its ends can be rounded (FIG. 1-19). It should be a sufficiently tight fit without glue, then if you ever need to take the holder apart, the rod can be knocked out easily.

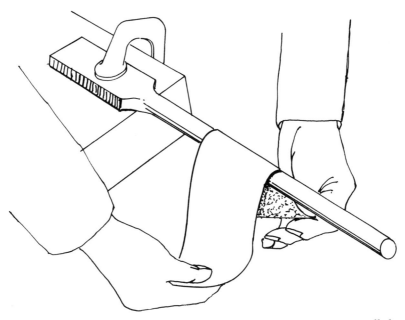

Fig. 1-19. *The arm of a towel holder can be rounded using abrasive paper pulled around it.*

Adding Machine Stand

Most of us use small adding machines at work or at home. If you use a desk-top machine, you might want to turn it about to the best direction, particularly if you change your position at your desk. Also, if there are other people who want to use the machine from the other side of the table, an easy way of turning the machine around will be welcomed.

The stand illustrated includes a turntable so the machine can be altered to any direction with minimum effort. This is a stand for a calculator (FIG. 1-20), but a stand for any other small business machine could be made in the same way, with sizes adjusted to suit.

The stand consists of a tray to take the machine and a square base, joined with a "lazy Susan" bearing. The base and the bottom of the tray could be solid wood or $1/2$-inch plywood. The rim of the tray is more prominent and might be

Materials List for
Adding Machine Stand

1 tray	$1/2 \times 9 \quad \times 11$
2 tray borders	$1/4 \times 1^{1}/8 \times 12$
2 tray borders	$1/4 \times 1^{1}/8 \times 10$
1 base	$1/2 \times 7 \quad \times 7$
1 lazy Susan bearing—3-inch size	

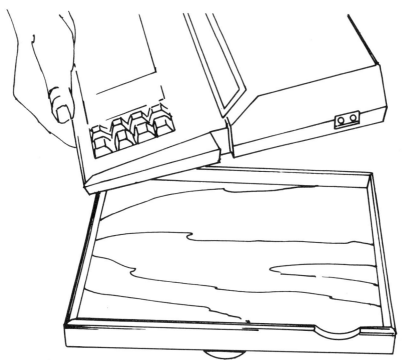

Fig. 1-20. This stand for a calculator can be moved in any direction on a turntable.

an attractive hardwood with a clear finish. Lazy Susan bearings are made in several sizes. For the tray shown, the 3-inch size should be adequate, but for bigger stands there are other sizes up to 12 inches.

Measure the machine and decide how high the rim should stand to keep it in place. An excessive height looks ugly, but some machine edges vary, and you must have enough rim all round to prevent the machine from slipping out. You also might have to allow for notching around a switch or an electric cable.

Cut the bottom of the tray (FIG. 1-21A) about 1/4 inch bigger than the machine. Cut the border strips with rounded tops (FIG. 1-21B). Make them to fit around the tray bottom with mitered corners (FIG. 1-21C). If there have to be any notches, shape them with rounded edges (FIG. 1-21D).

Attach the rim strips with glue and a few pins, which can be punched below the surface and covered with stopping.

The base (FIG. 1-21E) is a simple square block. Its edges and corners could be chamfered or rounded, but because it is almost hidden that is not necessary. The lazy Susan bearing is fitted in the same way as described for the lazy Susan bowls in chapter 11.

After you have drilled for screws and made a trial assembly, separate the parts and finish the wood with stain and polish. Reassemble with the lazy Susan bearing permanently screwed on. Glue a piece of cloth to the underside of the base to prevent slipping or marking a polished surface.

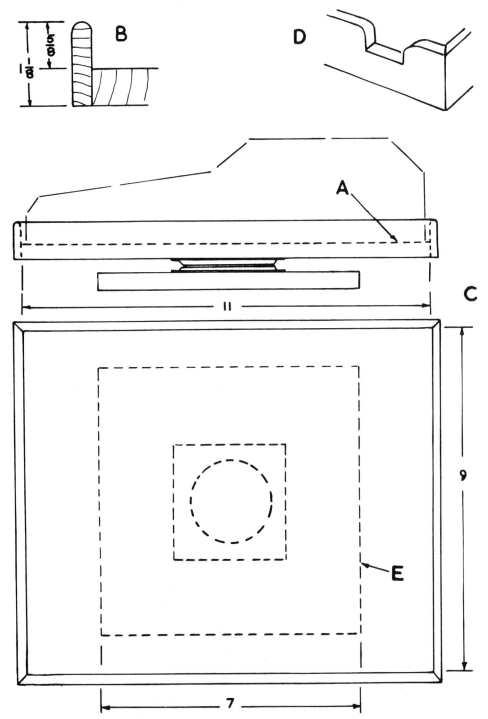

Fig. 1-21. Typical sizes of a business machine stand.

Hanging Telephone Table

If a telephone does not have its own place, it is liable to be put down in awkward positions where it might be knocked over or tampered with by children. In a roomy hall you might place a special telephone table or bench, but if you want to provide a proper place for the telephone that does not use up floor space and is out of reach of children or animals, the ideal solution is a small table hung on the wall (FIG. 1-22). This table has more than enough area for the instrument, so there is space to write notes. The rack beneath is large enough for more than one directory, plus your own telephone book and maybe a few magazines.

The suggested size (FIG. 1-23) should suit most equipment and directories, but measure what you have and modify, if necessary. All of the parts might be solid wood of about $5/8$ inch finished thickness. Or you can use veneered particleboard, with iron-on matching edging where it is cut.

Join with dowels, but counterbored screws with plugs make a strong construction (FIG. 1-23). If you have a plug cutter to use in a drill press, the plugs can

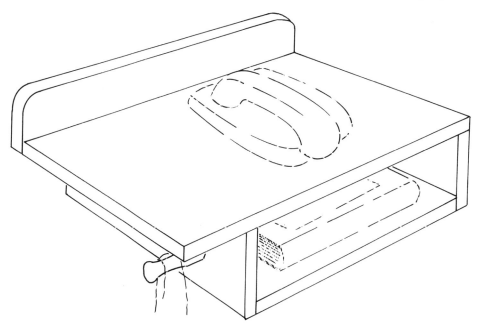

Fig. 1-22. *This wall-mounting telephone table has space for directories and a peg for keys or clothing.*

Materials List for
Hanging Telephone Table

1 top	$17 \times 8^{1}/4 \times {}^{5}/8$
1 back	$17 \times 2 \times {}^{5}/8$
2 ends	$10 \times 4^{1}/4 \times {}^{5}/8$
1 bottom	$13 \times 9 \times {}^{5}/8$

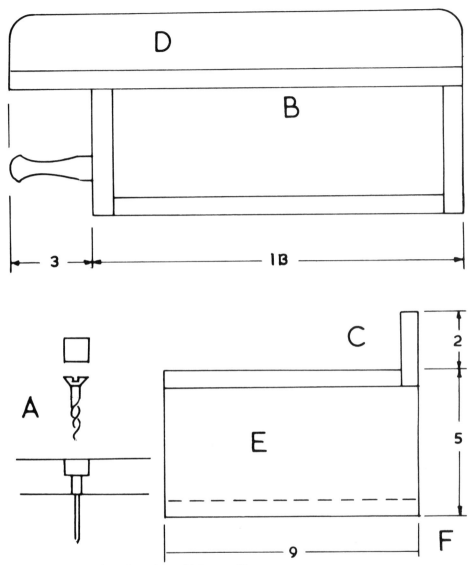

Fig. 1-23. Sizes of the hanging telephone table.

be cut cross-grained from scrap of the same wood so they will not be very obvious. Alternatively, you can choose a different wood, so the pattern of plugged screws are regarded as a design feature.

Cut the tabletop (FIGS. 1-23B and 1-24A) to size, allowing for the back to overlap it (FIG. 1-23C). Make the back (FIGS. 1-23 and 1-24) to fit behind it.

Screw the back to the top. In these and other joints you might use #8 × 1 inch or 1¼-inch screws. Make the two sides (FIGS. 1-23 and 1-24) and the bottom (FIGS. 1-23 and 1-24D) to fit between them.

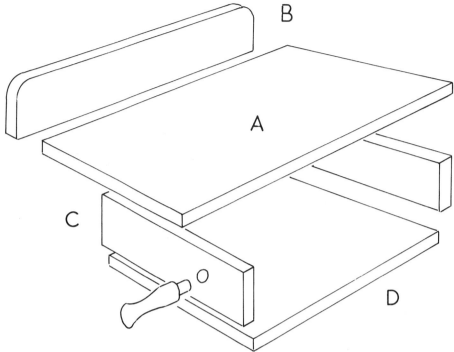

Fig. 1-24. Parts of the hanging telephone table.

The top is shown projecting to one side, but it could be either way. Drill for one or two Shaker pegs. If you turn your own, make them project 3 inches with a maximum diameter of 3/4 inch and a 1/2 inch in diameter dowel end.

Mark out the screw holes carefully, so you're sure to get a symmetrical and regular pattern. A spacing of 3 inches should be satisfactory. Do all drilling and counterboring at the same time, using a counterbore drill to suit the plugs your cutter produces. It docs not matter if the plug diameter is slightly more than that of the screw head.

Assemble all parts with glue and screws. Glue plugs over the screw heads, with grain direction matching. When the glue has set, plane the plugs level, and sand all over the hanging table.

If you have used an attractive hardwood, a clear finish might be best. Softwood can be painted. If you use particleboard with a plastic veneer, it will not need treatment, but if it has wood veneer, finish it in the same way as solid wood.

In most situations, two screws through the back should be all you need to hang the table. Check that it is level.

Garden Basket

A wooden basket with a central handle can have many uses—practical, decorative, or both. If made a reasonable size and given a painted finish it can carry

Fig. 1-25. This garden basket could be made large enough to carry things around the garden, or a small one could be used as a table decoration to hold flowers or a plant in a pot.

many small things during the planting season and be used for carrying fruit, flowers, or vegetables later in the year. If made of attractive wood and varnished, a small basket could be used as a table decoration, filled with fruit or containing a plant.

This basket is square with a laminated loop handle (FIG. 1-25). Some woodworkers are hesitant about laminating wood, but this handle is simple and can serve as an introduction to the process if you have not tackled it before. Most woods will bend in thin sections (in this case 1/8 inch), except if they are excessively dry—as they might be if over-seasoned or kept for some time in very hot, dry conditions. The basket could be made of the same wood throughout, or you might have to use a flexible wood—such as ash or hickory—for the handle and another wood for the other parts.

The sizes shown (FIG. 1-26A) will make a basket of average size, but other sizes are equally suitable without altering construction. The shape need not be square, but it would not be advisable to make the basket too narrow in the direction of the handle because this would tighten the curve and might make the handle more difficult to bend. There are two shaped ends, with side strips attached over a bottom and the handle fitting against the ends (FIG. 1-27). The main parts

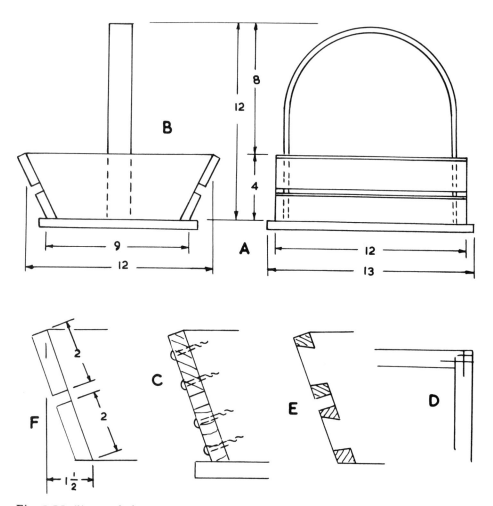

Fig. 1-26. Sizes and alternative construction for the garden basket.

Materials List for Garden Basket

2 ends	$1/2 \times$	4	$\times 13$
4 sides	$1/2 \times$	2	$\times 13$
1 bottom	$1/2 \times$	10	$\times 13$
3 laminations	$1/8 \times$	$11/2$	$\times 33$

are all $1/2$ inch thick. They can be solid wood or 112-inch exterior plywood for a painted finish, although the exposed ply edges might be more attractive under a clear finish.

Make the two ends (FIGS. 1-27A and 1-26B) to suit the chosen corner joints. The strips may be nailed or screwed on (FIG. 1-26C). You can make a stronger joint by letting the rails overlap with notches, then drive nails or screws both ways

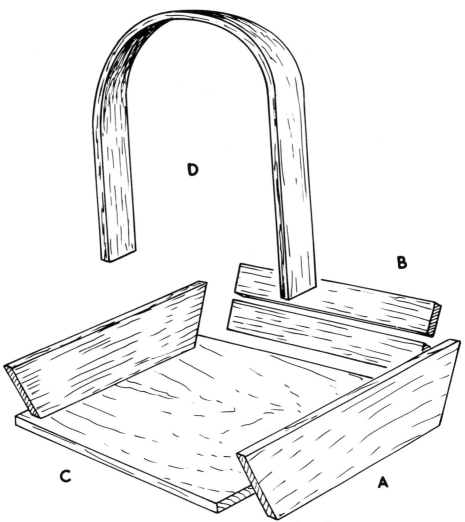

Fig. 1-27. How the parts of the garden basket are fitted together.

(FIG. 1-26D). The best joints—particularly if the basket is intended for display, is made in an attractive wood, and is given a clear finish—are dovetails (FIG. 1-26E). Although there is a slope, the angles of the sides of the tails should be related to the width of the end pieces and not tilted to the angles of the cut ends, which would result in a weak short grain.

Make the four side strips (FIGS. 1-27B and 1-26F). Bevel the bottom ones. Take the sharpness off all edges. Assemble the strips to the ends so the assembly is square when viewed from above.

Make the bottom (FIG. 1-27C) to extend 1/2 inch all around. Take sharpness off the edges and corners, then join it to the other parts with glue and nails or screws.

Make a former for bending the handle laminations (FIG. 1-28A). Allow for the handle width to fit against the ends (FIG. 1-27D), so the former width is this less the thickness of three laminations each side. The top is semicircular. The former and the strips could be a little longer than the finished handle because it is easier to get the handle size correct if there is enough at each end for trimming. The former can be any scrap wood, about the thickness of the handle. It could be made up of several pieces held together with temporary strips across.

The suggested laminations (FIG. 1-28B) are $1/8$ inch by $1^1/2$ inches, with three to make up the handle. They have to be coated with glue and held close around the former until the glue has set. It is possible to merely tie tightly in all directions, but you have better control with separate clamps. You can use cord through holes, tied tightly, then further tightened with wedges (FIG. 1-28C). Small strip steel clamps can be used through holes (FIG. 1-28D). Put wood pads against the laminations. At the end of the former you can put a bar clamp across (FIG. 1-29).

Another way of applying pressure is to fasten the former to a large board, then mount blocks with single stout screws so they will turn to match wedges driven against the laminations (FIG. 1-28E). This is probably worth setting up if you intend to make several baskets. It is difficult to do the laminating without getting glue where you do not want it. Newspaper under the laminations or anywhere that setting glue might stick them to other things can be pulled away and easily cleaned off.

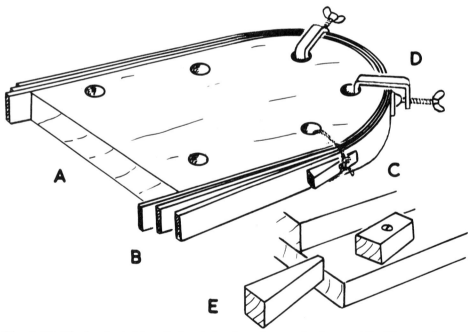

Fig. 1-28. The laminated handle has to be shaped around a former (A). Three strips are shown (B), held with clamps and wedges (C–E).

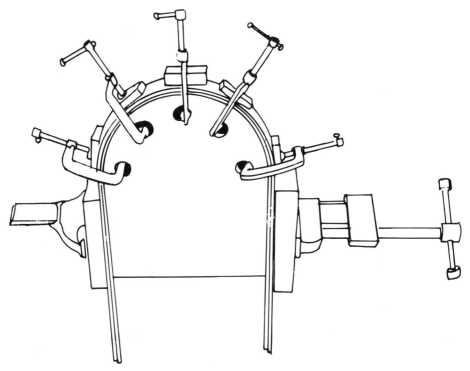

Fig. 1-29. These handle strips are held to the former with clamps, using blocks of scrap wood to spread the pressure.

When the glue has set, plane the edges of the handle level, and round the curved top. Trim the ends to length, and join the handle to the basket ends vertically, with glue and screws.

Check that all excess glue has been removed, sand all surfaces, and make sure there are no sharp or rough edges. Finish with paint or varnish.

Flowerpot Trough

Potted plants and flowers make an attractive show if brought together in a trough. The trough can be part of the indoor furniture, to stand under a window all year or just during the winter, then it can be moved outside for the summer.

This trough (FIG. 1-30) is shown on a stand, from which it can be lifted. In some situations, as when the plants are very tall, it could be made without legs and put on the floor.

If it is to be indoor furniture, the trough and its stand could be made of hardwood and finished with stain and polish. For outdoors, or to match other furniture, it might be made of softwood and finished with paint.

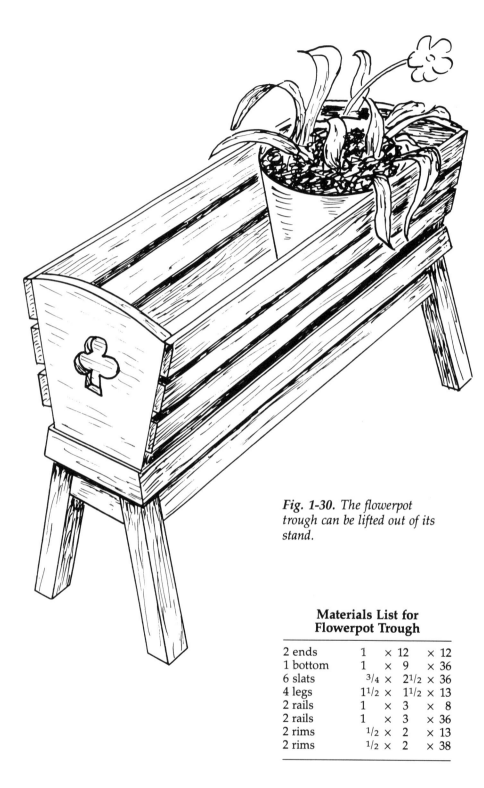

Fig. 1-30. *The flowerpot trough can be lifted out of its stand.*

Materials List for Flowerpot Trough

2 ends	1	× 12	× 12
1 bottom	1	× 9	× 36
6 slats	3/4 ×	2 1/2 ×	36
4 legs	1 1/2 ×	1 1/2 ×	13
2 rails	1	× 3	× 8
2 rails	1	× 3	× 36
2 rims	1/2 ×	2	× 13
2 rims	1/2 ×	2	× 38

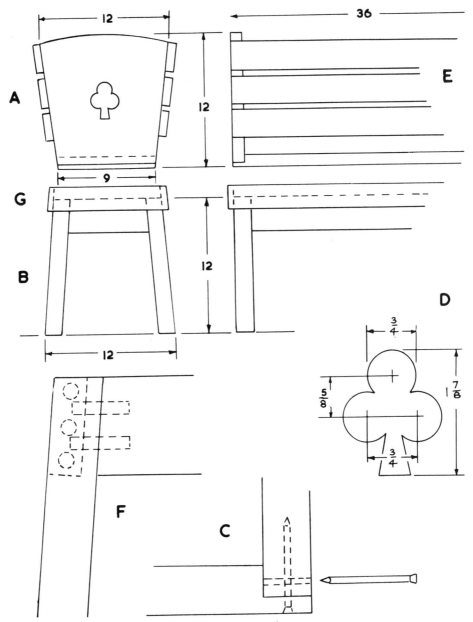

Fig. 1-31. Sizes and details of the flowerpot trough.

Decide on the pots to be used and make the trough to match. The sizes shown (FIG. 1-31) suit three containers about 10 inches in diameter and height.

Set out the trough end (FIG. 1-31A) and a stand with its top slightly wider than the trough (FIG. 1-31B). Let the legs spread to about the same width as the top.

Cut the two ends and the bottom. There are several possible ways of joining these parts. A simple way is to rabbet the bottom so nails can be driven both ways (FIG. 1-32C). Prepare these joints, but do not nail until the other parts are ready.

The ends could be decorated. You can make the shamrock design (FIG. 1-31D)

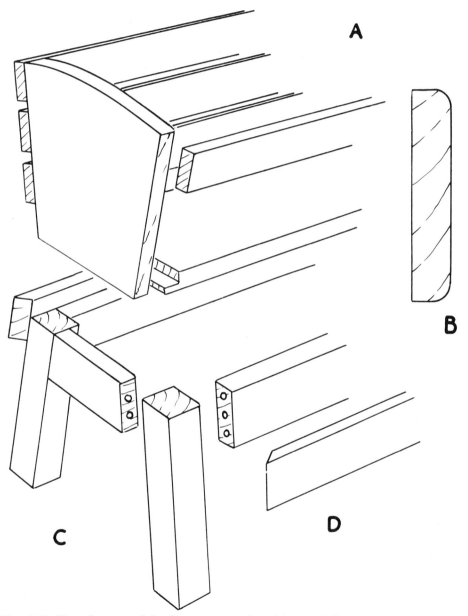

A

B

C

D

Fig. 1-32. *How the parts of the flowerpot trough and its stand fit together.*

go right through, or you can stop it about halfway by drilling and working with a router or chisel.

Prepare the lengthwise slats (FIGS. 1-31E and 1-31A), and round the outer edges (FIG. 1-32B). Drill four screws into the ends. Assemble the trough.

The stand is shown doweled. The rails and legs could have mortise and tenon joints. When marking out, arrange the dowel holes to miss each other (FIG. 1-31F). Use the full-size drawing to obtain the angles of the legs and end rails.

Make up the stand end assemblies first (FIG. 1-32C), and check that they match. Let the glue set before adding the parts the other way.

Cut the rim strips with miters at the corners (FIGS. 1-31G and 1-32D). Round the outer edges, and screw or nail them on.

Carry-All

One thing a table saw does well is cut any number of pieces of wood to the same size. If the project does not require long pieces, they can be cut from oddments that might otherwise be discarded. This carry-all (FIG. 1-33) could be used for magazines, knitting, or sewing items, or anything you want to keep together and carry about. The sides are made up of vertical strips like a small version of a paling fence.

The parts should be furniture-quality hardwood, but the pales need not be the same wood as the other parts. They are effective if in a contrasting darker or

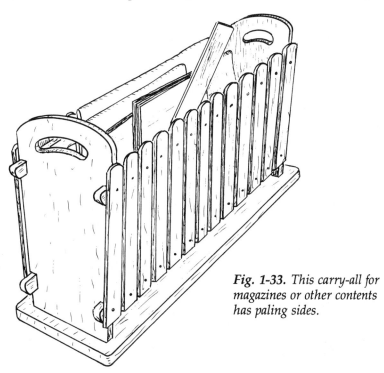

Fig. 1-33. This carry-all for magazines or other contents has paling sides.

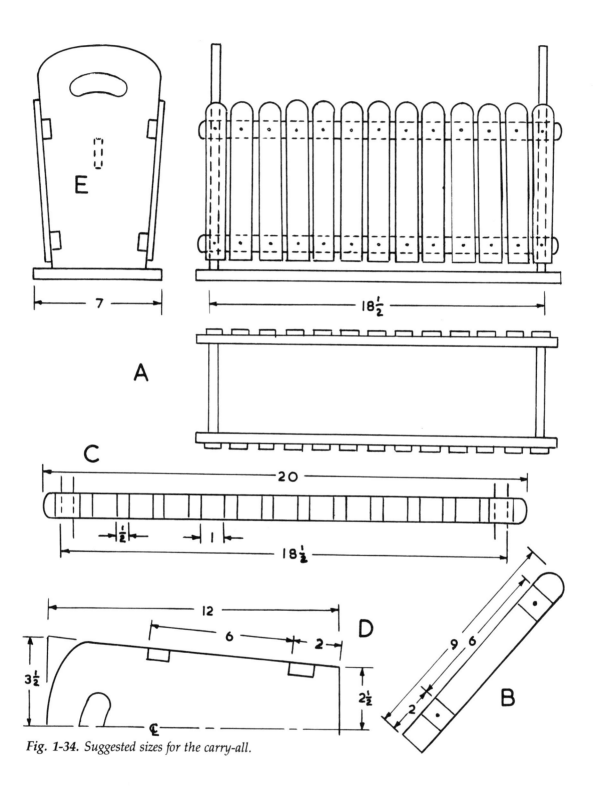

Fig. 1-34. Suggested sizes for the carry-all.

**Materials List for
Carry-All**

2 ends	$5/8 \times 7 \times 13$
4 rails	$1/2 \times 1 \times 21$
26 pales	$1/4 \times 1 \times 10$
1 bottom	$5/8 \times 7 \times 22$

lighter color. The pales are held in place with screws, which form part of the decorative design and may be roundhead brass or plated finish.

Select wood for the pales. They are shown $1/4$-inch-$\times$-l-inch finished section and could be cut through from a 1-inch board or brought to size both ways from oddments. If it would be more convenient to cut your wood to another section, you may do so, but you might have to adjust the sizes of other parts to give an even spacing (FIG. 1-34A).

Make sufficient pales, planed and sanded, with rounded tops and the screw hole positions marked (FIG. 1-34B). Mark out the four rails (FIG. 1-34C). They go through the ends and extend a little, so the end pales overlap the trough ends and are screwed through to hold the rails as well.

Mark out the pair of ends (FIGS. 1-34D and 1-35A). Cut notches for the rails. Shape the tops and the hand holes and round their edges well.

Make the bottom to overlap the other parts. Round its edges, and drill it for screwing on.

Join the pales to the rails squarely, leaving the outer ones to be added when you join the ends. Make sure that the assembly is square and screw on the bottom. Use glue in the joints and and make the end screws through the pales the same diameter as the others, but long enough to hold in the trough ends (FIG. 1-35B).

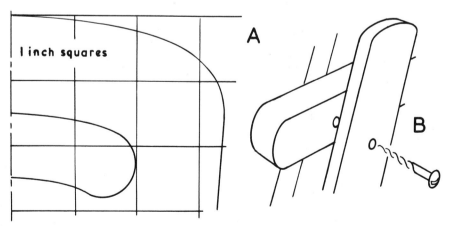

Fig. 1-35. The end shape and assembly details for the carry-all.

You might want to leave the underside bare. Much depends on where the carry-all will be used. You can screw on four rubber feet to the bottom or cover it with cloth.

The carry-all is described without anything built inside. However, if you plan to store magazines in it on edge, a central rail (FIG. 1-34E) prevents them falling over.

Box/Roll Holder

This is a wall-mounting storage box with a rail below for paper towels that you can use in the kitchen, although it could find a place in a garage, your garden store, or anywhere else you want to store small items or use a paper towel (FIG. 1-36). As drawn in FIG. 1-37A, the project will hold any paper roll up to 11 inches

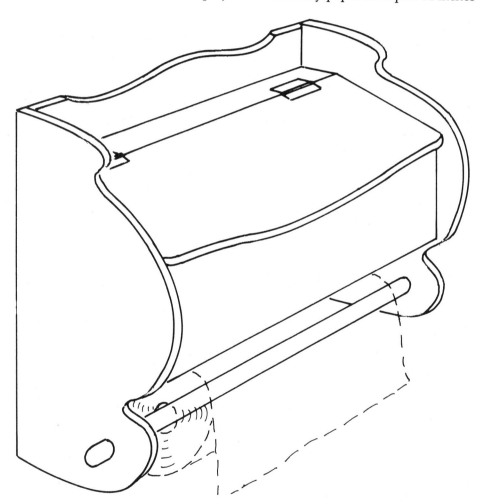

Fig. 1-36. This wall-hanging box has a rod for a paper roll underneath.

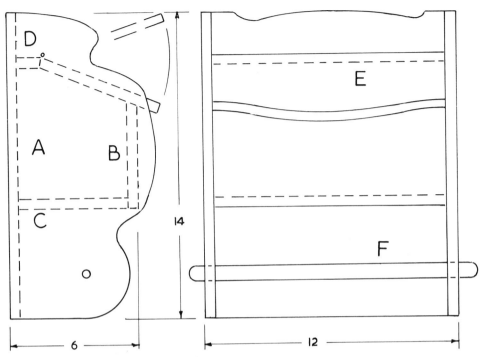

Fig. 1-37. Sizes of the box/roll holder.

Materials List for Box/Roll Holder

2 sides	7	× 14 × 1/2 plywood
1 front	5	× 11 × 1/2 plywood
1 bottom	5	× 11 × 1/2 plywood
1 top	1 1/4 × 11 × 1/2 plywood
1 lid	6	× 11 × 1/2 plywood
1 rod		14 × 3/4 diameter

long and 6 inches in diameter on a 3/4-inch rod. You can easily modify sizes if you want to accommodate a different roll.

All parts are 1/2-inch plywood. You could glue and nail or screw them, although dowels no thicker than 3/16 inch might be used if you want to avoid heads showing outside. All crosswise parts come between the sides, which should be made first.

Set out the two sides (FIGS. 1-37A and 1-38A) with the positions of the other parts marked on them. Drill to suit a 3/4-inch dowel rod. Cut and round the shaped edges.

Make the back the same height as the sides and to fit between them, and shape the top (FIG. 1-38B). You could shape the bottom similarly, but it will be hidden by the paper towels, so you might decide to leave it straight. Use the width of the back as a guide when you cut the other parts so their lengths match.

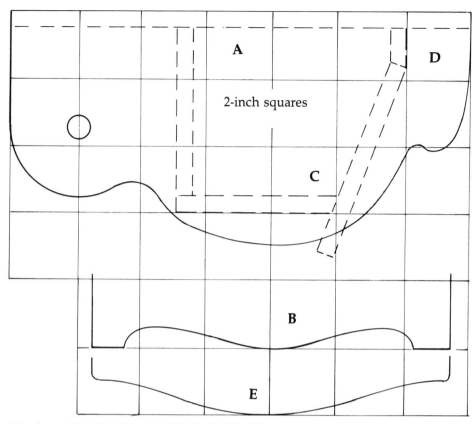

Fig. 1-38. *The shaped parts of the box/roll holder.*

Cut the front (FIG. 1-37B) and the bottom (FIG. 1-37C) to fit behind it. Use the grid drawing as a guide to the angle of the top edge of the front (FIG. 1-38C).

Make the top (FIG. 1-37D) and the lid (FIG. 1-37E). Bevel them to match where they meet (FIG. 1-38D) and shape the front of the lid (FIG. 1-38E). Round that edge.

Join these parts between the sides, and hinge the lid along its rear edge. If there is any risk of dampness, use brass hinges.

The rod (FIG. 1-37F) should project at the ends, for ease in pushing it out. Doming the ends in a lathe will improve appearance.

The best finish will probably be paint, possibly with a lighter color inside than out.

Under-Bed Storage Box

If a bed stands on legs, there is space underneath that is often not used because it is not easily accessible without crawling on the floor. This box on casters (FIG. 1-39) can be pulled out easily to use the under-bed space for storing spare bedding, children's toys, and other things you want to keep, yet only need to use occasionally.

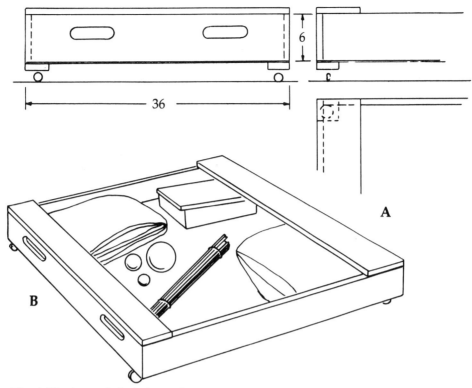

Fig. 1-39. *An underbed storage box on casters.*

Sizes obviously depend on the bed and the clearance below the mattress. It might not be wise to make one box to fit the maximum space. You must consider space around the bed as well as under it. Two or more boxes fit the space better. In some rooms the box can pull out sideways. In others, there might be more outside floor space to fit it in endwise.

The drawing offers size to suggest proportions. The boards on top (FIG. 1-39A) help to stop the contents from rising and catching on the mattress or other obstructions. The casters are small because they do not have to carry much load. If they are shallow, more height is available for storage.

Construction can be anything from nails to dovetails. I have assumed here that screws are being used. Staining and varnishing will make a box look better

Materials List for
Under-Bed Box

4 sides	$3/4 \times 6 \times 36$
2 tops	$3/4 \times 6 \times 36$
4 blocks	$3/4 \times 3 \times 3$
1 bottom	$36 \times 40 \times 1/8$ or $1/4$
	hardboard or plywood

among other furniture. Obtain the casters first so you can allow for their height and the size blocks needed to fix them.

Make the four sides. There could be handles for pulling out, but slots about 1 1/2 inches by 6 inches are simpler and provide a good grip without projections (FIG. 1-39B). They could be cut in one side, in opposite sides, or in all four sides, depending on how you expect to move the box. Make them by drilling their ends and sawing between the holes. Then round their edges.

Screw the sides together. Square the bottom so it will bring the assembly square as you screw it on. Screw on the top strips over opposite sides, then screw on the blocks under the corners and attach the casters.

Knife Box

A deep tray with a central handle is traditionally called a knife box, but it can have many other uses. Although it was (and still could be) used for cutlery, it might be used around the home for cleaning materials, in the garden for small tools and packets of seeds, or in the shop or elsewhere for carrying tools. This box (FIG. 1-40) is a size that will suit many purposes but dimensions can be altered to suit your needs without affecting constructional methods.

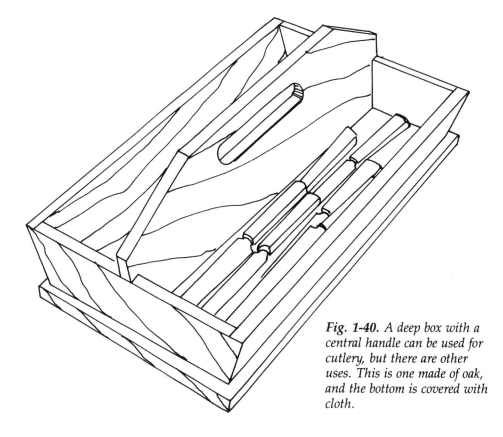

Fig. 1-40. A deep box with a central handle can be used for cutlery, but there are other uses. This is one made of oak, and the bottom is covered with cloth.

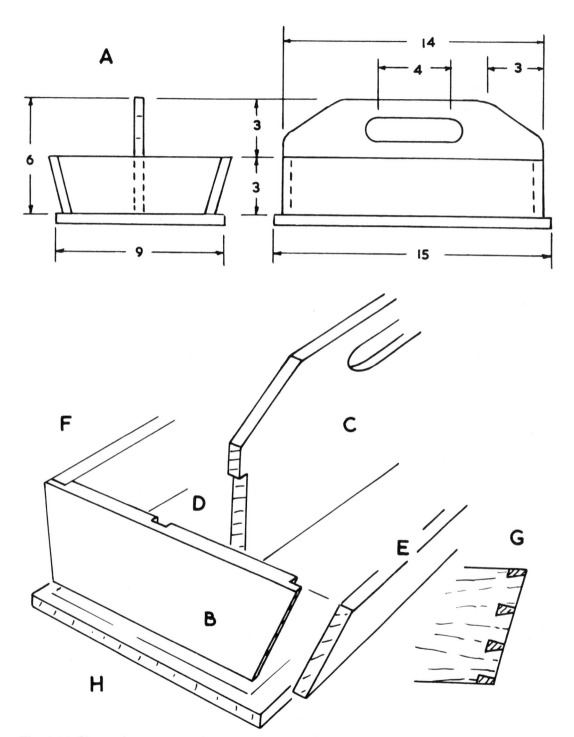

Fig. 1-41. Sizes and construction details of a knife box.

Materials List for Knife Box

2 ends	1/2 × 3	× 10	
2 sides	1/2 × 3½	× 15	
1 division	1/2 × 6	× 15	
1 bottom	1/2 × 9	× 16	

The wood chosen depends on the use the box will have. For cutlery it would best be an attractive hardwood given a clear finish. For garden use it could be any wood, including exterior-grade plywood, given a painted finish. In the shop it again might be any wood, possibly without any finish applied.

Construction can range from simple nailed joints to notched or dovetailed corners. Dovetails give a quality appearance under a clear finish.

Mark out the pair of ends (FIG. 1-41). The slopes are drawn at 15 degrees, but the exact angle is unimportant, providing the box is symmetrical.

Mark out the wood for the division/handle (FIG. 1-41C). In the simplest construction, ends could be nailed to it, but it is better to notch into dado slots (FIG. 1-41D).

Make the handle hole by drilling the ends and sawing away the waste. Shape the outside of the wood and round all edges that the lifting hand will touch.

Make the two sides (FIG. 1-41E) slightly too long. Bevel the edges to match the angle of the ends. You can notch the ends over the sides (FIG. 1-41F), then drive thin nails both ways to make strong corners. If the nails are set below the surface and covered with stopping, they will be inconspicuous under any finish.

If you use dovetails (FIG. 1-41G), keep in mind that their angles should be related to the sides of the wood and not tilted to the angle of the side, which would not be as strong due to the shortening of the grain at one side of each tail.

Assemble these parts. Check squareness, and if necessary, level the lower edges. Make the bottom (FIG. 1-41H) so it extends about 1/2 inch all around. Screw and glue it to the other parts.

Box with Shelf

A hanging box can have a shelf below. The shelf might be for matches, knives, or various small items. One modern use for a box would be for shoe-cleaning materials, with brushes in the box and polishes on the shelf.

The box could be made with a simple outline similar to the other boxes in this chapter, but this one is shown with curved decoration (FIG. 1-42A). Sizes

Materials List for Box with Shelf

1 back	1/2 × 9	× 18		
2 crosspieces	1/2 × 3½	× 10	× 11	
2 sides	1/2 × 4	× 14		
1 front	1/2 × 10			

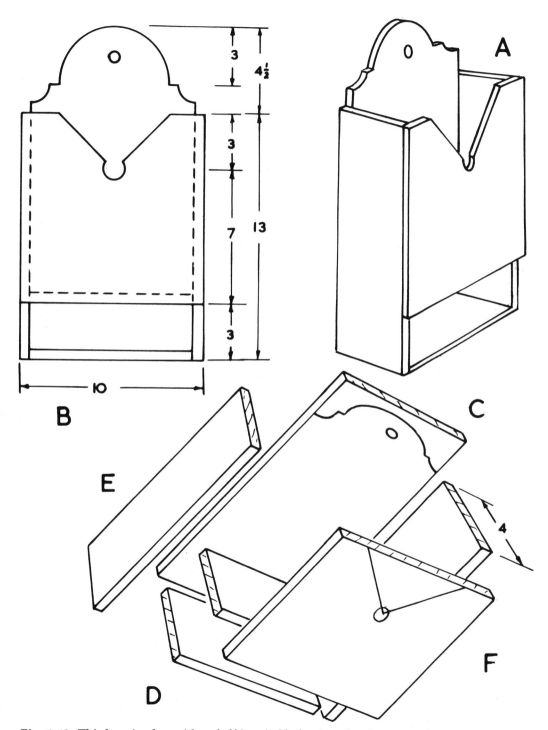

Fig. 1-42. This hanging box with a shelf is suitable for shoe-cleaning materials.

can suit your needs or available wood. Those shown should suit many purposes (FIG. 1-42B).

Mark out the back first (FIG. 1-42C) with the positions of the other parts and the shape of the top. Make the two crosspieces, the two sides to overlap them, and the back (FIG. 1-42E). Cut the top of the back to shape, and drill the hanging hole. Nail together the parts made so far.

Mark out the front (FIG. 1-42F) to match these assembled parts. For the notch, mark the center of the hole and draw lines to it, then drill a 3/4-inch hole and saw into it. Nail the front on and trim level any excess wood at the edges.

Tote Box

Boxes with central carrying handles are made in a great variety of sizes and designs and used for carrying small tools, nails, garden requirements, cutlery, and household cooking and cleaning materials. These tote boxes were often hastily made by nailing together offcuts of wood. The better ones, which have survived through time, have been more carefully made. Such a box is worth having, and the suggested design (FIG. 1-43) is an example that could be adapted to suit your needs. Most joints are dado, which might depend only on glue, or pins could also be driven and covered with stopping. Parts are 1/2 inch thick or slightly thicker; joints

Materials List for Tote Box

2 ends	1/2 × 5 × 14	
2 sides	1/2 × 5 1/4 × 14	
1 handle	1/2 × 8 1/2 × 14	
2 divisions	1/2 × 5 1/2 × 8	
1 bottom	1/2 × 12 × 14	

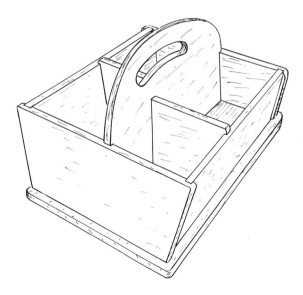

Fig. 1-43. A tote box can be used for garden or kitchen materials. In the shop it will hold tools or nails. This one has a central carrying handle.

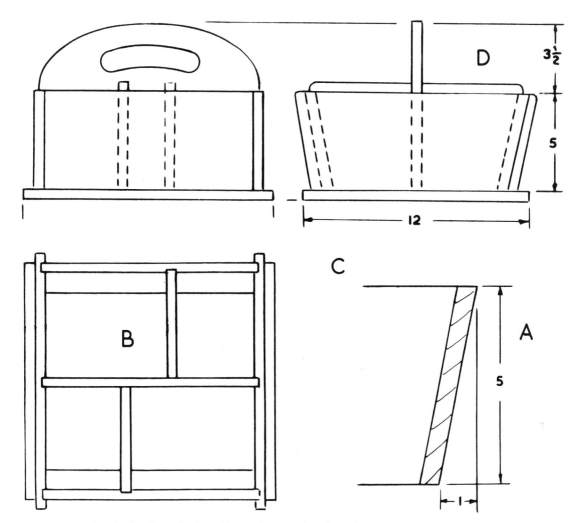

Fig. 1-44. The tote box has sloping sides and vertical ends.

are about one-third of the thickness (FIG. 1-45A). The sides slope 1 inch in the 5-inch depth, (FIG. 1-44A). Divisions are shown staggered (FIG. 1-44B).

Mark out the pair of ends (FIGS. 1-44C and 1-45B) and the handle (FIGS. 1-45C and 1-45D). From these parts, obtain the shapes of the sides (FIG. 1-45E) and divisions (FIG. 1-45F), which stand 1/2 inch above the sides (FIG. 1-44D). Cut all the dado grooves.

Round all exposed corners and those edges that will be handled. Assemble the parts, and mark the bottom from them to extend 1/2 inch all around. Glue and pin it on. If the box is for table use, glue cloth underneath after polishing the wood.

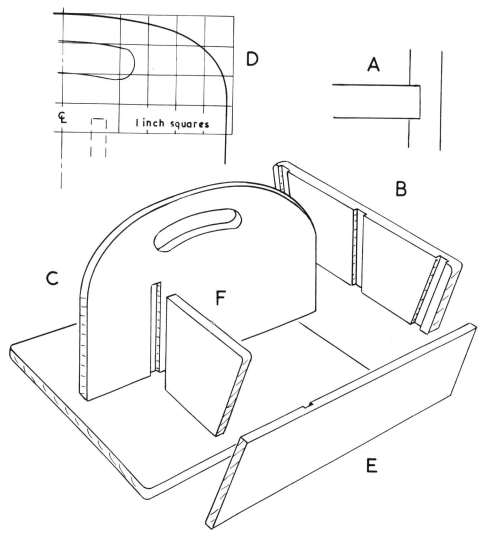

D

A

C

F

B

E

ℓ 1 inch squares

Fig. 1-45. Most parts of the tote box are joined with dado joints.

Take-Down Book Rack

In times past, wedged tusk tenons were used for furniture that had to be disassembled for transporting. This book rack (FIG. 1-46) is typical of the method of construction. It is angular, but you could soften the outline of the ends with curves. The suggested length is 18 inches, and most usual book sizes can be accommodated (FIG. 1-47A). A compactly grained hardwood is advised.

The two lengthwise shelves are the same. Reduce the 4-inch width at the ends to 2 inches (FIG. 1-47B). The wedges go through holes about 1/2 inch square.

Fig. 1-46. *A tabletop rack can be taken apart when the wedges are knocked out.*

Materials List for
Take-Down Book Rack

2 shelves	$^5/_8 \times 4 \times 22$
2 ends	$^5/_8 \times 11 \times 12$

Make the wedges $^1/_2$ inch thick, tapering from $^5/_8$ inch to $^1/_2$ inch (FIG. 1-47C). Taper each hole to match its wedge, and cut back the inner edge of the hole so it comes inside the thickness of the end and the wedge does not bear on it when it is pushed in. Trim the ends of the tenons leaving enough wood outside the wedge holes to take the thrust.

The drawing shows books tilted at 15 degrees, but that angle is not crucial. Use the grid as a guide to the end shape (FIG. 1-47D). Draw the book lines, then mark mortises to suit the tenons against them, followed by the outlines.

Round all exposed edges of the ends and shelves. Make a trial assembly before polishing the wood.

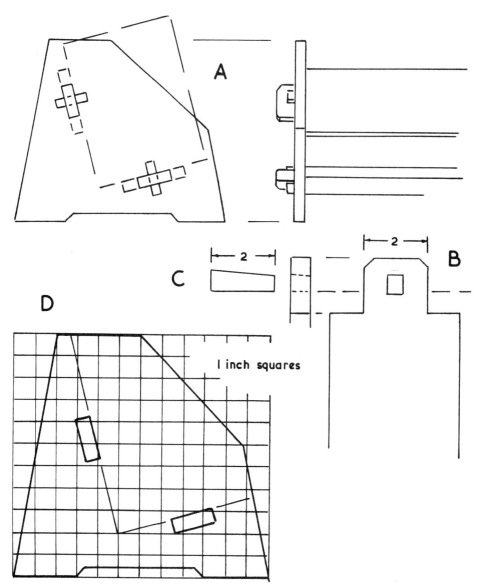

A

B

C

D

1 inch squares

Fig. 1-47. Assembly details and end shape of the take-down book rack.

2

Light Furniture

Much of the output of the shop of an enthusiastic woodworker may be called "light furniture"—somewhere between the simple one-weekend project and the occasional piece of large furniture which involves more skill and more working time.

It is difficult to decide what is light furniture and what is not, but in this section are gathered some interesting pieces of furniture which appear to fit into this category. They will test your skill and result in pieces of furniture that both you and the eventual user will find pleasing. This might also apply to projects described elsewhere in this book and in the original books from which the projects were extracted. The selection is large—you could be busy for a long time.

Modular Units

If your bathroom already has a washbasin and it is a pedestal-type unit or is bracketed to the wall, it probably has curves in all directions. Therefore, you would face careful scribing if you tried to fit a cabinet to it. A better solution is to simply provide cabinets in the vicinity of, but not attached to, the washbasin. You could have cabinets with tops at counter height and others, possibly joined by a shelf, on the wall above—all fairly close to the washbasin, but not joined to it.

The design shown in FIG. 2-1 is for basically similar modular units which can be brought together to form a pleasing and useful pattern around the washbasin. The counter units extend farther from the wall than those higher up, but are made in the same way. The upper ones could be independent, but they could have a common bottom which forms a shelf. You could join the tops in the same

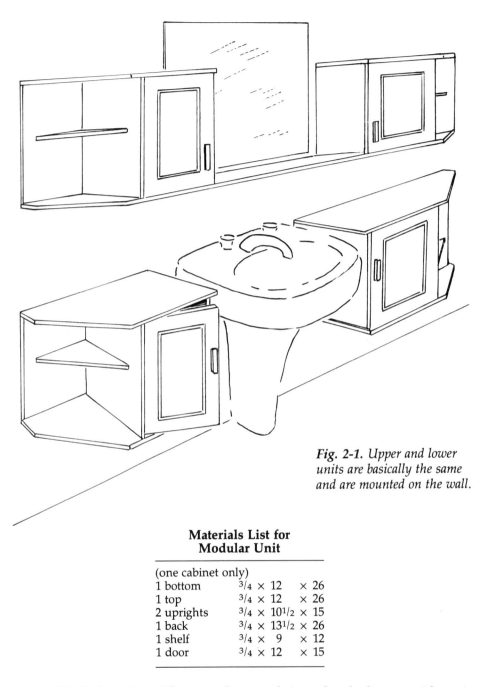

Fig. 2-1. Upper and lower units are basically the same and are mounted on the wall.

Materials List for Modular Unit

(one cabinet only)

1 bottom	$3/4$	$\times$ 12		$\times$ 26
1 top	$3/4$	$\times$ 12		$\times$ 26
2 uprights	$3/4$	$\times$ $10^{1/2}$		$\times$ 15
1 back	$3/4$	$\times$ $13^{1/2}$		$\times$ 26
1 shelf	$3/4$	$\times$ 9		$\times$ 12
1 door	$3/4$	$\times$ 12		$\times$ 15

way and include a mirror. These are shown only joined at the bottom with a mirror independently mounted.

You could use plywood or veneered particleboard, although solid wood might be good for many parts. As shown, doors are single pieces with half-round molding applied to give a paneled effect. Backs extend over the other parts. If you want to use thin plywood backs, you will need rabbets in the other parts. The joints are all doweled; 1/4-inch or 5/16-inch-diameter dowels at 3-inch intervals should be satisfactory, with slightly closer spacing for strength near the front edges (FIG. 2-2A). The instructions below are for making one side unit, but you could easily make another to match. You could make a pair of higher units in the same way, with the projection from the wall reduced and the bottoms continued in a one-piece shelf.

Make the top and bottom, which are the same (FIG. 2-2B), except that you might wish to give the top a surface of laminated plastic. Mark the positions of the other parts on them. The back comes inside, and it and the ends may be set in 1/2 inch so the top and bottom overlap (FIG. 2-3A). When marking the positions of the two uprights, allow for the thickness of the door. In the finished unit the door is between the top and bottom and should be set back about 1/8 inch. The two upright pieces and the back must all be the same height. The inside and outside shelves are at the same level (FIG. 2-2C).

Mark the shelf positions on the uprights (FIG. 2-3B), and prepare the two shelves. The triangular one (FIG. 2-2C) should be parallel to the edges of the top and bottom.

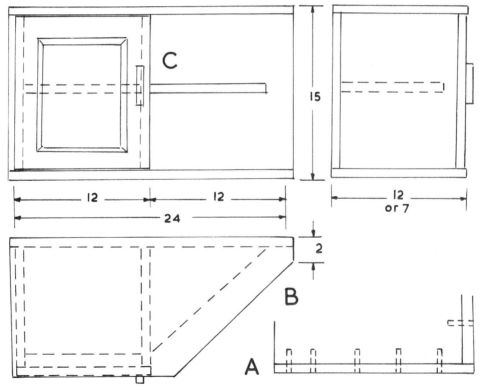

Fig. 2-2. Details of a modular unit.

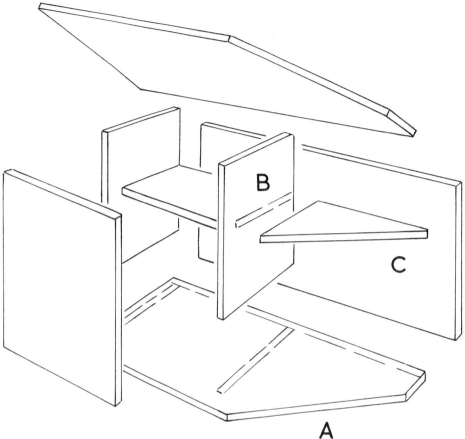

Fig. 2-3. Main parts of the modular unit.

Drill all parts for dowels. You can use screws in a few places, provided that their heads would not show. Elsewhere, stop all dowel holes. Where the two shelves meet, you can take dowels through into both edges.

Drill the back for screws to the wall. Glue all parts together, and check squareness, particularly at the door opening.

Make the door so that it swings easily between the top and bottom. Glue and pin on the half-round molding. Provide a knob or handle. Hinge the door at either side, and fit a catch.

If you want a pair of units, make all parts for both at the same time, to ensure uniformity.

In general, upper units should not project as much from the wall as lower units. A projection of 7 inches is suggested, but it could be as little as 5 inches. Except for that difference in measurement, construction of the top and bottom units is the same. If you plan to have a shelf connecting the upper cabinets, however, make their bottoms as one with the space between to suit your needs.

Vanity Unit

The vanity unit shown in FIG. 2-4 is ideal for bathrooms in which the washbasin has to be a short distance from a corner. The unit takes advantage of the space between to provide a block of drawers. As shown, the top is made of thick particleboard bought with a laminated plastic top that curves over the front edge. It is cut to width and intended to fit against a tiled wall, but you could add a splashback.

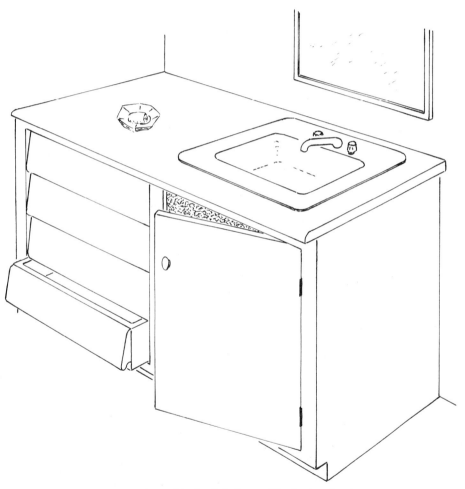

Fig. 2-4. This vanity unit has a block of shelves with sloping fronts.

The basin provides space underneath enclosed with a door, and the drawer fronts do not require handles, so anyone with soap in his eyes can reach anywhere along a drawer front to pull it out.

Materials List for Vanity Unit

2 ends	20 × 33	× 3/4 plywood
1 division	20 × 30	× 3/4 plywood
1 bottom	20 × 48	× 1 plywood
1 door	22 × 28	× 1 plywood
1 back	32 × 50	× 1/4 plywood
8 crosspieces	1 × 2	× 22
1 back strip	1 × 2	× 50
1 toe board	3/4 × 4	× 50
1 front frame	1 × 2	× 50
3 front frames	1 × 2	× 30
1 front frame	1 × 1	× 50
8 drawer fronts	1 × 6	× 24
4 drawer backs	5/8 × 5 1/2	× 24
8 drawer sides	5/8 × 6	× 21
4 drawer bottoms	21 × 24	× 1/4 plywood

Inset basins vary in size, so get yours before making the top and other parts. The basin in the example is 18 × 24 inches overall but the hole needed is smaller. A top height of 32 inches will probably suit your needs.

Start by setting out the end that will be against the wall (FIG. 2-5). Allow for the thickness of the top, and cut out for the toe board. The drawers are shown all the same depth, but you can make them different depths to suit your needs.

So the drawers will have ample clearance near the wall, pack their guides out a little. The amount depends on the width of the upright of the front frame. Check this and prepare strips to go across (FIGS. 2-5B and 2-6A), with their bottom edges level with the bottoms of the drawers. Put another strip to go under the bottom of the cabinet and another on edge at the top to take screws upward into the countertop.

Make the opposite end in the same way, but without the drawer strips (FIG. 2-6B). The outer surface of this piece will be exposed, so if you are using plywood it should have a suitable veneer.

Make the division that fits above the cabinet bottom (FIGS. 2-5C and 2-6). Put a strip at the top for screwing upward into the countertop. Mark the drawer positions to match the wall end piece, but do not put strips across, as the drawer guides can fit directly to the surface. Notch the division for the rear top strip to go through (FIG. 2-6D).

The bottom (FIG. 2-6E) fits between the ends. The location of the division depends on the space needed for the bowl, but here it is at the center. Join the ends and the division to the bottom—with screws where the heads will not show, and stopped dowels elsewhere. Fit in the rear top strip (FIG. 2-6F) to hold the parts vertical. Nail or screw on the back (FIG. 2-6G). Its edges will be hidden everywhere except at the end away from the corner wall. You can let in a narrow strip of thin wood there, or cover the end with a narrow half-round molding.

Fit the toe board (FIG. 2-6H). The parts should now be square if the assembly is stood on a flat surface.

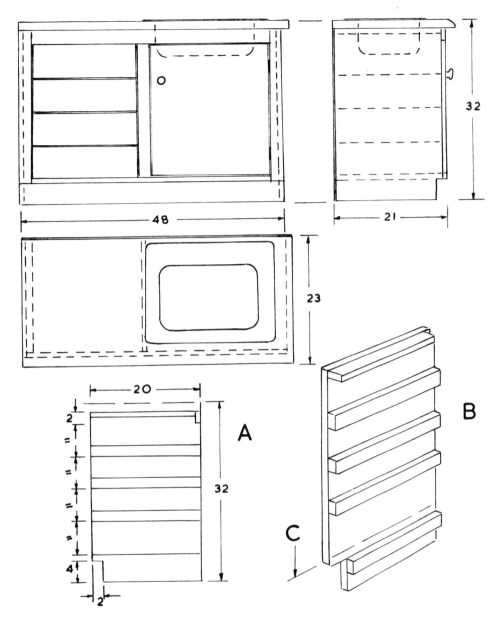

Fig. 2-5. Suggested sizes for the vanity unit.

Make a front frame (FIG. 2-6J). The piece that covers the division should be level with the surface on the drawer side, and its other edge should project into the compartment under the basin. Attach the frame to the other parts.

The door (FIG. 2-6K) is shown flush, but you can put it on the surface. It should be plain, with a suitable veneer on the front, and you should cover the edges with solid wood or veneer. You can use decorative hinges on the surface or

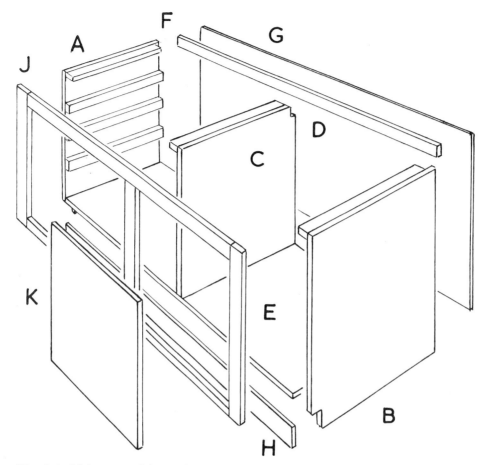

Fig. 2-6. Main parts of the vanity unit.

ordinary brass hinges let in. Open from either side to suit the situation. Fit a catch and handle to the opposite side. You could put a shelf in the compartment, but make it removable for easy access to the plumbing.

If the drawers fit flush with handles or knobs, have fronts overlapping the frame. Or, as shown in FIG. 2-7, have false fronts providing a grip and fitting within the frame so there is no projection. This last arrangement could be ideal for a confined space.

If you use metal or plastic drawer guides or runners, allow for their thickness (about $1/2$ inch) on each side of the drawer, but make the false fronts to extend over them and make a comfortable fit within the width of the front frame.

Make each false front tapering in section from 1 inch to $1/4$ inch (FIG. 2-6A). Round the narrow front and shape the underside of the thick edge to provide a finger grip (FIGS. 1-7B and 1-7C).

You can make the drawers by any of a number of methods, with the width reduced to allow for the guides. The drawer front-to-back length should allow for

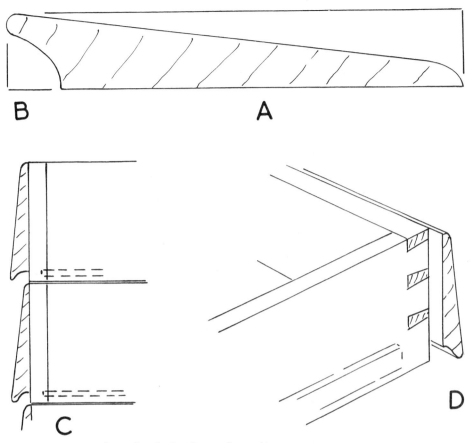

Fig. 2-7. Drawer-front details for the vanity unit.

the false front coming just inside the front frame when closed. Fit each drawer front behind its false front (FIG. 2-7D), and attach the guides to the drawer and the cabinet sides.

Prepare the top by cutting the opening for the basin and covering the outer end with laminated plastic. You should probably screw the carcass to the wall after cutting out any spaces for pipes, and then screw the top on from below.

Laundry Box

A table saw will cut grooves for panels, and this laundry box (FIG. 2-8) uses four corner posts with grooves as the main parts of the assembly. With the sizes suggested (FIG. 2-9), the box is suitable for use in a bedroom or bathroom for items to be washed, but it can be made to other sizes for different purposes—including a small box to stand on a table to contain small articles or a much larger version for use in the garden or shop. Even if you alter section sizes, construction will be the same.

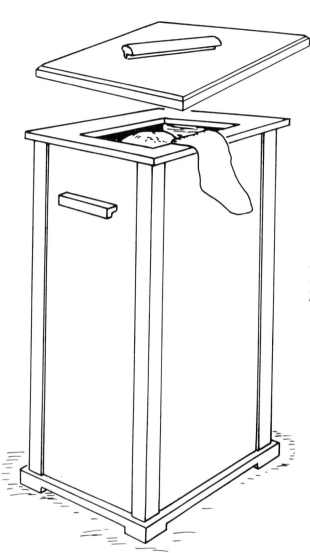

Fig. 2-8. *A laundry box with lid, made with plywood panels.*

Materials List for Laundry Box

4 posts	$1^{1}/_4 \times 1^{1}/_4 \times 27$
4 panels	$27 \times 14 \times {}^{1}/_4$ plywood
8 rims	$^{1}/_2 \times 1^{7}/_8 \times 17$
8 fillets	$^{1}/_2 \times {}^{1}/_2 \times 15$
4 feet	$^{1}/_2 \times 1^{7}/_8 \times 1^{7}/_8$
4 lid frames	$^{7}/_8 \times 1^{1}/_4 \times 15$
1 lid panel	$14 \times 14 \times {}^{3}/_8$ plywood
1 bottom	$14 \times 14 \times {}^{3}/_8$ plywood

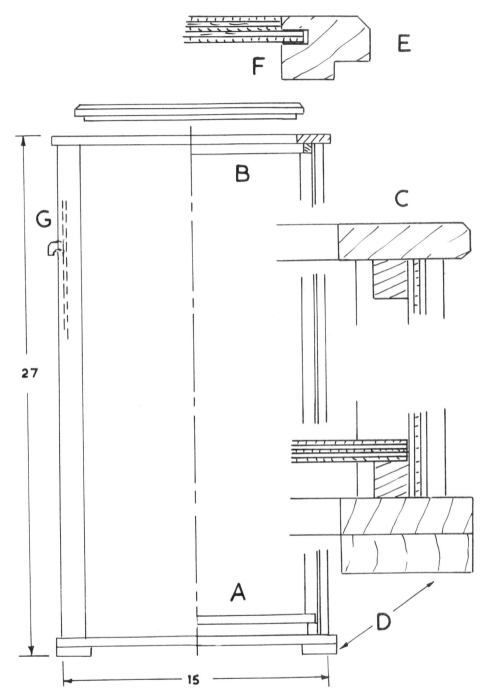

Fig. 2-9. Sizes and sections for the laundry box.

The laundry box may be made of softwood, with plywood panels, although a light hardwood will be more satisfactory. In any case, the finished box should be painted, so wood of mixed colors or textures will not matter. Exact sizes are not critical, but grooving must suit the panels chosen. If the box will be used in wet conditions, use a water-resistant glue and an exterior-grade plywood.

Prepare the wood for the corner posts, with grooves to suit the panels (FIG. 2-10), made with several adjoining straight cuts or with a wobble saw.

Cut the panels to size. They determine the box's size, but need not reach the bottoms of the grooves. The box is shown square, but the length and width may differ if you wish or if the box is to fit into a certain space.

Assemble the panels in the posts with glue, and add square strips at top and bottom between the posts (FIGS. 2-9A, 2-9B and 2-10B). Make up opposite sides, then cut and fit the bottom (FIG. 2-10C), which would be difficult to fit in if all four sides were brought together first. This will hold the assembly square while the glue sets.

Top and bottom rims are similar. Cut strips to miter on top of the posts (FIGS. 2-9C and 2-10D). Round or chamfer top and bottom outer edges of the box top strips, but only round the upper edges of the bottom strips. Fit the strips in place with glue and pins. You might want to set them below the surface and cover them with wood filler before painting.

Use the saw to cut square feet (FIG. 2-9D). Fit them in place with glue and pins, and take sharpness off edges that will come into contact with a carpet.

The box can be used with an open top, but a lid is shown, with a plywood panel framed all around. Prepare sufficient strips to the section shown (FIG. 2-9E). Make the groove to about half the thickness of the plywood to be used. Cut rabbets to fit into the box top.

Miter the corners to a size that will allow the lid to fit easily into the box. You don't need a very close fit; it should be possible to turn and fit the lid at any position.

Make the plywood panel to fit into the lid frame. It is important that the top finishes level and close to the frame. It does not matter if the wood does not reach the bottoms of the grooves (FIG. 2-9F).

Chamfer or round the outer edges of the lid. Glue alone should be sufficient to hold the lid parts together, but you can drive pins across the miters if necessary.

You can fit the box by its rim, or screw handles to opposite sides (FIG. 2-9G). Make the handles shown by rabbeting a strip. Chamfer the edges and bevel the ends (FIG. 2-10E).

Fit a matching handle for the lid diagonally. It has two rabbets and surface chamfering to match the side handles (FIG. 2-10F). Finally, remove all sharp angles and edges before sanding and painting.

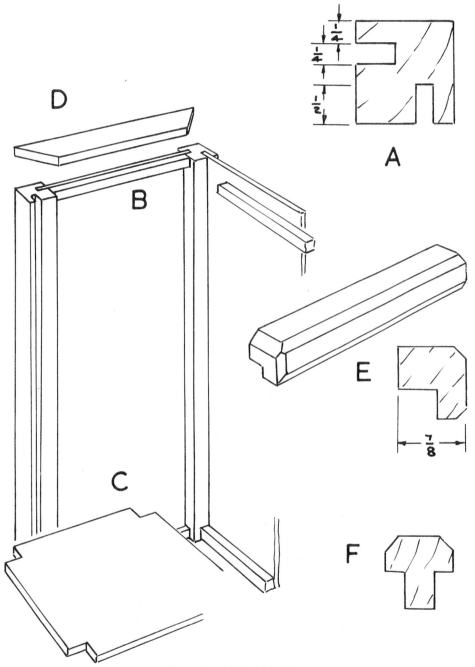

Fig. 2-10. Laundry box assembly and sections of parts.

Wall Drying Arms

Arms that pivot can fold flat against a wall, then be turned outwards when needed. There could be any number of arms, but three is a reasonable maximum number. If there are more, they would have to be made shallower and might then sag after long use, as some early examples do. A single arm is shown (FIG. 2-11) but the drawing of two arms (FIG. 2-12A) could be extended to three.

I recommend using a close-grained hardwood that has a reasonably straight grain to reduce the risk of warping.

Make the arms (FIGS. 2-12B and 2-12C) tapering from $3/4$ inch deep 4 inches from the inner end to about $5/8$ inch round at the tip. Leave the thick ends with square edges but well round the extending parts.

The support (FIG. 2-12D) has mortise-and-tenon joints. Drill for screwing to the wall and for a $1/4$-inch hardwood dowel as pivot. Use a drill press or a drill guide to make the holes squarely through all parts. If the dowel rod is allowed to project slightly, it is easy to withdraw if you ever need to take the assembly apart.

Materials List for Wall Drying Arms

2 arms	$3/4 \times 1 1/2 \times 18$
1 back	$1/2 \times 2 \times 9$
2 blocks	$1/2 \times 2 \times 4$
1 pivot	$6 \times 1/4$ round

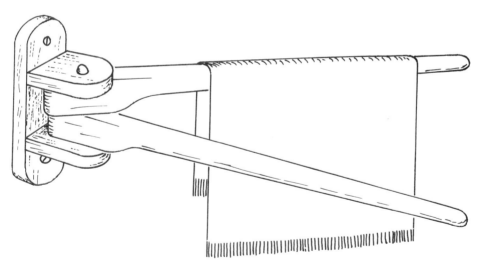

Fig. 2-11. A wall-mounted drying arm. There could be one, two, or three swinging arms.

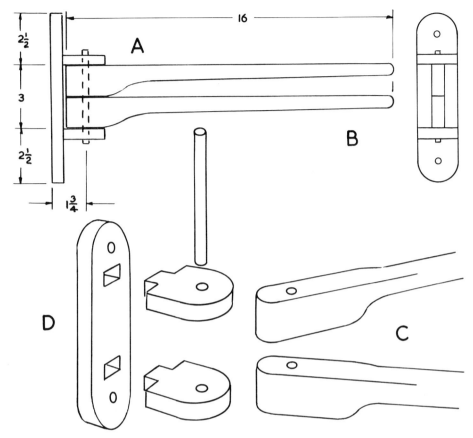

Fig. 2-12. The drying arms (A,B,C) pivot on a bracket screwed to the wall.

Drop-Arm Drying Rack

The alternative to folding, swinging arms is to arrange for them to drop down. This four-arm wall rack is based on one made as a full-circle herb-drying rack seen in a Cape Cod home. It was on a central post with feet and had eight arms. This rack (FIG. 2-13) is only half of that shape and more suitable for any hanging or drying purpose in a modern home.

**Materials List for
Drop-Arm Drying Rack**

1 main part	1	× $4^{1}/_{2}$ × 10
4 arms	1	× 1 × 19
1 top	$^{1}/_{2}$ × $3^{1}/_{2}$ × 8
1 back	$^{3}/_{4}$ × 4 × 14

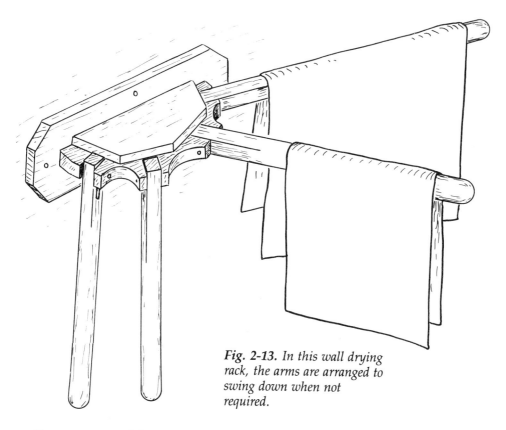

Fig. 2-13. In this wall drying rack, the arms are arranged to swing down when not required.

Because some of the cuts in the main part have to be across the grain, use a dense hardwood for strength. The top can be any wood, and the arms can be straight-grained hardwood. If you alter sizes, be careful to arrange the shape so the pivot rods can be fitted in clear of the next projection.

Mark out the shape of the main part (FIG. 2-14A). The arms are at a 45-degree angle to each other, with the rear ones 22^1/$_2$ degrees to the back. First draw their centerlines. Draw curves at the following radii: 2^1/$_4$ inches (inner ends of slots), 4 inches (centers of pivot rods), 4^5/$_8$ inches (outsides). With these lines as guides, complete the outline. Check that there will be clearance for the drill when you make the pivot holes (FIG. 2-14B). Cut the shape and lightly round edges (FIG. 2-14C). Drill for ^{1}/$_4$-inch pivots.

Make the top (FIG. 2-14D) to overlap the sockets by ^{3}/$_4$ inch, or a 3-inch radius (FIG. 2-14E), and glue it to the main part. Cut the back to shape and join to the main part with glue and screws (FIG. 2-14F). The assembly should be square or tilted up slightly, not down.

The four arms must fit in the grooves and can be 18 inches long. At each inner end, cut a slot (FIG. 2-14G). When on a pivot rod, it should come clear of the top when pulled out and allowed to swing down. When pushed in, the slot must allow the arm to go under the top to the end of the groove.

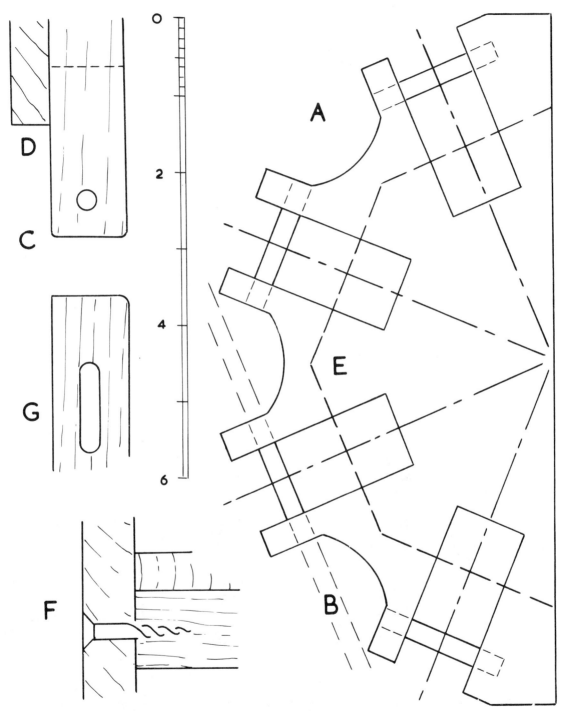

Fig. 2-14. *The layout of the top of the rack (A – E). The back is screwed on (F). Each arm is slotted (G).*

Portable Umbrella Stand

A large umbrella stand or one that is part of another piece of furniture is valuable, but a stand of light construction can be used in a hallway or porch. Then if you need it elsewhere, you can pick it up—with its contents, if necessary—and carry it easily to a new position.

This stand (FIG. 2-15) is intended for use with umbrellas and canes, but it could also hold fishing poles, golf clubs, and other long and narrow games equipment. You might have to modify sizes to suit special contents, but those shown (FIG. 2-16) will suit most uses in your home.

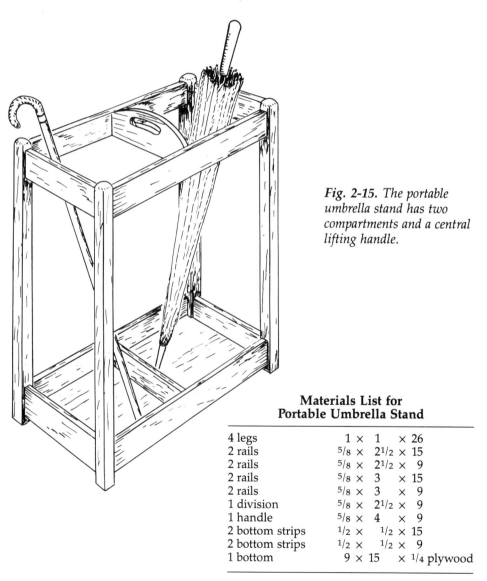

Fig. 2-15. The portable umbrella stand has two compartments and a central lifting handle.

Materials List for Portable Umbrella Stand

4 legs	1	×	1	×	26	
2 rails	5/8	×	2 1/2	×	15	
2 rails	5/8	×	2 1/2	×	9	
2 rails	5/8	×	3	×	15	
2 rails	5/8	×	3	×	9	
1 division	5/8	×	2 1/2	×	9	
1 handle	5/8	×	4	×	9	
2 bottom strips	1/2	×	1/2	×	15	
2 bottom strips	1/2	×	1/2	×	9	
1 bottom	9	×	15	×	1/4	plywood

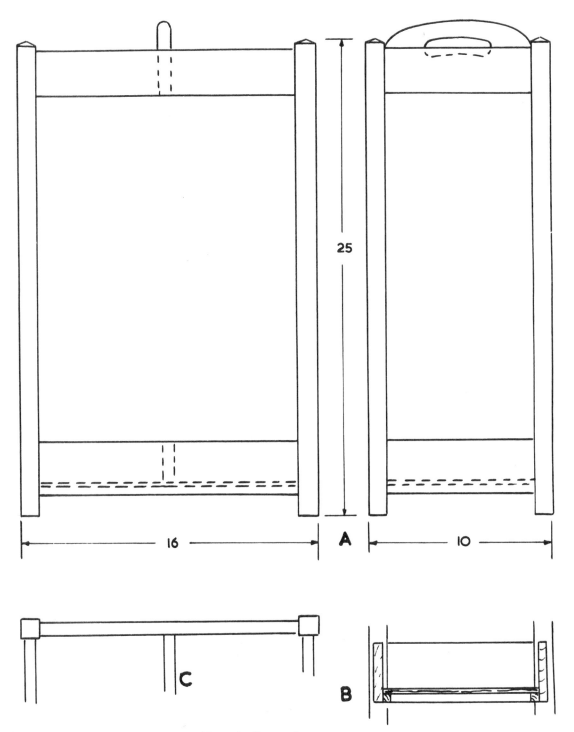

Fig. 2-16. Main sizes of the portable umbrella stand.

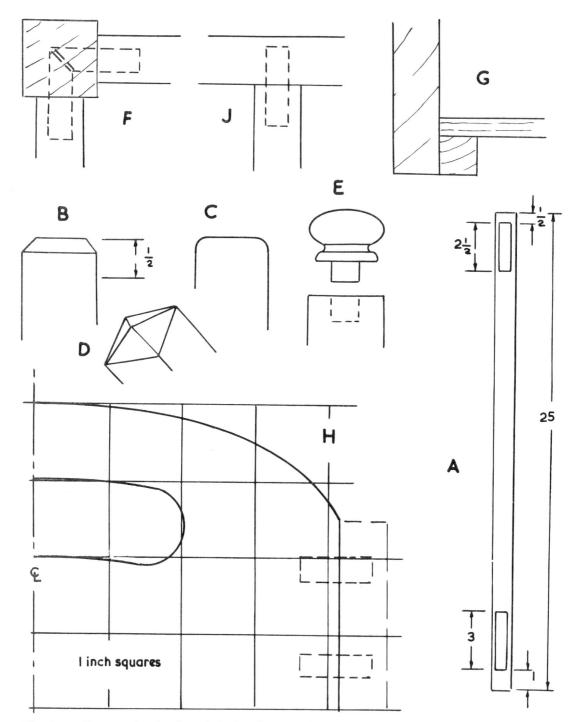

Fig. 2-17. Construction details and the handle shape for a portable umbrella stand.

An attractive hardwood is advisable, but choose straight-grained pieces for the fairly slender legs so there is little risk of warping. The joints could be all mortises and tenons if you wish, but the instructions and drawings show dowels.

Mark out the four legs together. They are the same, and the markings should be on two adjoining faces (FIG. 2-17A). The tops of the legs extend above the rails. These are prominent and should be decorated. Allow for the design you prefer.

The simplest top has the end squared, then chamfers cut all around (FIG. 2-17B). Alternatively, you could round the tops completely. Tapering in a shallow cone to a central point (FIG. 2-17D) looks attractive if cut neatly. You could also add finials or knobs—tall ones would be inappropriate, but a shallow broad design (FIG. 2-17E) could be used.

Make the rails both ways. See that the ends are square and lengths match. Then mark the rails and legs for dowels. Two $5/16$- or $3/8$-inch dowels in each joint should be sufficient. To provide sufficient glue area in the legs, drill the holes to meet and miter the dowel ends (FIG. 2-17G).

Put strips inside the bottom rails (FIG. 2-17G) to support the plywood bottom (FIG. 2-16B). Make the division (FIG. 2-16C) a suitable depth to fit over the plywood bottom when that has been fitted.

Make the handle to fit between the top rails (FIG. 2-17H). Round the edges of the curved top and the hand hole well. Mark and drill for dowel joints in the division and handle (FIG. 2-17).

Shape the tops of the legs if this has not been done already. Take the sharpness off the lower ends to prevent splintering on a rough floor and to avoid marking your floor covering. Round the upper edges of all rails slightly, if you like. In any case, take the sharpness off all edges and sand the parts before assembly.

Join the legs with the short rails. Check squareness, and be sure that the assemblies match as a pair.

Cut the plywood bottom. Notch its corners to fit around the legs. You can leave it slightly oversize and trim it to a close fit during assembly.

Join the end assemblies with the long rails. At the same time, fit the handle between the top rails and the plywood bottom and division between the bottom rails. The plywood will keep the lower parts square, but check squareness at the top and sight from above to see that there is no twist.

Finish in any way you wish, but if you expect the stand to hold wet things, be sure to use exterior or boat varnish.

Hall Mirrors

A mirror near an outside door allows anyone passing in or out to make a quick check on his or her appearance. It can include some provision for hair and clothes brushes and perhaps coat hooks.

Mirrors with Shelves

A simple mirror with a shelf is shown in FIG. 2-18A. The exposed edges are cut with curves, which give the piece a more graceful effect than straight lines.

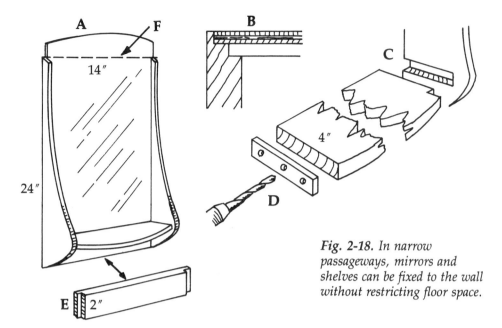

Fig. 2-18. In narrow passageways, mirrors and shelves can be fixed to the wall without restricting floor space.

Because the mirror determines the sizes of other parts, buy it first. Suggested sizes are given. You can frame the top of the mirror, but if you decide not to, be sure to grind and polish the exposed mirror edges.

The sides (FIG. 2-18B) are cut with two rabbets—one for the mirror and one for the backing plywood. Because of this, you can affix the assembly to the wall without the glass, using screws through the plywood, and then slide the mirror in from the top. If there is not enough clearance to do this, insert the mirror before fixing it to the wall and use some brass mirror plates at the sides. The glass makes the unit quite heavy for its size, so there should be two or more stout screws fairly high and one or more farther down.

You can fit the shelf into a dado joint at each end (FIG. 2-18C) or you can use dowels and a simple template (FIG. 2-18D) to make the holes.

A filler piece (FIG. 2-18E) goes below the mirror and shelf. Cut the plywood backing to match the top of the mirror or take it straight across between the sides (FIG. 2-18F). Check that the rabbets for the glass will allow it to slide in easily yet be free from wobble after the glass is inserted, then stain and varnish the wood-work. If there is any risk of dampness, use a coat of varnish on the back of the mirror itself to reduce the risk of moisture damage to the silvering.

A variation on this mirror/shelf (FIG. 2-19) involves hooks for brushes. It can be made in the same way as the first mirror, with extra backing at one side. The simple design shown gets its beauty from the grain of the wood rather than shaping of the sides.

The basic part is the plywood back. The shape of the back is determined by the size of the mirror (FIG. 2-19B), and the shelf is thickened at the back for stiff-ness. Tapering from below avoids a heavy look (FIG. 2-19C).

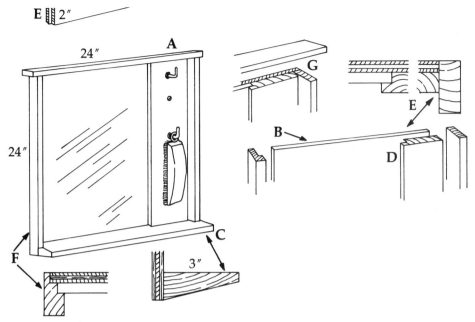

Fig. 2-19. *One variation of the mirror has hooks for brushes (A). The back conforms to mirror size (B) and the shelf is tapered to avoid a heavy look (C). The rabbeted strip for brush hooks (D) has a lip that conceals the plywood (E). Final framing includes installing the other side and top (F and G).*

The strip for the brush hooks has a rabbet to suit the glass (FIG. 2-19D). A lip on its edge covers the plywood and provides a support for the top (FIG. 2-19E). At the opposite side a rabbeted strip projects the same amount (FIG. 2-19F). The single rabbet is sufficiently deep for the glass as well as the plywood.

The top is a strip of wood that fits over side strips and the back after the glass has been fitted (FIG. 2-19G). Mounting is done with screws through the plywood.

If there is not enough space above to slide the mirror in after the woodwork has been fixed to the wall, you can make the assembly swing if one of the upper screws is through the side wood. Drive in the screw that will come behind the glass and swing the assembly on this to allow the glass to be fitted (FIG. 2-20). Then position the unit and drive the other screw.

Mirror with Clothes Hooks

Clothes hooks may be mounted on wings extending from each side of the mirror frame (FIG. 2-21). The mirror is fully framed, and it can be held in place with a plywood back and fastenings in the same way a picture is framed (FIG. 2-21B).

The woodwork can be doweled together. The traditional method would be to use mortise-and-tenon joints (FIG. 2-21C), but it is possible to have some parts and supplement glue with screws driven from the back (FIG. 2-21D). If you have

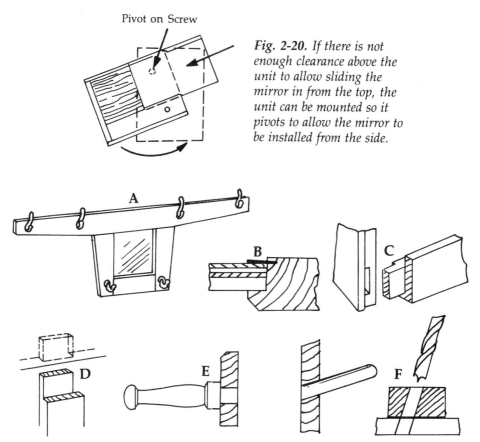

Pivot on Screw

Fig. 2-20. If there is not enough clearance above the unit to allow sliding the mirror in from the top, the unit can be mounted so it pivots to allow the mirror to be installed from the side.

A

B

C

D

E

F

Fig. 2-21. A hall mirror can be extended to provide clothes-hanging space.

access to a power molding tool, you can finish the edges by working a mold around the outline.

You can buy coat hooks or turn wooden pegs on a lathe (FIG. 2-21E). You could also insert pieces of dowel in holes at an angle. If the holes cannot be made on a drilling machine with a tilting table, make the holes at a uniform angle by drilling freehand through a block of wood with a suitable hole (FIG. 2-21F).

Television Turntable

Which is the best seat for viewing television? If you want to view from a different position, can you turn the set? A turntable under the set makes it easy to alter the screen to face any way you want it, with a minimum of trouble.

This turntable (FIG. 2-22) consists of a board under the set, joined to a base with a "lazy Susan" bearing. These turntable bearings turn smoothly on a circle of balls and are available in several sizes. You could use a 4-inch bearing for a small set, but most table models will use a 6-inch size. Sizes shown (FIG. 2-23)

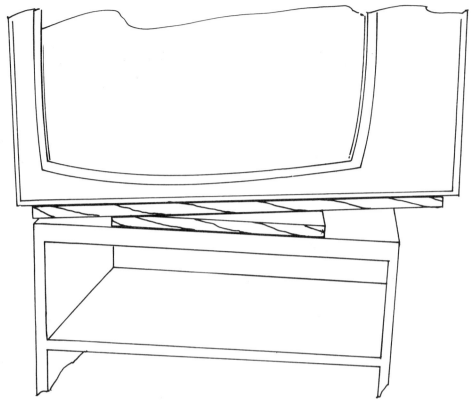

Fig. 2-22. A turntable allows a television set to be moved for the best viewing position.

serve as guides only and should be adapted to suit your television set. The base can be square, octagonal, or round, but it must be wider than the top.

Solid wood may be used—either a cheap wood stained, or a hardwood to match other furniture. Veneered particleboard is also suitable. Obviously, not much will show when the set is in position.

Make the top (FIG. 2-23A) to fit under the television case. It need not extend to the full length of the case, but if the set has feet, be sure to take the turntable past them and drill it so the feet go through and the two surfaces are in contact. Otherwise, the turntable top might bend after a time if the weight is taken only at the ends under the feet.

Make the base (FIG. 2-23B), and shape it if you wish. Mark the centers of both parts and draw on the outlines of the lazy Susan bearing (FIG. 2-23C). The largest ones are round, but others are square. The shape does not affect the method of fitting.

The turntable can be allowed to turn a full circle, but in most circumstances you will want to limit the movement. This can be done with projecting dowels. Two dowels can extend down from the top (FIGS. 2-23D and 2-23E). On the same circle are four dowels projecting up from the base (FIGS. 2-23F, 2-23G, and 2-23H).

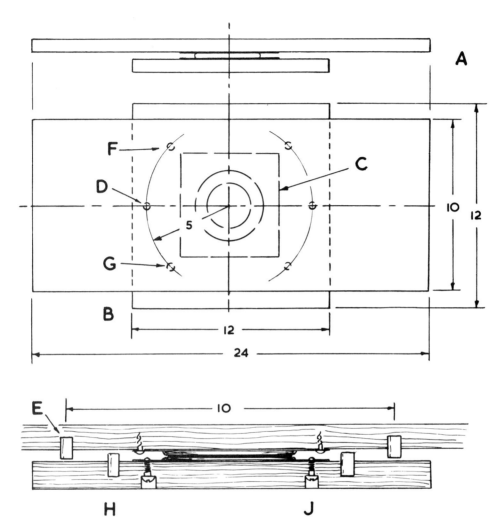

Fig. 2-23. Suggested sizes for the parts of a television turntable.

**Materials List for
Television Turntable**

1 top	³/₄ × 10 × 25
1 base	³/₄ × 12 × 12
1 lazy Susan bearing—6-inch size	

On the turntable shown, the pitch circle for the dowel positions is 5-inch radius. The top dowels are on the centerline. The bottom dowels are shown at 45 degrees, to give a movement just under 90 degrees, but you can space them to allow whatever movement you require. Measure the thickness of the lazy Susan

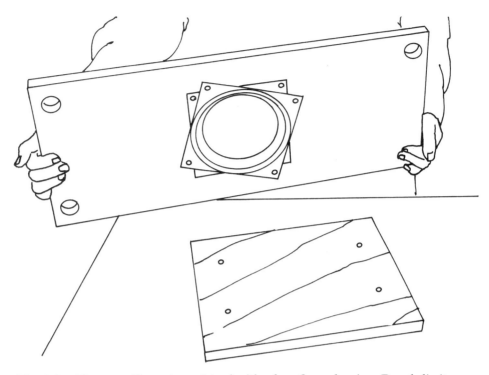

Fig. 2-24. The turntable parts are joined with a lazy Susan bearing. Dowels limit move-ment.

bearing, and have the dowels project enough to hit each other but not so far as to rub on the other part (FIG. 2-24).

The usual lazy Susan bearing does not come apart, so it is impossible to drive screws through it into the wood both ways. Instead, drive wood screws upwards into the top, but drive self-tapping screws (or screws into already-threaded holes) through the base into the bearing plate. One plate has small holes for the self-tapping screws or threaded holes. Position that plate on the base and mark through for small pilot holes to give you the positions on the other side, where you can enlarge the holes to suit the screws (6-gauge self-tapping should suit a 6-inch bearing plate). Counterbore so the screw heads are below the surface and their ends enter the plate far enough (FIG. 2-23J), but not so far as to touch the other plate.

If you have made a trial assembly of the base, remove the screws and position the lazy Susan bearing on the underside of the top. Drill for wood screws (6-gauge should suit a 6-inch bearing plate). Screw the bearing permanently to the top board.

Finish the wood with polish or varnish. Put a little oil on the balls in the bearing. Then put the base in place and attach it with the self-tapping screws.

If there are no feet under the television case to locate it in holes in the turntable top, glue cloth or thin rubber all over or only at the corners of the wood. Similar material under the base will prevent slipping and damage to a polished tabletop.

Plant Pot Container

You will probably grow plants in pots of many sizes, which you want to display in the yard or on a deck, but what about when you might want to bring them indoors? The usual plant pot is not a thing of beauty, but you can disguise it in a more attractive container.

Fig. 2-25. A plant pot container for use on the patio or indoors.

This container (FIG. 2-25) is all wood. You can give it a quality finish for use indoors, or an outdoor finish with paint. The sizes suggested (FIG. 2-26) will suit a pot about 9 inches in diameter and height. The same method might be used to make a container of almost any size; any wood could be used.

There are four slotted posts, into which the sectional sides are fitted. Pieces on the top and bottom close the slotted posts. Strips on bearers inside support the pot. Of course, the container is not intended to be watertight. For indoor use, there would have to be a bowl or tray inside under the pot. Outdoors, any surplus water can drain away between the bottom strips.

Make four identical posts and cut grooves in them (FIG. 2-26A) to suit the wood which will be used for the sides.

There are three sections in each side, so you have to make 12 pieces. Cut them all to the same length and hollow their lower edges to come between the

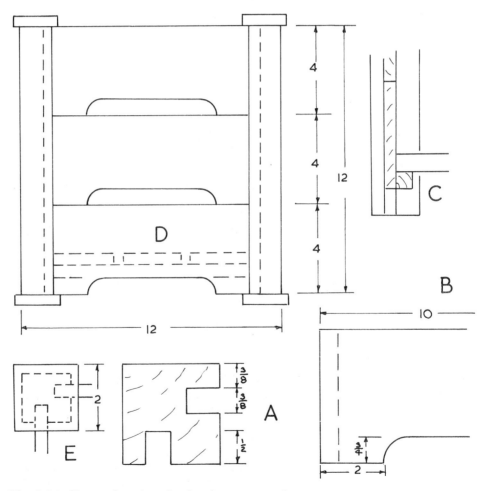

Fig. 2-26. *Sizes and sections for the plant pot container.*

**Materials List for
Plant Pot Container**

4 posts	$13 \times 1^{1}/_{2} \times {}^{1}/_{2}$
12 sides	$11 \times 4 \quad \times {}^{3}/_{8}$
2 bearers	$10 \times \quad {}^{1}/_{2} \times {}^{1}/_{2}$
3 strips	$11 \times 3 \quad \times {}^{1}/_{4}$
8 ends	$2 \times 2 \quad \times {}^{1}/_{2}$

posts and support the bottom strips (FIG. 2-26D). Use waterproof glue to fix the side sections into the slots. You can avoid the complications of damping if you drive a nail through each joint from inside to hold the parts while the glue sets. Assemble two opposite sides first; then bring them together with the other sections. Check squareness as viewed from above.

Fit bottom strips on the bearers inside. Exact widths do not matter, but leave drainage gaps.

Make 2-inch-square pieces for the top and bottom (FIG. 2-26E), and nail or saw them on. Finish to suit your requirements.

Step Stool

The cook might be glad of a seat a little higher than a normal chair—one that has steps to reach high shelves. There is an advantage in combining the two functions in one piece of furniture, particularly if the kitchen is compact. This step stool (FIG. 2-27) provides a seat 10 inches by 16 inches and 18 inches above the floor, with a step that swings out at half that height. Climbing to the top is safe when the steps are equally spaced. The stool is substantially framed and should withstand hard use. The folding step stows upside-down wholly within the stool. It swings out to rest on the floor, but if the stool is lifted with it out, it does not drop further.

Stool construction is straightforward. Position the rails accurately to pivot the step as shown in FIG. 2-28A so it will swing in and out without touching other parts.

Parts could be made of hardwood or softwood. The seat, tread sides, and top are plywood. Joints could be doweled or mortised and tenoned. Tenons are stronger in all joints. While dowels are adequate for most of them, the rails are better tenoned into the plywood sides of the step.

Set out a full-size end view of the stool (FIG. 2-28B) symmetrically about a centerline. Mark on it the positions of the top and bottom crosswise rails (FIGS. 2-29A and 2-29B). These are upright, although the legs slope. Also mark the top and bottom end rails (FIGS. 2-29C and 2-29D).

Join the top and bottom rails to the legs. There can be two, $^{1}/_{2}$-inch dowels in each bottom joint and three at the top. Otherwise use stub tenons (FIG. 2-29E).

Check that opposite ends match. Make the four crosswise rails and join these with dowels or tenons to the legs (FIG. 2-29F).

Fig. 2-27. The lower part of this step stool folds into the main part.

Materials List for Step Stool

1 top	10 × 16	× 1/2 plywood
1 step	6 × 12	× 1/2 plywood
2 step sides	8 × 9	× 1/2 plywood
4 legs	1 × 2	× 18
2 top rails	1 × 3	× 8
4 stool rails	3/4 × 1 1/2	× 14
3 step rails	3/4 × 1 1/2	× 12

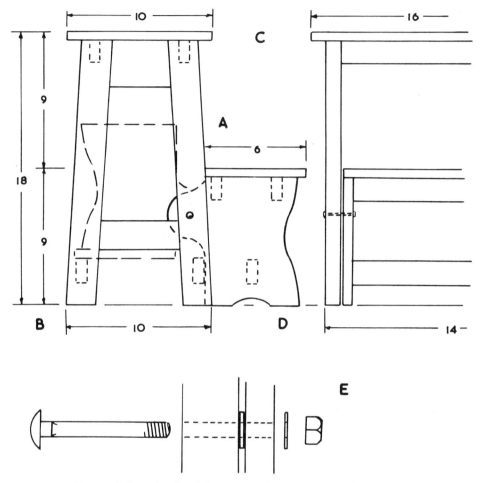

Fig. 2-28. *Sizes and pivot details of the step stool.*

Level the top of the framing and make the plywood top to fit (FIG. 2-28C). Round the edges and corners. For this stool, you might want to glue and screw down through the top into the rails. If you do not want screw heads showing, however, drive them upwards from pockets inside the rails.

Make the two sides for the step (FIGS. 2-28D and 2-29G). The pivot allows the side to swing to rest against a stool rail in the open position when the step top is horizontal. Mark the positions of the three step rails and the pivot hole. Cut the step sides to shape. Smooth all edges and around those that will be exposed.

Drill small holes to take nails at the pivot positions in the side. Use these as guides to check the pivot positions on the legs. Try the action of the step sides when swung fully in and out on nails.

Make the step rails a suitable length to allow the step sides to fit easily between the stool legs. They could be screwed through the plywood. Dowel

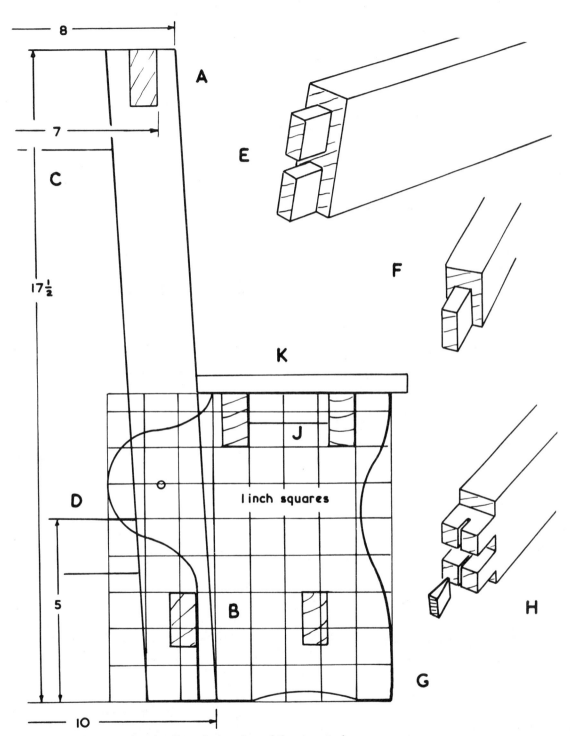

Fig. 2-29. Construction details and step sizes of the step stool.

joints in plywood would not work very well but tenons could be taken through and wedged (FIG. 2-19H). Put short strips between the ends of the top rails to take screws into the tread (FIG. 2-29). Make the tread (FIG. 2-29K) ends level with the plywood sides, and round the long edges. Glue and screw it in place.

The pivots may be 1/4-inch coach bolts. Enlarge the holes to suit. Include a washer at each side between the wood parts (FIG. 2-28E). You'll also want to add some form of locking nut to prevent the pivot from loosening.

A painted finish is appropriate, or you can varnish or paint the lower parts if you have used a suitable wood. In this case, paint only the tread and top. You might want to cover the top and tread, both for comfort and to reduce the risk of slipping. Upholstery is inappropriate, but plastic-coated fabric, pieces of carpet, or vinyl floor covering may be attached.

Rolling Tilt Bin

The bin in FIG. 2-30A is a container that tilts into its case, which is a table-high cabinet. When tilted out far enough to lift away, the bin can be rolled about on the floor. If you use it for trash in the kitchen or shop, you will be able to wheel it away instead of having to lift what might be a heavy load. Although this one is a self-contained unit, you could use the same kind of bin under a kitchen counter.

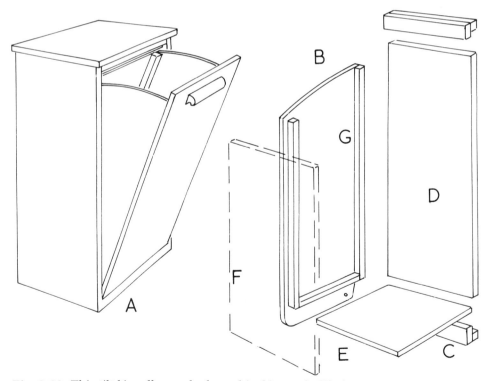

Fig. 2-30. This tilt bin rolls on wheels, and its bin can be lifted out.

The cabinet and bin front are 3/4-inch plywood. The other parts of the bin are 1/2-inch plywood. Strengthening pieces are 3/4-inch-square strips. The wheels are 2-inch diameter, which you can buy or make yourself on a lathe. (An alternative to wheels is to add a roller across.) A 1/4-inch steel rod will serve as an axle.

The front of the bin hooks over a two-part crosspiece at the bottom of the cabinet (FIG. 2-31A). Each side is cut so that the bin bottom comes above the cabinet crosspiece, then slopes down to within 1/4 inch of the bottom of the cabinet (FIG. 3-31B). The wheels or roller then fit on their axle through the sides, so they clear the bottom of the bin (FIG. 2-31A).

At the top, the bin front closes against a similar two-part crosspiece (FIG. 2-31). There is no need for a fastener because the bin will stay closed under its own weight.

The cabinet is box-like, with an overhanging top and an open bottom. Make the two sides 14 × 29 1/4 inches. Make the back the same length and 11 1/2 inches wide. Make the front crosspieces from 1- and 2-inch pieces of 3/4-inch plywood 11 1/2 inches long. Cut the top 15 inches square.

Join all the cabinet parts with 5/16-inch dowels at about 4-inch centers. Set out the bin sides (FIGS. 2-30B and 2-31). Sides come against the 3/4-inch front. At the back, sides should clear the inside of the cabinet by 1/4 inch. Cut the sides to hook over the crosspiece (FIGS. 2-30C and 2-31B). Bevel slightly and round the wood so they clear the crosspiece when tilted. Round rear corners (FIG. 2-31F).

The top edge of the side has to clear the cabinet crosspiece as the bin is swung out. To draw this curve (FIG. 2-31G), use the bottom front corner as a center and draw a curve from this to clear the crosspiece. Use an awl through a strip of wood and a pencil against the other end as a compass.

Make the bin front/door (FIG. 2-30D) to fit easily in the cabinet front opening. The bin bottom (FIG. 2-30E) fits above the level of the front notches in the sides. The back (FIG. 2-30F) fits between the sides and above the bottom. Round its top edge.

Put 3/4-inch-square strips on the sides to suit the positions of the other parts using glue and pins (FIG. 2-30G). Assemble the bin parts after checking their sizes in relation to the cabinet.

Materials List for Rolling Tilt Bin

2 cabinet sides	14 × 30 × 3/4	plywood
1 cabinet back	11 1/2 × 30 × 3/4	plywood
2 crosspieces	2 × 12 × 3/4	plywood
2 crosspieces	1 × 12 × 3/4	plywood
1 cabinet top	15 × 15 × 3/4	plywood
1 bin front	11 1/2 × 28 × 3/4	plywood
2 bin sides	12 × 28 × 1/2	plywood
1 bin bottom	12 × 12 × 1/2	plywood
1 bin back	11 × 23 × 1/2	plywood
4 strips	3/4 × 3/4 × 24	
4 strips	3/4 × 3/4 × 12	

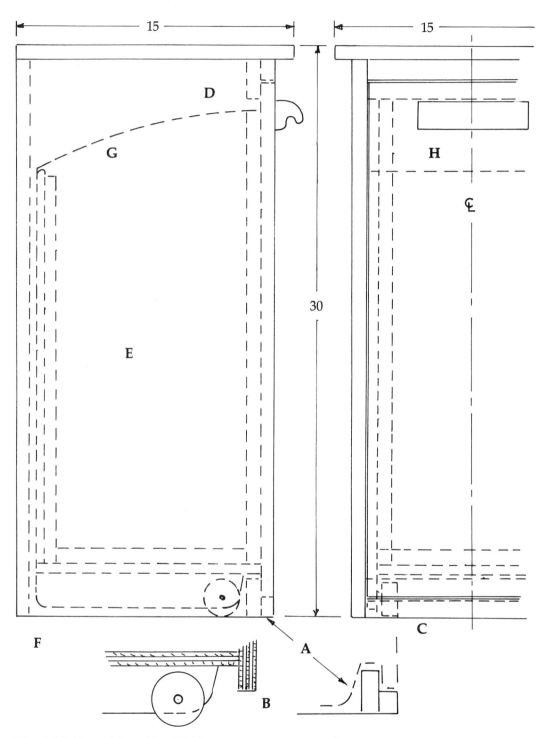

Fig. 2-31. Sizes of the rolling tilt bin.

Add a handle near the top of the front. You can make or buy one. A strip handle is shown in FIG. 2-31H, but you could use a knob.

Fit the wheels or roller and the axle. Try the action, then remove sharp edges and corners before finishing with paint.

Small Wall Cupboard

Most early homes used small wall cupboards. One with perforated metal panels served for food storage in the kitchen, while others with solid doors served in the living and bedrooms. Many developed from hanging shelves, to which a door was added in front. The example here is typical of many variations on a basic theme (FIG. 2-32A). In effect, it is a box with a door at the front.

On the sides, you can place rabbets for a rear panel and dadoes for the shelves. The dadoes can be either cut through or stopped for neatness at the front (FIG. 2-32B). Attach a bar across the inside of the top to take the main load when hanging. Deepen the rabbets in the sides to take the bar (FIG. 2-32C). Use screws through the bar into the wall to support the cupboard. You can supplement them with one or two other screws through the back panel lower down.

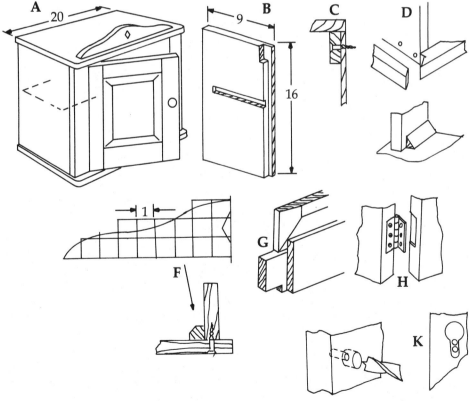

Fig. 2-32. Small wall cupboard.

Make the top overlap the sides. The bottom can overlap, but it is stronger if it fits between the sides and is notched around, with a mitered strip at each side (FIG. 2-32D). Attach stiles to each side of the door with nails or screws through them, and cover them with stopping or plugs. If you want a smooth front appearance, glue them with small fillets added to increase the glue area inside (FIG. 2-32E). When you assemble the cupboard, be careful to check squareness. The door opening must be true; a door only slightly out of square soon becomes very obvious.

To break up the plainness of the cupboard, fit a shaped piece to hold it above the front of the top (FIG. 2-32F). Use glue and screws from below. You can also place a glued fillet behind it.

A single-paneled door is shown with fairly wide framing for stiffness. The corners are mortised and tenoned in the way just described, and the panel shows the bevels at the front (FIG. 2-32G).

You can set the hinges on the surface for a kitchen cupboard or into the edges if the cupboard is made of attractive hardwood and polished. Traditionally, hinges were let into both surfaces (FIG. 2-32H), but it is less trouble to let into one edge only, adjusting the depth to suit the clearance needs.

You must usually do some fitting when you hang a door. Make the door near to its final size, but hang it with one screw in each hinge. Note what needs to be planed off, then remove the door, plane it, and try again until the clearance all around is the same and you can drive all the hinge screws.

You can use a turned wooden knob at the side opposite to the hinges. There is no need for a door stop because the door touches the shelves. You might be able to use the cupboard without a door fastener, but an appropriate type would be a knob with a shaft passing through to a turn button inside.

Cupboards had locks that screwed to the inside, and the lock bolt went behind the door frame as the key was turned. Use care in cutting the escutcheon hole. Give it enough clearance for the key, but do not make it too large. Measure the size of the key. Press the lock into position inside. The point of the post the

Materials List for Small Wall Cupboard

1 top	11	× 20 ×	$5/8$
1 bottom	11	× 20 ×	$5/8$
2 sides	9	× 16 ×	$5/8$
2 fronts	2	× 16 ×	$3/4$
1 back rail	2	× 18 ×	$5/8$
1 back, to make up	18	× 16 ×	$3/8$
1 shelf	6	× 18 ×	$5/8$
1 top decoration	3	× 18 ×	$5/8$
or from molding	$1^{1}/2$	× 40 ×	$3/4$
4 door frames	2	× 16 ×	$3/4$
1 door panel	11	× 11 ×	$1/2$

key fits on will make a dent in the wood. Drill through to remove some of the waste, (FIG. 2-32J) and clean out the slot with a chisel and file (FIG. 2-32C).

Some locks are supplied with a brass escutcheon liner, which makes a neat finish to the hole. This has a slight taper. If you cut the wood to match the smaller side, forcing the liner in will tighten it as it compresses surrounding wood fibers slightly. Escutcheon plates, which fix on the surface over the keyhole, are usually made of brass and held with small brass pins. For good-quality work, you can purchase matching sets that include hinges, knob, and escutcheon plate in an antique brass finish.

The furniture fashion in early Victorian days and before for moldings also was felt in America. You can make a variation of this basic cupboard with moldings around top and bottom (FIG. 2-33A). Make the framing at the front with moldings all around instead of only at the edges. Ideally, you should use mortise-and-tenon joints for the corners of the frame, but it would be satisfactory to use cross-lap joints (FIG. 2-33B).

Make the front edges of the top and bottom level with the sides and fit the front frame assembly against this. See that the front frame is carefully squared, but make its outer edges slightly oversize, and plane them level with the sides after fitting (FIG. 2-33C).

Any of the standard patterns of machine-made moldings will be suitable. Place the molding around the top and bottom edges, with mitered front corners (FIG. 2-33D), then add further strips with rounded or molded edges to give an appearance of greater bulk (FIG. 2-33E).

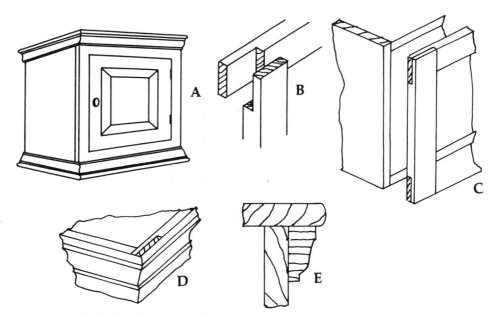

Fig. 2-33. Molded wall cupboard.

Corner Display Cabinet

The corner of a room is a good place to display valuable or interesting items, such as crockery and trophies, which will look better behind glass. These items can be in a case that hangs on the wall or stands on another piece of furniture. Various sizes are possible, but if the items to be displayed are few and not very large, a compact cabinet looks neat and will fill a space that otherwise would be vacant.

This cabinet (FIG. 2-34) has storage on three levels and has a glass door. It could be screwed to the wall so the contents are at eye level, or it could stand on the corner cabinet (see previous project) to make an attractive piece of combined furniture.

You can vary the sizes to suit the intended contents. The door opening, as drawn, is about 11 inches wide, and the greatest height that can be accommodated is about 10 inches. The best appearance is when the cabinet is tall in relation to its width. Some edge molding will improve the look. You can make all of the profiles with one router cutter, or you can combine square edges with simple rounding.

This cabinet (FIG. 2-34) has storage on three levels and has a glass door. It could be screwed to the wall so the contents are at eye level, or it could stand on the corner cabinet (see previous project) to make an attractive combined piece.

Check the squareness of the corner of the room. If it is out of square, make a template at least as large as the cabinet bottom out of scrap hardboard or plywood, and use that instead of a square for parts that have to fit into the corner. Set out the bottom (FIGS. 2-35A and 2-36A), allowing the extension for molded edges. Mark on the bottom where the other parts will come. Use this as a guide when preparing parts that connect to it.

Make the two backs (FIG. 2-36B). One is narrower than the other by the thickness of the wood, so projections along the walls will be the same when they overlap. Make dado grooves for the shelves (FIG. 2-36C). Prepare both ends for dowels. Overlap the backs, and glue and screw them together.

Materials List for Corner Display Cabinet

1 top	$5/8$	× 15		× 27
1 bottom	$5/8$	× 15		× 27
2 sides	$5/8$	× $14^{1}/_{2}$		× 29
2 shelves	$5/8$	× 12		× 20
2 fronts	$3/4$	× 4		× 29
2 fronts	$3/4$	× 2		× 29
1 front above door	$3/4$	× $1^{1}/_{2}$		× 12
1 molding	$5/8$	× 1		× 17
2 moldings	$5/8$	× 1		× 6
2 door parts	$3/4$	× $1^{1}/_{2}$		× 28
2 door parts	$3/4$	× $1^{1}/_{2}$		× 12
2 beads	$5/16$	×	$3/8$	× 25
2 beads	$5/16$	×	$3/8$	× 9

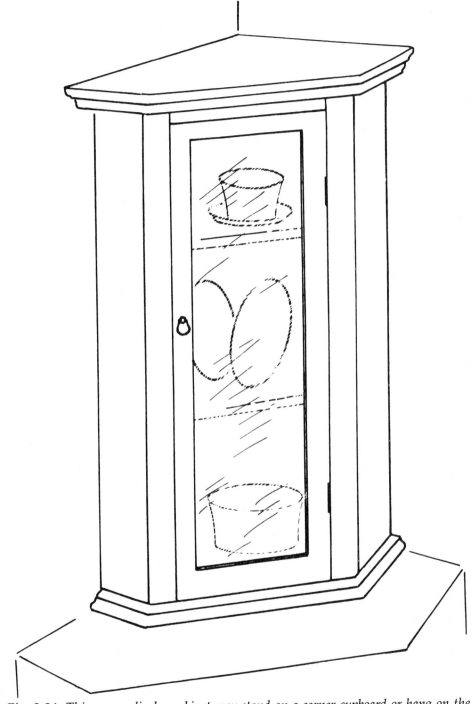

Fig. 2-34. This corner display cabinet may stand on a corner cupboard or hang on the wall.

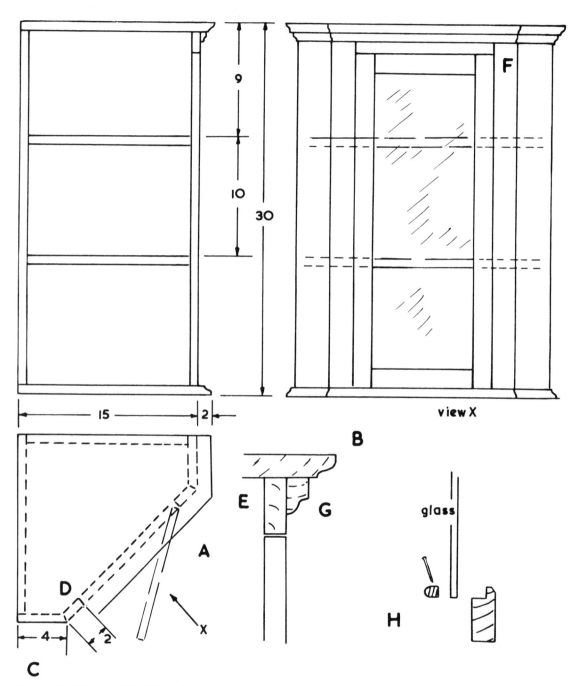

Fig. 2-35. Sizes and details of the corner display cabinet.

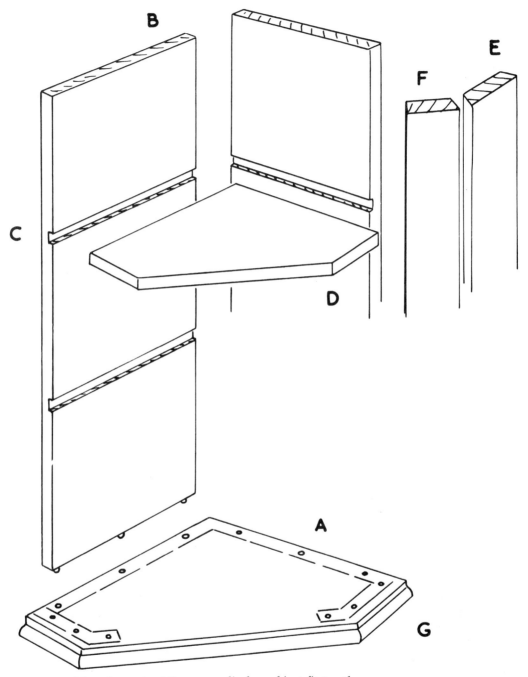

Fig. 2-36. How the parts of the corner display cabinet fit together.

Make the two shelves (FIG. 2-36D). They extend the full width of the back. The front piece will fit against them. Check with the marked bottom that the shelves follow the correct outline. If necessary, veneer or put a lip on the edge of each shelf that shows inside the door. The shelf edges act as door stops.

Make the top to the same outline as the bottom. Mold both parts on the exposed edges (FIG. 2-35B).

Prepare the fronts the same height as the backs. The wider pieces (FIGS. 2-35C and 2-36E) cover the edges of the backs and fit against the walls. The narrow pieces (FIGS. 2-35D and 2-36F) have their square edges forming the door opening. Miter the two sets of parts to fit against each other, then glue and dowel them.

When the cabinet has been assembled, there is little strain on most joints. To help locate the parts correctly during assembly, however, set a few thin dowels into the top and bottom (FIG. 2-36G) and between the fronts and the shelves. At the top of the door opening, include a strip across (FIGS. 2-35E and 2-35F) with dowels to the fronts.

Fit the shelves to the backs, then the fronts to them, followed by the top and bottom. The top overhang can be further decorated with a narrow strip carried around and cut with a similar molding (FIG. 2-35G).

Prepare the door parts with a rabbet. Its size depends on the thickness of the glass, but leaving about 3/16 inch at the front will usually be satisfactory.

Make the door with mortise-and-tenon joints. Let in hinges. You can use a spring or magnetic catch and handle. The handle might be the type with a shaft through to operate a catch inside.

To fit the glass, make narrow beads with mitered corners to go inside the rabbet. The strips could be square, but they look better if the inner surface is rounded (FIG. 2-35H). Before you fix the strips with pins, stain and polish the wood so you do not risk marking the glass.

If the cabinet is to stand on the corner cabinet, screw into each wall near the top to prevent tilting. If the cabinet is to hang without other support, fasten four or six screws into the walls through the backs.

Chairside Magazine Rack

This is a unit with space for magazines and books or other items and a flat top to form a small table. The unit stands beside a chair and is either on casters so it can be moved or given a plinth (FIG. 2-37). The main parts might be solid wood, veneered particleboard, or plywood (for a painted finish). The slats could be in a contrasting color. Varnished light hardwood looks good when the other parts are given a dark finish.

The sizes shown (FIG. 2-38) will suit most magazines, but if you have particular books or magazines to accommodate, alter the sizes. Doweled construction can be used for the main parts. The slats are screwed on.

Make the ends and divider (FIGS. 2-39A, 2-39B, and 2-39C) all the same height, but round the magazine end to slat level. Make the lengthwise divider (FIG. 2-39D). Mark and drill it and the adjoining parts for dowels.

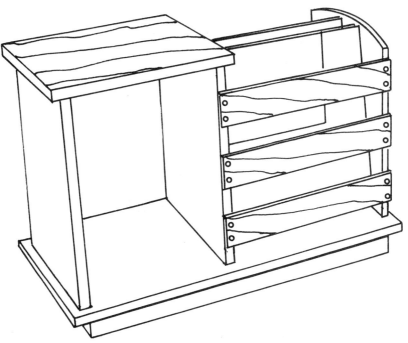

***Fig. 2-37.** This chairside magazine rack has space for books as well as magazines and newspapers and a small tablecloth.*

Materials List for
Chairside Magazine Rack

2 ends	$5/8 \times$	8	$\times 12$
1 divider	$5/8 \times$	8	$\times 12$
1 divider	$5/8 \times$	10	$\times 12$
1 bottom	$5/8 \times$	9	$\times 21$
1 top	$5/8 \times$	9	$\times 12$
3 slats	$3/8 \times$	2	$\times 20$
3 slats	$3/8 \times$	2	$\times 12$
2 plinths	$3/4 \times$	$1^{1}/2 \times$	20
2 plinths	$3/4 \times$	$1^{1}/2 \times$	8

The bottom (FIG. 2-39E) projects $1/2$ inch all around and may have its corners rounded. The top (FIG. 2-39F) should have its edge level with the divider but projecting $1/2$ inch on the other three sides. Round the corners to match the bottom.

Mark and drill all the main parts for dowels ($1/4$-inch dowels at about 3-inch intervals should be satisfactory). Assemble these parts tightly and squarely.

The laths extend the full length of the back (FIG. 2-39G), but only over the magazine rack at the front (FIG. 2-39H). Round all the exposed edges. Fit the slats with two screws at each crossing. They could be made a design feature by using plated roundhead screws.

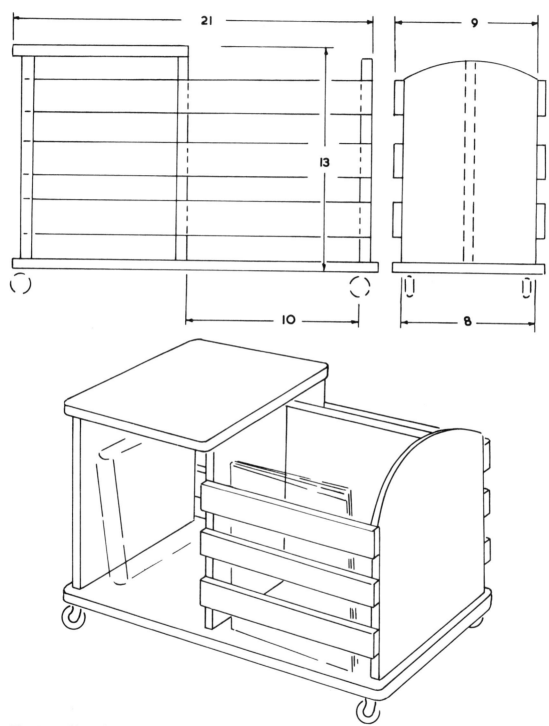

Fig. 2-38. Sizes of the chairside magazine rack.

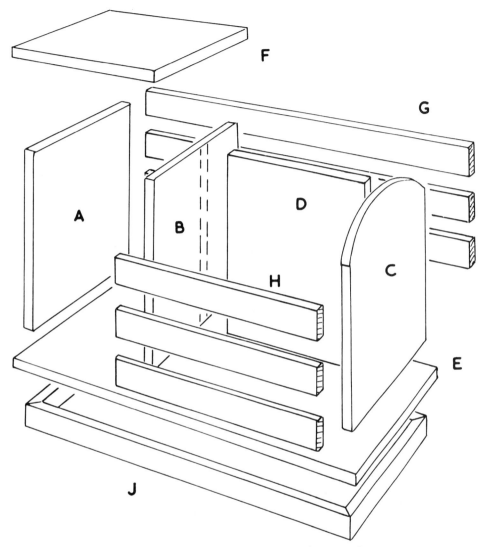

Fig. 2-39. How the parts of the chairside magazine rack go together.

If you want to use casters, choose the type with a drilled plate fitting to screw on. If you want to use a plinth (FIG. 2-39J), make it from strips mitered at the corners.

Corner Whatnot

Display shelves separated by turned posts can be made as four-legged long stands to any height and are often termed *whatnots*. A corner version can have three supports, and the rear one need not be turned. This project has three shelves (FIG. 2-40), but you could add more and vary the spacing. The square corner post pro-

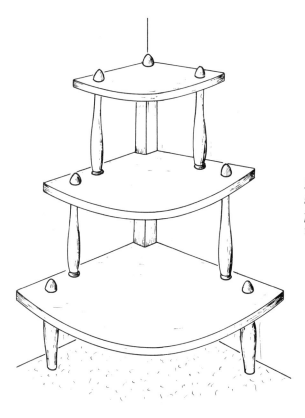

Fig. 2-40. A corner whatnot serves as a display unit in a part of the room that might not otherwise be used.

Materials List for Corner Whatnot

1 corner post	$1^{1}/_{2}$	×	$1^{1}/_{2}$	×	38
1 shelf	$^{3}/_{4}$	×	18	×	26
1 shelf	$^{3}/_{4}$	×	15	×	23
1 shelf	$^{3}/_{4}$	×	12	×	20
2 legs	2	×	2	×	10
2 spindles	2	×	2	×	17
2 spindles	2	×	2	×	18

vides rigidity by going through in one piece. The shelves are reduced in size, and there are separate spindles supporting the front corners. All of the spindles are within the capacity of a small lathe.

The total height is 36 inches (FIG. 2-41A). The largest shelf is 18 inches along the side. The others are 15 inches and 12 inches. They could be solid wood with the grain lines diagonal, or plywood covered at the edges with veneer. The wood for the other parts could be stained the same color or contrasting colors.

Make the corner post (FIG. 2-42A) with notches $^{1}/_{4}$ inch deep on two surfaces for the shelves. At the top, drill a $^{1}/_{2}$-inch hole centrally for a finial.

Make the shelves (FIG. 2-41B) with circular outlines and notched to fit into the corner post. Drill $^{3}/_{4}$-inch holes to take the spindles below and above (FIG. 2-42).

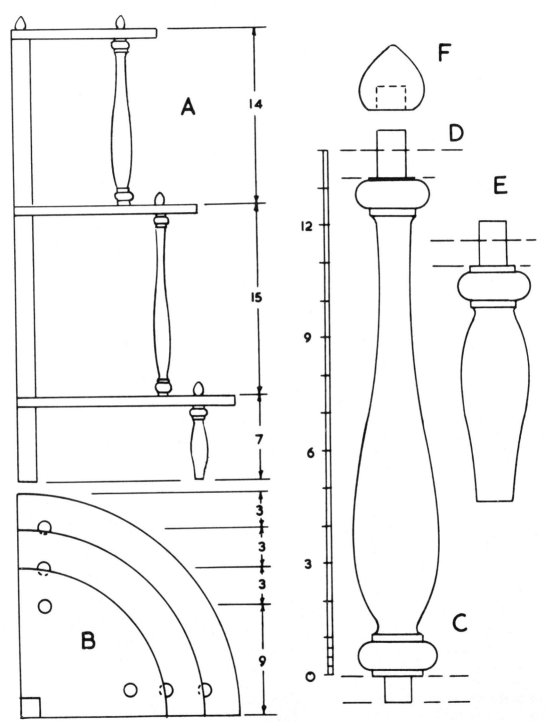

Fig. 2-41. Sizes of the corner whatnot and patterns for the turnings.

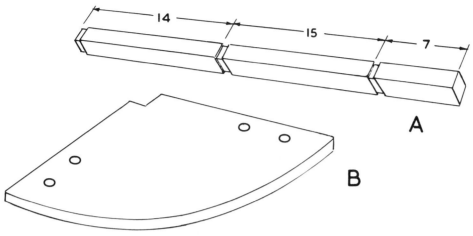

Fig. 2-42. Details of the corner post (A) and shelf (B).

When making the spindles, use the spacings on the corner post as a guide to lengths between shoulders. Turn the spindles between shelves (FIG. 2-41C) with ³/₄-inch-diameter dowel ends. At the bottom, the length is the thickness of the shelf, but at the top, the dowel projects through ¹/₂ inch (FIG. 2-41D). Make the two feet project in a similar way (FIG. 2-41E).

Turn tops to glue on the projections (FIG. 2-41F). Make a matching one with a dowel end to fit in the hole at the top of the corner post.

When you assemble, the joints to the corner post can have screws or nails driven diagonally upwards. Start assembly from the bottom up, and check squareness in all directions at each stage. Do not put the tops on the turned projections until you are satisfied that the assembly is correct.

Stiffened Shelves

When a block of shelves is made with an open back, any twisting strains have to be taken by the joints at the ends of shelves. One way to provide extra strength is to add a back, which is usually done today with plywood. Because plywood was not available to early furniture makers and solid wood cut thin and in sufficient width meant considerable extra work, they stiffened in other ways. A board above the top shelf provided rigidity and formed a back where it was wanted.

The example in FIG. 2-43 has a 5- and 8-inch shelf with shaved end pieces. There is a back at the top (FIG. 2-44A), and you can fit a strip below the lower shelf to take additional screws to the wall (FIG. 2-44B). If you want to keep things on that shelf away from the wall, arrange the strip above instead of below it.

Mark out the pair of ends (FIG. 2-45). Prepare the wood for the shelves and back. Cut dado grooves for the shelves (FIG. 2-44C) and make rabbets for the back to the same depth (FIG. 2-44D). If you fit a strip against the lower shelf, that could also be rabbetted or just cut to fit between the ends.

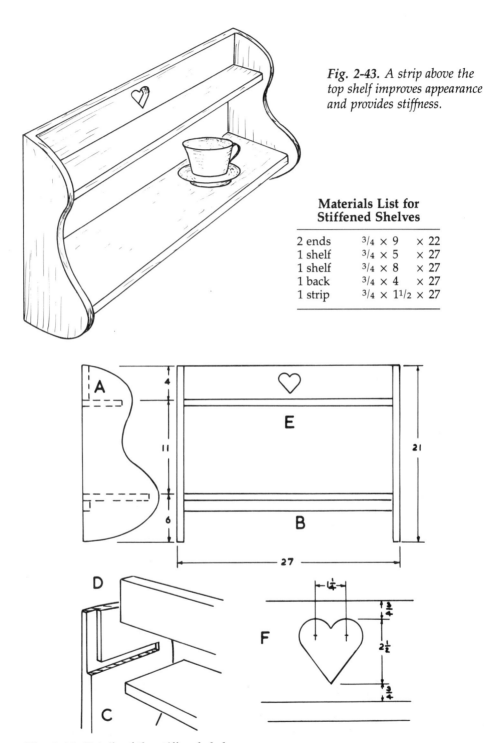

Fig. 2-43. A strip above the top shelf improves appearance and provides stiffness.

Materials List for Stiffened Shelves

2 ends	$3/4 \times 9$	$\times 22$
1 shelf	$3/4 \times 5$	$\times 27$
1 shelf	$3/4 \times 8$	$\times 27$
1 back	$3/4 \times 4$	$\times 27$
1 strip	$3/4 \times 1^1/2$	$\times 27$

Fig. 2-44. Details of the stiffened shelves.

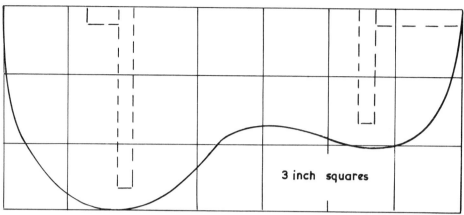

Fig. 2-45. The shape of the shelf ends.

Many early pieces of furniture were decorated with cutout hearts, and one is shown on the back (FIG. 2-44E). Drill two holes with sufficient overlap to make the top shape, then cut from them to the point (FIG. 2-44F).

When you assemble, use a few screws upwards through the top shelf into the back, as well as glue.

Nesting Trays

Trays have always been useful in the kitchen and dining room. A set of three that will fit into each other for storage or easy transport when empty are attractive. These three trays (FIG. 2-46) are the same, except that two of them nest into the large one. When they are in that position, the handle holes are in line to allow you to still push your fingers through and carry them.

The sizes suggested (FIG. 2-47A) for the large tray are 5 inches high, 14 inches wide, and 21 inches long. All parts are 1/2 inch thick. The frames should be a close-grained hardwood. The bases could be the same or you could use 1/2-inch plywood, as its edges will be hidden. It might be veneered, or you could cover it with cloth.

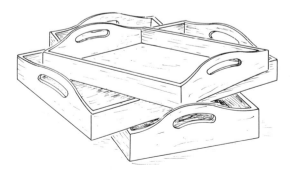

Fig. 2-46. These three trays fit into each other and can be lifted together when not required for separate use.

Materials List for Nesting Trays

2 ends	$1/2 \times$	5	$\times 15$
2 ends	$1/2 \times$	$4^1/2$	$\times 14$
2 ends	$1/2 \times$	4	$\times 13$
2 sides	$1/2 \times$	$3^1/2$	$\times 22$
2 sides	$1/2 \times$	3	$\times 21$
2 sides	$1/2 \times$	$2^1/2$	$\times 20$
1 bottom	$1/2 \times$	13	$\times 21$
1 bottom	$1/2 \times$	$11^1/2$	$\times 20$
1 bottom	$1/2 \times$	10	$\times 19$

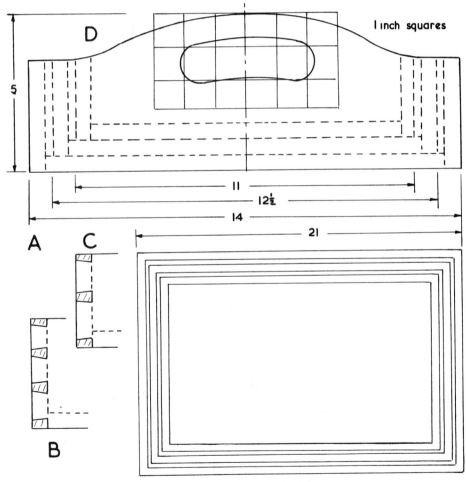

Fig. 2-47. Details of the tray ends and joints.

There are several, possibly more modern corner joints, but an early crafts-man would have used dovetails. For the large tray, arrange three tails (FIG. 2-47B), but the other trays need only have two at each corner (FIG. 2-47C).

Draw at least half an end view of the large tray (FIG. 2-47D). From that make the two ends and use them as templates for marking the ends of the other trays. Allow 1/4-inch clearance at the sides and enough for the thickness of each bot-tom, so the hand holes will come level.

Make the sides and cut their corner joints. Round the top edges of all parts and the insides of the hand holes. Make the bottoms to fit inside. Be careful that all corners are square so the trays will fit neatly. Hold the bottoms in with glue and pins through the sides and ends.

3

Seating

None of us are prepared to stand indefinitely. We are not built that way, so seats of many types are needed in and around the home. These can range from simple stools to chairs that might be used while eating or working to others designed for relaxation.

Seats of many types have been described in several of the books from which projects have been selected. Those included in this section are considered good examples of their types, are very fit for each purpose, and are good examples of projects which are satisfying to build.

Some woodworkers believe that chair making is a difficult process, but you can achieve worthwhile results if you follow the step-by-step instructions.

Three Stools

A stool has to perform two main functions. First, it should be fit to be used as a seat, or even a table, by a child. Secondly, it should provide you with something to stand on if you want to reach higher than you can when standing on the floor. These requirements have to be considered when deciding on sizes. You can vary sizes quite widely without affecting the method of construction. Sizes shown on drawings and in materials lists should suit many conditions. Stability is an important consideration. The area covered by the extremities of the stool feet should not be much less than the area of the top. If you allow much overhang, anyone stepping near an end could tip the stool, with unfortunate results. An overhang up to 1 inch would not matter.

Almost any wood can be used. A good furniture hardwood will be best, but much depends on the intended use. A good general-purpose stool can be of softwood finished with paint. But a stool made from hardwood with a clear finish can take its place with your best furniture. For a child's stool, choose a wood that does not splinter easily.

The three stools described here all fulfill similar functions; your choice of design depends on the appearance you prefer. The work involved in making them is about the same, and all are straightforward. If you are unsure of your ability to make more advanced furniture, building one or more of these stools will serve as a good introduction. The designs are simple enough to be quickly made, and you could soon produce a quantity for your friends or for sale.

First Stool

The first stool (FIG. 3-1) might be considered the basic nailed or screwed design. It is intended to be made of 1-inch softwood boards, although you could use slightly thinner hardwood. The legs are splayed a little in the length and width to improve appearance and provide stability. As shown (FIG. 3-1A), the stool is twice as long as it is wide.

Set out the leg slope (FIG. 3-1B). This gives you the angles to trim the tops and bottoms of the legs and the length down the slope—although you will probably not bother about the slight difference if you work to the vertical height.

Make the two legs with their grain vertical and tapering from 12 to 10 inches (FIG. 3-1C). The top is a simple rectangle. Mark on it where the legs will come, and round the corners.

The brace (FIG. 3-1D) has a top edge length to fit between the leg positions marked on the underside of the top. Take the angle for the ends from the leg setting out. The cutouts under the legs and the brace are the same. They are shown as parts of a circle (FIG. 3-1E). They form feet on the legs to help the stool stand level. The curve under the brace can be used as a hand grip, so round its edges.

Materials List for Three Stools

First stool

1 top	1	×	10	×	21
2 legs	1	×	12	×	12
1 brace	1	×	5	×	18

Second stool

1 top	3/4	×	7	×	17
2 legs	3/4	×	7	×	9
2 braces	3/4	×	2 1/2	×	17

Third stool

1 top	1	×	12	×	22
2 legs	1	×	10	×	12
3 braces	1	×	2	×	21

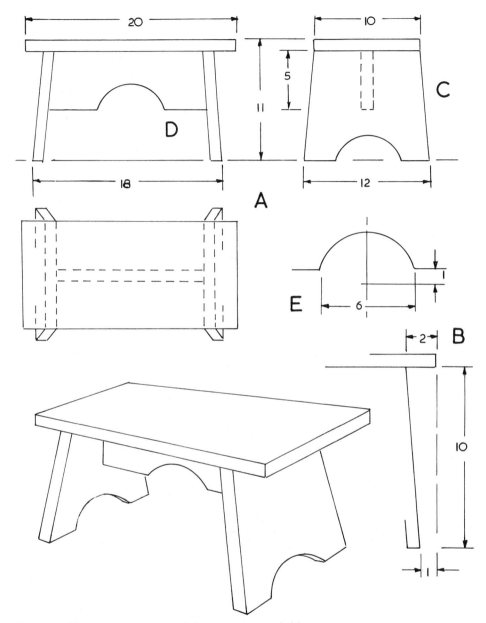

Fig. 3-1. This small stool is useful as a step or a child's seat.

Mark the brace positions on the legs, then drill for nails or screws, and use glue as you join these parts together. Drill the top in a similar way and join it on, using the guidelines to see that the parts are assembled squarely.

Round all exposed edges. Check that the stool stands without rocking. If necessary, plane a little off a foot. Finish with paint or varnish.

Second Stool

The second stool uses 3/4-inch wood and is shown here smaller overall than the first (FIG. 3-2A), but you could make it any size. This stool has some decorative shaping, but you could make it with straight edges. Much early furniture had shaped edges for the sake of appearance, but also to disguise errors in shaping

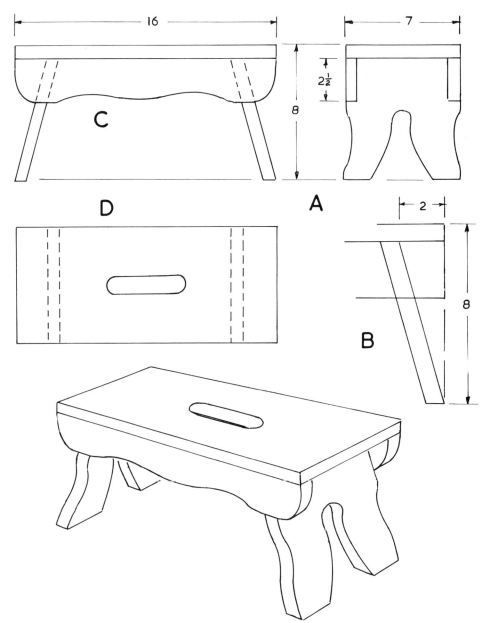

Fig. 3-2. This stool has more shaping than the first one, and a hand hole.

the wood, which might have been rough and probably not fully seasoned. Errors in curves are not so obvious as in an edge which should be straight, but tore up or split under the plane. Again, you can choose softwood with a painted finish or hardwood with a clear finish.

Set out the slope of a leg (FIGS. 3-2B and 3-2C). This will give you its length and the angles to cut the notches and ends (FIG. 3-3A). Make the two legs identical (FIG. 3-3B). Cut the notches to suit the actual thicknesses of the side braces (FIG. 3-3B). Alternatively, you could cut dado joints, as described for the third stool. However, for a small stool, glued and nailed or with screwed joints should be adequate.

The braces (FIG. 3-3C) are parallel where they meet the legs, but otherwise the lower edges are shaped (FIG. 3-3D). Take sharpness off all curved edges of the legs and braces. Assemble the legs and braces, being careful to maintain squareness and to avoid twist.

Make the top to match the lower parts. It is shown with a hand hole at the center (FIG. 3-2D) for carrying. This could be 1 × 5 inches, made by drilling its ends and sawing away the waste.

Round all exposed edges and corners. Correct any tendency to wobble by planing feet, if necessary, before applying your chosen finish.

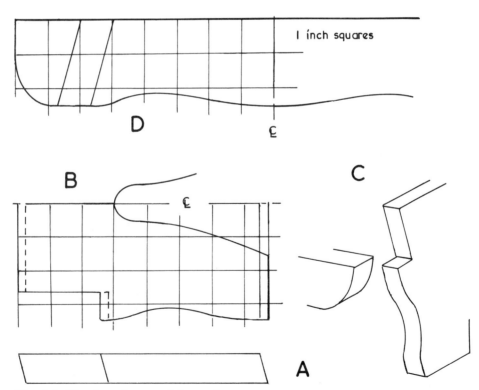

Fig. 3-3. The shaped parts of the stool.

Third Stool

The third stool (FIG. 3-4) is braced by three lengthwise pieces of comparatively reduced depth, so the effect is a rather lighter appearance, but with no reduction in strength. In some ways the stool is similar to early tables. The suggested sizes (FIG. 3-4) are for a stool made of 1-inch softwood boards, but oak with a waxed finish would give a contemporary appearance with some tables. Keep in mind,

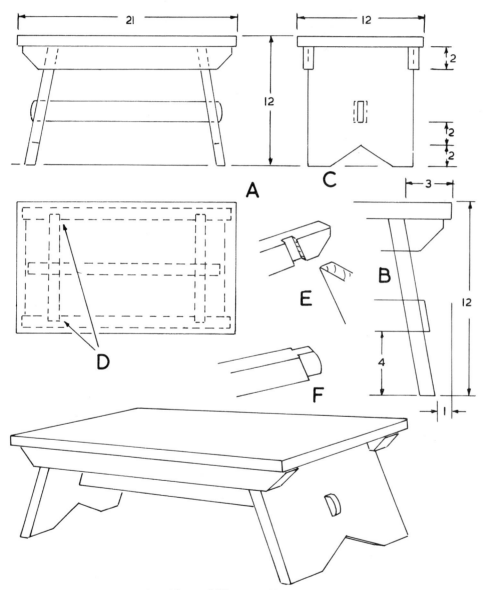

Fig. 3-4. *This stool is made with a rail like a small table.*

though, that a hardwood stool might be rather heavy if it is intended to be moved frequently.

The top overlaps the other parts by 1/2 inch. The legs fit into dado grooves in the top braces. The lower brace has tenons through the legs, and they may extend with rounded ends. The method of construction provides more strength in itself than in the other stools, but the parts should be glued and nailed or screwed.

Set out an end (FIG. 3-4B) to get the angles and lengths of the legs and braces. Make the two legs. The bottom cutout is shown as a simple V (FIG. 3-4C), but you could curve it. Mark the positions of the mortises, but do not cut them until you prepare the brace tenons. The legs will fit into dadoes in the top braces, without themselves being notched (FIG. 3-4D).

Make the top braces and cut the dadoes to match the thickness of the legs (FIG. 3-4E). The length is 1 inch shorter than the top. Bevel the ends.

Use your end setting out to get the length between the shoulders of the bottom brace. Mark tenons 1/2 inch thick and long enough to go through the legs and project 1/2 inch. Cut the tenons and round the projections (FIG. 3-4F); then make mortises in the legs to match.

Glue the parts and clamp them tightly while nails or screws are driven. Check squareness and freedom from twist. Cut the top to overlap 1/2 inch all around. This allows you to round the edges and corners well. The edges of the lower brace could also be rounded; it might be used as a handle for carrying the stool upside-down. Finish the wood with paint, varnish, or wax.

Woven-Top Stool

A stool with interwoven cord forming a flat pattern on top can have a dual purpose. If made at the right height, it can serve as a seat in front of a dresser or a worktable, or as a bar stool. The slightly flexible top is more comfortable than a plain wooden seat. With a close weave, the stool can also serve as a table beside a bed or elsewhere.

Several materials can be used for the top. There are many attractive cords manufactured from man-made fibers, and the appearance of some natural cords also suit stools. Suitable cords made especially for stool seating are sold by craft shops, or you can find other cords available in shops catering to boating needs. Seagrass is an attractive seating cord obtainable either in natural color or already dyed. Most materials are available in several thicknesses. There is more work in weaving thin cord, and the result might not be as rigid when you have completed the project. Thick cord can be woven quickly, but if there are not many over-and-under tucks, the result is not so attractive. This stool was made 13 inches square (FIG. 3-5), and cord between 1/8- and 3/16-inch diameter should be satisfactory. Some cord is supplied in metric sizes; the near equivalents are 3 millimeters and 5 millimeters.

Fig. 3-5. *A tall stool with a flat woven top can also be used as a bedside table.*

The frame is best made of strong hardwood. The joints should be mortise and tenon, because sections are not large enough for satisfactory dowel joints. If the stool is used as a seat, it must withstand the tendency of some users to rock on two legs. The combination of suitable wood, double lower rails, and good joints provides a good resistance to strain.

The frame can be stained and polished to match other furniture, and the colors used in the top can match other fabrics. If there is no particular color needed, a natural cord one way and a colored one the other way suits most situations. Natural in both directions will give a traditional effect.

The framework has square rails at the top for the woven seat, and they must be at the same level. The other rails can be higher one way than the other to allow

4 legs	$1^{1/2} \times 1^{1/2} \times 24$
4 top rails	$1 \times 1 \times 13$
8 lower rails	$^{3/4} \times 1 \times 13$

tenons of greater length and strength. For maximum strength those rails have barefaced tenons, allowing thicker wood for maximum rigidity. The sizes suggested make a stool that is a compromise between a seat and a bedside table.

Cut the wood for the legs overlong at first. Mark them together (FIG. 3-6A) so the sizes match, but pair them in twos for the different heights of the lower rails (FIG. 3-6B).

The stool does not have to be square, although that will suit most needs. It is shown 13 inches square over the legs, but it could be 12 × 15 inches, or any size you wish. Mark the length between shoulders of all rails together if square, or all together each way if not square. It is the length between shoulders that is important. The actual tenons can be left long until the joints are cut.

Mark the top tenons long enough to almost meet (FIG. 3-6C). This will be about 1 inch, although the mitered ends reduce the effective length (FIG. 3-6D). Tenon thickness can be 1/2 inch. Mark and cut the tenons and their mortises at the same time.

For the lower rails, cut away one side to leave tenons about 1 inch long (FIG. 3-6E). Mark mortises to suit. Round the top rails slightly (FIG. 3-6F). Except for taking the sharpness off edges, leave the lower rails as they are.

Cut the legs to length. The tops could be rounded, shaped to a shallow cone, or beveled all round, as shown (FIG. 3-6G). In the finished stool, the tops of the legs are prominent; make sure shaping is even and surfaces are smooth.

The legs can be left square, but if some decoration is required, do this in the gaps between the bottom rails and the top. With a lathe you could do some turned decoration. Another way is to put a chamfer or bevel on the outer edges or on all edges. A router would make a chamfer with rounded ends (FIG. 3-6H). The traditional wagon beveling has triangular ends (FIG. 3-6J). The name comes from the decoration done on the edges of wood in old-time wagons. A router bevel could be converted by handwork with a chisel. A further step is to make little nicks beyond the main bevels (FIG. 3-6K).

Any lack of squareness will be very obvious, so assemble carefully. Make up two opposite sides squarely and without twist. See that they match. Add the rails the other way, again checking squareness and measuring diagonals. It helps to assemble on a flat surface where you can stand back and look at the stool from several directions. If it looks right, you have a good stool.

To get tight joints, you should clamp them. If you do not have many clamps, pull the joints tight one way, then drive fine nails through the tenons from the inner surfaces of the legs. You can then move the clamps to the next joints.

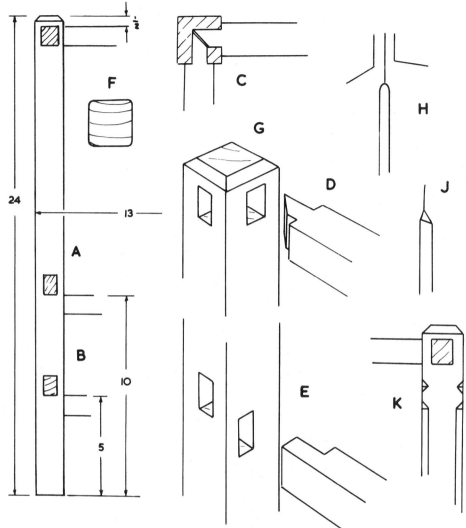

Fig. 3-6. Sizes and details of the woven top stool.

For most stools, it is advisable to stain and polish the wood before weaving the top. You might want to give a final coat of polish or varnish after the top has been worked because it is difficult to avoid some abrasion of the wood as you move the stool around during weaving.

Weaving

The top is woven with groups of strands across and wraps around the rails between them, with the same arrangements both ways. Several combinations are possible, but four across and two wraps will make a pleasing top.

Make two or three shuttles from scrap wood (FIG. 3-7A). Exact sizes are not important; these are for winding cord used in putting on the pattern in the first direction.

Knot the end of the cord and tack it into a leg under a rail (FIG. 3-7B). Put on four turns across the stool with only a moderate tension; how tight depends on the stretch in the cord. Weaving the other way will tighten these turns. You have to judge the amount of tension needed to get a taut top.

Wrap around the rail opposite to where you started (FIG. 3-7C). Return underneath and wrap twice around the near rail (FIG. 3-7D). Take four more turns across and so on until you have covered the rails that way. Always wrap at the far side before the near side or you will get a diagonal crossing on top. Press the turns close together along the rails, but adjust the spacing so you get a full set of four across on completion. Finish by tacking to a leg underneath a rail in the same way as at the start.

If you have to join cords, make the knots underneath. Almost any joining knot will do, but the traditional one is a weaver's knot. Bend one end back and work the other around it (FIG. 3-7).

In the other direction, you cannot use the shuttles. Instead, cut the cord into lengths as long as you want to handle. To weave them, make a wooden needle. Ash or hickory is best, but almost any wood will do if you are making one stool. Keep the needle thin—1/2 inch wide and 1/8 inch thick will do. The length should be more than the distance across the top. Put two holes in the end for the cord (FIG. 3-7H). With it you need a pointed rod, which could be a 1/2-inch dowel rod or a square piece about the same section (FIG. 3-7J). Make the rod as long as the needle.

Tack the knotted end of the cord as you did in the first direction. Push the pointed rod through to separate the up and down groups. Pass the needle through, pulling the turns tight as you go. After four turns, push close together, wrap at the far side, and return underneath to wrap on the near rail. There is no need to work the pattern underneath. However, merely going across without tucking is also unsatisfactory. A large interweave (FIG. 3-7K) will work to hold the cords together.

Pull out the rod and insert it in the opposite arrangement of cord groups, then pass the needle again (FIG. 3-7L). Continue in this way, pushing the turns close along rails and straight across the top. They will tend to curve. Use the point of the rod or needle to pull earlier groups of tucks back into straight lines.

As you get some way along with the tucking, tension will make it difficult to use the rod, so tuck with the needle as far as possible. Towards the end, you cannot use the wood needle and might have to pass the cord end alone, but it is useful to have a steel needle (FIG. 3-7M) to pick your way across. It will help to pull earlier rows slightly hollow to make more space for the final tucking.

Check with a straightedge in both directions and use the point of the rod to pull the rows straight. Finally, tack underneath in the same way as at the start.

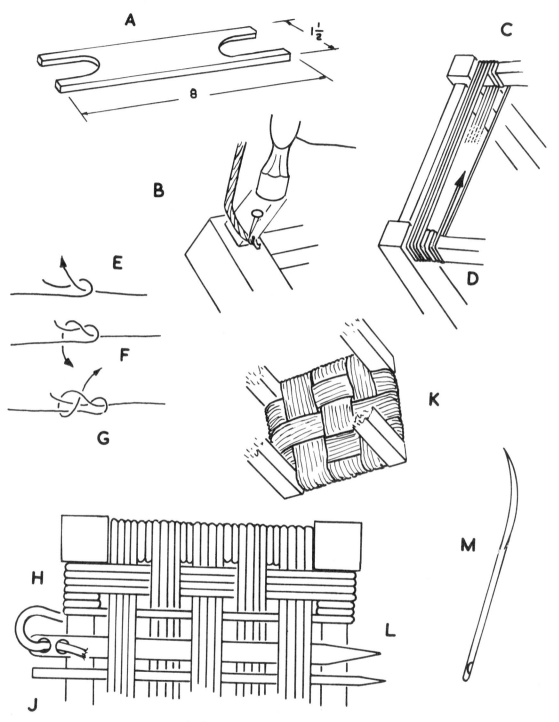

Fig. 3-7. Tools, knots, and method of weaving the top of the stool.

Bathroom Stool

It is convenient to be able to sit rather higher than chair level when drying yourself in a bathroom. It is also better to have a soft seat against bare skin. If the stool can also provide somewhere to put odds-and-ends, its value is further increased. This stool (FIG. 3-8) satisfies all these requirements. It is 19 inches high and has an upholstered seat and a tray/shelf underneath.

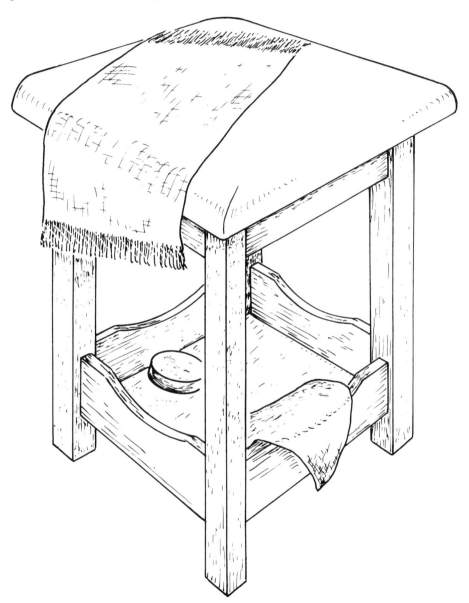

Fig. 3-8. This bathroom stool has a padded top and a deep shelf.

The stool could be made of softwood, but it would be stronger if made of a close-grained hardwood that would stand up well to rocking onto two legs and taking the other rough treatment unintentionally meted out by a bather with soap-filled eyes.

Joints are shown doweled, using $1/4$- or $5/16$-inch dowels. They could be tenoned for added strength, but close-fitting joints and well-glued dowels should be adequate. The stool is square, so the sizes are the same both ways (FIG. 3-9A).

Mark out the four legs together with the positions of the rails (FIG. 3-9B). Mark out the eight rails together, making sure they match and the ends are square. Groove the four lower rails for the tray bottom (FIG. 3-9C). This could be oil-tempered hardboard or thin, exterior-grade plywood.

Mark out the dowel positions on the rails and legs (FIG. 3-9D). They can be evenly spaced for the top rails, but for the lower rails, the hole positions must miss the grooves. The dowels will meet in the legs, and their ends should be mitered to allow maximum penetration.

Hollow the top edges of the lower rails (FIG. 3-9E), and round all edges that hands might touch.

The tray bottom fits into the grooves in the rails, but at the corners it could be notched around the legs. However it will be better to notch the legs in line with the grooves, so the bottom can be cut across (FIG. 3-9F). Do not cut the notches any deeper than necessary to avoid weakening the legs.

Remove all sharpness from the legs and rails. Sand everything, then assemble two opposite sides. See that they are square and match each other as a pair. Use them as a guide to the size of the tray bottom, which need not reach to the bottoms of the rail grooves, or it might prevent rail joints closing tightly. Fit in the tray bottom and assemble the rails the other way. Check that the assembly is square in all directions and that it stands upright on a level surface.

When the glue has set, check that the top rails and legs will present a flat surface to the top, which is plywood and should overlap about $1^1/2$ inches all around (FIG. 3-9G).

Round its edges and corners slightly, then screw down through it into the rails. Drill a few holes to allow air in and out of the upholstery.

Padding is a piece of rubber or plastic foam. For this purpose a thickness of 1 inch should be enough, but you can make it thicker if you wish.

Cut the foam slightly larger than the top. How much depends on the softness of the foam, but $1/2$ inch all around should be satisfactory. Cut away the underside (FIG. 3-9H) so the edge will compress to a curved shape.

Materials List for Bathroom Stool

4 legs	$1^1/4 \times$	$1^1/4 \times 19$	
8 rails	$5/8 \times$	3×12	
1 bottom	$11 \times$	$11 \times 1/8$	oil-tempered hardboard
1 top	$15 \times$	$15 \times 1/2$	plywood

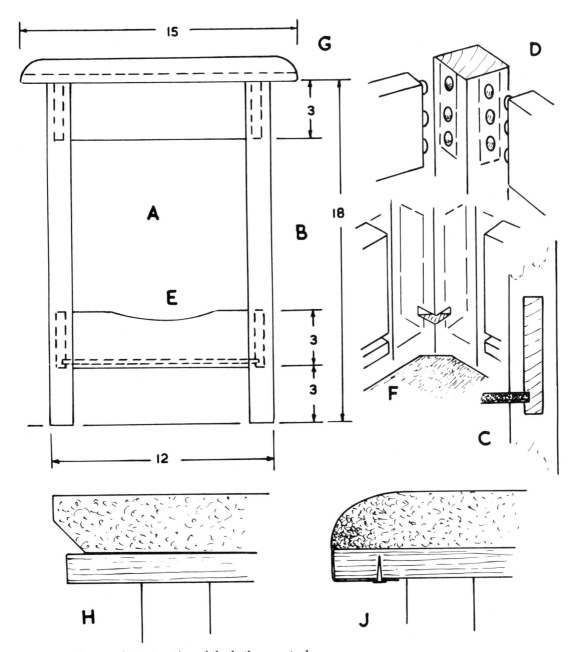

Fig. 3-9. Sizes and construction of the bathroom stool.

The covering should be waterproof; plastic-coated fabric is suitable. Cut a piece large enough to go over the foam and tuck underneath.

Use $3/8$-inch copper tacks. First pull across the center one way and tack underneath (FIG. 3-9J). Do the same across the center the other way, then work towards the corners at a suitable interval to pull the covering to a smoothly curved edge. With most materials, a spacing of 1¹/₂ inches should be satisfactory.

At the corners, fold the material under so as to show a smooth curve on top. Trim the edges of the fabric inside the line of tacks underneath. Finally, give the woodwork a water-resistant paint or varnish finish.

Kitchen Stool

A busy cook will be glad of something comfortable to sit on. However, a kitchen stool might also be needed to stand on, and this cannot be done on an upholstered top without risk of damage to the seat or to the user. This stool (FIG. 3-10) is a square, at a comfortable height for sitting at a table and with two alternative seats. For normal use, there is an upholstered seat and a plywood shelf, but for standing or using the stool as a small table, the seat can be removed and the shelf put in its place.

Hardwood is advisable for the framework. Softwood would probably not have enough strength in the joints for rough use. It would be possible to dowel the joints, but mortises and tenons are described here. The stool will take a standard seat pad 12 inches square; however, any plastic or rubber foam about 1¹/₂ inches thick might be cut to suit.

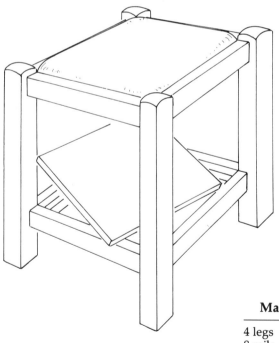

Fig. 3-10. This kitchen stool has a top and shelf which can be changed over when you need a firm top in place of the upholstered one.

Materials List for Kitchen Stool

4 legs	19 ×	1¹/₂ ×	1¹/₂	
8 rails	15 ×	1¹/₂ ×	³/₄	
8 bearers	13 ×	1 ×	¹/₂	
2 seats	13 ×	13 ×	¹/₂ plywood	

Mark out the four legs together with the positions of the rails (FIG. 3-10). Round the tops when the mortises have first been cut.

The eight rails are the same (FIG. 3-11B). Mark them together so the lengths between shoulders are the same. Allow 3/4 inch at each end for the tenons.

The tenons are barefaced, which means they have shoulders at one side only (FIG. 3-11C). Mark them and the mortises at the same time, so they match. Cut the mortises so they meet in the legs, and miter the ends of the tenons so they almost meet. This will give the maximum glue area (FIG. 3-11D).

Round the tops of the legs. Sand all parts and take sharpness off the edges.

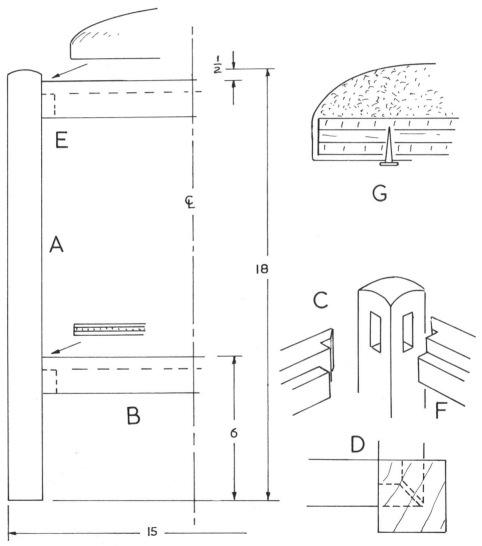

Fig. 3-11. *Sizes and details of the kitchen stool.*

Assemble opposite sides first to get them square and matching, then, join them with the rails the other way. Check squareness in all directions.

Glue and screw strips inside the rails, 1/2 inch down from their top edges (FIGS. 3-11E and 3-11F), to form bearers for the seat and shelf. The seat and shelf are squares of 1/2-inch plywood that will drop easily into position; they should fit into either place.

Use cloth or plastic-faced material to cover the foam pad for the seat. If you cut foam from a larger piece, make it about 1/4 inch too large, and bevel the underside all around. This allows for compressing and curving the edges. Pull the cloth underneath, and tack far enough in for the tacks to come inside the bearers (FIG. 3-11G). Pull over near the centers of opposite sides first; then work outwards towards the corners, where you may have to make V cuts in the cloth underneath. In this way, it can be neatly tacked with an overlap. Trim surplus cloth away below. Make the plywood base a suitable size to allow for the thickness of the cloth around the edges, so the seat will fit in without force or undue slackness. Finish with paint or a clear varnish.

Peasant Chair

Many European countries—notably Germany, Austria, and Switzerland—favor a stool-type of seat with a solid back having its decoration provided by shaping around the edge. The Pennsylvania Dutch remembered their German origin and produced chairs of this type in the early days of settlement when most available wood was in thicker sections. The example chosen here (FIG. 3-12A) should be kept to thick wood to retain authenticity and to provide sufficient strength in the joint between the seat and the back. If thinner wood is used, there would not be sufficient rigidity without additional brackets or other strengthening.

The seat is a plain slab with its grain running front to back. You can make the sides parallel or slightly wider at the front with the corners taken off (FIG. 3-12B). You can leave the edges square or round them, preferably with more rounding on the top edge than the bottom (FIG. 3-12C). Some chairs were molded (FIG. 3-12D). At this stage, leave the rear edge too wide and untreated.

There can be considerable load on the angle between the seat and the chair back when the sitter leans back, so the joint must be secure. The best is a multiple mortise-and-tenon joint, with tenons on the back passing through a series of mortises in the seat. Because both parts are meeting with their grains in line, arrange the tenons so their greater lengths are in the direction of the grain (FIG. 3-12E). This design is stronger than having the tenons wider. Mark out and partly cut the joint before you fit the legs and cut the outline of the back.

The back should slope at about 10 degrees. Set an adjustable bevel to this slant and use it instead of a try square when marking across the edges of both pieces of wood to transfer the joint details to the other sides (FIG. 3-12F). Cut the tenons carefully, watching the lines on both sides and tilting the saw. Similarly, drill out waste with the bit at a slight angle and trim the mortises from both sides

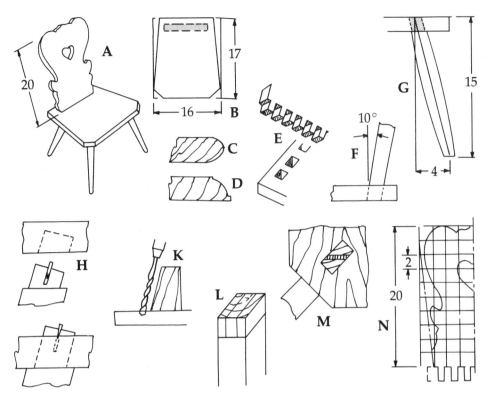

Fig. 3-12. Peasant chair.

toward the center of the thickness of the wood. Let the tenons be slightly too long so they can be trimmed level with the underside of the seat after the final assembly.

With the joints cut, but not finally fitted, you can undertake the rest of the work on making legs and shaping the back. Fixing the back to the seat should be done as the last assembly process. When you reach this point, do any final trimming with a chisel, and drive and glue the tenons into the mortises. Make saw cuts in the tenons so you can drive wedges from below. Leave the glue to set before trimming off the ends of the tenons and finally truing the back of the seat, which should be allowed to project enough for the end grain to resist the load on the joint. If the chair is made of softwood, the seat should project about 2 inches behind the joint, but this can be reduced to nearer 1 inch for a hardwood such as birch, beech, or maple.

Materials List for
Peasant Chair

1 seat	16	× 17 × 1¹/₂
1 back	16	× 22 × 1¹/₂
4 legs	2¹/₂	× 16 × 2¹/₂

The legs do not have rails, so make them fairly stout. You can turn them on a lathe with a simple outline and a dowel top (FIG. 3-12G). Early examples made this way were either fit into the seat with foxtail edging in blind holes (FIG. 3-12H), or taken right through and wedged on top (FIG. 3-12J) before being planed off level. It is important that all four legs splay the same amount. You might be able to set up a tapered support to make the holes uniformly on a drill press, but if you drill by hand, use an adjustable bevel or a piece of wood cut to the angle as a guide (FIG. 3-12K).

Make the legs with a tapered square section, taking the sharpness off the corners to produce an irregular octagon section. Although it would be possible to use dowels into the seat, a stronger joint is made with a tenon. Cut the tenon with its shoulders at an angle. Marking and cutting the tenon is done most easily before the legs are tapered or beveled (FIG. 3-12L).

You will need to cut mortises in the seat. As with the holes for dowels, you can have them go only part way and tighten the tenons with foxtail wedges, or you can have them go right through and wedge them on top. Saw cuts for the wedges should be at right angles to the grain of the seat and not at right angles to the tenons. This puts the spread of the tenon against the seat in the direction best able to resist it (FIG. 3-12M).

The back is shown with a typical outline (FIG. 3-12N). The hollows suit the cords of cushions tied on. It might be advisable to make a template of half the back so you can cut both sides uniformly. The band saw would be the best tool to cut the outline, but the first makers did the work by hand, and a bow saw or jigsaw will get around the outline, even if your muscles have to be exercised to the full. Clean the edges with a surform tool and plenty of sanding. Cut the hole at the center with a jigsaw or saber saw.

Many of these chairs have the outline left square across in section with the sharpness taken off the edges. Others have the front edge well rounded. Some have the outline thoroughly rounded to a semicircular section.

When assembly is completed, stand the chair on a level surface and trim the legs so it stands without wobbling and with the seat parallel with the floor. Round the bottoms of the legs so they will not mark carpets or other floor covering.

Dresser Seat

This vanity seat is to be used in front of a dresser (FIG. 3-13), although you might use it at a piano or with a desk or worktable. It has a hollowed top made of three strips (FIG. 3-14A) that can be used as is or with a cushion. The seat is rigidly braced with rails, and the ends have hand holes for lifting. The design shown is angular, but if a rounded shape would be a better match for other furniture, you could round the tops of the ends and the cutouts.

All parts are 3/4-inch plywood, which could be hardwood, with iron-on strips on the edges, then a clear finish. You could also use softwood plywood and paint it. It is the pair of ends that controls the other sizes, so make them first.

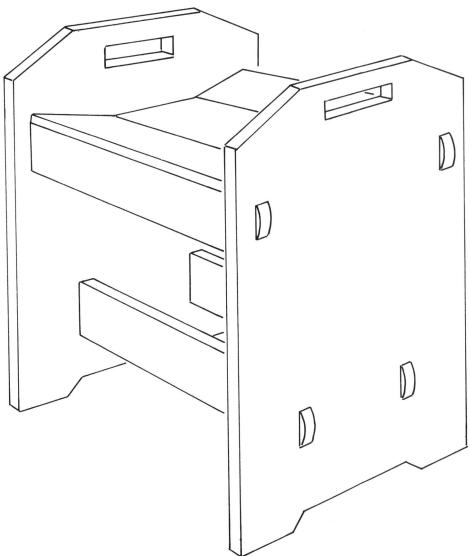

Fig. 3-13. This dresser seat has a shaped top that can be used with or without a cushion.

Mark out the ends (FIGS. 3-14 and 3-15A). Mark on the shape and position of the seat. Two rails (FIGS. 3-14B and 3-15B) fit each side of the seat support (FIGS. 3-14C and 3-15C). Two similar rails brace the sides lower down (FIGS. 3-14D and 3-15D).

Shape the outlines. Cut the hand holes, and round the edges. Mark the mortises.

Make four rails 16 inches between the shoulders (FIG. 3-15E), with tenons that will project through the sides a little with rounded ends (FIG. 3-15F). Cut the mortises in the ends to match the tenons.

Materials List for Dresser Seat

2 ends	18 × 22 × 3/4 plywood
4 rails	4 × 19 × 3/4 plywood
2 seat supports	4 × 15 × 3/4 plywood
3 seat strips	5 × 17 × 3/4 plywood

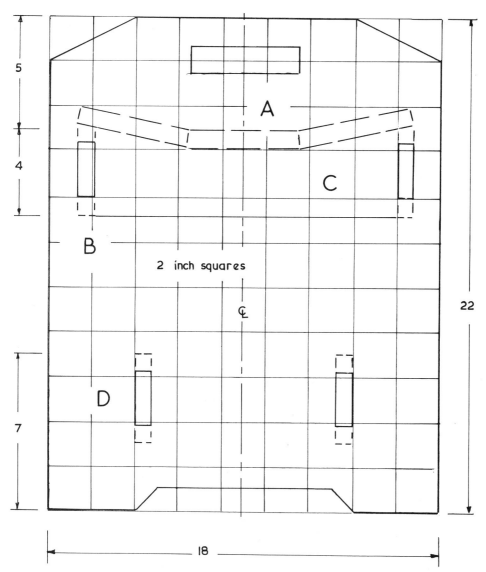

Fig. 3-14. Details of the end of the dresser seat.

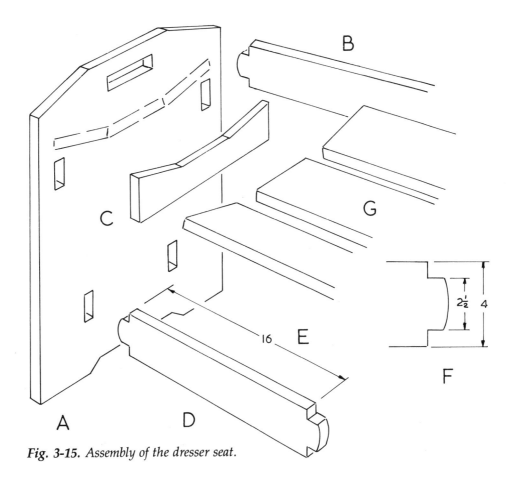

Fig. 3-15. *Assembly of the dresser seat.*

Cut the seat supports to fit between the top rails, with 1-inch rise at the sides. Glue and screw them to the ends. Join the ends with the four rails. Check for squareness and lack of twist, and clamp tightly.

Cut the three seat strips (FIG. 3-15G). Miter them to fit closely or to leave narrow gaps, if you wish. Round the exposed edges of the outer ones. Glue and screw the strips to their supports. Round exposed edges well before applying a finish.

Spindle Chair

Many Colonial chairs were made almost entirely by turning the parts on a lathe. It seems that having bought or made lathes, the furniture makers looked for projects that would make the fullest use of them. Probably a point in favor of turning was the comparative ease with which a competent craftsman could produce a good surface on round work, yet getting as good a surface with the planes and sanding equipment of the day was much more difficult. This applied particularly to wood that had not been fully dried during seasoning. Turned work in "green" lumber can be brought to a reasonable finish, yet the same wood worked under a plane would be liable to tear up and leave a poor surface, no matter what direction it was planed. Because sufficient time could not be allowed between felling trees and converting their wood into furniture, these qualities associated with the lathe must have had considerable appeal.

The ladderback chairs have turned parts, but their outlines are plain and utilitarian. Other chairs were given decorative turnings along the lengths of spindles. If made in attractive hardwood and polished, these chairs were attractive pieces in a dining room and could still be used for that purpose. Most followed the early tendency to make the backs upright. Seats were often made of rush, worked in the manner of ladderback chairs, but some were given lift-out panels that either supported a cushion or were upholstered. The example shown in FIG. 3-16A has this type of seat, but giving it a rush seat instead would only involve the substitution of suitable seat rails.

The main motif in all the turned parts is a series of large beads, with very few small quirks of angular sections. The lower parts of the rear posts were left plain, except for the feet, but they could be turned like the front legs if the back of the chair was likely to be visible in normal use.

Make the front legs. Note that the parts that will be drilled for rails are parallel (FIG. 3-16B). Mark the rail positions with lightly penciled rings while the wood is rotating in the lathe. Make the rear posts (FIG. 3-16C) using the front legs as a guide to the centers for drilling rails. As with the legs, keep the parts that will be drilled parallel. Some of these chairs had quite tall spindles projecting at the tops of the posts, but the more squat finial shown in FIG. 3-16D was typical of a more compact decoration. You should turn this finial as part of the post, but if the post length is near the capacity of the lathe, you could drill its end and make the finial separately with a dowel for plugging in.

The front legs and rear posts stand upright, so the side joints are at right angles. When viewed from above, the front of the chair is wider than the back. This means that you must use care when drilling to always have the drill at right angles to the length of the spindle being drilled, although it might need to be a few degrees away from a right angle in relation to other holes because of the

Materials List for Spindle Chair

2 legs	$1^3/4 \times 17 \times 1^3/4$
2 posts	$1^3/4 \times 42 \times 1^3/4$
7 rails	$1^1/4 \times 18 \times 1^1/4$
2 back rails	$1^1/4 \times 16 \times 1^1/4$
4 back rails	$1^1/4 \times 10 \times 1^1/4$
4 seat rails from	$1^1/2 \times 18 \times \quad ^3/4$
1 seat	$18 \quad \times 18 \times \quad ^1/2$
or 4	$1^1/2 \times 18 \times \quad ^5/8$

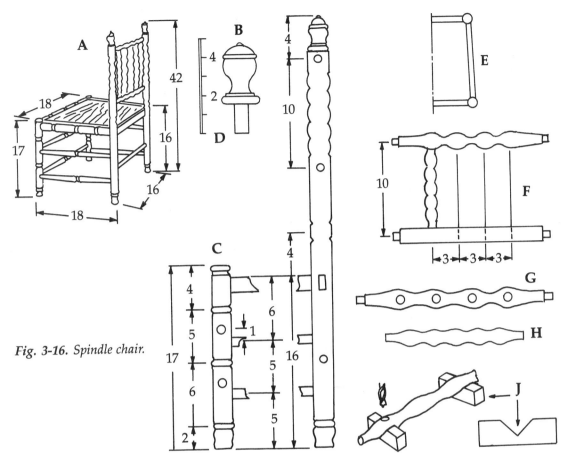

Fig. 3-16. Spindle chair.

taper of the seat. As with the ladderback chairs, draw the seat shape full size to get the corner angles (FIG. 3-16E).

Instead of slats, the back is made up of two horizontal spindles and four upright ones (FIG. 3-16F). Make the horizontal spindles with the same distance between shoulders as the lower rails, and space the beads to suit the upright spindles (FIG. 3-16G). Pencil around where the holes are to come, although some chairs have a line cut around with the long point of a turning chisel.

Turn the upright spindles without shoulders at their ends (FIG. 3-16H). In this way, you can make some adjustment in the joints to allow for slight errors in the diameters of the horizontal spindles or the spacing between the holes for them in the posts.

If you drill the horizontal spindles by hand, hold the wood in a vise and stand a try square beside each hole in turn so the drill is always as near upright as possible. If you drill the spindles in a drill press, it is helpful to use V-blocks. They can be a metal engineering type or made of wood. Accuracy in the V is not important, as long as both blocks are identical, as they should be if cut together on a band saw (FIG. 3-16J).

Drill the holes in the legs and posts at the correct angles in relation to each other, either with an adjustable bevel alongside for hand drilling or on a drill press with a packing.

The chair rails could be a rabbeted square section (FIG. 3-17A) to take the seat panel. An alternative is to fasten one piece inside another (FIG. 3-17B). If you want a turned effect alongside the seat, you can use a split turning.

Make two opposite parts at the same time. Prepare two strips that will make up a square when put together (FIG. 3-17C). Glue them with paper between (FIG. 3-17D) and let the glue set. Turn this spindle to the pattern for the seat rails. Avoid very great differences in diameter between parts of the spindle (FIG. 3-17E). Let the ends of the design be straight and leave a little excess length for trimming to make joints. Remove the wood from the lathe and split the pieces apart along the paper line with a knife or chisel. Scrape and sand away any remaining paper.

Glue on a strip to form the ledge inside the turned part (FIG. 3-17). Join whatever type of seat rails you use to the legs and posts with mortise-and-tenon joints. Assemble the chair as shown. Make up the assembly of spindles in the back and join them to the posts with the lower rails before the glue in any joint has set, then the upright back spindles can adjust to the other parts. Check diagonals and flatness, then allow to set—under weights, if necessary. Do the same with the chair front, then join with the side rails, checking that the chair stands upright and does not wobble.

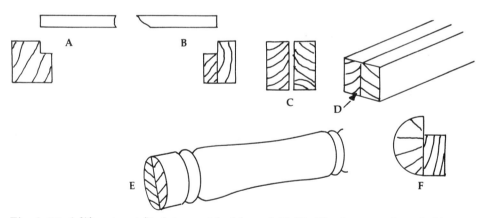

Fig. 3-17. A lift-out seat fits into a notched framed (A,B). The frame can have half-turning made by jointing two pieces (C) to make a square with paper glued between (D) and the pieces separated (F).

In its simplest form, the seat is a plain board, making a loose fit on the rails (FIG. 3-18A). In modern furniture, it would be plywood, but if you use a board as in an original chair, you can place battens across the grain below and cut them back to fit inside the rail frame.

The plain wooden seat can support a loose cushion, or you can give it its own padding. Originally, this would have been sheep wool or pieces of cloth, but

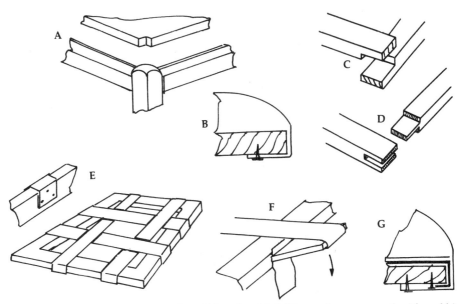

Fig. 3-18. A lift-out seat (A) can be solid and padded (B) or a frame covered with webbing (C–F) and then upholstered (G).

a modern version would be better with plastic or rubber foam. Stretch cloth over and tack it underneath (FIG. 3-18B), neatly folding the corners of the cloth around the corners of the board.

Such padding only gives limited comfort. A further step was to use an open frame with the padding supported on strips of canvas, webbing, or leather. Make the frame a loose fit in the recess, and crosslap the corners (FIG. 3-18C) or join them with open mortise-and-tenon joints, sometimes called *bridle joints* (FIG. 3-18D).

Interlace the straps tightly, and tack them below (FIG. 3-18E). You can put tension on with one of the modern upholstery webbing stretchers, but the simplest way is the original one: levering with a piece of wood (FIG. 3-18F). Tack a piece of cloth, such as burlap, above the webbing. Then put the padding on, pull the cloth cover over, and tack it in the same way as for a plain board bottom (FIG. 3-18G).

Shaker Rocking Chair

The construction of some chairs is rather complicated, but the Shakers simplified designs, so construction is fairly easy. They produced a range of chair designs; this example shows a rocker (FIG. 3-19). The rear legs slope in use to give comfort without having to curve them, and the legs all fit over comparatively narrow runners. There is some plain turning, but all of the parts can be made on a lathe with 30 inches between centers. Original seats were made in several ways; alternatives are suggested later in this chapter.

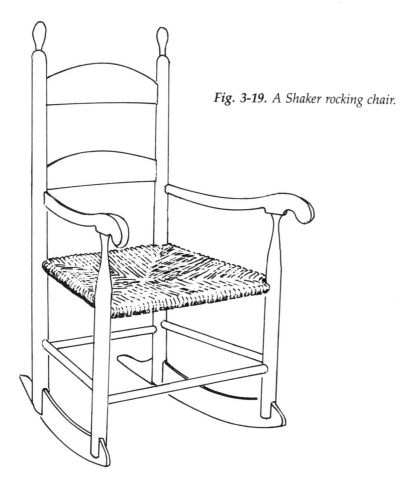

Fig. 3-19. A Shaker rocking chair.

The sizes suggested (FIG. 3-20A) are for a chair suitable for use in a living room or on a porch. All parts need not be made of the same hardwood, but if you mix the woods, you might need a painted finish to give an even appearance. Choose a wood with a compact grain that will grip strongly at the joints, where rails have to go into rather shallow holes.

Make the legs first. From 2-inch stock, turn as large a diameter as possible—at least $1^{3}/_{4}$ inches. The Shakers lightly scribed lines around at the hole positions while the wood was in the lathe, so you can do this, too. Aim to leave just the lightest cut showing after sanding.

The rear legs are shown 30 inches long (FIG. 3-20B) to come within the capacity of most lathes, but if your lathe has a long bed, add a further 6 inches so you can have three slats at the back, which will be closer to the original design. All other sizes and arrangements remain the same. Note that the lower rail holes are staggered enough for the holes one way to just miss those the other way. At the seat they have to be at the same level both ways.

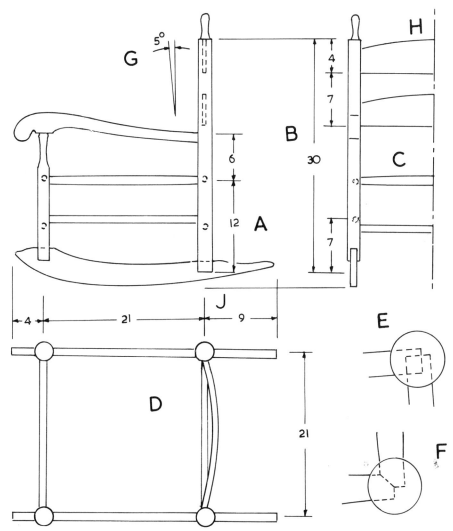

Fig. 3-20. *Main sizes of the Shaker rocking chair.*

Materials List for Shaker Rocking Chair

2 legs	2	× 2	× 32
2 legs	2	× 2	× 19
4 rails	23	× 1 diameter	
4 rails	23	× $3/4$ diameter	
2 slats	2	× 4	× 23
2 arms	$1^{1}/4$	× 4	× 28
2 runners	1	× 5	× 36
2 finials	$1^{1}/4$	× $1^{1}/4$ ×	7

Turn the front legs (FIG. 3-21A) in similar way. Do not cut the notches for the runners yet, but round the ends slightly in readiness. Reduce to a slender curve above the seat level, with a ³/₄-inch dowel to join the arm.

The lower rails are parallel, ³/₁₄ inch in diameter. Turn them from wood to match the other parts, or use hardwood dowel rod. The seat rails need to be thicker or they will tend to bend inwards and downwards eventually. Turn them a full 1 inch in diameter for most of their length, but taper towards the ends to fit into ³/₄-inch holes (FIG. 3-20C).

The chair is shown with a square seat (FIG. 3-20D), but at this stage you can check what sizes you need and alter width or depth to suit. You could make the back narrower than the front, but in a rocker this adjustment was never as much as might be allowed in an ordinary chair.

Check rail hole sizes by drilling scrap wood first and trying the rails. Strength will depend on a good fit. At lower rail level, drill so the holes overlap (FIG. 3-20E), but get all depths the same. At seat level, drill so the rails meet and can be mitered (FIG. 3-20F). Although the chair is intended to settle at an angle of about 5 degrees when unoccupied (FIG. 3-20G), all parts are square to each other. Use a drill press or a guide to ensure that holes are drilled squarely.

The arms (FIG. 3-21B) are prominent in the finished chair, so they must match and be well finished if they are to look right. Perform steps to make both at the same time. Allow for flat surfaces that will be drilled for the dowels on the front legs, and cut tenons to fit into the rear legs.

After cutting the profiles, round the shaped surfaces well, particularly at the front. Delay drilling for the dowels on the front legs until the rails have been joined to the legs, to allow for slight variations during assembly.

The back slats (FIG. 3-20H) should match the lengths of the back rails. They have to be given a curve for comfort (FIG. 3-21C). It would be possible to bend thin wood around a former, but such a method is more suited to quantity production. In this case, it might be better to cut from solid wood. Allow for tenons at the ends. Smooth all surfaces and round the edges. Cut matching mortises in the legs.

Turn finials, or decorative tips, for the tops of the rear legs (FIG. 3-21E). Drill the legs for the finial dowels and glue them in.

Do not make the runners (FIG. 3-20J) less than 1 inch thick, as they have to spread the load on the floor covering. Cut the outline (FIG. 3-21D), leaving flat surfaces where the legs have to fit. Take the sharpness off the corners, but do not round the edges much. Cut slots in the legs to fit over the runners.

You have two options: Put together the two side assemblies first and then join them, or assemble the back and front before completing the chair frame. It is probably easier to make up the two sides first. Check for squareness and see that legs are parallel. Match one side over the other as you assemble them. When the rails and arms have been fitted, join in the runners. Besides gluing them in place, drill for ³/₈-inch dowels across the joints.

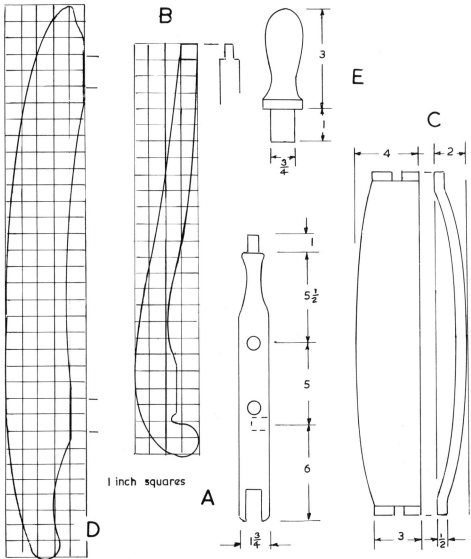

B

E

C

3

3/4

4

2

1 inch squares

1

5 1/2

5

6

A

1 3/4

3

1/2

D

Fig. 3-21. Details of parts of the Shaker rocking chair.

As you assemble the other way, besides checking squareness and parallel legs, stand away and look from front to back to ensure there is no twist in the chair. Front and rear legs should be in line with each other when viewed from a distance.

The chair frame could be finished with paint. In fact, that might be your best choice if you have used woods of different colors. Alternatively, the chair would look lighter and show your skill better, as well as probably be a more suitable match for other furniture, if given a clear polish or varnish finish.

Rush Pattern Seat

Original rush seats were made from natural rushes, used damp and twisted into rope as the seating progressed. This requires practice, and it can be rather messy. Suitable rushes might be difficult to find. Fortunately, there are satisfactory alternatives, with several cord-like materials, both natural and synthetic. One of these is seagrass, in the form of a rope under 1/4 inch in diameter which, in its undyed

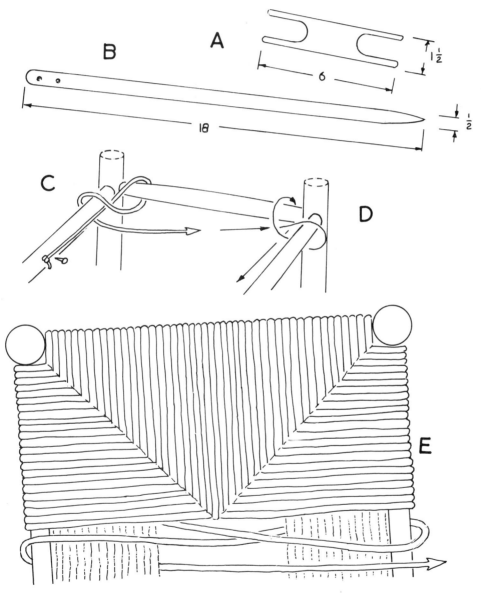

Fig. 3-22. How to weave a rush-pattern seat.

form, looks very much like rush. Because seagrass comes in long lengths and can be used dry, weaving a rush pattern seat becomes a fairly simple task.

Prepare a few shuttles to wind the seagrass on (FIG. 3-22A); cut them from plywood or thin solid wood. Towards the end of forming a seat you need a wood needle (FIG. 3-22B) to pull the line through. Make this of hardwood, because you might have to lever with it.

The finished chair seat shows a pattern, above and below, with lines of seagrass pointing inwards to a mitered joint (FIG. 3-10). How this is obtained appears a mystery. However, the actual technique of making the pattern is simple.

With a shuttle full of line, knot an end and tack it inside one rail. Take the line over the adjoining rail back around the leg to go over the first rail, so the shuttle is brought under in the direction of the next corner (FIG. 3-22C). That is the entire action, to be repeated at the next leg (FIG. 3-22D), and so on. When you get around to the first corner again, put the new turns inside the first. Continue round and round the chair until the seat is filled.

Maintain a good tension all the time. If you have a helper, work at opposite sides, with one person holding the tension gained while the other works the line around the next corner. You will see the pattern build up at the corners, while the lines between corners will become hidden. When you join in new line, have the knots here, where they will not show. Press the turns close together on the rails and see that the pattern, as it builds up, is square to the rails.

If the seat is square, the pattern should build up equally both ways. If you have made the frame wider at the front than the back, go around the front legs twice occasionally as you progress, until the remaining bare wood at the front is the same as at the back; then continue normally.

If the seat is wider than it is deep, fill the side rails before the other rails. This also might happen in one direction with a tapered seat. When you have as many turns as you can put on covering the side rails, fill back and front rails by a figure-eight action (FIG. 3-22E) until the rails are tightly covered.

As you progress you will reach a stage where you will not be able to pass a shuttle through the center. Use a loose end as far as possible; then for the final turns, put the line in the holes in the needle. Use its point to lever a gap. When you have packed in as many turns as possible, tack the line under a rail and hide the end inside the pattern below.

Checker Tape Seat

Some Shaker chairs had seats formed of cloth tape, woven in a checker pattern. They wove the tape themselves as a fairly coarse material about 1 inch wide. If you can get a comparable tape with very little stretch, use it.

Wrap the tape over the frame one way; then wrap in the other direction, over and under, to make the pattern underneath as well as on top. To get a good tension without reaching a stage where it is impossible to make the final tucks, judge the degree of slackness to allow in the wraps in the first direction. The cess of this procedure depends on the type of tape, its stretch, and your experience with it.

The only special tool you need is a pointed stick longer than the distance across the chair. You might use a seagrass needle or a piece of 1/2-inch-square wood with rounded corners (FIG. 3-23A).

Tack the end of the tape securely under the back rail, and wrap on turns (FIG. 3-23B) sufficient to fill the width. It might help to get the tension right to put the pointed stick or a larger piece of wood under the turns. To join in a new tape, tack the end of one piece over the other on the underside of a rail.

In the other direction, you cannot use the tape in a roll. You have to use a convenient length, then join in another by tacking under a rail. Use the pointed stick to lift alternate turns so you can tuck the tape across (FIG. 3-23C). Do the same on the return underneath. After each set of tucks, pull tight and press the tape along the rails as close as possible to the previous turn. Towards the end, you will not be able to use the pointed stick across, but will have to lever the turns one at a time. A broad screwdriver or a blunt chisel will work (FIG. 3-23D). Tack the final end underneath.

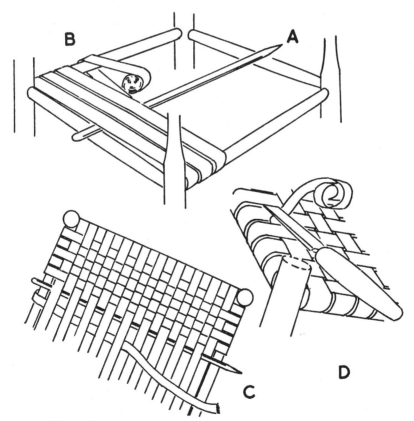

Fig. 3-23. Making an interwoven tape seat.

In an original seat of this type, the space between might have been filled with cloth as padding. In a modern version, it would be better to use a slab of plastic foam if you wish to add padding. Such padding could be held in place with adhesive tape while you work the tape seat pattern over it.

Firehouse Armchair

Armchairs shaped to fit around the body are sometimes loosely referred to as Windsor chairs, but the true Windsor chair has an arched back, while the Firehouse Armchair gets its name from its common use in early days in the quarters of volunteer fire departments. There are a great variety, but I have chosen the specimen shown in FIG. 3-24A because it can be made without steaming wood.

Some chairs had flat seats, others were shaped fully, and others were shaped from back to front, while remaining straight across (FIG. 3-24B). The front edge is straight, the grain is across the seat, and the back is a part of circle (FIG. 3-24C).

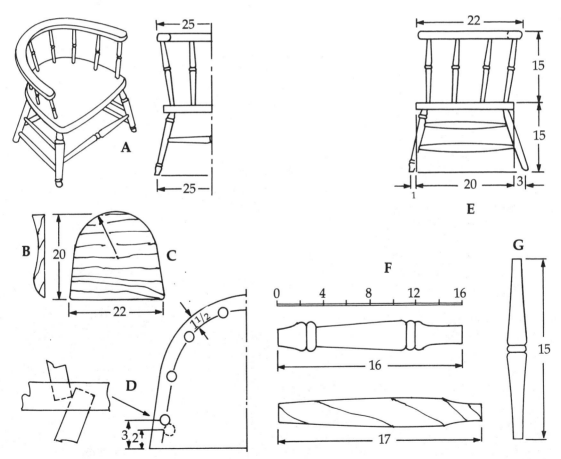

Fig. 3-24. Firehouse armchair.

Materials List for
Firehouse Armchair

4 legs	2	×	17 ×	2
7 rails	1½ ×		22 ×	1½
1 seat	20	×	22 ×	1½
1 arm from	5	× 180 ×		⁵/₈
8 spindles	1¼ ×		15 ×	1¼
1 back from	5	× 100 ×		⁵/₈
3 back spindles	1½ ×		5 ×	1½

The seat is the key member of the assembly; make it first. Locate the leg positions on the underside. On the top, pencil a line around parallel with the edge, and position the spindle locations on this line. Note there is an even number, and spacing is uniform (FIG. 3-24D).

The front legs are upright when viewed from the side, but are splayed when viewed from the front. The rear legs have the same splay as the front legs when viewed from the front, but from the side they are seen to have considerable splay toward the rear (FIG. 3-24E). It is difficult to arrive at the exact sizes of the legs, so turn the tops with parallel parts to adjust in the seat holes, and arrange the bottoms so that final trimming to length will not affect their appearance (FIG. 3-24F). In this case, the front legs are decorated with beads, but the rear legs are plainer.

Turn the spindles with thicker centers. You can use beads to match the front legs (FIG. 3-24G). In effect, the underassembly and seat can be regarded as a stool and be put together without reference to the parts above the seat. You can assemble these parts before proceeding with the arms and spindles, if you wish.

Laminate the combined arms and back with two or three thicknesses. The shape must match the seat, and the inner edge should be just within the outline of the seat (FIG. 3-25). Use any convenient lengths of wood. Let them abut, and arrange joints to come at different places in each layer (FIG. 3-25B). Cut each piece to shape with a little to spare. Glue the parts together, and put them under pressure until set. After that, you can treat the laminated part as a single piece of wood. Trim its profile, but do not do any cross-sectional shaping at this stage.

Transfer the spindle locations from the seat to the arm. The spindles will flare out slightly. Let the front pair flare in the width but be upright when viewed from the side, then space the hole positions for the others around the centerline of the arm piece (FIG. 3-25C).

The eight spindles are all the same. Allow a little excess length, and keep the ends parallel and to the hole size, so they will still fit if trimmed to length.

You can complete the armchair at this stage, but many chairs were given an extension backrest. A modern method of construction would be to laminate many thin pieces of wood around a mold, but the older glues were not suitable for this method, so the backrests were built up by laminating more flat pieces in a similar way to the arm piece (FIG. 3-25). You can work the backrest with spokeshave and plane to a comfortable section. Mount it on top of the arm piece (FIG. 3-25E), with dowels or screws from below.

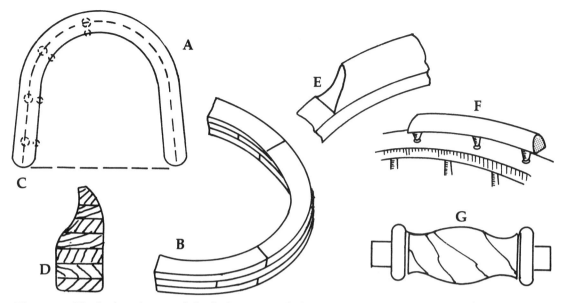

Fig. 3-25. The back and arms of the firehouse armchair.

This method of mounting does not give high support to the back. Another method of mounting the backrest is to use short spindles located above and between the main spindles (FIG. 3-25F). Turn these with dowel ends (FIG. 3-25G) and stand them upright between the two parts.

The front ends of the arms should be well rounded. Most of the rest of the shape also should have a rounded section. Drill the holes for the spindles connecting to the seat at angles judged by eye, with appropriate adjustment later with gouge and chisel, if necessary.

When the arm is to be attached to the seat, have all the spindle ends glued and lightly inserted in place in the seat. Bring the arm into place, and get the spindle ends located in their holes. Use a piece of scrap wood under a hammer or mallet to work around the arm a little at a time, driving the parts together. When all of the spindles have entered a short distance, check that the arm is parallel with the seat and that the assembly when viewed from the front is not flaring more one way than the other. Continue driving progressively around the arm until all the joints are fully closed and the chair looks symmetrical.

Easy Chair

For relaxing, a fully overstuffed chair might seem the ultimate in comfort, but making it is more an exercise in upholstery than a woodworking project, as the wood is usually almost entirely hidden. For a basic woodworking project, you can make a chair which is sprung and uses loose cushions to achieve almost the same degree of comfort. Moreover, it can show your woodworking skill instead of obscuring it.

This chair (FIG. 3-26) is not as complicated to make as it might first appear, if the step-by-step instructions are followed. Note that it is built up of several independently made units; there is a frame for the seat and another for the back, both carrying rubber webbing to support cushions. These join together and fit between the two sides, which are made completely before assembly.

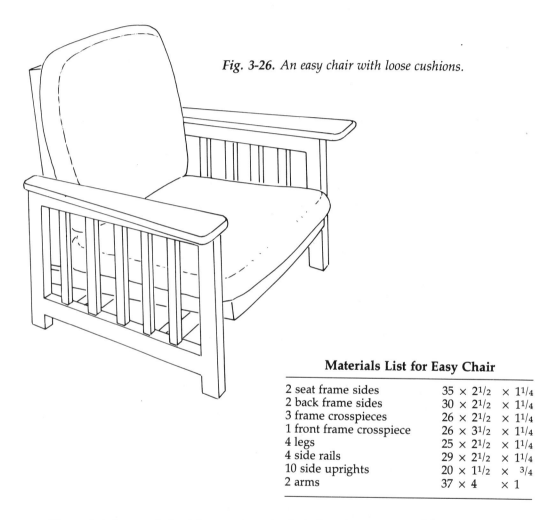

Fig. 3-26. *An easy chair with loose cushions.*

Materials List for Easy Chair

2 seat frame sides	35 × 2¹/2 × 1¹/4
2 back frame sides	30 × 2¹/2 × 1¹/4
3 frame crosspieces	26 × 2¹/2 × 1¹/4
1 front frame crosspiece	26 × 3¹/2 × 1¹/4
4 legs	25 × 2¹/2 × 1¹/4
4 side rails	29 × 2¹/2 × 1¹/4
10 side uprights	20 × 1¹/2 × 3/4
2 arms	37 × 4 × 1

Finger joints are advised for some parts, but elsewhere you could use mortise-and-tenon joints or dowels. Construction should be of hardwood, although, if you want to match pine furniture, softwood is possible. A clear finish on the wood and suitably colored cushions should make an attractive piece of furniture.

Sizes (FIGS. 3-27 and 3-28) are based on two cushions, 24 inches square and about 3 inches thick. You can get rubber or plastic foam cut to this size and cover it yourself, or you can buy cushions close to these sizes. Remember to adapt the

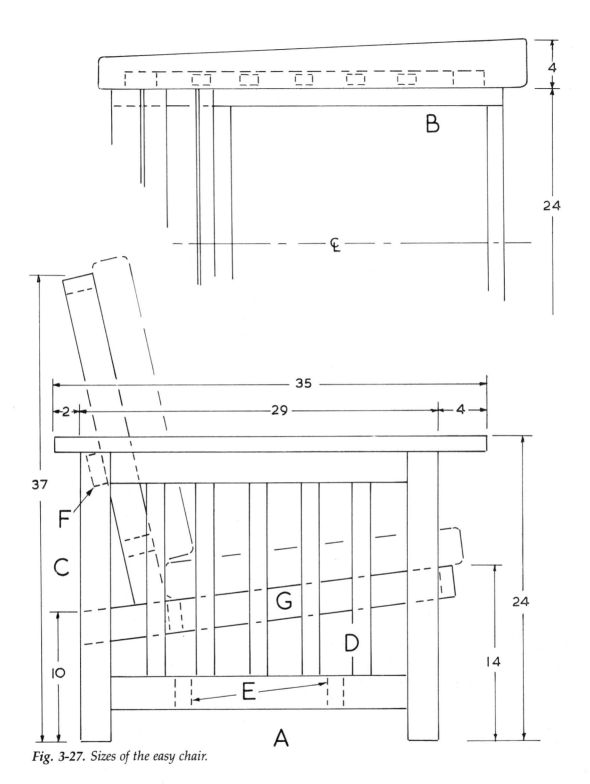

Fig. 3-27. *Sizes of the easy chair.*

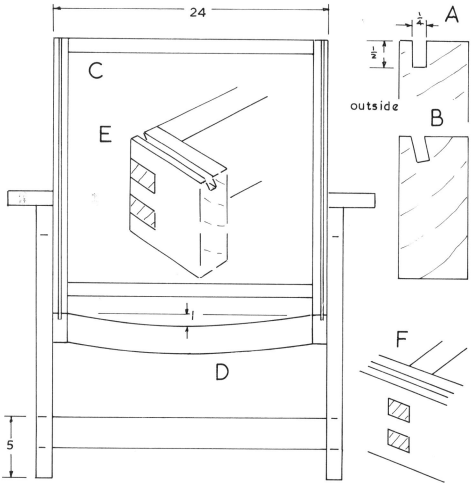

Fig. 3-28. Constructional details of the easy chair.

suggested sizes to suit. In any case, you might find it worthwhile to check the general sizes with your needs, or compare them with a favorite existing chair. Slight alterations to the dimensions will not affect the methods of construction.

Once you have decided whether the cushions are to be made or bought, get the rubber webbing and the metal clips for its ends (FIG. 3-30A). A clip is squeezed over the cut end of webbing (FIG. 3-30B), but if you can cut it at an angle (FIG. 3-30B), that will give it a slightly better grip (FIG. 3-30). If you get the clips first, tailor the groove size to suit, although a probable size is shown (FIG. 3-28A). Start with the two frames that make the seat and back (FIG. 3-29A). Cut the wood long enough for the two pairs of sides (FIGS. 3-29B and 3-29C). Cut grooves to take the webbing clips.

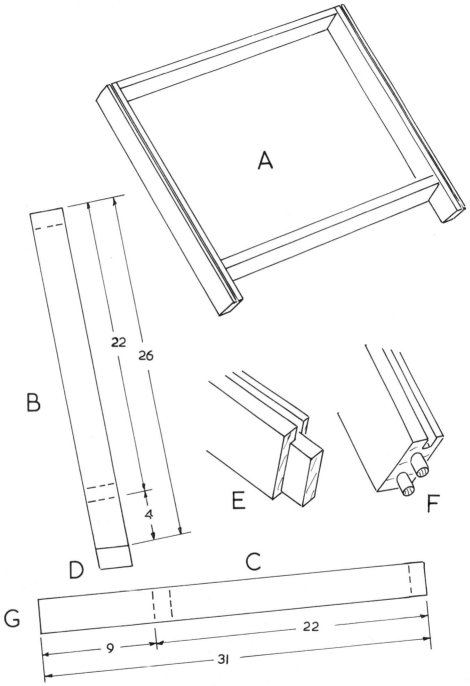

Fig. 3-29. Parts of the easy chair.

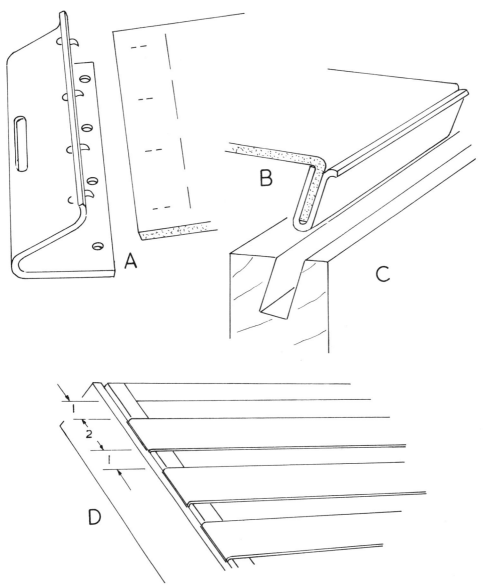

Fig. 3-30. *How to fit rubber webbing to the easy chair.*

Mark the positions of the crosspieces. The bottom of the back side pieces meet the seat at 97 degrees (FIG. 3-29D). Allow for tenons (FIG. 3-29E) or two 1/2- or 5/8-inch dowels (FIG. 3-29F). Leave the ends of the seat sides overlong at present (FIG. 3-29G); they will be trimmed to the leg edge during assembly. Prepare the joint where the back piece meets each side piece.

Cut the crosspieces. Three of them are straight (FIG. 3-28C), but the one at the front of the seat is better cut to a curve (FIG. 3-28D) to give you leg clearance when the cushion and the webbing sag under your weight. This will have to be cut to a curved section from a wider board.

Finger joints can be used at the corners (FIG. 3-28E). Adapt these to mortise-and-tenon joints at the other meeting places (FIG. 3-28F).

Assemble the two frames squarely. They could be joined together now, but you might prefer to make a dry trial assembly, then finally glue these parts together when joining them to the other parts.

The two sides (FIG. 3-27A) make a pair, framed with uprights and flat tops (FIG. 3-27B), which are parallel to the floor and wide enough to take a cup or plate (FIG. 3-31).

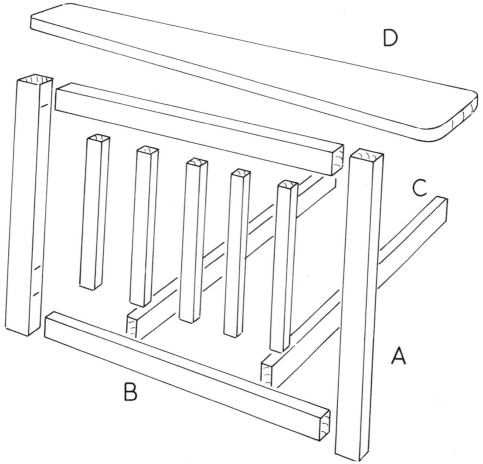

Fig. 3-31. Details at the side of the easy chair.

The framing of the sides may be tenoned or doweled. In any case, the arms should be doweled to the top rails.

Cut the legs to length and mark on them the positions of the rails (FIGS. 3-27C and 3-31A). Cut the rails to fit between them (FIG. 3-31B), allowing for tenons or dowels at the ends.

Mark equal spacings for the uprights. As shown (FIG. 3-27D) the gaps are 3 inches. It would be unwise to reduce the number of uprights, as the spacing might then be wide enough for a child to get his head caught. Use dowels or tenons for joining the uprights to the rails.

Mark the positions of the two crossbars (FIGS. 3-27E and 3-31C). Make these crossbars and cut their joints to the rails. Make a similar bar to go behind the seat back (FIG. 3-27F), but delay cutting the joint for it into the rear legs until you make a trial assembly.

Assemble the side frames and see that they are square and match as a pair. Make the two arms (FIG. 3-31D). Their inner edges are parallel to each other and level with the side rails, but the outsides taper to about half width. Round all edges. These are the most prominent parts of the woodwork of the chair, so do the rounding carefully, and thoroughly sand all over.

Join the arms to their side frames with 1/2-inch dowels at about a 6-inch spacing.

Put the seat and back assembly against one side frame in the position indicated (FIG. 3-27G). This will allow you to mark on the rear leg the position of the crossbar that supports the seat back (FIG. 3-27F). You might have to move the assembly or alter the tilt of the back slightly to get this bar positioned. When you have it correct, mark this joint and where the seat side crosses the legs. Transfer the markings to the other side frame. Cut the mortises or drill for dowels for the rear crossbar, and drill for screws to be driven from inside the seat sides into the legs. Two or three screws with glue at each place should be sufficient.

Have the crossbars ready. Glue the joints between the back and seat frames. Screw and glue the seat frames to the side frame legs, and at the same time join the crossbars to the sides. The frames should pull the chair square, but check that it stands level without twist. Screw the rear crossbar to the back frame. Trim the rear ends of the seat frame at the legs.

The spacing and tension of the webbing depends on its choice. If it is not very elastic, you might space wider and not stretch as much in fitting as you would with more flexible material. With the usual 2-inch rubber webbing you can space pieces 1 inch apart across both frames (FIG. 3-30).

To get the tension you want, experiment with one piece; then cut all pieces to the same length. On this 24-inch width of frame, you will probably cut the webbing between 1 inch and 2 inches short of the distance between the grooves. Because there is more weight on the seat than the back, make the seat pieces shorter than the back pieces (for more tension), but keep all pieces in a frame the same. Cut sufficient pieces of webbing, and fit the end clips tightly; squeezing in a vise is suggested.

Apply stain and a clear finish to the woodwork before finally fitting the webbing and adding the cushions to complete the chair.

Tenoned Armchair

The tenoned armchair is substantial, and most of the parts are joined with mortises and tenons. It should have a long life and not suffer much if left outside for most of the year. The suggested wood sections can be softwood, providing you protect it well with paint. A rot-resistant hardwood would be better, and you could paint or varnish it, or leave it untreated and allow it to weather to blend in with its surroundings. In that case, you should secure the joints with a boat-building-quality waterproof glue and drive dowels across the tenons of the main structure.

The chair shown in FIG. 3-32 is at a size that could be used as it is or with cushions. The ends also could be used to make a longer bench seat. The sections of lengthwise wood suggested should be satisfactory for a bench up to about 5 feet long to seat two or even three people close together.

The important shapes are the ends (FIG. 3-33A). In front view, the legs are upright, but from the side, both lower parts flare out a little. Cut the slope of the back into the extension of the back legs. The arms slope slightly because they are

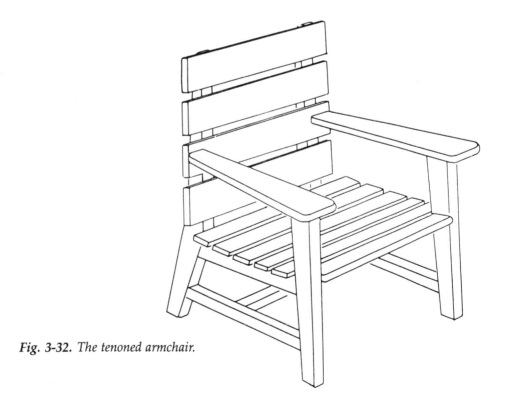

Fig. 3-32. The tenoned armchair.

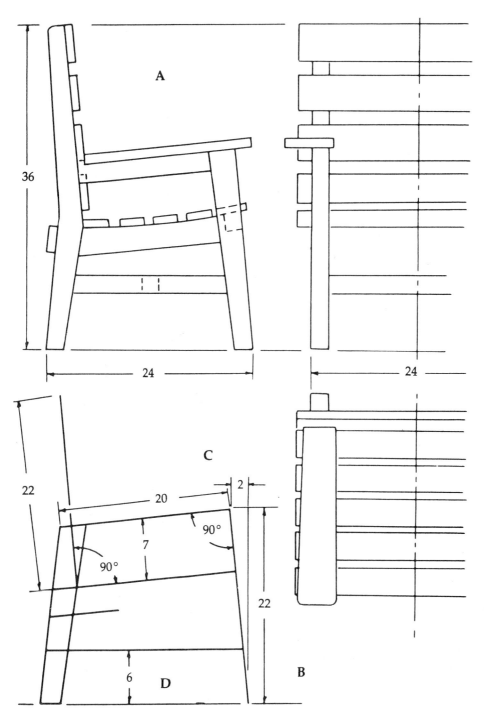

Fig. 3-33. Main sizes of the tenoned armchair.

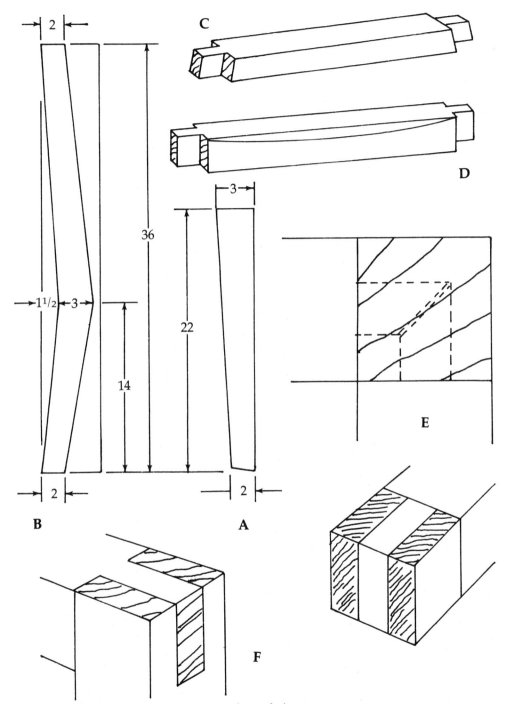

Fig. 3-34. Details of parts of the tenoned armchair.

higher at the front. The seat also slopes at about the same angle. Give it a slight hollow in the top so that the slats across make a little concession to body shape. Make up the ends as identical units and fit the other parts between them, with the bottom rail jointed. Otherwise, the parts screw on.

Draw the main lines of the end shape to full size (FIG. 3-33B). The arm is square to the front leg (FIG. 3-33C), and the rake of the back is about the same angle as the front leg. Allow for the slope of the seat, but make the bottom rail (FIG. 3-33D) come parallel with the floor.

Taper the widths of the front legs (FIG. 3-34A). The front edge of the rear leg is in straight lines, but the change of shape at the back can follow a curve (FIG. 3-34). Do not go too thin near the center of each leg. It is worthwhile examining the grain formation of the wood. Grain is not usually straight along the wood. If you can mark out the wood so that a curve in the grain follows the shape of a leg, it would be stronger than if your cuts go across grain lines.

Mark where the other parts come on the legs. Prepare the pieces that will come under the arms and the lower rails (FIG. 3-34C). Cut the pieces for the seat rails (FIG. 3-34D). The ends for the tenons will be straight, but hollow the top edges so the pairs match. Do not weaken the wood by going too thin at the center.

All of the parts are the same thickness. Mark with the face sides outward and make the tenons $5/8$ or $3/4$ inch wide. They should go about $1^1/2$ inches into the legs (FIG. 3-34E). The exploded view of an end shows the joint arrangement (FIG. 3-35). The top front joints will be covered by the arms. It will be simplest to use open, through, mortise-and-tenon joints there (FIG. 3-34F). At this stage, the two ends are the same except for the mortises in the lower rails, which must face inward.

Pull the joints tight with clamps, if possible, and then drill and fit dowels across them. See that each end frame remains flat. Check the second frame over the first to see that it matches.

Make the bottom lengthwise ran or stretcher (FIG. 3-36A) and the front rail.

Materials List for Tenoned Armchair

2 front legs	3 × 23 × 2
2 rear legs	5 × 37 × 2
2 seat rails	3 × 21 × 2
2 arm rails	2 × 18 × 2
2 lower rails	2 × 23 × 2
1 stretcher	2 × 24 × 2
1 front rail	3 × 24 × 2
1 backrail	3 × 25 × 1
5 seat slats	3 × 28 × 1
4 back slats	4 × 28 × 1
2 arms	5 × 24 × 1

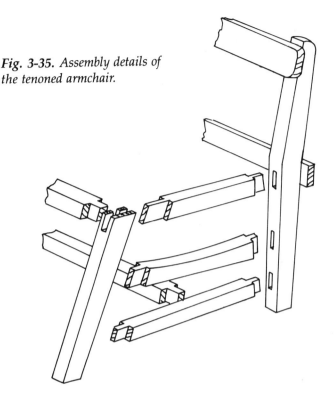

Fig. 3-35. Assembly details of the tenoned armchair.

They must be pulled tight at the ends so they determine the lengths of other parts. Make the back rail that screws to the back legs (FIG. 3-36B). This and the stretcher and front rail will hold the ends in the correct relative positions for the slats to be added. Check squareness and that the assembly is without twist before you add the slats.

The back slats are wider than the seat slats. Make the seat slats, with rounded top edges and well-rounded ends that overlap the supports by $1^{1}/_{2}$ inches. An exception is that the front slat comes between the front legs and is supported by the front rail (FIG. 3-36C). Space slats evenly around the curved supports and screw them down. For a neat finish, counterbore and plug over the screw heads.

Prepare the back slats in the same way as the seat slats and to the same lengths. The space between the bottom back slat and the rear seat slat should be about the same as the spaces between the back slats. The lower back slat must be notched around the arm rail (FIG. 3-36D).

The arms mount on top of the side frames and are best held with counter-bored and plugged screws. Round the forward ends. The arms look best if kept parallel on the inner faces, but tapered outside toward the rear. Round the upper surfaces well. Take the sharpness off all exposed edges of other parts before painting or varnishing.

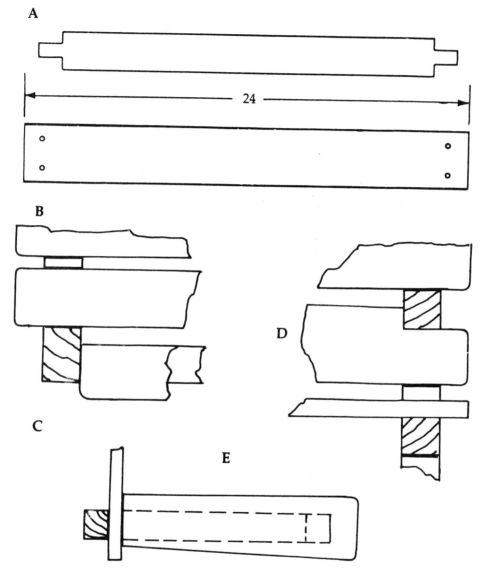

Fig. 3-36. Slat and arm details of the tenoned armchair.

Sofa

A two-place sofa or love seat is a useful addition to the seating of a room. It is only a little more complicated to make than a chair and does not involve extra strengthening like a longer seat. Some similar furniture is fully upholstered, with only the feet showing the wooden construction.

An alternative is to make a wooden sofa where most of the wood is exposed and the padding is with loose cushions. This project (FIG. 3-37) is of this type and is intended to be used with four 20-inch-square cushions about 4 inches thick. The cushions could be made or bought as a standard size. Get the cushions first in case measurements of the sofa have to be altered to suit the exact sizes of available cushions.

The seating is sprung with rubber webbing (taken from the sides to the center, not interwoven), but the back cushions rest against vertical dowel rods. Construction has been simplified as far as possible, without sacrificing comfort or appearance. Although the complete assembly appears complicated, the work is straightforward if tackled one step at a time.

The sofa is heavier and more stable than a chair and not likely to be abused by tilting in use, but it should still be strongly made, preferably with a good hardwood. The design allows for doweled joints, except for tenons on the bottom rails

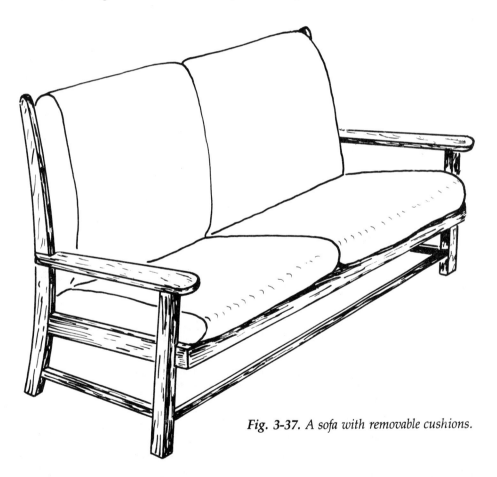

Fig. 3-37. A sofa with removable cushions.

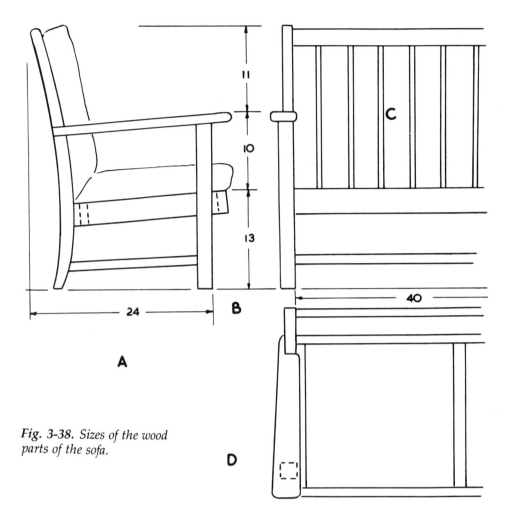

Fig. 3-38. *Sizes of the wood parts of the sofa.*

where there is insufficient space for two dowels. There could be tenons in place of dowels elsewhere.

The design can be used to make a matching lounge chair, if the lengthwise parts are shortened to suit a single cushion width. All other construction is the same.

Set out the rear legs (FIG. 3-39). Cut them to shape, and mark on them the positions of other parts. Draw a full-size end view of the sofa, marking the rear leg shape around the one you have cut (FIG. 3-38A). This drawing will give you the sizes and angles of other parts.

The seat ends and center rail have to be grooved to take the metal ends of the rubber webbing (FIG. 3-39A). Obtain the clips and webbing, and squeeze one clip on to the end of a strip of webbing. Measure this for the size of groove needed,

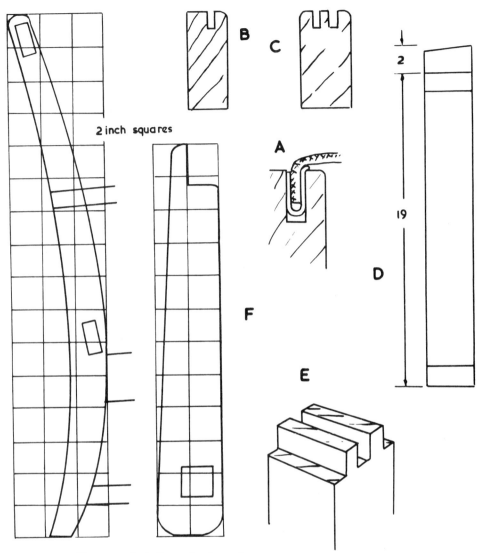

Fig. 3-39. Shapes and sections of sofa parts.

with enough depth for the lip on the clip to come level with the surface. Put a single groove in each seat end (FIG. 3-39B) and double grooves in the center rail (FIG. 3-39C). Round the edges of the wood where the rubber will cross.

Make the seat frame (FIG. 3-40A). The ends extend at the angle shown on the full-size drawing to attach to the rear legs (FIG. 3-39D). The long rails can be attached to the end rails with dowels, comb joints, or dovetails. Dowel the center rail in place. Drill for the dowels into the rear legs—three 1/2-inch diameters

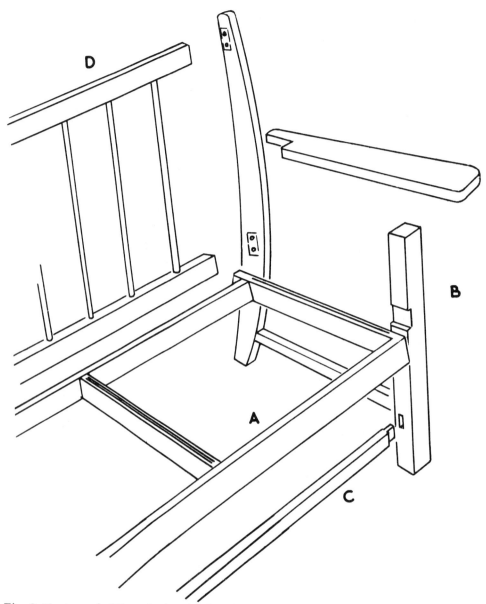

Fig. 3-40. *An end of the sofa showing how the parts fit together.*

should be enough. Make the two front legs (FIGS. 3-38B and 3-40B), using your full-size drawing to get the positions and angles of the other parts.

Allow for mortises for the bottom rails. Make shallow notches for the seat frame. When you assemble, you can screw into these joints from inside the seat

Materials List for Sofa

2 rear legs	$1^1/_4$	× 5	× 32
2 front legs	2	× 2	× 23
2 arms	1	× 4	× 24
2 seat ends	$1^1/_4$	× 3	× 24
2 seat rails	$1^1/_4$	× 3	× 44
1 seat center rail	$1^1/_2$	× 3	× 24
2 bottom rails	$1^1/_4$	× $1^1/_4$	× 23
2 bottom rails	$1^1/_4$	× $1^1/_4$	× 44
2 back rails	$1^1/_4$	× 2	× 44
10 back spindles	20	×	$^1/_2$ diameter dowel rods

frame. At the top, there could be four dowels or two stub tenons (FIG. 3-39E). These joints should be strong, as users tend to pull up on the arms.

Make the bottom rails (FIG. 3-40C) to fit all around with tenons into the legs. Use the seat frame, with an allowance for the front leg notches, as a guide to length between the shoulders of the long rails. The full-size drawing gives you the size of the end rails.

Make the two back rails (FIG. 3-40D), and prepare the ends for mortise-and-tenon joints or dowels. Drill the rails for the upright spindles (FIG. 3-38C) at about $3^1/_2$-inch spacing.

Mark out the two arms (FIG. 3-39F). Their inner edges come square to the front, but the other edge flares outwards (FIG. 3-38D). Delay completely cutting to size until after the other parts have been assembled, in case there are slight discrepancies. The front ends could be prepared for the joints to the front legs, but leave the notch to be cut at the other end as you fit each arm.

Fit the dowel spindles between the back rails, but check that the spacing between the rails suits their positions on the rear legs.

Join the back rails and the long bottom rails between the rear legs. See that the assembly is square so far and matches the length of the seat frame.

Join the front legs to the seat frame and the front bottom rail. Put in the end bottom rails. Check that the assembly is square and stands level.

Try the arms in position and cut the notches. Round the forward parts of the arms. Use dowels between the notched parts and the rear legs.

The 2-inch rubber webbing should be used with spaces about $1^1/_2$ inches. That means five or six strips each side for a total length of about 20 feet, plus 24 clips to squeeze on the ends. If you do not have a special tool, the clips can be squeezed to close them and make their teeth penetrate the webbing in a vise. Make a trial strip. Put a clip on one end and press that in the rail groove. Stretch the webbing across until you judge there is a suitable tension to give adequate springing under a cushion. Mark that length, with an allowance for the clip. Let this spring back, and use it as a guide to make all the other pieces the same length.

Fit all the rubber webbing strips, evenly spaced in their sections, and try the seating with all the cushions in position. If it is satisfactory, remove the webbing and cushions, and give the woodwork a final sanding before applying its finish.

4

Tables

Next to something to sit on comes the need for surfaces for eating and carrying out many of the activities of everyday life. Consequently, tables have been made in a great variety of patterns, from simple improvisations to very elaborate structures.

The choice of table designs available can allow you to match your skill and needs. There are light and folding tables, there are large dining tables, and there are many other table types in between.

The books from which the table designs in this section have been selected contain projects that cover all needs, ranging from the simplest to the most elaborate. In the following pages are details of tables of many kinds that are good examples of their types, and all the projects are interesting to build and satisfactory in use. Like chairs, tables are liable to get rough treatment, so you shouldn't rely on quick and nonstandard methods of construction. The instructions for these projects cover accepted, craftsmanlike methods appropriate to the particular tables.

Classic Table

What may be regarded as the classic type of table has tapered legs without lower rails. Rigidity comes from the joints between the legs and the top rails, which must be fairly deep to give adequate width in the joints. The top overlaps and has molded edges.

You can cut the tapered legs with a table saw, either by following a line or, preferably, with the aid of a wedge-shaped jig or push stick, which keeps the wood at the correct angle to the fence. This might be cut for the particular job or, if you expect to cut tapers frequently, you could make an adjustable guide.

The wood should be a good hardwood that will have an attractive grain when polished. Joints between rails and legs can be dowels, but if you want to follow tradition in this table, use mortises and tenons, which are described in these instructions. The top is held on with buttons, in the traditional way, to allow for expansion and contraction without the risk of the top splitting. The sizes shown (FIG. 4-1) are for a light side table, but the method of construction could be used for tables of other sizes.

Mark out the legs (FIG. 4-2A) before cutting the tapers. Leave a little extra wood at the tops for trimming level after the framework is assembled.

Cut the rails to size. Make grooves near the tops of the inner surfaces (FIG. 4-2B) to take the buttons. Mark and cut the joints between the rails and the legs (FIG. 4-3A). To get maximum glue area, take the tenons in to meet and miter their ends (FIG. 4-2C).

Fig. 4-1. A classic table for use in the home.

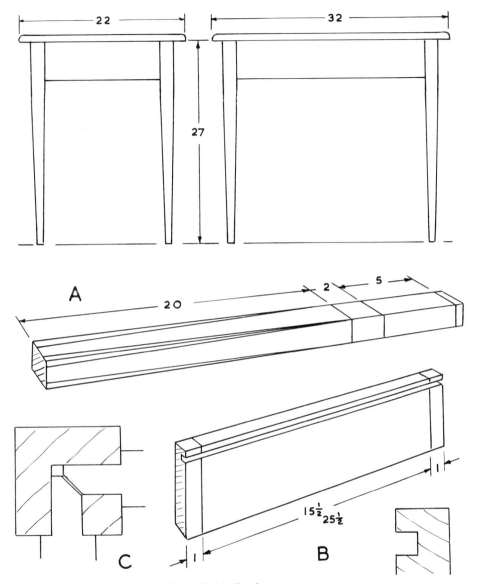

Fig. 4-2. Sizes of the classic table and details of parts.

Materials List for Classic Table

4 legs	$1^3/_4 \times 1^3/_4 \times 28$
2 rails	$^7/_8 \times 5 \times 29$
2 rails	$^7/_8 \times 5 \times 19$
Buttons from	$^3/_4 \times 1^1/_2 \times 24$
1 top	$^3/_4 \times 22 \times 33$
	joined boards

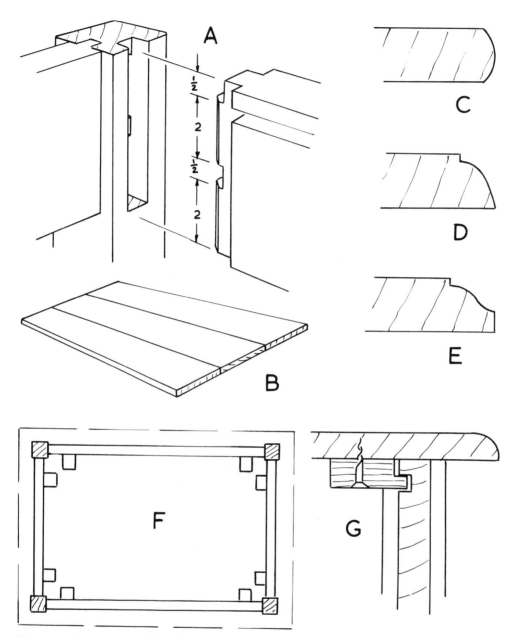

Fig. 4-3. *Construction of the classic table and sections of its top.*

Cut the tapers on the legs. They go from the full 1³/₄ inches square below the rail positions to 1 inch square at the foot. Follow sawing with planing. If the saw leaves a reasonably smooth surface, light hand planing will be better than power planing.

Sand the wood, and take sharpness off the lower edges of the rails, which can be molded, if you like. Assemble the long sides. Because there will be no lower framing to hold the assembly true, careful squaring is important. Check also for lack of twist.

Assemble the rails the other way, again checking squareness. Compare diagonal measurements across the tops of the legs for squareness that way.

Make the top by gluing sufficient boards (FIG. 4-3B). The final size should overhang the legs by about 1½ inches all around. The edges may be left square, be rounded (FIG. 4-3D), or be molded (FIGS. 4-3D and 4-3E).

Make buttons. On the size table suggested here, two in each side towards the legs should be sufficient (FIG. 4-2F). Make each so that when it is screwed to the top, its projecting tongue will pull up on the groove (FIG. 4-3G).

Invert the frame work on the underside of the top and locate it centrally. When you screw the buttons, allow clearance so any movement of the top is not restricted.

See that the table stands level. If necessary, adjust the bottoms of legs. Take sharpness off them, so as not to mark carpets.

Refectory Dining Table

This table of traditional form is made in the traditional way (FIG. 4-4). The name *refectory* comes from the massive tables used in the refectories, or dining halls, of the great monasteries of Europe, where the end supports were trestles made in this way. Some of the large tables were joined with wedged tusk tenons so they could be disassembled, which was probably necessary to get the tables from room to room. However, this table is not intended to take apart, and it is of a size that could pass through modern doorways.

The table has a top 30 inches wide × 42 inches long, standing 29 inches above the floor. It will accommodate four people comfortably or six rather closely, but make the table any length if you want it to regularly suit six or more people. Keep height and width the same—or check the sizes of doorways if you want to make it much wider.

Fig. 4-4. A refectory dining table of traditional form.

Materials List for
Refectory Dining Table

2 pedestal tops	$28 \times 3 \times 1^1/_2$
2 pedestal feets	$28 \times 4 \times 1^1/_2$
2 pedestal uprights	$26 \times 10 \times 1^1/_2$
2 rails	$28 \times 5 \times 1^1/_2$
1 top	$44 \times 30 \times 1^1/_4$
Buttons from	$33 \times 2 \times {}^3/_4$

Although it would be possible to use softwood to match other furniture, this is really a table to be made in a quality hardwood, and given a good finish by polishing. It would then be a piece of furniture to be proud of and worth the cost of the fairly large pieces of wood needed.

The structural joints are mortises and tenons. This is not an assembly where dowels might be substituted for satisfactory results. Sizes are given for joints, which might be cut by hand or machine. Alter them to suit your equipment, but do not vary sizes too much. There is some stopped chamfering, or grooving, which could be worked by hand, but this is most easily done with a suitable cutter in a router. A tabletop of this width is liable to expand and contract enough to matter, even if you start with properly seasoned wood, so it is held down by buttons which can slide.

Construction is done in stages. First, make the two pedestals completely; then prepare the lengthwise parts, and assemble them to the pedestals. Finally, make the top and attach it. It is best to sand and prepare each part for finishing as it is made, taking care not to damage joints, rather than to wait until after assembling sections or the whole table before thinking about the finish.

Make the tops of the pedestals (FIGS. 4-5A and 4-6A). Taper and round the ends. Cut grooves for the buttons along what will be the inside top edges (FIG. 4-6B). Mark where the upright will come (FIG. 4-6C).

The feet are very similar (FIGS. 4-5A and 4-6A). Cut similar tapers to rounded ends. Mark where the mortises will come on the top surface. Mark where the cutout will be underneath (FIG. 4-6E), but it will probably be better to leave this uncut until after you have made the mortises, so as to have a flat supporting surface.

On the uprights (FIG. 4-5C) allow for tenons $1^1/_2$ inches long at each end (FIG. 4-6F). Mark where the rails will come. The lower rail is 2 inches up from the joint (FIG. 4-6G). The top rail has to overlap the pedestal top (FIG. 4-6H).

Mark out the tenons on both ends of the upright. There are four tenons with a wider gap at the center (FIG. 4-5D) in order to give clearance for the tenon on the top rail; use the same arrangement at the bottom. Make the tenons one-third the thickness of the wood.

Be careful to have clean lines on the shoulders when you cut the tenons. Mark the line with a knife cut; then the joints will close neatly.

Cut the mortises to match; then do the shaping under the feet.

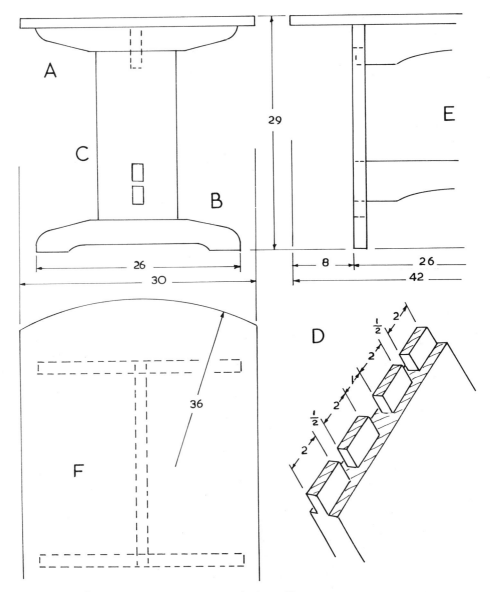

Fig. 4-5. *Sizes and a joint of the refectory dining table.*

Chamfering edges lightens the appearance and gives a high-quality effect. It is not essential, but if you have suitable equipment, it is worth doing. A chamfer or groove, about 3/8 inch, is appropriate. Go all around the projecting curved ends and up to 1 inch of the joint. Do the same on the edges of the upright (FIG. 4-7A). Assemble the pedestals, and see that they match.

The two lengthwise rails (FIG. 4-5E) are the same between shoulders (FIG. 4-7B), but they differ in the tenon arrangements. They have curves on the undersides;

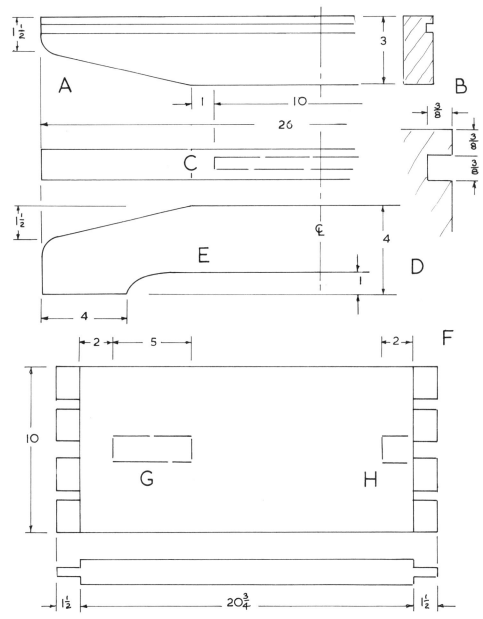

Fig. 4-6. Sizes of parts of the refectory dining table.

these might have chamfers worked to match those on the pedestals, but do not carry the chamfers along the parallel parts.

Cut grooves for buttons along both sides of the top rail (FIG. 4-7C), the same size as those on the pedestal.

The tenons on the bottom rail will go right through the pedestal upright.

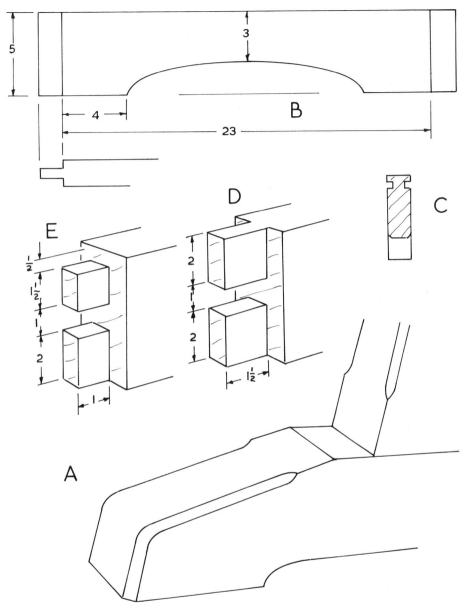

Fig. 4-7. Shaped parts and joints of the refectory table.

Mark and cut them as shown (FIG. 4-7D). Make them slightly too long at first to allow for leveling with the uprights after assembly.

The tenons on the top rail will enter the pedestal top and the upright and not go through. Cut them as shown (FIG. 4-7E); the top tenon will be entirely in the crosspiece between the upright tenons; the other tenon comes at the top of the upright.

Cut matching mortises in the pedestals. Those at the top are the same sides as the button grooves. Mark and cut the mortises for the lower rail on both sides of the upright to reduce the risk of grain breaking out during cutting.

Join the rails to the pedestals. Check that the assemblies are square and remain so while the glue is setting. It might help to lightly nail or clamp temporary strips across the ends of the pedestal tops.

Although a modern glue will make secure joints, the lower exposed joints will look traditional and be stronger if there are two wedges in each tenon (FIG. 4-8A). Put saw cuts across the tenons before fitting them; drive in glued wedges, and cut them level after the glue has set.

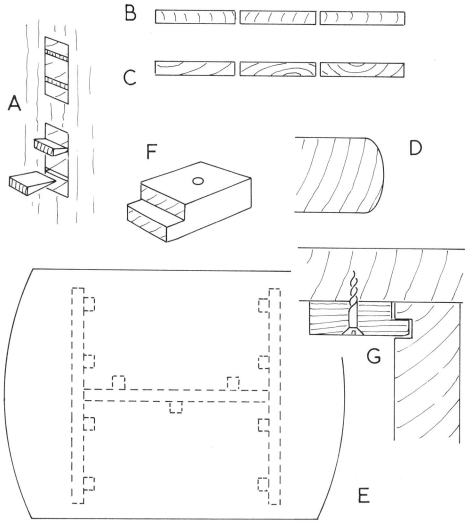

Fig. 4-8. Leg joint (A) and details of the top (B−E) and buttons (F and G).

The top (FIG. 4-5F) has parallel sides and curved ends. Prepare it by gluing together sufficient boards. Reduce any risk of warping by using boards which are radially cut showing the end grain lines through the thickness of the board (FIG. 4-8B). Otherwise, cancel any risk of warping by joining boards with the end grain in opposite directions (FIG. 4-8C). Try to assemble the top so there is an interesting grain pattern showing, if it is that sort of wood. Using a good glue should be sufficient. Earlier tops with poorer glues would have had some dowels in each joint.

Cut the outline of the top to shape. Level and sand the upper surface. Leave the edges of the top square or mold them. If you want to follow tradition, round them to half an elliptical section (FIG. 4-8D).

Prepare sufficient buttons to screw under the top and hold it to the center rail and the tops of the pedestals. Much depends on the rigidity of the top or any tendency to warp, now or later, but the arrangement shown (FIG. 4-8E) should be sufficient. If the table is lifted by its top, all the load comes on the screws through the buttons, so allow enough.

Cut the buttons (FIG. 4-8F) so each pulls against the top of the groove when the screw is fully tightened (FIG. 4-8G). Allow for possible movement by arranging them so there are spaces between the bottoms of the grooves and the edges of the wood.

Assemble the inverted framework on the inverted top. Center it and screw on the buttons. Locate the buttons and their holes; then keep the top away from the framework until after you have applied a finish.

Sawbuck Table

Many ecclesiastical tables and chairs in Europe incorporated crossed legs. Many old monasteries and cathedrals have examples of crossed-leg furniture many hundreds of years old, although their users would not recognize the term *sawbuck*. Many settlers in America would have known these tables and chairs, which were usually large and of quite heavy construction, so when they were faced with the need to make furniture for public buildings and churches, they reproduced these designs. A modern reproduction of this type might be regarded as a reproduction of a reproduction.

Much of the beauty of these tables was in the legs. Exact reproductions of many of them would be too large to use in a modern home, and they would also require sizes of wood that might be almost impossible to obtain, but lighter versions can be attractive. The full-size version was usually a refectory table, the communal table around which the monks sat to eat a meal. A smaller version makes a good dining-room table with plenty of character (FIG. 4-9A).

Tenoning of the legs into the top rails was usual and is advisable today because maximum strength is needed for a heavy table that could put excessive strain on joints if mishandled or dropped when moving. The type of decoration shown in FIG. 4-9B comes from an ecclesiastical table, but it is appropriate to a dining room.

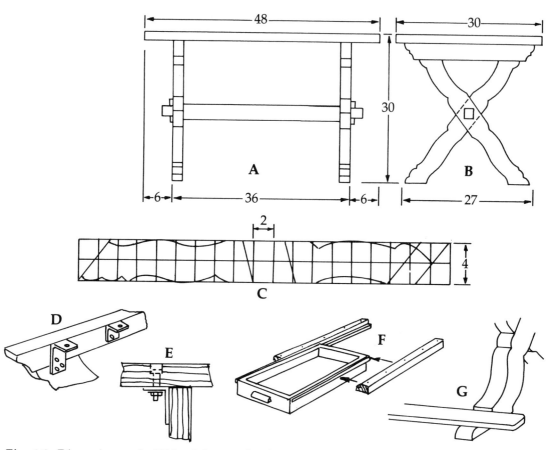

Fig. 4-9. Dimensions and additional features for the sawbuck side table.

**Materials List for
Sawbuck Side Table**

1 top	30 × 48 × $1^{1}/_{2}$
4 legs	4 × 40 × $1^{3}/_{4}$
2 rails	3 × 28 × $1^{3}/_{4}$
1 stretcher	3 × 42 × $1^{3}/_{4}$

A full-size drawing would give the angles of joints and cuts, but it is probably advisable to make a template for marking the shaping so all four legs are identical (FIG. 4-9C). They are most simply cut with a band saw, but you can remember the hard labor and skill of the original craftsmen by using hand tools. Make sure all signs of machine sawing are removed from the decorated edges. In addition to sanding, scrape with a metal scraper or the edge of a broken piece of glass to remove saw marks from the more awkward parts of the design.

The tabletop must be fairly thick, and you will need to build it up from several boards glued edge to edge. As much as possible, select wood where the end grain of one board is the opposite way to the next, to minimize any overall tendency to warp. With modern glues and even clamping, a simple edge-to-edge joint will suffice, but for further security you can use dowels between boards or work the edges with tongue-and-groove joints. Even if the boards have all been machine-planed, you will need to hand-plane the top surface. Something might be done with a power sander, but be sure there are no signs of its action in the finished surface. You will need to spend some time getting the top smooth, but this and the shaping of the legs are the outstanding features of the design.

Because of the weight of even this lightened version, it is unwise to depend only on wood screws to hold the top to the leg rails. Instead, it is advisable to follow what was customary in the heavier originals. Iron angle brackets go inside the top rails (FIG. 4-9D). Those above the legs should overlap onto them so two or three stout wood screws can be driven. The original brackets would have been made by a blacksmith, but you should be able to adapt iron shelf brackets that will look sufficiently authentic. The originals would have been black from forging, so bright modern brackets would not look right. The number of brackets depends on their size, but four should be enough.

To hold the top, bolt through these brackets, but before drilling any holes, invert the assembled legs and stretcher over the reversed top. Get its position correct, and check that the framework is square and the legs are upright. When you are certain everything is as accurate as you can get it, mark through the bolt holes in the brackets. Drill through with an undersize drill from the underside. This will give the location on the top without the risk of grain breaking out, which might happen with a larger drill.

Use carriage bolts to fix the top. Counterbore enough to sink the head far enough below the surface to allow for plugging, then follow through the small pilot hole with a drill to suit the bolt (FIG. 4-9E). Insert all the bolts, then tighten progressively all around until the top is tight. Make the plugs from the same wood as the top. Their grain should be across to match the top.

Some refectory tables were fitted with shallow drawers for cutlery. Because there was no framing between the legs immediately under the top, they were easy to fit. One type of drawer could be opened from either side, and this would be useful in a modern dining table version. Make the drawer in the usual way, but with what amounts to two fronts. Dovetail the two fronts and fit them with handles.

Hang the drawer from slides fixed under the tabletop. Attach square strips along the top edges of the drawer sides. Screw rabbeted pieces below the tabletop as runners (FIG. 4-9F). On a long table, you could have more than one drawer, but keep them shallow so as not to impede the knees of sitters.

Other additions to some refectory tables were footboards (FIG. 4-9G). These were intended to provide somewhere to put the feet a few inches above the ground. There is no real need for footboards on a reproduction, but you could provide them if you like.

Take-Down Trestle Table

The original idea, used by traveling noblemen, of making tables and other furniture to take apart for storage or transport can still be used today. A table made in this way will pack flat when not needed, yet it will make a more substantial piece of furniture than many modern tables made to fold or disassemble for camping and similar purposes. Even where the table is kept in constant use for long periods, it is convenient to be able to reduce its size when not needed temporarily, as when rearranging the furnishings of the home or when moving.

This table is of fairly light construction, although it is of sufficient size for dining. It also would make a useful table in a child's room. It could be made of hardwood, but if you plan to take it down and move it frequently, it is better to use a softwood, such as yellow pine, for lightness. Much depends on the intended use. Softwood will have a good life with careful use, but hardwoods will take a better finish and might be needed to match existing furniture. They will also stand up to rougher use. This type of table can be used outdoors on a patio, but a durable wood must be used if it is to stay out in all weather.

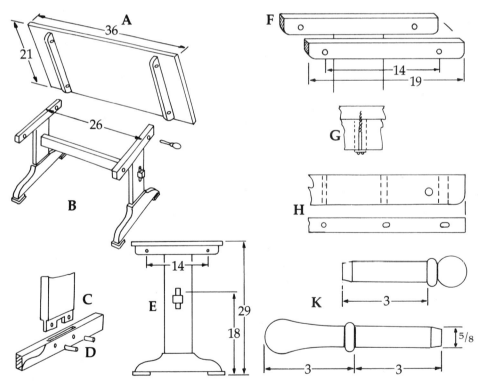

Fig. 4-10. *Takedown trestle table.*

Materials List for
Take-Down Trestle Table

1 top	21	× 36 × 1
2 braces	2	× 19 × 1
2 leg rails	2	× 19 × 1$^1/_2$
2 posts	6	× 25 × 1$^1/_4$
2 feet	4	× 19 × 1$^1/_2$
4 pads	2$^1/_2$ ×	4 × $^5/_8$
1 stretcher	2	× 30 × 3

The feet and top rails could have many different outlines. Those shown are easy to cut. Instead of the feet tapering toward the floor directly, they are given an upward curve, then pads are added to bear on the floor. This appearance of solidity around the feet prevents the table from looking excessively light (FIG. 4-10B).

Match the uprights with the parts they tenon into. Prepare and cut the joints before doing any shaping (FIG. 4-10C). Keep the tenons thick, and let them come to the extreme width of the wood to get the benefit of maximum resistance to bending. The tenons may go through the top rail, or only part way, as in the feet, but a tenon length of about 1$^1/_2$ inches is needed for adequate strength, particularly in softwood. Original tables of this type usually had pegs through the tenons. These pegs often were rounded only roughly from the square section, then driven into round holes. Their uneven outline can be seen on the surface of some old furniture. You can still make and use pegs in this way, but it will be simpler to use pieces of dowel (FIG. 4-10D).

The framed ends are held in place by a rail with wedged tusk tenons, then the top is attached with four pegs through braces under it and the crossbars of the end assemblies (FIG. 4-10A). If the pegs and wedges are removed, the table can be reduced to four almost flat pieces.

Fit the stretcher above half the height (FIG. 4-10E). Shape its ends as wedged tusk tenons. Fit the joints carefully so the assembly stands with the trestle legs upright when the wedges are tightened. Put the assembly on a flat floor and sight across the top rails to check for twist.

The top is a plain rectangle, which can be made up of several boards if necessary. The braces need not be as thick as the top rails of the trestles, but they should have similar outlines (FIG. 4-10F).

A pine top is likely to expand and contract in its width more than most hardwoods might. You should allow for this process in fitting the braces by using slot screwing. Expansion and contraction is most noticeable near the full width and is less obvious near the center of the board. This means that movement which must be allowed for is slightest close to the middle. With slot screwing, slot holes are made in the brace, usually by drilling two holes and cutting away the waste between them. Screws go through the slots into the top and have washers under their heads, so any movement of the top causes the screw to slide along its slot (FIG. 4-10G).

In this table, there is one screw through a round hole at the center, two others with slots about $1/2$ inch long, and two farther out about $3/4$ inch long (FIG. 4-10H). Locate the braces on the underside of the top so they fit easily over the tops of the trestles. Check the whole table for squareness, particularly that the trestles are upright in relation to the top, before fixing the braces.

Hold the top to the trestles by pegs, or trunnel pins, through holes. It might be possible to have only one central peg at each end, but wear might cause the top to wobble. It is better to have two pegs in each place, spaced fairly widely. The pegs could be pieces of dowel given a slight taper at one end for ease in driving. If a lathe is available, however, you can turn pegs with knobs (FIG. 4-10K)—either round ends for gripping to pull, or longer handles that might be better for twisting to remove. In either case, it probably will be necessary to use a hammer or mallet to drive out the pegs when they have been in place for a long time.

Only in exceptionally accurate work or by a great deal of luck will the top reverse on the framework and the peg holes line up properly again. It is better to mark the way the peg holes were drilled, so the table is always assembled the same way. An X-cut with two crossing chisel cuts on the adjoining brace and trestle will be better than a mark with a pencil or pen.

Matching Table and Benches

A table large enough for a meal for several people has to be made of fairly stout wood, but if your table saw is able to cut hardwood up to $13/4$ inches thick, most of the cuts can be done on it, if your wood is obtained already machined to thickness. This table (FIG. 4-11) could be made alone, but it is shown with matching benches, made in the same way, although of lighter-section wood. If made of a good quality hardwood and finished by polishing, these items are suitable for use indoors. A similar set, made of a durable wood or treated with preservative, could be used on a deck or patio and left outside for most of the year.

Materials List for Matching Table and Benches

4 table pedestals	$13/4$	×	3	×	23
2 table pedestals	$13/4$	×	8	×	25
4 table feet	1	×	$13/4$	×	5
2 tabletop rails	1	×	3	×	45
1 table rail	$11/2$	×	5	×	45
1 tabletop	$11/4$	×	27	×	56
8 bench pedestals	$11/2$	×	2	×	12
4 bench pedestals	$11/2$	×	6	×	13
8 bench feet	1	×	$11/2$	×	4
2 bench rails	$11/2$	×	4	×	32
2 bench tops	$11/4$	×	12	×	40

Fig. 4-11. *A table with matching and stowing benches.*

Assembly is described with mortise-and-tenon joints for the main parts, for a traditional construction, but dowels could be used. Tenons can be cut accurately on the table saw and mortises shaped mostly with a drill. Solid wood is used for all parts, but the top could be made of framed plywood, for economical production.

This type of refectory table is made with end pedestals, which are built as units, then joined with one or more rails. The is added last. The benches are made in the same way to a reduced size.

As shown (FIG. 4-12A), the table has a top 27 inches wide and a length of 54 inches. If the benches are made with tops 12 inches wide and a length that fits easily between the table pedestals, they will push under the table until stopped by the lengthwise rail, and will then be completely under the table and out of the way (FIG. 4-12B). The tabletop is 29 inches high and the seat tops are 16 inches high. These are common heights, but you might want to check the heights of

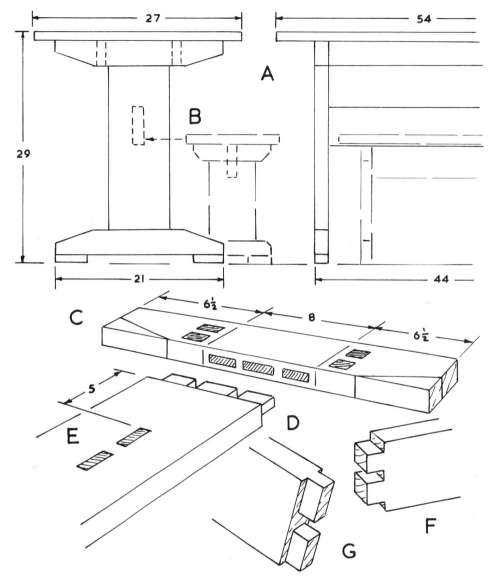

Fig. 4-12. Sizes and constructional details of the table.

existing tables and seats, if you wish them to match. If you alter heights very much, make sure the vertical rail between the table pedestals is in a suitable position to act as a stop when the benches are pushed in.

Prepare the wood for the table pedestals. All parts are 1³/₄ inches thick. Top and bottom have the same outlines, but rails tenon into the top, and there are blocks forming feet under the bottoms.

Mark out the tops (FIG. 4-12C). Allow for the uprights tenoning into the edge and mortises for the top rails $1/2$ inch outside the upright position, then taper to half thickness at the ends.

Mark out the bottoms in the same way, but without the mortises for the rails. Feet 1 inch thick and 4 inches long will go under the ends.

Mark out the uprights (FIG. 4-12D) with tenons 1-inch long to match the mortises. Mark the position of the main lengthwise rail and the mortises (FIG. 4-12E).

Make the two top rails, with tenons cut across to suit the direction of the grain of the pedestal tops (FIG. 4-12F). Make the main lengthwise rail with tenons to suit the vertical grain of the upright part of the pedestal (FIG. 4-12G). Tenons in all rails could be 1 inch long.

Cut the mortises to match the tenons, and finish shaping the pedestal parts. Glue them together, including the feet. See that they match.

Prepare the top rails for counterbored screws upwards into the top (FIG. 4-13A), at about 12-inch intervals. Drill near the ends of the pedestal tops similarly. After assembly, you may glue plugs in the holes, but because they are underneath, they don't really matter.

Join the pedestals with the rails. Check that the pedestals are upright and that the assembly is square by comparing diagonals. Stand it on a level surface while the glue sets.

Make the top by gluing sufficient boards to make up the width. A traditional refectory tabletop has square edges, but you could round or mold them, if you wish.

Invert the framework on the underside of the top, and locate it centrally. Screw through the holes, but do not use glue. The top might then expand and contract slightly without the risk of cracking.

The benches have a generally similar appearance to the table, but there is only a single rail between the pedestals (FIG. 4-13B).

Make the two pairs of pedestals in the same way as for the table, except allow for the mortise-and-tenon joints both ways under the top.

Mark out a rail so there is one tenon into the top of the pedestal and one into the upright (FIG. 4-13C). Arrange the tenons from the uprights into the top of a pedestal far enough apart to clear the mortises the other way (FIG. 4-13D).

Drill for screws upwards into the rails and ends in the same way as for the tabletop. Assemble the bench frameworks, checking squareness and freedom from twist.

When you cut the boards for the tops, make the length an easy fit inside the table pedestals. A clearance of 1 inch at each end will allow the benches to be pushed in without trouble.

Lightly round all exposed edges of the table and benches before applying a finish. Make sure there is no sharpness on the bench feet so floor covering will not be damaged.

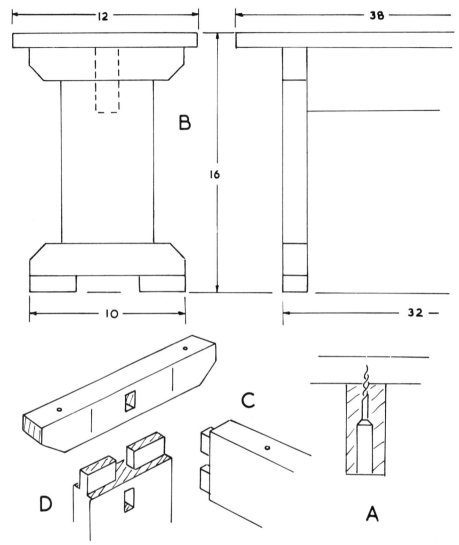

Fig. 4-13. Sizes and details of the benches to match the table.

Drop-Leaf Table

Some tables that can be adjusted in size are intended for sitting around, whether they are fully extended or in their reduced size. Another type is normally in its larger form for use, but the top can be reduced in size so the table occupies less space when not in use. There are several ways of arranging this, but usually part of the top is arranged to fold down. When it is hanging down, there is no space for a sitter's knees, so it is unsuitable for eating when folded, though it can still serve for storage as a side table. The example shown in FIG. 4-14A is based on an Appalachian original, but the type was common to many early households.

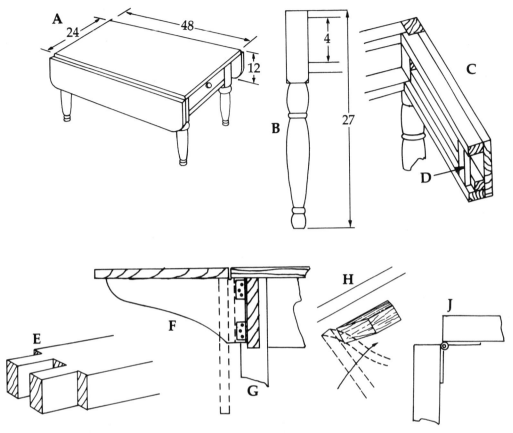

Fig. 4-14. Drop-leaf table.

Make the table framework in the same way as for a plain table. Legs could be square and tapered, but lathes came early so many legs on the originals were turned. The drawing is of an original type (FIG. 4-14B). A drawer at one end is useful and easily incorporated.

Attach upper and lower drawer rails at one end, extending them for at least the distance the drawer is to go with runners and kickers. Make the guides level with the inner surfaces of the legs (FIG. 4-14C). Use small blocks of wood on the runners to stop the drawer at the right position (FIG. 4-14D). Delay fitting these until the drawer is made and put in position, then locate the blocks to come against the drawer. It helps in stiffening the table to make the lower drawer rail wide, with twin tenons (FIG. 4-14E). A large table might have a rail across the center, which could also act as a drawer stop.

The main part of the top is a simple rectangle with a reasonable overhang at the ends, but only slightly wider than the distance across the tops of the legs. You can use brackets on hinges to hold up the drop leaves (FIG. 4-14F). The amount of overhang of the top should be enough to allow the leaves to hang with some clearance over the brackets when folded (FIG. 4-14G).

If you make the brackets to a right angle you might theoretically expect them to hold the leaves level when swung out, but wear and slackness in the hinge knuckles, as well as the need for clearance to allow for moving the brackets, cause the leaves to sag slightly, unless something is done about it. Where a bracket comes under the leaf, fit a small wedge, longer and going deeper than you expect at first (FIG. 4-14H). The bracket swings on to this and can be moved as far as is necessary to level the top. There could be a stop on the wedge, but usually it is sufficient to continue the deep part of the wedge parallel for a short distance.

In the simplest arrangement, the leaves hang on hinges and have square edges (FIG. 4-14J). Locate three hinges so they do not come in the way of the brackets when the brackets are swung out.

Although square-edged boards might have been practical, the joint was not beautiful, and many cabinetmakers brought with them knowledge of what was usually called a *rule joint* as the normal way of dealing with boards in a drop-leaf tabletop. In Europe, extended hinges, called *back-flap* hinges, were used to give stronger joints. The name *rule joint* comes from a similarity of the section to the joint used in some two-fold rules (FIG. 4-15A).

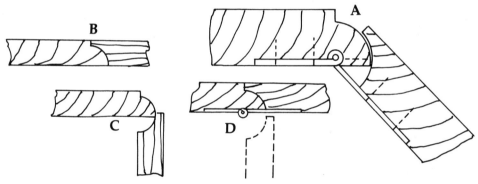

Fig. 4-15. *Rule joint for a drop flap, showing the relative positions of the parts.*

Materials List for Drop-Leaf Table

1 top	24	× 48 ×	1
2 leaves	12	× 24 ×	1
4 legs	3	× 27 ×	3
2 side rails	$6^{1/2}$ × 47 ×		1
1 end rail	$6^{1/2}$ × 23 ×		1
2 drawer rails	$2^{1/2}$ × 23 ×		$1^{1/4}$
4 brackets	6	× 12 ×	1
4 drawer runners	2	× 24 ×	$1^{1/4}$
2 drawer guides	1	× 24 ×	1
1 drawer front	4	× 18 ×	1
2 drawer sides	4	× 24 ×	$5/8$
1 drawer back	4	× 18 ×	$5/8$
1 drawer bottom	18	× 24 ×	$1/4$

For the traditional method of making the joint, there had to be hollow and round planes, but a modern way of forming the shapes could be with a spindle molder or suitable router cutters. When the tabletop is up, the edges should meet closely. The leaf should follow the curve as it swings down so there is little gap showing and the meeting surfaces have a molded look (FIG. 4-15B). A backflap hinge is designed to be used with its knuckle upward and the two parts can swing back to a right angle, which is further than normal hinges will go. Notch the knuckle into the wood so it comes at the center of the curve molded on the edge (FIG. 4-15C). If you use an ordinary hinge, it will have to be arranged with the knuckle downward, and the action will not be quite as accurate when the parts move in relation to each other (FIG. 4-15D).

Swivel-Top Table

One way of arranging a tabletop with drop leaves—without brackets, gatelegs, or other supports for the leaves—is to have the top swiveling on the framework, which is narrow and long. The leaves hang down when the top assembly is crosswise, but if the leaves are lifted level and the top turned through a right angle, they will be held up by resting on the ends of the framework. The top parts are best joined with backflap hinges, but if ordinary hinges are used, the top can be raised on packings so the hinges clear the framework as it is turned. Metal pivots were originally made, and modern versions can be bought, but a bolt type and a wooden pivot are described here.

Although this type of table could stand on upright legs, a more stable form has the legs splayed in both directions. The example shown is a small side table, but the method could be used for a table of any size. This example gets its stiffness from wide top rails only. With straight-grained wood for the legs and good mortise-and-tenon joints, preferably doweled through, the result is a graceful, rigid table (FIG. 4-16A).

The compound angles resulting from splaying the legs both ways need not cause difficult work if you tackle them systematically. The angles in both directions need not be the same; there could be more splay in the width than the length. Setting out is simpler, though, if the angle is the same both ways.

Make a full-size drawing of a leg and one corner. It is helpful if the top line is at least as long as half the length of the side rail.

When a framework is splayed in two directions, the view of a leg from above remains a right angle, but the actual section becomes a diamond. With a wide splay, this becomes increasingly important if joints are to fit properly, and you must use geometry to find the angles to which the legs must be planed. With a double splay of only a few degrees, as in this example, the difference between a theoretically correct section and a square section is very slight. By using bare-faced tenons in the rail joints, you avoid the slight difference between the fit of front and back shoulders of each joint, so you can make the legs to square sections.

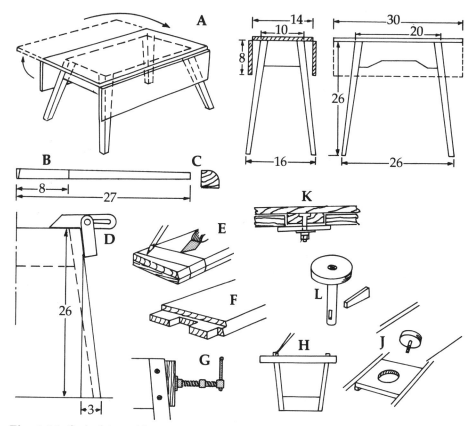

Fig. 4-16. Swivel-top table.

Each leg is square and parallel to a point below where the rails will come, then there is a slight taper on each side to the bottom (FIG. 4-16B). The legs look even more graceful if you round the outer corner, starting with only a slight curve at the top of the taper and continuing to a quarter circle at the foot (FIG. 4-16C). Allow a little excess length at top and bottom of each leg.

Set an adjustable bevel to the angle shown in FIG. 4-16D, and lock it at that. It is the only angle other than a right angle you will need to test, but it should be the same throughout.

Mark the wood for the two side rails. Plane the top edges to the angle of your adjustable bevel. The bottom edges can remain at right angles. Put the two pieces together, and mark across their edges the length between shoulders and a further 1 inch at each end for the tenons. Mark the shoulders on the outer surfaces with a knife and the ends of the tenons with a pencil, using the adjustable bevel (FIG. 4-16E). Cut the pieces to length mark the widths of the tenons, and cut away the waste. Then shape the tenons (FIG. 4-16F).

Materials List for Swivel-Top Table

1 top	14	× 30 × 1
2 leaves	8	× 30 × 1
4 legs	1½	× 27 × 1½
2 rails	6	× 20 × ¾
2 rails	6	× 10 × ¾
1 center pad	6	× 10 × ¾
Rotating gear as required		

Mark the mortises to match the tenons, and cut them. Do the same with the short rails. Do not try any of the joints at this stage. The rails must be fairly deep to provide stiffness. You can leave them full width or reduce their central areas, either by cutting back with plain curves or with a decorative outline. You might want to leave the end rails full depth and only reduce the side rails. In any case, leave a good width of full-depth ends so as not to weaken the joints with short grain.

The best way to tackle assembly is to first make up the two sides, ignoring the splay in the other direction, then add the short rails to join the sides. You must pull the joints tight and make two packing blocks for the bar clamp to squeeze on. While the clamp is still on, drill through for a dowel into each extending tenon (FIG. 4-16G). Check the two side assemblies on each other. Turn one over on the other. This will show if the splay is the same at each corner. Let the glue set before proceeding.

Make all four joints the other way at the same time since the meeting surfaces will not be quite at right angles due to the double splay. Make a dry trial assembly with the tenons only entered a short distance. This will show that they are not entering quite squarely and it might be necessary to pare the side of each tenon slightly with a chisel to get a neat fit. Apply glue and clamp the joints, preferably pulling each end tighter a little at a time to keep the shape uniform. Dowel through in the same way as at the sides, and check that the corners at the top are at right angles by using a try square and checking diagonals.

The beveled top edges of the rails will show how much to cut off the tops of the legs. Measure down each leg the same amount, and make a mark on the outer corner for the foot. Use a long, straight board as a guide to mark where the legs are to be cut (FIG. 4-16H). Round the edges of these cuts.

You can make up the top from three boards, preferably with rule joints and backflap hinges, but you can cut the meeting edges square and use plain hinges for a simpler construction. If you use sizes different from those given here, make the center part long enough to have a slight overhang on the framework, but wide enough to allow the leaves to hang without touching the splayed legs. The proportions are best if the ends of the framework come more than halfway under the raised leaves when the top is turned to give the full area.

The top shown has square corners and plain edges, but you could treat it in any of the ways described for the tops of earlier tables. Many of these tables had round tops; others were elliptical. Hanging, curved leaves have a pleasing appearance. You can round or square edges. Much shaping goes better with turned legs, and a plainer treatment is all that is needed with the legs shown.

Glue and screw a disk to the underside of the center of the top. The disk fits in a hole in a board fitted between the framework sides. Bevel its ends to fit, and support it by strips screwed to the sides (FIG. 4-16J). You can turn the disk, but perfection in its outline is not essential to its functioning, so a handcut circle will do. This also applies to the hole it fits. Providing the disk will turn in the hole, a small amount of slackness is unimportant and preferable to parts that bind against each other at some points.

Another, larger disk goes below the disk in the hole and overlaps the hole. In modern construction, this would best be made of plywood, considering it does not show. But if you want complete authenticity, you could use any thin wood that is unlikely to crack or split.

The best way to arrange the pivot is to use a bolt with its head let into the top disk. Attach the bolt through both disks to two nuts with a washer (FIG. 4-16K). Glue and screw the disk to the underside of the top after you insert the bolt. Adjust the nuts to allow the top to turn without undue slackness, then lock them by tightening them against each other. An original blacksmith-made bolt would have had a square head and square nuts, but you might need to use modern machine-made screws and nuts.

Some of these tables were made with wooden pivots. Drill a hole in both disks. Make a stout round wood rod and slot it at the bottom to take a long wedge (FIG. 4-16L). Glue and wedge the rod in the hole in the top disk. This must be a secure fit, and you can drive two glued wedges into the top across each other to resist the downward pull that will come later. Fit the rod through the lower disk, and drive a wedge in the slot, so it will stay in place to get the best tension on the assembly.

Magazine Rack/Table

A rack for magazines and newspapers keeps these things tidy and is often positioned beside a chair, where it also would be useful to have a small table for books and refreshments. This unit combines the two functions (FIG. 4-17). In the lower two compartments, there is space for a reasonable number of newspapers and magazines. Above this is a top 12 inches × 24 inches.

The suggested construction is plywood for all the lower parts and solid wood for the top. Attractive hardwood with a clear finish for the top might be set off by having all the other parts painted. The sizes shown should suit most needs, but if you check such things as armchair height and sizes of the usual papers that come into your home, you can modify the measurements to match. The compartment divisions and the bottom fit through the ends with tenons, and these pro-

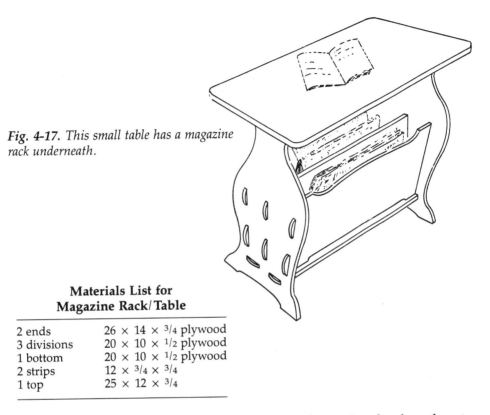

Fig. 4-17. *This small table has a magazine rack underneath.*

Materials List for Magazine Rack/Table

2 ends	26 × 14 × 3/4 plywood
3 divisions	20 × 10 × 1/2 plywood
1 bottom	20 × 10 × 1/2 plywood
2 strips	12 × 3/4 × 3/4
1 top	25 × 12 × 3/4

vide rigidity. A scroll saw would be the ideal tool for cutting the shaped parts, but you could also use a band saw or jigsaw.

The two ends (FIGS. 4-18 and 4-19A) are the key parts which will settle several sizes of other parts. Mark them about centerlines to get them symmetrical. Although 3/4-inch plywood is suggested, you might be able to use 1/2-inch plywood if it is stiff.

Cut the outlines; smooth and round the shaped edges. Wait to cut the mortises until you can match them to the tenons.

The three divisions (FIGS. 4-18 and 4-19B) are basically the same, but only the outer ones need shaped edges. The cutouts in the lower edges allow easy cleaning out of dust or paper scraps.

Make the divisions the same length and match their tenons with the mortises on the ends, then cut the joints.

Make the bottom (FIGS. 4-18C and 4-19C) to the same length, with straight rounded edges. Well round the exposed ends of the tenons. Put strips across for attaching the top (FIGS. 4-18D and 4-19D).

Round exposed edges of all parts, and sand the surfaces; then glue the parts together. Clamp the joints tightly, and see that there is no twist.

The top (FIG. 4-19E) can be one piece of solid wood or several pieces glued to make up the width. It would be possible to use framed plywood or veneered

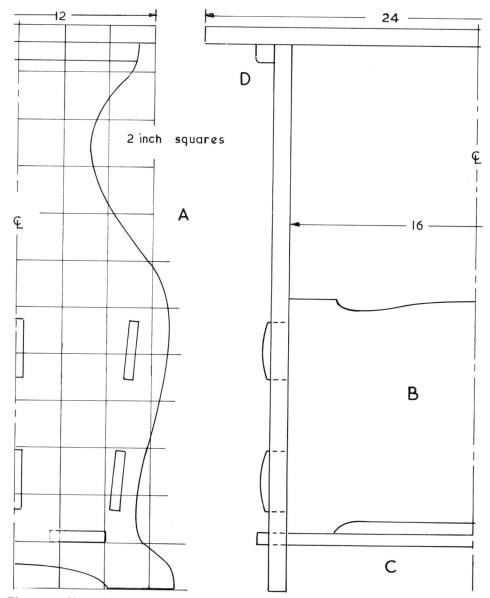

Fig. 4-18. Sizes of the magazine rack/table.

particleboard with suitable edging. A hardwood top could have its edges molded or rounded.

Attach the top with screws up through the end strips. Work with the assembly upside-down, and check that the parts are correctly centered.

Complete the project with a clear finish appropriate to the wood on the top and several coats of paint on the lower parts. You could have a lighter color inside the compartments.

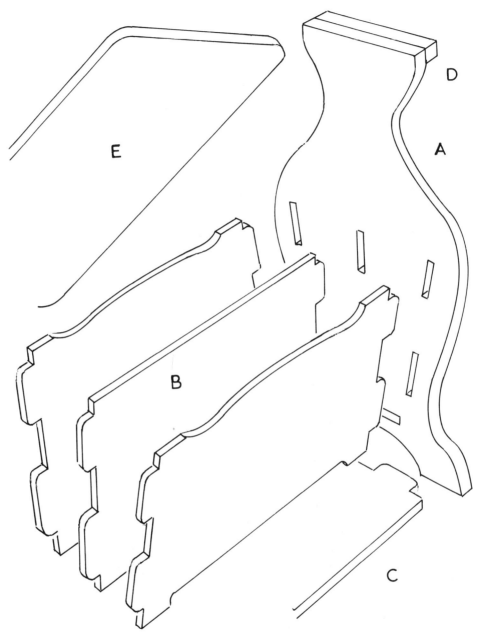

Fig. 4-19. Parts of the magazine rack/table.

Magazine Table

A coffee table with a rack underneath will keep magazines tidy and provide a top to spread them on. Because most magazines will fit into a 15-inch space, that should be the minimum size for the width of a rack under a table. The little table in FIG. 4-20 is shown 30 inches long, but it could be adapted to suit your needs or available space. The top might be solid wood or manufactured board or, as suggested, made of plywood faced with an attractive veneer and surrounded by a solid wood frame. The legs could be square or turned. The magazine rack is made with spaces between slats, so it is easily cleaned.

Materials List for Magazine Table

4 legs	$1^1/_2$	×	$1^1/_2$	×	18
2 rails	$^3/_4$	×	3	×	28
2 rails	$^3/_4$	×	3	×	18
2 rails	$^3/_4$	×	$1^1/_2$	×	28
2 rails	$^3/_4$	×	$1^1/_2$	×	18
4 slats	$^1/_2$	×	4	×	18
2 top frames	$^7/_8$	×	$2^1/_2$	×	30
2 top frames	$^7/_8$	×	$2^1/_2$	×	20
1 top	$^3/_8$	×	18	×	28 plywood

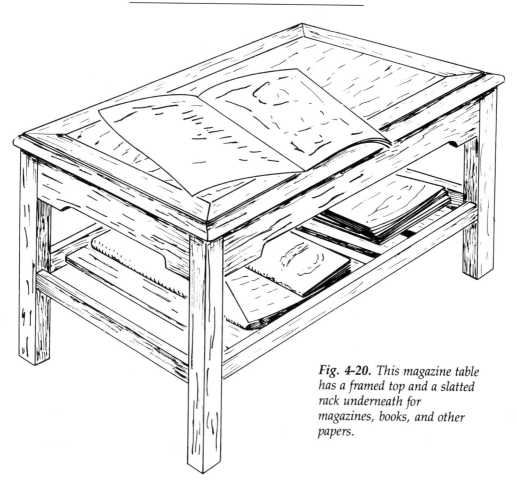

Fig. 4-20. This magazine table has a framed top and a slatted rack underneath for magazines, books, and other papers.

Mark out the four legs (FIG. 4-21A), leaving a little extra at the ends until after the joints have been cut. These could be tenons (FIG. 4-22A) or dowels (FIG. 4-22B).

If you want to turn the legs (FIG. 4-21B), mark the limits of the square parts before mounting the wood in the lathe. The legs could be left square and the same size throughout. They look better, though, with a light taper below the lower rails (FIG. 4-21C).

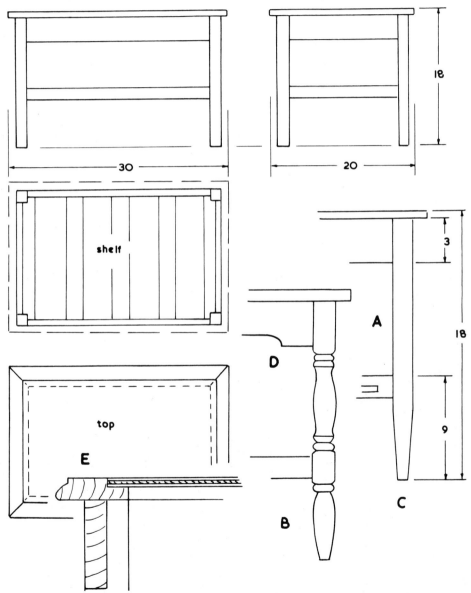

Fig. 4-21. Sizes and alternate leg details for the magazine table.

Prepare the wood for the top rails. The lower edges can be cut away (FIG. 4-21D) to give easier access to the magazines.

Make the bottom rails. They could be doweled, but with the smaller section, the joints are better tenoned (FIG. 4-22C). Plow grooves 1/4 inch wide and deep on the long rails to take the ends of the slats.

Reduce the ends of the four slats to fit the rail grooves (FIG. 4-22E).

Assemble the table ends first, checking for squareness and match against each other.

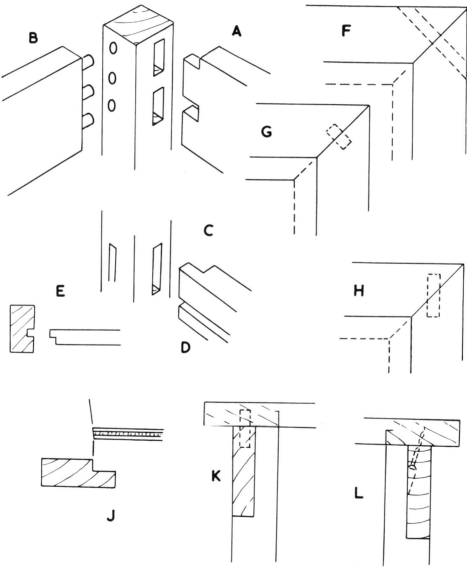

Fig. 4-22. Joints between parts of the magazine table.

Have the long parts and the slats ready, then assemble them completely. Check for squareness and lack of twist. See that the legs stand level.

Make the top so it is 1 inch outside the legs all around. Prepare the border strips (FIG. 4-21E) with rabbets to suit the plywood. Make them 3/4 inch wide to give a broad glue area.

Cut the miters so the length of the inner edges of these pieces come over the inner surfaces of the legs.

If you plan to leave the edges of the top square or rounded, use dowels diagonally across the joints (FIG. 4-22F). If you mold the edges, it would be better to use short dowels square to the miter (FIG. 4-22G) or parallel with one side (FIG. 4-22H).

Assemble the top frame, then cut the plywood to fit. For the closest fit, give the plywood edge a very slight taper (FIG. 4-22J). The top can be held with dowels in the rails (FIG. 4-22K) or with pocket screws (FIG. 4-22L).

Round Plywood Table

This little table is suitable for drinks and snacks (FIG. 4-23). It is of light construction and is easily carried. The main parts are 1/2-inch plywood, with the legs formed by two pieces notched together. The parts (FIG. 4-24) could be prefabricated for several tables at one time. This is a table for almost any room, but is particularly suitable as a side drinks table in a den.

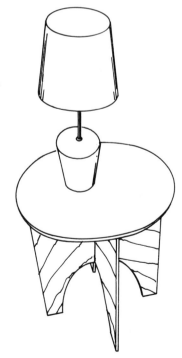

Fig. 4-23. A plywood table with a round top.

Materials List for
Round Plywood Table

2 legs	14 × 18	× 1/2 plywood
1 top	15 × 15	× 1/2 plywood
2 rails	3/4 ×	11/2 × 14

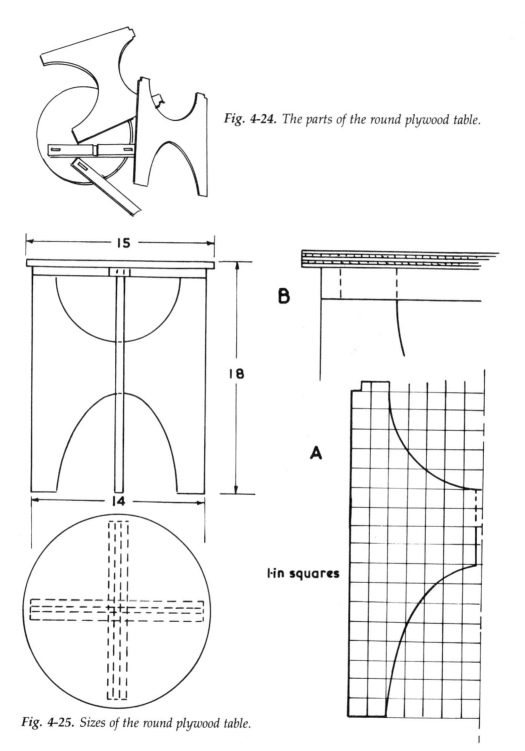

Fig. 4-24. The parts of the round plywood table.

15

18

14

B

A

l·in squares

Fig. 4-25. Sizes of the round plywood table.

If you choose a hardwood plywood, the table could be varnished. The top might have an attractive veneer left clear, while the edge is darkened. This table has a Formica top, and the edge is painted black. If fir plywood is used, a painted finish would be better.

For stability, the top shouldn't overhang very much. It is shown 1 inch bigger than the legs (FIG. 4-25).

Set out the shapes of the leg parts (FIG. 4-25A). If several tables are made, a hardboard half template would ensure uniformity.

Cut the curves, but do not cut the tenons until the rails are made. Cut the matching slots to be a tight push fit. The legs should assemble square and level (FIG. 4-26A).

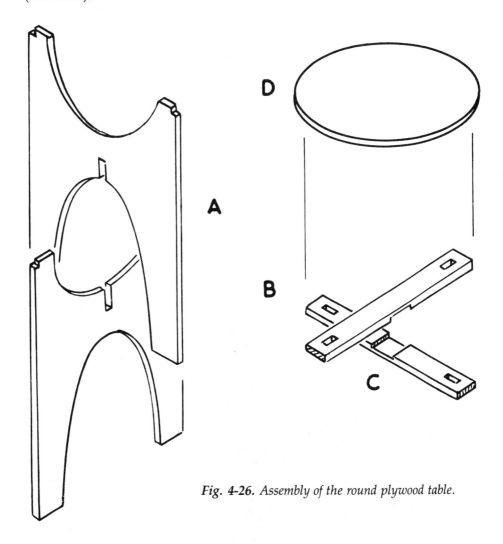

Fig. 4-26. *Assembly of the round plywood table.*

Make the two top rails (FIG. 4-26B). Their length is the same as the width of the legs. Cut a halving joint at the center so the surfaces finish level (FIG. 4-26C). Mark the mortises to fit the tenons on the legs. Cut these joints (FIG. 4-25B).

Remove all saw marks and round all edges, except where joints come. Glue the rails together, checking that they are square. Glue the legs together and to the rails. Check that the assembly stands level.

The top is shown with square edges (FIG. 4-26D). It could be rounded or molded, but plywood will not take fine detail on its edge. There could be plastic or veneer glued around as a lip. Cut the shape of the top as accurately as possible because discrepancies will be obvious. The outline could be octagonal if you wish.

Drinks Table

A chairside table that will hold bottles in its base is obviously convenient, but it also has the advantage of stability. Some small, light tables are easily knocked over, but up to four bottles low down will make the table very steady, even when the bottles are only partly full.

Size has to suit the bottles. Fortunately, many soft drink and wine bottles are all similar sizes, but if you want to use unusual sizes of bottles, adjust the table

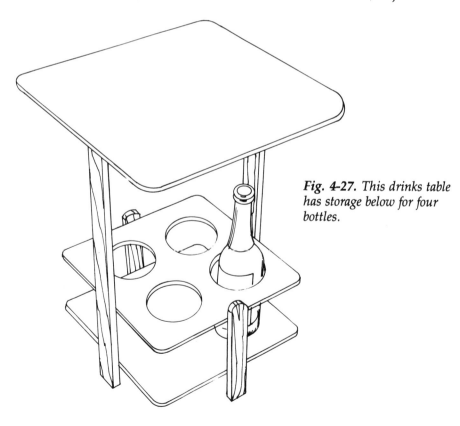

Fig. 4-27. This drinks table has storage below for four bottles.

sizes to suit. This table (FIG. 4-27) is designed to hold four bottles about 4 inches diameter and 15 inches high, and to give clearance for their removal. Smaller bottles and slightly larger ones would fit also (FIG. 4-28A).

The suggested materials are 1 × 2-inch softwood with 1/2-inch plywood. You could use Formica or other material on the top. With these materials, a painted finish is advised. If you want a better-quality furniture finish, use hardwood and veneered plywood.

The key parts that control other sizes are the long legs and the shelf with holes. Make them first.

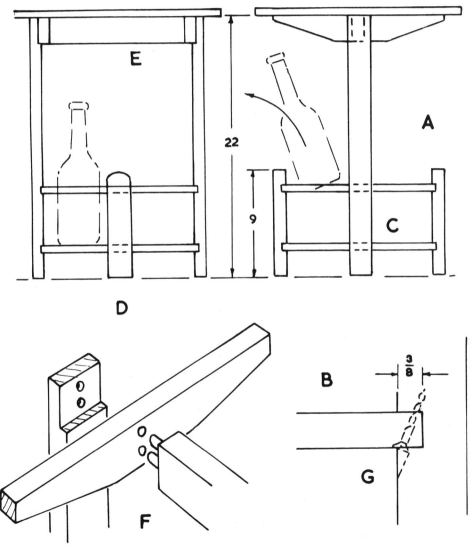

Fig. 4-28. Layout of the drinks table and construction details.

Choose straight-grained strips for the long legs (FIG. 4-29A). All of the notches are ³/8 inch deep (FIG. 4-28B). At the top, allow for the depths of the rails, and check the lower dadoes with the thickness of the plywood.

Make the shelf square (FIG. 4-29B) with curved corners. Mark out the positions of the bottle holes. You might be able to drill these with an expansive bit, but otherwise you will have to drill many small holes and saw and shape the

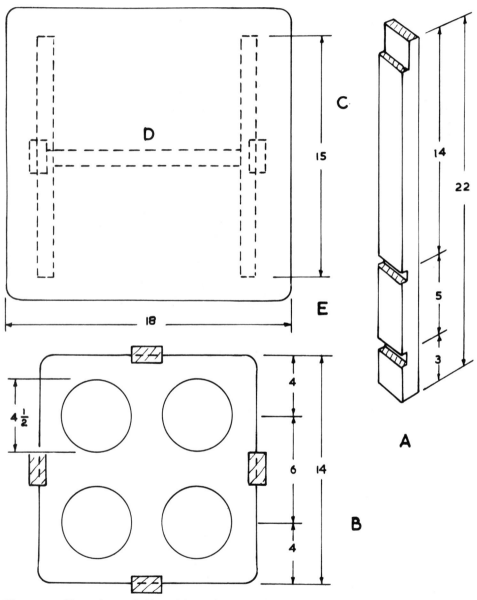

Fig. 4-29. Sizes of top, shelf, and legs of the drinks table.

Materials List for Drinks Table

2 legs	$1 \times 2 \times 23$
2 legs	$1 \times 2 \times 10$
2 rails	$1 \times 2 \times 16$
1 rail	$1 \times 2 \times 14$
1 shelf	$14 \times 14 \times 1/2$ plywood
1 bottom	$14 \times 14 \times 1/2$ plywood
1 top	$18 \times 18 \times 1/2$ plywood

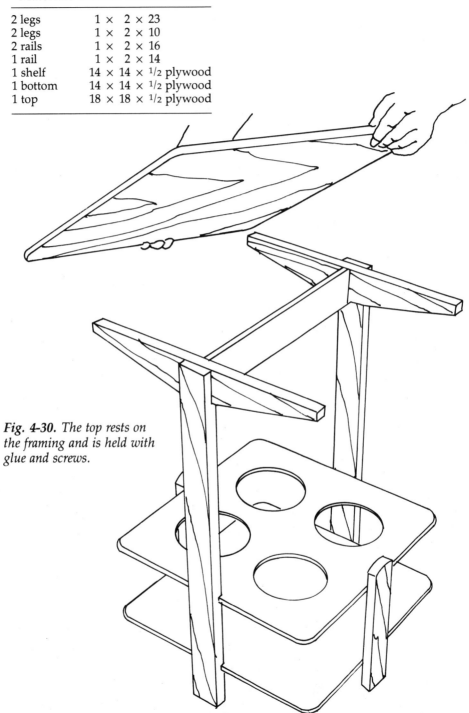

Fig. 4-30. The top rests on the framing and is held with glue and screws.

large hole outlines. Round the edges of the bottle holes and the exposed outer edges of the shelf.

Make the bottom (FIG. 4-28C) the same size as the shelf, but without the holes.

Make the two short legs (FIG. 4-28D), getting the notch spacing from the long legs. Round the extending tops of these legs.

Make the two top rails (FIG. 4-28E) to fit into the leg notches, but there is no need to notch the rails. Let them extend 15 inches (FIG. 4-29C) with tapered ends.

Make the crosswise rail (FIGS. 4-28E and 4-29D), checking the length so the legs will stand upright when the shelf and bottom are tightly in their notches.

Drill for two 1/2-inch dowels in each end of the crosswise rail, through the top rails, and as deep as possible in the legs without going through.

Assemble the parts, taking care to get the plywood pieces central. At each leg, drive a screw diagonally up through the bottom to strengthen each leg joint (FIG. 4-28G). See that parts are square to each other and that the table stands upright.

Cut the top to size 1 1/2 inch outside the legs and rail ends, which should be about 18 inches square (FIG. 4-29E). Round the corners. If the table is to have Formica or other covering, add that now and true the edges. The edge could be left square or given a slight rounding. Most plywood is unsuitable for a molded edge.

The top can be glued to the rails, but this can be reinforced with screws driven diagonally upwards near the tapered ends of the rails (FIG. 4-30). Remove surplus glue and sand the wood, if necessary. Finish with paint.

Take-Down Coffee Table

The take-down coffee table in FIG. 4-31 is a small, octagonal table that could be made as a permanent assembly, but it is designed to separate into three pieces that can store flat. The two leg pieces notch into each other and fit into strips under the top.

Make the top from 1/2-inch plywood and the legs from 3/4-inch plywood. If you use softwood plywood, you might paint the table. The top can be veneered with a choice hardwood or covered with a melamine plastic to protect it from heat and liquids. You can then paint the legs, although clear varnish on hardwood plywood also will look good.

Mark out the top first as a square (FIGS. 4-32A and 4-33A). Divide its underside centrally across the leg positions. If you measure the diagonal distance from the

Materials List for
Take-Down Coffee Table

1 top	24 × 24 × 1/2 plywood
2 legs	14 × 24 × 3/4 plywood

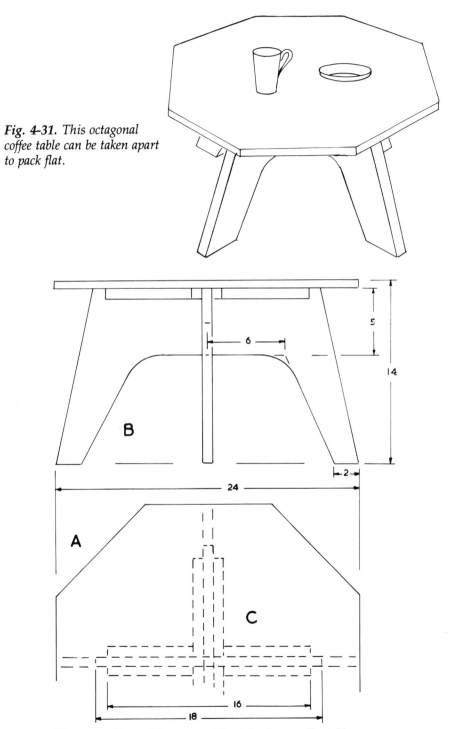

Fig. 4-31. This octagonal coffee table can be taken apart to pack flat.

Fig. 4-32. Sizes of the parts of the take-down coffee table.

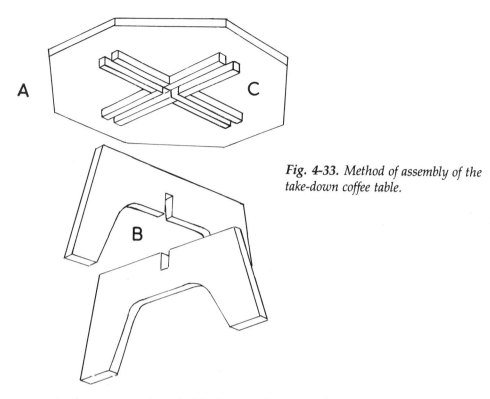

Fig. 4-33. Method of assembly of the take-down coffee table.

corner to the center and mark this distance from the corners along each side, you will get the points from which to mark the octagon. Cut the outline.

Mark out a pair of legs (FIG. 4-32B). The feet extend as far as the top and slope to 3 inches in. Cut the outline and mark the second leg from it.

Notch the centers of the legs' pieces to fit each other (FIG. 4-33B). Mark the thickness of the legs on the underside of the top. Fit strips across outside these marks (FIGS. 4-32C and 4-33C) so the assembled legs can be pressed in. The outer ends of the strips are 1 inch from the outsides of the legs. Round the outer edges of all parts.

When you are satisfied with the fit of parts and their ability to disassemble, apply your chosen finish.

Small Dresser

In a large bedroom, the facilities for combing your hair, applying make-up, or leisurely preparing your appearance can be quite a large dresser, either free-standing or built-in. If the room is more compact, however, so must be the dresser. This dressing table or vanity is intended for use where space is limited (FIG. 4-34). It is a table with classical lines, without lower framing, so a stool can be pushed underneath, or you can sit without your legs being obstructed. The mirror in its frame is supported on shaped pillars, so the general effect is traditional Victorian.

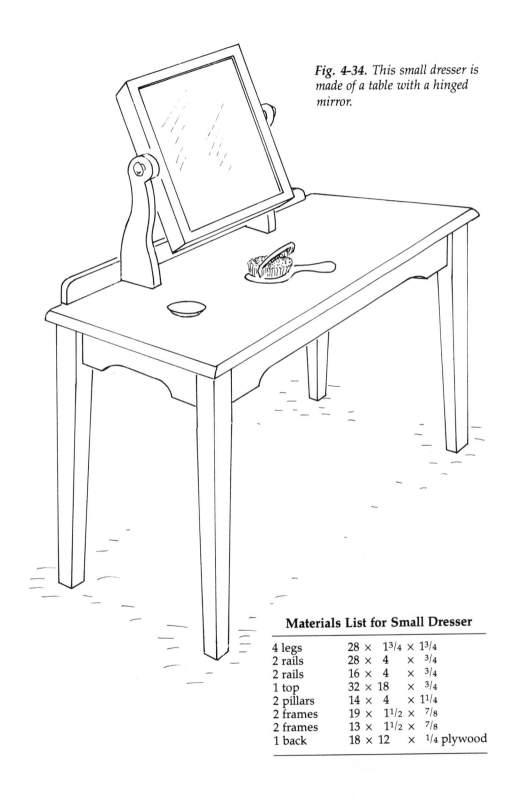

Fig. 4-34. This small dresser is made of a table with a hinged mirror.

Materials List for Small Dresser

4 legs	28 ×	1³/₄ ×	1³/₄
2 rails	28 ×	4 ×	³/₄
2 rails	16 ×	4 ×	³/₄
1 top	32 ×	18 ×	³/₄
2 pillars	14 ×	4 ×	1¹/₄
2 frames	19 ×	1¹/₂ ×	⁷/₈
2 frames	13 ×	1¹/₂ ×	⁷/₈
1 back	18 ×	12 ×	¹/₄ plywood

Construction should be hardwood, preferably matching existing furniture. With a traditional appearance it would be appropriate to use traditional mortise-and-tenon joints, but no one will see the leg joints, so you could use dowels between rails and legs. The pillars could also be doweled to the tabletop, but tenons are better there.

Exact sizes are not important. The tabletop will have to be made by gluing boards together. If this results in a slightly different width, it does not matter,

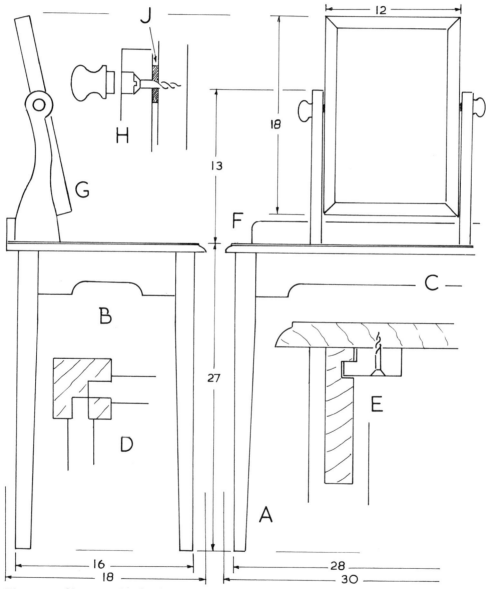

Fig. 4-35. Sizes and details of the small dresser.

unless your table has to fit a particular position. You can use a mirror of a different size, unless it is vastly different. However, if you make a frame and take it to a glass merchant, he will have stock mirror glass and will cut what you need. Check the thickness of available mirror glass before cutting rabbets in the frames.

The suggested sizes (FIG. 4-35) are for a table with its top 16 inches × 28 inches, standing 27 inches above the floor. The tilting mirror projects about 20 inches above the tabletop. If your situation requires the table to be a different size, alter measurements at this stage. Do not make the top too narrow, or the table will be unsteady.

Prepare the wood for the four legs (FIG. 4-35A). Mark their lengths, but leave a little extra at the tops until after the joints have been cut. They are shown with tapers on the inner surfaces only, so the outsides will be square to the top in both directions. Mark the tapers from 6 inches down. Reduce to $1^{1}/_{4}$-inch squares at the feet. Cut the tapers both ways.

Mark out the rails (FIGS. 4-35B and 4-35C). If they are to be doweled to the legs, cut the ends square to fit against the legs. If you want tenons, allow for about $5/_{8}$ inch into each leg (FIG. 4-37A). Use double tenons $3/_{8}$ inch thick (FIG. 4-37B).

Mark matching mortises on the legs. Cut them to meet (FIG. 4-35D) or be slightly deeper, so the tenon corners will have to be mitered. If you use dowels, they can be $3/_{8}$ inch or $1/_{2}$ inch, arranged three on each rail end. Drill the legs, so the dowels meet and are mitered.

Cut away the lower edges of each rail (FIG. 4-37C), 3 inches from each leg. Take sharpness off all edges that will be exposed.

It will be best to hold the top on with buttons, to allow for expansion and contraction, so cut grooves on the inner surfaces of the rails (FIG. 4-35E). A suitable size is a groove $3/_{8}$ inch wide and deep, $3/_{8}$ inch from the rail edge.

Assemble two long sides first. Pun the joints tight, and check that the legs are square to the rails, and the outside measurements are the same at top and bottom. If necessary, to hold the shape while the glue sets, nail strips across under the feet. See that the two assembled sides match.

Join the rails in the other direction in the same way. Check squareness of the assembly when viewed from above.

Trim the tops of the legs level with the rails. Sight across the rails to look for high spots or twist.

Glue and level boards to make the top. Make it to extend 1 inch outside the legs all round.

Leave the rear edge square, where the ledge will fit, but mold the other three edges. A simple rounding might be all that is needed. The molding could match other furniture, or use any molding cutter available (FIG. 4-37D).

Make the rear ledge (FIGS. 4-35F and 4-36A). Round its outer corners and take sharpness off the upper edges. Mark its lower edge and the rear edge of the tabletop for $3/_{8}$-inch dowels at about 6-inch intervals. Do not join yet.

The mirror frame has to be rabbeted in two steps (FIG. 4-36B). The deeper one takes the mirror; then there is strong card, either all over or just around the

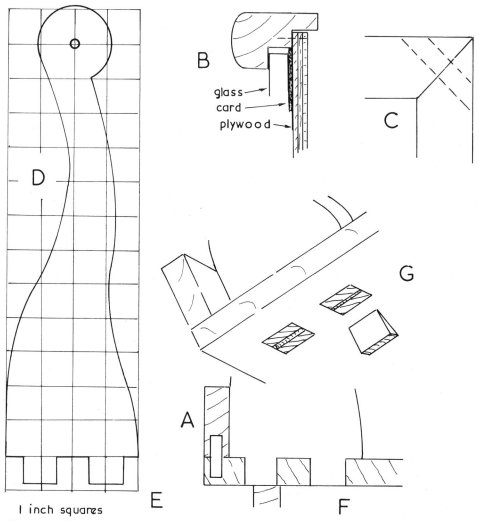

I inch squares

Fig. 4-36. The mirror supports and joints for the small dresser.

edges. A piece of thin plywood goes into the second rabbet, where it is held with thin screws. The front edge could be molded, but it is shown with a curved section. Make enough molding for the frame.

The mitered frame corners will need strengthening. They should be glued; the back plywood will provide some strength, but one way of reinforcing is with 1/4-inch dowels arranged diagonally (FIG. 4-36C). Glue them in and plane the ends level after the glue has set.

Cut the two pillars (FIGS. 4-35G and 4-36D). Use straight tapered pillars, if you wish, but those shown enhance appearance. Remove all saw marks from the shaped edges and take the sharpness off, or fully round them. Tenons are advised (FIG. 4-36E); or arrange three, 1/2-inch-diameter dowels in each pillar.

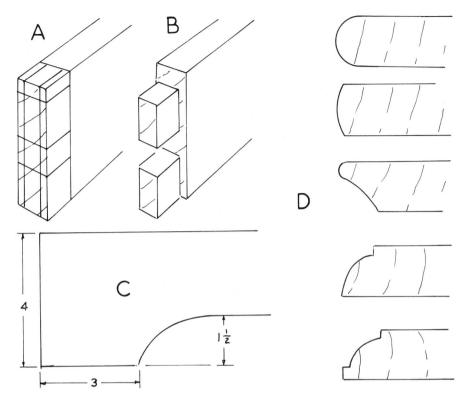

Fig. 4-37. Joints and edge moldings for the small dresser.

At the top of each leg, drill for a stout screw; #10-gauge would be suitable. Counterbore to about half thickness (FIG. 4-35H).

To hold the mirror at any angle by friction, you could use rubber or soft fiber washers between the pillars and the mirror frame (FIG. 4-35). Allow for the thicknesses of these when arranging the spacing of the pillars on the tabletop.

Mark the mortises in the tabletop (FIG. 4-36F) at a spacing that will allow the pillars to be upright when the screws are tightened through the rubber washers into the mirror frame.

Cut the mortises. Join the ledge strip at the same time as the pillars. Put saw cuts across the tenon ends; then drive wedges from below when you glue the joints (FIG. 4-36G). Check that the pillars are upright, and match the mirror before the glue has set.

Attach the top to the leg and rail assembly with buttons (FIGS. 4-38F and 4-38G). There might be three on each long rail and one at each end. Assemble the table inverted, so you get the overhang the same all around.

Make knobs with dowel ends that will press into the counterbored holes over the screws through the pillars. They should be left as push fits without glue, so you can withdraw them if you need to tighten the screws. Do not finally assemble and fully tighten the screws until after you stain and polish the wood.

Tray Table

At one time the butler brought in food or drink on a tray that fitted onto its own stand and became a serving table. In these days when we do our own waiting, something similar can be very useful, particularly if the whole thing can fold away to take up little space when out of use. You can have the stand ready and bring in the tray of food to fit on it, then if you want to pick up the tray to take to guests, or to remove used things, it can be lifted off again.

This tray table (FIG. 4-38) has a tray 15 inches wide and 21 inches long. It stands about 23 inches from the floor and there is a removable shelf underneath that provides extra space and keeps the legs in place when the tray is removed. When the tray and shelf are removed the stand folds flat.

The sizes shown (FIG. 4-39A) depend on the crossing arrangement of the legs. The width (FIG. 4-40A) could be altered without affecting the action of the table.

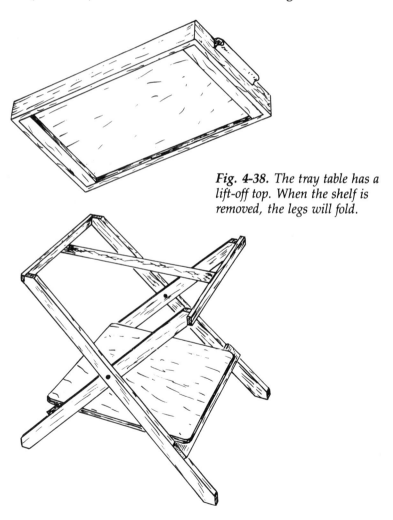

Fig. 4-38. The tray table has a lift-off top. When the shelf is removed, the legs will fold.

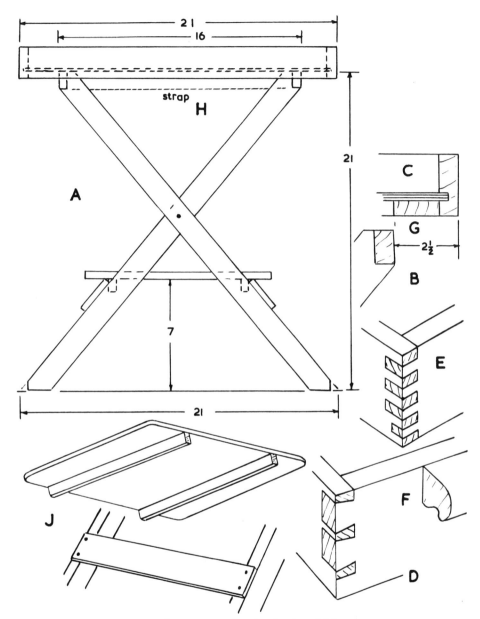

Fig. 4-39. Sizes and alternative construction for the tray table.

To set out the leg sizes, draw a square with 21-inch sides (FIG. 4-40B), mark in 3¼ inches from the top corners, and join these points to the bottom corners. These lines are the upper edges of the legs (FIG. 4-40C). The drawing also gives you the angles to cut on the legs.

   Make the four legs (FIG. 4-40D). Cut the tops to the angles, and notch them to take the crossbars (FIG. 4-38B). At the bottom, the extreme points might be fragile,

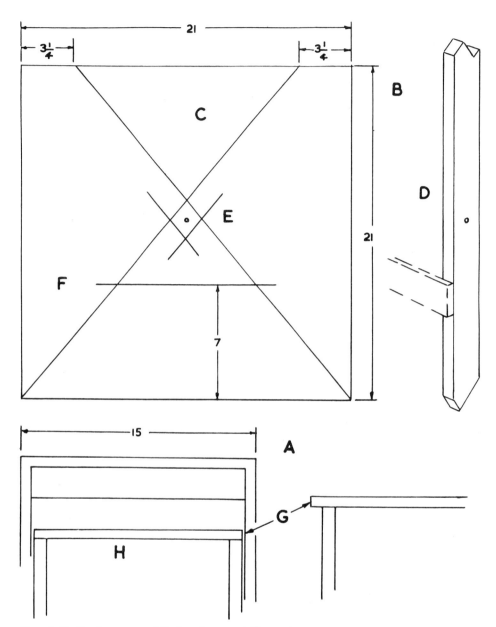

Fig. 4-40. *Laying out and fitting the tray table parts.*

so cut them back about 3/4 inch. On your drawing, mark the widths of the legs so you can get the locations of bolt holes (FIG. 4-40E). A line 7 inches up will show you the position of the top edges of the leg braces (FIG. 4-40F).

Make the crossbars and the leg braces. One pair of legs crosses inside the other pair, but the crossbars at the top should be the same length (FIG. 4-40G).

Materials List for Tray Table

2 tray sides	$5/8 \times$	2	$\times 22$
2 tray ends	$5/8 \times$	2	$\times 16$
2 tray handles	$1 \times$	1	$\times 8$
1 tray base	$15 \times$	21	$\times 1/4$ plywood
2 tray stops	$3/8 \times$	$17/8$	$\times 15$
4 legs	$3/4 \times$	$11/2$	$\times 30$
2 crossbars	$5/8 \times$	1	$\times 15$
2 leg braces	$3/8 \times$	2	$\times 15$
1 lower shelf	$12 \times$	12	$\times 1/2$ plywood
2 shelf guides	$5/8 \times$	1	$\times 12$

Have these pieces prepared, but slightly too long, so they can be adjusted to suit the tray after that has been made.

The tray is made as a box with the base let into grooves (FIG. 4-39C). Cut the grooves $3/8$ inch from the bottom edges.

Corners could be dovetailed (FIG. 4-39D) with the part from the groove down mitered to hide the groove. You could use a comb joint (FIG. 4-39E), with the groove enclosed in the next comb to the bottom.

It would be possible to put hand holes in the ends of the tray, but lifting handles are shown (FIG. 4-39F). They could be glued and doweled if you want to avoid screw heads showing inside the tray. Alternatively, you could use metal or plastic handles.

Assemble the tray. Put two stops under the ends (FIG. 4-39G). If all other parts are to size, these will be $17/8$ inch wide, but you might want to wait until after a trial assembly before settling on their widths and fitting them.

Check the lengths of the crossbars, which should be an easy fit between the tray sides (FIG. 4-40H). Drill the legs for $1/4$-inch bolts. Glue and screw the crossbars to the legs, and screw on the braces so the assemblies are square and parallel and the inner pair of legs fit between the outer pair.

Make a trial assembly. The crossbars should come upright against the tray stops, and the feet should be flat on the floor.

When the wood has been stained and polished, pivot the legs permanently with $1/4$-inch coach bolts with their shallow heads outside. Put washers between the legs and under the nuts. If possible, use lock nuts.

Although the leg assembly will remain in shape while the tray is in place, it could spread if nothing is done to hold it when the tray is removed. Make a strap across the crossbars. (FIG. 4-39H). This could be webbing, stout tape, or a leather strap. Attach it with screws through washers. Arrange its length so it holds the crossbars at the right distance to fit into the tray.

For the lower shelf (FIG. 4-39J), cut a piece of plywood to fit easily between the inner pair of legs. Round its edges and corners. On its underside, fit guides to go between the leg braces when the tray table is in use. The strap will prevent the legs spreading, while the shelf will prevent them closing and hold the assembly square when the tray is lifted off.

Folding Hall Table

Many entrance halls are small, and there is little room for furniture, yet there is often a need for a table. Even a small rigid table can take up too much room when it is out of use. The answer might be a table that folds back to the wall when out of use. The size will have to be adjusted to suit your requirements and the available space, but this one (FIG. 4-41) is 24 inches long and projects 15 inches from the wall when in use, but drops to only 3-inch thickness (FIG. 4-42A).

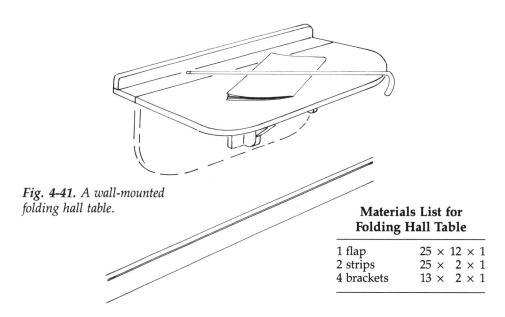

Fig. 4-41. A wall-mounted folding hall table.

Materials List for Folding Hall Table

1 flap	25 × 12 × 1
2 strips	25 × 2 × 1
4 brackets	13 × 2 × 1

If you use this design to make a table of a different size, it should be about twice as long as the top of the supporting bracket, if that is to be arranged centrally and hidden when the table is folded. If the table has to be relatively shorter, the bracket will be just as effective if mounted off-center, so when it is folded it will be covered by the hanging tabletop.

It will be best to make the parts of solid wood, but it would be possible to use veneered particleboard or plywood for the flap, except these would have to be edged. The usual adhesive edging is difficult to fit around curves; therefore, you might have to make the flap with square or beveled corners.

Make the flap (FIG. 4-42B) and the strip behind it (FIG. 4-42C). Edges may be left square, rounded, or molded.

The backboard (FIG. 4-42D) could have a similarly molded edge, but it is shown with rounded corners and square edges. Join it to the horizontal strip with glue and screws driven upwards.

The bracket assembly has a strip to attach to the wall (FIG. 4-42F) and the bracket itself, which hinges to it so it can be turned flat to the wall or brought out square to it to support the flap.

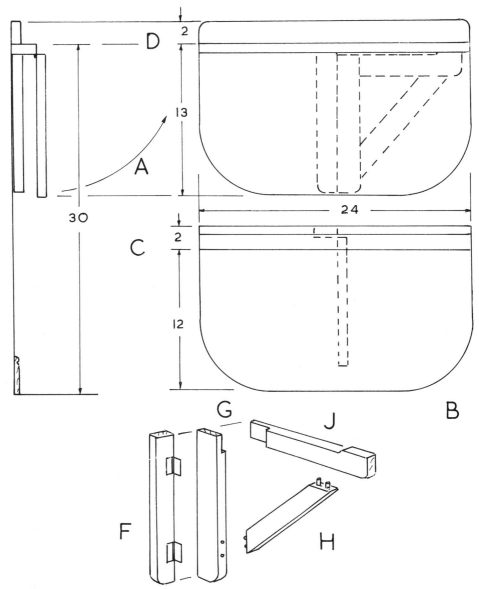

Fig. 4-42. Sizes of the folding hall table.

The bracket parts could be joined in several ways but they are shown with a halved joint at the corner (FIG. 4-42G) and dowels on the diagonal (FIG. 4-42H).

Use screws as well as glue in the halved joint. Round outer corners and all exposed edges. Check that the assembled bracket is square, as a sagging tabletop will be very obvious.

Join the bracket to its upright with two 2-inch hinges, arranged so when the bracket closes to the wall, there is only a minimal space between the wood edges.

It should be satisfactory to use three 2-inch hinges to join the flap to its strip, but arrange clearance for the bracket to swing back.

Notch the top of the bracket enough to clear the hinge knuckles (FIG. 4-42J). The hinge away from the folded bracket can be 3 inches in from the end. The one the other way should be inside the folded bracket end, and the other as near the center as the swinging bracket allows. When the hinges on the undersurfaces are opened so the flap is up, the edges should meet closely for a good appearance.

Mount the table on the wall so the top surface is 30 inches above the floor. Three screws through the backboard should be enough to hold it, and two screws through the bracket support will be adequate. The bracket does not have to be exactly central, if you can get a better wall attachment to one side of the middle.

No stop for the bracket is shown under the flap. You might find it satisfactory to merely swing the bracket to about a square position, but you can screw a small block under the flap to limit the movement of the bracket.

The finish should be appropriate to the wood and might match other furniture.

Hexagonal Candle Stand

This design is based on an early original created when cabinetmakers probably did not have access to a lathe (FIG. 4-43). The top was arranged to tilt, but a fixed alternative is also shown.

The central hexagonal piece is parallel in the length, but a little decoration is provided above and below the leg joints in the shallow V-shaped cuts. Make them with a backsaw, using two guidelines (FIG. 4-43B). You can bevel the projecting bottom, but cut the top carefully so it is at right angles to the sides.

The legs sweep upward, and the outer curves are sufficiently near parallel over the joints for clamps to be used over scrap wood. Use a template, or make one leg and use it as a pattern for the others (FIG. 4-43C) if you cannot cut all of them at one time on a band saw. Arrange the wood so the grain is diagonal. If there is any curve in the lines of grain, arrange it to follow the shapes of the legs. Be careful that the edge which meets the pedestal is at right angles to the foot of each leg.

Because the grain in the legs would come across any tenons, thus reducing their strength, it is better to use dowels in these leg joints (FIG. 4-43D). Prepare the joints, but wait to put the parts together until work at the top of the pedestal has been finished.

For a tilt top, fix a square block to the top of the pedestal. In some originals the top was nailed on, but screwing would be better. You can also glue in four small dowels (FIG. 4-43E). The square block supports the top when the top is raised or lowered. Even if the rest of the table is a softwood, it would be better if this and the pieces that frame it are made of close-grained hardwood.

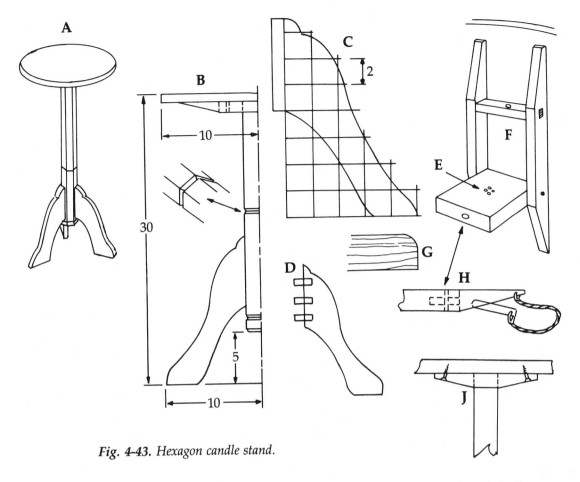

Fig. 4-43. Hexagon candle stand.

Glue the pedestal assembly and test that it stands upright. If the legs are identical and carefully fitted, there should be no difficulty, but check with the feet on a level surface, and use a large try or set square in three directions. You can make corrections by planing the bottom of a leg.

The top can be round, elliptical, or hexagonal. Curves were more popular than angular shapes, possibly because there was slightly less risk of anyone passing and knocking the table over. A circle is shown in FIG. 4-43A. You can make up the top from several boards, then arrange the underframing across its grain to provide some resistance to warping.

Fix two braces to the top, parallel and on each side of the supporting block on the pedestal. They should be across the grain of the top and in the same direction as the grain of the pedestal block. Taper the ends almost to nothing so they are not obvious when the top is down. Tenon into these braces another piece between them (FIG. 4-43F). When the top is central on the pedestal, this piece

1 post	$2^1/2$	× 25	× $2^1/2$
3 legs	6	× 17	× 1
1 top	20	× 20	× 1
1 support	3	× 3	× $1^1/2$
2 braces	$1^1/2$	× 18	× $3/4$
1 brace	$1^1/2$	× 6	× $3/4$
1 peg		$5/8$ round	× 4

comes loosely over the block. Fix the parts to the top with glue and counterbored and plugged screws.

Mark for pivot screws, and drill small pilot holes through the braces into the block. The points marked on the block are the centers the curve of the top edge of the block. Use a compass to draw the curves, then round the top edge (FIG. 4-43G) to allow the top to tilt. Enlarge the holes to suit large roundhead screws. For a larger table, the pivots could be dowels or iron rods.

There are metal catches available to hold the tabletop in the down position, and fittings of this type were available quite early, so using one is not necessarily a departure from authenticity. A simpler and older method of locking the top in position was a peg (FIG. 4-43H) pushed into a hole. This could be turned or hand-whittled. It might have a hole in the end for a cord to another hole in a brace so it does not become lost.

For a fixed tabletop, the support does not need to be square, so you can make a round or hexagonal piece of wood to fit on the top of the pedestal. Tapering toward its edges will improve its appearance and allow for screws upward into the top (FIG. 4-43J).

Bookcase and Table

An older child usually has a need for plenty of book storage. This desk or table (FIG. 4-44) is of a unit construction with two bookcases as supports that might have enough stiffness in themselves. A drawer unit fits centrally between the supports. If the units are screwed together from below, the whole thing will be a rigid piece of furniture. It will be possible to disassemble it, however, so that there are two bookcases that could be used alone, a top that might serve as a drawing board, and a drawer unit that could be put under another table.

The height shown would suit a child of 12 years old and yet could still be useful for an adult. For a young child the whole thing could be made lower, although if the bookcases are first made to stand without plinths, these can be added later to give an extra 2 inches or more when needed. If you anticipate this, make the plinths at the same time as the other parts so they can be finished with paint, stain, or varnish to match the other parts. They can then be kept and screwed on when needed.

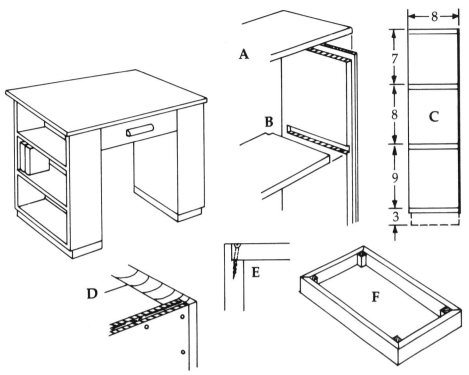

Fig. 4-44. *A table for an older child can be made with bookcase ends and a wide drawer:
(A) rabbets at top and bottom; (B) dado joints for shelves; (C) marked four sides; (D) overlapping plywood backs; (E) screwing the sides; (F) strengthening blocks.*

Several joints can be used in the bookcases, but those shown are rabbets at
top and bottom (FIG. 4-44A) and stopped dado joints for the shelves (FIG. 4-44B).
Mark out the four sides together (FIG. 4-44C). You might have to adjust the spacing of the shelves to the actual books. There is no need for the two bookcases to
have the same spacings, although overall lengths should be marked across all
four pieces together to get the heights uniform.

The plywood backs fit into rabbets in the sides and can overlap the top and
bottom (FIG. 4-44D). These rabbets and those across the ends of the side pieces
are deeper than the dadoes. Make the tops and bottoms and put them temporarily in position so the lengths of the shelves can be measured.

When the bookcases are assembled, pull the sides to the tops and bottoms
with clamps, while gluing and screwing into the sides (FIG. 4-44E). The screw
heads will be hidden so there is no need to sink and plug them. The shelves
should be a good fit, but be careful of making them overlong, forcing the sides to
become bowed outwards when they are forced in. Glue alone should be sufficient in the dadoes, but if a shelf is loose, it can be screwed from below.

If the plywood backs of the bookcases are carefully squared, you should have
no difficulty in getting the bookcases assembled true, but try one on the other to

Materials List for a Bookcase and Table

4 uprights	8 × 27	× 3/4
8 shelves	8 × 20	× 3/4
4 plinths	2 1/4 × 20	× 3/4
4 plinths	2 1/4 × 7 1/2	× 3/4
2 backs	20 × 27	× 1/4 plywood
4 drawer rails	1 1/2 × 18	× 3/4
4 drawer rails	3/4 × 20	× 3/4
2 unit sides	5 × 20	× 1/4 plywood
1 unit back	5 × 18	× 1/4 plywood
1 drawer front	3 1/2 × 18	× 5/8
1 drawer front	5 × 18	× 5/8
1 drawer back	3 × 18	× 5/8
1 drawer bottom	18 × 20	× 1/4 plywood
1 top	20 × 36	× 3/4 solid wood or framed plywood

see that they match. Put the plywood in the rabbets with glue and drive light nails into the sides and the crosswise parts.

The plinths have mitered corners with strengthening blocks inside (FIG. 4-44F). They are set in from three edges of the bottoms of the bookcases, but are level with the plywood backs. Attach them with pocket screws inside.

The top can be made of solid wood, with several pieces glued to make up the width. The top shown (FIG. 4-45A) is made of thick plywood with a frame of the same thickness. It could be faced particleboard treated in the same way.

Plow a groove all around the top and fit a solid wood edging into it with a tongue (FIG. 4-45B). Then miter the framing pieces at the corners. To allow for slight errors in cutting the matching parts, make the edging pieces a little too thick, so they can be planed and sanded level after gluing.

It is possible to assemble the top to the two bookcases and use the table, but there might be some lack of stiffness (that might not matter) and the appearance of the comparatively thin top without framing below would not be very attractive. Besides its usefulness, the drawer unit provides stability in the assembly and improves appearance.

The drawer unit is made like a box with an open top and bottom and plywood sides and back. The drawer has a false front that overlaps the plywood sides of the box and the top and bottom rails.

First, make the plywood sides. Their length should be the same as the width of the bookcases and deep enough to accommodate the drawer and its guides (FIG. 4-45C). Four rails fit between the pieces of plywood. At the rear they are set in enough to take the plywood back, but at the front they are level with the edge (FIG. 4-45D). Screw through the plywood into the ends of the rails and nail on the back. Put guides between the rails (FIG. 4-45E), making sure to get the surfaces that will come next to the drawer level. Check that the whole assembly is square.

The drawer is given a false front, but it could be made with dovetails. A simplified method is described here. There are grooves for the plywood bottom in

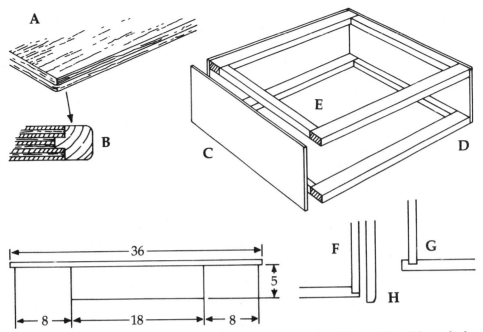

Fig. 4-45. Details of the tabletop and drawer compartments: (A) top; (B) solid wood edging with tongue; (C) drawer; (D) front guides are level with edge; (E) guides between rails; (F) front rabbets; (G) dado grooves for back; (H) large false front.

the sides and the front, and the sides are screwed into rabbets in the front (FIG. 4-45F). The back goes into dado grooves above the plywood grooves (FIG. 4-45G). The complete drawer at this stage should fit into the box with its front level.

The wood you use for the drawer parts need not be as good quality as for the other parts, but make the false front of wood to match the rest of the table. It should be large enough to overlap the plywood sides (FIG. 4-45H) and the top and bottom rails. Round the exposed edges. Attach it with glue and screws from inside the drawer. If the handle you choose has to be attached with screws through the wood, it might be better to fit the handle to the false front before fitting that to the drawer.

Hexagonal Table

Tables do not have to be rectangular. There is a certain attraction about sitting around a symmetrical table. If you want to use an umbrella shade on a central support, it is logical to shape the table around that central rod or tube. The table shown in FIG. 4-46 has a hexagonal top and three splayed legs, with a shelf underneath, so the top and the shelf provide bracing for the umbrella pole. With the three legs, there is the property of steadiness on an uneven surface. This will be an advantage if the umbrella is caught in a wind. Although the top is shown hexagonal, it could be made round with very little modification. The size and height

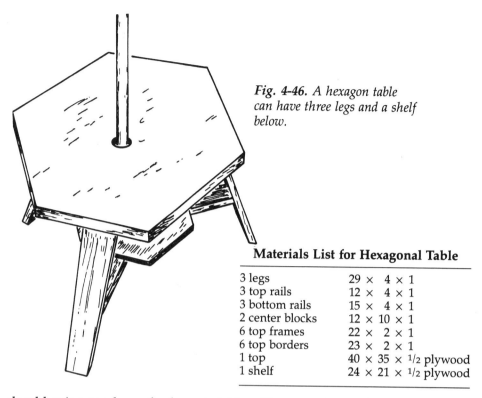

Fig. 4-46. A hexagon table can have three legs and a shelf below.

Materials List for Hexagonal Table

3 legs	29 × 4 × 1
3 top rails	12 × 4 × 1
3 bottom rails	15 × 4 × 1
2 center blocks	12 × 10 × 1
6 top frames	22 × 2 × 1
6 top borders	23 × 2 × 1
1 top	40 × 35 × 1/2 plywood
1 shelf	24 × 21 × 1/2 plywood

should suit a meal or refreshments table with up to six people using chairs of normal height.

The top and shelf are made of exterior-grade or marine-grade, 1/2-inch plywood. The other parts are all 1 inch thick. Construction should be easy with hand tools if power tools are unavailable. With a regular hexagonal shape, all the angles that have to be cut for the top framing are 60 degrees. Leg joint angles will be found on the drawing.

It will help in getting the sizes of many parts to have the top piece of plywood set out so that the underframing can be marked out on its underside. Its outline is obtained by drawing a circle, stepping off the radius around the circumference, and then joining these points. The plywood is bordered with wood 1 inch thick (FIG. 4-48A). A suitable circumference for the circle is about 38 inches.

On the underside of the top, mark another hexagon on a 12-inch circle (FIG. 4-47A). From this, draw the outlines of the top rails to the centers of three sides (FIG. 4-47B).

Make a center block to this hexagonal shape. It is 1 inch thick, but you can use pieces to make up its size if you do not have a single piece of wood large enough. It will be glued and screwed to the top, which will reinforce any joints needed to make up width.

Fit the block to the top plywood, and drill through for the umbrella pole. Make it an easy fit; 11/2 inch will probably suit most poles (FIG. 4-48B).

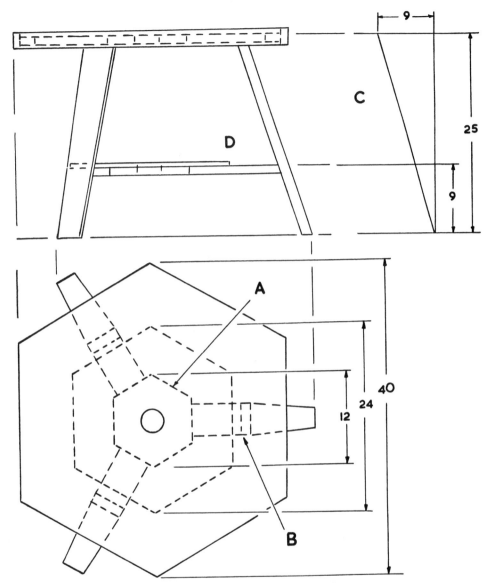

Fig. 4-47. The table shape is set from a pattern of regular hexagons.

Frame around the plywood top with strips underneath (FIG. 4-48C). Miter their corners. If you do not get a perfect fit, it does not matter. Aim to get the outer corners tight.

Cut the top rails (FIG. 4-48D) to fit in place, but do not fix them yet.

To obtain the shape and slope of the legs, set one out (FIG. 4-47C). From this, cut the wood for the legs. Allow a little extra at the top for tenons. Taper the legs from just below the tenon shoulders to 3 inches wide at the bottom. Mark the

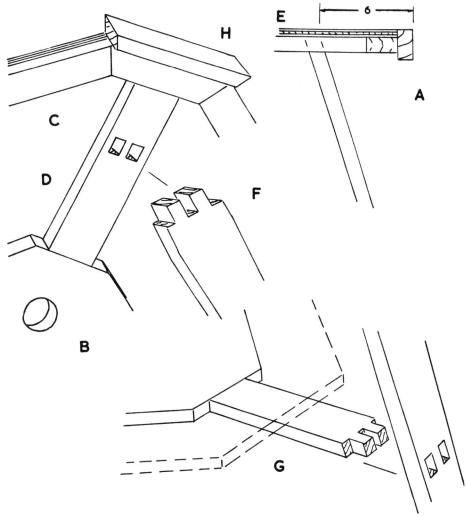

Fig. 4-48. Constructional details of the top and shelf of the hexagon table.

mortise positions at what will be 6 inches in from the outside of the top (FIG. 4-48). Mark and cut the mortise-and-tenon joints. A pair of tenons is advised (FIG. 4-48F). Do not assemble these parts yet.

At the shelf level, mark out in a very similar way to the top. Make the shelf (FIG. 4-47D). It can be left unframed unless you want to add a lip to prevent things from falling off.

On the underside of the shelf, fit a center block the same as that under the top, and drill through with the same size hole.

From the leg setting out, get the length of the bottom rails. Each bottom rail has to fit against the center block and be tenoned to the leg in a similar way to the top joints (FIG. 4-48G).

Frame around the outside of the top with mitered strips (FIG. 4-48H). Attach them with glue and screws. Make sure the edges of the plywood are thoroughly glued so water is unlikely to enter the end grain of the veneers. Round the outer edges of the top when the glue has set.

With all the joints prepared, assemble the legs and rails. It is advisable to first join the legs to the top rails. Wedge the tenons from above and plane level before fitting the rails to the top. The bottom rail tenons can also be wedged, but you can do that during assembly.

Check that all legs splay the same amount by comparing the angles they make with the top or shelf. Before the glue has set, view the table from above to see that all legs project the same amount. Stand back and look at the table from several directions to check its symmetrical appearance. A painted finish is most appropriate.

Screwed Slatted Table

A light table will make a suitable companion to many armchairs. It is of simple construction, with all of the joints nailed or screwed, without the need to cut and fit any piece into another. Most of the wood is of the same section. (See TABLE 6-2.)

The slatted top is enclosed (FIG. 4-49) to make a neat surround and to give an impression of a more stout construction than would be obvious without the border. The legs are splayed and steadied by struts that also brace the top without

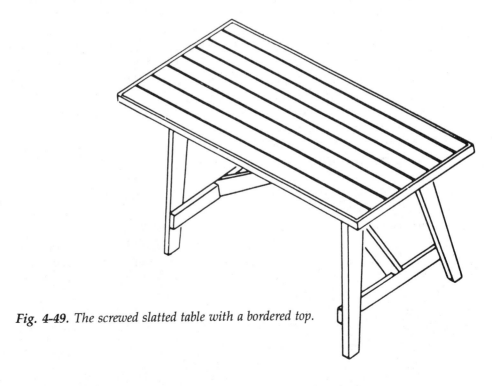

Fig. 4-49. The screwed slatted table with a bordered top.

Materials List for
Screwed Slatted Table

8 top slats	3	× 60 ×	3/4		
4 crossbars	3	× 32 ×	3/4		
2 borders	1 1/2	× 61 ×	3/4		
2 borders	1 1/2	× 33 ×	3/4		
4 legs	3	× 28 ×	1 1/2		
4 leg rails	3	× 32 ×	3/4		
2 struts	3	× 38 ×	3/4		

getting in the way of a sitter's legs. The sizes give a reasonable table for at least four people to use (FIG. 4-50A).

If the top slats are not a full 3-inch width, you should lay them out so as not to have excessive gaps. Then make the overall width of the table to suit the result you get. Spaces should be 3/8 or 1/2 inches. Wider gaps might interfere with things put on the table or cause a tablecloth to sag between.

Make up the top by screwing the slats to crossbars at the ends (FIG. 4-50B) and to others that also will take the bracing struts (FIG. 4-50C). For neatness you could screw upward so that the top surface remains smooth. Fit the outside slats, and check that the assembly is square by measuring diagonals before adding the other slats. Level the ends, and then frame around with strips (FIGS. 4-50D and 4-51A).

Make the crossbars at the tops of the legs (FIG. 4-51B) to fit into the frame and against the end crossbars. Bevel the ends to the frame, but do not fit the crossbars into the frame yet.

To get the slope of the legs, draw a half section of an end (FIG. 4-50E). The legs taper from 3 inches at the top to 2 inches at the bottom. Make them all the same, and cut the ends to the angles obtained from the half-section drawing. Mark where the lower rails will cross.

Assemble the legs to the top crossbars and to the rails. Note that these pieces cross on opposite sides of the legs. Make sure the assemblies are symmetrical by checking diagonals, and see that opposite ends match. Screw the leg assemblies inside the end crossbars (FIG. 4-51C).

The two struts cross and must be notched around the leg rails and crossbars under the top. It is important that they hold the legs upright when viewed from the side. Invert the table. If necessary, nail on temporary pieces of scrap wood at the sides to hold the leg assemblies square to the top. You should get the shapes of the struts on scrap wood and use them as templates for marking the final pieces of wood. Screw the notched ends and the crossing of the struts (FIG. 4-51D).

See that the table stands level. Round the ends and corners of the top before finishing with paint.

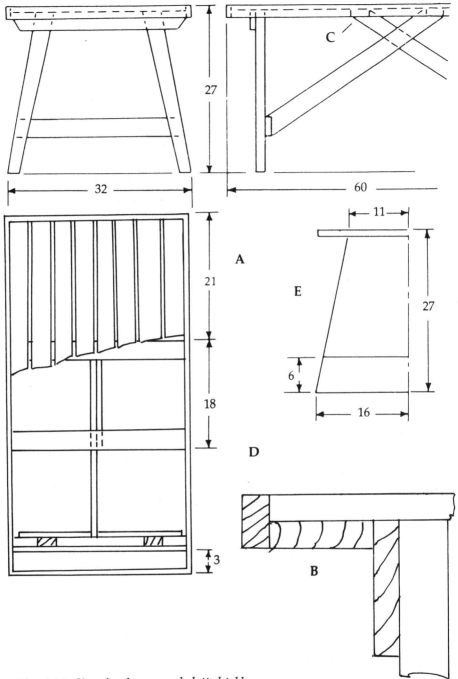

Fig. 4-50. Sizes for the screwed slatted table.

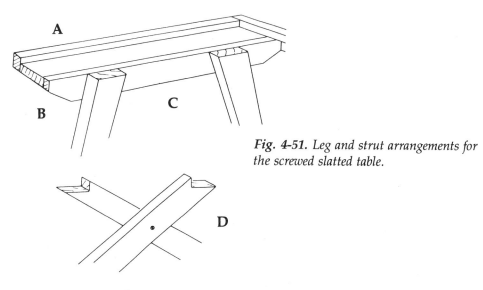

Fig. 4-51. Leg and strut arrangements for the screwed slatted table.

Round Patio Table

A round tabletop can be supported with three or four legs. The table shown in FIG. 4-52 has four legs and is intended to stand on a deck or patio where the surface is reasonably flat. It would, of course, be suitable for any level ground. It could be used as a table only, but there is a shelf below with a hole through the center of it as well as through the top to take the upright of an umbrella. The distance between the top and the shelf is enough to support the umbrella without it wobbling.

The top is made of several boards, with gaps between, and held to shape with strips across underneath. These strips also serve as attachments to the underframing which is made up as a straightforward square table. The sizes shown in FIG. 4-53 should suit most purposes. If you alter the table, arrange the top to an odd number of boards so that the central hole comes at the center of one and not at a gap.

The framework is best tenoned together, but you could also use dowels. The legs (FIG. 4-54) are all the same. Top rails (FIG. 4-54B) and bottom rails (FIG. 4-54C) are also in matching sets. The joints are on the same level. Allow for the tenons being mitered in the legs (FIG. 4-54D). The lower rail tenons can be the full depth of the rails, but at the top cut down a little and divide the tenons (FIG. 4-54E).

Make up two opposite sides first by carefully squaring and checking that they match. Pull the joints tight with clamps. If you do not have enough clamps, you can pull a joint tight and drive a nail from the inner surface of the leg through the tenon at each side to hold the parts while the glue sets. Then you can move the clamp to another position. Join the opposite assemblies with the other rails, and be certain that the table stands upright and squarely.

It is best to deal with in two stages. First cut the boards close to their final sizes. Wait to do the final curving of the edges until after assembly.

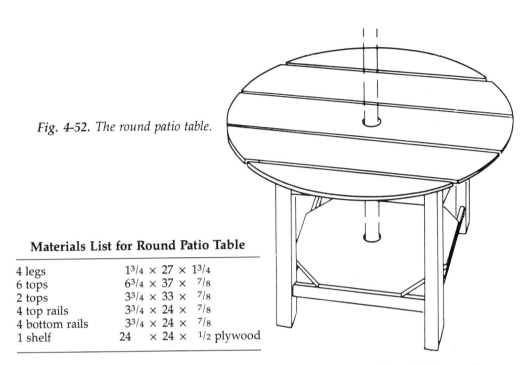

Fig. 4-52. The round patio table.

Materials List for Round Patio Table

4 legs	$1^3/4$	× 27	×	$1^3/4$
6 tops	$6^3/4$	× 37	×	$^7/8$
2 tops	$3^3/4$	× 33	×	$^7/8$
4 top rails	$3^3/4$	× 24	×	$^7/8$
4 bottom rails	$3^3/4$	× 24	×	$^7/8$
1 shelf	24	× 24	×	$^1/2$ plywood

Lay out the boards for the top and mark the center of the middle one. Improvise a compass with an 18-inch radius (FIG. 4-55A) so you can draw a circle of the right size. It might help to put temporary spacing pieces between the boards. They need not be full length; they can be short strips positioned near where the circumference of the circle will come. Cut fairly closely to the line, but leave a little for trimming after assembly.

One stiffening piece goes across centrally, and the other two must be positioned so that they will come over the top rails of the framework (FIG. 4-55B). Make all these pieces too long and then glue and screw them on from below. After assembly, cut the ends to the curve, trim the circle to the final shape, and bevel the cross pieces underneath (FIG. 4-55C).

Make and fit the shelf before attaching the top. The shelf is a regular octagon screwed to the lower rails (FIG. 4-55D). To get a regular shape, mark out the plywood to a square that matches the rails. Draw two diagonals and measure half the length of one (FIG. 4-55E). Use this distance to measure along each edge of the square from each corner in each direction (FIG. 4-55F), and join these marks. If you have laid it out accurately, you will have eight equal sides (FIG. 4-55G).

If the table is to support an umbrella or shade, drill centrally for the upright in the shelf before screwing it to the rails. The hole does not need to be a close fit on the upright because the upright should go in and out easily. As much as a $1/4$-inch clearance would be acceptable. Drill a matching hole at the center of the top. Most umbrella uprights are intended to go through to the floor, but if you have one that needs a stop, you can put another piece of wood under the hole in the shelf.

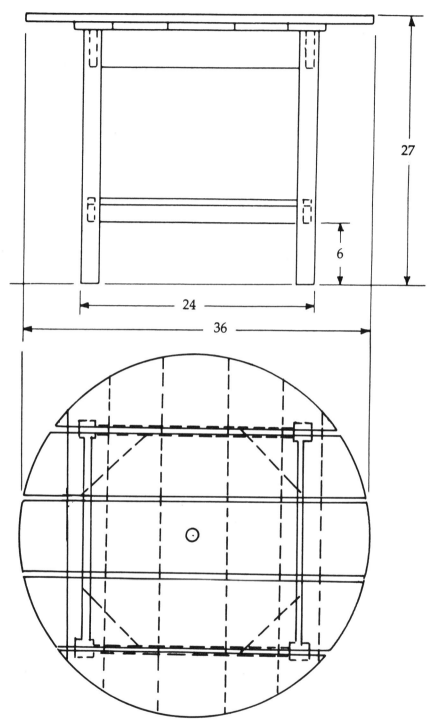

Fig. 4-53. *Sizes of the round patio table.*

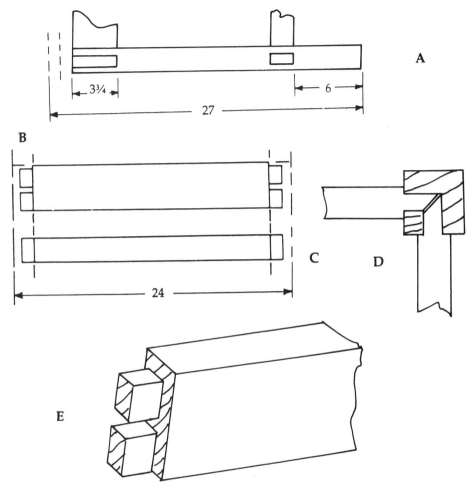

Fig. 4-54. Parts of the supports for the round patio table.

Be careful as you position the top on the framing. The two holes must line up to hold the umbrella upright. Where the two crossbars come over the top rails, screw downward in the gaps between top boards, into the rails and into the tops of the legs (FIG. 4-55H). Those four screws at each position might be enough, but you can put one or two more downward into the other rails where the central crossbar comes. There is plenty of thickness. Counterbore and plug over the screw heads.

As with most outdoor furniture, hardwood would be the best choice for this table, particularly if you expect to leave it outside in wet conditions. It would be lighter and easier to move if made of softwood, but then you would need to store it under cover. If it is well protected with paint, however, an occasional wetting would not matter. In any case, the plywood shelf should be exterior- or marine-grade plywood.

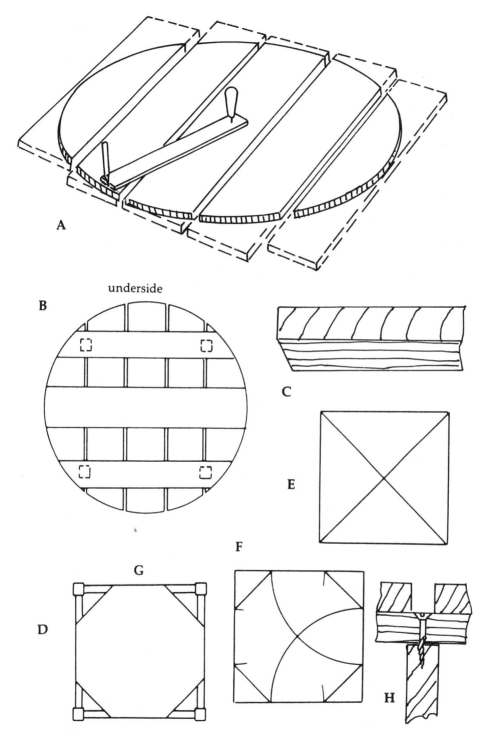

underside

Fig. 4-55. Shaping and constructing the top and shelf of the round patio table.

Strip-Wood Table

A very simple table can be made of strips of wood and with nearly all the joints screwed (FIG. 4-56). It is possible to prefabricate all the parts for later assembly. This design is suitable for offering as a kit for a customer to assemble or for producing a large quantity.

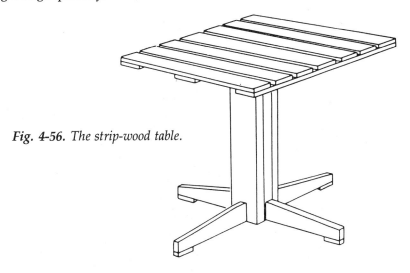

Fig. 4-56. The strip-wood table.

**Materials List for
Strip-Wood Table**

7 tops	3	× 31	× 1	
3 tops	4	× 31	× 1	
2 feet	3	× 27	× 1¹/₄	
4 feet	1	× 4	× 1¹/₄	
2 posts	4	× 27	× 1	
2 posts	1¹/₂	× 27	× 1¹/₄	
			or to suit umbrella	
2 cleats	1	× 5	× 1	

The top pieces have gaps between and crosspieces below. The central pillar is hollow, and the upright of an umbrella can pass through it. The feet are formed by two crossed pieces (FIG. 4-57).

If you have the umbrella or shade that will be used, check the diameter of its shaft and make the thickness of the spacers in the column to suit.

Prepare the feet (FIG. 4-58). They are halved where they cross. Add the pieces under the ends (FIG. 4-58B) and glue the crossing. Hold it square with weights or with other means while the glue sets.

Make the parts for the column (FIG. 4-58C). Notch the 4-inch pieces to suit the feet. In the other direction, notch the filler pieces if they are thick enough (FIG. 4-58D). If you have not needed to thicken them to suit an umbrella, you can cut them short and use packings on each side of the feet, if necessary (FIG. 4-58E). At

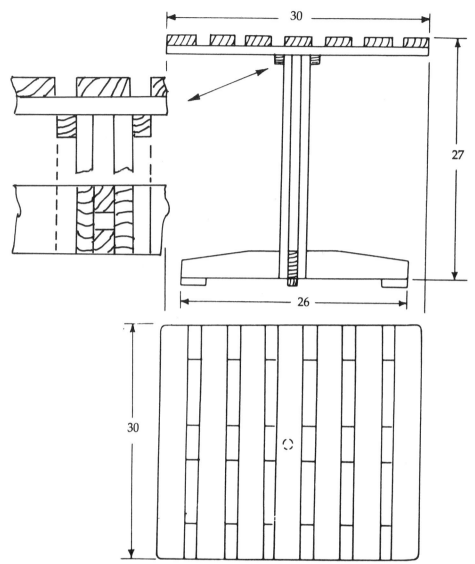

Fig. 4-57. Sizes for the strip-wood table.

the top, check that the parts are cut squarely because this will affect the level of the tabletop. Assemble the column parts with glue and screws. Add cleats on the 4-inch pieces (FIG. 4-58), and make sure the whole top surface is flat as well as square to the sides.

Assemble the tabletop after cutting or marking all pieces to length. You can drive screws upward so that the exposed surface is not marked by screw heads. At this stage, leave out the center top piece (FIG. 4-59) but have it ready. Screw and glue the parts together. Then level edges and round the outer edges and corners.

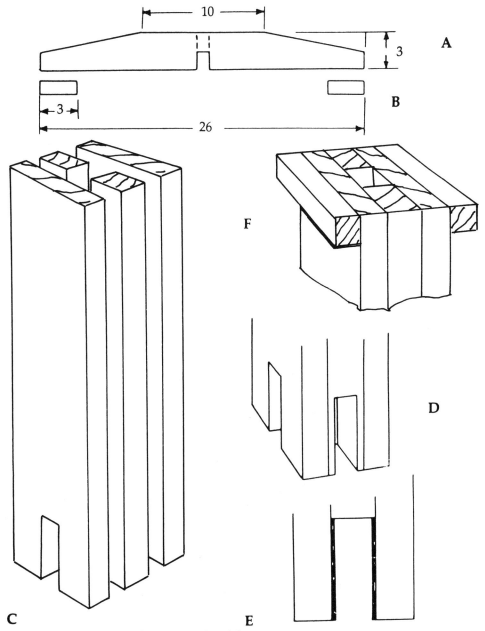

Fig. 4-58. Construction of the pedestal and feet.

Mark where the column comes under the top on the central crossmember. Drill for screws downward into the column. Use 3-inch screws into the end grain and 2-inch screws into the cleats (FIG. 4-59B). Add the central top strip and then drill downward through the center to suit the umbrella.

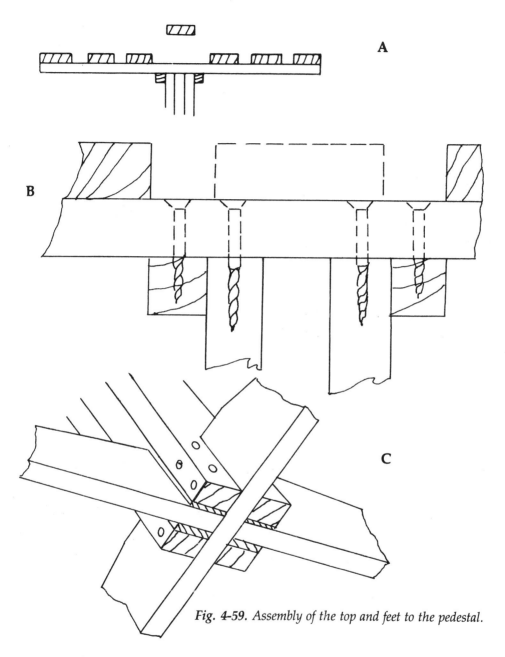

Fig. 4-59. *Assembly of the top and feet to the pedestal.*

Invert the table and check that the pillar is perpendicular to the top. Bring the crossed feet into their slots and check their fit. If the fit is satisfactory, drill for screws each way (FIG. 4-59C), and then glue and screw in the feet. At the same time, measure from the underside of the top to the ends of the feet to see that these parts are parallel and that the table will stand level. Try it the right way up, and allow the glue to set. Finish with preservative and varnish or paint.

Butcher-Block Table

A tabletop in the butcher style could be made of thick pieces, but the result would be quite heavy, which might be an advantage in a permanent situation. If the table is to be used for outdoor hobbies, then a stiff solid top would be an advantage. For the more common outdoor use of a table, it would be better to lighten construction, while retaining the typical butcher-block appearance, so it could partner benches or chairs made the same way.

The table shown in FIG. 4-60 is of a moderate size, with the usual sturdy butcher-block appearance, but with a top that is not as heavy as it appears. The sizes given in FIG. 4-61 are suggestions. They can be varied according to needs and available wood. Most of the parts are 2-inch-square and 1-×-2-inch sections. They are shown without allowance for planing, but the wood should be planed all around. The final sizes will be less than shown.

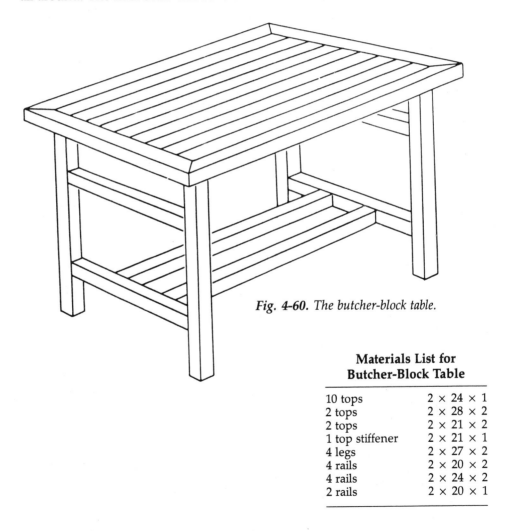

Fig. 4-60. The butcher-block table.

Materials List for Butcher-Block Table

10 tops	2 × 24 × 1
2 tops	2 × 28 × 2
2 tops	2 × 21 × 2
1 top stiffener	2 × 21 × 1
4 legs	2 × 27 × 2
4 rails	2 × 20 × 2
4 rails	2 × 24 × 2
2 rails	2 × 20 × 1

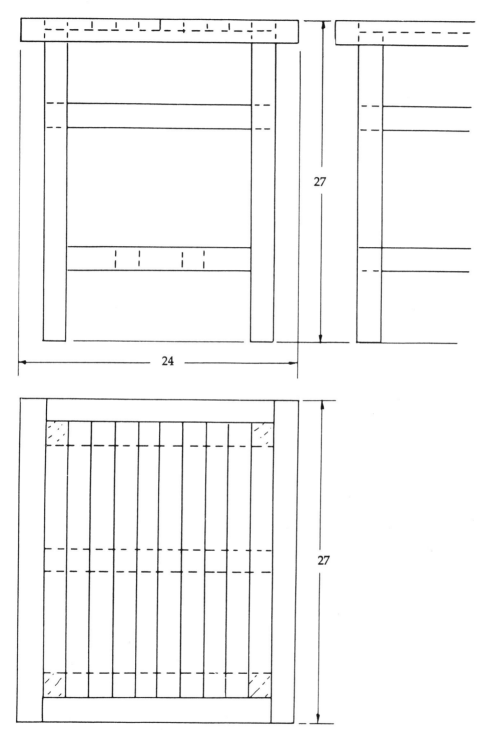

Fig. 4-61. Sizes for the butcher-block table.

It is the central area of the top that controls other sizes. Make this part first. If you work the other way and need to fit the top into a frame, you will need to cut the width of one strip. Join enough strips together (FIG. 4-62A). It might be sufficient to rely on glue only. If so, assemble all the parts of the top face-downward on a flat surface covered with paper to prevent the glue sticking to it. Pull them together with bar clamps. You will need to put weights on the assembly to prevent it from buckling. A safer way of keeping it flat is to assemble the strips in groups of two or three that have their tops planed true before joining them to other groups.

You could use nails between the parts in predrilled holes or dowels across in a similar way. Three along each joint should be enough. Have all the pieces too long at this stage so that you can trim the whole assembly as if it is a single board. The way you deal with the ends depends on your equipment. The best way is to rabbet across so that a tongue goes into a plowed groove in the frame (FIG. 4-62B). For this task, you could use a router, two passes on a table saw, or a hand fillester plane.

Alternatively, you can use dowels in square-cut ends (FIG. 4-62C). At the sides, you can glue the joints or use a few dowels there. In the 1-inch thickness, the dowels could be 3/4 inch in diameter.

There are three ways of making the frame. You can make the ends go right across with the sides taken into the same plowed grooves (FIG. 4-63A). You could carry the sides through so that the ends are covered, and use dowels in the joint (FIG. 4-63B), going either partly into the sides or taken through. (Exposed dowel ends can be regarded as a design feature in this type of construction.) You also could miter the corners and take dowels through diagonally (FIG. 4-63C).

The top should be stiff enough as it is, but you could place a piece across under the center, tenoning it into the sides (FIG. 4-62D). Complete the top before you start on the framing. Clean off surplus glue where the legs and their top bars will come underneath.

The legs and rails are all square to match the solid appearance of the top. Four rails go around the table a short distance down from the top. Then there are two rails between the legs at the ends and lengthwise rails between them. At the tops of the legs, there are rails across to take screws upward into the tabletop.

Mark out the legs (FIG. 4-62). Use mortise-and-tenon joints for the rails. The tenons can go about halfway through the legs. You will need to miter the lower ones where they meet. You could use doweled joints if you prefer, but tenons are more appropriate. You can tenon the thinner top rails to take screws, but they are better dovetailed into the tops of the legs (FIG. 4-62F). Drill for screws before assembly, but angle them slightly so that there is clearance for your screwdriver past the main rail. Make the rails of a length that allows the legs to come closely inside the top frame.

Make up the two end leg and rail assemblies. See that they are square, flat, and match as a pair. Join them with the rails the other way, and fit the framework to the tabletop.

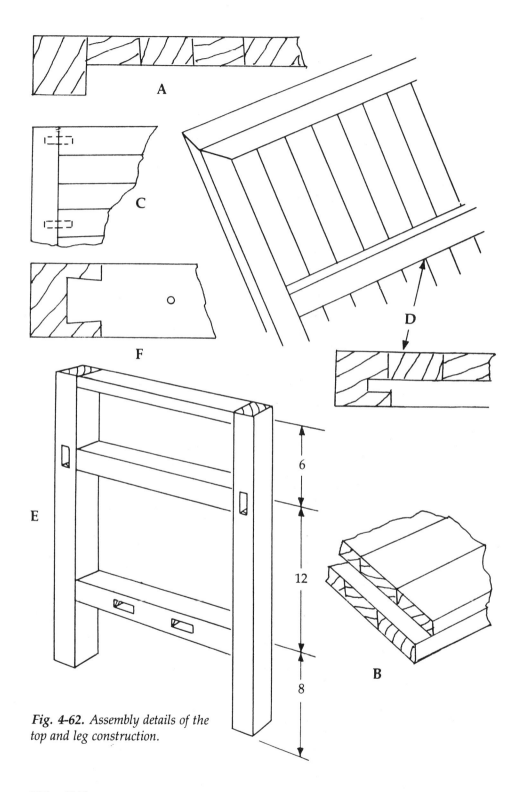

Fig. 4-62. *Assembly details of the top and leg construction.*

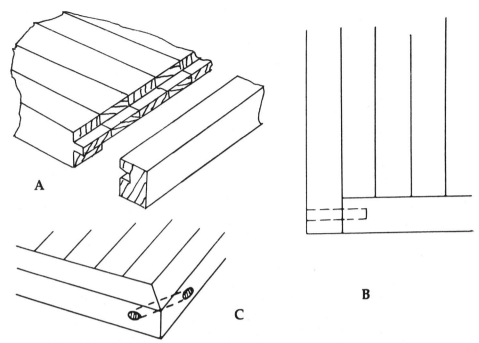

Fig. 4-63. Constructional details of the tabletop.

Radial Tabletops

Butcher-block tops do not need to be just parallel strips. You can make interesting tables with the tops divided into segments that are all in the same wood or in alternating colors of woods. You can show your skill by making tops using narrow strips and a large number of segments. For the usual purposes of an outdoor table, however, a more simple arrangement would be appreciated just as much. It will usually be sufficient to divide the top into four segments.

An example is a square top with or without a border (FIG. 4-64A). This is shown with 2-×-4-inch pieces, with the greater width on the top, but you could also use 2-inch-square pieces or even narrower ones. Join enough pieces to make up the width of a side with the outside edge cut squarely, but extended enough to mark the miter (FIG. 4-64B). The safest way to get an accurate shape is to set out the final square, with diagonals, full size on a piece of scrap plywood or hardboard, then cut and plane the miter edges to that shape. In any case, you will need to do some careful planing for final close fitting. Mark adjoining surfaces so that they go back in the same place, then drill for a few dowels.

Exposed ends of hardwood look attractive with their different grain patterns, particularly if woods are mixed and the ends are sealed with varnish. Softwoods are better covered. You can make a border (FIG. 4-64C) with mitered or lapped corners. You can attach the top to legs and framing made in the way described for the previous table.

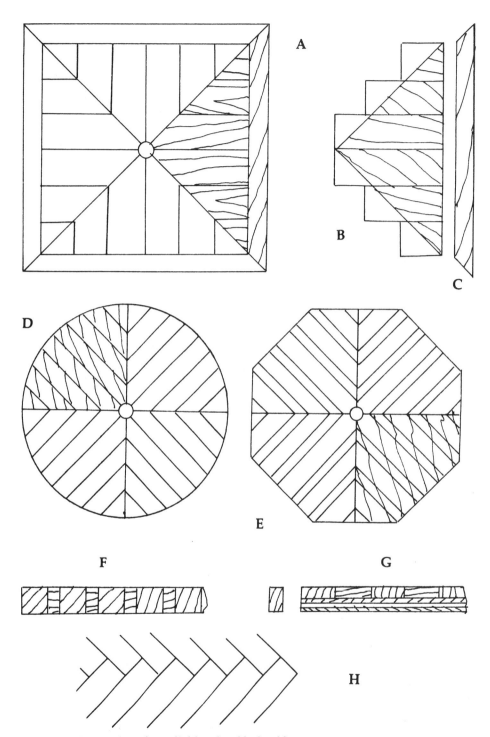

Fig. 4-64. Suggestions for radial butcher-block tabletops.

A very similar top is easily converted to round (FIG. 4-64D). This is shown with square strips. The best plan to get a good shape is to start with the outline of a square table and draw the circle when the parts are joined. You could draw curves on each segment, but cut oversize so there can be a final trimming to a true circle later.

The strips used do not all need to have the same widths. You can obtain an interesting effect by using random widths. This is a way of using up oddments left from other work. You can alternate wide and narrow pieces. Dark narrow pieces between lighter colored ones can be very attractive. An example is shown with an octagonal outline (FIG. 4-64E), but you could use the design in other shapes.

You can border any top having straight edges with strips glued and nailed or screwed on. An alternative to a square, unbordered edge is to make it semicircular or to bevel around top and bottom edges.

The usual assembly is with pieces to the full thickness of the top (FIG. 4-64F), but there is an alternative way of getting a similar top appearance using thinner wood. For the base, mark or cut a piece of stout exterior-grade plywood to the shape the table is to be. On the plywood, place thinner strips of wood to make up any pattern you prefer (FIG. 4-64G). You can use any of the patterns suitable for solid wood, but in this case you can put the pieces in place over a penciled pattern on the plywood. You can glue the parts or drive screws from below as well. Glue is advisable, in any case, because it seals the gaps and prevents water from becoming trapped between and under the strips.

A variation in pattern that would be difficult with solid pieces but that is easier to do on a plywood base is to arrange the meeting pieces in a herringbone pattern (FIG. 4-64H) instead of straight miters. Add a border, bedded in glue, to prevent moisture from being absorbed by the exposed end grain of the plywood veneers.

5

Kitchen

An expert chef prefers wood to plastic or metal for much of his or her kitchen equipment. You can follow this example and provide many wooden items for food preparation or serving. These can range from small items for use on a worktop, to tables and counters or storage for equipment.

There is a need for plenty of storage space if working areas are to be kept clear for their real purpose. You can make shelves and cupboards custom-fit to use available space to the fullest.

Some food-serving items will go from the kitchen to the dining room. Besides having a utilitarian function, these can be attractive pieces of furniture. Although the projects described in this chapter are primarily for use in the kitchen, many of them could find a place in other parts of your home.

Kitchen Boards

Despite the advent of plastics for nearly everything, no enthusiastic cook will accept anything but wood for a surface on which to cut, chop, or roll. A professional chef often has many boards of different sizes and for different purposes. Such a board could be just that—a simple, flat piece of wood. However, there are many developments and variations you can make with a table saw. One attraction is the opportunity to use up oddments of wood that might otherwise be discarded.

Modern waterproof glues allow wood to be joined positively and with no need for complex jointing. Such joints will remain secure under wet conditions; something which could not be claimed of the glues from not so many years ago.

Make sure the glue you obtain is described as *waterproof* and not just *water-resistant*. If it is suitable for boat building, you have the best.

Avoid resinous wood or wood that is greasy or has an odor. A light color is more hygienic. A close grain is easier to clean and less likely to splinter. Sycamore is typical of the wood to choose. If you are laminating, you could use different woods for the sake of the resulting pattern, but beware of different hardnesses, which will result in an uneven surface after much use.

If you wish to use a single wide board, it should be radially cut from the log (FIG. 5-1A). You can check this by looking at the end grain lines, which will be fairly straight through the thickness (FIG. 5-1B). If you cut elsewhere from the log, the lines will be curved in varying degrees (FIG. 5-1C). If your wood gets wet, particularly more on one side than the other, as it might in kitchen use, it will warp. The effect is for grain lines to try to straighten. The radially cut board might get a little thicker, but it will remain flat (FIG. 5-1D). The board with curved lines will go out of shape (FIG. 5-1E).

A board may be held flat or given feet with cleats underneath (FIG. 5-2A). If the cleats are at the ends, there will be less risk of tipping (FIG. 5-2B). A further development is to make one cleat deeper with a notch, so it can be steadied over the edge of a table (FIG. 5-2C). Nailing or screwing are inadvisable, even if you use noncorrosive fastenings. Glue between the surfaces might be sufficient, but a few dowels (FIG. 5-2D) will lock the parts together more securely.

The risk of warping is removed if you laminate the wood by gluing strips together to make up the width (FIG. 5-2E). This is often described as *butcher block*, but the true butcher block uses end grain squares (described later). For a laminated board, saw strips in random widths, then saw them all to the same thickness. Your board width can be made up of three or four pieces, or a much larger number—it does not matter. Examine the end grain, and alternate the grain lines as much as possible, then any tendency to warp will cancel out.

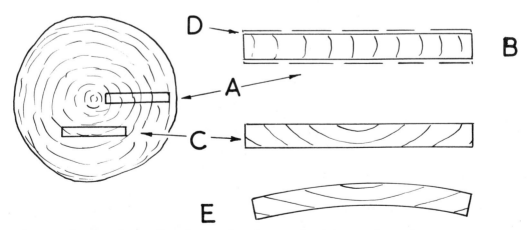

Fig. 5-1. How boards are affected when they dry out after being cut from a log.

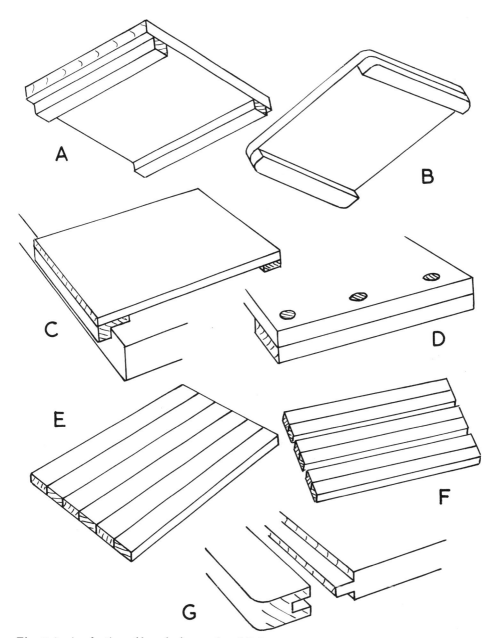

Fig. 5-2. *A selection of boards for use in a kitchen.*

The board you make should be about 3/4 inch thick and 10 inches square for chopping and cutting, or it could be 20 inches by 30 inches for rolling pastry. It is inadvisable to try to glue all the strips at the same time. It is easier to clamp and keep surfaces level if you first join strips in pairs and then bring pairs together after the first glue lines have set (FIG. 5-2F).

A board of lengthwise laminations should remain flat in use, but if you want to secure the board, or one made from a wide piece, and do not wish to put cleats underneath, there could be strips across the ends in the traditional pastry-board manner. This involves cutting a tongue on the board ends, with a matching groove in the end pieces (FIG. 5-2G). Take the tongue into the other piece at least 1/2 inch, for stiffness. It will be easier to make the board finish level on both sides if the end pieces are slightly too thick at first, so you can plane and sand them level.

The true butcher-block pattern is made of pieces of wood with their end grain on the surface (FIG. 5-3A). This provides the best long-lasting cutting surface. The board has to be made slightly thicker than the other boards, about 1 inch is satisfactory. The wood should be close-grained hardwood with little tendency to split.

Although it is possible to arrange a pattern with different sizes, you should make your first board from square stock all the same section. Suppose you have wood suitable for cutting to 1 1/2-inch squares: A board 9 inches one way and 12 inches the other way would need 48 squares. At a final thickness of 1 inch, that means preparing a strip, or several oddments, totaling a length of 48 inches, with

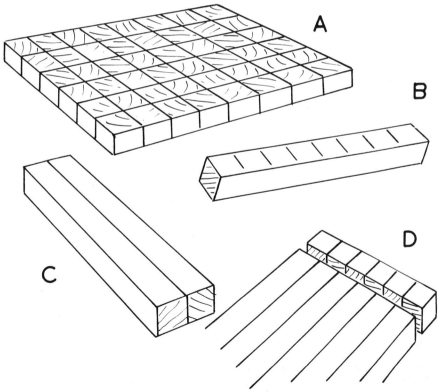

Fig. 5-3. Construction of butcher-block boards.

maybe a further 12 inches to allow for cutting. Start by gluing together pieces long enough to cut into eight blocks (FIG. 5-3B). These will make up the short way, so you need six strips, but it is safer to glue in pairs (FIG. 5-3C) before gluing the final joints.

Square one end. Remove surplus glue. True the surfaces flat, if necessary, but do not take off any more wood than you have to. Saw the block across into 1-inch pieces (FIG. 5-3D). Glue these pieces together, starting with pairs. When the glue has set, plane and sand the surfaces level, trim the edges, and round the corners.

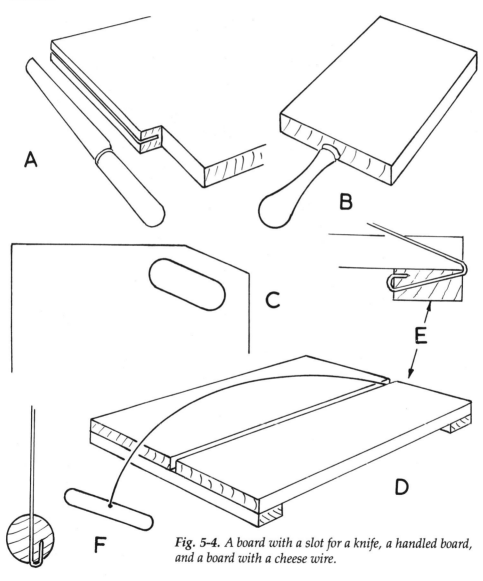

Fig. 5-4. A board with a slot for a knife, a handled board, and a board with a cheese wire.

Before using the board, soak the end grain butcher block in vegetable oil and repeat the treatment occasionally during its life to reduce water absorption. Boards made in other ways may be treated in the same way, but side grain surfaces are not so absorbent.

There are many variations on the plain boards. A knife could be kept in one edge, if you recess for the handle and make a saw cut that is a push fit on the blade (FIG. 5-4A).

You also could provide a handle. It might be turned with a dowel to fit into the edge of a board (FIG. 5-4B). A finger hole may be provided, either across one end or at the corner (FIG. 5-4C). Make it by drilling two 3/4-inch holes at least 3 inches apart, then saw between and around the edges. Some kitchen boards that have survived from pioneer days have complicated decorative handles, but it is important to remember that any shaping of the board reduces the useful working area.

The old-time grocer always cut cheese with a wire and not a knife. You can make a wire-cutting cheeseboard in two parts (FIG. 5-4D). Arrange a gap of about 1/8 inch. Use stainless steel wire, about 20-gauge. At one side, take it through a hole and turn its end over to drive into the wood (FIG. 5-4E). Allow a sufficient length to loop over the largest piece of cheese, then take the wire through a piece of 1/2-inch dowel rod 4 inches long (FIG. 5-4F). Position the board near the edge of a table so you pull downwards over the edge as the wire cuts through the cheese.

Magnetic Cheeseboard

This is a leaf-shaped cheeseboard where the knife fits into a groove in the leaf stem handle (FIG. 5-5). It is held there by a magnet gripping the blade. A simpler board could be made without provision for the knife, if you wish.

You can use any wood, but because the board should not be polished or varnished, softwood (because of its porosity) is not suggested. A light-colored hardwood looks hygienic, but a darker wood shows up attractively on a light-colored tablecloth. Cutting will be done on the board, so a close-grained wood is preferable. The completed cheeseboard can be left untreated, but rubbing it with vegetable cooking oil will emphasize the grain markings, allow safe contact with food, and prevent the wood from absorbing water when it is washed.

The board could be cut from one piece of wood 8 inches wide, but to reduce the risk of warping it might be better made of two or three pieces glued to make up the width—preferably with the curves of end grain in opposite directions.

The knife will have to be provided with a shaped handle, so you may have to obtain an unhandled knife or remove the handle from an existing one. Most suitable knives have tangs about 1 inch long, and that suits a wood handle you can make. Obtain the knife and a small round magnet. A magnet diameter of 3/8 or 1/2 inch and a depth of 1/4 inch would be suitable. Some stainless steels are nonmagnetic; make sure this is not the case with the knife you use.

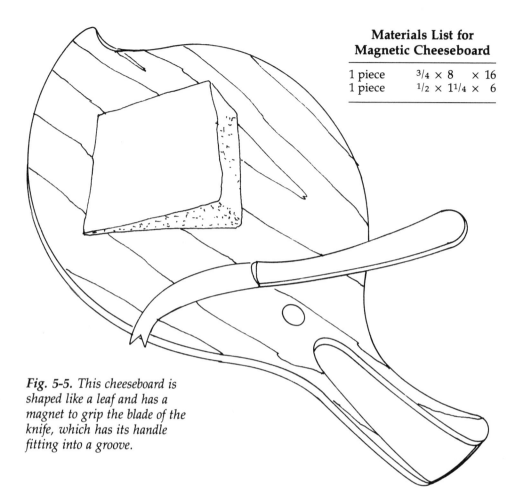

**Materials List for
Magnetic Cheeseboard**

1 piece	$3/4 \times 8 \times 16$
1 piece	$1/2 \times 11/4 \times 6$

Fig. 5-5. This cheeseboard is shaped like a leaf and has a magnet to grip the blade of the knife, which has its handle fitting into a groove.

Draw and cut the outline of the board (FIG. 5-6A). Cut the profile of the knife handle (FIG. 5-6B). Drive the knife tang into an undersize hole in the handle (FIG. 5-6C) and coat it with epoxy glue for extra security. Round the handle, if you wish.

Draw around the handle on the board handle, with the knife handle end extending a short way. Allow about 1/6 inch each side of the knife handle for the width of the slot.

Cut the slot in the board for the knife handle. Its depth (FIG. 5-6D) should allow the blade to rest flat on the surface of the board. The ends of the groove are flared open slightly. This, with the slight overhang of the handle end, makes it easy to remove and replace the knife.

The main part of the board could be left with square edges, but it looks better if the underside is rounded (FIG. 5-6E) or beveled (FIG. 5-6F). At the angle end, thoroughly round underneath (FIG. 5-6G) so fingers can be slipped under to pick up the knife.

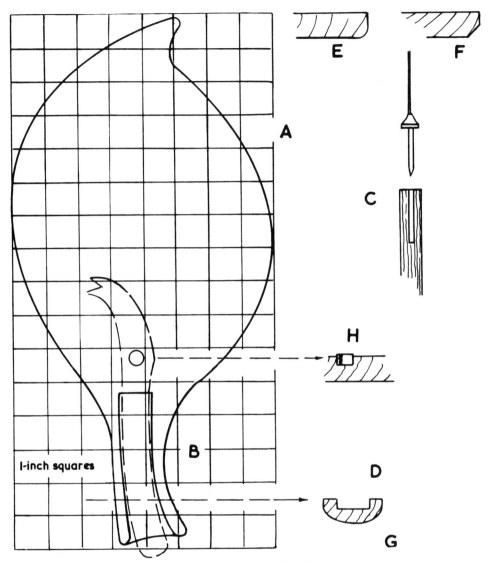

Fig. 5-6. Shape and details of the magnetic cheeseboard.

Drill for the magnet and secure it with epoxy glue so its top is slightly above the wood surface (FIG. 5-6H).

Sand all over. The knife handle may be varnished. Treat the board with vegetable oil, preferably by immersing and draining.

Cook's Tool Cabinet

Cooks who take their work seriously accumulate a large number of tools. Some may be stored quite satisfactorily in a drawer, but others need more careful storage, as they could be damaged by close contact with other tools. This is particularly true of knives, which need to be sharp to do their job. Tossing them all together in a drawer or tray will soon blunt them. Moreover, this storage method increases the risk that someone will cut himself looking for a certain knife.

Knives should be stored individually. You can get knife blocks that stand on the countertop, but these blocks can get in the way. A better solution is a rack, with individual slots, located away from the worktop. Better still, you could build a cabinet for the rack and include storage space for other tools.

The tool cabinet shown in FIG. 5-7 has a knife rack that can be tilted forward for easy storage and removal. The blades are protected, but you can see them

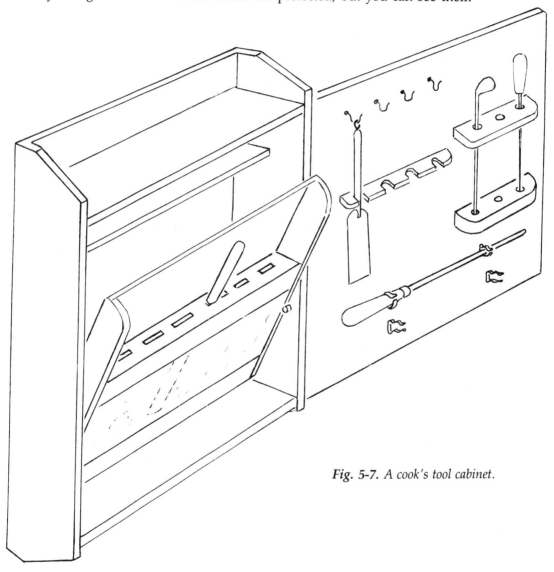

Fig. 5-7. *A cook's tool cabinet.*

Materials List for Cook's Tool Cabinet

1 knife rack	$7/8 \times$	$2^{1}/2 \times 21$
1 knife rack	$1^{1}/8 \times$	$2^{1}/2 \times 21$
1 knife rack bottom	2×2	$\times 21$
2 knife rack ends	$1/2 \times 2$	$\times 19$
1 knife rack back	17×21	$\times 1/2$ plywood
2 cabinet sides	$3/4 \times 6$	$\times 23$
1 cabinet top	$3/4 \times 6$	$\times 23$
1 cabinet bottom	$3/4 \times 6$	$\times 23$
1 shelf	$5/8 \times 5$	$\times 23$
1 back	21×24	$\times 1/4$ plywood
1 back	$3/4 \times 3$	$\times 3$
1 back	$3/4 \times 4$	$\times 23$
1 door	21×25	$\times 3/4$ or 1 plywood
4 door edgings	$1/2 \times 1$	$\times 26$

through a transparent plastic front. Whatever else goes in the cabinet is up to the cook, but there is space for many hanging tools inside the door. You can use spring clips (preferably plated or covered with plastic) for some tools, while others can hang outside the cabinet.

Figure 5-8 shows suggested sizes that you can adapt when you have sorted and measured the tools to be stored. The cabinet could be much bigger than shown, with double doors. Increasing its depth would allow you to fit drawers or trays. A rail below the bottom could take several hanging tools, or you could use it for a towel (FIG. 5-8B). If your main concern is the safe storage of knives, count and measure them first. Allow for one or two spare slots. Based on this information, you can settle the sizes of the unit.

Start with the knife rack. Use close-grained hardwood for the thick pieces. The back could be plywood. There is no need to make slots to fit knife blades closely; you might be able to decide on one, or perhaps two, slot sizes that will serve all knives. In FIG. 5-9A, all slots are 1/4 inch wide. Slot length should be slightly more than the width of the largest blade. The rack shown takes blades up to 9 inches long with handles up to 6 inches long (FIG. 5-9B).

You could cut slots through a solid block, but it is easier to get accurate results by using two parts. The diagram shows a flat back piece (FIG. 5-9C) glued to a front piece in which the slots are cut (FIG. 5-9D).

The bottom block (FIG. 5-9E) is solid. Cut rabbets in both pieces to take 1/8-inch plexiglass or similar transparent plastic. Put uprights across the ends, and close the back with plywood.

Use the knife rack as a guide to internal sizes. Mark out a pair of sides (FIG. 5-8C), with rabbets at the rear edge for plywood and widening parts for solid pieces at the top and bottom. Cut stopped grooves for the cabinet top and bottom and for a shelf, if you wish to fit one. Make the cabinet top and bottom with notches to fit the stopped grooves. Make the shelf the same length. Cut the solid back strips.

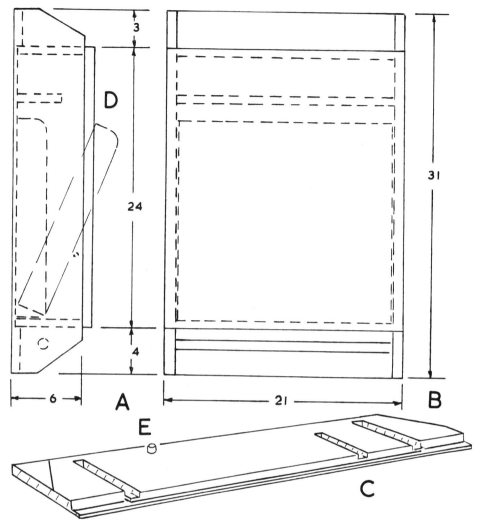

Fig. 5-8. Suggested sizes for the cook's tool cabinet.

Try the knife rack against one side before assembly, and decide how much you want it to tilt forward (FIG. 5-8D). Based on this test, position a short, 1/2-inch dowel on each side to act as stops (FIG. 5-8E).

Have the plywood back ready, then assemble all the parts of the cabinet made so far.

Make the door from thick plywood, with solid wood lips all around (FIG. 5-10A). Figure 5-10 suggests ways of hanging cooks' tools. Several will hang on hooks, but you could add a notched strip lower down to limit their swaying when the door is moved (FIG. 5-10B).

Some tools can pass through holes with their ends resting in other holes drilled only partly through another block (FIG. 5-10C). Some tools are better held

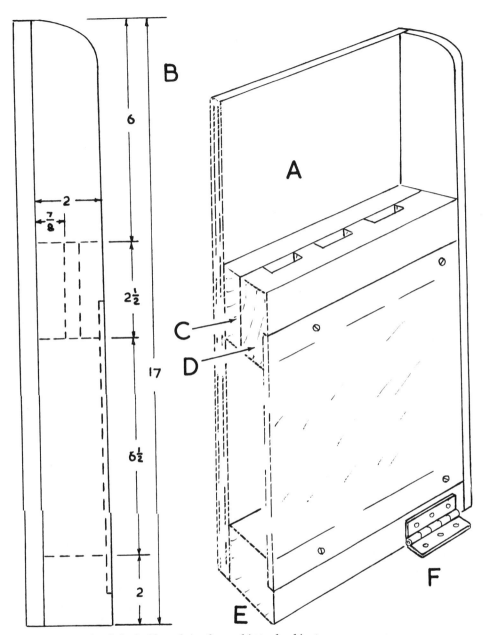

Fig. 5-9. *Details of the knife rack in the cook's tool cabinet.*

with spring clips (FIG. 5-10D). Try laying the tools on the door (lain flat) to get the best arrangement.

Fit the knife rack with hinges on its front edge (FIG. 5-9F). The rack's own weight will keep it upright, and you can pull it forward by gripping its edge or a knife. Hinge the door at one side, fit a catch at the other side, and add a handle.

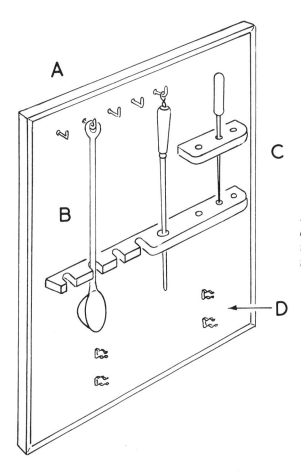

A

B

C

D

Fig. 5-10. A sample arrangement of tools on the inside of the door of the cook's tool cabinet.

Writing-Flap Cabinet

A cook might be glad to have a special rack for personal notebooks, recipe cards, and other such things. If the same unit has a pull-down flap for writing on, the cook can make notes away from the mess of the worktop.

The cabinet shown in FIG. 5-11 has a divided top section for notebooks and papers. The compartment below includes a flap front that provides a writing area over 12 inches square. There is space behind for pads, pens, and many other small things. Figure 5-12A suggests sizes, which you can modify to suit your needs. When planning this unit, allow enough of the flap to go under its shelf when lowered to support the surface in normal use. A quarter of the amount projecting should be about right. In the drawing, there is about 3 inches under the shelf for a flap projection of 12 inches.

You could make most of the parts with plywood or veneered particleboard, with suitable edging, but the instructions are for solid wood. Even if you make nearly all the parts of solid wood, you might want to use plywood for the flap

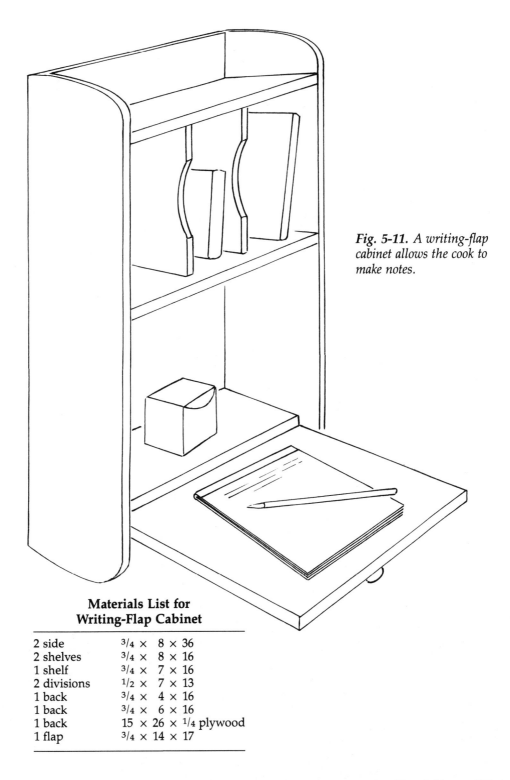

Fig. 5-11. A writing-flap cabinet allows the cook to make notes.

Materials List for Writing-Flap Cabinet

2 side	$3/4 \times 8 \times 36$
2 shelves	$3/4 \times 8 \times 16$
1 shelf	$3/4 \times 7 \times 16$
2 divisions	$1/2 \times 7 \times 13$
1 back	$3/4 \times 4 \times 16$
1 back	$3/4 \times 6 \times 16$
1 back	$15 \times 26 \times 1/4$ plywood
1 flap	$3/4 \times 14 \times 17$

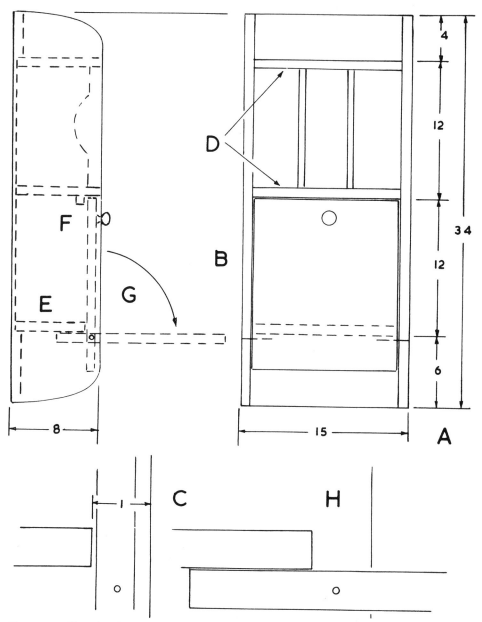

Fig. 5-12. Sizes for the writing-flap cabinet.

because it does not warp or shrink. As shown, the unit has solid wood pieces across at top and bottom of the back, with thin plywood between.

Mark out the pair of sides (FIGS. 5-12 and 5-13). Rabbet the rear edges for plywood, and increase the width of the rabbets for the top and bottom solid strip backs, as described for other projects in this chapter. The two top stopped

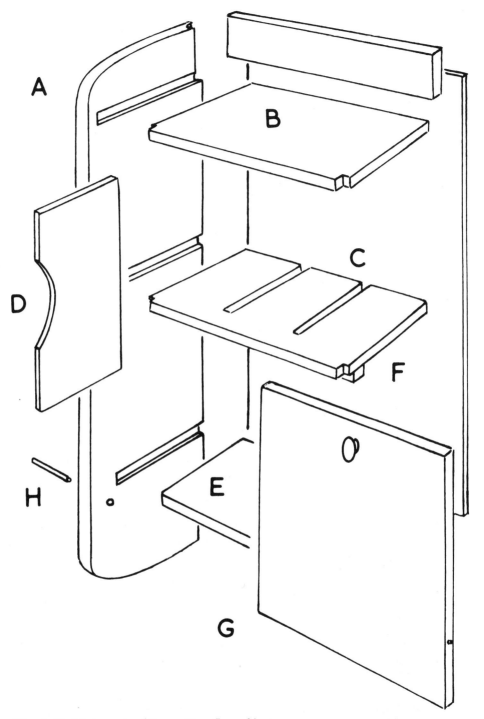

Fig. 5-13. Main parts of the writing-flap cabinet.

grooves across are for shelves that will come flush with the front edges of the sides. The groove for the lower shelf allows for it being set back to clear the flap when raised (FIG. 5-12C). Shape the top and bottom ends of the sides as shown or to match other cabinets.

Make the top two shelves (FIGS. 5-12D and 5-13B) notched to fit the grooves in the sides. Divide the widths into three, and cut grooves for the divisions, which can stop 1 inch from the front edge (FIG. 5-13C). The divisions can have hollowed front edges (FIG. 5-13D) and should be well rounded.

Make the bottom shelf (FIGS. 5-12 and 5-13) to match the grooves in the sides. Put a strip across under the middle shelf at the same distance from the back as the width of the bottom shelf, to act as a stop for the flap when raised (FIGS. 5-12 and 5-13F). Prepare the solid and plywood back parts.

Join the divisions to their shelves, then the shelves to the sides. Add the back parts. Check squareness, and make sure that the sides are parallel for a good fit on the flap.

Make the flap (FIGS. 5-12 and 5-13G) to fit easily between the sides. Round the top and bottom edges if you wish. Fit a knob or handle near the top edge.

The pivot point on each side has to be located so that the flap will be upright when closed and it fits under the shelf when open (FIG. 5-12H). The pivots could be stout screws (2 inches long by at least #12 gauge), but it is better to use pieces of noncorrosive metal rod, 3/16-inch diameter (FIG. 5-13H).

Mark and drill the sides. Put the flaps in position and mark and drill through. Drill a short distance into the flap and insert the rods, so you can try the action. If necessary, you can relocate the holes slightly as you drill the full depth.

Drive in the rods until the ends are level with the surface. If you want to be able to remove the rods, however, let project a little, preferably with rounded ends for the sake of appearance. A small ball catch at one side will hold the flap in its up position.

Side Shelf Unit

Having shelves at the end of an island unit might not be the best arrangement for your kitchen, particularly if the end faces a little-used wall or a narrow or congested part of the floor. Shelves at one or both sides can make the things they store more accessible. And if the shelves are also intended for display, placing them at the side will probably better serve that purpose.

Several variations are possible. The unit shown in FIG. 5-14 has a block of drawers at one end, a double-door cupboard at the other, and back-to-back shelves in the middle. Suggested sizes are only a guide (FIG. 5-15A); you will have to adapt them to suit your needs and space. If shelves are not needed on both sides, one side could have doors. The suggested unit has a plinth all around and a tiled top, but any other top would suffice.

The unit is made as one assembly—not in sections to be brought together after making. This means that there are no double thicknesses. It also means that

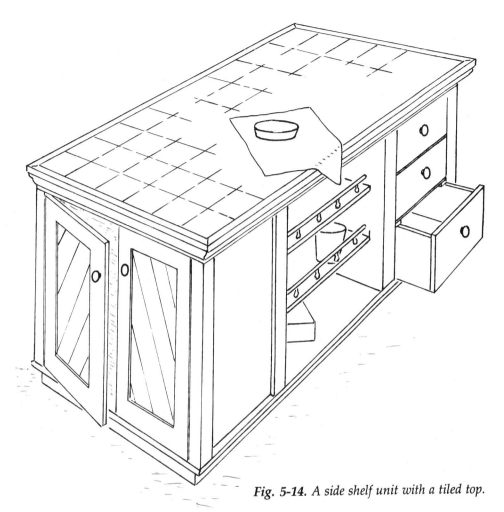

Fig. 5-14. A side shelf unit with a tiled top.

you must check access sizes to ensure that a unit made in your workshop can pass through doorways on its way to the kitchen. If necessary, you can save a few inches of width by leaving the top off until the unit is in place.

Most parts are 3/4-inch plywood. Some moldings are included, and there are turned pillars under the rails on the shelves. You could simplify the design, however, if a plainer finish would better match other cabinets in the kitchen. If you decide on a tiled top, you can reduce work if you arrange the top to take whole tiles. Start with those measurements and relate other sizes to them. Doors are shown with diagonal tongue-and-groove board panels, but you could make doors and drawer fronts to match the doors of other cabinets. The height is the same as the wall cabinets, but you could reduce it if your cook prefers a lower work area.

Mark out the bottom first (FIG. 5-16A). The upright parts are 1 inch in from the edge, which will be covered later with a half-round molding.

Materials List for Side Shelf Unit

1 bottom	28 × 48	× 3/4 plywood	
1 top	32 × 54	× 3/4 plywood	
3 uprights	26 × 30	× 3/4 plywood	
1 division	21 × 30	× 3/4 plywood	
3 uprights	13 × 30	× 3/4 plywood	
4 shelves	13 × 22	× 3/4 plywood	
3 strips	1 × 2	× 27	
2 top strips	1 × 2	× 48	
1 top strip	1 × 2	× 27	
2 side frames	1 × 3	× 52	
8 side frames	1 × 2	× 30	
2 end frames	1 × 3	× 28	
4 end frames	1 × 2	× 30	
2 top moldings	1 × 2	× 52	
2 top moldings	1 × 2	× 30	
2 bottom moldings	3/4 × 52 half-round		
2 bottom moldings	3/4 × 30 half-round		
4 shelf moldings	3/4 × 22 half-round		
2 top edgings	5/8 ×	1 1/2 × 56	
2 top edgings	5/8 ×	1 1/2 × 34	
4 shelf edge rails	3/4 ×	3/4 × 22	
16 shelf edge spindles	3/4 ×	3/4 × 4	
4 door frames	1 × 2	× 30	
2 door frames	1 × 2	× 14	
2 door frames	1 × 3	× 14	
Door panels to suit			
1 drawer front	3/4 × 10	× 12	
2 drawer fronts	3/4 × 9	× 12	
1 drawer back	5/8 × 9	× 12	
2 drawer backs	5/8 × 8	× 12	
2 drawer sides	5/8 × 9	× 29	
4 drawer sides	5/8 × 8	× 26	
3 drawer bottoms	12 × 26	× 1/4 plywood	

Make the three crosswise uprights (FIG. 5-16B). They are the same overall size. Fit notched strips across the top edges to take the lengthwise strips (FIGS. 5-16C and 5-16D). On upright #1 (FIG. 5-16E), cut away the plywood notches and mark for both sides of the cupboard on the side with the top strip. Mark for the central division and the shelves on the other side. Mark upright #2 in the same way, but without a piece connecting at the fronts of the drawers. Mark the inner surface of upright #3 as a pair to #2, but do not cut away the plywood notches.

Make the division (FIGS. 5-16E and 5-17A) to fit between uprights #1 and #2. Cut plywood for the shelves (FIGS. 5-16F and 5-17B). If you want to have rails and spindles at the front of the shelves, make them now, and allow for small tenons on the rail ends into the plywood (FIG. 5-18A). Use bought spindles or turn your own with dowel ends.

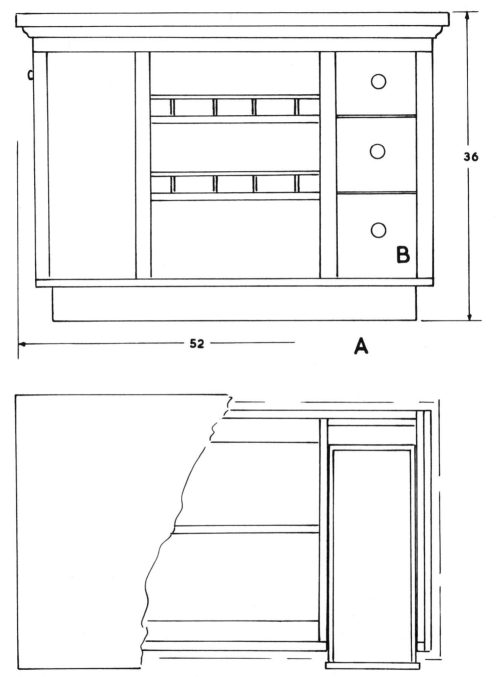

Fig. 5-15. Details of the side shelf unit.

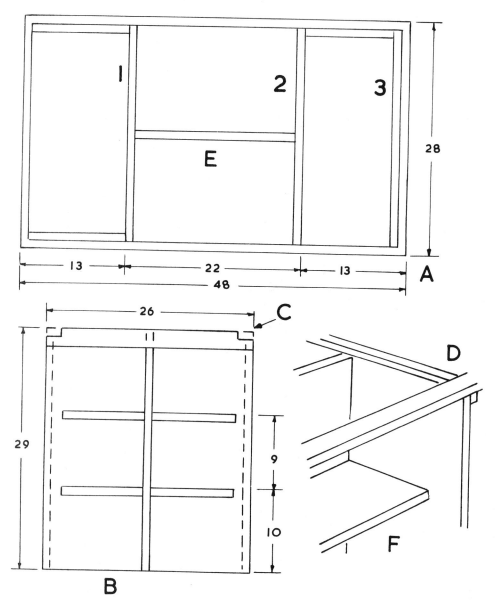

Fig. 5-16. Sizes of parts of the side shelf unit.

Make the two sides of the cupboard (FIG. 5-17C) and the piece at the back of the drawers (FIG. 5-17D). The tops of these parts come against the underside of the lengthwise strips.

Prepare all the meeting edges for dowels—3/8-inch dowels at about 4-inch intervals should be satisfactory.

Cover the front edges of the shelves and all edges of the bottom with half-round molding (FIG. 5-17E). Fit drawer runners to uprights #2 and #3. Three

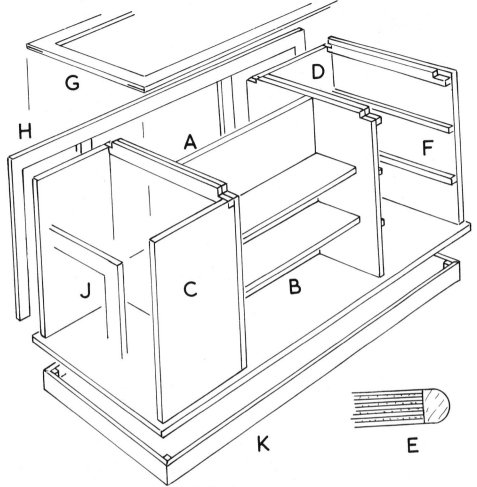

Fig. 5-17. Main parts of the side shelf unit.

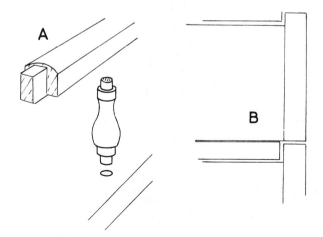

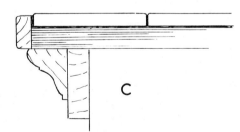

Fig. 5-18. Details of the rail drawers, and top of the side shelf unit.

drawers are shown (FIGS. 5-15 and 5-17F), but you could have four or more. Assemble the parts made so far.

Fit lengthwise strips in the top notches, with a piece across the top of the cupboard (FIG. 5-17G).

Make frames to cover the back and front, with 3-inch-wide strips at the top and 2-inch-wide pieces for the uprights (FIG. 5-17H). There are no pieces across the bottoms of the frames. The intermediate upright pieces should be level with the edge of the shelf openings and cover the edges of the plywood crosswise uprights.

Make frames for the ends (FIG. 5-17J) in a similar way. The frame on the outside of the end with the drawers is only there for appearance, but the one at the other end will hold the doors, which can be flush or set on the surface. Match the doors to others in the kitchen. As there are no drawer rails across the front, you should make the fronts extending upward enough to hide the ends of the drawer runners (FIG. 5-18B). They could be flush inside the frames, or they could overlap.

If the top is to be tiled, make its base with a good overhang and edge it to contain the tiles. You could put a molding underneath the edges (FIG. 5-18C).

Make the plinth like an open box, with blocks inside mitered corners (FIG. 5-17K). Fit the plinth with screws downward and the top with screws upward.

Display Rack

Some racks intended to display your treasures and collectibles are so enclosed and heavy in appearance that attention is drawn to the stand rather than to what it contains. It is better to have the rack as light and open as is possible, providing there is sufficient strength. This rack (FIG. 5-19) is lightly framed so the items put on it are in view in any direction. Besides display, it could have uses for storing pots and pans in the kitchen. Also, it would take care of books and papers in a den or office, or take folded linen and blankets in a bedroom. In short, you could find a use for it in any room.

The sizes are for a rack with four shelves (FIG. 5-20) which could be solid wood. They might be plywood with solid wood edging, or you could use veneered particleboard. The rest of the rack should be straight-grained hardwood. For these parts of light section, avoid twisting grain, which might lead to warping. The dowel rods across the back should also be hardwood.

The key parts are the shelves (FIGS. 5-20 and 5-21A), which should be identical.

To ensure accuracy in locating the uprights, cut notches 1/8 inch deep (FIG. 5-21B) at the rear corners, and 1 inch back from the front edge (FIG. 5-21C). Round the front corners, and round the edges as far back as the notches. Leave the edges square at the ends.

Mark the shelf positions on the uprights together, to avoid slight errors. At each shelf position, cut notches 1/8 inch deep to engage with the shelf notches (FIG. 5-21D).

Fig. 5-19. This display rack provides shelves for books, plants, and many other items in a living room.

**Materials List for
Display Rack**

4 shelves	22 ×	11	× 3/4
2 uprights	45 ×	1 1/2	× 3/4
2 uprights	54 ×	1 1/2	× 3/4
1 crossbar	21 ×	3	× 3/4
7 rails	22 ×	3/8 diameter	

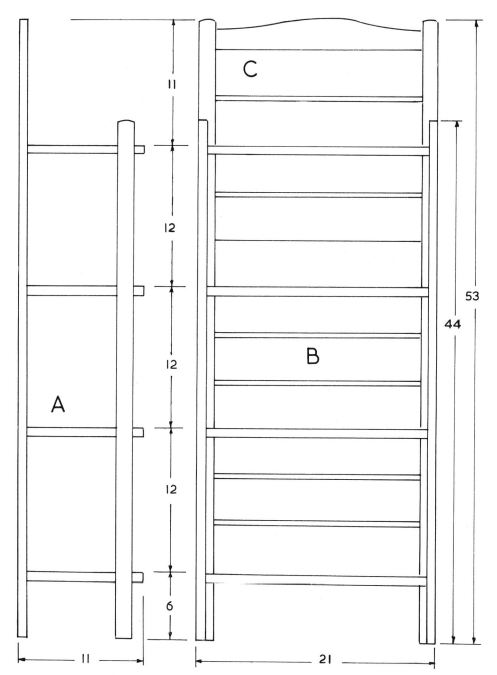

Fig. 5-20. Sizes of the display rack.

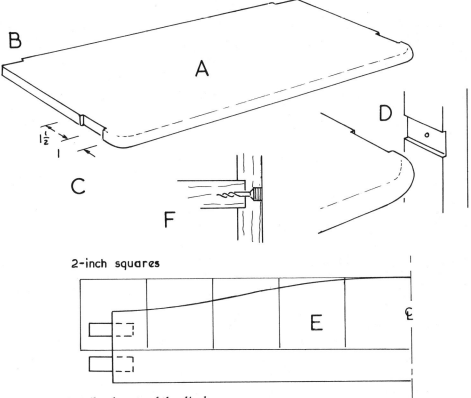

Fig. 5-21. Details of parts of the display.

Mark and drill for dowel rods (FIG. 5-20B) in the rear legs. Space them at 4-inch intervals between the shelves. Cut the front legs to length and round their tops.

The crossbar at the top of the back (FIG. 5-20C) has a shaped edge(FIG. 5-21E), and the ends are joined to the uprights with dowels.

The crossbar and the shelves set the spacing of the rear uprights. Be careful that the dowel rods are not cut too long, so they prevent the uprights being brought into position. They do not have to reach the bottoms of their holes.

Join the uprights to the shelves with counterbored and plugged screws (FIG. 5-21F). These could be #8 gauge by 1¹/4-inch screws. The plugs can be cross-grained matching wood, or you might prefer wood of a contrasting color as a design feature.

If you have used an attractive hardwood, you will probably prefer a clear finish, but if you have used different woods, it might be better to use paint. Painted shelves with the other parts clear might offer the best display for some items.

Tall Shelves

If the base of a block of shelves is on the countertop in a kitchen, you must keep it reasonably shallow back-to-front so as not to take up too much of the working area. However, if the block is tall, you can make the upper part extend farther out from the wall without interfering with normal food preparation. This is often done with wall cabinets, but you can arrange shelves in the same way.

The block of tall shelves shown in FIG. 5-22 is a self-contained unit, but you could arrange it between cabinets or alongside one cabinet. With its shaping, it would make a good end to a series of cabinets.

The whole unit could be solid wood, mostly 3/4 inch thick, but some parts could be plywood with solid-wood edging. You could make the two sides of solid wood and other parts of lipped plywood. If the sides are plywood, the brackets between the narrow and wide parts would have to be matching solid wood. The top that extends over the sides and front and will look best with molding underneath. The vertical divisions are intended to support magazines as well as cookbooks. Figure 5-22 shows one drawer, but you could omit this in favor of extra shelving, or you could put a shelf at the bottom of the narrow part.

Check the suggested sizes (FIG. 5-23A) to your available space and to see if the cook will be able to reach everything that will be stored on these shelves.

Make a pair of sides (FIGS. 5-23B and 5-24A). A piece 7 inches wide goes right through. Glue on a 5-inch piece to make up width, but before adding it, shape the bracket end (FIGS. 5-23C and 5-24B). Rabbet the rear edges to take the plywood back.

You could fit the horizontal part with dowels, but the drawing shows dado joints (FIG. 5-24C) stopped at the front edges.

At the top, there is a piece across at the front (FIG. 5-23D) and one at the back inside the plywood (FIG. 5-23E). The back piece provides strength for screwing what could be a heavy weight to the wall. You can dowel or tenon these pieces (FIG. 5-24D). Cut the mortises (FIG. 5-24E).

The shelf at the bottom is notched around the sides and could have a rounded front (FIG. 5-23F). Secure the strip across below with glue, or use dowels.

The two wide shelves should be the same length as the bottom shelf, but notch them to finish flush with the front edges of the sides (FIG. 5-25A).

One shelf is plain, but the other has to take the divisions, which could be doweled. They stop 3/4 inch from the front edges of the shelf and can be fitted into dado grooves (FIG. 5-25B).

Make the two strips (FIGS. 5-23D and 5-23E), with tenons to fit the side mortises.

Prepare the top. You can use plywood, even if other parts are solid wood, but you will have to cover its edge with half-round molding. How much extension you allow depends on the molding you will fit under it. The diagram assumes that the molding will be about 1 1/2 inches on the vertical face and 1 inch wide. The top can then overlap 1 1/2 inches at the sides and front.

Fig. 5-22. *A block of tall shelves can rest on the countertop, with the upper part extending farther out from the wall.*

The two divisions could have straight front edges, but as shown they are cut away to give easier access to books and magazines (FIG. 5-25C). Make them to fit into the grooves at the bottom. They could go into grooves at the top, but it is easier just to screw downward into them.

Assemble all the crosswise pieces to the sides, except the top. Fit the divisions and glue and nail or screw the back into the rabbets.

Screw the top onto the framework and the divisions. Add the molding, mitered at the front corners.

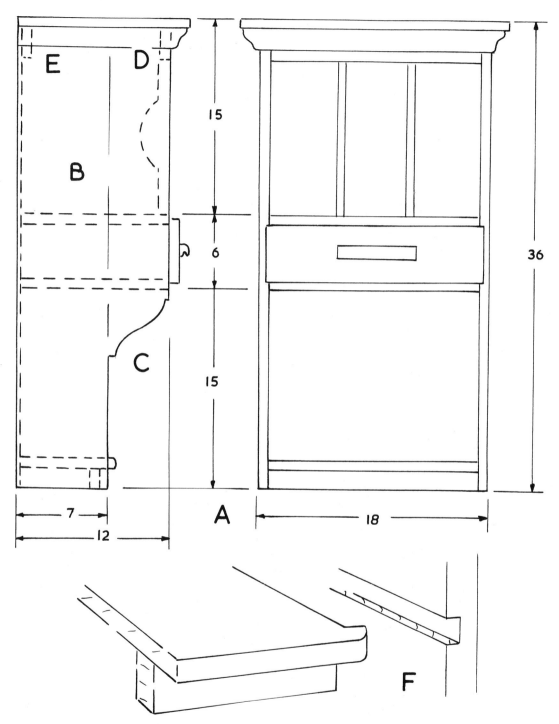

Fig. 5-23. Sizes and details of the tall shelves.

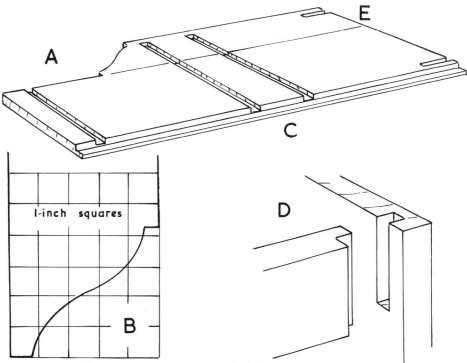

Fig. 5-24. *Making a side of the block of tall shelves.*

Materials List for Tall Shelves

2 sides	$3/4 \times$ 7	$\times$ 38
2 sides	$3/4 \times$ 5	$\times$ 28
1 shelf	$3/4 \times$ 8	$\times$ 20
1 strip	$3/4 \times$ $1^{1}/2$	$\times$ 20
2 shelves	$3/4 \times$ 12	$\times$ 20
2 top rails	$3/4 \times$ 3	$\times$ 20
2 divisions	$5/8 \times$ 11	$\times$ 16
1 back	18×36	$\times$ $1/4$ plywood
1 top	14×22	$\times$ $3/4$
1 molding	1 $\times$ $1^{1}/2$	$\times$ 22
2 moldings	1 $\times$ $1^{1}/2$	$\times$ 14
1 drawer front	$5/8 \times$ $4^{1}/2$	$\times$ 18
1 drawer front	$5/8 \times$ $5^{1}/2$	$\times$ 18
2 drawer sides	$5/8 \times$ $4^{1}/2$	$\times$ 13
1 drawer back	$5/8 \times$ 4	$\times$ 18
1 drawer bottom	13×18	$\times$ $1/4$ plywood

Make the drawer, but allow the false front to overlap all around to about half the width of the surrounding front edges.

Try the block of shelves in position. Drill for screws to the wall, then stain and polish or paint the wood before finally fixing the unit in place.

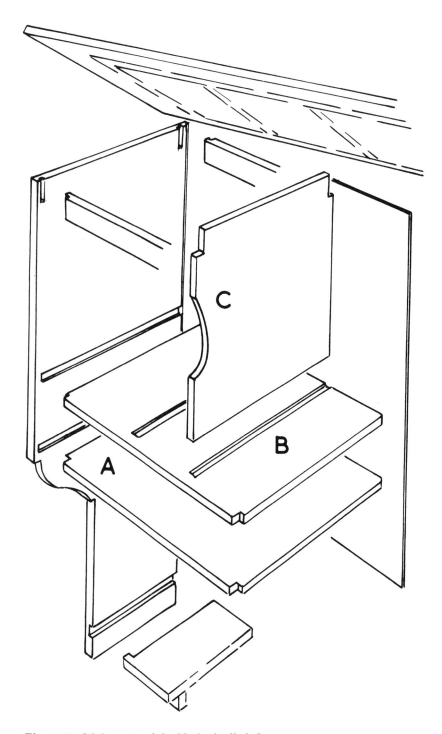

Fig. 5-25. Main parts of the block of tall shelves.

Dough Trough

After dough for bread is mixed and kneaded, it is left to rise before being formed into loaves and baked. A dough trough was a form of chest once used for flour and for holding rising dough. Sizes varied, from those to be carried and put on a table to others that were large enough to require a permanent place. A feature of all of them was *flaring*. The ends might be upright, but the sides opened outward to make the box wider at the top. In some examples, the sides were upright and the ends flared. In a few examples, there was flare both ways. To put the larger troughs at a convenient working height, they were given legs or arranged to mount on a stool or low table. Lids then became working tabletops.

Some small dough troughs were made in the same way as boxes with flared sides. Handles or knobs were needed for lifting. Another type had the sides extended to provide four handles (FIG. 5-26A). There was a slight flare both ways, and they were simply nailed. Larger troughs were usually dovetailed, with vertical ends dovetailed into flared sides (FIG. 5-26B).

After you prepare the boards, lay out the ends first, and mark out lengths and angles together (FIG. 5-26C). Note that dovetail angles are arranged in relation to the length of the wood and not to the angled cuts, so the sides of the dovetail

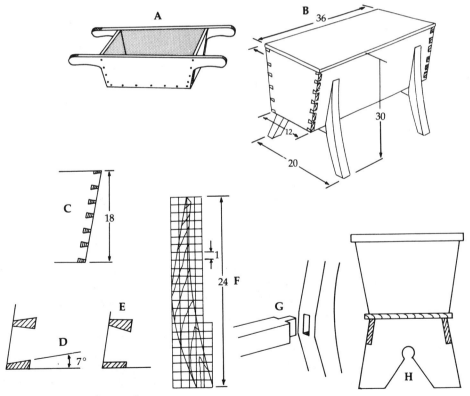

Fig. 5-26. Dough trough.

Materials List for
Dough Trough

Small		
2 sides	5 × 20 × 1/2	
2 ends	5 × 6 × 1/2	
1 bottom	7 × 10 × 1/2	
Large		
2 sides	15 × 36 × 1	
2 ends	15 × 18 × 1	
1 lid	18 × 36 × 1	
1 bottom	10 × 34 × 1	
4 legs	5 × 24 × 2	
2 rails	2 × 16 × 2	

are at about 7 degrees to the sides of the wood (FIG. 5-26D) and not at 83 degrees to the edge (FIG. 5-26E). This arrangement gives greater strength. It might not be very different with a moderate flare, but when there is much of an angle, cutting dovetails in the second way results in too much weak "short" grain in each dovetail. Except for this step, lay out and cut the joints in the same way as for a square corner—preferably with the dovetail part first and the other marked from it.

Give the lid a slight overlap all around, and position battens across the ends to locate the lid on the trough. If you are building in legs, they must stand wide enough to hold the trough steady for use as a working table. One type is cut from stout solid wood, extending up the sides (FIG. 5-26F). You can cut the shapes with a band saw. Chamfer the tops of the extensions and the outer edges.

Crossbars share the weight of the box, so tenon them into the legs. On each leg, arrange the part that will be mortised at right angles to the crossbar, to simplify marking and cutting the joint. Mortises might have gone right through in some early specimens, but if you are making a dough trough with a good finish to serve as a side table in modern surroundings, it might be better to have stub tenons finishing within the thickness of the leg (FIG. 5-26G).

Another way of supporting a trough to put the top at table height is to have a stool under it. This might be a separate item or you can make it so the bottom of the trough is also the top of the stool. It is important that the stool's feet stand wide enough to be steady under the wider top, so some flaring of the legs is required (FIG. 5-26H).

Instead of the stool construction, you can make the support more like a table. Although quite low if the trough is deep, this example can have table construction, but with the legs sloping outward to give a steady base. Although there is no need for a dough trough, as such, in a modern home, the pattern makes a convenient table with storage space underneath. If you do not need the full depth of a traditional trough, there could be a shallowed bow with longer legs. It might be more convenient to hinge the lid than to arrange it to lift off. For use with dough, the troughs were bare wood and scrubbed after use, but for use in a living room there could be a stained and polished finish.

Another use for a trough is outdoors to contain plant pots, or with soil and flowers planted directly in it. Of course, no lid is needed for this use. You can vary the shape considerably to suit the position the trough is to take and how many pots it is to accommodate.

Welsh Dresser

Dressers played an important part in the equipment of each early kitchen and dining room. With more settled conditions and the availability of specialist crafts-men with more time at hand, there came Welsh dressers of good quality that served as main features of dining rooms, as well as functional pieces. A characteristic of some Welsh dressers is a curved top, but others kept to a generally square outline and got their decoration from shaped edges.

The specimen described here is of the second type, and the method of construction given is of cabinetmaking quality (FIG. 5-27A). You can obtain the same general appearance with a simpler construction, but a cabinetmaker always preferred fitted and glued joints to nailed or screwed ones. Although counterboring

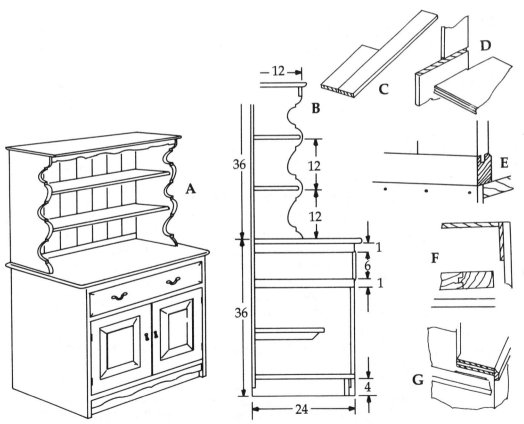

Fig. 5-27. Fine Welsh dresser.

Materials List for Fine Welsh Dresser

2 sides	12	× 72 × 1	
2 sides	12	× 36 × 1	
1 tabletop	26	× 36 × 1	
1 tabletop	2	× 40 × 1	
2 tabletops	2	× 26 × 1	
1 bottom	24	× 36 × 1	
1 cupboard shelf	18	× 36 × 1	
2 shelves	11	× 36 × 1	
1 top	14	× 38 × 1	
1 top rail	2	× 36 × 1	
4 drawer dividers	$1^{1}/_{2}$	× 36 × 1	
4 drawer dividers	$1^{1}/_{2}$	× 24 × 1	
1 plinth	4	× 36 × 1	
1 plinth	2	× 36 × 1	
1 drawer front	7	× 36 × 1	
1 drawer back	6	× 36 × $^{3}/_{4}$	
2 drawer sides	6	× 24 × $^{3}/_{4}$	
4 door sides	4	× 23 × 1	
4 door rails	4	× 18 × 1	
2 door panels	16	× 21 × 1	
1 upper back rail	2	× 36 × 1	
1 upper back, to cover	36	× 36 × $^{5}/_{8}$	
1 lower back, to cover	34	× 36 × $^{5}/_{8}$	

and plugging over screw heads might be found in some early furniture, the better pieces normally had no sign of this procedure, except where there was no alternative. Instead, the craftsman cut joints that fit so external surfaces were not marred by screws, nails, or plugs.

Make a drawing of one end to a fairly large scale, with details of shelves, drawers, dividers, and other horizontal members on it (FIG. 5-27B). From this drawing, mark all the important positions on the edge of a straight piece of wood to use as a rod for marking all upright parts so they match.

Some dressers were made so the top with shelves lifted off the other part, or they were made in two parts and doweled together. This one is made with the sides to the full height without a break. Make each side from two boards glued together (FIG. 5-27C). Also glue the tabletop to width from narrower boards. Make its ends to pass over the lower part of the sides, but to fit into dado grooves across the higher part (FIG. 5-27D). At the back, nail the boards covering the lower part to the top, but cover the upper part by a molded strip that takes the tongued ends of the exposed boards behind the shelves (FIG. 5-27E).

Frame the tabletop around the front and ends. Groove its edges for tongued pieces that go around, and miter them at the front corners (FIG. 5-27F). Where the end pieces overlap the higher ends, cut off the tongue (FIG. 5-27G).

The bottom of this dresser should be flat on the floor with a plinth fitted around it. Do not cut back any part, but do not continue the rear edge to the floor. Fit the bottom of the cupboard on to battens to increase the bearing area (FIG. 5-28A).

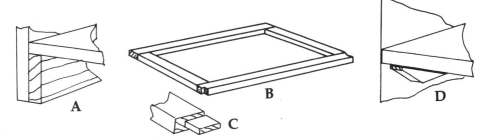

Fig. 5-28. Bottom (A), shelf (B), and drawer divider (C) details of the fine Welsh dresser.

Above and below the drawer, there are two identical frames (FIG. 5-28B). Tenon their corners. The upper one goes directly under the tabletop. Fix it with glue and screws into the ends and the top. Screw the other one into the ends—although for the best work, make it extra long to fit into dadoes on the ends (FIG. 5-28C). Assemble the two frames, and check their squareness by measuring diagonals. Let the glue set before fitting them. They govern the shape of the drawer and should be carefully fitted if the drawer is to slide freely.

The shelf in the cupboard rests on battens (FIG. 5-28D) and is probably best left loose so it can be removed for cleaning. You could choose another shelf arrangement to suit your needs.

At the front, make the edges of the frames above and below the drawer and the edge of the bottom to come level with the edges of the side (FIG. 5-29A). Set back the plinth under the bottom (FIG. 5-29B). It will carry a decorative overlay. Place the ends of the plinth to fit against the ends of the battens under the bottom, which you need to cut back to suit. Notch the plinth into the sides or cut it to fit closely in the final assembly.

Check dimensions and squareness of the lower body, but do not assemble the pieces yet. Avoid a trial assembly because that might cause loosening of joints. You can give the overlay on the plinth an undulating edge pattern or make

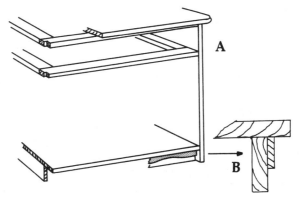

Fig. 5-29. Front details of the fine Welsh dresser.

it to a similar shape to the rail under the top. When the dresser is finished, you can stain the overlay darker than the rest of the wood to emphasize its shape.

Decorate the upper part of the dresser with scalloped edges. Some early furniture makers drew curves with a compass and left the shape at that (FIG. 5-30). A step between reversed curves was usual. A better artistic appreciation is shown by asymmetrical curves between the shelves (FIG. 5-30B), with comparable curves around the fronts. A paper template is helpful.

Round the front edges of the shelves, and cut them back to fit into stopped dado grooves (FIG. 5-30C). Groove them to hold plates. At the top, place a rail with a shaped lower edge (FIG. 5-30D). Shoulder its ends to fit into grooves in the sides (FIG. 5-30E).

The top is one part where a skilled furniture maker might resort to screws, since this is not normally visible, but the best way of attaching it would be with a series of short tenons (FIG. 5-30F). In this case, cap the dresser with a fairly wide overhang on top.

Make the back of the top of several vertical boards, which you can tongue-and-groove, or halve thin boards (FIG. 5-30G). With halving, there is a risk that a board warping might open its joint with its neighbor, but tongued-and-grooved boards will limit each other's warping tendencies.

At the sides, fit the board into rabbets in the ends. At the top, nail or screw the boards to the back of the top board. At their bottoms, tongue the boards into the strip across the tabletop. These are the only parts that are not glued in the final assembly, since they must be able to expand and contract.

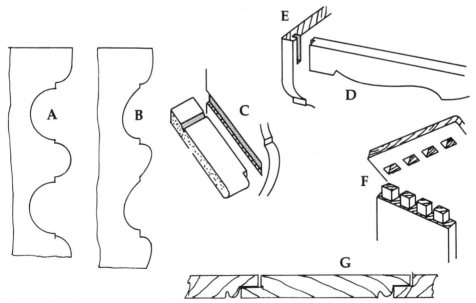

Fig. 5-30. Side shaping (A,B), shelf assembly (C), top joint (D – F), and back joints (G) in the fine Welsh dresser.

Up to this stage, you can make up certain subassemblies, but do not make any final assembly until it is certain that fixing parts together will not interfere with work to be done later to another part of the same assembly. For instance, you should do all the grooving for shelves and the making of joints for the upper part before you assemble the cupboard. You should fit the frames and the bottom of the cupboard between the sides before you add the tabletop or upper shelves.

When you have assembled the frame, check it in all directions for squareness, and leave it standing level for the glue to set.

Make the pair of doors in the same way as previously described, with the frame joints mortise and tenon and grooves for the panels. In better work, the panels are not merely thinned to fit the grooves, but they are fielded and raised. This means that the center part has a definite edge so it shows a clean line, instead of a blend from flat to a bevel (FIG. 5-31A). You can use a suitable tool in a power spindle or router for this step, but to make a panel by hand, cut in the outline of the raised part, either with a cutting gauge working from the edge, or with a sharp knife along a steel straightedge. This is important if you are to avoid disfiguring by grain tearing out. The amount of raising can be slight—1/16 inch might be enough. You can pare away some of the waste wood with a chisel (FIG. 5-31B), then use a rabbet plane to reduce the waste thickness (FIG. 5-31C).

A low-angled shoulder plane is the best tool for working across the grain. With the depth worked, tilt the plane to make the bevel (FIG. 5-31D). Then thoroughly sand the lowered and tapered part, with the abrasive paper around a flat piece of wood to get an even surface. Try not to round the raised edge.

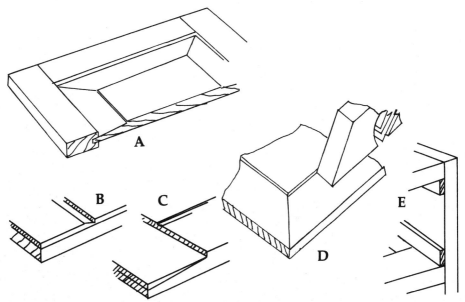

Fig. 5-31. *Steps in fielding panels (A – D) and arranging drawer guides in the fine Welsh dresser.*

You must have drawer guides fit inside on the runners, which are formed by the sides of the frame (FIG. 5-31E); otherwise, there are no special preparations to take the drawer. Fit stops for the drawers.

The drawer for this piece of furniture has an overlapping front (FIG. 5-32A), otherwise its construction is similar to drawers described for earlier items. Prepare the front by working rabbets across the top edge and the ends (FIG. 5-32B). When this has been done, the projecting part of the back surface should fit in the opening in the frame. Dovetail the drawer sides into the front (FIG. 5-32C). Cut the bottom dovetail high enough to allow for a groove for the bottom to follow through the sides into the front (FIG. 5-32D).

You can dovetail the drawer back (FIG. 5-32E), or fit it in dadoes above the bottom (FIG. 5-32F). Slide the bottom in the groove from the back, and screw it under the back.

Hinges for the doors could be ornamental ones on the surface, or they could be a butt type fit into the space between the doors and their stiles.

Knobs for doors on this type of dresser were nearly always turned wood, and they followed a fairly uniform pattern (FIG. 5-32G). They might have been screwed from the inside of the drawer, but it was more usual for them to be turned with a dowel to glue into a hole.

You can provide separate catches for the doors, but one original wooden combined catch and knob was used here. Extend the dowel inside the door and mortise it to take a wedge, which can be turned to overlap the stile and hold the door (FIG. 5-32H).

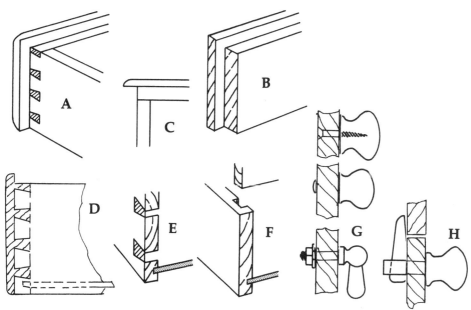

Fig. 5-32. *Drawer construction (A–F), with suitable knobs and catches (G,H) for the fine Welsh dresser.*

Folding Food Trolley

A trolley to carry food from the kitchen to the dining table or patio saves a lot of steps. It can also be a serving table or a food preparation surface. When not in use, however, most food trolleys take up precious space. This food trolley (FIG. 5-33) has two lift-out trays. When they are removed, the trolley folds to a few inches thick. The lift-out trays increase the usefulness of the trolley.

The whole trolley is best made of a good hardwood, but if lightness is important, the trays could be of softwood. Rigidity of the frame depends on the strength of the joints, and this will be greater with hardwoods. Exact sizes are not important, but those shown will make a trolley of useful proportions.

The wheels are casters with plastic or rubber-tired wheels suitable for use on carpet. Wheel diameters of 2 or 3 inches are suitable. Get the type with a stem

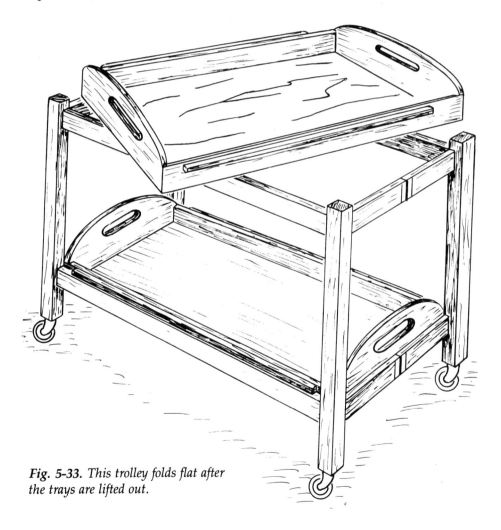

Fig. 5-33. This trolley folds flat after the trays are lifted out.

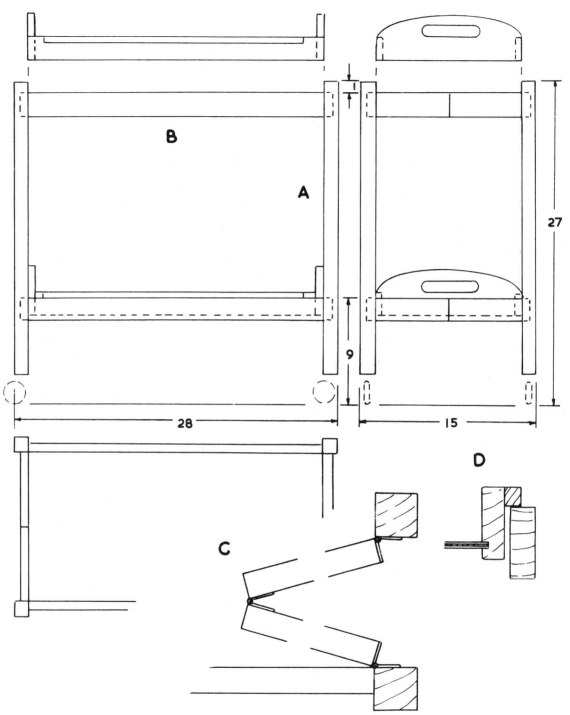

Fig. 5-34. Sizes of the folding food trolley.

Materials List for Folding Food Trolley

4 legs	$1^1/4 \times$	$1^1/4 \times$	27
4 rails	$^3/4 \times$	2 $\times$	28
8 rails	$^3/4 \times$	2 $\times$	7
4 tray sides	$^5/8 \times$	2 $\times$	26
4 tray side strips	$^1/2 \times$	$^1/2 \times$	24
4 tray ends	$^5/8 \times$	4 $\times$	13
2 tray bottoms	13 $\times$	26 $\times$	$^1/4$ plywood

that pushes into a hole in the bottom of its leg. Obtain the casters first because their size controls the lengths of the legs.

Mark out the four legs (FIG. 5-34A) with the positions of the rails. Prepare the long rails (FIG. 5-34B). The joints are shown with tenons (FIG. 5-35A), but there could be dowels. The inner surfaces of the legs and rails should be level.

Cut the joints, then shape the tops of the legs. These will be prominent in the finished trolley and should be shaped neatly. Three possible shapes are shown: simple bevels (FIG. 5-35B), a shallow cone (FIG. 5-35C), or rounded (FIG. 5-35D).

Drill the bottoms of the legs for the casters, then assemble the legs and long rails, making sure the assemblies match as a pair.

Cut all the end rails, which are divided at the middle (FIG. 5-34C). Use hinges the full depth of the rails. At the center, screw on hinges with the rails flat and tight together. At the corners the screws have to go into the end grain in the rails. To increase their grip, $^1/4$-inch dowels can be let in for the threads to penetrate cross grain (FIG. 5-35E). They need not go right through to show on the outside.

The trays have to fit between the rails. Make them with enough clearance to lift in and out easily. Since projecting handles would be a nuisance, the ends of the trays are given finger slots. Several types of corner joints are possible, but a simple rabbet is shown (FIG. 5-35F), with the sides screwed into the ends.

Make the tray sides. Plow grooves for the rails (FIGS. 5-34D and 5-35G). These could be full length or just short pieces near the corners.

Cut the ends to shape (FIG. 5-35H), with grooves to match those in the sides. Round the top edges and finger slots.

Check the tray sizes against the trolley frame, then assemble them. Check that the trays lock the trolley in shape and that the ends hinge correctly for the trolley to fold flat. Polish or varnish the wood, and add casters.

Wine Trolley

If you have to move food and drink from the kitchen to the dining room, the patio, or further, some sort of trolley will be helpful to avoid a large number of trips carrying trays. A plain trolley with two or three trays on it is functional, but not necessarily an attractive piece of furniture. This wine trolley (FIG. 5-36) is intended to transport plenty of food and drink, but it might also stand in the dining room to fit

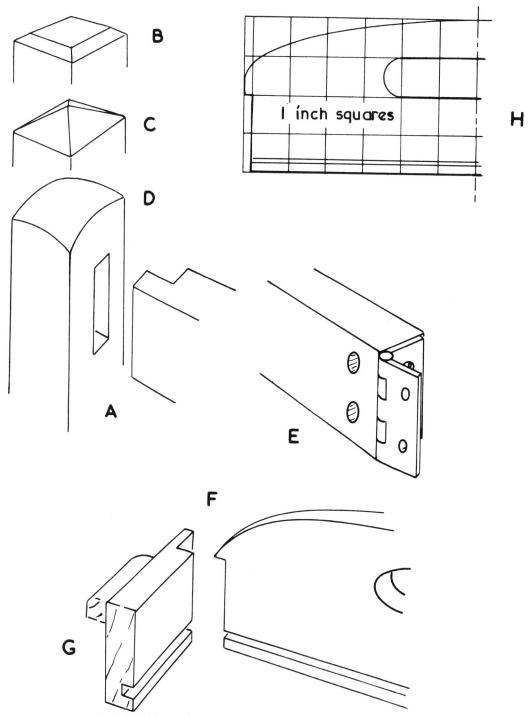

Fig. 5-35. *Details of the folding food trolley.*

Fig. 5-36. *This wine trolley has three shelves and a cupboard. It it mobile, but it is at a height for use as a serving table.*

Materials List for Wine Trolley

4 legs	28 ×	$1^1/2$ × $1^1/2$
4 rails	32 ×	$1^1/2$ × 1
7 rails	18 ×	$1^1/2$ × 1
2 uprights	22 ×	$1^1/2$ × 1
2 frame strips	18 ×	$3/4$ × $1/2$
2 frame strips	22 ×	$3/4$ × $1/2$
2 frame strips	14 ×	$3/4$ × $1/2$
2 door frames	22 × 2	× 1
2 door frames	14 × 2	× 1
Knobs from	14 ×	$1^1/2$ × $1^1/2$
2 tray panels	32 × 18	× $1/2$ plywood
1 tray panel	17 × 18	× $1/2$ plywood
4 cupboard panels	18 × 12	× $1/4$ plywood
1 cupboard back	20 × 14	× $1/4$ plywood
1 cupboard shelf	14 × 12	× $1/2$ plywood

in with other furniture. Also, it functions as a serving table. The top is about the same height as a dining table. The glass-fronted cupboard will hold plenty of soft and alcoholic drinks, and the trays are quite roomy. The upper two have ledges around, but the bottom one is without projecting edging, so heavy containers can be slid in or out. There are casters on the legs. In short, the whole trolley is mobile as well as attractive and functional.

Construction should be of a furniture-quality hardwood, possibly selected to match existing furniture. The plywood is best obtained veneered to match the framing, but you might be able to stain other plywood to match. The tray tops could be plastic-covered. Two inches are allowed for the depth of the casters, but you might have to alter this to suit the ones you have. Use wheels if you intend making the trolley suitable for pushing along outside paths. The tops of the legs are shown decorated with turned knobs, which you can make or buy, but the trolley would still look good with the leg tops just rounded.

Most of the joints are mortise-and-tenon. With the need for grooves and rabbets for the plywood, there is little space at the end of some rails for the two dow-

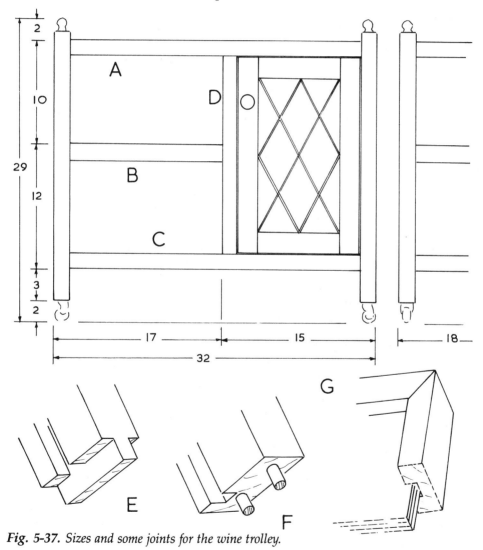

Fig. 5-37. Sizes and some joints for the wine trolley.

els that would be required as an alternative; moreover, dowels would not be as strong. There is considerable mutual support from the many parts when the whole trolley has been assembled, but care will be needed in handling some of the subassemblies.

Prepare sufficient wood for all parts before marking out and cutting joints. Use the actual plywood to get the sizes of grooves which have to be cut. The legs are $1^{1}/2$-inch-square pieces without grooves. All the rails and the intermediate uprights are $3/4$-$\times$-$1^{1}/2$-inch sections; each has one or more grooves to suit $1/2$-inch or $1/4$-inch plywood. Substitute $3/8$-inch plywood in both cases, but note that details on the drawings are for the first two sizes.

Cut all pieces a few inches longer than shown (FIG. 5-37). Cut the wood for the four legs, and mark on them the positions of the rails (FIG. 5-39A).

Groove the wood for the top and middle trays (FIGS. 5-37A, 5-37B, 5-38A, 5-38B). The grooves are $3/8$ inch deep and $1/4$ inch from the bottom edge.

For the bottom four rails, cut rabbets to let the $1/2$-inch plywood in $3/8$ inch (FIGS. 5-37C and 5-38C).

The rail that goes across the top of the closed end also needs a groove $1/4$ inch deep and $1/4$ inch from the outer edge (FIG. 5-38D). The rail that goes across the bottom of the closed end needs a matching groove (FIG. 5-38E).

Cut $1/4$-inch grooves $1/4$ inch from the edge in the rail that will hold the inner end of the middle shelf (FIG. 5-38F).

The outer panel is divided at the same level; this needs grooves at the top and bottom (FIG. 5-38G). When the trolley is finished, a shell can rest on these two rails.

The two uprights (FIG. 5-37D) have to be grooved for $1/4$-inch plywood (FIG. 5-38H), forming the inner side of the cupboard. The top and bottom of this cupboard side come against the plywood trays, which cannot be grooved. Instead, prepare strips of $1/2$-$\times$-$3/4$-inch sections with $1/4$-inch grooves (FIG. 5-38) to glue to the plywood and take the edges of the panels.

A piece of plywood forms the back of the cupboard. If you have the means of making stopped grooves, you can let the plywood into the rails, legs, and uprights. Otherwise, it will be simpler to use similar strips to those across the plywood trays (FIGS. 5-38K and 5-38L).

The joint between the rails and the legs are barefaced tenons on the rams into mortises in the legs arranged so the inner surfaces of the rails meet at the corners (FIG. 5-38M). Allow for the mortises meeting (FIG. 5-38N), so the tenons can be as long as possible and meet with miters. When you assemble, the plywood must have small notches around the legs.

Mark out all parts in each direction together to ensure that they match. It is the length between shoulders which is important, but allow extra for the tenons.

All rails across the trolley between legs are the same length (FIG. 5-39A). The intermediate center rail is longer, to allow for the uprights being thinner than the legs.

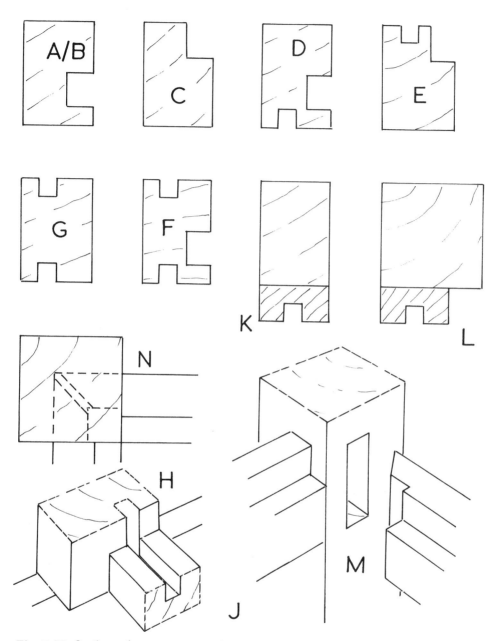

Fig. 5-38. Sections of parts to prepare for constructing the wine trolley.

Mark all the lengthwise rails the same (FIG. 5-39C), with the positions of the uprights marked. The middle side rails reach the upright (FIG. 5-39D).

Cut all the tenons that will join the legs, and miter their ends. Cut matching mortises in the legs.

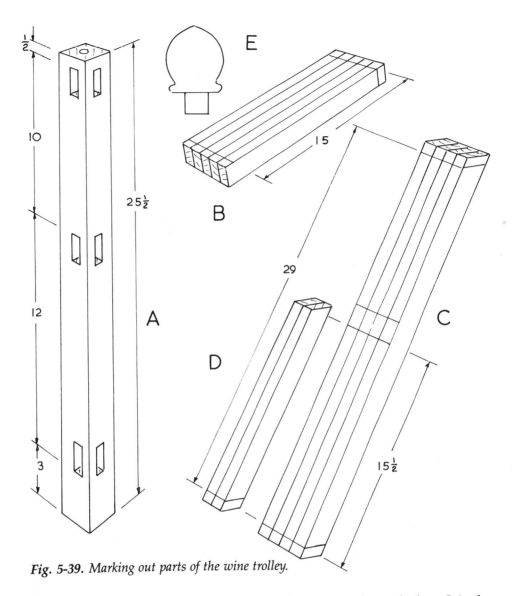

Fig. 5-39. Marking out parts of the wine trolley.

Get the lengths of the uprights from the relevant marks on the legs. Join the uprights into the rails with thin central tenons (FIG. 5-37E), or use 1/4-inch dowels (FIG. 5-37F). Join in the middle side rails, using one of these ways.

Prepare the decorative knobs for the tops of the legs (FIG. 5-39), and drill the legs to suit. Prepare the bottoms of the legs for the casters, which may screw on or fit into holes.

Ready the two pieces of plywood for fitting into the closed end. When you fit them, plane their edges, so they go in without quite touching the bottoms of the grooves; then they will not tighten before frame joints are closed.

Lightly round the upper edges of tray rails, and sand all parts. The legs at the open part could be chamfered between the trays, if you wish. In any case, take sharpness off there.

Assemble the open end, then assemble the closed end with its plywood panels. Check that these ends are square, without twist; also, they must match each other as a pair.

Carefully fit the parts in stages as you assemble the rest of the trolley, which should be done in one operation. The back cupboard panel and its framing can be left until later and, obviously, the door also will come at a later stage. Have the plywood tray pieces ready, but slightly oversized, until you know the exact dimensions as assembly progresses.

Join the middle rail across the uprights and slide in its plywood panels, allowing for the grooved 1/2-×-3/4-inch strips that will come at top and bottom.

From the end frames and the long rails, get the sizes of the bottom plywood panel to fit in rabbets, and cut it to size, including the small notches at the corners. This will also provide a guide to the sizes of the other tray bottoms. Keep them a little undersize, so they do not quite reach the bottoms of their grooves when fully tightened.

Fit all three pieces of plywood, using glue and pins in the rabbets. Join with the uprights and their panels and grooved strips; then, bring this assembly into the legs, using clamps as much as possible for tighter joints. The end frames will ensure squareness in that direction, but check that the assembly is square when viewed from the front. It should stand level, without twist.

Make the back of the cupboard to fit in as one assembly. Miter the corners of the grooved strips (FIG. 5-37G), and cut the plywood slightly undersized. Bevel the outer exposed edges of the strips. Fit the assembly with glue and a few pins driven through the strips inside.

A shelf inside might be a loose piece of plywood resting on the rails. If you make it only about 10 inches wide, there will be space in front of it for tall bottles. However, if you are only storing canned drinks, you can make it wider.

The door could be made with a plywood panel, but a glass panel looks better, particularly if it is given a leaded pattern. Make the door to fit inside the opening (not on the surface) for the best appearance.

The door will be about 12 × 19 inches (FIG. 5-40A), but get the actual sizes from the opening. It should have square corners, but if your opening is slightly out of true, you must make the door to suit. Allow sufficient clearance for the door to fit easily. Remember that a test of good cabinetmaking is to make door clearances no more than is necessary.

Make the framing of the door of 1-×-2-inch section wood. Cut rabbets two-thirds of the thickness of the wood and 3/8 inch deep (FIG. 5-40B). Tenons should be one-third the actual thickness of your wood, or as near to that as your equipment will cut. The tenon edge should be in line with the rabbet, so check before rabbeting your strips (FIG. 5-40C).

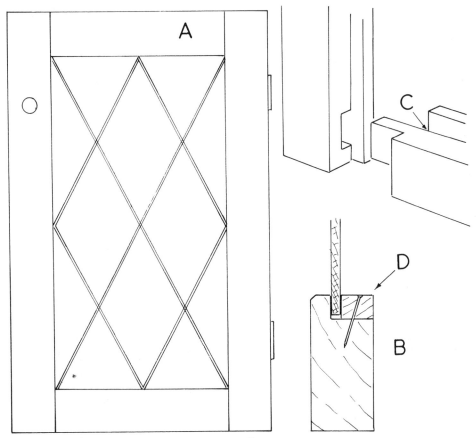

Fig. 5-40. Details of the door of the wine trolley.

The sides of the door are the full height; the other pieces tenon into them. Mark the lengths of the side pieces, but leave a little extra on the ends until after the mortises have been cut. The tenons need not enter the sides more than 1 inch.

Mark and cut the tenons. From them, mark the mortises and cut them. Join the door parts and cut off the side extensions after the glue has set. Remove any surplus glue inside the rabbets. Do any planing necessary to make the door fit the opening.

Cut glass to fit, and prepare fillets to go round the rabbets and hold it in place (FIG. 5-40D).

If you want to give the door a leaded appearance, use self-adhesive strip lead about $3/16$ inch wide. Draw the outline of the opening on a piece of paper, and find the middle of each side. Join these points and the corners to obtain the pattern. Put this under the glass, and stick on strips of lead over the lines. Stop the ends of the lead at the edges of the wood.

Fit the glass in the door with just enough pins to hold the fillets and no glue; then if the glass ever has to be replaced, you can remove it without difficulty or damage to the frame.

Let in two 2-inch hinges, preferably brass. Add a knob or handle, fairly high so it is easy to reach. Use a spring or magnetic catch. If the trolley is to be used over a rough surface, make sure the catch is strong enough to resist the contents falling against the door and opening it, or fit a lock to the catch. If the catch does not also act as a stop, put a small block of wood on the upright near its center.

Choose the finish to suit the wood and any other furniture it has to match. Start with stain, especially if the plywood is a different color; then use several coats of a clear finish.

Kitchen Table

In earlier days the kitchen table was the center of activities. For similar reasons, a modern cook might prefer a table to an island counter. This table needs to be more substantial than a dining table and be functional rather than decorative. The table shown in FIG. 5-41 satisfies these requirements. It could be made with leg space or with a shelf underneath. The shelf framing adds stiffness, but even without a shelf, the table should be rigid enough for normal use. Carried edgewise, you should be able to get it through a normal doorway, but check first. It would be frustrating to make a table in your shop and not be able to get it into the kitchen!

Large drawers can weaken rails, but the table in the example has a moderate-size drawer going right through, to be pulled out from either side (FIGS. 5-41 and 5-42). The sizes suggested are a guide; adjust them to suit your kitchen. The wood sections specified are for the common furniture hardwoods, but if you want to use softwood, you will have to increase sections slightly.

Rail-to-leg joints are shown with traditional mortises and tenons, but you could use dowels. Drawer guide ends should have dowels. As the drawer is double-ended, you will have to treat both ends as fronts. As shown, the table has a shelf on lower rails, but you could omit this.

Mark out the four legs (FIG. 5-43A) together to ensure that they match. The top tenons are divided (FIG. 5-42B), but they are plain for the lower rails (FIG. 5-42C). You could leave the legs parallel, but they look better tapered on the outer two surfaces (FIG. 5-42D). That way, the inner surfaces are parallel between opposite legs. Mark the tapers, but do not cut them until after the mortises have been cut.

Mark the top and bottom rails together, so the lengths between the shoulders are the same (FIG. 5-43B). Mark and cut tenons to suit the leg mortises.

If the top is to be plywood or particleboard, which does not expand or contract in width, drill the top rails diagonally for screws and cut pockets for their heads (FIG. 5-43C). If you are making the top from boards or butcher-block strips, which might expand or contract, plow grooves near the top edges of the top rails to take buttons (FIG. 5-43D).

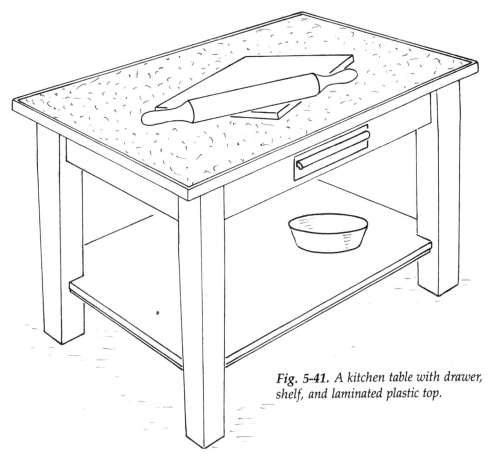

Fig. 5-41. A kitchen table with drawer, shelf, and laminated plastic top.

Materials List for Kitchen Table

4 legs	4	× 4	× 31	
2 rails	1¹/₄ ×	6	× 44	
2 rails	1¹/₄ ×	6	× 26	
2 rails	1 ×	2	× 44	
2 rails	1 ×	2	× 26	
1 top	30	× 48	× 1 plywood	
1 shelf	30	× 48	× ¹/₂ plywood	
2 thickeners	¹/₂ ×	1¹/₂ ×	48	
2 thickeners	¹/₂ ×	1¹/₂ ×	30	
2 edgings	³/₈ ×	1¹/₂ ×	50	
2 edgings	³/₈ ×	1¹/₂ ×	32	
2 shelf edgings	³/₈ ×	1	× 40	
2 shelf edgings	³/₈ ×	1	× 22	
2 drawer guides	1 ×	6	× 22	
4 drawer guides	1 ×	1	× 22	
2 drawer ends	1 ×	4	× 12	
2 drawer sides	³/₄ ×	4	× 30	
1 drawer bottom	12	× 30	× ¹/₄ plywood	
2 drawer handles	1¹/₄ ×	1¹/₄ ×	12	

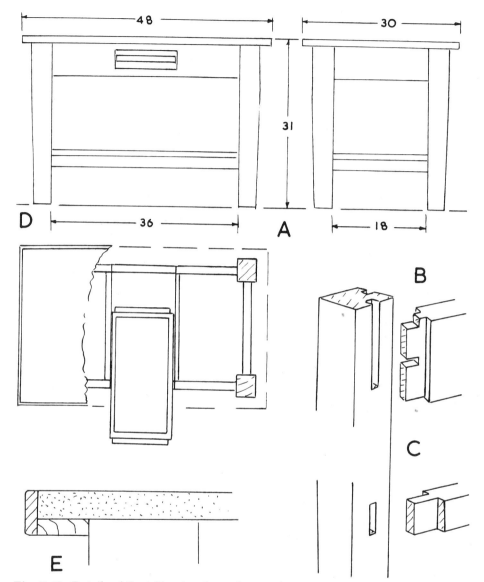

Fig. 5-42. Details of the table, showing a drawer that opens both ways.

Mark and cut the drawer openings in the long top rails (FIG. 5-43E). Make the drawer guides to fit between the rails, with strips top and bottom, level with the openings (FIG. 5-43F). Prepare the ends and the rails for dowels.

Assemble the two long sides. Check squareness by comparing diagonal measurements, and see that the two sides match and do not twist. When that glue has set, join the sides with the drawer guides and the other rails. Again, check squareness in all directions.

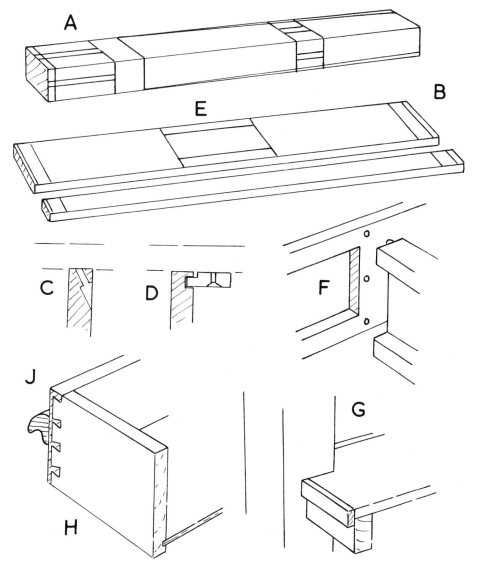

Fig. 5-43. *Marking out legs and rails (A,B). Attaching the top (C,D). Shelf corner (G) and drawer (F,J,H) details.*

If the top is plywood or particleboard (at least 3/4 inch thick), with a laminated plastic surface, you should thicken the edges and add a wood edging (FIG. 5-42E). Avoid a molded edge if you expect the table to have to accommodate any clamp-on appliances. Attach the top with glue, and screw through the pocketed holes in the rails. If the table is very wide, one or two similar screws in each drawer rail might be advisable. If the top is solid wood, use buttons screwed to the top at about 12-inch intervals so they engage with the grooves in the top rail.

As shown, the bottom shelf is plywood notched around the legs. It could overhang the rail to the edges of the legs, or you could cut it level with the rails and cover the edges (FIG. 5-43G).

Make the drawer by any of the usual methods. The ends must be flush with the rail surfaces because you cannot have overlapping fronts on a drawer that has to go both ways. The best construction method is with dovetails, with the bottom fitted into grooves (FIG. 5-43H). Handles should probably extend the width of the drawer, so the cook can find the handle easily by feel (FIG. 5-43J). You cannot fit stops to the drawer, so you might have to settle for merely pushing it into a level position. You could, however, let small ball catches into the undersides or edges of the ends—to engage with plates on the rails—to hold the drawer end level when closed but allow for easy pulling either way. This will likely be used for longer cook's tools, but it could have divisions at each end to accommodate small items and cutlery.

End Table

In many kitchens, the most convenient place to put a permanent extending table is at the end of a row of cabinets. It could serve as a dining area away from the immediate cooking area and as a divider if another part of the room is used for other purposes. The table could be stepped down from the counter level for use with ordinary chairs, or it could continue at counter level for use with high stools. The table shown in FIG. 5-44 is at the lower level and has ample leg room because there are no drawers, shelves, or cabinets built in below. Chairs can fit at the end as well as at the sides, so four people should be able to eat here in comfort.

The cabinet next to this table should have a level end, although the worktop may overhang in the usual way. You can let the cabinet back extend behind the table or use separate plywood there, but extending the back would contribute to strength. You could also add a table to an existing cabinet end, but it is better to treat the assembly as a whole in new work.

The size of the top determines many other sizes, so make it first (FIG. 5-45A). It is shown as plywood covered with laminated plastic, with the corners angled and with a wood edging (FIG. 5-46A), but you could use any other type of tabletop to match the countertop.

Stiffen the underside of the top with strips parallel with the edges (FIGS. 5-45 and 5-46). If you can fit these strips before adding the laminated plastic, you can drive screws downward. Otherwise, screw upward with counterbored holes in the strips.

Where the table comes against the cabinet end, cut away the top to notch around (FIGS. 5-45C and 5-46C). The simplest approach is to cut back to the supporting strip, but if the overhang would then interfere with a door or drawer on the cabinet, cut back less and include a packing when you screw to the cabinet.

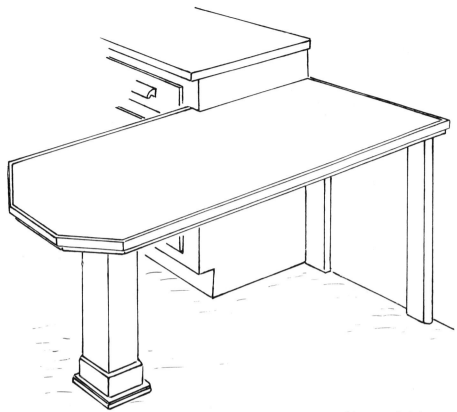

Fig. 5-44. This end table is stepped down from the countertop and has a pedestal support.

Materials List for End Table

1 top	24 × 54	× 1	plywood
1 top edging	3/8 × 11/4	× 50	
1 top edging	3/8 × 11/4	× 30	
3 top edgings	3/8 × 11/4	× 12	
2 top stiffeners	1 × 2	× 50	
3 top stiffeners	1 × 2	× 12	
2 legs	1 × 3	× 30	
1 top piece	1 × 3	× 24	
1 leg edge	30 × 11/2	half-round	
2 pillars	3/4 × 5	× 30	
2 pillars	3/4 × 31/2	× 30	
4 pillar tops	1 × 1	× 10	
4 pillar bottoms	1 × 3	× 10	
1 pillar base	1 × 10	× 10	

At the wall end, make two legs and a crosspiece to screw to the top (FIG. 5-45) and with either its own plywood backing or the extension from the cabinet back. Arrange the width across the legs to fit inside the top stiffeners.

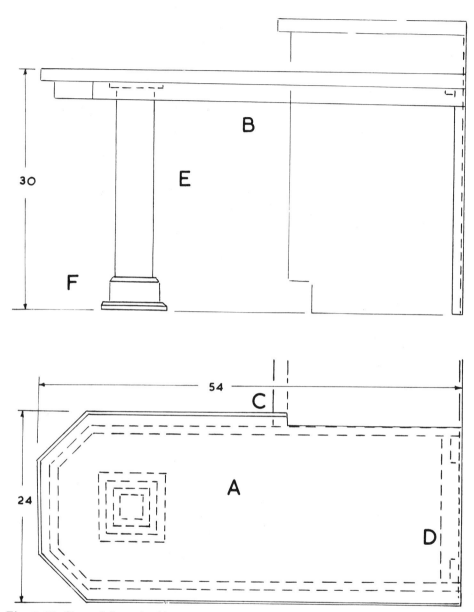

Fig. 5-45. Sizes of the end table.

The pillar (FIG. 5-45E) is square and attached to the tabletop. It could be screwed to the floor, but you might find that unnecessary. Join pieces to make a 5-inch-square section (FIG. 5-46E). At the top add square strips (FIG. 5-46F), which can be drilled for screwing upward into the tabletop. Be careful to finish the top square in both directions, as this affects the final attitude of the pillar. If it is out of vertical, it will be visually obvious.

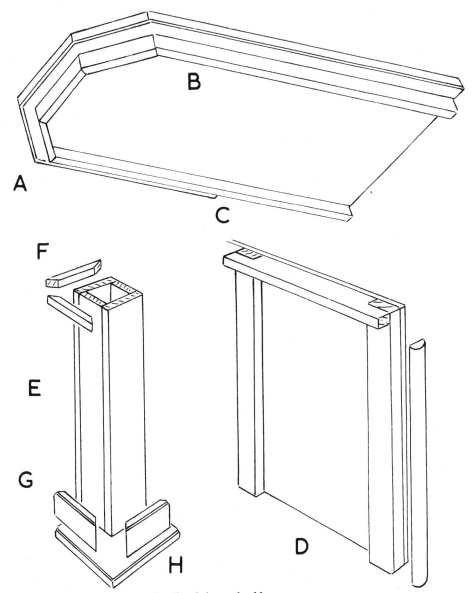

Fig. 5-46. Constructional details of the end table.

At the bottom, miter four pieces around the pillar, and then add a square below to extend an additional 1 inch (FIG. 5-45F). Bevel the top edges of the upright strips (FIG. 5-46G) and the edges of the base (FIG. 5-46H).

Mark the position of the table on the cabinet end, then make a trial assembly to make sure that the top will be level and the parts fit squarely. For finishing, the best approach is to stain and polish or paint the parts before final assembly with glue and screws.

Raised End Cabinet

Another way of making a positive and decorative kitchen cabinet end is to build a higher and deeper compartment there. This could be closed with a door, or you could combine drawers with a cupboard or make the whole thing a block of drawers. What you do depends on your needs. Do not arrange drawers so high that it is difficult to see or reach into them. You can continue design features into the enlarged end, but you probably cannot continue door or drawer lines.

The example in FIG. 5-47 has a full-depth door and a removable tray. It is 6 inches higher and 6 inches deeper than the adjoining cabinet. Therefore, the top is not too high to be used when standing, and the cabinet can store wider and taller items. The top can be a place to put food or packages, away from the main counter work space.

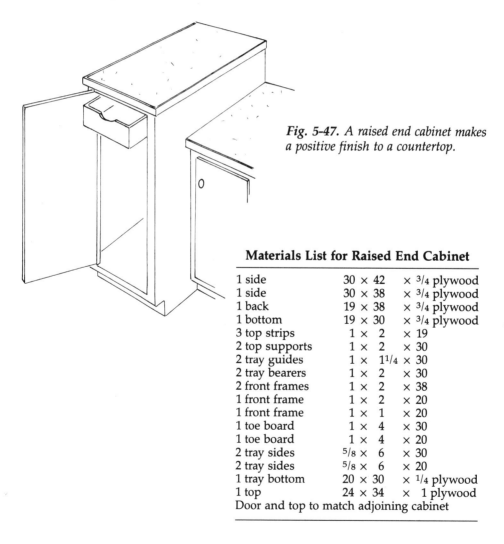

Fig. 5-47. A raised end cabinet makes a positive finish to a countertop.

Materials List for Raised End Cabinet

1 side	30 × 42	× 3/4 plywood
1 side	30 × 38	× 3/4 plywood
1 back	19 × 38	× 3/4 plywood
1 bottom	19 × 30	× 3/4 plywood
3 top strips	1 × 2	× 19
2 top supports	1 × 2	× 30
2 tray guides	1 × 1 1/4	× 30
2 tray bearers	1 × 2	× 30
2 front frames	1 × 2	× 38
1 front frame	1 × 2	× 20
1 front frame	1 × 1	× 20
1 toe board	1 × 4	× 30
1 toe board	1 × 4	× 20
2 tray sides	5/8 × 6	× 30
2 tray sides	5/8 × 6	× 20
1 tray bottom	20 × 30	× 1/4 plywood
1 top	24 × 34	× 1 plywood
Door and top to match adjoining cabinet		

Build this assembly as a unit to fit against the end of a normal cabinet that has its top finished level with its side. Panels can be 3/4-inch plywood or particleboard, with a suitable veneer on exposed surfaces. Parts are screwed where the heads will not show and doweled elsewhere. Doors and top should match adjoining cabinets. Figure 5-48 shows suggested dimensions.

Make the pair of sides (FIG. 5-48), with notched strips for the three top crosspieces.

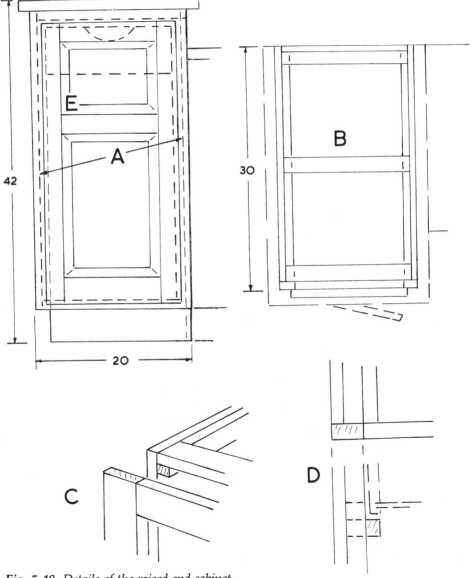

Fig. 5-48. Details of the raised end cabinet.

The exposed side (FIG. 5-49A) stops above the toe-board line whereas, the inner side (FIG. 5-49B) continues behind the toe board to the floor, to match the bottom of the adjoining cabinet.

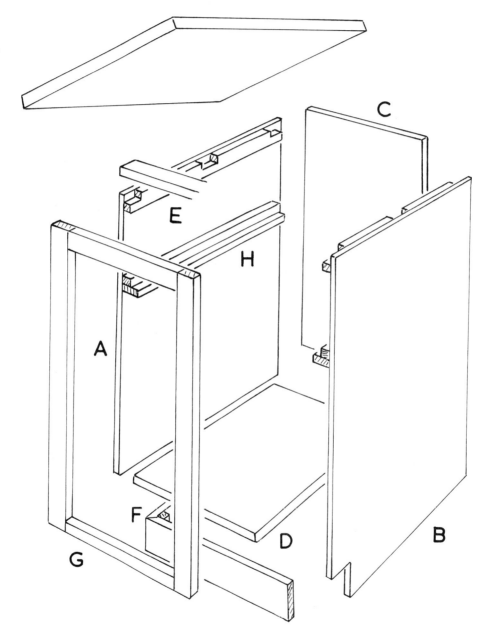

Fig. 5-49. *Parts of the raised end cabinet.*

Make the back (FIG. 5-49C) and bottom (FIG. 5-49D) to fit between the sides. Make the top crosspieces (FIGS. 5-48B and 5-49E) the same length as the bottom.

Drill for screws and dowels, then assemble the parts made so far. Placing the back and bottom between the sides should keep the assembly square, but check that there is no twist in the open front. Fit toe boards under the end and across the front, with a mitered corner (FIG. 5-49F).

Make a frame to cover the front. It should be 2 inches wide at the sides and top, and of a thickness to match the plywood at the bottom (FIGS. 5-48C and 5-49G).

The bearers for the tray should have guides level with the edges of the front frame, but they should then extend about 3/4 inch past that point (FIGS. 5-48D and 5-49H). You could fit any number of trays and shelves, but remember to leave room for taller items. Make each tray like an open box, with a hollowed front to provide a grip (FIG. 5-47).

Make the top in the same way as the adjoining cabinet: level at the back and overhanging the same amount at the sides and front. Fit matching edging.

You could also fit a tiled top. To avoid having to cut tiles, get the tiles first and then arrange the size of the cabinet and its top to accommodate whole tiles.

Make the door to match those near it. If they are paneled, however, this taller door might look better with a dividing rail across it (FIG. 5-48E).

Enclosed Two-Drawer Cabinet

If you plan to build a cabinet completely as a unit before putting in position, you will have to make ends and a back. A cabinet butt in this way should not be too large to be moved from the shop to where it is to be used. An alternative is to build several units, to be linked in position and covered by a continuous top.

The cabinet shown in FIG. 5-50 is intended to stand anywhere against a wall, but it could be adapted to fit into a corner or against an appliance. It could have full-depth doors, but as shown it has drawers above the doors and shelves between (FIG. 5-51). The carcass stands on a plinth, and the top may be fitted during construction or after the other parts are attached to the wall. Construction is mainly of 1-inch plywood, although particleboard could be used for some parts. The top is made in the same way as in the fitted cabinet discussed earlier, but other forms could be used. If you use a standard worktop that is already surfaced, check its width before making the carcass and other parts.

Make the pair of ends (FIGS. 5-51 and 5-52A). The outer face should be veneered or be suitable for painting. Rabbet the rear edges to take the back (FIG. 5-52B).

Put strips across. Notch the top one to take three lengthwise strips that will support the worktop (FIGS. 5-51 and 5-52C). At drawer bottom level there is a 2-inch strip with a 1-inch-square strip attached to act as drawer guide and runner (FIG. 5-52D). (If your drawer-fitting method does not prevent the drawer from tilting, you could fit a similar piece on the top strip as a kicker. However, you could save that step until you fit the drawers.) Complete the ends as a pair.

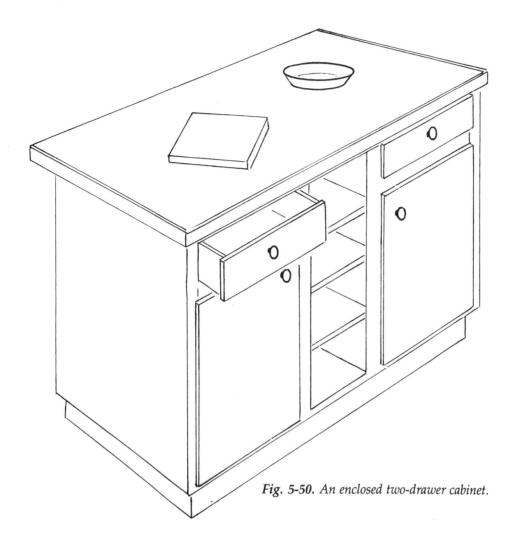

Fig. 5-50. *An enclosed two-drawer cabinet.*

Make the pair of divisions (FIG. 5-52E), which are placed above the bottom and inside the back. On the outward surfaces, fit strips across the top the same as at the ends.

Fit a single strip across at drawer level. Put cleats on the inner surfaces to support shelves (FIG. 5-52F). Make the bottom to fit between the ends. Use dowels at the ends. You could use dowels for the divisions, but it is simpler to screw up through the bottom (FIG. 5-52G).

The three lengthwise strips at the top are the same length as the bottom. Have them and the bottom ready for assembly to the ends and divisions. Glue and clamp the dowels at the bottom, and screw the top strips in place. With the carcass face-down, compare diagonal measurements to see that the assembly is square before the glue sets.

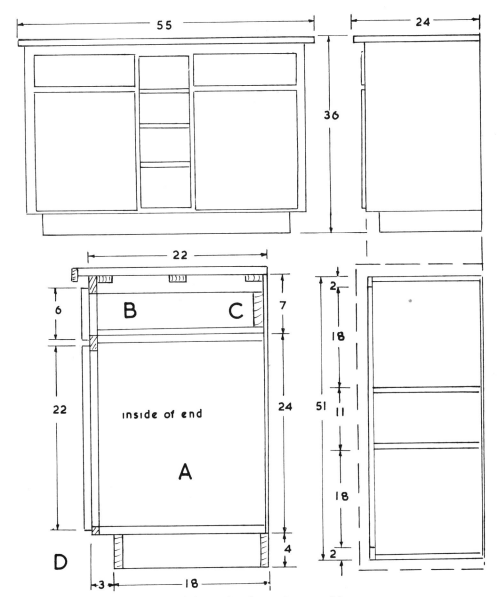

Fig. 5-51. *Sizes and sections of the enclosed two-drawer cabinet.*

Make the nail rail to fit between the ends and into the notches in the divisions (FIGS. 5-51C and 5-52H). Fit the back into the rabbets and to the other parts with glue and ample screws or nails. The nail rail and back will keep the carcass in shape.

Make the plinth as a separate unit (FIG. 5-53A). Let it stand back 3 inches from the front and ends and come level at the back (FIG. 5-51D). Miter the front corners,

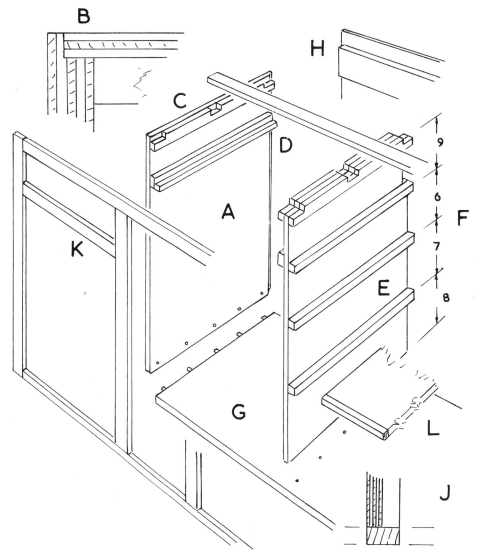

Fig. 5-52. Main parts of the enclosed two-drawer cabinet.

but have the ends overlap the back (FIG. 5-53B). You can avoid screw or nail heads outside if you fit blocks inside the corners. Join the plinth to the carcass with screws downward through the bottom.

Make a frame to fit over the front in a fashion similar to that of the fitted cabinet discussed earlier. The top rail covers the crosswise pieces. Make the bottom rail to match the carcass bottom. Fit uprights over the divisions to cover the ends of the shelf supports, but leave the ends of the drawer runners open (FIG. 5-52J). Let the rails below the drawers (FIG. 5-52K) come level with the tops of the drawer runners.

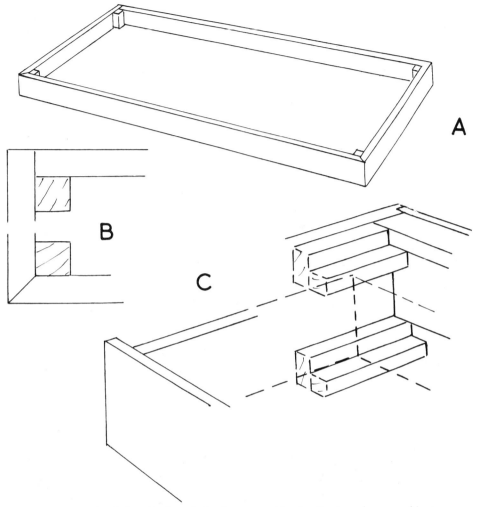

Fig. 5-53. Details of the plinth and the drawer guides for the two-drawer cabinet.

Make the shelves with solid-wood front edging (FIG. 5-52). Screw the shelves to their supports, with front edges level so they will come inside the front frame. Start with the bottom shelf, or you might have difficulty using a screwdriver.

Attach the front frame to the carcass. Check that the top surfaces of all parts finish level. Treat the inside of the cabinet with paint or other finish.

You can make and fit the two drawers in any of the ways described earlier. If you use metal side tracks, you will have to put pieces across inside ends to suit them, and you will have to make the drawers narrow enough to admit the tracks. With the carcass made as described, you can make the drawers to fit the opening and run on their bottom edges (FIG. 5-53C). The nail rail will act as a backstop, although an overlapping front will also stop the drawer. The false front can overlap 1/2 inch all around.

2 ends	1	× 22	× 32 plywood
4 end frames	1	× 2	× 24
2 end frames	1	× 1	× 24
2 divisions	1	× 22	× 32 plywood
6 division frames	1	× 2	× 24
6 division frames	1	× 1	× 24
1 bottom	1	× 22	× 51
3 top strips	1	× 2	× 51
1 back	1/2	× 32	× 51 plywood
1 nail rail	1	× 4	× 51
3 shelves	1/2	× 11	× 24
3 shelf edges	1/2	× 1/2	× 11
4 front frames	1	× 2	× 52
2 front frames	1	× 2	× 22
1 front frame	1	× 1	× 52
1 top	1	× 24	× 56 plywood
1 top edging	3/4	× 1	× 56
2 top edgings	3/4	× 1	× 26
2 doors	1	× 20	× 24 plywood
2 drawer fronts	1	× 6	× 20
4 drawer sides	5/8	× 4	× 24
2 drawer fronts	3/4	× 4	× 20
2 drawer backs	5/8	× 3 1/2	× 20
2 drawer bottoms	1/4	× 18	× 24 plywood

The doors and drawer fronts should match. Use a 1/2-inch overlap all around. Fit knobs or handles to match.

Make the top with laminated plastic over plywood and a hardwood edging. You can make the top completely before fitting it, but as you have room to work all around this cabinet, you might prefer to fit the plywood top by screwing downward, put on the laminated plastic, and trim its edges in position, then add the edging at the front and ends.

Finish the outside of the cabinet in any way you wish, but the top edging will probably look best varnished.

Barbecue Table/Trolley

When you set up a barbecue outdoors, you need a place to put food and equipment as well as a place for serving. Quite often you put together temporary arrangements, but they are not always satisfactory. The piece of outdoor furniture in FIG. 5-54 provides a working top or serving table that is 36 inches long, 16 inches extending to 24 inches wide, and 34 inches high. Underneath, there is plenty of storage space behind an open front. There are wheels at one end and towel rails at both ends. The rail at the opposite end to the wheels also serves as a handle when you want to move the trolley.

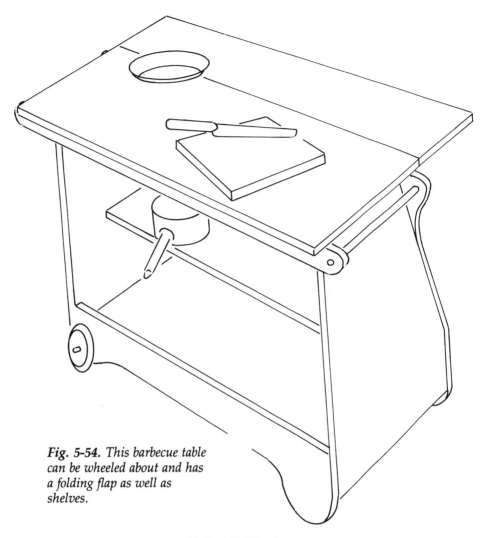

Fig. 5-54. This barbecue table can be wheeled about and has a folding flap as well as shelves.

Materials List for
Barbecue Table/Trolley

2 ends	$16 \times 30 \times \frac{3}{4}$ plywood
1 back	$24 \times 40 \times \frac{3}{4}$ plywood
2 bottom parts	$10 \times 32 \times \frac{3}{4}$ plywood
1 front	$5 \times 40 \times \frac{3}{4}$ plywood
1 bottom	$15 \times 32 \times \frac{3}{4}$ plywood
2 shelves	$11 \times 32 \times \frac{3}{4}$ plywood
1 top	$16 \times 36 \times \frac{3}{4}$ plywood
1 flap	$8 \times 36 \times \frac{3}{4}$ plywood
2 brackets	$9 \times 9 \times \frac{3}{4}$ plywood
4 strips	$\frac{3}{4} \times \frac{3}{4} \times 32$
8 strips	$\frac{3}{4} \times \frac{3}{4} \times 16$
2 rods	$16 \times \frac{3}{4}$ diameter

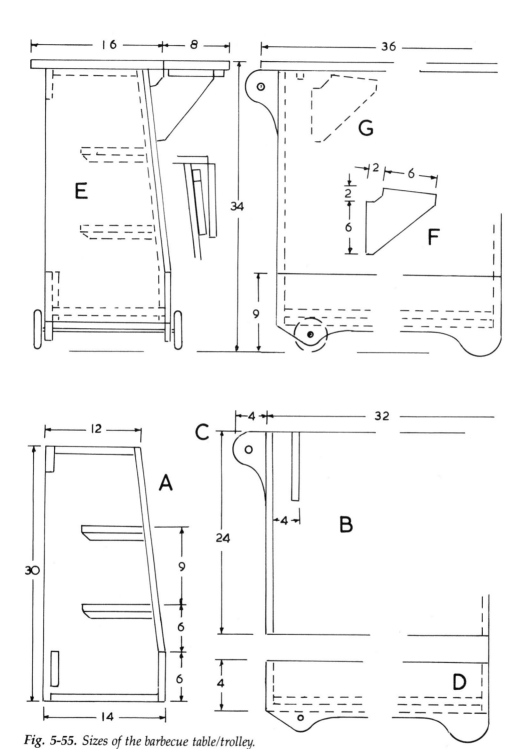

Fig. 5-55. Sizes of the barbecue table/trolley.

The main parts are ³/₄-inch plywood. Stiffening strips are ³/₄-inch-square solid wood. You could make plywood disc wheels, but store-bought, 4-inch diameter, metal-tired wheels on a ³/₈-inch steel axle are appropriate for the design. Towel rails are ³/₄-inch dowel rod. If you store the trolley in a dry place, you could use any plywood, but exterior grade is preferable. Use waterproof glue and nails or screws for joints.

Start by setting out the ends (FIG. 5-55A). The broadened bottoms give stability, particularly when pressure is put on the top flap. Attach framing strips (FIG. 5-56A). Allow for the bottom fitting under the upright strips.

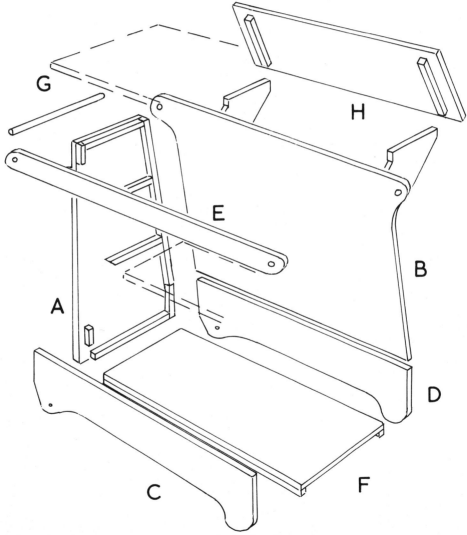

Fig. 5-56. *How parts of the barbecue table/trolley fit together.*

The back (FIGS. 5-55B and 5-56B) fits over the ends and extends to take the towel rails (FIG. 5-55C) at both ends. Mark on the positions of the brackets.

The two bottom parts (FIGS. 5-56C and 5-56D) are the same, except the front piece fits between the ends and the rear piece overlaps them. The wheel size will decide depths. When the wheels are in position, the extensions at the other end (FIG. 5-55D) should hold the table horizontal. Round the top edge of the front piece. Bevel the other piece to fit against the back.

Make the front piece (FIG. 5-56E) to match the top edge of the back. Drill both parts to take 3/4-inch dowel rods.

Place stiffening strips on the bottom (FIG. 5-56F) at the back and front.

Assemble all parts made so far. If necessary, put a strip inside the long joint between the two parts at the back.

Make the shelves (FIG. 5-56E). If the plywood is not stiff enough, put strips along the front edges. You might choose to leave the shelves loose, or you can attach them to the end cleats.

The top overhangs 2 inches at the ends and front and 2 inches at the back, but increase this if necessary to clear the folded brackets (FIG. 5-56G).

Make the flap (FIG. 5-56H) to match the main top. Mark where the brackets will come, and put stop strips there. Leave the top edges untreated if you will be using a painted finish, or you might prefer to add solid wood lips. You also could use Formica top or something similar.

Make the bracket angle to match the slope of the back (FIG. 5-55F). Hinge the two parts of the top. Four 2-inch hinges should be suitable, but keep the hinges away from where the brackets have to swing.

Put the top in position, and screw it to the other parts. Locate the bracket positions so that they swing against the strips on the flap and close towards each other (FIG. 5-55G). Two 2-inch hinges should be satisfactory on each bracket. The flap should hang over them when folded.

Glue the dowel rods in place. Fit the axle and wheels. A light-colored paint inside makes it easier to see what you have put there. A darker, durable color will be better outside.

6

Other Furniture

There are a great many pieces of furniture worth making that do not fall into particular categories, but are too large or involve too much work to be classed as weekend projects or light furniture. Most of these examples are different from anything you could buy. Because they are designed to suit special purposes, they are unique.

Divisions between projects in this section and those in other parts of the book cannot be defined exactly. A skillful and well-equipped woodworker might complete a project in a weekend. Another enthusiast might take much longer. The projects in this section range from useful, easily made furniture to more ambitious pieces that will exercise all the skill of an expert.

Display Shelves

If you want to display valuable plates or other tableware on a shelf, it must have a positive stop at the front. In some cases, a notch in the shelf or a shallow rail might keep items in place, but a higher rail on spindles is safer and more decorative, as well. If the shelves are part of a row of wall cabinets, you can leave the end plains, but if the display shelves hang independently, you might want to shape the extending parts. The display shelf shown in FIG. 6-1 will hang without touching other furniture.

For the sizes suggested in FIG. 6-2A, the main parts could be 5/8-inch hardwood. If you use softwood, increase thicknesses to 3/4-inch. The back between the shelves is 1/4-inch plywood, but there is a solid wood back above the top shelf, to provide stiffness and take the hanging screws. The plywood back can finish at the bottom shelf or continue to the ends of the sides.

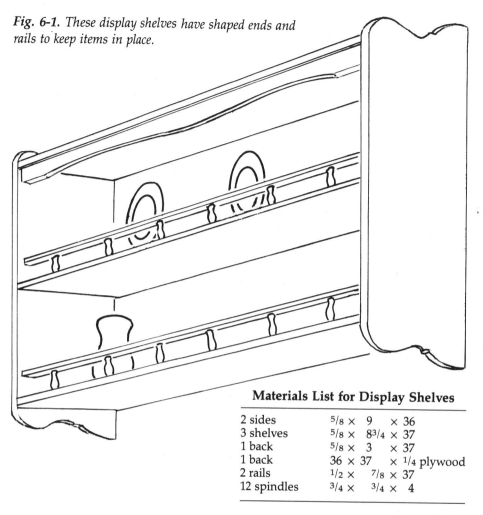

Fig. 6-1. These display shelves have shaped ends and rails to keep items in place.

Materials List for Display Shelves

2 sides	$^5/_8 \times$	9	$\times$ 36
3 shelves	$^5/_8 \times$	$8^3/_4 \times$	37
1 back	$^5/_8 \times$	3	$\times$ 37
1 back	$36 \times$	37	$\times$ $^1/_4$ plywood
2 rails	$^1/_2 \times$	$^7/_8 \times$	37
12 spindles	$^3/_4 \times$	$^3/_4 \times$	4

The key parts are two sides, so mark them out first (FIG. 6-2B). Continue the rabbet for the plywood to the end, if that is what you want, or stop it at the bottom shelf. At the top of each side, cut away to take the top solid back (FIG. 6-2C).

Prepare the wood for the shelves and cut the dadoes in the sides. Stop them $^1/_4$ inch back from the front (FIG. 6-2D), and cut the ends of the shelves to suit.

The shaped ends of the sides are the same (FIG. 6-2D). To ensure uniformity, cut a card template of the shape. Mark and cut the shapes. Remove saw marks and sand the ends. The top curves might be too high for surface details to be seen, but the bottom shaping should be smooth. If the top of the unit will be high, you might not have to worry about the edge of the solid wood back above the top shelf, but if it is visible you might wish to shape it (FIG. 6-3B).

You could add a strip under the front of the top shelf (FIG. 6-2) to improve appearance. It need not be tenoned to the sides; you could use dowels or depend only on glue. The strip should repeat the curve of the solid wood back.

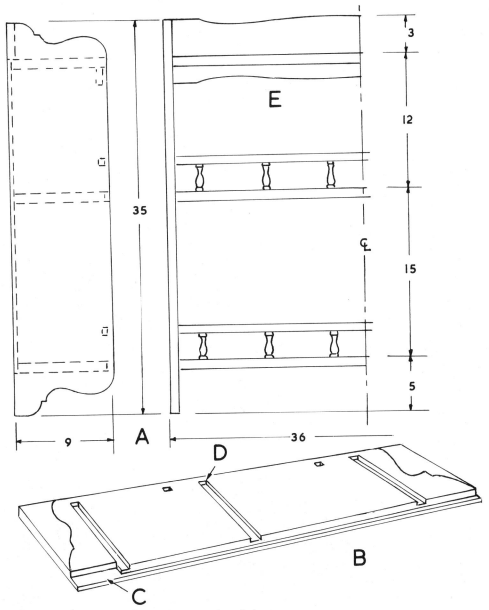

Fig. 6-2. Sizes and details of the display shelves.

You might have to relate the rail sizes to the spindles, depending on the dowel ends. If you turn them yourself (FIG. 6-3C), 1/4-inch dowel ends can go into rafts about 1/2 inch × 7/8 inch (FIG. 6-3D). Shape the raft sections, and cut small tenons to fit into the sides (FIG. 6-3E). Spindles at 6-inch centers should be satisfactory, but if the shelf will display smaller things, make the spindles closer together.

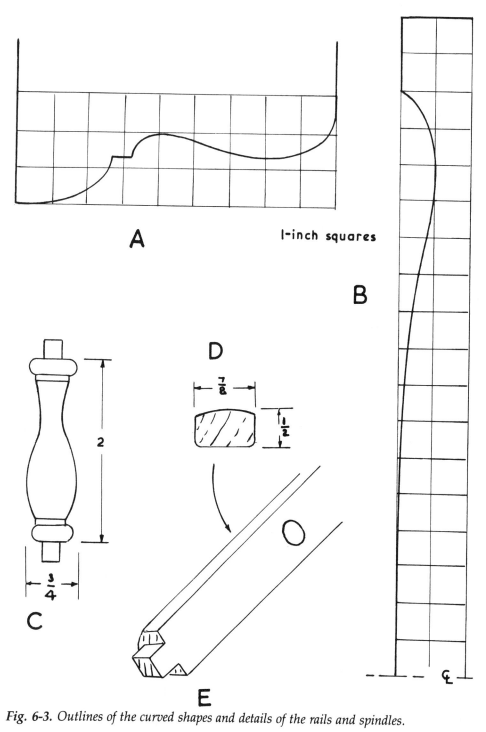

A

1-inch squares

B

D

$\frac{7}{8}$

$\frac{1}{2}$

C

$\frac{3}{4}$

2

E

Fig. 6-3. Outlines of the curved shapes and details of the rails and spindles.

When you assemble the unit, screw the ends of the top solid wood back into the sides, and put two or three screws upward through the shelf, into the back, before fitting the plywood, which goes over the top shelf and against the solid wood back. You will probably need to drive one or two screws diagonally upward through the ends of the bottom shelf to strengthen the dado joints.

Drill the solid wood top for the main hanging screws. You might need one or two more screws lower in the plywood to keep the unit close to the wall.

Hanging Shelves

Shelves or compartments can hang on the wall above a bed's headboard, over a desk or bench, or anywhere that books and other things should be kept together and off other furniture. This set of hanging shelves (FIG. 6-4) is used over twin beds to keep books and other things within reach.

The shelves shown are made of mahogany, but any hardwood can be used. Softwood might be suitable for a painted finish in a child's bedroom. Sizes may vary, but if you make the unit smaller, don't reduce wood thickness because it will weaken the joints. Likewise, a much larger assembly should be made with thicker wood.

Several different methods of construction are possible, depending on your wishes, skill, and the availability of power tools. The satisfactory use and appearance of the shelves is dependent on joints that will not fail.

Prepare the wood with all parts the same width and thickness. Mark out the top board (FIG. 6-5A) with the positions of the other parts. Leave some excess length until you have decided on the methods of jointing. Make the other lengthwise parts (FIGS. 6-5B and 6-5C) using the top board as a guide.

Mark the four uprights (FIG. 6-5D) together, but leave some excess length so you can cut the chosen joints.

The drawing shows the corners without extensions (FIG. 6-5E). It is possible to let the shelves or the uprights extend (FIG. 6-5F and 6-5G) in some forms of construction. Some of these variations are dependent on the choice of joints.

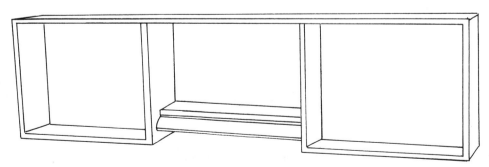

Fig. 6-4. This hanging shelf goes above twin beds and has a reading lamp at the center.

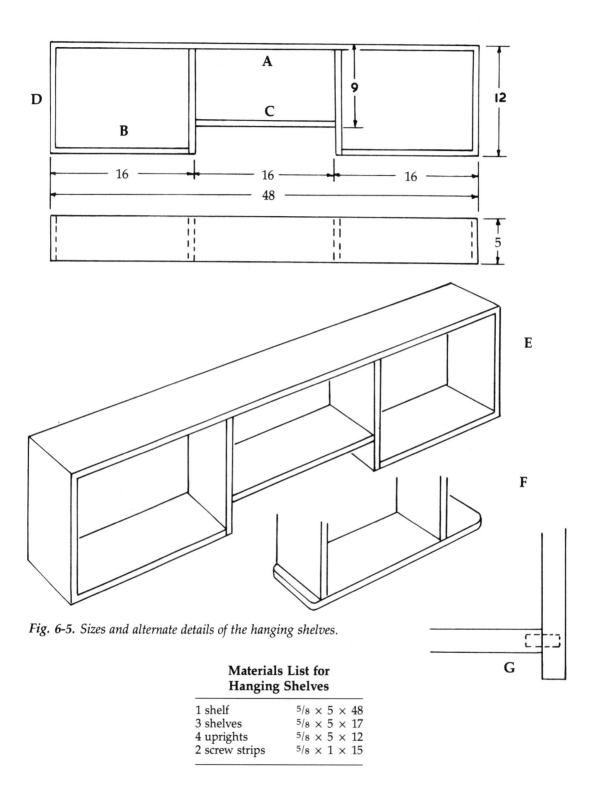

Fig. 6-5. Sizes and alternate details of the hanging shelves.

**Materials List for
Hanging Shelves**

1 shelf	$5/8 \times 5 \times 48$
3 shelves	$5/8 \times 5 \times 17$
4 uprights	$5/8 \times 5 \times 12$
2 screw strips	$5/8 \times 1 \times 15$

The shelves shown here have through dovetails (FIG. 6-6A), cut by hand. The exposed joint details can be regarded as decorative. Note the tails are vertical, to take the hanging load. Machine-cut dovetails are equally suitable, but these might not have the narrow pins that are a feature of handwork.

A simpler joint uses a rabbet (FIG. 6-6B) about two-thirds of the thickness of the top piece. This allows the upright piece to fit in and nails to be driven both ways to lock the joint. You can use glue, but remember that it is not very strong on end grain, so much of the load has to be taken by the fastenings. Screws are too conspicuous, but finishing nails can be set below the surface and covered with filler. If you have the equipment to cut the joint, a rabbet and tongue (FIG. 6-6C) will join the wood without nails.

As with most furniture, it is possible to join the parts with dowels. Using these at corners without an overhang, however, does not leave much wood outside the dowel holes and the short grain can break out. It is better to extend the overlapping part (FIGS. 6-5G and 6-6D). If you want the shelves to extend outwards, the doweling will have to be downwards (FIG. 6-5F).

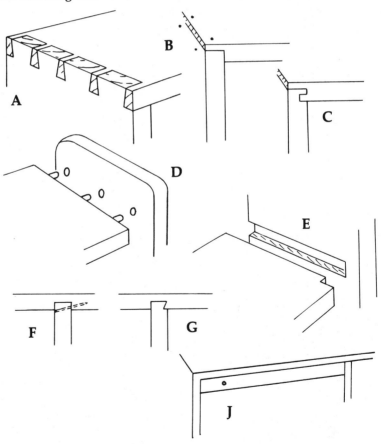

Fig. 6-6. Joints at the corners and divisions of the hanging shelves.

The raised shelf (FIG. 6-5C) can be fitted to the uprights with dowels, although a better joint is a stopped dado (FIG. 6-6E). Taking it through to the front would expose the end of the shelf unattractively.

Where the inner uprights join the top shelf, you can use dowels. Tenons are an alternative, but they would have to go through for sufficient strength, and their exposed ends might be regarded as ugly. A simple stopped dado, as at the ends of the middle shelf, might not be strong enough because of the weakness of end-grain gluing, unless nails are driven diagonally (FIG. 6-6F). A dovetail-stopped dado (FIG. 6-6G) will take downward loads without the help of nails.

The shelves could be attached to the wall with metal plates screwed to the backs of at least two uprights, with holes in extensions for the screws to the wall. Another way is to glue strips under the ends of the top shelf and screw through them (FIG. 6-6J).

Spindle-Supported Shelves

Turned wood parts always add a decorative feature to an otherwise plain design. They tend to look tighter than plain square parts, and they give an open feeling to an assembly. Used between shelves, they provide an open effect on units that would otherwise need solid ends or brackets. Such shelves can suit bathroom or kitchen. In a compact bathroom, shelves with spindles give a more spacious feeling than shelves that are more boxed in.

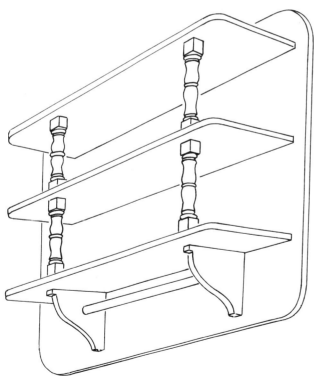

Fig. 6-7. Shelves with wood brackets and spindle supports.

Materials List for
Spindle-Supported Shelves

3 shelves	$3/4$ ×	$91/2$ ×	36
2 brackets	1 ×	7 ×	12
4 spindles	$13/4$ ×	$13/4$ ×	14
1 back	36 ×	40 ×	$3/4$ plywood
1 rail	30 ×	1 round	

The shelves shown in FIG. 6-7 have brackets under the bottom shelf and turned spindles to support the other. As shown, the brackets could also carry a rail for towels.

The back could be plywood with a suitable face veneer, but you might want to paint edges black to hide the plies, or frame around the back with solid wood. If you cannot turn your own spindles, you can buy suitable ones with square ends; they are intended to be used for making stools. The square ends allow you to cut the parts to length within quite a wide range.

Make the three shelves (FIG. 6-8A) with rounded front corners and edges. Mark the positions of the brackets and posts.

Cut back the plywood carefully to avoid splintering. Round the corners and sand the edges. Mark the positions of the shelves. The lower gap is 1 inch larger than the top gap, to provide a balanced appearance.

Mark out the two brackets (FIG. 6-9A) with the grain diagonal. Mark the hole position if you want to fit a rail.

Make sure that the wood edges of the bracket are square. Remove saw marks from the front edges.

The spindles all have turned parts the same size (FIG. 6-9B), but those in the lower space are 1 inch longer overall. Turn the set of four spindles with some excess left at the ends. Mark out the mortises on the shelves and the tenons on the spindles (FIG. 6-9C).

At the middle shelf (FIG. 6-8B) the mortise goes through and the tenons enter from opposite sides, so their length should be less than half the thickness. At the top and bottom shelves, the mortises do not go through, so cut the tenons to suit.

To ensure squareness, start assembly at the bottom. Join the bottom shelf to the back with glue and screws. Position the brackets, and fit them with glue and screws through the back. One screw driven downward through the shelf into each bracket, just behind the spindle position, should suffice. You could counterbore and plug the hole if you do not want the screw head to show. Include the towel rail, which could be a piece of 1-inch dowel rod or plated metal tube, in holes drilled about halfway through each bracket.

Add the next shelf with screws through the back, and position the two spindles as you assemble. Do the same with the top shelf.

Two screws through the back above the top shelf will hang the assembly, but another screw lower down will keep the back close to the wall.

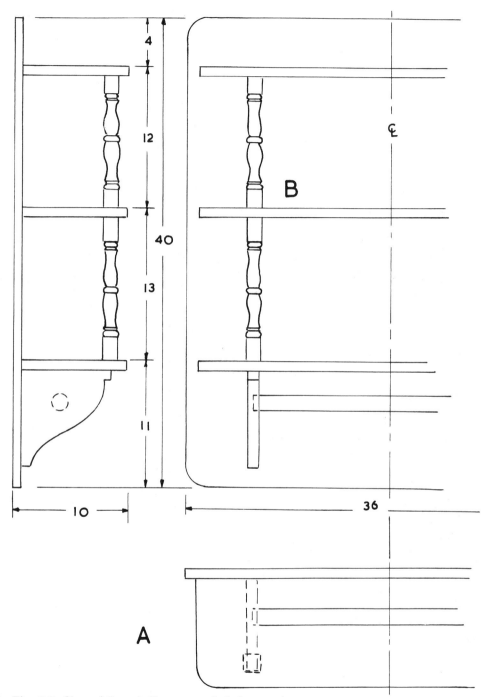

Fig. 6-8. Sizes of the spindle-supported shelves.

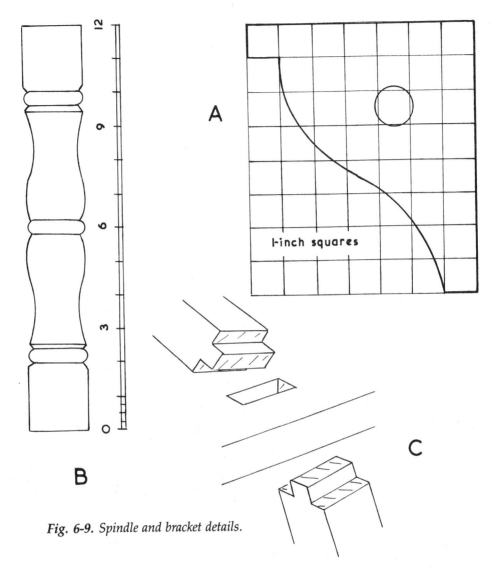

I-inch squares

C

B

Fig. 6-9. Spindle and bracket details.

Wall Desk

If floor space is limited, a desk or work surface supported on the wall and able to fold back has many attractions. This desk (FIG. 6-10) could be used for writing or typing, but it would also serve as a bench for a light hobby. It would not withstand heavy hammering, but for such things as paper modeling and fabric crafts, it makes a work table that can be swung out of the way when not needed.

The design suggested is 28 inches square (FIG. 6-11); when closed, the unit projects 5 inches from the wall and does not reach the floor. When opened, the

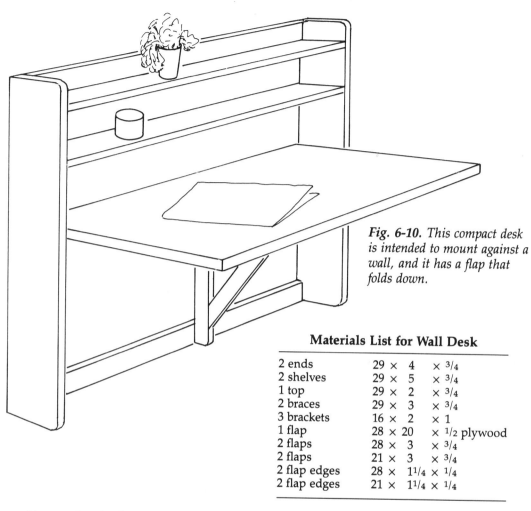

Fig. 6-10. *This compact desk is intended to mount against a wall, and it has a flap that folds down.*

Materials List for Wall Desk

2 ends	29 ×	4	× 3/4	
2 shelves	29 ×	5	× 3/4	
1 top	29 ×	2	× 3/4	
2 braces	29 ×	3	× 3/4	
3 brackets	16 ×	2	× 1	
1 flap	28 ×	20	× 1/2	plywood
2 flaps	28 ×	3	× 3/4	
2 flaps	21 ×	3	× 3/4	
2 flap edges	28 ×	11/4 × 1/4		
2 flap edges	21 ×	11/4 × 1/4		

working surface is about 26 inches wide, extends 20 inches, and is supported by a substantial bracket. There are two shelves shown, but you could alter the unit height and put in more shelves or compartments.

Most parts are solid wood 3/4 inch thick. The working surface is framed plywood. Construction is with 5/16-inch or 3/8-inch dowels.

Mark out the pair of sides (FIG. 6-12A) with the positions of the other parts, including the flap in up and down positions, so you can see where the pivot holes will come.

Mark and cut the crosswise parts to the same length with square ends. There are two lower braces (FIG. 6-11A), two shelves (FIG. 6-11B), and a top (FIG. 6-11C).

Mark the ends for dowels (FIG. 6-12B). Glue and dowel the top to its shelf.

Round the front corners of the sides. Take sharpness off the exposed edges of all parts and do any necessary sanding. Join the crosswise parts to the sides with glue and dowels. Measure diagonals to check squareness.

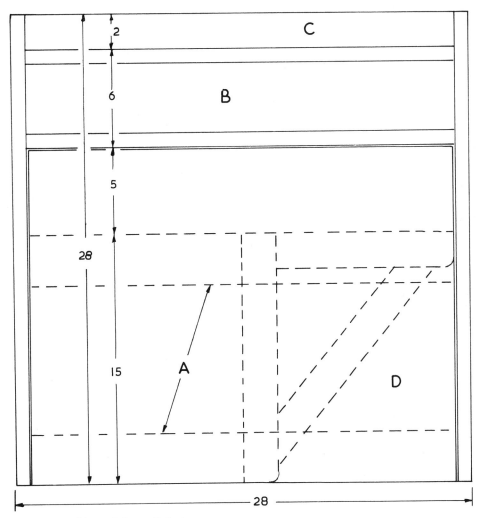

Fig. 6-11. Sizes of the wall desk.

The flap could be made to suit the intended use. Veneered particleboard might be suitable. It is shown as ¹/₂-inch plywood framed with ³/₄-inch strips and edged (FIG. 6-12C). Make the overall width to fit easily between the sides. The depth, when folded down, should go under the shelf and reach the bottom of the sides (FIG. 6-12D).

When the flap is opened horizontally, its rear edge should rest on the brace at the back. Try the flap in this position, and drill the sides in the screw position. However, first drill a ¹/₈-inch hole each side for nails to be pushed through. When you are satisfied with the action on nails, drill out for the pivot screws, which should be fairly large. Roundhead screws #12-gauge × 2¹/₂ inches would be suitable. Put clearance holes through the sides, and drill undersize holes in

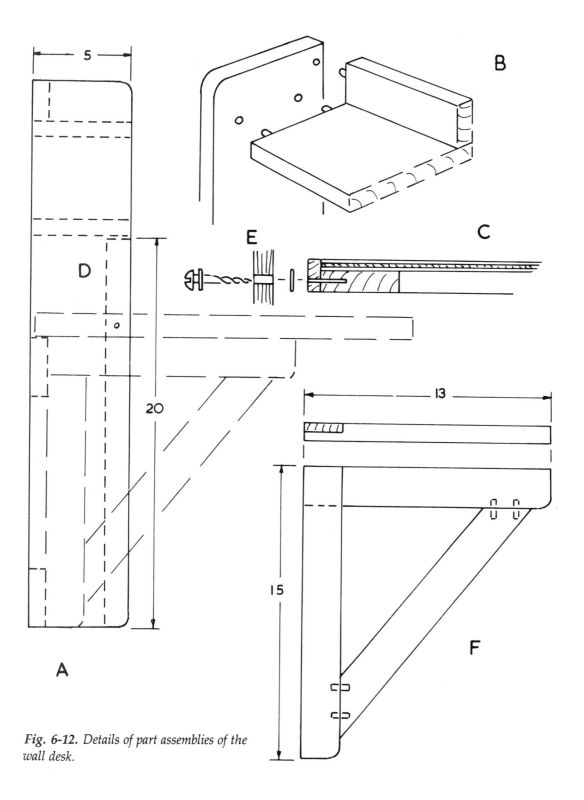

Fig. 6-12. Details of part assemblies of the wall desk.

the flap to prevent splitting. When you finally assemble, include washers on the screws (FIG. 6-12E).

The bracket (FIG. 6-12) is built up from strips. Cut a halved joint at the corner, and temporarily assemble this squarely, so you can mark the size and shape of the strut. Dowel the strut joints.

Position the bracket so it will fold inside (FIG. 6-11D). Attach it to the braces with 2-inch or larger hinges. The bracket should stop under the flap when it is about square, but if you think it is necessary, put a stop block under the flap.

Finish the wood in a way to match the surroundings. The working surface might be best without a gloss.

Mount the unit on the wall so the working surface will be at a suitable height, probably between 27 and 31 inches.

Wall Units

Combined units that cover most of one wall are useful for multipurpose, built-in furniture. Total needs should be assessed beforehand, as several different layouts might be possible. If you use solid wood available in sufficient lengths, it might be simplest to carry horizontal lines right through (FIG. 6-13A).

Manufactured board is not usually available in lengths greater than 8 feet. This is usually more than enough for heights, but might not be enough to carry through the whole width. If you use this material, it is best to carry vertical lines through, too (FIG. 6-13B)

Careful work will let lines in the opposite direction of the followed-through lines match, but the risk of slight discrepancies showing will be reduced if different sections are staggered (FIG. 6-13C).

Usually, wall units project uniformly from the wall. This simplifies construction, as all parts are the same width. Breaking up the front line, however, can improve appearance as well as provide better storage. For instance, a sewing machine might need more back-to-front space than other things, so a section of the wall unit can be made wider (FIG. 6-14A). This will also apply if a drop-front desk is built in or a chair out of use is to be pushed under a desk (FIG. 6-14B). Alternatively, it might be better to reduce the width in cramped quarters where chairs have to be pushed under (FIG. 6-14C).

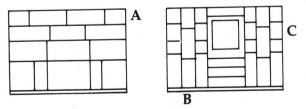

Fig. 6-13. For convenience in construction, a large wall unit should be given shelves going right through, or uprights going right through, but not both.

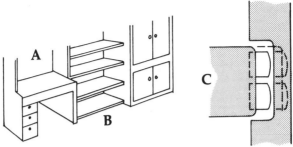

Fig. 6-14. Side units can be connected by shelves.

If horizontal lines are to follow through, the first parts made should be the shelves, base, and anything else that runs the full length. Mark these together so distances match. The only place where there might be slight deviations is in an end that comes against a wall at a corner. Check the wall with a level or plumb line. If it is out of vertical, allow for this when making the end parts.

Elsewhere in the unit, upright parts should be truly vertical, and not parallel with a faulty wall. Adjust the ends of horizontal parts accordingly. In an old house with very inaccurate walls, it might be neatest to recess a piece at the front to give a truly vertical start to the new work (FIG. 6-15A).

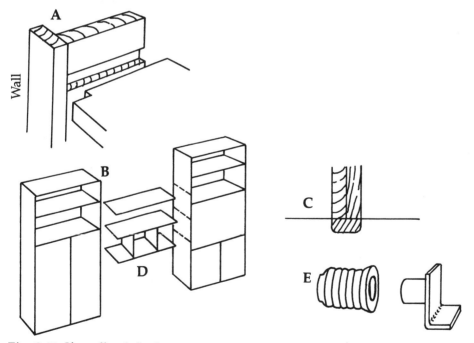

Fig. 6-15. If a wall unit fits into a corner, it might be necessary to cover inequalities there (A). Subunits can be made and brought together (B through D). Shelves can be made adjustable with special hooks (E).

With the followed-through lines vertical, the method of construction will depend on the overall width. If this is little more than the height, the whole thing can be prefabricated, and there should be no difficulty in erecting and attaching the entire assembly satisfactorily.

If there is a large expanse of wall to be covered, it might be better to work in sections. Each section can then be treated separately (FIG. 6-15B). This does mean duplication of some uprights where the sections come together. Actually, this double thickness can aid the appearance by emphasizing solidity. You could add molding over the joint or just a strip with rounded edges (FIG. 6-15C).

A method of prefabricating is to make up alternate sections and add what comes between after these are in position (FIG. 6-15D). In this case, it is best for the more complicated parts to be in the prefabricated sections.

Much of the construction will be the same as described elsewhere in this book using dado, doweled, or manufactured joints for the main assembly. For shelves, the joints can be permanent, which will help to stiffen the whole unit; but there are places such as bookshelves where height adjustments might be desirable.

There can also be metal strips that recess into the uprights and allow supports to be located in several places. Alternatively, there can be hooks on metal dowels that fit into holes in the wood or into plastic sockets (FIG. 6-15E). These can also be used for glass shelves, which then can be taken out for cleaning.

The front view is a multitude of crossing lines. This can be attractive, but if the line effect is to be reduced, doors and flaps can overlap the framework (FIG. 6-16A). This also applies to drawers (FIG. 6-16B) with the fronts hiding the runners.

If a cocktail or drink cabinet is included, this can be lined with Formica and given glass shelves. Doors can accommodate glasses, either standing in racks or hung by their stems (FIG. 6-16C). You can make the door to pivot centrally so everything housed there is brought to the front on semicircular racks (FIG. 6-16D).

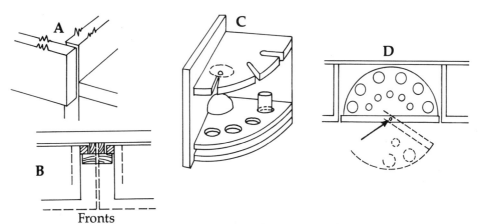

Fronts

Fig. 6-16. The severity of a wall unit can be broken up by drawers, doors, and special storages.

Wall Fitment

To break up the shelf lengths of a long bookcase, you can change the depth to suit different sizes of books (FIG. 6-17A). The number of changes made will depend on the overall length and the number of different sizes of books. For very wide books or magazines laid flat, the shelves can project forward from the uprights. For the neatest joints, the dados can be cut through and the shelf end allowed to overlap (FIG. 6-17B).

The sides can also project below the bottom shelf. In this case, dado joints can be used. It would be better if the side did not go below the shelf level: There has to be a stronger joint to take the load. A through dovetail is best (FIG. 6-17C).

The stepped arrangement, if taken below, can be adapted to another use. There can be a rail, made from a piece of dowel rod, fitted into holes, (FIG. 6-17D) to serve as a rack for ties, belts, and other items of clothing.

A part of the rack can be fitted with a door and the enclosed space arranged above or below the bookshelves. It might be at one end or could be between open shelves.

The simplest door is a piece of thick plywood cut to fit over the surrounding edges (FIG. 6-17E), with hinges behind one edge and a fastener that fits into the other side. Another door fits inside the frame. It could be similar plywood or framed with thinner plywood in a plowed groove (FIG. 6-17F). This might be also a good place for a mirror fitted into rabbeted wood (FIG. 6-17G).

In the common bookcase assembly, the shelves are supported by the ends. It is possible to make an assembly with one or more shelves, since the strength members and upright divisions are dependent on them. In the example (FIG. 6-18A) there is a main shelf, which can be hung from the wall with metal mirror

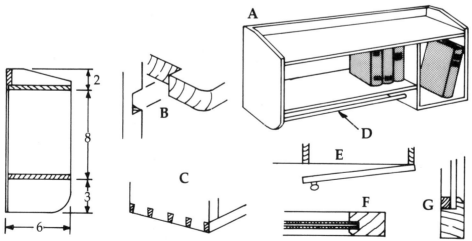

Fig. 6-17. Shelves can be at different levels and fitted with doors and racks: (A) depth changes; (B) overlapping end; (C) through dovetail; (D) rail; (E) door; (F) plowed groove; (G) mirror rabbeted into wood.

plates (FIG. 6-18B), or there can be a strip of wood under the rear edge (FIG. 6-18C) to take screws into the wall.

The other parts are joined with dowels. Four dowels 5/16-inch or 3/8-inch diameter in each joint should be strong enough. Cut the ends of the wood accurately, and mark the joints together (FIG. 6-18D), or use a dowel jig. Cut the shelf ends and other exposed ends at a slope with a rounded front corner (FIG. 6-18E). Use a template to get them all the same, or cut one end and use that as a template at the other places. Where the ends are cut squarely, they could come level with the part joining, but they are shown with slight projections (FIG. 6-18F). Although they appear square, take off all sharpness before assembly.

At the end where there are uprights above and below the shelf, take dowels right through (FIG. 6-18G). Elsewhere put the dowels about three-quarters of the way through the shelf. Be sure to make the holes in the uprights slightly too deep (FIG. 6-18H) so the joint can be squeezed tight with a clamp.

A horizontal rail behind the top space (FIG. 6-18J) will strengthen the assembly and provide another place for screws to the wall. For a child's collection of small, decorative figurines, the extending parts might be taken a little further to provide space for displaying them.

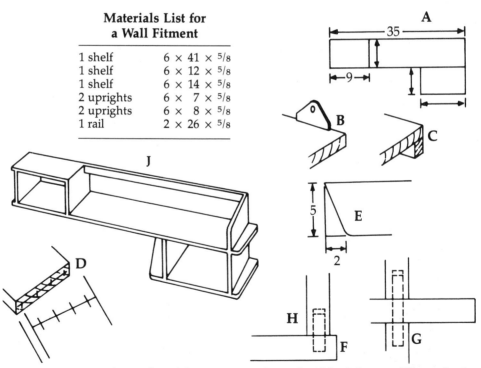

Materials List for a Wall Fitment

1 shelf	6 × 41 × 5/8
1 shelf	6 × 12 × 5/8
1 shelf	6 × 14 × 5/8
2 uprights	6 × 7 × 5/8
2 uprights	6 × 8 × 5/8
1 rail	2 × 26 × 5/8

Fig. 6-18. Interesting and useful patterns can be made with shelves at different levels. This unit has doweled construction: (A) main shelf; (B) metal mirror plates; (C) strip of wood; (D) marked joints; (E) rounded front corner; (F) slight projections; (G) dowels; (H) deep holes; (J) horizontal rail.

Television Stand with Magazine Rack

With television there is usually a video recorder and a large number of tapes, all needing storage. You will also have newspapers and magazines that would benefit from a neat storage. This unit (FIG. 6-19) functions as a stand for the television set, with storage below for video equipment and racks at each end for magazines and newspapers. The unit can be on casters or glides, so it can be moved about or turned to give the best angle of viewing.

Arrange the sizes to suit your own equipment, but some sizes are suggested as a guide (FIG. 6-20). If you alter sizes very much, keep the proportions so the unit will be stable and have a fairly broad base in relation to the height.

As described, construction is almost completely of veneered particleboard, which might already have a satisfactory finish, or you might treat it as wood and

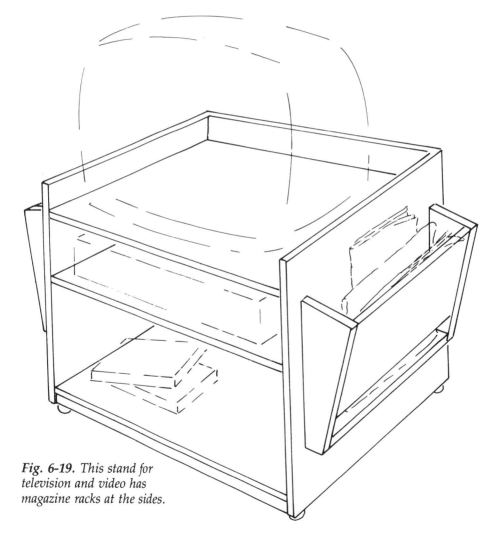

Fig. 6-19. This stand for television and video has magazine racks at the sides.

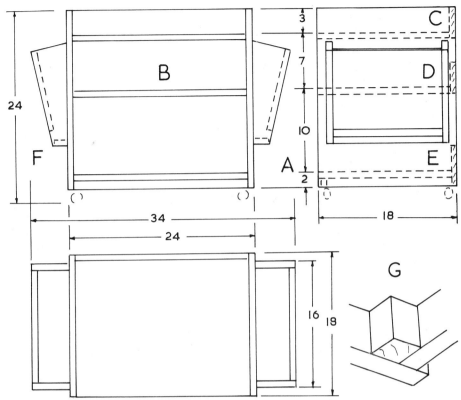

Fig. 6-20. Sizes of the television stand with magazine racks.

**Materials List for
Television Stand with
Magazine Rack**
(All ³/₄-inch veneered
particleboard)

2 sides	24 × 18
3 shelves	24 × 18
3 backs	25 × 5
1 base	24 × 1¹/₄
4 rack sides	14 × 6
2 rack fronts	16 × 10
2 rack bottoms	16 × 2

give it a clear finish. In any case, cut and exposed edges must be covered with iron-on veneer strips. It would be possible to use plywood of the same thickness; either edge it with solid wood, or give it a painted finish. Solid wood is possible, but it could be expensive. Also, you would have to glue pieces to make up the width.

All of the joints can be doweled, except in some places where their heads will not show; then, you can use screws. If you choose to use screws elsewhere in place of dowels, their heads must be counterbored and covered with wood or plastic plugs, which might then be regarded as a decorative feature. Use 3/8-inch dowels, and space them about 3 inches apart on most joints. For narrow parts, do not have fewer than two dowels.

Cut the pair of ends (FIGS. 6-20A and 6-21A). Mark on them the positions of the other parts. The shelves come level at the front, but at the back edge they are covered with upright strips. The base is set back 1/4 inch.

The three shelves are the same (FIGS. 6-20B and 6-21B). Allow for the covering pieces at the back.

Make the base strip (FIG. 6-21C) the same length as the shelves. Make the top back piece (FIGS. 6-20C and 6-21D) to cover the back of the shelf and come level with the top of the sides. The one behind the middle shelf (FIGS. 6-20D and 6-21E) can be the same, unless you would prefer it deeper to retain something larger on the shelf.

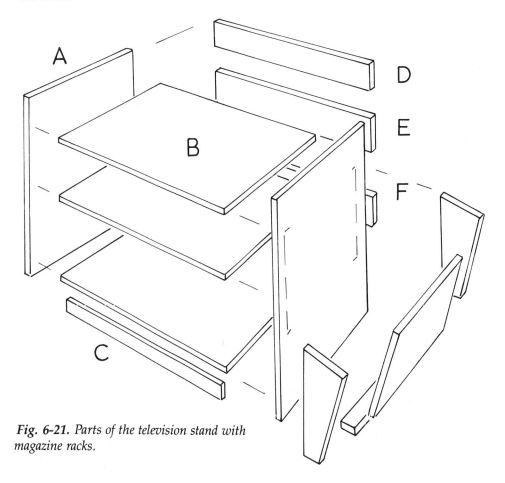

Fig. 6-21. *Parts of the television stand with magazine racks.*

The piece behind the bottom shelf (FIGS. 6-20E and 6-21F) should stand high enough above the shelf and reach to the lower edges of the sides.

Mark and drill all these parts for dowels. A few widely spaced parts can go between the base and its shelf. Do not assemble these parts yet, as the magazine racks are more easily fitted to the sides before the main parts are assembled.

Mark out and cut the sides of the magazine racks (FIGS. 6-20F and 6-22A). The sizes given here should be adequate, but if you want to accommodate special papers or books there is room for larger racks. The top outer corner is shown at 90 degrees.

The piece across the front of each rack (FIG. 6-22B) does not reach the bottom (FIG. 6-22C), so there is space for cleaning out. Join these parts with dowels, while the back edges are on a flat surface, to prevent twisting.

Mark the positions of the magazine racks on the outside of the sides and drill through for screws from the inside. Glue and screw on the racks.

Prepare sufficient dowels for all the joints. Join the back strips to their shelves and the base to the bottom shelf. Allow the glue to set in these joints before joining to the ends. Position the assembly on a flat surface when you join on the sides. Clamp tightly; the parts should pull themselves square without twist.

The arrangements for fitting casters or glides will depend on their design, but for most types it should be satisfactory to increase the corner areas below the bottom shelf with blocks screwed in the corners (FIG. 6-20G). Make their sizes to suit the casters. Remove any excess glue and apply your chosen finish.

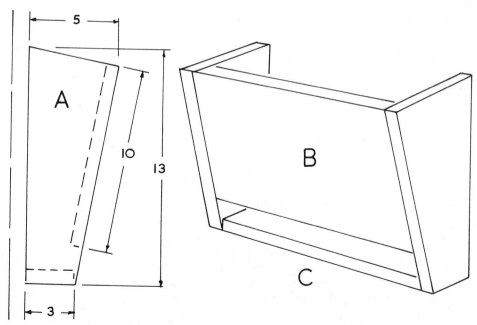

Fig. 6-22. Details of magazine rack.

Double-Door Cabinet

Dust was a problem in early homes, and one reason for doors was to keep it out. The problem might not be as acute today, but reasonably dustproof doors are still worth having. In this cabinet or cupboard (FIG. 6-23), the top overlaps the pair of doors, which overhang the bottom. At the center, the doors fit into each other.

Fig. 6-23. A wide cabinet needs double doors. These are arranged to give the contents good protection against dust.

Materials List for Double-Door Cabinet

2 sides	$5/8$	×	7	×	32
1 bottom	$5/8$	×	$6^3/4$	×	26
2 shelves	$5/8$	×	6	×	26
1 top	$5/8$	×	8	×	26
1 upper back	$5/8$	×	6	×	26
1 back	$1/4$	×	24	×	24
1 dust strip	$5/8$	×	$5/8$	×	24
3 door stiles	1	×	2	×	26
1 door stile	1	×	$2^3/8$	×	26
2 door rails	1	×	2	×	12
2 door rails	1	×	3	×	12
2 door panels	$1/4$	×	$11^1/2$	×	27

The suggested sizes (FIG. 6-24A) will make a useful cabinet for many purposes, but the same construction could be used for other sizes. Any wood could be used. A softwood might be painted, but a clear finish on a good hardwood would be attractive. The back is shown as plywood, but if you want to be more authentic in the reproduction, use thin, vertical boards.

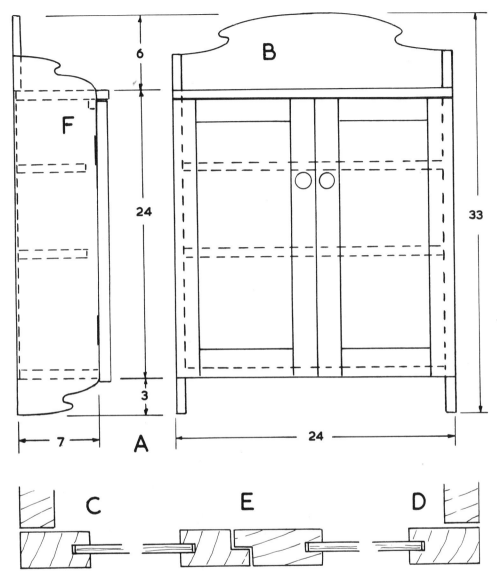

Fig. 6-24. Sizes and door sections for the double-door cabinet.

Mark out the sides first (FIG. 6-25A). Rabbet the rear edge for the plywood, and widen the rabbet above the top shelf for the upper back. The dado grooves for the top go across, the two shelf grooves stop at 6 inches, and the bottom fits into a stopped grove.

Make the bottom level with the front (FIG. 6-25B) and the shelves the same length. Make the top (FIG. 6-25C) wide enough to overhang the doors slightly, and cut it around the sides. The upper back (FIG. 6-24B) fits above the top, to which it

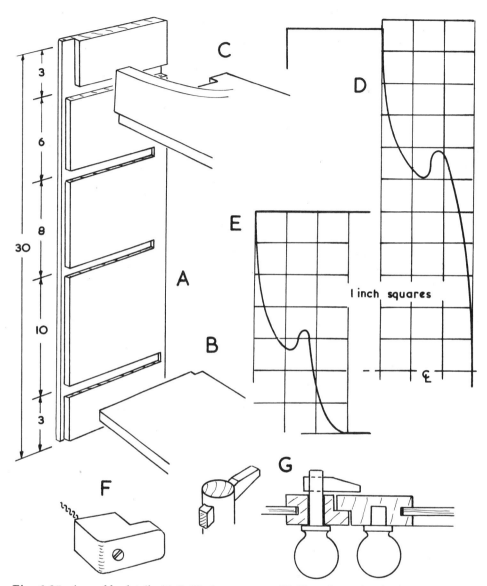

Fig. 6-25. *Assembly details (A,B,C) shapes to cut (D,E) and wooden fasteners (F,G).*

can be screwed from below. Shape it (FIG. 6-25D) and cut the ends of the sides to match (FIG. 6-25E) .

When you assemble, use screws or nails diagonally up through some joints to supplement the glue. Have the back ready so it can be fitted to keep the assembly square.

The framed doors could have plywood panels (FIG. 6-24C), or you could make raised panels from solid wood, particularly if you are using an attractive hardwood. Make the doors to come under the top with a little clearance. At the bottom, it would be better for the doors to extend about $1/8$ inch below the cabinet bottom than for part of it to show. At the sides, allow for the doors fitting over (FIG. 6-24D), and let in two 3-inch hinges.

On the front surfaces, the sides and top of each door are 2 inches wide. The bottom looks better 3 inches wide. At the center, the door stiles have overlapping rabbets. To keep the 2-inch front width, one stile has to be wider by the amount of overlap (FIG. 6-24E).

Groove the wood for the panels, and cut the rabbets so the front surfaces will close level. Use mortises and tenons at the corners. The doors will shut against the cabinet bottom. Put a strip across at the top (FIG. 6-24F) to act as a dust stop.

To fasten the doors, you can use a metal bolt inside the door with the wider stile, downwards into a hole, then the other door can have a knob with a catch to turn and hold it.

You can make wooden catches similar to those often used on early doors. Instead of the bottom bolt, make a turn button on a screw at the top (FIG. 6-25F) to close behind the dust strip. For the other door, turn a knob with a dowel long enough to go through and have a catch slotted in (FIG. 6-25G). Make a matching knob without the extension for the other door.

Corner Fixtures

A corner is a good place for displaying china or trophies, so a glass-fronted cabinet is appropriate. The lower part can have a wooden door (FIG. 6-26A).

Although a traditional corner cupboard of this type would have been made of solid wood, this is probably best made today out of manufactured board with veneered faces and lipped edges of matching wood (FIG. 6-26B). The piece is shown with a step between the two levels, which necessitates a special joint in the lipping if you wish to avoid exposed end grain (FIG. 6-26C).

After the two main parts are lipped along their exposed edges, they are joined in the angle, and the other parts are made to fit between them. If the corner of the room is less than a right angle and the cupboard is made a right angle, the front will fit closely and the gap at the back will not show. If the corner is wider than a right angle, a gap at the front will show. Put the main parts in position and temporarily fasten them, then check the angle that will have to be used for the parts between them.

Wings extend from the main parts, and the doors hang on the wings. Shelves inside can reach the wings, but they should be cut back to give clearance to the doors (FIG. 6-27A). If glass shelves are used in the upper part, they can rest on narrow battens or hooked studs (FIG. 6-27B). The glass-paneled doors should have tenoned joints to resist any tendency to flex and possibly break the glass. The glass is held by a rabbet with beads (FIG. 6-27C).

If you use the usual manufactured board, about $5/8$ inch thick, the door framing should be about $1^7/8 \times 7/8$ inches and the wings should be this size or slightly thicker to provide stiffness where they support the door hinges.

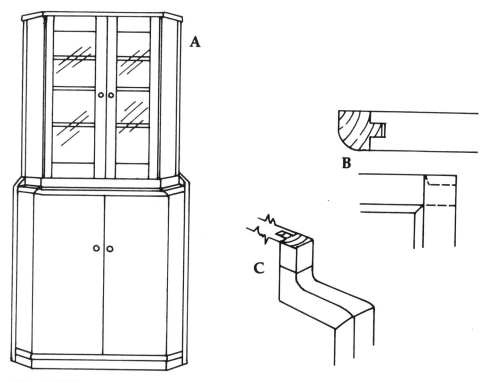

Fig. 6-26. The corner of a room is often wasted; a display cupboard is attractive and useful.

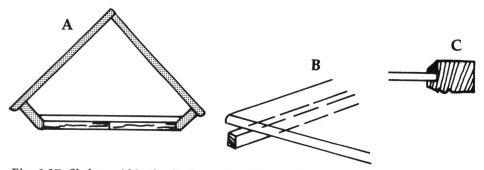

Fig. 6-27. Shelves within the display cupboard have to be cut back to clear the doors (A). If glass shelves are used (B), they can be cut back to clear the doors (C) resist flexing.

It is sometimes possible to extend a corner cabinet along one or both walls. The capacity of a corner cupboard with short wings is slight, but this increases as the wings become wider (or deeper). The door size is reduced, however. If there are extensions, you can enlarge the wings until they and the door are about the same width (FIG. 6-28A).

How the extensions are arranged depends on the room and the purpose. Such an assembly can often be made to accommodate a record player and its speakers. It can also serve as a sideboard or bookcase. If you have things that you would like to display, some of the doors can be sliding glass. A possible layout is shown in FIG. 6-28B. Although there could be the usual plinth, this example is shown on short legs.

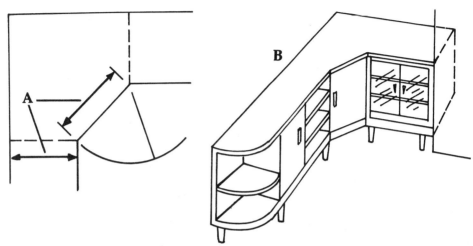

Fig. 6-28. *In a corner assembly, access to the corner has to be considered, the feet have to be high enough for cleaning, and a member to tie parts together should be included.*

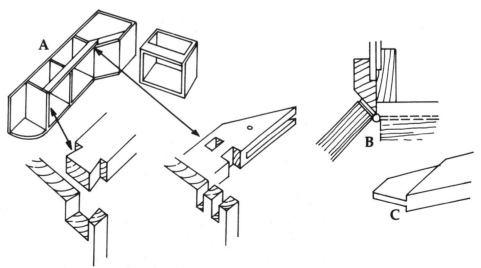

Fig. 6-29. *In this example the glass-fronted case is built as a separate unit.*

This sort of built-in furniture can be prefabricated in units—the corner and two separate extensions, or the corner as part of one side and the other extension separate (FIG. 6-29A). In any case, the top is best treated as a whole and applied after the lower parts are fixed. The meeting parts of units can be faced with hardboard or plywood, providing front edges will be covered to hide this. A point to watch with a corner door and extensions is that there is sufficient clearance for the door to swing back without fouling. It is advisable to set back the extension on the hinge side slightly (FIG. 6-29B).

With this sort of assembly, it is always good practice to arrange some of the structural parts to tie the assembly together. In the case of an extension-and-corner assembly, a front rail can be recessed and screwed in place, or it can be dovetailed at its end. Double tenons can come at intermediate vertical parts. The strength can be carried around the corner with a bridle joint (FIG. 6-29C).

Chest with Trays

In some communities, particularly the Pennsylvania Dutch, there were bride's chests, or hope chests, in which a girl put the things she had made in anticipation of marriage. Similar chests were used for general storage. Smaller boxes made in the same way could be used on a table for jewelry. Painted decoration was used by the Pennsylvania Dutch, but other chests were made of good-quality wood and finished by polishing. The stark outline of a rectangular box was broken by shaped feet and some molded edges.

The specimen in FIG. 6-30A is of moderate size, but originals were in all sizes, from those to be carried in one hand to blanket boxes. You could nail corners and hide the holes with stopping, but dovetails are better. Enclose the bottom within the sides and ends. You can use plywood or other manufactured board for the bottom since its edges are covered and it would not be easily identified. Thinner material might have supporting battens underneath (FIG. 6-30B).

A plinth goes around the bottom with a small overlap and with much of the lower edge cut away to leave supports at the corners. Miter corners and put blocks inside to strengthen the joints and provide extra bearing surfaces on the floor (FIG. 6-30C). You can mold the top edge of the plinth or fix a separate strip of molding around with glue and thin nails or pins (FIG. 6-30D).

The lid can be a single stout board, preferably cut with the end showing grain lines vertical, so there will be the minimum of risk of warping. Mold the edge and place strips around below it to provide a dust seal to the box; the whole top should have enough overlap on the carcass of the chest to allow for this (FIG. 6-30E).

The rear edge of the top is not molded, but it should finish level with the box back so it will swing up on its hinges.

Some of these chests had a single fixed compartment inside at one end. This did not interfere with reaching into the bottom of the box, but it provided a place for small items (FIG. 6-30F). In the best construction, the side and bottom of the compartment are let into the sides and end of the chest (FIG. 6-30G). You must

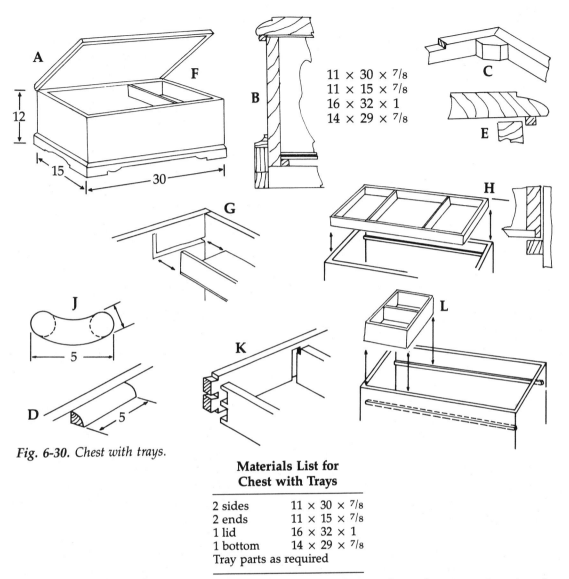

A

12

15 — 30

B

$11 \times 30 \times \frac{7}{8}$
$11 \times 15 \times \frac{7}{8}$
$16 \times 32 \times 1$
$14 \times 29 \times \frac{7}{8}$

F

C

E

H

G

J

5

D

5

K

L

Fig. 6-30. Chest with trays.

**Materials List for
Chest with Trays**

2 sides	$11 \times 30 \times \frac{7}{8}$
2 ends	$11 \times 15 \times \frac{7}{8}$
1 lid	$16 \times 32 \times 1$
1 bottom	$14 \times 29 \times \frac{7}{8}$
Tray parts as required	

make the grooves before you assemble the chest and put the compartment parts in before you fit the second side. The side of the compartment should have its top edge well rounded in cross section. You can hollow it at the center.

An alternative arrangement has a lift-out tray. In some chests, this was full size, so it had to be lifted out to get at the lower part of the box (FIG. 6-30H). You can arrange compartments in this tray to suit the contents. If you can arrange divisions conveniently, you can cut handholds in them for lifting (FIG. 6-30J); otherwise you should make in the ends of the tray or fix blocks there for lifting (FIG. 6-30K). The tray rests on strips of wood across the ends or the sides—there is no need to fit them all around.

Another arrangement has one or two trays resting on lengthwise strips, so a tray can slide along or be lifted out to aid access to the bottom of the box (FIG. 6-30L). In addition to household use, this was a common arrangement in tool chests. Dovetail the corners of trays if possible, and round the top edges of the trays and any dividers. Bottoms of trays would have been solid wood cut thin, but they could be plywood if they have their edges hidden by letting into rabbets. For jewelry or precision tools, you can line the bottoms of trays with cloth or rubber.

Paneled Chest

Early settlers were fortunate in finding trees of sufficient thickness to cut broad boards. The equipment they had for cutting was more appropriate to producing heavy stock, so most early chests are of quite stout construction, with parts often thicker than might really be justified if strength was the only consideration. The wood had to be prepared that way, however. As people became more established and towns were set up with more of the amenities of civilization, the plain and sometimes crude furniture was not wanted. Along with the demand for better furniture came better woodworking facilities. Sawmills were set up and wood of more delicate section could be provided. The cabinetmaker was able to equip his shop with more than the basic hand equipment, although for a very long time nearly all of the operations he performed depended on hand or foot power.

The newer furniture had to be lighter and better looking. Chests were still important in the home, and cedar in particular was valued for making chests to store blankets and clothing.

One type of chest that evolved had the sides and ends paneled. This was not new; medieval furniture had many examples of paneled construction. Without our modern plywood for wide panels, there was an everpresent problem of wide pieces of wood expanding and contracting with changes in moisture content resulting from atmospheric variations. Panels in a frame, however, could be arranged so expansion and contraction across the grain could take place without affecting appearance. Variations in the direction of the grain were so slight as to be negligible.

The making of paneled furniture by hand called for a considerable amount of skill and some hard work. With a modern table saw, much of the work can be done with greater precision and much less labor. Other power tools also have their uses in this type of work, but a modern hand plow plane will do much of the grooving better than the earlier tools could.

The chest shown in FIG. 6-31A has single panels at the ends and sides made up of three similar panels. It would be possible to overlap assembled side panels on the ends in the same way as chests made from solid boards. Some chests were made this way, but this chest has corner legs. If you make variations, be sure that the faces of the legs, the upright stiles, and the top rails are all the same width on each side or end of the chest, and that the bottom rail is wider. If you make the bottom rail the same width as the other faces, an optical illusion will make it look

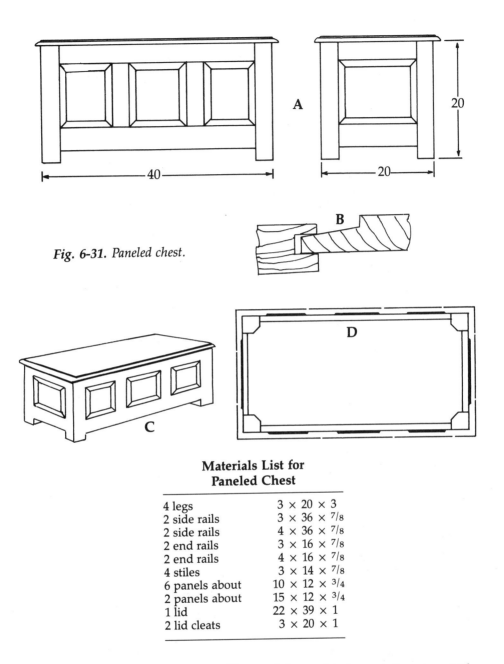

Fig. 6-31. Paneled chest.

A

B

C

D

**Materials List for
Paneled Chest**

4 legs	$3 \times 20 \times 3$
2 side rails	$3 \times 36 \times 7/8$
2 side rails	$4 \times 36 \times 7/8$
2 end rails	$3 \times 16 \times 7/8$
2 end rails	$4 \times 16 \times 7/8$
4 stiles	$3 \times 14 \times 7/8$
6 panels about	$10 \times 12 \times 3/4$
2 panels about	$15 \times 12 \times 3/4$
1 lid	$22 \times 39 \times 1$
2 lid cleats	$3 \times 20 \times 1$

narrower and spoil the appearance. There might need to be variations to suit the widths of wood available for panels. Having a center side panel wider than the two that border it looks good, but a narrower center panel between wider panels is not as attractive.

The panels have raised centers. Do not cut these until after you prepare the other parts. It is necessary, however, to examine the wood available and decide on sizes. The raised center of each panel is surrounded by what was called fielding. This slight taper is fit into a groove made deeper than needed for a close fit (FIG. 6-31B). As the wood expands or contracts, it moves in and out of the groove. If the panels are 3/4 inch thick, it should be satisfactory to settle on grooves 3/8 inch wide throughout the assembly.

The design is shown with all edges square. It is unwise to try to incorporate molding around the framing as this complicates the joints. All that is needed is for the sharpness (the arrises) to be sanded off just before assembly, particularly along those edges that will frame the panels.

The top is the only part that can have its appearance relieved by molding (FIG. 6-31C). The legs are square, but inside the chest it looks better if they have the inner angle taken off (FIG. 6-31D). You can cut this angle right through so the feet are the same shape, or stop at the bottom to leave the projecting feet square.

Like any other cabinetmaking project consisting of a great many parts, tackle the preparation systematically. It is advisable to collect the wood for all parts, then cut and plane at least the vital structural parts to width and thickness. There will be a few parts, like the bottom and panels, that you will not work to size until they can be fit into other parts, but you can prepare them to thickness.

The next work should be grooving. The legs, rails, and stiles have similar grooves, which all need to be at the same distance from the front (face) surfaces (FIG. 6-32A). Joints could be doweled, but the early cabinetmaker always used mortise-and-tenon joints. If you choose 3/8 inch for the width of the groove, you can simplify the marking out and cutting of the joints by also using that measurement for the width of the mortise. The top rails go about 1 1/2 inches into the legs. Haunch them to fit the grooves (FIG. 6-32B). The joints for the bottom rails can be similar, although a 4-inch width is better arranged with two tenons (FIG. 6-32C). Where the stiles go into the rails, that tenon is the width between the bottoms of the grooves (FIG. 6-32D).

With grooves cut where needed, place parts requiring similar distances together and mark across them with a try square, so all distances that have to match actually will do so. Put the legs together. Mark across their length, but do not cut the ends close to the marks until after other work has been done. Use the ends of rails as guides to their widths and mark the positions of the mortises (FIG. 6-32E). You can use marks on the legs as guides for marking the stiles for their tenons—it is the distance between the shoulders that is important (FIG. 6-32F).

Mark the edges of the four lengthwise rails together and do the same with the four end rails. In all of these parts, it is the distances between shoulders that are important, and you should cut these around the wood with a knife. Slight variations in overall length affecting the tenons are not so important. Cut the tenons by hand or with a table saw. Drill out some of the waste from the mortises and chop them to shape with a chisel. It is best to not make a complete trial assembly because this might cause wear in the joints, and they might not fit as closely in the final assembly.

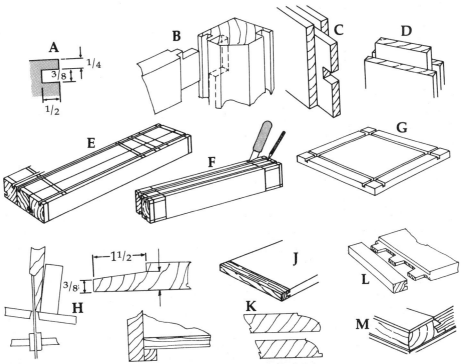

Fig. 6-32. *Constructional details of the paneled chest, showing frame joints (A – F), panel details (G,H), the bottom (J), and lid shaping (K-M).*

Measurements from these parts will give the overall sizes of the panels. In the widths, allow for the panels to have approximately a 1/8-inch clearance above the bottoms of the grooves. Lengths can be similar, but as later variations along the grain will be slight, the wood can be a closer fit that way.

How to cut the fielding around the panels depends on the available equipment. The outline of the raised part of the panel is best cut around with a plowed groove (FIG. 6-32G). It might be necessary to cut deeply across the grain with a knife and make the groove on the waste side of this to avoid grain fibers breaking out. You can then cut the fielding with a table saw having a tilt arrangement (FIG. 6-32H). Leave a little to be removed by handwork with a shoulder plane, followed by sanding with abrasive paper wrapped around a wood block. You must remove machine marks, and uniformity of the four sections of fielding around a panel are important for appearance. Corners then will show neat miters between the bevels. These panels are the main decorative features of the chest, so they should be given as good a tool and sanded finish as possible.

If you plan to stain the chest, deal with the panels before assembly; otherwise, shrinkage after assembly could show plain wood at the edges.

It is advisable to deal with assembly in two stages. Glue alone should be adequate, provided sufficient clamps are available. Some early chests had the joints secured with pegs or dowels. This can be done, particularly if it is necessary to move a clamp on after pulling a joint together. The dowel ends can be regarded as a design feature.

Put the panels and stiles between the lengthwise rails, then add the legs. With all these joints pulled close, check squareness by measuring diagonals before leaving the back and front for the glue to set. Sight along to check for twisted assembly. If you place the back over front in the relative positions they will eventually be, you can check them to match and hold them flat with boards and weights over them. Put newspaper between in case any glue oozes out and joins the two parts.

When the glue has set, clean off any surplus, particularly inside. If there is any unevenness inside, level the surfaces. It is easier to deal with inner surfaces at this stage than after the ends have been added. Put the end panels in place between their rails and assemble to the legs. Check the end assemblies for squareness. Have the chest standing so the four legs rest on a surface known to be flat. Measure diagonally across the tops of the legs to see that the chest is square in plain view. Stand well back and sight across the two ends and then the two sides to see there is no twist; then leave the assembly for the end glued parts to set.

The bottom fits inside. Solid wood was arranged with several boards having their grain across the box and resting on strips inside the bottom rails (FIG. 6-32J). If the rest of the chest is made of cedar for storing blankets or linen, it would be advisable to use thin cedar boards for the bottom, but for other purposes you can use plywood.

The lid could be a plain board, but it would need battens underneath to reduce warping, and this might be considered a rather crude method that would not match the more refined construction method of the rest of the chest. The better method is to tenon on cleats across the ends. A *cleat* is a strip of wood with its grain across the direction of the grain of the top (FIG. 6-32K).

A groove across the cleat has a matching tongue on the top, which extends in two or three places to deeper tenons (FIG. 6-32L). The number of tenons depends on the width, but in this case three should suit. To get a good fit, it is simplest to have the cleat too long and too thick; then you can work it to exact size after fitting. Molding around the top has to be carried around the cleat (FIG. 6-32M), which calls for care where lengthwise grain changes to end grain at the joints.

The lid should swing on three strong hinges, preferably of the strap type, bent to bring their knuckles outside. Although earlier chests rarely had locks or were fitted with staples, this later type might have a proper box lock let into the front to engage with a plate under the lid. This ties in with the more advanced cabinetmaking standard of this chest compared with the earlier ones.

Paneled Cabinet

Framed plywood allows attractive furniture to be made economically and without using very much solid wood. Grooves must be made for the plywood with a table saw or by other means. If you have facilities for doing that, construction is straightforward. The framed panels may be joined with dowels for a strong assembly.

This cabinet (FIG. 6-33) is made by assembling several framed plywood panels, then joining them with dowels. The top, shelf, and bottom are solid wood or thicker plywood with solid wood edging. All of the framing is 1-inch × 2-inch section, and the plywood panels are 3/8-inch thick.

The sizes (FIG. 6-34A) are for a cabinet at table height and of a suitable size for use in the home or shop, but variations would not affect the method of building. A furniture-quality hardwood and veneered plywood would make a cabinet to

Fig. 6-33. *This floor-standing cabinet makes use of framed plywood panels.*

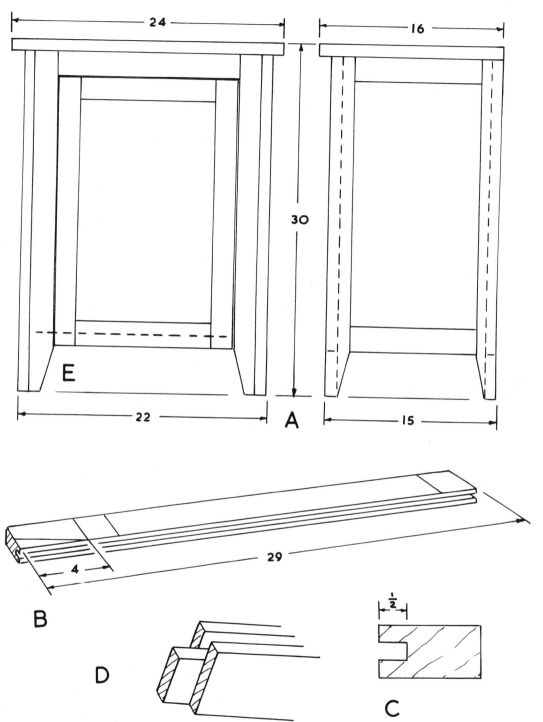

Fig. 6-34. Sizes and frame details of the paneled cabinet.

Materials List for Paneled Cabinet

8 legs	1 × 2 × 30
4 rails	1 × 2 × 15
3 rails	1 × 2 × 22
2 shelf bearers	1 × 2 × 15
1 top	1 × 16 × 25
2 door sides	1 × 2 × 24
2 door rails	1 × 2 × 14
2 panels	13 × 24 × 3/8 plywood
1 panel	18 × 24 × 3/8 plywood
1 panel	14 × 22 × 3/8 plywood
1 shelf	10 × 22 × 3/4 plywood
1 bottom	13 × 22 × 3/4 plywood

match other furniture. Softwood may be used for a painted finish. A cabinet with a strong, solid top can form the base for a machine in your shop.

The back, front, and side panels all have similar legs (FIG. 6-34B), except that the front legs do not need grooves. Make the grooves to suit your plywood and 1/2 inch deep (FIG. 6-34C). Cut the shaped feet on the legs.

Make the rails to fit between the legs, with tenons to fit tightly in the grooves (FIG. 6-34D). Start with the pair of side framed panels (FIG. 6-35A). Cut the plywood to size and assemble the sides to match each other.

Cut the rails for the back. Make a similar one without a groove for the front. Front and back fit between the sides (FIGS. 6-34E and 6-35B). Assemble the back. Cut mortises for the rail in the tops of the front legs. Mark and drill for 3/8-inch dowels, at about 6-inch intervals, where the legs will meet.

If there is to be a shelf, put bearers on each side, cut back to clear the front and back legs (FIG. 6-35C). Make the bearers this length, even if the shelf is to be narrower.

Prepare the bottom (FIG. 6-35D) to fit between the bottom rails of the sides and back and inside the front legs. If you use 3/4-inch plywood, put a solid wood lip across the front for the sake of appearance in better quality work. Drill for dowels into the rails and the front legs.

Glue and dowel the parts together. The bottom should hold the parts square, but see that the assembly stands level.

The shelf can just rest in place, if you want it removable, or it can be screwed to its bearers to provide additional stiffening.

Make the top (FIG. 6-35E) level with the back, if the cabinet is to come close to a wall, and overhanging about 1 inch on front and sides. Plywood can be lipped with solid wood. For a solid top, glue together sufficient boards. Edges can be molded, if you wish. Fit the top with glue and dowels. One dowel in each leg top and one or two intermediately on each rail are enough.

Make the door in a similar way to the main panels. Its size should allow it to fit easily between the front legs and overhang the cabinet bottom. Use two 2-inch hinges at one side, and fit a handle and fastener at the other side.

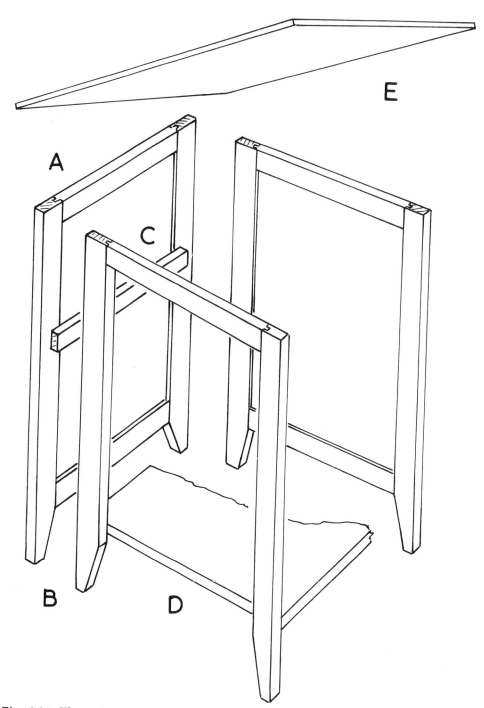

Fig. 6-35. *The main parts of the paneled cabinet.*

Angled Bookcase

Do you get frustrated when trying to read the title, or pull out a book from the bottom shelf of the usual upright bookcase? The only way to identify some books is to crawl on the floor. This problem can be solved by making the racks at angles, which bring the backs of the books into positions where the titles are more easily read; then you can remove the one you want with no difficulty.

This bookcase (FIG. 6-36) has its bottom rack tilted at 30 degrees, the middle rack at 15 degrees, and the top rack level. The bottom shelf is intended for books up to 8 inches × 10 inches; the middle rack will take them almost as big; and the top rack will suit page sizes of 6 inches × 8 inches. Above that is a shelf to take all the other things that most people want to put on a bookcase.

To accommodate books of these sizes and at the specified angles, the ends have to be fairly wide. If your books are smaller or if different angles would suit your need, you can lay out the pattern to use narrower ends. This design is intended for solid wood. Construction is with dowels.

Materials List for Angled Bookcase

2 ends	48 × 15 × 1
1 top shelf	30 × 8 × 3/4
1 top rack	30 × 6 × 3/4
1 top rack	30 × 5 × 3/4
1 middle rack	30 × 9 × 3/4
1 middle rack	30 × 6 × 3/4
1 bottom rack	30 × 9 × 3/4
1 bottom rack	30 × 7 × 3/4

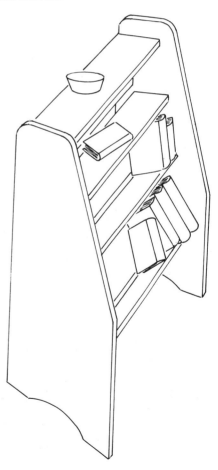

Fig. 6-36. This bookcase has its lower shelves angled so the contents are more easily seen.

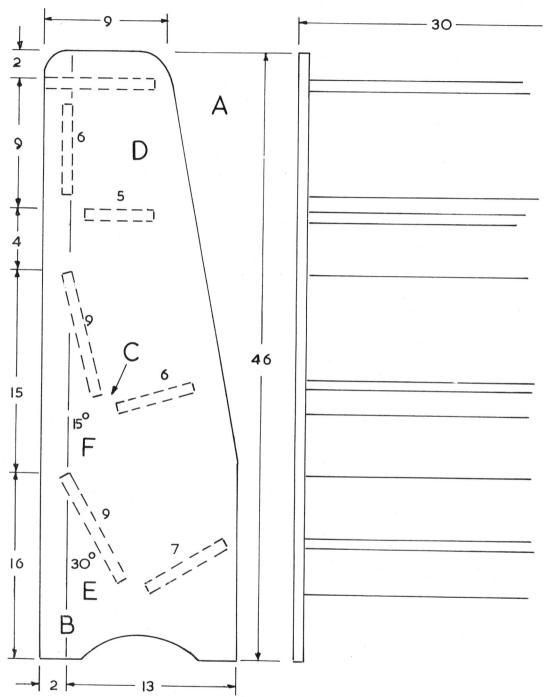

Fig. 6-37. Sizes of the angled bookcase.

The key part that controls the layout is an end (FIG. 6-37A). Work from the rear edge and have a square line at the bottom. Draw a line 2 inches from the rear edge, and mark on it the distances shown (FIG. 6-37B). Imagine the shapes of books and work from them. At the inner corners of a book, the rack parts are cut 1 inch from it (FIGS. 6-37C and 6-38A).

The top shelf and the rack below it are marked square (FIG. 6-37D). Draw in the full outlines of the ends of the pieces to avoid confusion when locating dowel holes.

For the other two racks, start by drawing lines at 30 degrees and 15 degrees from the marked points. Use these angled lines and the imaginary square-cornered book to draw in the outlines of the rack part (FIGS. 6-37E and 6-37F).

Mark the rack positions on both ends, then mark and cut the outlines. Round all edges, except those that touch the floor.

Make the lengthwise pieces, matching their widths to the marked positions on the ends. Keep all lengths exactly the same, if joints are to pull tight and assembly is to be square.

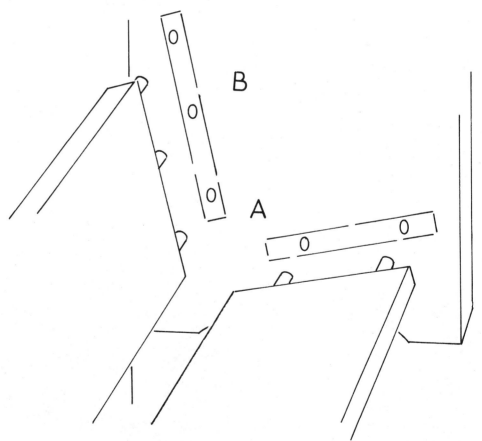

Fig. 6-38. Assembly details of the angled bookcase.

Mark and drill for 3/8-inch or 1/2-inch dowels (FIG. 6-38B). Clamp tightly when you glue the parts together. The assembly should pull square, but check that there is no twist and that the bookcase will stand firm on a level surface. Finish to suit the wood or to match other furniture.

Stepped Bookcase

The plainness of a block of shelves to hold books can be eased by arranging them in steps. This bookcase (FIG. 6-39) has one straight upright end. The other end is stepped so there are short ledges for vases or ornaments. Although intended to hold books, the shelves are equally suitable for other things. Because the back is not fully closed, there are strips to prevent books pushing through and to keep other articles in place. These strips also provide stiffness and prevent the bookcase from being pushed out of shape or the shelf joints from being strained. The stepped ends are arranged to extend slightly above the ledges to prevent anything from slipping off.

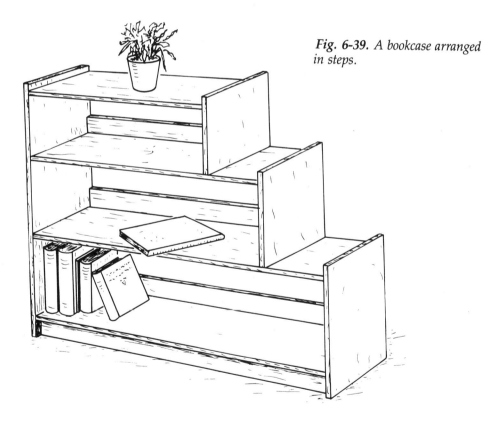

Fig. 6-39. A bookcase arranged in steps.

Materials List for
Stepped Bookcase

2 shelves	$3/4 \times 8 \times 30$
1 shelf	$3/4 \times 8 \times 25$
1 shelf	$3/4 \times 8 \times 20$
1 side	$3/4 \times 8 \times 35$
1 side	$3/4 \times 8 \times 16$
1 side	$3/4 \times 8 \times 12$
1 side	$3/4 \times 8 \times 10$
1 plinth	$3/4 \times 3 \times 30$
1 back	$3/4 \times 3 \times 30$
1 back	$3/4 \times 3 \times 25$
1 back	$3/4 \times 3 \times 20$

Sizes could be varied, or the bookcase could be made the other way around to suit your room arrangements. If it is made much larger, the shelf thickness should be increased to resist bending. A load of books can be quite heavy.

The bookcase could be made of solid wood, although this method of construction is particularly suitable for veneered particleboard. It would be possible to use dado joints in solid wood, but for particleboard and solid wood, dowels are more suitable. For most joints, 3/8-inch dowels spaced 3 inches apart are appropriate.

Mark out the tall side (FIG. 6-40A) with the positions and thicknesses of all parts shown. Use this as a guide when marking all other upright pieces.

Mark out the three stepped sides (FIGS. 6-40B, 6-40C, and 6-40D) from the tall side. Make sure all tops and sides stand the same amount above the shelves. If using solid wood, square and smooth the tops of the sides. Their corners could be rounded. If using veneered particleboard, veneer the tops to match the edges and surfaces.

Cut the shelving to length (FIGS. 6-40E, 6-40F, 6-40G, and 6-40H) and make the plinth (FIG. 6-40J) and back strips to the same lengths.

Mark where the upper two sides will stand on their shelves, using the shorter shelves as a guide to distances.

Locate where the parts will come in assembly (FIG. 6-41) and mark and drill for dowels. Drill as deeply as possible in the side surfaces.

Assembly can be done in one gluing session. It helps to drive and glue all the dowels into the ends of boards first. Work from the bottom of the bookcase upwards, fitting the shelves and other crosswise parts between sides.

Check squareness and sight across the back to see that there is no twist. Leave the assembly on its back or standing on a flat surface until the glue sets. Clean off surplus glue and apply a finish.

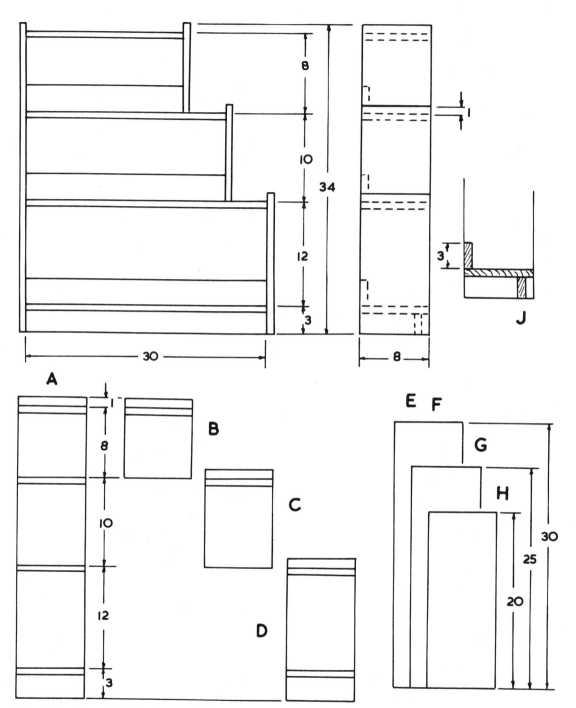

Fig. 6-40. Sizes of the bookcase with details of the stepped parts.

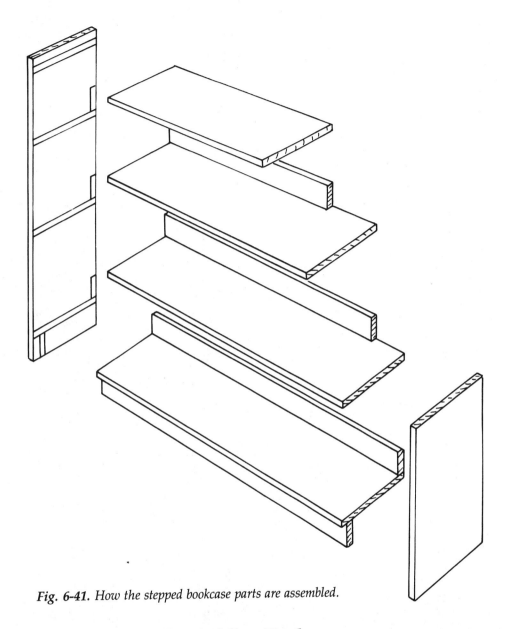

Fig. 6-41. How the stepped bookcase parts are assembled.

Folding Desk

A desk or work top is a useful piece of furniture for dealing with home accounts or doing school work, sewing, or a hobby. But when it is not in use, it might take up too much room. The desk in FIG. 6-47 has a pedestal cabinet with storage space and a long kneehole working area that can be folded with its leg against the side of the cabinet when it is not in use.

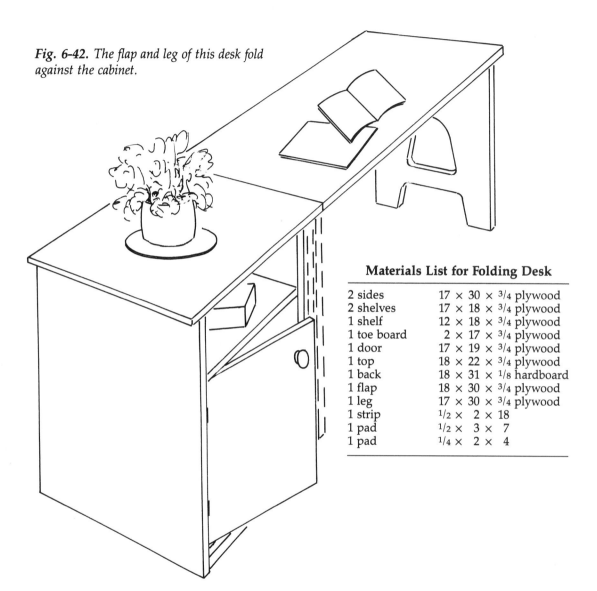

Fig. 6-42. *The flap and leg of this desk fold against the cabinet.*

Materials List for Folding Desk

2 sides	17 × 30 × 3/4 plywood
2 shelves	17 × 18 × 3/4 plywood
1 shelf	12 × 18 × 3/4 plywood
1 toe board	2 × 17 × 3/4 plywood
1 door	17 × 19 × 3/4 plywood
1 top	18 × 22 × 3/4 plywood
1 back	18 × 31 × 1/8 hardboard
1 flap	18 × 30 × 3/4 plywood
1 leg	17 × 30 × 3/4 plywood
1 strip	1/2 × 2 × 18
1 pad	1/2 × 3 × 7
1 pad	1/4 × 2 × 4

When opened for use, the top is 18 inches wide × 51 inches. When folded, the cabinet top area is 18 inches × 22 inches, with all the lower parts within that area. Height in both cases is 30 inches. The cabinet is described with an open shelf above a cupboard, but you could equip it with drawers or in any other way to suit tools or whatever you wish to store.

Most parts are 3/4-inch plywood. The back of the cabinet is hardboard or thin plywood. If the desk is to form part of the furnishings of a living room, the plywood for the top and exposed parts would look best if veneered with attractive wood or plastic, with matching edging ironed on. A wood lip on the top would be better able to keep its appearance after long use.

Joints could be glued and screwed, with the heads counterbored and plugged, or you could use 5/16-inch dowels at about 3-inch intervals. If you alter sizes, the length of the flap and its leg have to be related to the height of the cabinet. The cabinet is of straightforward construction and should be completed first. The depth is 17 inches from front to back, including the hardboard. The top overhangs 1 inch at one side and at the front, and extends 3 inches at the side where the flap will hinge (FIG. 6-43A), which could be on either side.

Make the two cabinet sides (FIG. 6-44A). Mark on the positions of other parts.

Cut the pieces that go crosswise to the same length. The shelf (FIG. 6-44B) and the cupboard bottom (FIG. 6-44C) are the same width as the sides. The middle shelf can be 12 inches wide (FIG. 6-44D). The toeboard is set back a little (FIG. 6-44E).

Mark dowel positions on the cabinet pieces or prepare them for screwing. Assemble with glue between meeting surfaces.

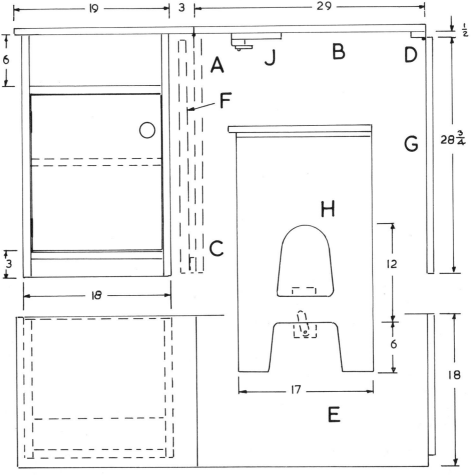

Fig. 6-43. Suggested sizes for the folding desk.

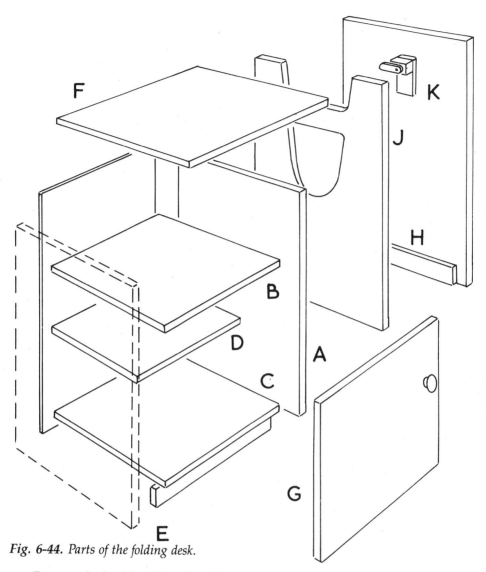

Fig. 6-44. *Parts of the folding desk.*

Prepare the back hardboard with enough at the top to go over the cabinet top later. Glue and screw it in position to keep the assembly square.

Prepare the cabinet top (FIG. 6-44F) with any surface veneer and edging. Fix it to the sides with dowels. Screw the hardboard to it.

The door (FIG. 6-44G) should be cut to fit in the opening easily. Use two 2-inch hinges at one side. Put a knob or handle at the other side, high enough to be reached comfortably. Fit a spring or magnetic catch, or you might prefer a lock.

Make the length of the flap 1/4 inch less than the cabinet height under its top (FIG. 6-43B), so it can swing down without rubbing the floor (FIG. 6-43C). It is a simple rectangular piece finished to match the cabinet top.

To give clearance for the leg to fold, it is necessary to thicken the outer end of the flap. A strip about 2 inches wide and $1/2$ inch thick will do (FIGS. 6-43D and 6-44H) and can be plywood or solid wood.

The leg is the same width as the cabinet. Its length must be sufficient to hold the flap level, yet it has to fold inside the flap (FIG. 6-43E and 6-43F). The $1/2$-inch packing on the flap allows the length to be $1/4$ inch less than the length of the flap (FIG. 6-43G).

Cut away the leg to form two feet (FIG. 6-43H). The exact shape cutout is not important, but include a crossbar (FIG. 6-44J).

When the desk is folded, the leg should be held to the flap, then gravity will ensure that it hangs vertically without fastening. Put a $1/2$-inch strip pad under the flap to come behind the folded leg and extend 2 inches for $3/4$-inch thickening piece (FIGS. 6-43 and 6-44K). Arrange the pad so you can use a thin wood turn button to secure the leg when the leg hinges under the flap.

Hinge the flap to the cabinet top and the leg to the thickening piece on the flap with two 2-inch hinges at each place, and test the folding action. You might wish to remove the hinges while you finish the wood. You could use a dark stain, followed by varnish or polish. You also could paint the lower parts and put a clear finish on the top, if it is attractively veneered.

You might find the leg stands upright without further support, but you could attach a folding metal strut to the rear edges of the flap and leg.

Divider with Table

A divider might also incorporate other things. There can be a flap to swing down to form a writing desk, with compartments for stationery hidden behind it. A cocktail cabinet can be built in. A stereo system can be permanently installed with speakers at the ends of the divider.

To include a table at a useful height, there has to be a part at about 30 inches above the floor (FIG. 6-45) big enough to provide space for the table. How the rest of the divider is made depends on requirements; it could be made in any of the ways already suggested, but the example shown provides some more ideas.

The main part of the divider is made as already described, with shelves securely fixed into the uprights. It can be treated as a unit, except for the extension of the top. The tabletop is round, with a center part wide enough to overlap the divider shelf sufficiently for the extension pieces to hang down when not required (FIG. 6-46A). Although it could be made from solid wood, it is probably better made of blockboard or particleboard with a suitable veneer.

At the center, there should be a bolt to pass down through the shelf. The bolt head can be recessed into the wood and secured with a plate. The bolt head must be prevented from turning. If it is carefully set into the wood, that might provide sufficient grip, or it can be brazed or welded to the plate. A locknut keeps the bolt from loosening.

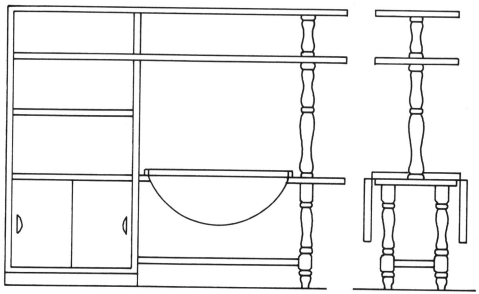

Fig. 6-45. A room divider can be embellished by turning. This divider includes a round folding table unit.

To ensure smooth action, affix a piece of stout cloth plastic or rubber sheeting with adhesive under the tabletop (FIG. 6-46B). This can cover the part of the shelf that will be under the tabletop. You could use a piece of about a 6-inch diameter around the bolt, and strips farther out towards the circumference of the tabletop. Having separate pieces is best if the hinges project at all under the top.

The hinges should be back flaps. These will swing back more than normal hinges so that the table flaps can hang down (FIG. 6-46C).

Traditional drop-leaf tables have the meeting edges worked with a rule-joint molding (FIG. 6-46D). (This can be done in solid wood, but manufactured boards cannot be shaped satisfactorily in this way.) If you want rule-joint molding, the total effect is improved if the table edge is also molded (FIG. 6-46E). To bring the table into use, the flaps are lifted and the top turned through a right angle.

In the example, the shelf supporting the table has rails underneath and two legs. The legs can be square, preferably with a slight taper, but turned legs complement the round tabletop (FIG. 6-47A). The legs are joined with a lower piece that takes the end of a central rail. This allows more leg room for anyone sitting at the table than if the divider had been continued full width.

What comes above the table depends on the design and size of the divider. If it is not very high, there need be nothing extending from the main block. A shelf extending above the table without plenty of clearance might seem overpowering, but if the total height is perhaps 5 feet, it is possible to let the top extend and have another shelf below it. A pillar to support these shelves should carry through the design of the legs (FIG. 6-47B).

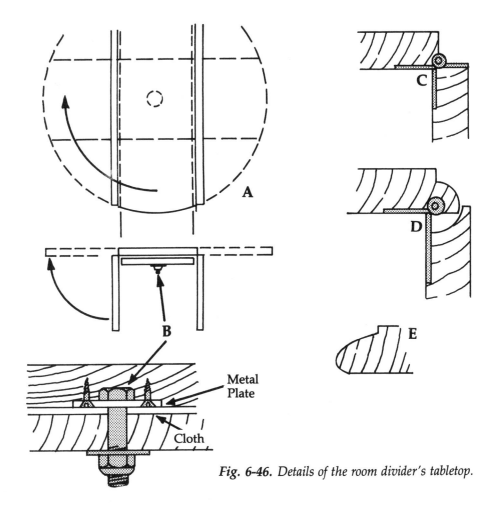

Fig. 6-46. Details of the room divider's tabletop.

In the example, sliding doors are shown. They could be plywood or glass. Sliding doors are often more convenient than swinging doors if space near the divider is restricted. However, swinging doors give better access to the interior, as sliding doors never expose more than half the inside.

For sliding doors in anything except the smallest sizes, it is best to buy a suitable door track and guides made of metal or plastic. Such guides provide a smoother action than anything that can be made from wood. If guides are made, pieces of hardwood can be grooved and screwed in place (FIG. 6-47C); then if the doors have to be removed, the screws can be withdrawn to release the guides.

Door edges, whether wood or glass, should be smooth and their corners rounded. The grooves should be sanded smooth and lubricated either with graphite (the end of a pencil) or candle wax—not oil or grease.

Although our ancestors probably never thought of room dividers, the effect of this piece of furniture with a round tabletop and turned legs and pillar is Jacobean. If this theme is to be carried through, the finish should be brown oak.

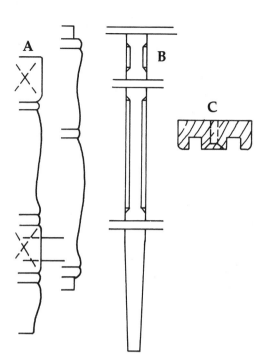

Fig. 6-47. *Turned legs complement the found tabletop; the design can be carried into the shelf supports (B). Guides that are screwed in allow easy door removal (C).*

Closed Backs

In most pieces of furniture the back is hidden and little care is lavished on its finish. If a divider is to have one side closed, the exposed side of the back paneling is at least as important as the side with shelves and doors. If it is to be hidden by wallpaper, it need not be of select veneer, but it should be flat and smooth. Even then, something might have to be done to break up the plainness of the surface.

At the top and wall edges, the plywood can merely overlap, but anywhere that this joint would show the edge of the plywood, it is best to have a rabbet (FIG. 6-48A).

The plainness of the back can be broken up by using moldings. You can cover the edge with molding, using mitered corners (FIG. 6-48B). If the finish is polish or varnish over veneer, a paneled appearance can be obtained by using another light molding (FIG. 6-48C).

Of course, there are other uses for a plain back. If there is a study or working area behind the divider, the back can have shelves and racks to suit what is being done there. In a bedroom this might be a place to hang clothing.

A divider gives the opportunity for a lot of new thinking about a room, and its design offers plenty of opportunity to express individuality.

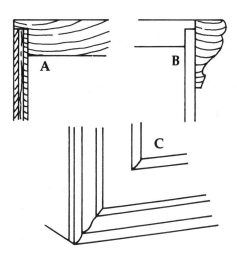

Fig. 6-48. A rabbeted joint at the top rear edge of the divider hides the plywood (A); the back can be made more attractive with molding (B). A paneled appearance could be obtained by using another molding (C).

Corner Dressing Table

In small bedrooms, consider the use of corners. In some arrangements there might be a little waste space in the point of the triangle, but this will be compensated for. A dressing-table mirror can come across the corner. It need not necessarily be at 45 degrees (FIG. 6-49A). If it is arranged at another angle, there could be some advantage in the use of limited light or space.

If you use a corner assembly, you must accept limitations of drawer shape and capacity. The dresser can have a front with the corners at right angles to the walls, then drawers can be taken as deep as the shape will allow (FIG. 6-49B)— narrow drawers going deeper than wide ones. If the corner is other than a right angle, the possible depth of a drawer becomes less, although this can be increased if the back of the drawer is cut on a slant (FIG. 6-49C).

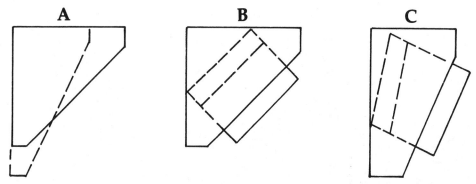

Fig. 6-49. A corner dressing table need not make a 45-degree angle with the walls (A). Drawers have to be arranged to make best use of the unusual geometry involved (B and C).

Check the angle of the room corner, and make either the actual top or a template to match. Never assume that the corner is truly a right angle.

If the dresser is to be removable, it can have a plywood back. Otherwise there need only be sufficient framing to support drawer guides and to take screws that fasten into the wall. If there is a base molding in the room, you can cut it back, or cut the dressing table to fit over it (FIG. 6-50A). It might also be pos-

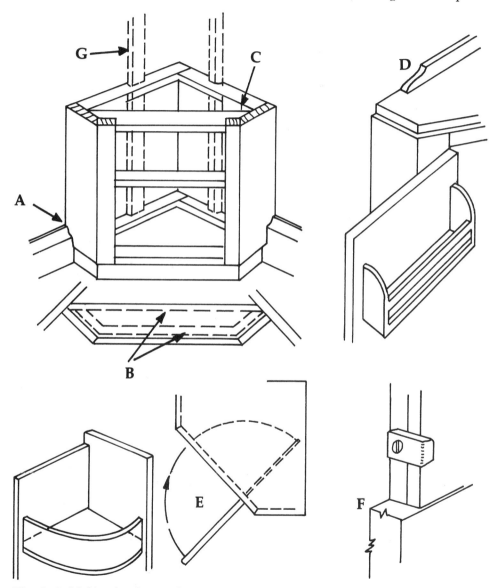

Fig. 6-50. Making furniture to fit a corner brings some special problems, but this dressing table takes up minimum space. It can be given drawers or doors.

sible to have the plinth at the same height as the base molding. It can follow the shape of the front or can be taken straight across (FIG. 6-50B).

The angular vertical joints at the fronts can be mitered and glued. Blocks can be glued in the angles, but if the joints are accurately cut and fitted, sufficient stiffening will probably be provided by drawer rails and other framing carried across these angles (FIG. 6-50C). Be careful to make the drawer guides at right angles to the front. The drawers are made in the usual way and can be fitted between the framing or arranged with overlapping fronts.

If you want maximum capacity, use doors instead of drawers. Whether to have one or two doors depends on the situation. The doors will swing back to the wall, and it is possible to fit racks or shelves inside to take toilet items, cosmetics, etc. (FIG. 6-50D).

If maximum capacity is not important, you can arrange curved shelf blocks on the doors (FIG. 5-50E). Transparent plastic sheet bent around the curved shelves will keep stored things in place, yet allow them to be seen when needed.

A mirror in a corner cannot be designed to tilt, so the common swinging arrangement cannot be used. This means that the mirror should be fairly tall to suit users of various heights and to allow a full-length view. Its lower edge may rest on the top surround (FIG. 6-50F). The mirror is clipped to a piece of plywood screwed to uprights, which are carried down the carcass to provide stiffness (FIG. 6-50G).

Because its triangular shape makes work on the table more difficult than with a rectangular piece of furniture, it is best to construct the table in its entirety before affixing it to the wall. You might need to make several trial fittings as work progresses. Complete all but the painting or polishing before screwing the dressing table in place.

Dresser

A dressing table should provide one or more mirrors at a convenient height to use when standing or sitting. It should also have a surface area suitable for many toilet articles. If it can also have drawers, it can store clothing and bedding. This dresser (FIGS. 6-51 and 6-52) is a solid piece of furniture that does all that a good dresser should, and it looks good, too.

The mirrors adjust so you can see yourself at several angles. The sunken top is shown with a glass cover. This and the two narrow drawers (FIG. 6-53) will hold a large accumulation of smaller items, while the full-width drawers have the capacity for almost anything, even folded blankets. The dresser proportions give an attractive appearance, but they could be modified to suit space or available materials.

The original dresser was designed to suit a quantity of mahogany already finished to a 3/4-inch thickness and 7-inch width. If wood is obtained in this section,

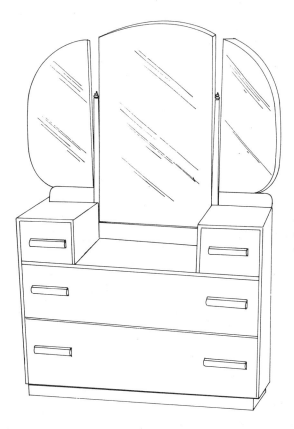

Fig. 5-51. *Sizes and sections of the enclosed two-drawer cabinet.*

it can be cut or made up to width so there is very little waste. The drawer interiors can be softwood. The handles shown are also mahogany, but this is a piece of furniture that might benefit in appearance from brass or other metal handles.

It is possible to use the design for other materials, with a few adaptions. Veneered particleboard could be used for all the visible parts. It should have any cut ends veneered to match the surfaces and edges (FIG. 6-54A). Plywood could be used, but it should have an attractive veneer unless you intend to apply a painted finish. Edges should be lipped (FIG. 6-54B). You can get an attractive effect by having lips on the front edge in a color that contrasts with the surface veneer.

The choice of material will affect some details of construction. With solid wood you have the choice of a variety of joints, or you can substitute dowels in some parts. With particleboard or plywood, many cut joints are not practical, and dowels must be used. Fortunately, dowels will give a satisfactory and sound construction, except the design might have to be altered slightly to accommodate them. The instructions assume the use of solid wood, with some guidance on what to do with other materials.

The top corners serve as examples of the variety of joints possible. The dresser has secret dovetails, so the construction is hidden, and only a miter

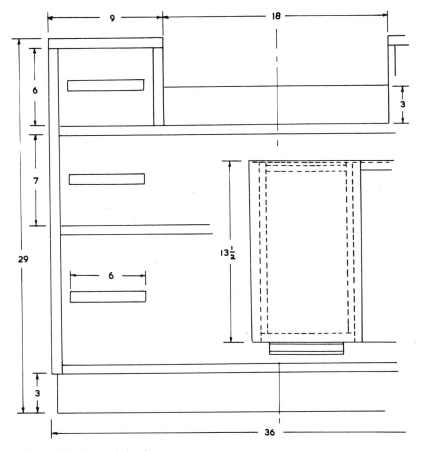

Fig. 6-52. Sizes of the dresser carcass.

Fig. 6-53. Each small drawer fits into a compartment at the side of the dresser.

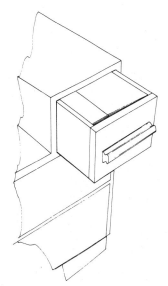

shows on the surface. If dowels are used, in any material, the top can be level with the side. It is better with a slight overhang (FIG. 6-54C), however, particularly if you are using particleboard. The overhang prevents holes breaking out and hides any lack of tightness between parts.

In solid wood, an alternative joint is a rabbet (FIG. 6-54D). In its simplest form, glue could be supplemented by pins driven both ways, then set below the sur-

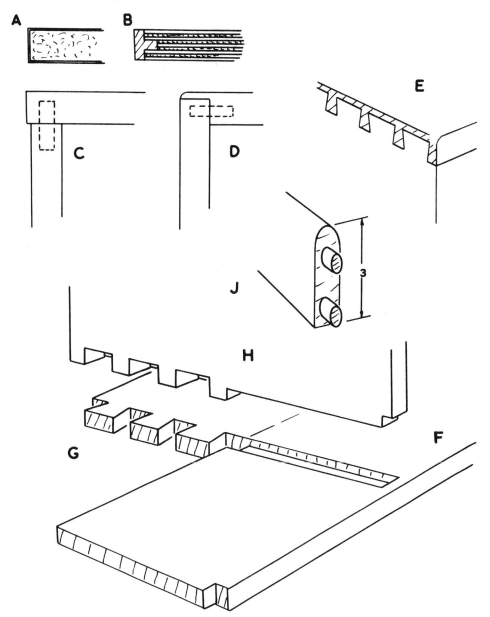

Fig. 6-54. *Construction details of parts of the dresser.*

face and covered with filler. As shown, thin dowels in the rabbet are hidden. If the overlap is rounded, the division between end and side grain will not be very apparent. This joint may be made with plywood, particularly if the plies are thick enough to make the overlap.

Materials List for Dresser

carcass

2 sides	$3/4 \times 13^1/2 \times 29$	
2 inner uprights	$3/4 \times 13^1/2 \times 8$	(grain short way)
2 tops	$3/4 \times 13^1/2 \times 9$	(grain short way)
1 top	$3/4 \times 13^1/2 \times 36$	
2 drawer rails	$3/4 \times 3 \times 36$	
2 drawer rails	$3/4 \times 2 \times 36$	
1 back rail	$3/4 \times 3 \times 18$	
2 back rails	$3/4 \times 1^1/2 \times 9$	
6 drawer runners	$3/4 \times 1 \times 8$	
1 plinth	$3/4 \times 3 \times 35$	
2 plinths	$3/4 \times 3 \times 13$	
1 back	$26 \times 36 \times 1/8$ or $1/4$ hardboard or plywood	

top drawers

2 fronts	$3/4 \times 6 \times 8$
4 sides	$1/2 \times 6 \times 14$
2 backs	$1/2 \times 6 \times 8$
2 bottoms	$8 \times 14 \times 1/4$ plywood

middle drawer

1 front	$3/4 \times 7 \times 35$
2 sides	$1/2 \times 7 \times 14$
1 back	$1/2 \times 7 \times 35$
1 bottom	$14 \times 35 \times 1/4$ plywood

bottom drawer

1 front	$3/4 \times 10 \times 35$
2 sides	$1/2 \times 10 \times 14$
1 back	$1/2 \times 10 \times 35$
1 bottom	$14 \times 35 \times 1/4$ plywood
6 drawer handles	$1^1/8 \times 1^1/8 \times 6$

mirrors

2 posts	$3/4 \times 2 \times 31$
2 finials	$3/4 \times 3/4 \times 3$
1 backboard	$17^1/2 \times 30 \times 1/2$ plywood
2 backboards	$10 \times 22 \times 1/2$ plywood

If you cannot make secret dovetails but want to show your skill at dovetailing, you could use stopped dovetails with the tails on the upright parts (FIG. 6-54E). The joints can be cut by hand or with the help of a power dovetail guide.

Where wide boards are required, it is probable they will have to be made by gluing narrow pieces—the 7-inch boards are convenient, but any pieces could be joined. As far as possible, match the grain. The pieces at the inside of the top drawer casing should have their grain vertical, although they are wider than they are deep. Prepare the pieces above the top drawers in the same way. The back can be hardboard or thin plywood.

Cut rabbets to suit the back on the rear edges of the sides, inner uprights, and the narrow tops. Mark out the pair of sides first as a guide to sizes when marking other parts (FIG. 6-55A). Allow for the actual thicknesses of wood, and mark the depths of the drawers, but let the lower drawer come where it will, which will be about 10 inches. Some of the joint details can be marked later when the other parts are prepared, but at this stage, you can determine their location. Leave a little excess wood at the ends.

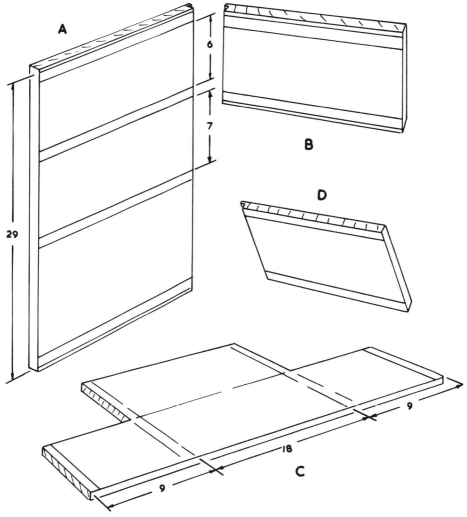

Fig. 6-55. Marking out the main parts of the dresser.

Mark the inner uprights (FIG. 6-55B) to match the sizes on the sides.

The piece across that comes under the narrow drawers and forms the center recess could go all the way as a full-width board. If you have to glue to make up the width, only the front need go all the way (FIG. 6-55C). With this as a guide, mark the two narrow tops (FIG. 6-55D). The part across the recess does not have a rabbet at the back as it comes inside the plywood or hardboard, and there will be a cover strip in the recess over that edge.

Between the two long drawers, there are strips across. At the front is a piece level with the edges of the sides. Cut it to fit into a stopped dado (FIG. 6-56A). There is a similar narrower piece at the back, but because its joint will be covered, there is no need for the dado to be stopped (FIG. 6-56B). After the two have been fitted, a drawer runner is screwed to each side (FIG. 6-56C).

At the bottom, make two similar pieces to come between the bottom drawer and plinth, but at their ends, dovetail into the sides (FIG. 6-56D). Fit drawer runners between these rails when the carcass is assembled.

The top piece across can fit into wide, stopped dado joints if it is taken full width across. If only half of it crosses, let it into narrower stopped dadoes (FIG. 6-56E), and screw on drawer runners behind it (FIG. 6-56F).

If the crosspiece is a full-width board, the inner uprights should be doweled to it, whatever the material. An alternative for solid wood would be dadoes with tenons taken through as well, for maximum strength. If only part of the crosspiece goes all the way, the best joint for solid wood at the inner uprights combines a dado and dovetails. For the width of the extended part make a stopped dado (FIG. 6-54F). For the rest of the board width make dovetails (FIG. 6-54G). Note how the dado joint meets a pin of the dovetails (FIG. 5-54H).

The strip at the back of the sunken top (FIG. 6-54J) should have its top rounded and be prepared with short dowels at the ends. When it is fitted, it will be level with the edges of the inner uprights, so it overhangs the back of the part it rests on and will cover the edge of the carcass back. It will probably be sufficient to glue its long edge, but there could be screws upwards into it, if necessary.

Prepare the joints for the short top pieces above the drawers. Trim any excess length from the sides. See that ends are cut square.

Have all the joints prepared ready for assembly. This is not a project suitable for assembling in separate steps. Where dowels are to be used, make sure all holes are ready and dowels cut. Check parts in relation to each other. Crosswise parts should all be the same length between shoulders. Work should flow smoothly because there is little opportunity to make adjustments or alterations if preparations have been overlooked.

Assemble the long crosswise pieces to the sides. The dovetailed strips at the bottom will hold the sides in at that level. At the higher positions you might need clamps. You could also hold the joints tight with a few screws driven diagonally upwards through the dado joints, particularly if you need to release clamps for use elsewhere. Fit the recess back strip between the inner uprights, and fit the uprights into the dadoes and dovetails of the main crosspiece. There can be screws through the dovetails, if needed to pull the joints tight, because they will be hidden in the finished dresser. Fit the short tops, and check squareness of the whole assembly by measuring diagonals and correcting the shape before the glue sets.

Make the back from one piece of plywood or hardboard to fit into the rabbets, across under the strip in the recess, and low enough to cover the rear strip below the bottom drawer. Glue and screw the plywood in place.

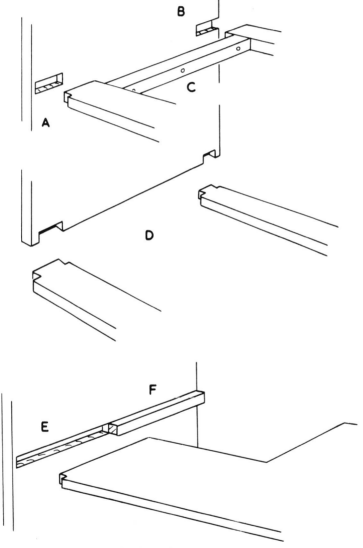

Fig. 6-56. *Fitting the horizontal parts into an end of the dresser.*

The plinth lifts the dresser off the floor and is set back at the sides and front by 1/2 inch for appearance and to make knocks from shoes less obvious. Unless the dresser is to stand in a position where it will be seen from all sides, there is no need for a back to the plinth. It is made of 3-inch-wide strips mitered at the front, with the joints strengthened by blocks inside (FIG. 6-57). Fix it with screws driven downwards through the front strip and the bottom drawer runners. Make sure no screw heads stand above the wood surface.

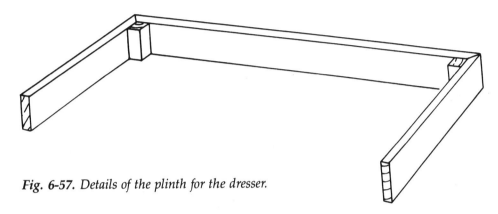

Fig. 6-57. Details of the plinth for the dresser.

It is suggested that the drawers (FIG. 6-58) are all made in the same manner in the traditional way, using dovetails. They could be made with simpler joints, but if you make this dresser in a good hardwood, you should use the best joints. The inner parts could be 1/2-inch softwood with thin plywood bottoms. Pieces will probably have to be joined to make up the width for the bottom drawer, but the others can be cut from 7-inch boards. The drawer fronts can stand forward about 1/8 inch from the framing and have rounded edges.

Prepare the material for a drawer. Groove the front (FIG. 6-59A) and sides for the bottom. The drawer back will come above the bottom. Cut the front to be a close sliding fit into its opening. Cut the width of the drawer sides so they slide easily, although with minimum slackness in their openings. At this stage, leave them too long. Make the back and bottom later.

Mark and cut the front joints. Cover the groove at the bottom of the front with a half dovetail at each side (FIG. 6-59B).

Make the sides short enough so they do not quite touch the carcass back when the front is in the right position. Mark and cut the joints for the drawer back (FIG. 6-59C) so the bottom half dovetail is high enough to take the bottom groove and the lower pin of the back (FIG. 6-59D).

Check the sizes of the drawer parts in the positions they have to fit. There can be some adjustment after they have been assembled, but the thickness of wood does not allow a great amount to be planed off.

Assemble a drawer with all the joints clamped tight. Make the bottom a little undersize so it will slide in easily from the rear under the drawer back. Leave it loose until the glue in the drawer joints has set. Clean off any excess glue, and

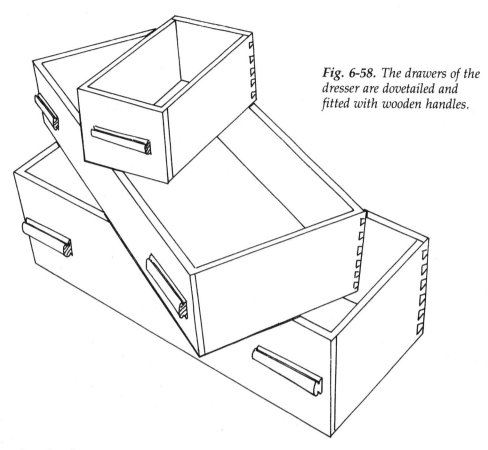

Fig. 6-58. The drawers of the dresser are dovetailed and fitted with wooden handles.

plane level any projecting parts of joints. Try the drawer in position, and plane if necessary. When it is satisfactory, slide in the bottom, and fix it by screwing upwards into the back.

Make all the drawers in the same way. Arrange stops under the rails at the front (FIG. 6-59E), centrally for the top drawers and a pair spread towards each side for the others. These should stop the drawer fronts when they are projecting about 1/8 inch from the carcass front. The drawers should not come against the back when pushed in. A drawer can be inserted or removed by tilting the front upwards so the back clears the stop.

Suggested sections for handles are shown in FIG. 6-59F. Make them in long lengths and cut off. Fix with glue and screws from inside. Center the handles across the top drawers, and fit the others in line under them. To avoid the optical illusion of appearing too low, position each handle a little above the center of its front.

The supports for the mirrors have to be rigid because glass is heavy. The posts can be the same wood as used in general construction, but see that it is straight-grained. Cut the posts long enough to screw into the lower drawer

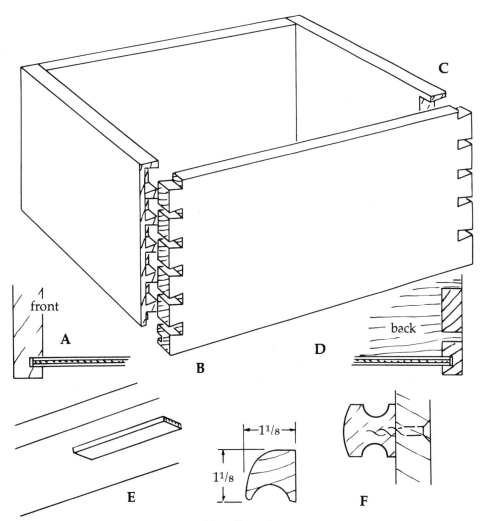

Fig. 6-59. Drawer construction and handle sections.

dividers (FIG. 6-60A). Reduce that part to 1 inch thick. From 4 inches above the carcass top, taper to a 3/4-inch square (FIG. 6-60B). For extra strength, put a 1/4-inch dowel downwards into the top (FIG. 6-60C).

At the top of each post, drill for the dowel from a finial (FIG. 6-60D), which you can turn or buy. Round the tapered edges of the posts, which must be fitted exactly vertical or the mirrors will exaggerate any discrepancies.

At the rear edges of the tops outside the posts, fit short strips (FIG. 6-60E) with rounded edges and outer corners. Two dowels downwards will supplement glue.

Cut the plywood backboards for the mirrors, and use them as templates when cutting or ordering the mirrors. The central mirror is a plain rectangle with

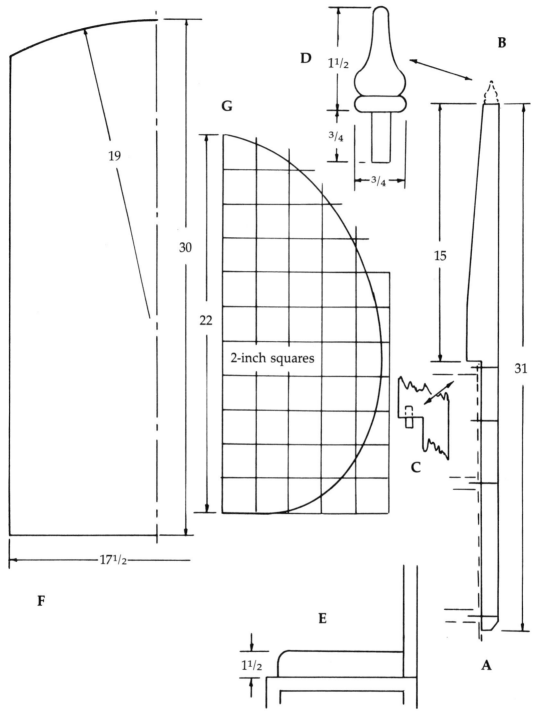

D 1¹/₂

³/₄

³/₄

G

19

30

B

22

15

31

2-inch squares

C

17¹/₂

F

E

1¹/₂

A

Fig. 6-60. Dresser mirror shapes and pedestal details.

a rounded top (FIG. 6-60F). Before deciding on its exact width, check the clearance needed for the pivots (as explained below). Set out the shapes of the side mirrors on a pattern of squares (FIG. 6-60G). If you modify the sizes, do not make the top angles of these mirrors too acute, or they would be difficult to cut and liable to break in use.

Mount the mirrors to the backboards with metal clips over the edges. There will be a tendency for gravity to make the glass slide down, so have ample clips at the bottoms—four under the large mirror, then two at each side and top should be enough.

For the center mirror, the pivots should screw to the posts and the curved pieces on the mirror backboard drop in. There should be a limited range of move-

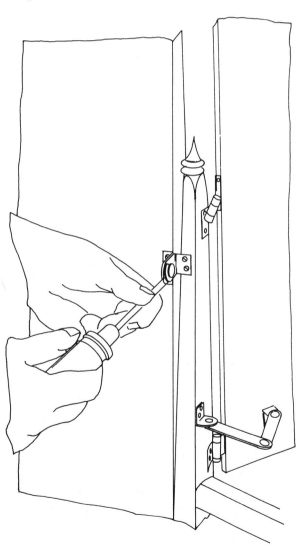

Fig. 6-61. The central mirror has fittings that allow it to swing. The side mirrors are on vertical pivots. This side mirror has a friction arm to hold it in position.

ment. These should provide enough friction to hold the mirror at any angle. If not, there can be a folding strut from the bottom of the backboard to the center of the rear rail below.

There could be ordinary hinges on the side mirrors. A neater one has a part with a pin on the mirror backboard dropping into a socket in a part on the post (FIG. 6-61). Fit two hinges on each side mirror.

Small Chest of Drawers

Particleboard in standard widths with veneer on surfaces and edges allows simple and effective construction. This chest (FIG. 6-62) is made mainly with 4-inch, 6-inch, and 15-inch widths. The dimensions can be modified to available stock sizes to avoid cutting to widths. The chest looks attractive if the main parts are covered with wood or wood-grained plastic, and the drawer parts have a plain, white plastic veneer. Strips of matching veneer will be needed for covering cut edges.

Fig. 6-62. A small chest of drawers alongside a bedside cabinet.

Dowels with a 3/8-inch diameter and spaced about 3 inches can be used for joints. Use a stop on the drill to get the maximum depth of holes in the thickness, but you can drill slightly deeper in the ends.

The drawer fronts are the controlling sizes (FIG. 6-63A). Cut them to size and veneer their ends.

Materials List for
Small Chest of Drawers

(all veneered particleboard unless marked)

3 drawer fronts	$3/4 \times 6 \times 29$
6 drawer sides	$3/4 \times 4 \times 14$
3 drawer backs	$3/4 \times 3 \times 28$
3 drawer bottoms	$14 \times 29 \times 1/8$ hardboard
2 chest ends	$3/4 \times 14 \times 22$
1 chest top	$3/4 \times 15 \times 30$
1 chest plinth	$3/4 \times 3 \times 29$
1 chest back	$21 \times 28 \times 1/8$ hardboard
6 drawer runners	$3/8 \times 3/4 \times 14$ hardwood
2 back fillets	$3/8 \times 3/8 \times 22$ hardwood
1 back fillet	$3/8 \times 3/8 \times 29$ hardwood

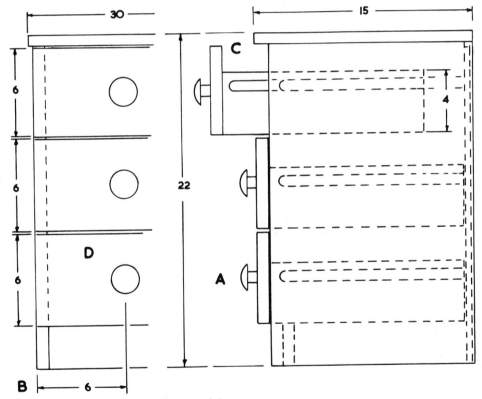

Fig. 6-63. *Sizes of the small chest of drawers.*

Mark out the pair of ends (FIG. 6-63) allowing $1/8$ inch between drawer fronts and under the top. The difference in depth is made up at the bottom by the plinth. Mark across where the bottoms of the drawers will come.

Fit strips near the rear edges (FIG. 6-64A) to take the back.

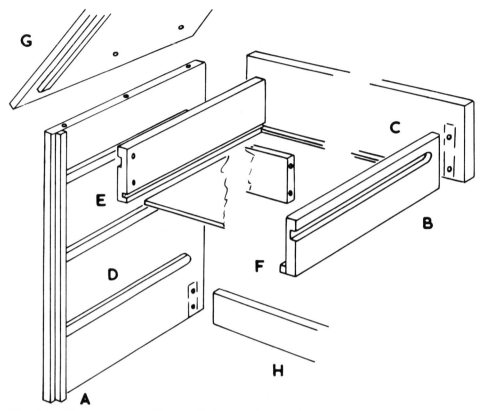

Fig. 6-64. *How the parts of the small chest of drawers fit together.*

Cut the drawer sides (FIG. 6-64B). Allow a little clearance inside the rear strips on the sides. Use a router to groove the outside of each drawer 1/2 inch deep and 1/2 inch wide, to within a 1/2 inch of the front (FIGS. 6-63C and 6-64C).

Screw and glue runners to suit on the chest sides (FIG. 6-64D). Allow a little clearance at the chest front.

Groove the drawer sides for the drawer bottom (FIG. 6-64E). If you do not have a suitable cutter, use strips for the bottom to rest on (FIG. 6-64F).

A router can be used to groove the drawer fronts for the bottoms, but the grooves should stop within the thickness of each drawer side so its end does not show. Alternatively, put strips across for the bottom to rest on.

When the chest is assembled, the drawer fronts should come level with the outer surfaces of the sides. Mark the length of the top to allow for this and to overhang about 1/2 inch (FIG. 6-64G). Put a strip under the rear edge to take the back, and match the strips on the sides.

Make the plinth (FIG. 6-64H) to fit between the sides. Mark its position on each end 3/4 inch back from the front.

Mark and drill all the dowel holes, and prepare enough dowels.

Assemble the top and plinth to the sides. Have the back ready, and glue and tack it to the strips to hold the assembly square. Check that the chest stands level.

Join the drawer sides to the fronts. Fit each drawer bottom loosely, and check the drawer action on its slides. If it is satisfactory, add the drawer backs and fit the bottoms permanently. Make sure the drawer fronts close tightly against the chest sides. The rear ends of the drawer sides should not hit the strips at the rear of the chest sides.

Knobs are shown (FIG. 6-63D), but you could use long handles on the drawers. Most types are fitted with screws from inside.

Small Bedside Cabinet

A cabinet that occupies a minimum space, yet has a reasonable capacity, might be all that can be put beside a bed in a small room. This one (FIG. 6-65) is made of

Fig. 6-65. A small bedside cabinet made from veneered particleboard.

Materials List for
Small Bedside Cabinet

(all veneered particleboard unless marked)

2 sides	$3/4 \times 12 \times 22$
3 shelves	$3/4 \times 12 \times 12$
1 door	$3/4 \times 12 \times 12$
2 back fillets	$3/8 \times 3/8 \times 11$ hardwood
2 back fillets	$3/8 \times 3/8 \times\ \ 7$ hardwood
1 back	$12 \times 19 \times 1/8$ hardboard

veneered particleboard, either all one type of veneer or, if the cabinet is to match the small chest of drawers, wood-grained plastic veneer for most parts and white plastic veneer for the door. All main parts are joined with 3/8-inch dowels. The back is hardboard.

Mark out the pair of sides (FIG. 6-66A), with the top shelf 1/2 inch down and the other shelf positions marked. Cut the three shelves to the same length and take 1/4 inch off the backs of the lower shelves to allow for the hardboard back (FIG. 6-67A).

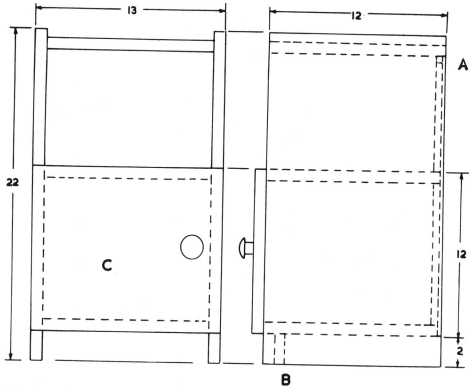

Fig. 6-66. Sizes of the small bedside cabinet.

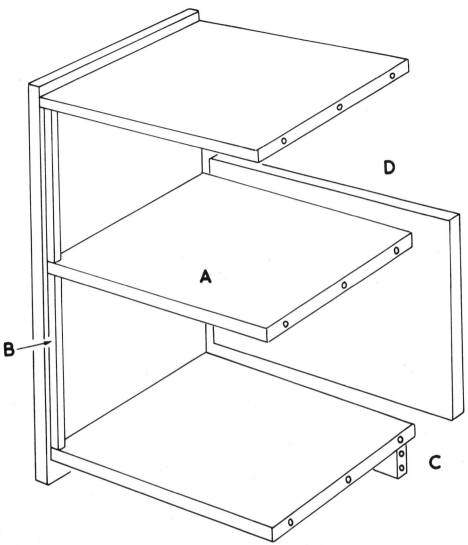

Fig. 6-67. Rear view of part of the bedside cabinet showing how the parts assemble.

Make and fit strips to go between the rear edges of the shelves (FIG. 6-67B). Make the plinth (FIGS. 6-66B and 6-57C), and drill for and prepare sufficient dowels.

Join the parts together. Fit the back to hold the other parts square. Check that the assembly will stand level.

Make the door (FIGS. 6-66C and 6-57D). It should be level at the sides and middle shelf, but it can overhang at the bottom. Veneer any cut edges.

The door can swing on two thin hinges, or you can fit throw-clear types inside (FIG. 6-68). If spring hinges are used, you might not need a catch, otherwise, fit a spring or magnetic fastener. Add a knob for opening.

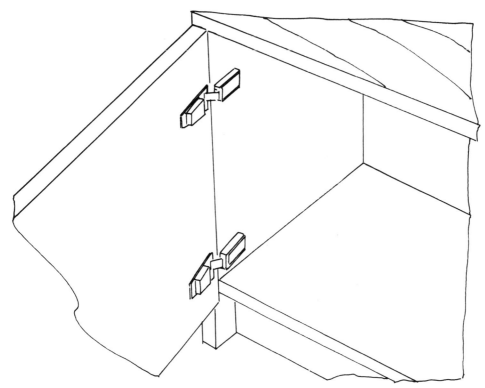

Fig. 6-68. Throw-clear hinges allow the door to open, even if close to a wall or other piece of furniture.

Independent Headboard

If there is space in a room for a headboard unit that stands out from the wall and so causes the bed to project farther, it is possible to make a unit into a piece of furniture in its own right that can stand unaided when the bed is removed. This allows the headboard plenty of storage capacity. One way of doing this is shown in FIG. 6-69. You could make it with an extension at one side only for a corner situation, or make one side a different size from the other. A further possibility is to make one side entirely a bookcase or other sort of storage unit.

The unit is in one piece, but you could make it in three pieces if this would be better for transport or possible rearrangement at a future date. There would then be a central part slightly wider than the bed and side pieces with their own sides fitting against the sides of the central part.

In the arrangement shown, the central part that projects above the bed level slopes back, so it could be used as a pillow support when sitting in bed. This features sliding doors for access while in bed to a large storage space behind. Below that the front is arranged as a removable panel. It would not be accessible when the bed is in position, but when the bed is pulled away the front can be lifted out for getting at a blanket store.

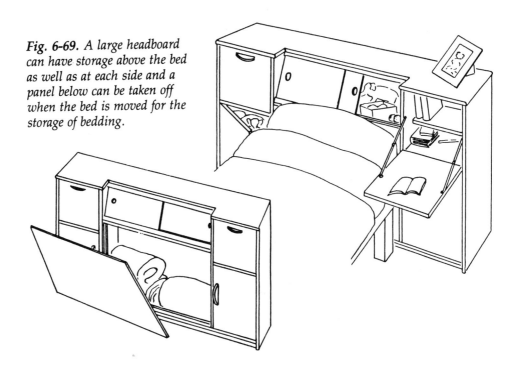

Fig. 6-69. A large headboard can have storage above the bed as well as at each side and a panel below can be taken off when the bed is moved for the storage of bedding.

**Materials List for
an Independent Headboard**

2 ends	12	× 42 × 3/4
2 uprights	12	× 40 × 3/4
1 bottom	12	× 76 × 3/4
1 top	12	× 78 × 3/4
1 divider	12	× 41 × 3/4
2 dividers	12	× 18 × 3/4
4 shelves	9	× 18 × 1/4 plywood
4 shelves	1	× 18 × 1
1 plinth	2	× 76 × 3/4
2 flaps	18	× 18 × 3/4 plywood
2 doors	18	× 22 × 3/4 plywood
2 doors	15	× 22 × 1/4 plywood
1 panel	25	× 40 × 1/4 plywood
2 panel frames	1 1/2	× 25 × 1/2
2 panel frames	1 1/2	× 40 × 1/2
2 panel stops	1/2	× 25 × 1/2
2 panel stops	1/2	× 40 × 1/2
1 back	42	× 76 × 1/4 plywood

The side parts have doors to the bottom sections and flaps to the top sections. The doors can be arranged to support the flaps in the same way as in the previous example, but the design shows them with folding stays. The insides of both parts can be arranged with one or more shelves.

Sizes are dependent on the bed. The center section should be a few inches wider than the bed, and the bottom of the top compartment should be above the mattress level and preferably nearly as high as the pillow. Other dimensions will have to be adjusted around these measurements.

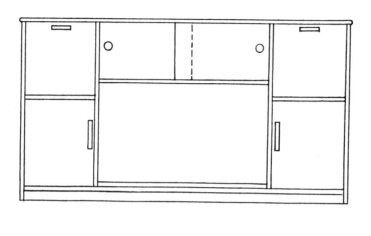

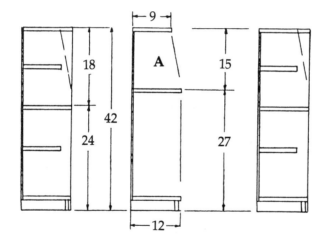

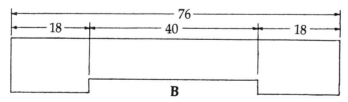

Fig. 6-70. Sizes of the large headboard: (A) uprights; (B) top.

To make the headboard, use solid wood, thick plywood, or faced particleboard. Plywood panels should be lipped on their exposed edges for a clear finish. Particleboard should have suitable edging added where it is not already on manufactured edges.

The four uprights are almost the same. Mark one outer upright (FIGS. 6-70A and 6-71A) with the positions of parts that will be attached to it and the location of center section parts, so that it can be used as a pattern for marking the other uprights. The outer uprights go to the floor to act as feet, but the intermediate ones stop at the bottom board.

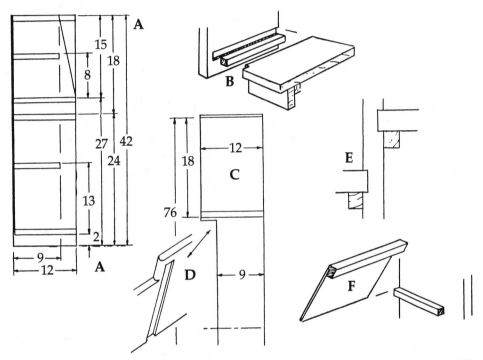

Fig. 6-71. Sizes of headboard parts and some of the joints: (A) uprights; (B) bottom; (C) top; (D) stopped dado joints; (E) battens; (F) solid front.

The bottom goes right through and can fit into dados or rest on battens that fit behind the front plinth (FIG. 6-71B). Rabbet the backs of the outer uprights to take the thin plywood back, and make the intermediate uprights narrow enough for the plywood to pass over them.

The top goes right through but is cut back over the center section (FIGS. 6-70B and 6-71C). The simplest satisfactory joints are made by letting the top overhang for stopped dado joints to be used (FIG. 6-71D). The alternatives are any of the corner joints, such as dovetail or notched.

The central divider and those for the side parts can be joined with dado joints, but for the sake of rigidity there should be battens below (FIG. 6-71E). They should be kept back at the front to clear the flaps and doors.

The shelves can also be fitted into dados, although it might be better to rest them on battens so they can be removed to allow storage space for large items. One way of making the battens unobtrusive is to put a solid front on a thin plywood shelf (FIG. 6-71F).

The doors and flaps do not involve cutting into the main parts before they are assembled, so it is best to finish and sand the parts described so far and assemble them. Make the back out of one piece of plywood if possible, but if this is an opportunity to use up smaller pieces where joints will not show, you can butt edges over the solid framing. If there is any doubt about whether the floor is level or the wall upright, the bottoms of the sides can be cut away to form feet or their angles adjusted to suit.

It is better for the headboard to tilt slightly towards the wall than away from it, if you cannot make it stand vertically. Check squareness, but if the back plywood is carefully shaped, this should keep the assembly accurate.

The flaps can be made in one piece, or you can let plywood flush into rabbets in a frame to give a paneled effect when closed and a flat surface when lowered (FIG. 6-72A). The doors can be made in the same manner.

Another way to provide a thicker door without excess weight would be to use plywood on each side of a frame, mitered on the top corners, but allowed to overlap where it would not show at the bottom (FIG. 6-72B). Provide matching handles on the flaps and doors.

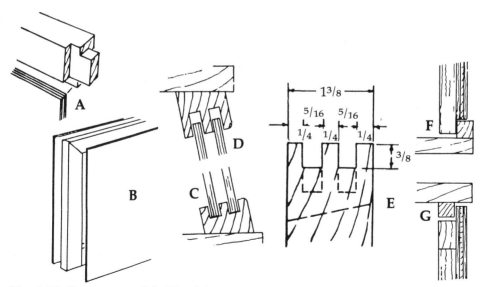

Fig. 6-72. Parts are paneled. The sliding doors move in grooves: (A) paneled effect; (B) thicker door; (C) lower grooves; (D) doors; (E) door guides; (F) headboard bottom; (G) top edge of panel.

Hinge the doors on the outer uprights, and put stops and catches at their other edges. The flaps swing down on hinges and are arranged with two folding stays each, so there is less risk of distortion with uneven pressures. It might be necessary to try the action of the stays before fitting shelves to allow for their movement as they fold.

The sliding doors on the sloping center section are pieces of plywood. Projecting handles would interfere with their movement. Finger holes are all that are needed, although these could be lined with a type of flush handle intended for the purpose.

The doors slide in plowed grooves. They rest against the bottoms of the lower grooves (FIG. 6-72C) but at the top the grooves should be deep enough to allow the doors to be lifted clear of the bottoms for removal or insertion (FIG. 6-72D). The clearance in the top grooves should be only just enough to release the doors; otherwise there is a risk of unintentionally lifting a door free when sliding it.

The best way to make both door guides is to plow the grooves on a rectangular piece and bevel it afterwards (FIG. 6-72E). Sand the insides of the grooves with abrasive paper wrapped around a thin piece of wood or a door edge. The sliding action should be easy, so allow for the slight thickening of a coat of paint or varnish. Fit one of the guides in place and make a trial assembly of the other guide and the doors, to check that the action is correct and that one guide is not twisted in relation to the other.

The lower removable panel is a piece of plywood that rests against stops in the opening, which should be taken all around the sides and top. Put strips of wood inside the panel edges and across the bottom, with the upright pieces long enough to fit inside a strip across the headboard bottom (FIG. 6-72F). There can be a strip across the top edge of the panel to fit easily inside the stop (FIG. 6-72G), then there can be two catches arranged to hold the panel in place. To remove it, tilt outwards and lift.

No shelves are shown in the example inside the lower compartment, but if folded blankets and similar things are to be stored there, the space might be better left unimpeded.

Bed with Drawers

Space under a bed is often wasted, yet this is a useful area that can be put to good use in a small or overcrowded bedroom. Putting things loosely under a bed that stands on legs is untidy, difficult to get to, and certainly not a place to put clothing or bedding, unless they are in bags or containers. It is better to make a bed that encloses the space with drawers.

This can be done in several ways. You have to relate the drawers to the space around the bed. It is no use fitting drawers if other furniture prevents them being pulled out. The size and shape of a bed will allow long drawers, but there has to be the space to use them. A drawer usually pulls across the bed, but a drawer at the foot of the bed might be more accessible. Under a narrow bed, the drawers can be full width and pull from either side, as in FIG. 6-73. If the narrow bed is near a wall or if something prevents movement one way, leave that side blank. With a wide bed, space to pull out a long crosswise drawer is unlikely, so there can be shorter drawers working against stops. Under a very wide bed there can be drawers on both sides.

One problem with an enclosed bed with drawers is its bulk compared with a normal bed on legs. To avoid the nuisance of moving the bed, it helps if the bed is in two parts with a joint (FIG. 6-74A). The bed can then be taken apart at the center to form two boxes. With the headboard removed and the drawers pulled

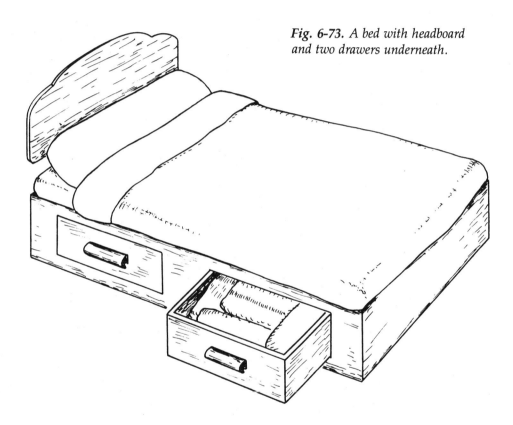

Fig. 6-73. *A bed with headboard and two drawers underneath.*

out, the individual parts are easy to manage and will pass through doorways or up stairs.

The bed drawn is made in the form of two inverted boxes, open towards the floor. It is intended to take a mattress 36 inches wide and 78 inches long, but could be modified to other sizes. If made much wider, some additional stiffening

Materials List for Bed with Drawers

4 sides	12	× 39	× 1/2 plywood
4 ends	12	× 36	× 1/2 plywood
2 tops	36	× 39	× 1/2 plywood
8 side frames	1	× 2	× 39
16 side frames	1	× 2	× 8
8 end frames	1	× 2	× 34
16 drawer strips	1	× 2	× 34
4 drawer fronts	8	× 27	× 1/2 plywood
4 drawer sides	8	× 36	× 1/2 plywood
2 drawer bottoms	27	× 36	× 1/2 plywood
8 drawer front frames	1	× 1	× 27
8 drawer front frames	1	× 1	× 7
4 drawer bottom frames	1/2	× 1	× 36
1 headboard	15	× 36	× 1/2 plywood
2 headboard supports	11/2	× 11/2	× 18

might be needed under the plywood top. They are two, almost identical boxes. The only differences are in the bolt holes for the headboard supports and for joining the boxes. As drawn, the drawers are arranged to pull out from either side. If that does not suit the surroundings, the drawers could be arranged to work one way. It would be quite simple to arrange the drawer in the box at the foot of the bed to pull out endwise.

The major parts of the bed are made of 1/2-inch plywood framed around with 1-inch-by-2-inch strips, which could be softwood. All of these parts can be glued and held with finishing nails, either painted over or set below the surface and covered with filler, if a varnished finish is to be used. Although the plywood prevents the wood from warping, start with straight pieces, particularly for the drawers and their guides.

Joints could be cut between some parts of the framing, but it is satisfactory to use glue and nails for most parts and screws where endwise parts have to be secured.

Start by marking out the four sides (FIG. 6-74B). They are all the same if you are fitting drawers of the same size that operate both ways. Cut the drawer openings. Their depth is controlled by the framing strips. If these are not exactly 2 inches deep, it will not matter, but you should make the openings to match the actual wood.

The toll framing strips go the full length of each side (FIG. 6-75A). Other short strips fill the gap at the ends and beside the drawer openings (FIG. 6-75B).

Cut and fit the four ends (FIG. 6-75C). The plywood is attached to the sides, and the top and bottom edges are stiffened. See that the assemblies are square. You could cut the top pieces of plywood to size and use them for squaring, but do not attach them yet. Check that the two boxes match.

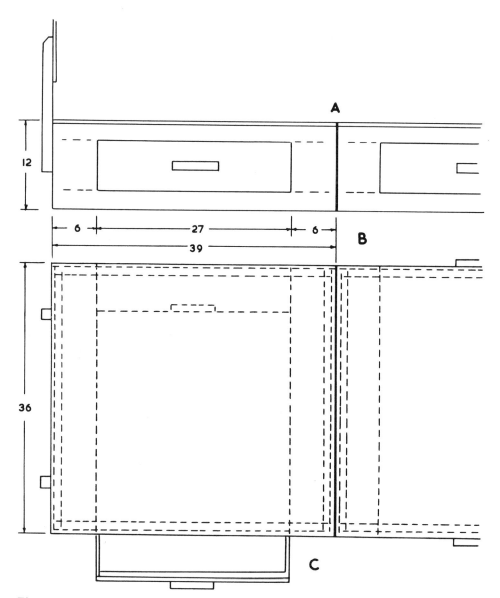

Fig. 6-74. Suggested sizes for a bed with drawers.

Where the drawers are to come, fit strips across at the top and bottom in line with the openings (FIGS. 6-75D and 6-75E). Because they will form runners and kickers for the drawers, they should be absolutely straight and with their surfaces in line with the edges of the openings.

Attach strips outside these pieces, overlapping half their width, to rub against the sides of the drawers and act as guides (FIGS. 6-75F and 6-75G). As you assemble these parts, check squareness across the bed.

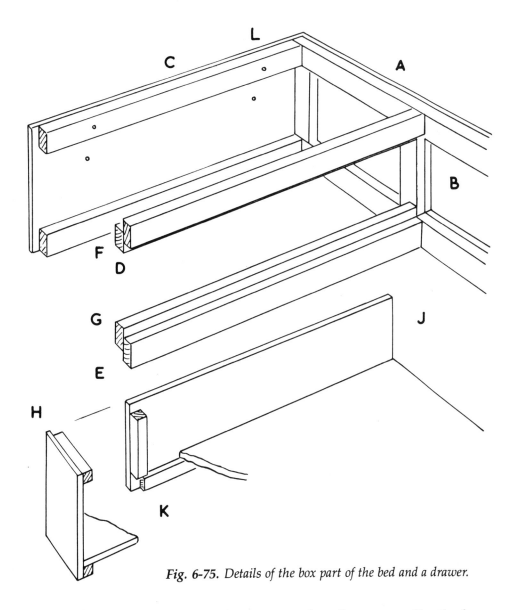

Fig. 6-75. *Details of the box part of the bed and a drawer.*

Attach the top pieces of plywood. Trim edges if necessary. Put the boxes together, and drill for two widely spaced bolts to hold them together—3/8 inch by 4 inches through the framing, or 2 inches through the plywood only should be suitable. Put washers under the nut and bolt heads to prevent pulling into the wood. If you expect to move the whole bed much, four bolts are preferable.

As the drawers have to pass through the bed both ways, the opposite fronts must be the same size as the drawer section (FIG. 6-74C). If you are making a drawer that will only work one way, the front could overlap the opening. In this case, you do not have to be so careful about the fit of the drawer because the opening is hidden.

Cut the drawer fronts to fit the openings (FIG. 6-75H). Leave just enough clearance to permit easy movement.

Make the drawer sides the same depth (FIG. 6-75H).

The drawer framing can be wood 1 inch square or smaller—2-inch strips cut down the middle will do. Frame across the top and bottom of each drawer front. Make the drawer sides of plywood with strips to go between the front strips (FIG. 6-75K), but allow for the thickness of the bottom plywood. The side supports for the plywood bottom could be reduced to $1/2$ inch thick.

Assemble the two sides and one drawer front, and put the plywood bottom temporarily in position. You would not be able to put it in place with both fronts attached to the sides. Try the temporary assembly through a box to see if it runs

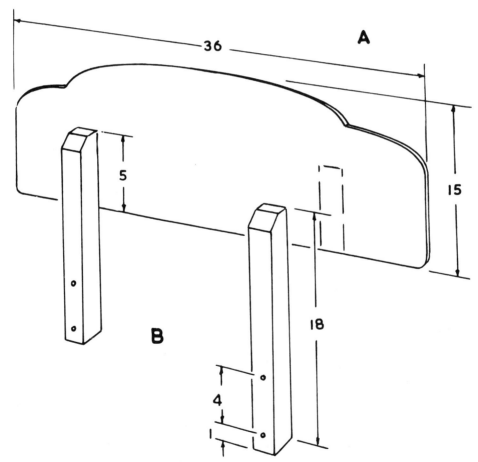

Fig. 6-76. Suggested design for a headboard on the bed with drawers.

smoothly. If there is any lack of symmetry, you might be able to correct it by planing the plywood. Complete the assembly of both drawers.

The drawer handles can be any type you wish. There will be less projection for bare legs to knock against if you choose bail handles that swing down.

Because the drawers are intended to be pulled out from either side, there cannot be any stop to hold them in the closed position. Spring ball catches can be used at the sides or bottom front edges. A ball set into the edge of the opening will then hit a catch plate on the edge of a drawer.

The headboard could be any design you wish, but a simple shaped piece of plywood on two supports is suggested (FIG. 6-76A). Make the plywood to match the width of the bed. If you shape the top, draw half the pattern full size on paper and turn it over to make the outline symmetrical.

The headboard supports (FIG. 6-76B) are square strips glued and screwed to the headboard, then bolted to a box. Two holes in each support match two more in the box. For the strongest hold, secure the top bolts through the box framing (FIG. 6-75L) Coach bolts 3/8 inch in diameter are suitable, with washers on each side. To adjust the headboard height, alternative sets of bolt holes could be drilled in the supports.

Victorian Bed

Victorian furniture is characterized by curves, and this bed head (FIG. 6-77) is modified from a Victorian example. You might not favor very ornate work, but this design uses Victorian features without going to excess. The bed is shown without a visible foot, in the way preferred today, but you could make a lower version of the head, in the same way as the previous beds. They could be made with hidden foot ends similar to this one, if you wish.

Mark out the long legs with the positions of the rails (FIG. 6-78A)and the low rails with matching heights. Make rounded, domed tops on the long legs. Moderately round the tops of the short legs.

Make all the crosswise rails with tenons or dowels into the legs. The ends of the top rail reduce to 2¹/₂ inches for the tenon (FIG. 6-79A). Mark and cut its shape and the hole (FIG. 6-79B). Round all edges.

Make the central slat (FIG. 6-79C) and the three each side of it. They reduce in width and are shown 3 inches, 2 inches, and 1 inch, with 2-inch spacing, but you might have to adjust widths and spaces to suit the actual width of your bed (FIG. 6-78B).

Prepare the ends of the slats with barefaced tenons (FIG. 6-78C). The wider central slat will be better with double tenons (FIG. 6-79D). Cut mortises in the rails to suit so the slats finish central in the thickness of the rails. Use ¹/₄-inch dowels instead of tenons, if you wish.

At the foot, rigidity comes from two rails across (FIG. 6-78D). One is at bed level at the outside, and the other is centered (FIG. 6-78E).

Fig. 6-77. This Victorian bed is without an exposed foot, which is generally preferred today.

Materials List for Victorian Bed

2 legs	$2^1/_2$	×	$2^1/_2$	× 35
2 legs	$2^1/_2$	×	$2^1/_2$	× 17
1 rail	$1^1/_2$	×	6	× 38
1 rail	$1^1/_2$	×	3	× 38
2 rails	1	×	3	× 38
1 rail	1	×	4	× 38
1 slat	$5/_8$	×	8	× 12
2 slats	$5/_8$	×	3	× 12
2 slats	$5/_8$	×	2	× 12
2 slats	$5/_8$	×	1	× 12
2 sides	1	×	4	× 80
2 sides	1	×	3	× 80
13 slats	1	×	4	× 38

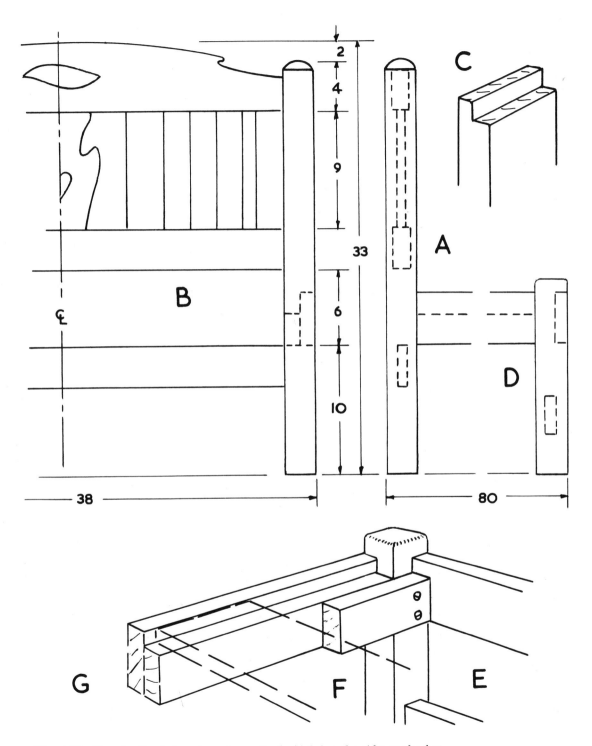

Fig. 6-78. Sizes for the bed parts and a method of joining the sides to the foot.

The sides could be attached to the legs at the head with any of the methods described at the start of this chapter. The joints at the foot might be the same, but a screwed block is a simple alternative (FIG. 6-78F). Support the mattress with slats across (FIG. 6-78G) or with plywood.

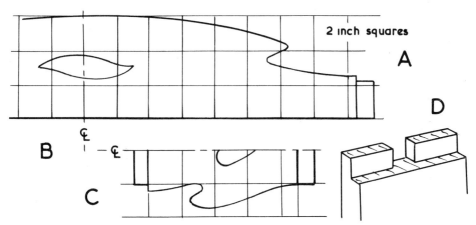

Fig. 6-79. *Make the crosswise rails with tenons or dowels into the legs.*

7

Outdoor Woodwork

The home-owning woodworker with a yard and garden can find a considerable amount of work to do on his property. There are many things you can make for use outdoors. Some are strictly utilitarian, being of use in gardening or maintenance of your property. Some might be necessary to define and protect your property. Some are for relaxing and enjoying outdoor life in comfort. Possibly the largest woodworking projects are small buildings, varying from simple shelters to workshops and summer houses. Although large and involving a fair amount of time and materials, these are not necessarily the most difficult woodworking tasks undertaken.

Outdoor woodwork, possibly more than any other branch of woodworking, improves the home and land you own, both in amenities and actual value. You use your skill with tools in a way that is both satisfying and with a value that is immediately obvious.

The selection of projects in this section are only a few drawn from several books. Some projects described in other sections could also be made for use outdoors.

Sun Shelter

Something with a more decorative appearance than a simple shelter will look better in a yard or garden, if you intend to sit in it, screened from wind and sun. You can also use it to store outdoor furniture or garden tools.

As shown in FIG. 7-1, the back and the front are parallel and upright, but the side walls slope inwards. The top and back of the door opening are curved, and

Fig. 7-1. The sun shelter has sloping sides and decorative bargeboards.

the front bargeboards are given shaped edges to avoid an austere appearance. This design includes a wooden floor, so the shelter could be self-contained and not attached to the ground, making it easier to move it to a different location. With the usual softwood construction, it should be possible for two men to carry the whole assembly a short distance.

The sizes suggested in FIG. 7-2A allow for occupying a ground area about 48 inches × 60 inches, but you can modify the sizes to suit your needs, providing you do not increase the size excessively. The skin suggested is shiplap boarding, but you can use plywood or other sheet material. You can use boards or plywood for the roof, then cover it with roofing felt or other material. Nail the bargeboards on after you have covered the roof. You can build in any seating or you can rely on separate chairs.

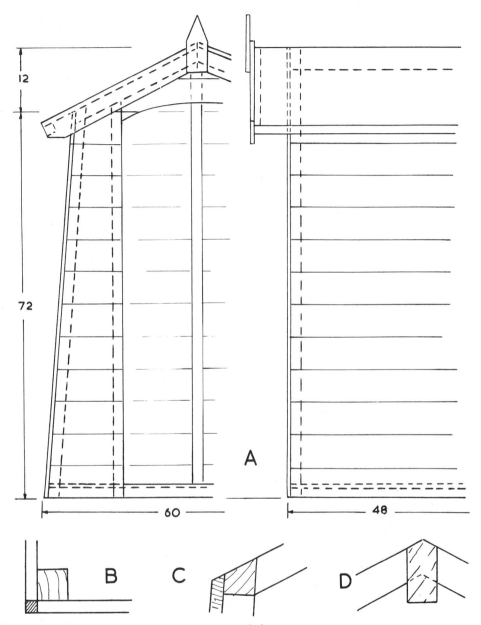

Fig. 7-2. Sizes and corner joints of the sun shelter.

The key assembly is the back (FIG. 7-3A). Set this part of the building out symmetrically about a centerline. With the usual covering, one central upright should be all that you need to supplement the outside framing, which you can halve together (FIG. 7-3B). Cover the back with boarding, working from the bottom up.

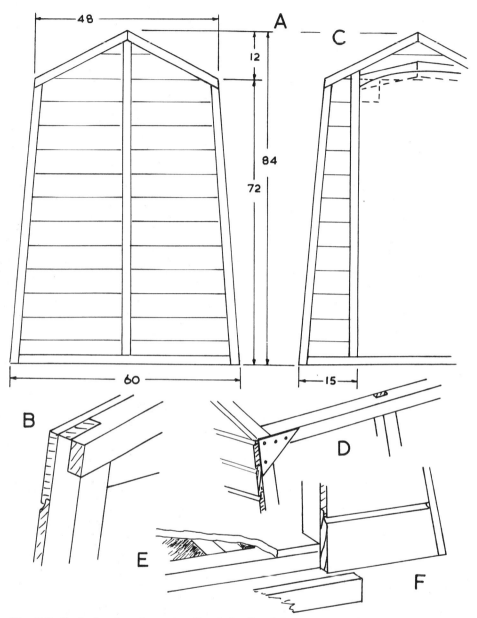

Fig. 7-3. Back, front, and constructional details of the sun shelter.

Use the back as a pattern for getting the shape of the front (FIG. 7-3C). Arrange uprights for the doorway sides. Cover with boarding. At the top of the opening, nail stiffening pieces inside and cut the curve through them and the boarding, preferably with a jigsaw. Round all edges of the doorway.

Materials List for Sun Shelter

8 uprights	2	× 2	× 75	
1 upright	2	× 2	× 86	
4 tops	2	× 2	× 30	
2 bottoms	2	× 2	× 62	
2 bottoms	2	× 2	× 50	
2 bottom supports	2	× 2	× 50	
2 top rails	2	× 2	× 50	
4 corners	1	× 1	× 75	
2 roofs	36	× 72	× $3/4$ plywood	(or boards)
4 roof edges	$1^1/2$ ×	$1^1/2$ ×	36	
2 roof edges	$1^1/2$ ×	$1^1/2$ ×	74	
1 ridge	2	× 4	× 50	
4 bargeboards	$3/4$ ×	5	× 36	
2 bargeboard ends	$3/4$ ×	4	× 15	
1 floor	48	× 60	× $3/4$ plywood	or particle board (or boards)

Covering: shiplap boards about $3/4$ × 6

You can make the two sides as separate units, with bolts into the back and the front, if you want to prefabricate the shelter or arrange it to take apart for removal to another site, but it is compact enough for you to move it bodily by truck. Consequently, you might find it simpler to assemble it completely and permanently. If so, put pieces across at top and bottom and central uprights at each side (FIG. 7-3D). The easiest way to join to the front and back is with sheet-metal gussets. When you have nailed the side boarding on, you will strengthen the joints further. For the neatest corners, stop the board ends at the uprights, and fill the corners with square strips (FIG. 7-2B).

You might consider it satisfactory for your purpose for the eave's strips to be left with square edges, but it will be better to plane them to the slope of the roof (FIG. 7-2C), and make a ridge piece with matching slopes (FIG. 7-2D).

Square the assembly as you fit the floor. What stiffening you provide depends on the materials. Two pieces from back to front should be sufficient (FIG. 7-3E). Over these strips might come particleboard, plywood, or 6-inch-wide boards. Cover the front edge with a strip to match the thickness of the shiplap boarding (FIG. 7-3F).

Allow for a 6-inch roof overhang all around. You can use plywood or arrange boards from back to front. Stiffen all edges with strips below (FIG. 7-4A). Take the roof-covering material over the top without joints. Turn in the edges and tack underneath (FIG. 7-4B). Use more large-head nails elsewhere on the roof, if necessary. Make the bargeboards to stand about $1/2$ inch above the roof covering and to project at least 1 inch at the eaves. Leave the lower edges straight, or give them a regular pattern of deckle edges.

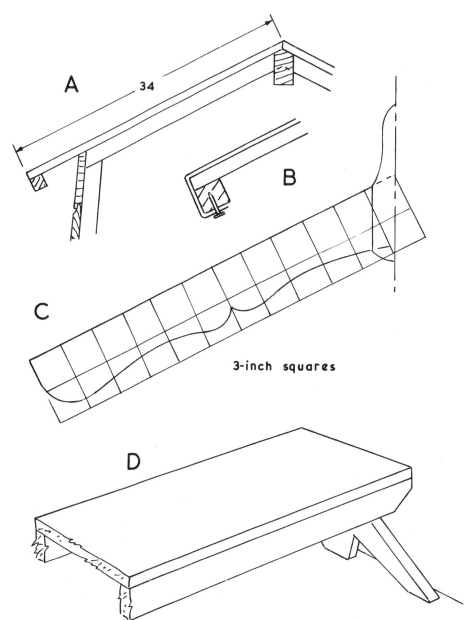

A

34

B

C

3-inch squares

D

Fig. 7-4. Roof, bargeboard, and seat details for the sun shelter.

The pattern shown is distinctive (FIG. 7-4C), and you can cut it with a portable jigsaw. Cut one and use it as a pattern for marking the others. The central piece might have a simple point or might be curved to match the other decoration.

If you put strips across the sides at seat height, you can place one or more boards across as a seat and move them to stand on end if you want to use the shelter as a store. Another idea would be to make a bench with its feet arranged to come between the sides (FIG. 7-4D), then you can lift it outside when you prefer the open air.

If the sun shelter is to stand on soil or grass, soak the lower parts, at least, with preservative. For a permanent position, you should place it on a concrete base. You can leave the inside untreated, but it would look best if you finished it in a light-color paint, even if you paint the outside in a dark color.

Simple Shed

A storage shed with enough space inside for tools and a small bench on which to deal with seed trays and similar things need not be complicated. The shed shown in FIG. 7-5 is intended to be made in sections and bolted together. It is shown covered with plywood, but you can use any of the other methods of sheathing. There is a wooden floor, but a concrete one would be just as suitable.

Fig. 7-5. A simple shed covered with plywood.

Materials List for Simple Shed

2 roof frames	96 ×	2	× 2
4 roof frames	48 ×	2	× 2
6 end frames	44 ×	2	× 2
2 end frames	84 ×	2	× 2
2 end frames	78 ×	2	× 2
4 side frames	90 ×	2	× 2
4 low side frames	78 ×	2	× 2
3 high side frames	84 ×	2	× 2
3 window frames	28 ×	2	× 2
4 window frames	28 ×	2	× 5/8
4 window frames	28 ×	1	× 5/8
2 door frames	72 ×	3 1/2	× 5/8
1 door frame	31 ×	3 1/2	× 5/8
2 door frames	90 ×	4	× 2
4 floor frames	40 ×	4	× 2
6 door boards	72 ×	5	× 3/4
3 door ledgers	30 ×	5	× 3/4
2 door braces	48 ×	5	× 3/4

1/2-inch plywood:

2 ends	84 × 42
3 low sides	78 × 30
1 high side	84 × 48
1 high side	84 × 42
1 floor	86 × 38
1 roof	96 × 48

The sizes suggested in FIG. 7-6A allow you to make the plywood covering with the minimum of joints. You can use the same method for a shed of other sizes adapted to suit your available space. Although this is a freestanding shed, you can make it as a lean-to against an existing wall.

Several ways exist for dealing with frame corners. Bridle (or open mortise-and-tenon) joints might appeal to a true craftsman (FIG. 7-7A), but with plywood providing some strength, simple nailing will do (FIG. 7-7B). For that or other covering, you could include a block to give extra nailing surface (FIG. 7-7C). Another way of strengthening for any covering is to nail on triangles of galvanized sheet steel or aluminum (FIG. 7-7D). In general, let uprights overlap horizontal and sloping members.

The ends provide the key shapes. Make the back first (FIG. 7-6B). Trim the covering level at the edges. If there is to be a wooden floor, let the plywood extend below the edges, enough to at least partially cover it. If you are using shiplap boards, allow for the bottom one to go over the edge of the floor, but you do not need to fit it yet.

Assemble the other end over the back so that it makes a pair (FIG. 7-6C). Include the framing for the door, and check this opening for squareness as you join the strips.

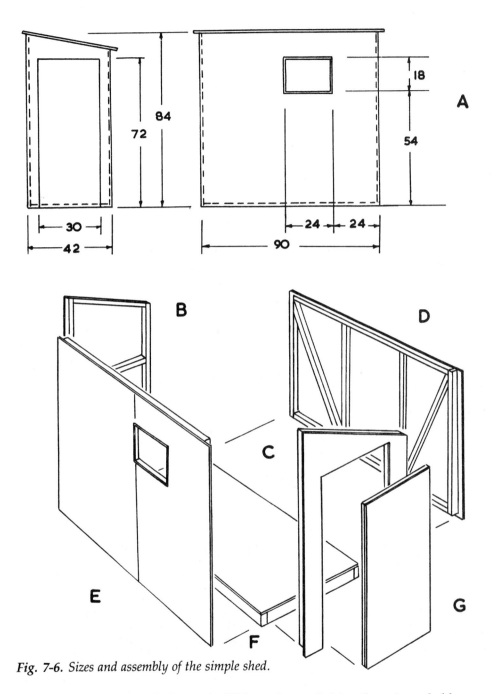

Fig. 7-6. Sizes and assembly of the simple shed.

Make the low side (FIG. 7-6D). With a plywood skin, there is probably no need for diagonal bracing. With other sheathing, it is advisable. This is especially important if the shed will be exposed to high winds.

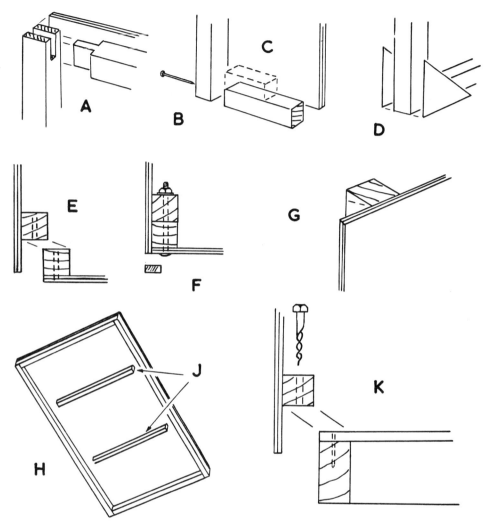

Fig. 7-7. *Methods of framing and assembling parts of the simple shed.*

At the corners, allow for the uprights to bolt together and the side skin to overlap (FIG. 7-7E). Use three or four coach bolts at each corner. Cover the skin edges with a batten after assembly (FIG. 7-7F). Allow for the sheathing to go over the floor in the same way as at the ends. The top edge could be left square, but for the best construction, cut it to the same angle as the ends (FIG. 7-7G).

Make the high side (FIG. 7-6E) with its length to match the low side and height to match the ends. Frame the opening for the window, and cut the sheathing level with it. If there is a vertical joint in the plywood, cover it with a batten. Treat the edges of the assembly in the same way as the back.

The roof could be prefabricated. If you will be assembling the shed straight away, wait until after you erect the four walls in case you must allow for slight errors of size or squareness. This size plywood roof requires little framing. Allow the plywood sufficient overlap and frame it all round (FIG. 7-7H). Two other strips across inside the walls should give sufficient stiffness (FIG. 7-7J).

You can make a wooden floor of plywood or particleboard on framing (FIG. 7-6F) . Nailed construction is all that is needed, but it is important that the overall sizes match the sizes of the assembled walls. Attach the walls to the floor with coach screws or long nails, and nail the sheathing around the outside (FIG. 7-7K).

If you are covering the plywood roof with asphalt roofing, screw it down to the wall framing first. Wrap covering over the roof edges, where appropriate.

The window can be a single piece of sheet glass or stiff plastic. You can fit it with strips around the opening to project over the sheathing outside. Other strips hold the glass from inside (FIG. 7-8A). If you lightly nail the inside strips, you can remove them easily if you have to replace glass. Frame the doorway with strips that overlap the sheathing slightly (FIG. 7-8B).

The door (FIG. 7-6G) can be plywood or vertical boards with framing inside (FIG. 7-8C). Hinge it on whichever side is convenient, and fit a latch and lock.

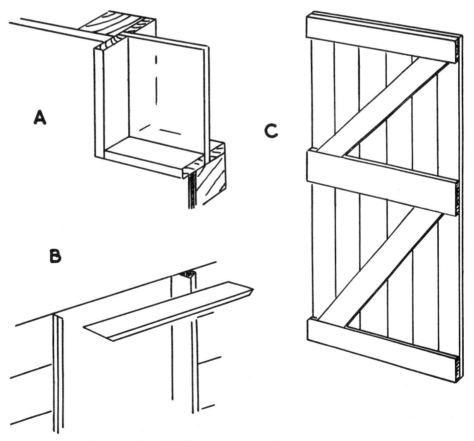

Fig. 7-8. *Window and door details.*

For the most durable shed, treat the wood with preservative either before or during assembly so that you can reach parts that would be inaccessible later. This procedure would also apply to painting. Paint the meeting surfaces before they are brought together, and then paint the finished shed all over.

Although a painted plywood roof might seem adequate, you will get a longer life out of using asphalt sheet materials over it. Arrange any overlaps in the direction the water will run. Use plenty of galvanized roofing nails.

Greenhouse

A greenhouse is a gardener's workshop. Besides being a place to grow some things completely and start others before putting them in the ground, it is also a shelter to work in when conditions outside are uncomfortable, and it is also a place to plan new horticultural projects. It extends the gardener's season for his occupation or hobby. For an enthusiastic gardener, a greenhouse is almost essential. A second stage in preparing plants to be put outside is to place them in a cold frame to harden them off. Quite often, that structure is a crude improvisation. In this building, a cold frame is included as part of the same unit, so you can efficiently tackle that stage of gardening (FIG. 7-9).

Construction of a greenhouse can be very similar to that of any other building of the same shape, except you cover large areas of the walls and roof with glass instead of wood. You can prefabricate this building to a large extent, with

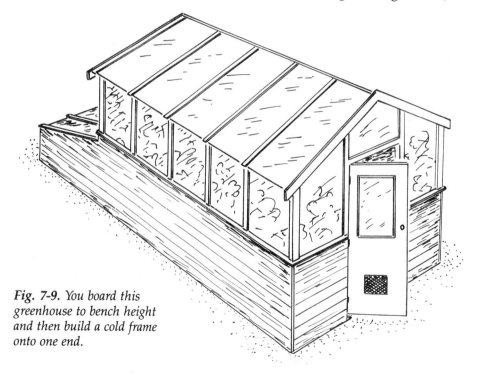

Fig. 7-9. You board this greenhouse to bench height and then build a cold frame onto one end.

Materials List for Greenhouse

Ends

4 uprights	2 ×	2 ×	78
4 uprights	2 ×	2 ×	90
3 rails	2 ×	2 ×	96
7 rails	2 ×	2 ×	34
4 rafters	2 ×	2 ×	60
2 sills	1 ×	4 ×	34
1 sill	1 ×	4 ×	100

Sides

12 uprights	2 ×	2 ×	78
2 rails	2 ×	2 ×	124
2 rails	2 ×	2 ×	172
2 rails	2 ×	4 ×	124
4 uprights	2 ×	2 ×	20
2 strips	2 ×	2 ×	24
2 strips	2 ×	2 ×	56
2 sills	1 ×	4 ×	128

Cold frame

3 rails	2 ×	2 ×	96
2 rails	2 ×	3 ×	96
2 covers	1 ×	4 ×	56
1 cover	1 ×	4 ×	96
5 glazing bars	2 ×	2 ×	56

Roof

1 ridge	2 ×	6 ×	124
12 glazing bars	2 ×	2 ×	66
4 bargeboards	1 ×	6 ×	70

Door

2 sides	1 ×	2 ×	80
6 rails	1 ×	2 ×	30
2 window posts	1 ×	2 ×	40
2 edges	1/2 ×	2 ×	80
2 edges	1/2 ×	2 ×	32
2 window edges	1 ×	2 ×	40
2 window edges	1 ×	2 ×	26
2 panels	30 × 78 × 1/4 plywood		

Cladding

	1 × 6 shiplap boards
Rabbets and fillets	3/4 × 1

ends and walls ready to bolt together. You make the roof on-site and glaze after erection, although a careful worker might prefer to fit some glass while the walls are flat on the floor. One problem is flexing, which could loosen putty or even break glass. In most cases, it is better to leave glass until you are satisfied that you have finally, and rigidly, assembled the greenhouse.

The sizes suggested are for a building of modest size (FIG. 7-10A,B), but you can use the same method for other sizes. Most of the structure is made from 2-inch-square wood, with some wider pieces where extra strength is needed.

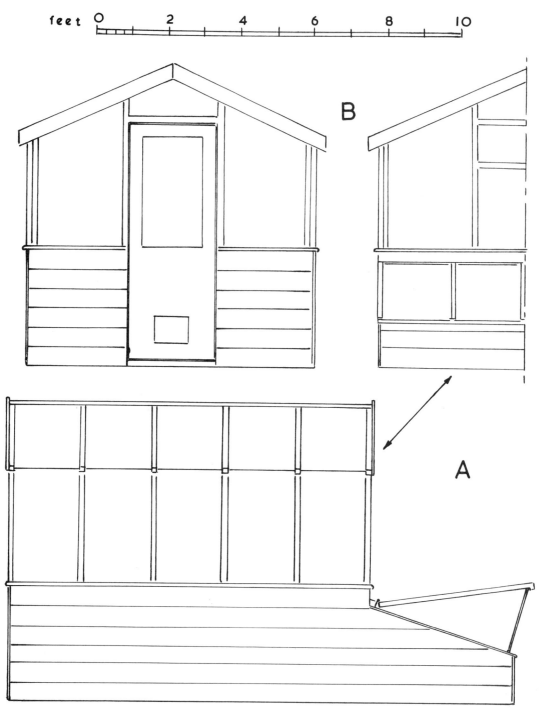

feet 0   2   4   6   8   10

B

A

Fig. 7-10. *Four views of the greenhouse, showing sizes and proportion.*

Use shiplap boarding outside to near bench level. Above that, use glass. The door is at one end.

A shuttered hole provides control of ventilation. Locate this hole low in the door and another one high in the opposite end. Make the cold frame by extending the sides, so you can finish it with access via a lifting top. It does not have any connection through to the inside of the greenhouse. As a result, it is not affected by any heating in the greenhouse and if you put soil into it, it is kept away from the floor of the main building.

The greenhouse could have a wooden floor, but because of water often running about, it would be better to lay a concrete base. The concrete base could go under the cold frame, but you might want to use soil base for that. You can cut drainage channels in the concrete and lead them under the greenhouse walls to take away surplus water.

The two ends fit between the sides. For an overall width of about 96 inches, you can arrange the uprights to be 30 inches between centers. This spacing gives a suitable width for the door, and you simplify glass cutting by making all panes the same width (FIG. 7-11A).

Joints in the upper parts of the frames will be without the additional strength of boarding. It is advisable to use open mortise-and-tenon (or bridle) joints with waterproof glue, and drive either nails or dowels across each. The lower joints can be the same or the simpler, halving joints.

Start with the door end (FIG. 7-11B). The bottom rail goes right across. Other short rails mark the height of the doorway and the cladding. At the apex, leave a gap to take the 2-inch × 6-inch ridge standing 2 inches above the framing (FIG. 7-11C), and put a short rail below the opening to brace the rafters and support the ridge (FIG. 7-11D).

Let the cladding project on each side to go halfway over the side posts (FIG. 7-11E). You will fill the space with a strip when you assemble the building. There will be a sill above the cladding (FIG. 7-11F). Because the sill looks best if you miter it around the corner, you might want to install it after you have assembled the walls.

The opposite end has a matching outline, but the rail at the top of the cladding should be taken right across and another short rail put 12 inches below the one in the door top position. The space between the railings is the ventilation opening (FIG. 7-11G). Clad that end across, up to the same level as the opposite end. Let the board ends extend to fully cover the side uprights. Make rabbets in all the openings for the glass with strips nailed in. Use 3/4-inch × 1-inch pieces making them level with the inside edges of the framing (FIG. 7-11H). At cladding level, allow for the sill to be fitted. The sill will have its own strip.

Arrange the uprights on the pair of sides so they are 24-inch centers and, as a result, you can cut all glass the same width (FIG. 7-12A). Put cladding up to the same height as at the ends. Include the cold-frame extensions, boarded to the top (FIG. 7-12B). The top member is a 2-inch × 4-inch section. Rafters have to rest

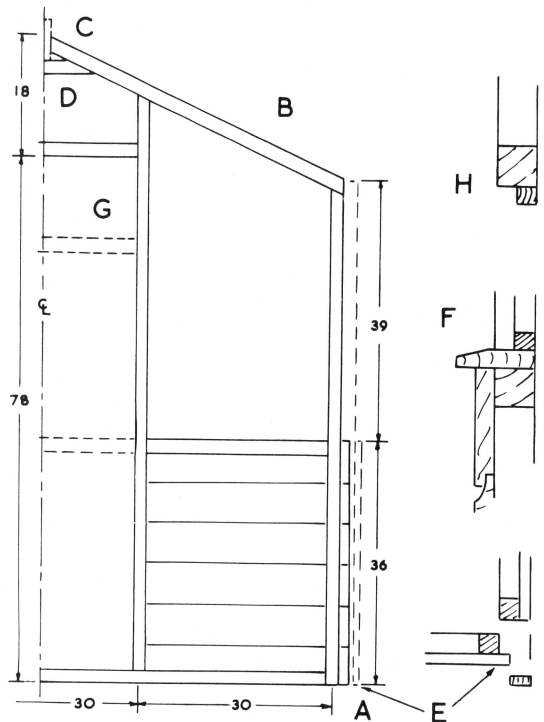

Fig. 7-11. The door end of the greenhouse and sections through windows and corners.

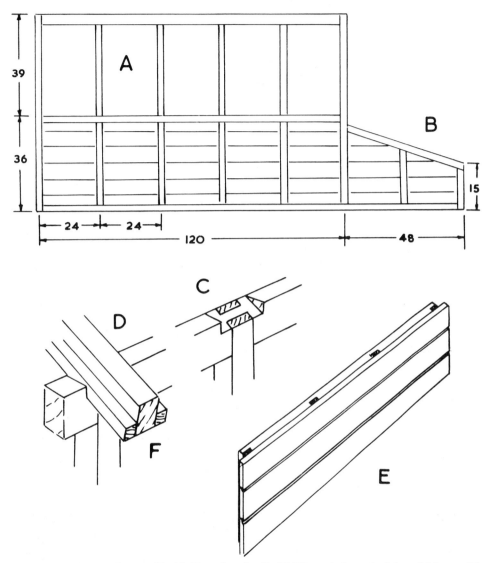

Fig. 7-12. *A greenhouse side (A,B), rafter details (C,D), and the end of the cold frame (E).*

on it. Instead of cutting its top to suit the roof slope, leave it square, except for notches at the roof angle where the rafters will come directly over the uprights (FIG. 7-12C,D). After you assemble the building, you can put filler pieces on the squared tops to close the gaps between the wall and the roof glass.

Cut off the ends of the cladding boards level with the end uprights. At the end of the cold frame, make a piece the same width as the greenhouse ends so it fits between the sides (FIG. 7-12E), with cladding to the top. Cut the cladding at the same angle as the sides. Let the ends extend to cover the side uprights in the same way as the door end (FIG. 7-11E).

Assemble all the parts made so far, using 3/8-inch bolts at about 15-inch intervals through the posts. Put filler pieces in the corners of the, cladding. Check squareness and fasten the bottom frame members down to the base.

Fit a sill all around. Level the sill inside and taper it from just outside the edges of the uprights (FIG. 7-11F). You can extend it a few inches inward if you want to make it into a shelf. You can make the sill in sections, but you will obtain the neatest finish by making it continuous on the sides and ends. For the strongest construction, notch the sill into the uprights about 1/4 inch (FIG. 7-13A). At the corners, extend the sill parts to miter together (FIG. 7-13B). Put rabbet strips in place.

Make the 2-inch × 6-inch ridge to fit in the slots in the ends and be level outside. Mark on it the positions of the rafters, to match the positions of the slots on the tops of the building sides. Prepare the rafters with rabbet strips on each side of the intermediate ones (FIG. 7-12F) and on the inside edges only of the end ones. Using the angle of a building as a guide, cut the tops of the rafters to fit against the ridge (FIG. 7-13C). Make the length of a rafter enough to overhang the walls by 6 inches. Prepare all twelve rafters so they match.

Nail the end rafters on top of the frame ends (FIG. 7-13D). At the other positions, put a supporting strip underneath (FIG. 7-13E) as you position each rafter. Nail the lower end into its recess. Make rabbet strips with sloping tops to go between the rafters (FIG. 7-13F).

This procedure completes the assembly of all parts that you must glaze. Putty and the alternative compounds do not bond well with untreated wood, so either paint all the woodwork or just the rabbets, so they will dry while you work on other parts.

Glaze the door to the same level as the walls. A ventilation hole is in its bottom panel. The suggested construction has 1/4-inch plywood panels on each side with a frame of 1-inch × 2-inch strips inside (FIG. 7-13G).

Make the door an easy fit in the doorway, with its bottom above the bottom framing strip. The plywood could go to the edges without further protection, but it will be better to cover with 1/2-inch strips (FIG. 7-13H). Allow for this covering when marking out the plywood panels. Make one plywood door panel first and check its sizes. Glue and fix with thin nails the framing strips around the edges and openings (FIG. 7-13J). When you are satisfied with this panel, make the other panel slightly oversize, so when you have fixed it, you will have true edges.

Line the window and ventilation openings with strips that are level inside but project with rounded edges at the front (FIG. 7-13K). Because movement of the door, particularly if it is slammed, might loosen putty, it will be better if the door glazing is held between two fillets (FIG. 7-13L). Use jointing compound to embed this glass tightly.

Cover the ventilation opening with fine-mesh wire gauze, to keep out vermin. To control ventilation, hinge a flap on the inside of the door, with a cord to a hook above to regulate the amount of air allowed to pass (FIG. 7-13M). At the other end of the building, arrange a similar flap inside the high opening there, with a cord up to a ring or pulley and down to a cleat within reach.

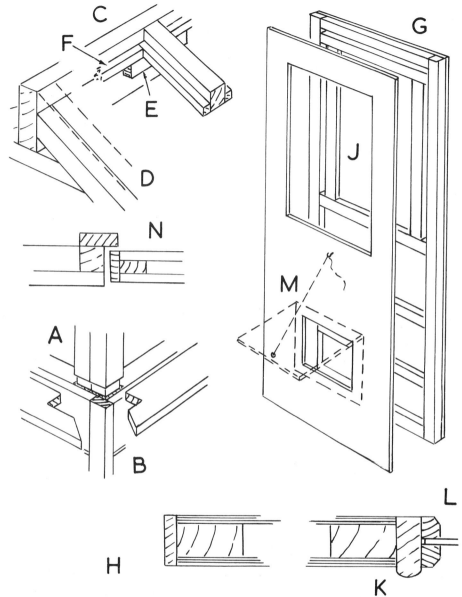

Fig. 7-13. Constructional details of the greenhouse and the way you assemble its door.

Strips inside the doorway framing (FIG. 7-13N) will act as stops. Hang the door to swing outwards on three 3-inch hinges, and fit a handle and catch or lock.

Although pieces of glass could be as large as the openings each panel has to fit, you might prefer to use shorter pieces, with the upper pieces overlapping the lower ones, to shed water. This design might be more economical, and the first fitting might be handled easily. It also might be easier and cheaper if you ever have to replace a broken pane. Embed the glass in putty with fine nails (sprigs) holding the glass, then neatly putty over them (FIG. 7-14A).

At the cold frame, cover the top edges with strips (FIG. 7-14B). At the end of the greenhouse, fit a piece of 2-inch-×-3-inch wood over the cover strips and bevel it to fit close to the cladding on the greenhouse (FIG. 7-14C,D). Make the lifting cover to fit against this strip of wood overhang with a 6-inch overhang at the bottom. This cover is built up with a 3-inch-wide piece at the top and all other parts are 2-inches square, with 3/4-inch-×-1-inch rabbet strips (FIG. 7-14E).

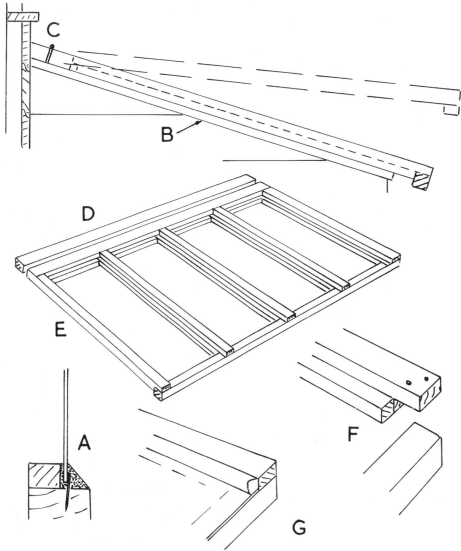

Fig. 7-14. The cold-frame cover and its construction and mounting.

Mortise-and-tenon joints are best for the joints to the top rail, but the 2-inch-square bottom piece has to be kept down below the glass level, so water will run off. Halve the ends of the sloping pieces, and glue and screw the crosspiece to them (FIG. 7-14F). When you glaze the frame, carry the glass to the edge of the bottom piece (FIG. 7-14G).

The frame with glass will be fairly heavy. Use four strong, 4-inch hinges at the top. Arrange a strut to hold the top open.

Finish the ends of the greenhouse with bargeboards. They need not be elaborate, but they will improve appearances by covering the ends of the roof structure (FIG. 7-10B).

Basic Workshop

The size and arrangement of a building you make for use as a hobby shop will depend on many factors, including the available space and the situation. You will have to consider the actual craft or occupation and its needs. However, a building with about an 8-feet-×-12-feet floor area with working headroom and several windows will suit woodworking and metalworking, as well as many other crafts. The building shown in FIG. 7-15 is of basic, partly prefabricated construction. It

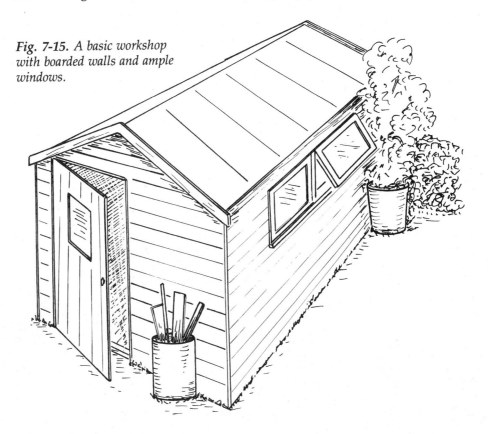

Fig. 7-15. A basic workshop with boarded walls and ample windows.

Materials List for Basic Workshop

Ends

5 uprights	2	× 3	×	80
2 uprights	2	× 3	×	100
3 uprights	2	× 3	×	90
4 rails	2	× 3	×	98
4 tops	2	× 3	×	54

Sides

10 uprights	2	× 3	×	80
8 rails	2	× 3	×	138
4 corners	1	× 2	×	80

Cladding

	1	× 6 shiplap boards	
		or 3/4 plywood	

Door

2 frames	1	× 4	×	80
1 frame	1	× 4	×	40
3 ledges	1	× 6	×	38
1 brace	1	× 6	×	45
7 boards	1	× 6	×	80
2 window sides	1	× 2	×	16
4 window frames	1	× 2¹/₂ ×		16
8 window fillets	1	× 1	×	16

Windows

6 frames	1	× 4¹/₂ ×		20
3 frames	1	× 4¹/₂ ×		36
1 sill	1	× 5¹/₂ ×		36
1 sill	1	× 5¹/₂ ×		74
6 stops	1	× 1¹/₂ ×		20
6 stops	1	× 1¹/₂ ×		36
6 window sides	1¹/₂ × 1¹/₂ ×			20
6 window rails	1¹/₂ × 1¹/₂ ×			36

Roof

1 ridge	2	× 6	×	160
2 eaves	2	× 4	×	160
2 purlins	2	× 2	×	160
16 battens	1/2 × 1		×	54
2 rafters	2	× 3	×	54
1 tie	2	× 3	×	40
4 bargeboards	1	× 5	×	60
Covering	1	× 6 boards or		
		3/4 plywood		

has a door wide enough to pass most pieces of furniture or light machinery and the suggested windows should give enough light if most activities are on a bench that you arrange at one long side.

At the entrance end, a window is shown in the door. The wall alongside it, then, would be available for shelves and racks. Two windows that open are shown over the long bench (FIG. 7-16A), and you might put another window that opens at the back (FIG. 7-16B). Besides providing ventilation, these windows

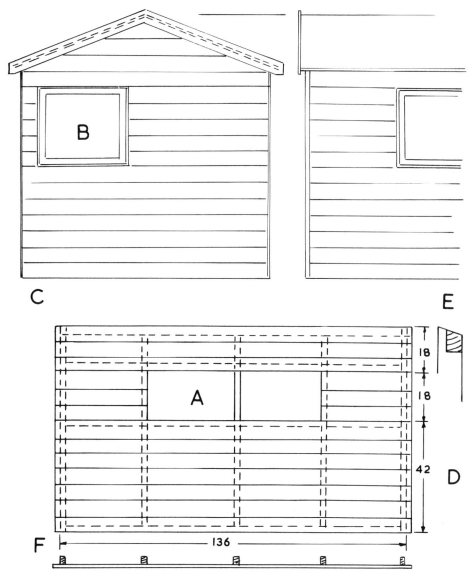

Fig. 7-16. Suggested sizes for the basic workshop.

allow long or awkward work to be extended outside, if that is the only way to handle it. You might leave the other long side without windows, but that will depend on your needs. If you want to have a lathe or table saw near that wall, arrange more windows there, not necessarily ones that open.

This structure is not intended to be a portable building; it is not intended to be moved once you have assembled it fully. However, you can prefabricate much of it. You can make the four walls elsewhere, then assemble them to each other on-site and add the roof. Nearly all the framing is made from 2-inch-×-3-inch section wood. The covering is shiplap boards about 6 inches wide, but you could use exterior plywood or other covering. As described, the building is not intended to be lined, but it would not be difficult to line and insulate the finished building. If you build in a full-length bench, it will give rigidity to the structure as well as help to brace the building. Fix shelves, racks, and other storage arrangements directly to the walls.

Start by making one end (FIG. 7-17A). Halve or tenon external-frame joints and halve or notch internal-meeting joints. Halve crossing parts. At the top, bevel the rafters to rest on the other parts and nail through. Check squareness by comparing diagonals—a door or window out of true will be very obvious.

Cover the end with shiplap boarding or other covering, starting at the bottom edge. Cut board ends level with the uprights. At the top, fit the covering under the roof (FIG. 7-17). Leave some excess here for trimming to fit later. At the apex, leave space for the 2-inch-×-6-inch ridge piece, with a supporting member under it.

Make the opposite end (FIG. 7-16C) to match the overall size. Arrange uprights at about 24-inch intervals. Put pieces across at window height, which might match the windows in the side (FIG. 7-16D). Cover this end in the same way, leaving a ridge notch and allowing for trimming of board ends later under the roof.

Make the side heights to match the ends, and bevel top edges to match the roof slope. Like the ends, all the side framing has the 2-inch width towards the outside, except for the top piece, which you arranged vertically (FIG. 7-16E). If the overall length is to be 12 feet, the constructed side length will be about 8 inches less (FIG. 7-16F) over uprights. Make a side frame with rails for the windows. If one side is without windows, arrange two intermediate rails equally spaced. Uprights are shown about 32 inches apart, but you might alter uprights and rails to suit benches and shelves you might wish to build in. Do not have fewer framing parts than suggested. Use joints similar to those in the ends for the side frame parts.

Check squareness, then cover the framework. Where the sides meet the ends, carry the boarding over so it will go far enough on the end uprights to allow you to put a filler piece in to cover the board ends (FIG. 7-17C).

Line the doorway sides and top with strips level with the inside and outside (FIG. 7-17D). Do the same at the sides and tops of the window openings, but let the outside edges project up to 1/2 inch (FIG. 7-18A). You can treat the bottom in the same way, but it will be better to make it thicker and extend it further to make a sill (FIG. 7-18B).

Make a door to fit the opening, with its boards overlapping the bottom frame member, with 1/2-inch ground clearance. Three ledges and one diagonal brace are shown in FIG. 7-19A. If there is to be a window, arrange it between the upper ledges, and frame the sides with strips (FIG. 7-19B). After covering with vertical boards (preferably tongue-and groove boards), line the opening with pieces that overhang a little (FIGS. 7-17E and 7-19C). You can make the window in the door

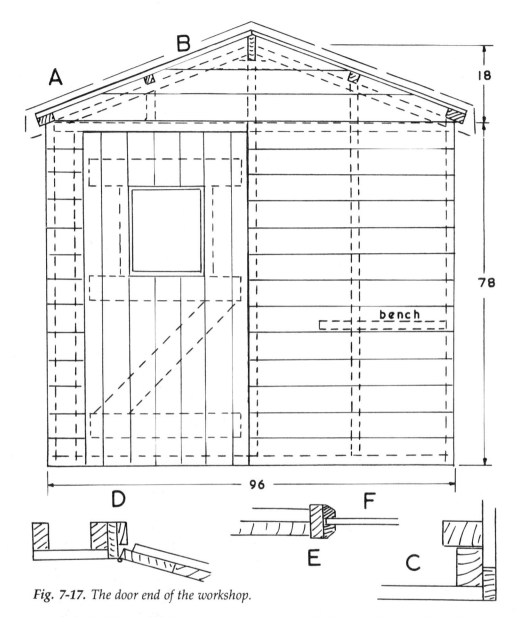

Fig. 7-17. *The door end of the workshop.*

simply by holding glass between strips (FIG. 7-17F). Cut the glass a little undersize to reduce any risk of cracking. Waterproof the window by embedding the edges in putty or a jointing compound.

Put strips around the doorway sides and top to act as stops and to provide draftproofing. Keep the ledges on the door short enough to clear them. You can put hinges in the edge of the door, or you might fit T hinges across the surface. Fit an ordinary door lock with bolt and key, if you want to secure the shop; otherwise a simple latch might be adequate.

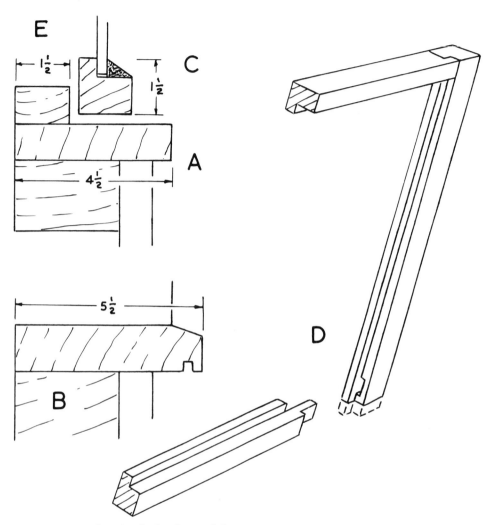

Fig. 7-18. Window details for the workshop.

You can make the windows with standard molding, but these windows might be a much lighter section than the usual house windows. It would be better to prepare simple, rabbeted strips (FIG. 7-18C). If you use a standard window molding, you probably will have to increase the width of the pieces around the window openings.

Make up the windows with mortise-and-tenon joints (FIG. 7-18D). Leave the sides too long until after assembly, to reduce the risk of end grain breaking out. Make the windows so they fit easily in their openings. Put stop strips around the inner edges of the framing (FIG. 7-18E). Hinge the windows at the top and arrange fasteners and struts inside at the bottom. You might want to lift the windows horizontal occasionally, but you can do that with a temporary strut or a cord from

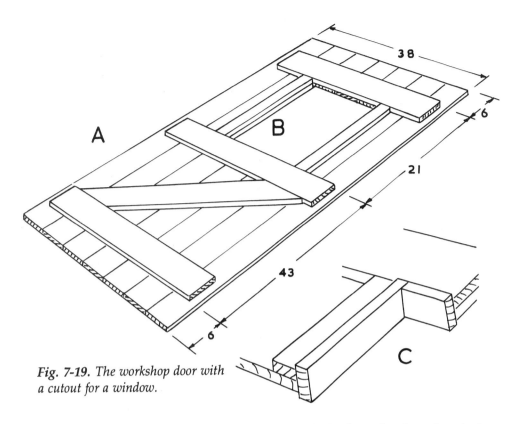

Fig. 7-19. The workshop door with a cutout for a window.

higher on the wall. When you are satisfied with the fit and action of a window, you can putty in the glass, although it might be better to putty after you have painted the wood. The building will look attractive if you paint the window frames and bargeboards a different color than the main parts, so you could paint the window frames and glaze them in advance of final assembly.

The roof is supported by the 2-inch-×-6-inch ridge, the 2-inch-×-4-inch eaves laid flat, and 2-inch-square purlins halfway down each side of the roof. Nail the eaves strips and purlins to the sloping top frames of the ends, and bevel the ridge to match (FIG. 7-20A). Let the ends project about 3 inches at each end of the building. Cut the shiplap covering boards around them and trim their top edges to match the roof (FIG. 7-20B).

On a 12-foot length, it should be sufficient to prevent sagging of the roof by having rafters only at the center. If you make the building longer or have doubts about the stiffness of the assembly, use two sets of rafters, spacing them equally. Cut a pair of rafters to fit between the top pieces of the side frames and the ridge (FIG. 7-20C). Check straightness of the sides while cutting. If you get the length of a rafter wrong, it could make the side bulge or bend in slightly. You can have a nailing block at one or both ends of each rafter. A block below the purlin will locate and support it (FIG. 7-20D). Put a strip across the rafters below the ridge (FIG. 7-20E). No other lower tie-down is needed.

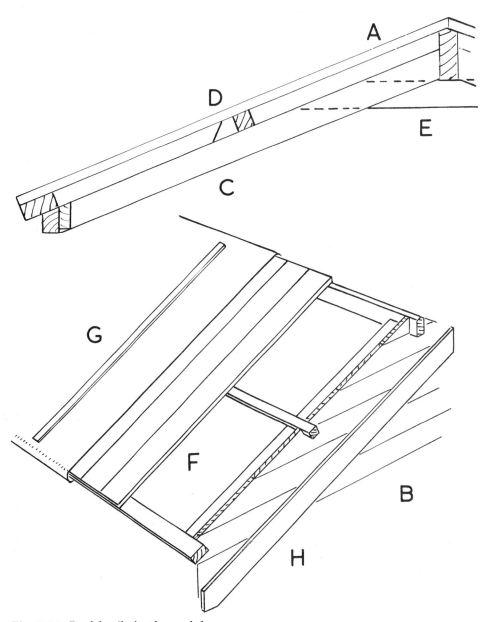

Fig. 7-20. *Roof details for the workshop.*

You can cover the roof with exterior-grade plywood, but FIG. 7-20 shows it boarded. Finish level at the eaves. Put covering material over the structure in single lengths from one eaves to the other, if possible, turning the ends under and nailing them. Any overlaps should be wide, and you should arrange them so water cannot run under. Nail on battens (FIG. 7-20G) at about 18-inch intervals to prevent the covering material from lifting.

Simple, narrow bargeboards are suggested in FIG. 7-20H, nailed to the roof ends after covering. You could make more elaborate ones, to use your own ideas. Make sure there is clearance for the door to swing open, at least to 90°.

Substantial Workshop

If you need a small building to use as a shop for year-round work, or if you want to install several machines or other heavy equipment, the construction ought to be more substantial than many shops which have sectional construction. The sectional-construction building is satisfactory for lighter or occasional use. If climatic extremes affect the contents, insulate the building adequately. This insulation also will improve your personal comfort. You probably will need to use plenty of electricity, which would include the accompanying switchgear and fuses or cutouts. Electricity is installed more safely in a building more like a house than in a temporary shed.

Such a substantial shop obviously will be more costly than one of lighter construction. Building it will involve more work, mostly on-site, but if you want a long-lasting shop of the best construction, this shop is it. Line and insulate the walls; you also might line the roof. A wooden floor covers a concrete base. You can place a simple, single door in one end, you can enlarge it to double doors, or you might fit double doors at the other end. Even if your normal activities do not need wide doors, make sure your door is wide enough for you to pass your largest machine through it. You can place windows in one side only, with more natural light coming from the opposite roof, or you can arrange windows to suit your needs, during the initial planning stage. You probably will have a bench at the window side for hand work, assembly, and the use of portable machines. Check the sizes of fixed machines. Locate them so you can move around them safely and so there is clearance to work with sheet and long material.

Think of storage. You might arrange racks inside, although a lower lean-to shelter could cover racks along one side. This design might be valuable for natural seasoning of wood.

Available space and access to it might control sizes. For example, it is assumed that the building is 10 feet wide, 14 feet long, and that there is a lean-to store 4 feet wide (FIG. 7-21). The height is 8 feet to the eaves. One wall and one end are solid. The solid wall gives firm and adequate attachments for machines which you need to mount on the wall, and plenty of space for shelves and cabinets. Windows and doors take away a surprising amount of wall space, and you will have to weigh the value of cutting through these walls against their use when left solid.

The building will be fairly heavy. The equipment and stock you add will represent more weight. If you add machines with plenty of cast iron in them, the total weight on the base might be more than you first visualized. If an inadequate base allows part of the building to sag, rectification at a later date will be difficult, if not impossible. Fortunately, you can prepare a concrete base of sufficient

Materials List for Substantial Workshop

Floor

10 joists	2	× 3	× 125	
20 boards	1	× 6	× 86	or equivalent area

Sides

12 uprights	2	× 3	× 98
7 rails	2	× 3	× 170
1 rail	2	× 3	× 120
4 sway bracings	2	× 3	× 36
4 sway bracings	2	× 3	× 56
6 fillets	2	× 2	× 34
4 fillets	2	× 2	× 48

Ends

4 uprights	2	× 3	× 98
4 uprights	2	× 3	× 118
5 rails	2	× 3	× 116
2 rails	2	× 3	× 38
4 sway bracings	2	× 3	× 48
4 top rails	2	× 3	× 66

Trusses

4 rafters	2	× 3	× 66
2 ties	2	× 3	× 100

Cladding

Cladding	1 × 6 shiplap boards or equivalent plywood
Lining	1/2 plywood or particleboards

Roof

6 purlins	2	× 3	× 180	
60 boards	1	× 6	× 72	or equivalent area
4 bargeboards	1	× 8	× 76	
3 finials	3	× 3	× 20	
4 roof-light linings	1	× 5	× 25	
3 roof-light frames	1 1/2	× 3	× 30	
1 roof-light frame	1	× 3	× 30	
18 battens	1/2	× 1 1/2	× 70	
2 cappings	1	× 3	× 180	

Door

2 linings	1	× 6	× 86	
1 lining	1	× 6	× 44	
5 boards	1	× 9	× 86	or equivalent area
3 ledges	1	× 6	× 40	
2 braces	1	× 6	× 42	
1 top	1	× 2	× 42	
2 stops	1	× 3	× 84	

Windows

6 linings	1	× 6	× 38
3 top linings	1	× 7	× 38
3 top-hinge rails	1	× 5	× 38
3 sills	1 1/2	× 7 1/2	× 38
12 window moldings	2	× 2	× 38

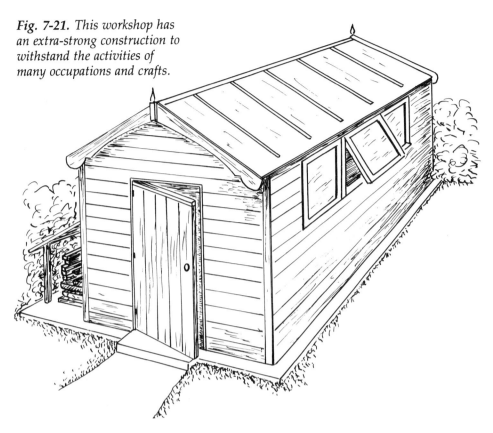

Fig. 7-21. *This workshop has an extra-strong construction to withstand the activities of many occupations and crafts.*

strength almost as easily as a thinner, poorly-supported base. Dig deep enough to fill under the base with compacted stone, then lay more than 4 inches of concrete on top of it, taking it about 6 inches outside the building area and keeping the top surface above the surrounding ground.

Although it is possible to put the wooden floor directly on the concrete base, it is better to raise it. Several ways are possible. You could cement bricks or concrete blocks in place. You might use railroad ties. If you use new wood, it should be pressure-impregnated with preservative. This of type wood would be advisable for the floor framing as well. Use 2-inch- × -4-inch wood, or larger. You can arrange the supports all around, but it would be better to have them only under the floor joists, so there is ventilation (FIG. 7-22A). Spike or bolt the wood to the concrete. Alternate bearers might be full-length. You could place short pieces intermediately, depending on the stiffness of the floor. Put polyethylene or other plastic sheeting between the wood and concrete to reduce the amount of moisture meeting the wood.

You could put the floor joists in position and nail full-length floor boards to them, but if you prefer to put the floor together away from its final position, it could be in two parts which you would bolt together (FIG. 7-22B). Boards might be plain, but tongue-and-groove boards will prevent gaps, if there is shrinkage.

Substantial Workshop **431**

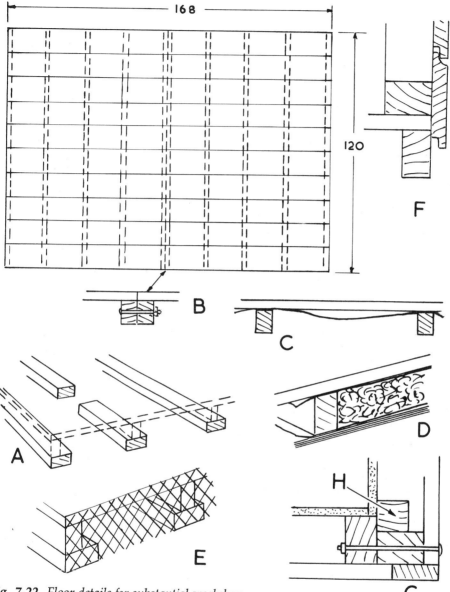

Fig. 7-22. Floor details for substantial workshop.

Alternatively, use particleboard or thick plywood. Polyethylene sheeting between the floor boards and the joists (FIG. 7-22C) will act as a vapor barrier. For maximum floor insulation, sandwich insulating foam between the floor boards and plywood from below (FIG. 7-22D).

The floor settles the shape of the building, so take care to get it and its supports square. Compare diagonal measurements. Before proceeding with the walls, be sure to fix fine, metal mesh at open ends (FIG. 7-22E) to keep out leaves and vermin, without restricting ventilation.

You can do much of the assembly of sides and ends flat on the floor. The square corners of the base will serve as guides in squaring wall assemblies. Make the walls so the outside of a frame comes level with the outside of the floor, and take the siding a little way below the floor level (FIG. 7-22F). As you mark out the frames, allow for the corner joints. Bolt the 2-inch-×-3-inch uprights together and cover the siding with an upright corner strip (FIG. 7-22G). Include a fillet (FIG. 7-22H) to support the lining. Joints between frame parts might be the same as in earlier buildings, preferably with open mortise-and-tenon joints at the corners. Shallow notches or halving joints are suitable elsewhere.

Diagonal strut-sway bracing is advisable in a building of this size, particularly if it will be exposed. This bracing resists wind loads and relieves the skin material of racking loads under strain that it might otherwise get. Covering with plywood sheets might provide stiffness without the need for diagonal struts, but with shiplap siding, they are advisable.

The two sides are rectangular frames the same length as the floor. They are shown 8 feet high, but if you will be covering with standard plywood sheets, you might reduce the height a little to allow for the sheets to project over the edges of the floor. For shiplap-board covering, you might keep the height to 8 feet, which will then suit the standard sheets you use for lining.

The closed side (FIG. 7-23A) has uprights at 24-inch intervals. and two equally spaced rails are halved to them. At the end, fit the cleats (FIGS. 7-22H and 7-23C), if you are going to line the walls after assembly. The four sway-bracing diagonals should fit closely, and you should securely nail them to the framing. You can arrange this bracing easily by putting blocks in the corners and cutting the diagonal ends to fit against them (FIG. 7-23D).

Cut the cladding boards level at the ends. Along the bottom edge, allow a projection to overhang the floor (FIG. 7-22F). You can finish the top board level with the top of the frame, or you might prefer to fit it after you have assembled the building, as you will have a gap to fill after you have boarded the roof, and you might continue upwards with a wide board. If you cut the boards flush with the frame, you can put filler pieces on top later.

The side with the windows has the same overall size (FIG. 7-23B). You can arrange the window opening to suit your needs, but the arrangement shown has three windows about 36 inches square, 48 inches above the floor. If you plan a different window layout, have sufficient uprights not more than 36 inches apart to support the cladding. Fit cleats and arrange sway bracing in the same way as on the other side. Put the cladding boards on in the same way. At the window openings, cut the boards level. You can cover their edges when you frame the windows.

The two end frames are almost the same (FIG. 7-24A). Make the closed end like the door end, but take the central rail right across (FIG. 7-24B). Although an

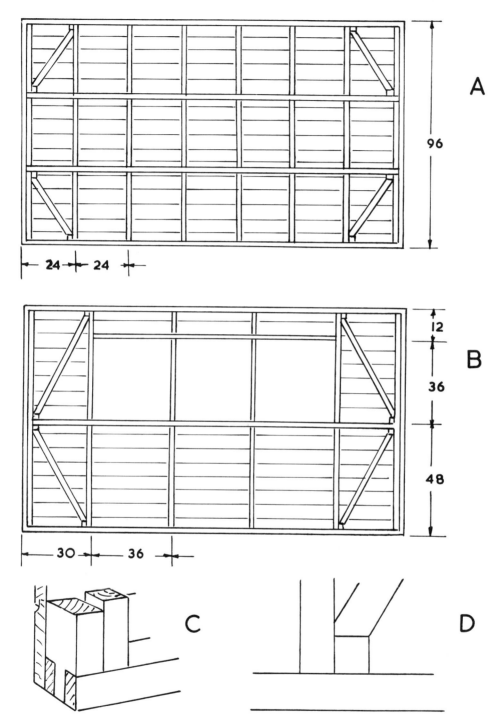

Fig. 7-23. *Walls of the substantial workshop.*

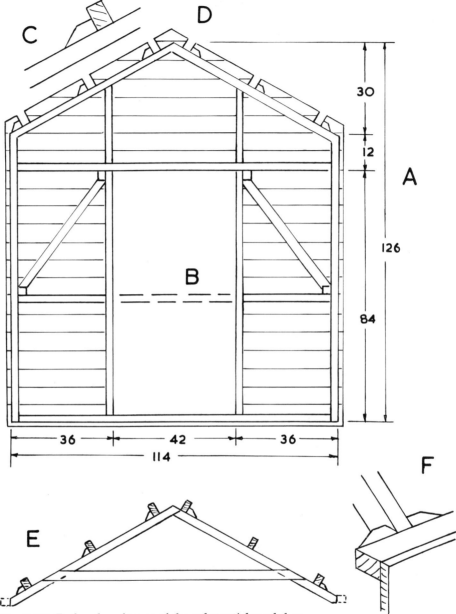

Fig. 7-24. End and roof truss of the substantial workshop.

overall width is given, it is important that the ends fit between the sides (FIG. 7-22G,H). Check on the floor that the ends will hold the sides the correct distance apart for you to take the cladding down outside the floor. Also check that the eave's height matches the sides.

Assemble the frames squarely. Halve the sloping tops to each other and to the uprights. The doorway is 42 inches wide, and the top is 84 inches above the floor. You could modify these sizes at this stage, if you wish. Include sway bracing similar to that on the sides.

Three 2-inch-×-3-inch purlins are on the edge at each side. In this building, there is no separate ridge. Instead, the top purlins are fairly close to the apex to support the roof boards there. Arrange lower purlins close to the eaves and the others midway. Put supporting cleats on the frame (FIG. 7-24C).

Cladding has to overhang on all edges. At the bottom, allow the same amount to go over the floor as at the building sides. At the vertical edges, let the cladding project 1 inch, so it will overlap the side uprights, and leave a space for a filler (FIG. 7-22G). At the top, the cladding has to fit around the purlins and extend high enough to be level with their top edges under the roof boards (FIG. 7-24D). You might trim these boards to shape at this stage, or leave fitting those above eaves level until after you have erected the building. Cut the board edges level with the framing around the door opening.

You need two roof trusses, spaced at about 56-inch centers, to support the purlins and prevent distortion of the roof or development of a sag. Make the trusses (FIG. 7-24E) with their 3-inch size vertical. Check that they match the ends and have matching cleats for the purlins.

Bolt or nail the ties to the surfaces of the truss rafters. During assembly of the building, check that the rafters are vertical and in line with the ends. Nail the rafter ends between supporting blocks on the tops of the side frames (FIG. 7-24F).

Nail the purlins to the end frames and trusses via the cleats. Let them extend about 6 inches at each end. Cover the roof with boards about 6 inches wide, preferably with tongue-and-groove edges. Cut the boards to fit closely at the ridge (FIG. 7-25A), and let them overhang about 5 inches at the eaves. Cover completely and tightly, except if you want to fit a roof light (directions to follow). Use roofing felt or other covering material (FIG. 7-25B), preferably taken from one eaves over the ridge to the other eaves in one piece. If you must make a joint in the felt or covering material, allow a good overlap arranged in the direction that will allow water to flow away from the joint. Turn under and nail at the eaves. If there is any tendency for the board ends to warp or go out of line, nail strips underneath before turning the covering material under.

You can nail another wide strip of the same material along the ridge (FIG. 7-25C) and put wooden capping strips over them (FIG. 7-25D). Nail battens down the slope of the roof (FIG. 7-25E) at about 18-inch intervals.

If you want to make one or more roof lights, arrange them most conveniently between the upper two purlins (FIG. 7-25F). Cut the opening in the boards. A width of 24 inches is the maximum advisable. Line the opening with strips which stand 1 inch above the roof level. It is important that the joints around the opening are waterproof. Use waterproof glue in the wooden joints, then cover the roof with felt. Turn the felt up the projecting frame, and embed it in jointing compound and nail it closely.

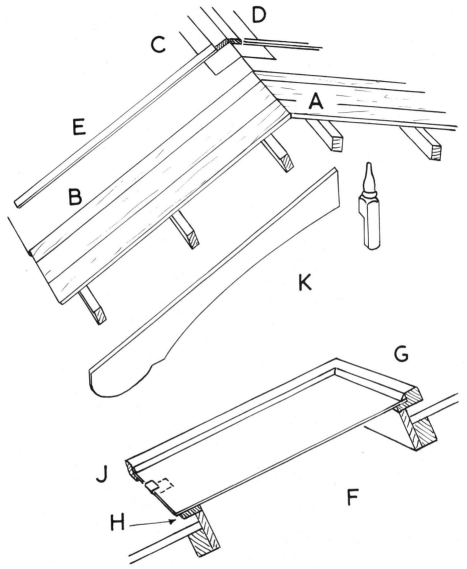

Fig. 7-25. *Roof, bargeboard, and roof light details for the substantial workshop.*

Make a frame into which you can putty glass. Allow ample depth for the glass, which might be a reinforced type about $1/4$ inch thick. The inside edges of the frame might come level with, or inside, the lining of the opening. Make the top and both sides of the frame with rabbets to take the glass and putty (FIG. 7-25G). So you will not trap rainwater, let the lower part of the frame only come under the glass, which might project there slightly (FIG. 7-25H).

Mount the frame in position by gluing and screwing it to the lining pieces. Complete painting this woodwork before embedding the glass in putty. If you have doubts about the putty being able to prevent the glass from slipping, nail two sheet-metal pieces to the lower part of the frame and bend their ends around the glass (FIG. 7-25J). Fit bargeboards to both ends of the roof. They could be straight or you can decorate them in the ways described for some earlier buildings. A different decorated pattern is suggested in FIG. 7-25K. With this pattern goes a turned finial on a square part notched over the apex of the meeting bargeboards.

Line the door opening (FIG. 7-26A) with strips at sides and top. Round the

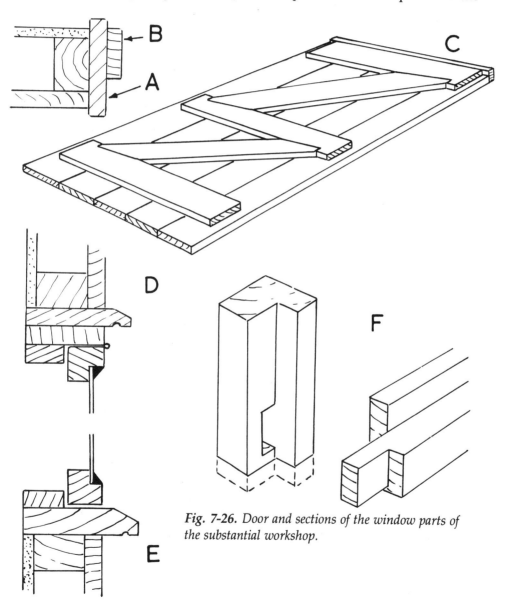

Fig. 7-26. Door and sections of the window parts of the substantial workshop.

projecting edges, and at the floor continue the lining pieces over the floor boards.

Ledge and brace the door in the usual way, except that there is a covering piece at the top with the brace immediately below it. At the bottom, the door overlaps the floor, as weatherproofing. Put stop strips in the sides of the doorway (FIG. 7-26B), but leave space at the top to clear the covering piece.

Use tongue-and-grove boards for the door. At the top, glue and screw the covering piece on (FIG. 7-26C). Make the ledges short enough to clear the stop strips, and fit the braces sloping up from the hinge side. Arrange hinges and fasteners over the ledges.

If you are going to line the building, you might do it before you fit the windows, so their framing can cover the lining boards, which might be plywood or particleboard. Include polyethylene sheet as a vapor barrier, if you wish. You can include insulating material in the space.

At the roof, close any spaces around the edges with cladding carried up to the roof boards or with pieces on top of the side frames. Nail lining material to the undersides of the purlins.

At the sides of the window openings, fit lining similar to that at the sides of the doorway. You can line the top in a similar way, but it would be more weatherproof if a piece extends and there is another strip below it for the window hinges, if you wish to make them open (FIG. 7-26D). At the bottom, make a wider sill to shed water (FIG. 7-26E).

Make the windows with rabbeted strips, with mortise-and-tenon joints at the corners (FIG. 7-26F). Fit hinges at the top and a stay and fastener at the bottom, if the window is to open. Screw other windows into their openings, preferably embedding them in jointing compound.

Because the shop floor is above the surrounding concrete base, you might make a wooden or concrete step at the doorway. If there is to be a storage lean-to along one side, you can make it with a roof similar in construction to the main roof, with open-frame supports and racks underneath.

Summer House

You can use a building with a sheltered porch for sunbathing or sitting out in chairs, even when the weather is not perfect, since the structure provides shelter from wind and rain. It can provide a peaceful retreat for anyone who wants to get away from activities inside the house. It might be a place for studying or a play center for children, although it is not primarily a playhouse. The enclosed part of the building will provide full shelter when you need it, and it makes a place to store chairs, tables, games, equipment, or gardening tools.

The summer house shown in FIG. 7-27 has a base which is 9 feet square, divided in half by a partition with a door and windows (FIG. 7-28). The upper part is open, with sheltering lower sides, and a rail front. The door is arranged to lift off, so you can put it inside instead of it swinging it and interfering with seating

Materials List for Summer House

Floor

7 joists	2	× 3	× 110
14 boards	1	× 6	× 110 or equivalent
2 ends	1	× 3	× 110

Partition and back

6 uprights	2	× 2	× 88
2 uprights	2	× 2	× 24
4 window uprights	2	× 2	× 32
5 rails	2	× 2	× 110
4 rails	2	× 2	× 36
4 tops	2	× 2	× 60

Sides

8 uprights	2	× 2	× 88
2 uprights	2	× 2	× 40
4 rails	2	× 2	× 110
2 top tails	2	× 2 or 3	× 120

Front

1 rail	2	× 2	× 110
2 rails	2	× 2	× 60
3 uprights	2	× 2	× 24
4 uprights	2	× 2	× 42
4 rails	2	× 2	× 28
4 posts	1¼	× 1¼	× 42
2 posts supports	2	× 2	× 24
2 rail tops	1¼	× 3	× 28

Edge covers

2 side-edge tops	1¼	× 4	× 54
2 side uprights	1	× 4	× 70
2 window sides	1	× 7	× 30
2 window sides	1	× 5	× 30
2 corner fillers	1	× 1	× 88

Windows

8 surrounds	1	× 4	× 28
8 stops	1	× 1	× 28
8 frames	2	× 2	× 28

Door

6 boards	1	× 6	× 80 or equivalent
3 ledges	1	× 6	× 36
2 braces	1	× 6	× 36
2 pegs	1½	× 1½	× 12

Roof

32 boards	1	× 6	× 60 or equivalent
2 battens	1	× 3	× 108
2 edges	2	× 1¼	× 120
4 ends	1¼	× 1¼	× 60
2 edge decorations	1	× 3	× 120
4 bargeboards	1	× 6	× 66
8 battens	¼	× 1	× 60

Cladding | 1 | × 6 shiplap boards or equivalent

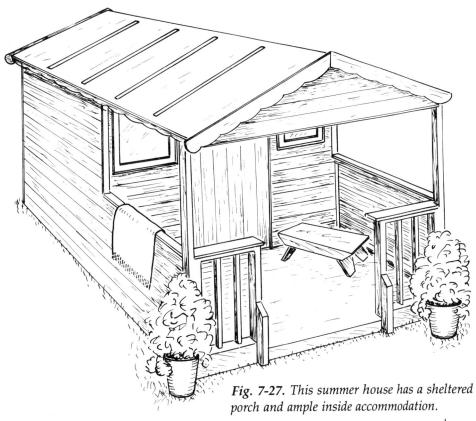

Fig. 7-27. This summer house has a sheltered porch and ample inside accommodation.

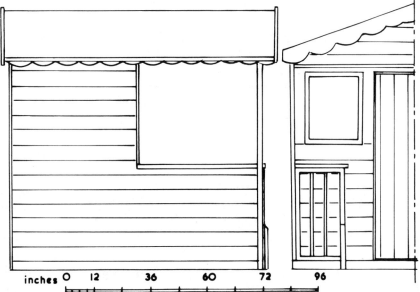

inches O   12   36   60   72   96

Fig. 7-28. Two views of the summer house of the suggested size.

on the porch. The exterior probably will look best with shiplap siding, but you could cover all the building or just the partition and door with plywood. The summer house is built on a floor, which forms part of the assembly.

Most of the framing can be 2-inch-square wood, although you could increase that to 2-inch-×-3-inch wood for greater strength. The roof is boarded, without separate purlins and is covered in the usual way. Much of the decorative appearance comes from the bargeboards and the matching eave's strips. The fence at the front has square uprights, but if you have the use of a lathe, they would look attractive if you made them as turned spindles with square ends.

Start with the floor, which should be 9 feet square. Use 1-inch boards and 2-inch-×-3-inch joists at about 18-inch centers (FIG. 7-29A). Close the joist's ends with strips across (FIG. 7-29B).

Make the building to fit the floor. Let the cladding overlap the floor—either just the top boards or to the bottoms of the joists. Use the floor as a guide to sizes when making the other parts.

Make the partition (FIG. 7-29C), and use it as a height guide when making other parts. It probably will be best to make the bottom part of the frame right across at first (FIG. 7-29D), then cut out the part for the doorway when you nail or screw the partition to the floor. Halve the frame parts or use open mortise-and-tenon joints. Make the frame width to fit inside the sides when they stand on the floor (FIG. 7-29E). The side cladding should go over the edge of the floor. At the apex, allow for a 2-inch-×-4-inch ridge to be slotted in (FIG. 7-29F) with a supporting rail underneath.

Vary door and window sizes, if you wish. When you have erected the building, the partition will fit between uprights on the side, with its covering overlapping, whether it is boards or plywood (FIG. 7-29G). Consequently, when you cover the partition, let the covering extend enough at the sides. At top and bottom, the covering should be level with the framing.

Make the back of the building the same as the partition, except leave out the door and windows and extend cladding over the floor edge. This procedure means the framing could be the same as the partition, with the center and bottom rails right across. Cover in the same way as you did the partition, since there is a similar overlap at the corners, which you will cover with a filler strip between the meeting boards.

The pair of sides could have windows, but these are shown closed (FIG. 7-30A). Cladding is taken to the front edge, but you could arrange open rails, similar to the front, if you wish. Cladding should be level with the frame all around, except you should allow for going over the floor edge and for going over the ends of the covering at the front of the partition. Cover pieces will be over this joint and along the top edge of the porch. Bevel the top edges of the sides to match the slope of the roof (FIG. 7-29H) . The top part of the frame extends 6 inches at the front and 3 inches at the back to support the roof. This top part also might be 3 inches deep for extra stiffness, and you could build small angle brackets into the front, open corners (FIG. 7-30B).

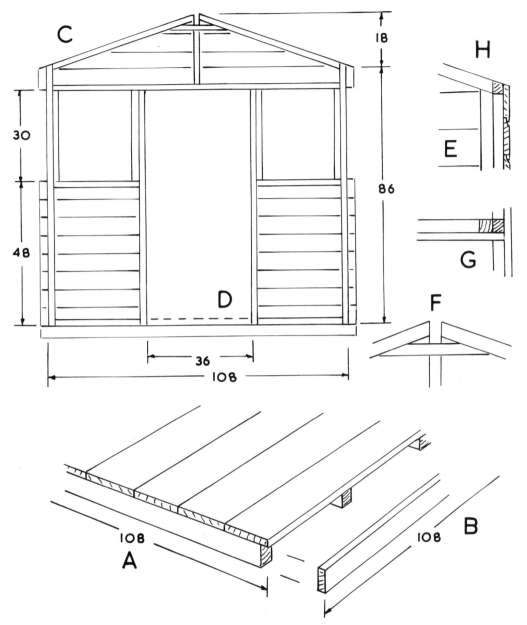

Fig. 7-29. *The summer house floor (A,B), its front (C,D), and constructional details (E,F,G,H).*

Use the top part of the partition as a guide when making the front, which fits between the side uprights (FIG. 7-30C), where you will nail and screw it. Extend its cladding over the side uprights. Slot the apex to take the ridge piece. Make its bottom edge 5 inches below the eaves. Fit a covering piece over this edge (FIG. 7-30D) and around its edges.

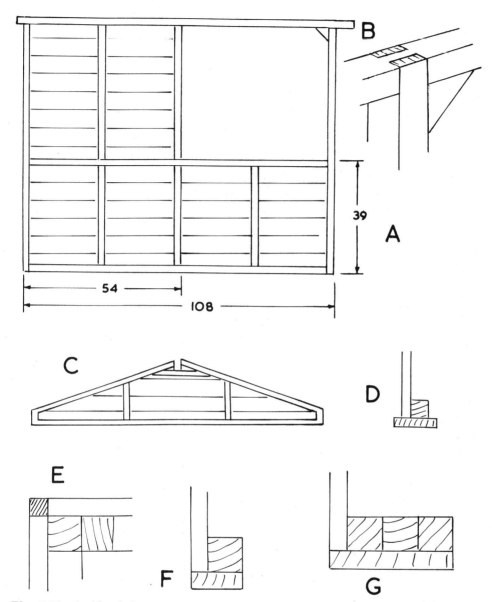

Fig. 7-30. *A side of the summer house (A,B), a roof truss (C), and assembly details (D,E,F,G).*

The rails or fence at the front are shown extending 24 inches from the sides, but you can make them any width. This width gives a good space for moving chairs and other things in and out, as well as for allowing several people to pass. Make two identical frames, with strong corner joints. Use planed wood and take the sharpness off the exposed edges. Two uprights about 1½ inch square should be enough intermediately (FIG. 7-31A).

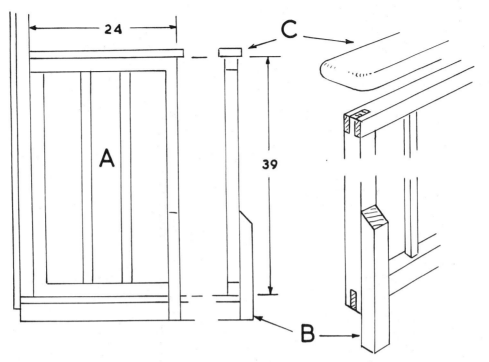

Fig. 7-31. Sizes and details of the fence at the front of the summer house.

Mount this assembly on the edge of the floor, and securely screw or bolt it to the floor and the side uprights . Arrange an overlapping piece to extend to the bottom of the floor (FIG. 7-31B) to stiffen the post at the open end of each piece.

Start erection of the building by bolting the two sides to the back and the partition—3/8-inch coach bolts at about 24-inch intervals should be sufficient. Square this assembly on the floor and nail the bottom edges down. Cut out the bottom piece across the doorway. Put square filler pieces in the rear corners (FIG. 7-30E). Cover exposed cladding edges at the partition and front (FIG. 7-30F). Put strips on each side of the window frames so they are the same thickness as the cladding (FIGS. 7-30G and 7-32A).

Fix the front rails and make an overlapping covering piece (FIG. 7-31C) with well-rounded edges. It will look best if you fix it with counterbored screws and cover them with plugs.

The two windows are shown fixed, but you could arrange for them to open, either with hinges at the top or on the outer edges. They are protected from the weather by the porch, so there is no need for a sill. Put strips all around the window openings (FIG. 7-32B), extending out a little and rounding all exposed edges. Make the window frames to fit closely (FIG. 7-32C), using rabbetted strips (FIG. 7-32D). You could screw the strips directly in place, but it will probably be easier to make a good, weather-tight fit with stop strips inside (FIG. 7-32E). Fit the glass with putty after you paint the woodwork.

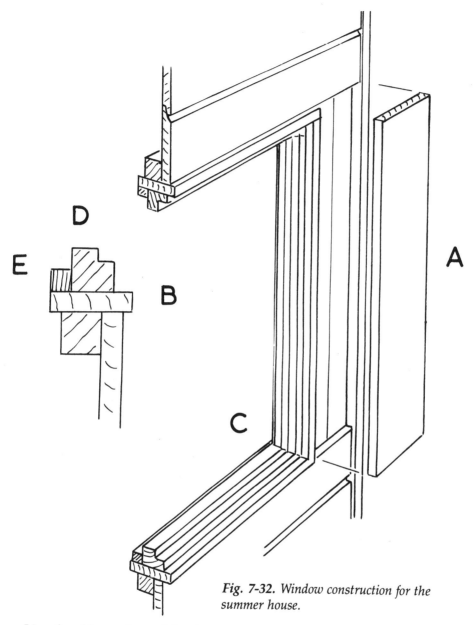

D

E

A

B

C

Fig. 7-32. Window construction for the summer house.

Line the sides and top of the doorway in the same way as the window openings. Put stop pieces near the inner edges (FIG. 7-33A). Make the door (FIG. 7-33B) an easy fit in the opening. Have the edge of the bottom ledge about 2 inches from the bottom of the door. If the top ledge has only a small clearance below the top stop strip in the opening, you can fit a lock with a keyhole there, or arrange a catch which turns with a knob. Place the other ledge centrally and arrange braces both ways.

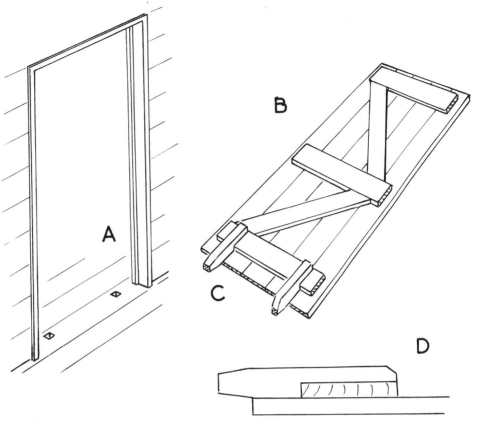

Fig. 7-33. The doorway and lift-out door for the summer house.

At the bottom, fit two pegs to go into holes in the floor (FIG. 7-33C). Notch over the bottom ledge and taper the extending ends slightly (FIG. 7-33D). Glue and screw these a few inches in from the sides of the door. Mark holes in the floor where you can drop the pegs in while you angle the door forward, so they hold it fairly close to the stop strips. When the top of the door is held with a lock or catch, the building will be secured.

Fit the ridge to extend 6 inches at the front and 3 inches at the back. If necessary, trim the ends of the eave's strips to the same length (FIG. 7-34A,B).

You can board the roof direct, using 1-inch-×-6-inch boards, preferably tongue-and-grooved. If you use boards with plain edges, there can be a central batten (FIG. 7-34C) to prevent the boards from warping out of line. You do not need to fix the batten to the back or partition.

Nail the boards to the ridge and to the eaves, where they should extend about 4 inches (FIG. 7-34D). At the eaves, put a strip underneath, with its edge and the ends of the boards cut vertically, if you are adding the side decoration (FIG. 7-34E). Put similar square-edge strips down the end boards (FIG. 7-34F) to support the bargeboards.

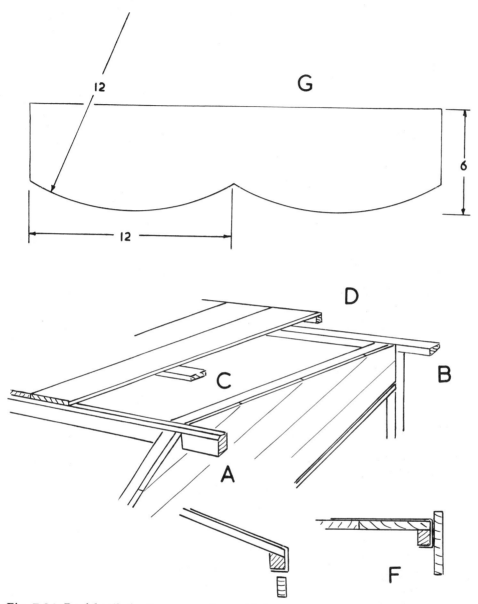

Fig. 7-34. *Roof details for the summer house (A,B,C,D,E,F) and a template for marking edge decorations (G).*

Carry roof covering over from eaves to eaves and turn under for nailing. Turn under at the ends. Allow ample overlap where there are any joints, and make joints in the direction that will let water run away from them. You could add capping strips, but they probably will not be necessary on this small roof. Nail battens down the slope at each side at about 18-inch intervals.

If the decoration on the lower edges of the bargeboards and eave's boards is to look right, the curves should be uniform. Make a template of at least two curves, using scrap plywood or hardboard (FIG. 7-34G). Use this template to mark all the shaped edges and to check them after shaping. Nail the boards to the roof to complete construction.

Barn

If you need to house larger animals, the building has to be bigger and stronger than most other small buildings. A horse or other large animal or group of animals might put considerable strain on the structure, so it has to be substantial. You need a good barrier inside to spread any load on the walls. If the barrier is a strong, smooth lining, that reduces any risk of damage to the animals and makes cleaning easier. The building should be high enough to allow for good air circulation. These facts mean that if the building is to be adequate for its purpose, you have to be prepared to build fairly large.

The barn shown in FIG. 7-35 has a double-slope roof and double doors. It is 11 feet square and 10 feet high. Opening windows are high in the back and shallow windows are at the sides, above the lining. A building this size provides room for

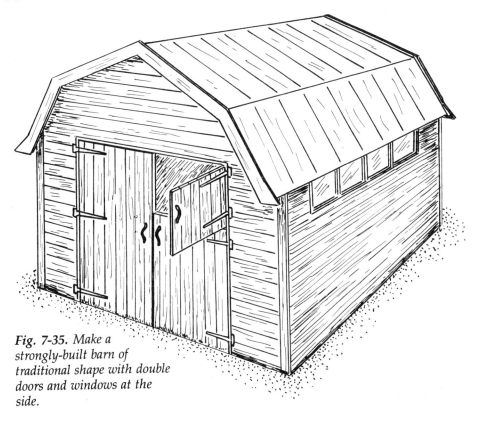

Fig. 7-35. *Make a strongly-built barn of traditional shape with double doors and windows at the side.*

Materials List for Barn

Front

2 corner posts	2	× 3	×	74
2 door posts	2	× 3	×	86
1 bottom rail	2	× 3	×	134
1 door rail	2	× 3	×	120
4 side rails	2	× 3	×	26
2 uprights	2	× 3	×	26
1 upright	2	× 3	×	36
2 rafters	2	× 3	×	84
2 rafters	2	× 3	×	60

Back

2 corner posts	2	× 3	×	74
2 posts	2	× 3	×	100
1 upright	2	× 3	×	36
3 rails	2	× 3	×	134
1 rail	2	× 3	×	12
1 rail	2	× 3	×	54
2 rafters	2	× 3	×	84
2 rafters	2	× 3	×	60
8 window linings	1	× 4	×	26

Sides

14 uprights	2	× 3	×	74
8 rails	2	× 3	×	130
8 window linings	1	× 4	×	24
16 window linings	1	× 4	×	18
8 window sills	1¼	× 5	×	24
4 corner fillers	1	× 2½	×	74

Roof truss

2 rafters				
2 rafters	2	× 3	×	60
1 tie	2	× 3	×	48
2 struts	2	× 3	×	120
3 gussets	2	× 3	×	60
	2	× 3	×	36

Roof

1 ridge	2	× 4	×	150
8 purlins	2	× 3	×	150
4 bargeboards	1	× 6	×	90
4 bargeboards	1	× 6	×	80
14 battens	½	× 1½	×	84
14 battens	½	× 1½	×	60

Doors

7 ledges	1	× 6	×	42
4 braces	1	× 6	×	70
Covering boards	1	× 6 tongue-and-groove boards		
3 door linings	1	× 5	×	86
8 edges	1	× 3	×	40

Cladding

Ends and sides	1	× 6 shiplap boards or equivalent	
Roof	1	× 6 plain or tongue-and-groove boards	
Doors	1	× 6 tongue-and-groove boards	
Lining	½ or ¾ particleboard or plywood		

a horse to be stabled, with space for tack and feed. If you are concerned with smaller animals, you can accommodate two or more. The barn would also make a good place to store all the many things you would use on a small farm. The building has an attractive appearance, and you might wish to use it for many purposes in your yard. With different window arrangements, it would make a good workshop. You can alter doors to suit your needs. As shown, the doors are big enough for small trailers or other wheeled vehicles. A motorcycle, trail bike, or even a small car could fit through them.

The drawings and instructions are for a barn framed with 2-inch-×-3-inch section wood covered with horizontal shiplap boards (FIG. 7-36). Suggested lining material is particleboard or plywood.

Measure your available space. Allow for laying a concrete base larger than the barn area. You must securely bolt down a building this size. You may prefabricate the ends and sides. Roofing is done in position after you have erected the walls.

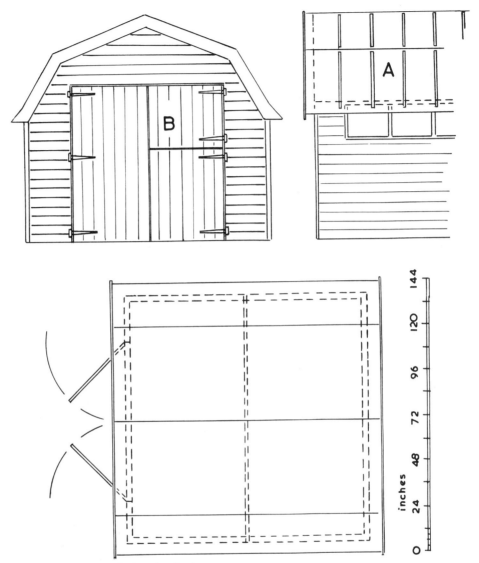

Fig. 7-36. Suggested sizes for the barn.

Start by making the ends (FIG. 7-37). The back (FIG. 7-37A) is closed, but the front has a 7-foot-square doorway (FIG. 7-37B). Assemble framing with the 3 inch way towards the cladding. Halve or tenon joints in the framing. Halve crossing parts of internal framing. The central rail is at the height intended for the lining. If that height does not suit your needs, alter its position. This height allows for shallow windows above the lining and under the eaves. Angles for the roof are shown (FIG. 7-37C). If you do not work exactly to these angles, it does not matter, as long as each end is symmetrical and they match.

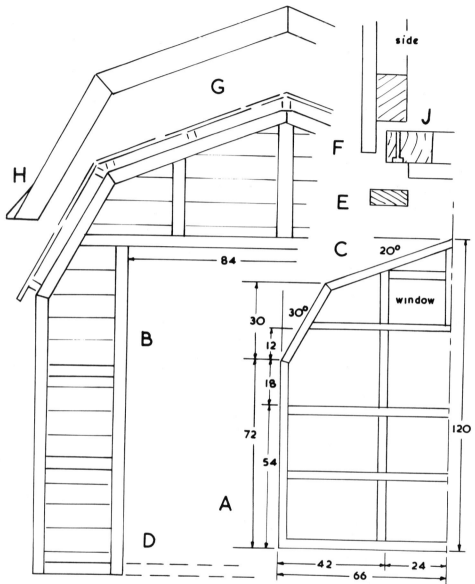

Fig. 7-37. Details of the ends of the barn, which you should make first.

Make the back and use it as a pattern for the outline of the front. Make the bottom rail of the front right across (FIG. 7-37D), but after you have erected the walls and anchored them down, you can cut it away to give a clear door opening. You can improve appearance of the ends if you add a broad filler piece at each corner (FIG. 7-37E). To allow for this filler piece, stop the shiplap boards over the center of the corner posts. Take them to the edges of the roof slopes.

The two sides are the same (FIG. 7-38A), unless you want to fit a side door or alter the number of windows. The drawing shows four window openings on each side (FIG. 7-38B), but you could reduce this to two or none. The tops of the windows are covered by the roof, so you cannot arrange them to swing outwards very much. They could open inwards, but it probably will be satisfactory to make them fixed.

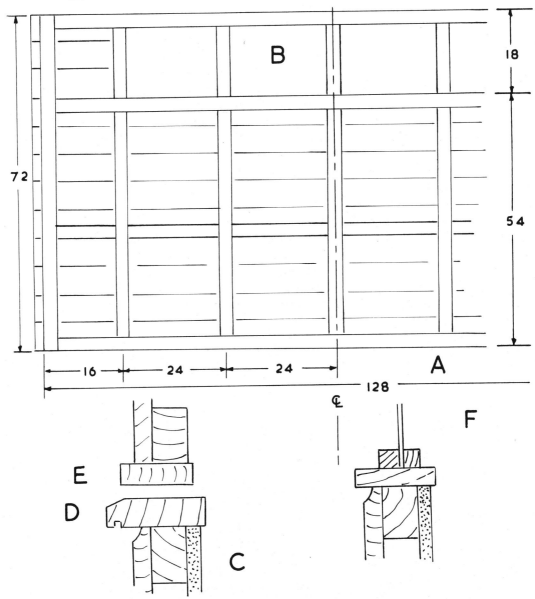

Fig. 7-38. A side of the barn and sections at the windows.

Allow for the cladding boards extending at the ends to cover the end-corner posts (FIG. 7-37F). Finish level at top and bottom. You do not have to bevel the top to match the slope of the roof.

You could add the lining at this stage or leave it until after erection. Take it to the window line (FIG. 7-38C). Cover it there with a sill extending outwards (FIG. 7-38D). Line the tops and sides of the openings (FIG. 7-38E). The roof will provide protection to the upper parts of the windows.

The roof needs a truss halfway along. This truss must match the ends of the building, so use one of the ends as a pattern for the shape. The outline is the same down to the top of the side panels. As no boards are across to strengthen the framing, securely nail or screw gussets under the angles (FIG. 7-39A). The tie is the same height as the rail above the doorway. From its center, take struts at 45 degrees to it, up to the rafters (FIG. 7-39B). Cut the rafters to rest on the tops of the side frames, with locating blocks there (FIG. 7-39C). The purlins are 2 inches × 3 inches and the ridge is from 2-inch-×-4-inch stock. Bevel the top of the ridge piece to match the slope of the roof (FIG. 7-39D). These slopes have to match the tops of the purlins. Measure their heights and cut down the tops of the ends and the truss, so the roof at the ridge will be the same height from the framing as it is at the purlins (FIG. 7-39E).

Make cleats to position and hold the ridge and purlins (FIG. 7-39F). At the angle of the roof, put the purlins as close together as possible. The top purlins are midway between the angle of the roof and the ridge. The lower purlins should come close to the joint with the sides.

Assemble the walls, using 1/2-inch bolts, and sink their heads so the cover strips will hide them (FIG. 7-37J). For ample strength in any circumstances, have

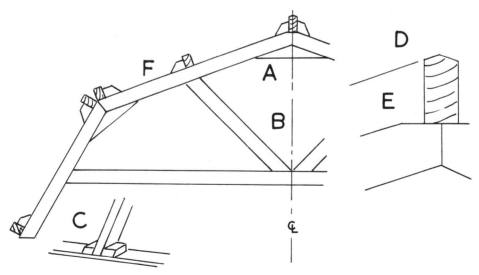

Fig. 7-39. Details of the barn-roof truss.

the bolts at about 12-inch centers. Check squareness and fasten down to the base. Cut out the bottom of the end frame under the doorway. If necessary, nail on temporary braces to keep the building square and to hold the truss upright until you fit the roof.

The purlins and ridge should extend 6 inches at each end. Fix them in position. The roof covering could be shingles over 1/2-inch plywood. However, it's best to use 1-inch boarding, covered by roofing felt or any of the sheet-roof material supplied in a roll, taken over the ridge and turned under the roof boards.

Cut the board ends to meet reasonably close at the ridge and at the angles. Take the ends of the boards to about 1 inch below the tops of the building sides. A gap will be all around under the roof boards. You can leave the gap entirely or in part for ventilation, or you can fill the narrow spaces against the lower purlins or the wider gaps between purlins at the ends.

Make bargeboards at the end (FIG. 7-37G). Take the ends a short distance below the roof edges. You can give a traditional appearance with triangles if you turn the board line outwards (FIG. 7-37H). Put battens down the slope of the roof, over the covering, at about 18-inch intervals (FIG. 7-36A).

The double doors are ledged and braced, but because of their size and weight, you must double them around the edges (FIG. 7-40A). Put lining strips around the door opening, covering the wall lining as well as the cladding (FIG. 7-40B). Make the doors with vertical tongue-and-groove boards. Put braces across level with the board ends, and fill in to the same thickness at the edges (FIG. 7-40C). So the diagonal braces take any compression loads which come on them without allowing movement, fit them closely at their ends, making sure there are no gaps that might cause the door to drop.

You could make one half in two parts for the usual stable door pattern (FIGS. 7-36B and 7-40D). A height of 48 inches would give a horse about 36 inches to put its head through, but the gap would not be big enough for most animals to jump through. Make each door part similar to the large door, with bracing upwards from the hinge side.

For hanging the doors, T hinges about 18 inches long would be suitable. Notch the lining strips around the doorway for the hinges, which should come over the ledges on the doors and be held with long screws in both parts. You can take bolts right through to nuts instead of screws. Arrange bolts upwards and downwards on the inner edge of one door, and place a lock on the other door to close it or a hasp and staple for a padlock. Put handles on the outside of both doors. If you make one door in two parts, put a bolt inside to hold them together when you want to use the parts as one.

How you make the windows depends on the use of the barn. If you want it to be weathertight, the windows should be made closely. The overhang of the roof, however, gives partial protection to the windows and you can use a simple construction if a slight risk of leakage is not important. With the window openings lined, you can hold glass in between double strips (FIG. 7-38F). You could

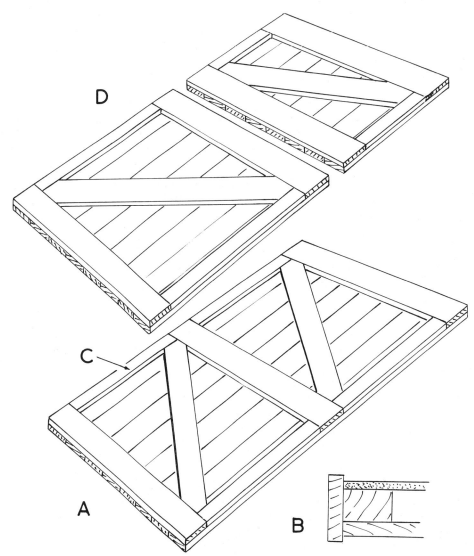

Fig. 7-40. Construction of the barn doors.

embed the glass in jointing compound, or you could put single strips around the glass and putty the glass against them.

For better windows, frame them separately to fit in the openings. If you want any windows to open by being hinged at the top, make them this way.

Play Barn

A traditional barn has an attractive appearance, and there is an appeal of the olden days to young people, which makes them want to use such a building in the ways they have read about. The scaled-down barn in FIGS. 7-41 and 7-42A has

Fig. 7-41. A child-size play barn can provide storage, inside play area, shelter for toys, and a porch to sit under.

the traditional shape with a mansard or gambrel roof. The door is the stable type, so children can close the bottom part and look out above it. A lean-to commonly used as a cart shelter in a full-size barn now stores toys up to the size of bicycles. You can use a lean-to at the other side as a porch for sitting out or for playing with toys. The barn is large enough for many children to play in it at one time, and it makes a good store for outdoor equipment and the toys which are too large to be taken indoors.

Most of the construction is with shiplap boards on 2-inch-square framing. Make the roof with boards on purlins, then cover with roofing felt or other similar material. The standard design has the door at one end and a window in the other end. You could have doors in both ends. There could be windows in one or both sides, and you might put a door from the barn into the lean-to.

Start with the two ends (FIG. 7-43A), which are the same, except in the closed end, the central rail is taken right across (FIGS. 7-42B and 7-43B). The boarding goes across below the central rail, and the space above becomes the window. The bottom rail across the doorway can remain in the finished barn, or you can cut it away after you have anchored the building. If you want to move the barn later, it is better to leave the bottom rail in place.

Materials List for Play Barn

Door

4 ledges	1	× 6	× 30
2 braces	1	× 6	× 34
2 sides	1	× 3	× 40
2 sides	1	× 3	× 30
6 boards	1	× 6	× 40
6 boards	1	× 6	× 30

Sides

8 uprights	2	× 2	× 62
6 rails	2	× 2	× 80
4 corner fillers	1	× 2½	× 62

Roof

8 purlins	2	× 2	× 10
8 bargeboards	1	× 5	× 24
10 battens	½	× 1	× 24

Covering

Cladding	1	× 6 shiplap boards
Roofing	1	× 6 plain or tongue-and-groove boards

Ends

4 uprights	2	× 2	× 90
4 uprights	2	× 2	× 64
2 uprights	2	× 2	× 24
4 rails	2	× 2	× 86
1 rail	2	× 2	× 40
8 rafters	2	× 2	× 30
2 door edges	1	× 4	× 74
1 door edge	1	× 4	× 40
4 window edges	1	× 4	× 40

Large lean-to

1 rail	2	× 3	× 86
1 rail	2	× 2	× 86
2 rafters	2	× 2	× 64
2 legs	2	× 2	× 52

Small lean-to

1 rail	2	× 3	× 86
1 rail	2	× 2	× 86
2 rafters	2	× 2	× 32
2 uprights	2	× 2	× 30
2 braces	2	× 2	× 32

Take the shiplap boards to the edges of the doorway. When you erect the barn, the boards from the sides will overlap the end uprights (FIG. 7-43C). For a neat end finish, cut back the boards on the end to the center of each upright (FIG. 7-43D) so you can put a filler piece in each corner (FIG. 7-43E) after you bolt the parts together. Carry the boards to the edges on the roof slopes. Nail the purlins

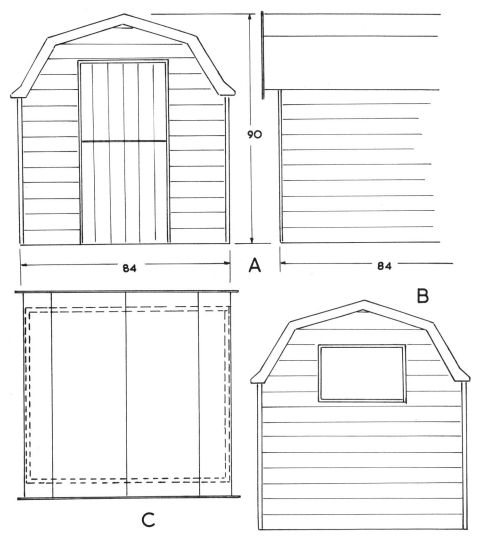

Fig. 7-42. Sizes and four views of the main building of the play barn.

to the edges of the end frames and locate them with cleats, which you can put on now or later (FIG. 7-43F).

If you are to line the building with plywood, handle the ends now. Edge the door and window openings (FIG. 7-43G), going over any lining and extending a short distance inside and out.

The barn sides are simple rectangular frames (FIG. 7-44A). Leave the top edges square. Have the cladding level with the framing at top and bottom, but at the ends, extend the boards enough to overlap the end uprights.

Assemble the ends and sides. Use 1/4-inch or 5/16-inch coach bolts at about 18-inch centers in the corners, and cover them with the filler strips. Square the

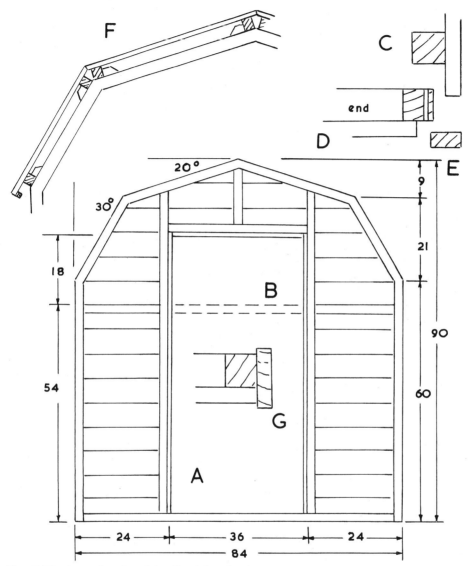

Fig. 7-43. An end and roof details of the play barn.

assembly by comparing diagonal measurements, then anchor the building to its base.

Fit the purlins against their cleats to extend about 5 inches at each end, so the bargeboards will be 6 inches from the barn ends (FIGS. 7-42C and 7-44B).

Place boards over the purlins with fitted ends where they meet on the ridge and at the angles. You will be covering these joints, but the covering will fit better if you avoid gaps. Boards can be plain or tongue-and-groove. As an alternative, you could use 1/2-inch or 3/4-inch plywood. Put strips of covering material along

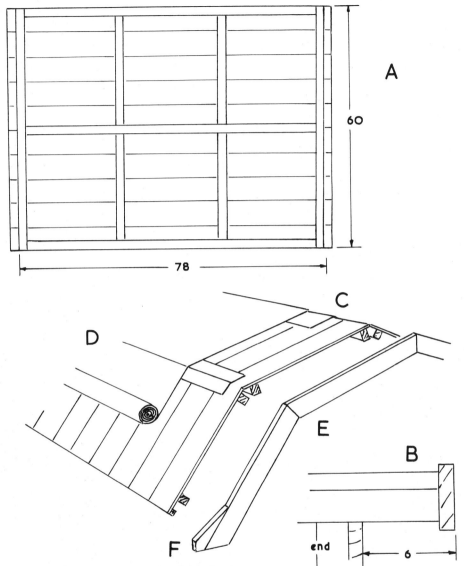

Fig. 7-44. *Side and roof details of the play barn.*

the joints (FIG. 7-44C). Roll the main covering material from eaves to eaves (FIG. 7-44D), where you should turn it under edge strips and nail it. Turn down at the ends so bargeboards will trap the material. Fit battens at about 18-inch intervals down the slopes on each surface to hold the covering.

Make the bargeboards to stand a little above the surface of the roof and extend below the purlins. Fit the boards to each other (FIG. 7-44E) and take the ends to a few inches below the roof level. Trim the ends parallel with the floor. Triangular additions (FIG. 7-44F) will give the traditional appearance. Gaps under the roof can be left as ventilation. To close them, you can fit pieces in or continue the cladding to touch the roof.

Make the door in the same way as the two-part door described for the barn, and hinge it in the same way. You can leave the window at the other end open. You could hinge a shutter over it, or you could glaze it, either with glass between fillets, as in the last building, or with a separately framed window that you can hinge open.

The barn is a complete unit. If you are going to add lean-tos, they fit against the cladding, and you can screw or bolt the parts through to framework inside.

If the barn would be full-size, the lean-to would form a shed for farm implements and be designed to suit that need. In this case, make the main lean-to as long as the barn and as high under the eaves as it can go. Then extend it 60 inches to its own eave's height of about 48 inches or 12 inches less than its higher edge. Two end supporting rafters will be sufficient (FIG. 7-45A). Use 2-inch-square strips, except for a 2-inch-×-3-inch piece against the barn wall. Screw this piece through the cladding or bolt it into the framing.

Make the lean-to length the same as the barn wall or take it to fit inside the bargeboards, if you want maximum roof length. Bevel the top of the 3-inch piece to suit the slope of the lean-to. Notch the rafters into it (FIG. 7-45B). At the other end, join in a matching lengthwise piece (FIG. 7-45C), and make legs to fit a short distance back from it (FIG. 7-45D). What you do with the bottoms of the legs depends on the ground or base. You can drive a leg into the ground or set it in concrete. It is shown with a broad base (FIG. 7-45E), which would spread the load on the earth or you could screw down to wood or concrete. The joints in the assembly could be open mortise-and-tenon or halving joints.

Allow for the lean-to roof to fit under the eaves of the main roof (FIG. 7-45F). You can board the lean-to in the same way as the main roof, or you could use plywood. For 1/2-inch plywood, there should be a supporting purlin between the ends, halfway down the slope. Cover the roof to match the main roof. At the outer end, turn the material under and nail it. At the upper end, take it through and nail it to the top of the barn side. Arrange battens down the lean-to slope to match those on the barn roof.

You can make a narrower lean-to in the same way, but if it is no more than 30 inches wide, you could support it with end brackets, so there are no posts to the ground. This lean-to should be wide enough if young people want to use it as a porch for sitting under. Arrange the brackets to come on the end uprights of the barn, but extend the roof over them. Place a 2-inch-×-3-inch piece along the barn wall, in the same way as for the large lean-to. It can come between the brackets, without being joined to them.

Make the two brackets (FIG. 7-45G) with halved or mortise-and-tenon joints. Allow for a lengthwise piece similar to that on the large lean-to. Use boards or plywood for the roof, and finish it in the same way as the other lean-to.

It is possible to add one or both lean-tos after you complete the barn, but if you intend to fit them at the same time as you build the barn, include them in the

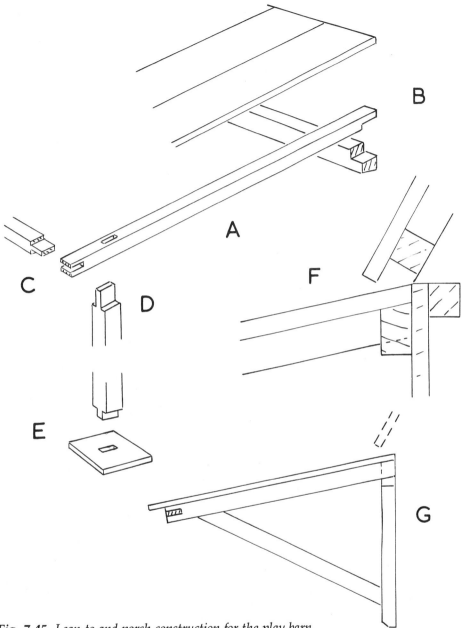

Fig. 7-45. Lean-to and porch construction for the play barn.

main work schedule and do their roofing as you do the main roofing. In that way, you can deal with the inner ends of some lean-to roof parts more easily.

How you finish the whole building depends on several factors. You can leave some woods, such as cedar, to weather without painting, or you could use a paint or a colored preservative. Traditionally, many of these barns were red, with a different color for the bargeboards. The roof probably will be black. The brighter colors might appeal to young users, but you might wish to choose them to fit in with the surroundings.

Studio

Anyone practicing an art form needs good, all-around light which doesn't glare. This fact applies to three-dimensional carving and sculpture as well as to painting. There should be plenty of windows that let in light where needed, as broadly as possible, so there is no glare and harsh shadows are not cast.

Sloping windows will pass light without glare better than upright windows, and they will spread the natural illumination. An artist usually wants one wall without windows. The size of a studio will depend on the work to be done and how many people are to be accommodated. The studio in FIG. 7-46 is designed for a single worker on projects of only moderate size. You can use the same construction for a studio of a different size. The suggested sizes are for an 8-foot-square floor space and the same size maximum height (FIG. 7-47). Lined walls and roof are advisable. The smooth interior, painted a light color, will help to disperse lighting evenly. Although you might use a concrete base, a wooden floor over it would be comfortable and kinder to dropped tools. Cladding is assumed to be

Fig. 7-46. This studio gets good light from sloping windows.

Materials List for Studio

Ends

6 uprights	2	× 2	×	80
2 uprights	2	× 2	×	90
2 uprights	2	× 2	×	50
2 uprights	2	× 2	×	56
6 rails	2	× 2	×	98
2 tops	2	× 2	×	98

Back

5 uprights	2	× 2	×	80
3 rails	2	× 2	×	92
2 corners	1	× 1	×	80

Lower front

5 uprights	2	× 2	×	50
2 rails	2	× 2	×	92
2 corners	1	× 1	×	50

Upper front

6 uprights	2	× 2	×	56
2 rails	2	× 2	×	92
1 sill	1	× 4$\frac{1}{2}$	×	92
2 cover pieces	1	× 5	×	56

End window

3 frames	1	× 3$\frac{1}{2}$	×	34
1 sill	1	× 4$\frac{1}{2}$	×	34
4 frames	2	× 2	×	34

Door

3 ledges	1	× 6	×	32
2 braces	1	× 6	×	40
6 boards	1	× 6	×	78

Roof

5 rafters	2	× 3	×	116
1 fascia	1	× 6	×	116
4 edges	1$\frac{1}{2}$	× 1$\frac{1}{2}$	×	116

Covering: boards 1 × 6 or $\frac{3}{4}$ plywood

Cladding

Shiplap boards 1 × 6 or $\frac{3}{4}$ plywood (approximately)

shiplap boarding, but you could use plywood. The 8-foot-square size makes for economical use of standard plywood sheets.

Start with one side that has a door (FIG. 7-48A). You can use any of the usual framing joints at most places. Where the sloping and vertical fronts join, use a halving joint, with screws both ways (FIG. 7-48B). Cover with boards, cut level at the back and front edges, but with enough left at the top to trim to the same height as the rafters (FIG. 7-48C).

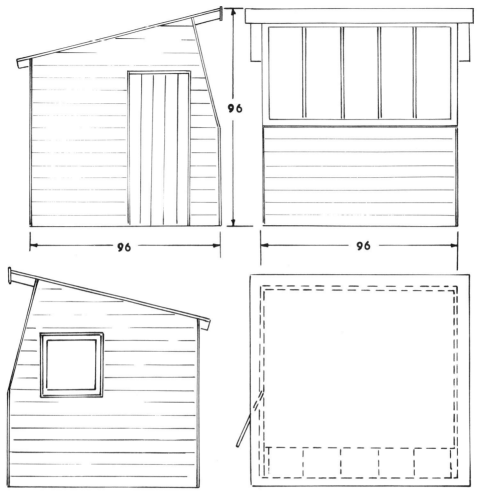

Fig. 7-47. Suggested sizes for the studio.

Make the opposite side identical, but instead of a doorway, you might allow space for an opening window, the same width as the door (FIG. 7-48D). Cover with boards in the same way as the first side.

The back is a simple, rectangular frame (FIG. 7-49A). Divide the width into four, and put a central rail across. Check the height against the matching parts of the sides, and bevel the top frame member to match the slope of the roof. At the top, let the covering boards project about 3 inches. When you assemble the studio on-site, notch the covering boards for the rafters and trim level with their top surfaces. At the sides, allow the covering to extend by the width of the end uprights. Then when you assemble, the board ends will overlap, and you can put a square strip in the corner (FIG. 7-48E).

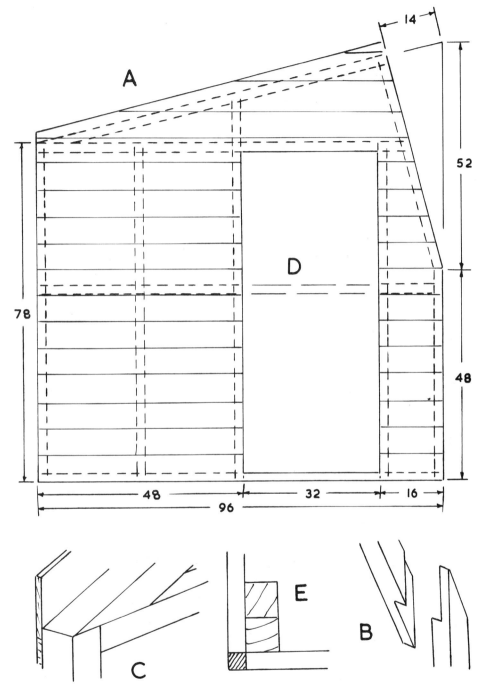

Fig. 7-48. The studio end.

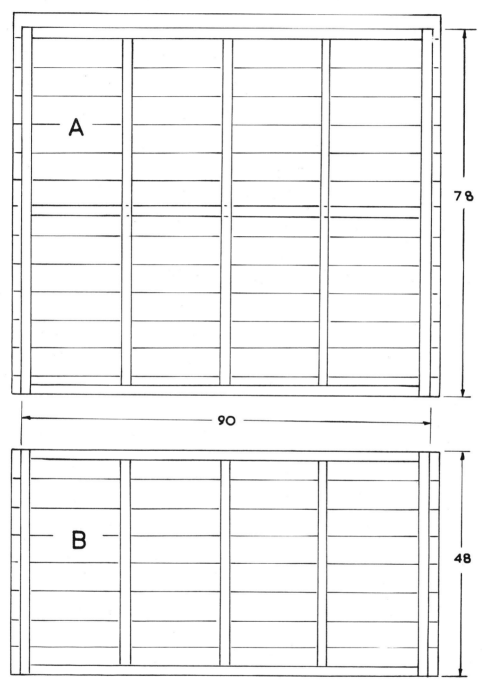

Fig. 7-49. Back and front of the studio.

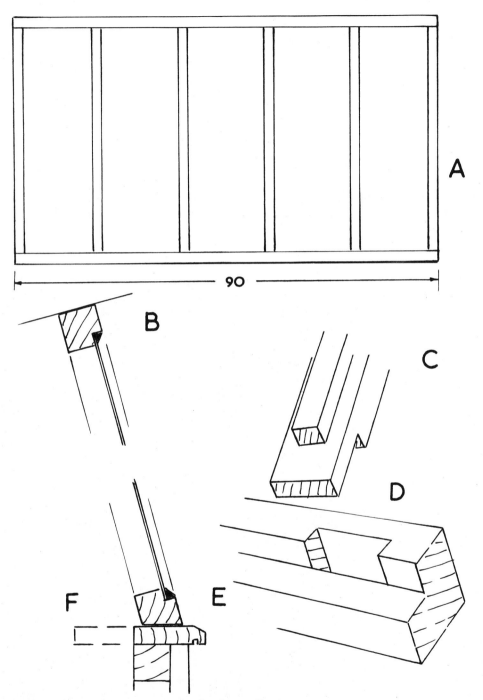

A

90

B

C

D

E

F

Fig. 7-50. Glazing arrangements for the studio.

Make the lower front (FIG. 7-49B) to match the back width. The covering boards are level at top and bottom edges, but they extend at the sides in the same way as on the back.

Fully glaze the upper front. Divide it into five glass panels (FIG. 7-50A). The overall length should be the same as the lower front, and the height must match the sloping parts of the sides. All of the parts are rabbeted—5/8 inch deep and 5/8 inch wide should be enough. The outside parts have rabbets on one edge (FIG. 7-50B). The intermediate pieces have rabbets on two edges (FIG. 7-50C).

It is possible to dowel parts together, but the best joints are mortises and tenons (FIG. 7-50D). Treat the corners similar to the intermediate joint shown, but reduce the width of the tenon at the outside. Do not fit the glass until after you have erected the building.

Arrange a sill on the lower front for the upper front to fit over (FIG. 7-50E). You can extend the sill inwards to make a shelf (FIG. 7-50F). It would be difficult to waterproof the joint between the upper frame and the sill with glue. It is better to embed it in jointing compound. Cover the ends of the upper front with strips over the edges of the studio ends when you assemble it.

Make the opening window in the end the same way as described earlier (FIGS. 7-18 and 7-26). Make the door with vertical boards and ledges and braces, as described (FIGS. 7-18 and 7-26). If you do not include a window, put a second brace across. Braces should slope up from the hinged side. Line the doorway and arrange stop strips in the way described earlier for the door you are using,

Make the roof with rafters laid from back to front (FIG. 7-51A). Let the rafters project about 6 inches at back and 12 inches at front. Notch the plywood at the back. At the front, fill the gaps between the rafters with 2-inch-×-3-inch pieces, level with the front of the glazed part (FIG. 7-51B).

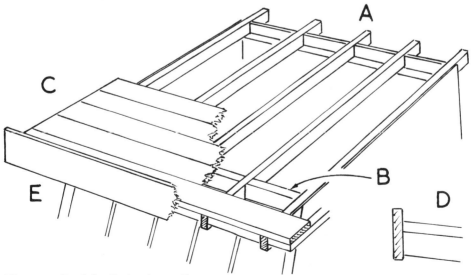

Fig. 7-51. Roof details for the studio.

Cover the rafters with boards across (FIG. 7-51C) to give a 6-inch overhang at the sides. Thicken all edges with strips underneath. Bevel the front so it is vertical (FIG. 7-51D). Turn the covering material under and nail underneath to the strips. Put battens on top from front to back.

At the front, put a fascia board across (FIG. 7-51E). Do not make it too deep or it will restrict light in the windows. You could give it a decorative shape if you wish.

When you have completed assembly, you can line the walls and under the rafters with plywood or particleboard. If you mounted the building on a concrete base, there could be a wooden floor. Place the boards over the bottom framing parts, and lay stiffeners across underneath at about 18-inch intervals. Fit the floor before lining the walls.

Dual-Purpose Playhouse

If you want to make a building that children can use for playing and that would be useful for storage for gardening tools as big as lawn mowers, it must be a reasonable size and stronger than anything intended purely as somewhere for younger children to play. It is likely to be permanent, so you must make it weatherproof. The requirements mean its construction will be very similar to other small buildings.

The dual-purpose building shown in FIG. 7-52 has a frontage with a porch that can be used as a play area. It is large enough for children up to young teenagers, who might use it as a base for games and activities in the vicinity. At the back is a large lift-out door, which gives access to a floor area about 60 inches × 72 inches, to use for storage when children no longer need the building.

As drawn in FIG. 7-53A, the door is almost up to adult height at the front, with a glazed window alongside it. A porch that projects 24 inches shelters the door and window. You can lock the door, so the building then becomes a storage place with wide access at the back. Construction is mostly of 2-inch square strips covered by shiplap boards.

No floor is shown, but you should place the building on a concrete base. You can put a board floor inside, made with 2-inch-square framing covered with 1-inch boards that project onto the bottom parts of the frames. The frame that crosses under the door is intended to be left in place, but you could cut it away after you have anchored the other parts of the building, if you want a clear floor for wheeling things in.

Start by making a pair of sides (FIG. 7-54A). You can use any of the normal framing joints, except two places need special treatment. At the apex, three pieces meet together. Miter the two sloping pieces together, then halve their meeting ends with the upright (FIG. 7-54B). Place a purlin halfway down the long slope (FIG. 7-54C). This placement requires cutting through the framing member. Put a piece under the cut (which does not go through the covering boards), and square its underside to meet the central upright (FIG. 7-54D).

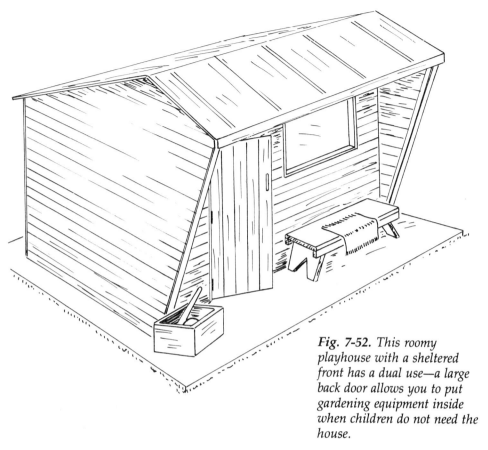

***Fig. 7-52.** This roomy playhouse with a sheltered front has a dual use—a large back door allows you to put gardening equipment inside when children do not need the house.*

The front (FIG. 7-55A) fits between the uprights under the apex, so check the height there as you put the frame together. All of the framing is 2-inch-square strips, except for the top, which forms the ridge. The top is 2 inches × 3 inches, and you must bevel to match the slopes of the roof (FIG. 7-55B). If you want the cladding to go close up, bevel that as well.

Carry the uprights to the full height, to give the best support to the horizontal shiplap boarding. Arrange rails between and across them for the doorway and the window. Check squareness by comparing diagonal measurements, as this frame controls the accuracy and symmetry of the building.

When you erect the building, the joints between the front and the sides will look best if the cladding of the front continues over the uprights on the sides (FIG. 7-55C). Allow enough boarding on each side of the frame to almost cover the adjoining upright.

You can line the building, but assuming it will serve your purpose without lining, edge the doorway and window opening with strips, allowing them to project a little inside and outside (FIG. 7-55D). When you make the back (FIG. 7-56A), its height must match the rear edges of the sides and its width should be

Materials List for
Dual-Purpose Playhouse

2 uprights	2	× 2 × 86
6 uprights	2	× 2 × 74
2 rails	2	× 2 × 74
4 rails	2	× 2 × 70
2 rails	2	× 2 × 30

Front

4 uprights	2	× 2 × 86
2 rails	2	× 2 × 80
1 rail	1	× 3 × 80
1 rail	2	× 2 × 42
2 window posts	2	× 2 × 30
4 window edges	1	× 4 × 24
8 glazing bars	1	× 1 × 24
2 doorway sides	1	× 4 × 70
1 doorway top	1	× 4 × 32

Back

4 uprights	2	× 2 × 68
2 rails	2	× 2 × 80
1 rail	2	× 3 × 80

Back door

3 uprights	2	× 2 × 58
1 rail	2	× 2 × 62
1 rail	2	× 3 × 62
2 diagonals	2	× 2 × 70

Front door

3 ledges	1	× 6 × 30
2 diagonals	1	× 6 × 40
6 boards	1	× 6 × 70

Roof

1 front strip	2	× 3 × 90
1 purlin	2	× 2 × 86
1 fascia	1	× 5 × 90
1 rear edge	1	× 1 × 90
Covering, boards about	1	× 6
5 battens	1/2	× 1 × 65
5 battens	1/2	× 1 × 26
Cladding, shiplap boards	1	× 6

the same as the front. Framing is 2-inch-square strips, except the top, which is 2 inches × 3 inches. The doorway is 60 inches wide and 55 inches high. This doorway takes quite a lot out of the back, so it is important that the remaining back is made strongly to prevent distortion of that part of the building. Bevel the top edge to suit the slope of the roof (FIG. 7-56B).

When you assemble the building, the covering boards on the back should overlap the uprights on the sides to leave a space for a filler piece (FIG. 7-56C). At the top of the doorway, take covering boards to the edge of the door. At the sides,

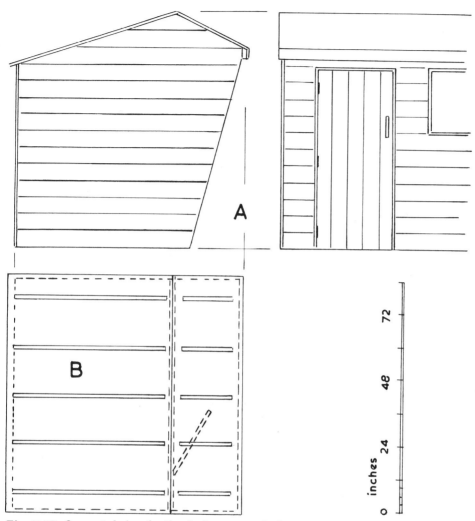

Fig. 7-53. Suggested sizes for the dual-purpose playhouse.

the covering boards on the door must overlap the uprights on the doorway, so cut back the ends of the shiplap boarding on the back to half the thickness of those uprights (FIG. 7-58D).

Make the door frame to fit easily in its opening (FIG. 7-56E). Use 2-inch-square pieces. The bottom, however, which is liable to get rougher use, should be 3 inches deep. Fit diagonals to keep the door in shape. Fit covering boards level at top and bottom, but at the sides, extend them to overlap the door uprights. When clearance of the rear of the building is important, cut the door boarding so its lines match the boarding around the doorway.

This extended boarding on the door will prevent the door being pushed

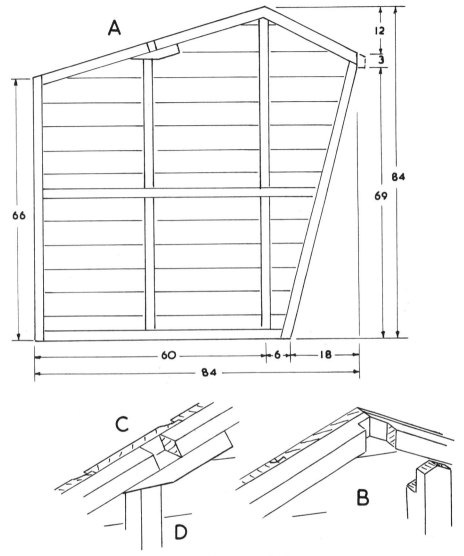

Fig. 7-54. *Details of an end for the dual-purpose playhouse.*

inwards. You now have to prevent it from pulling outwards. At the bottom, you can put a board across the width of the door, or make three pegs from l-inch-×-3-inch wood to hook over the bottom member of the back frame (FIG. 7-56F). Taper slightly for easy fitting. Glue and screw to the inside of the bottom of the door. The glue and screws retain the bottom of the door. What you do at the top depends on the degree of security you desire. The simplest arrangement is a large wooden turnbutton on the back to turn down over the center of the door. You could fit a hasp and staple for a padlock alongside the turnbutton.

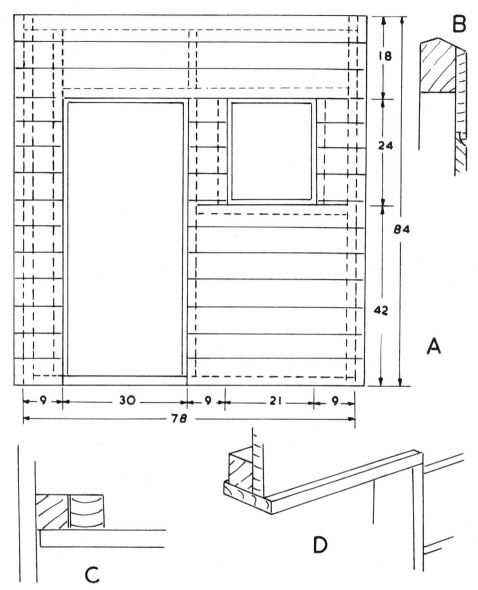

Fig. 7-55. *Details of the front of the dual-purpose playhouse.*

You can cover the roof in several ways. You could use corrugated metal or plastic sheets. Plywood would be satisfactory if you covered it with roofing felt or similar material. The method suggested here is to board and cover the roof (FIG. 7-57A).

Assemble the front, back, and sides, using 3/8-inch coach bolts at about 18-inch intervals. Square the assembly and fasten it down to the base before adding the roof. Fit purlins between the slots in the sides (FIG. 7-57B). Fit the front

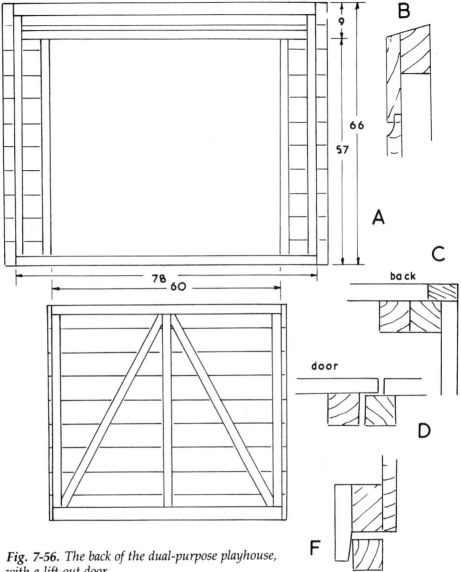

Fig. 7-56. *The back of the dual-purpose playhouse, with a lift-out door.*

piece to the ends (FIG. 7-57C). The roof boards extend 2 inches at each side, and the front piece should project the same amount. Cut the boards to meet closely at the ridge (FIG. 7-57D), and project 2 inches at the back. They could be plain boards, tongue-and-groove boards, or shiplap boards laid with the shaped parts underneath. Start at one side and allow for the overhang, then fit further boards tightly.

Put a strip under the ends of the boards at the back (FIG. 7-57E). Carry roof-covering material right over the ridge from front to back. Put a smaller piece over

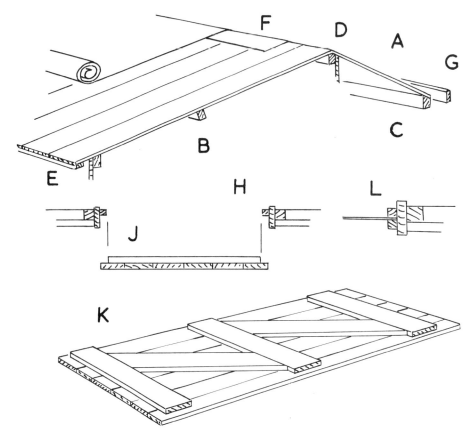

Fig. 7-57. *Roof and front door for the dual-purpose playhouse.*

the ridge area only (FIG. 7-57F) to give added protection there. Turn the covering material under and nail into the strip at the back. Turn it down at the front and nail there, then cover with a fascia board (FIG. 7-57G). Battens on the slopes (FIG. 7-53B) will prevent the covering material from lifting. It might be sufficient to turn the covering under at the sides, or you can nail battens on the edges there as additional security.

The front door may be ledged and braced, with vertical, plain, or tongue-and-groove boards. Put stops around the sides and top of the doorway (FIG. 7-57H), and cut back the ledges on the door to clear them (FIG. 7-57J). Make the door with the bottom ledge high enough to clear the strip across the bottom of the doorway (FIG. 7-57K) and the top ledge a few inches down. Slope the braces up from the hinged side. You can make the door to swing either way. Use plain or T hinges. Either fit a lock or make a turnbutton. Fit a handle on the outside. You might need a catch and handle on the inside. When using the building for storage, you might want a bolt on the inside of the front door, so the only access then is via the rear door.

You could make a framed window to swing open, but a simple fixed window has the glass held between fillets (FIG. 7-57L).

Double Arch

An arch based on four posts can be given thickness, and the plants climbing over it will make a more impressive display than they could on a simple two-post arch. How thick you make it depends on needs and the situation, but an arch of normal size might be 18 inches thick. It would be less attractive if made rather thin; 12 inches ought to be regarded as the minimum for most double arches. In some situations, you might want to give more of a tunnel effect, and the arch could be 36 inches or more thick.

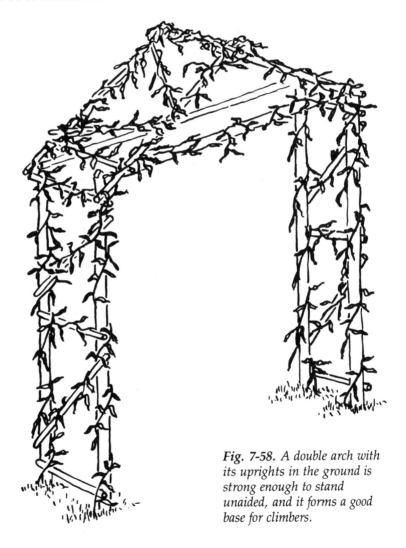

Fig. 7-58. A double arch with its uprights in the ground is strong enough to stand unaided, and it forms a good base for climbers.

As shown in FIG. 7-58, the arch is assumed to be about 84 inches under the crossbar, about 48 inches wide, and 18 inches thick. For that size, the posts could be 2 inches or 3 inches thick and the other parts thinner. Much depends on the type of wood. The diagonals need not be much more than 1 inch thick (providing they are without flaws). All of the wood should be stripped of bark (unless the bark is very tight), and it should at least be partially seasoned.

Select the wood for its locations. The main structures are made up of posts with the crossbars and rafters bolted through. Choose the best wood for these parts.

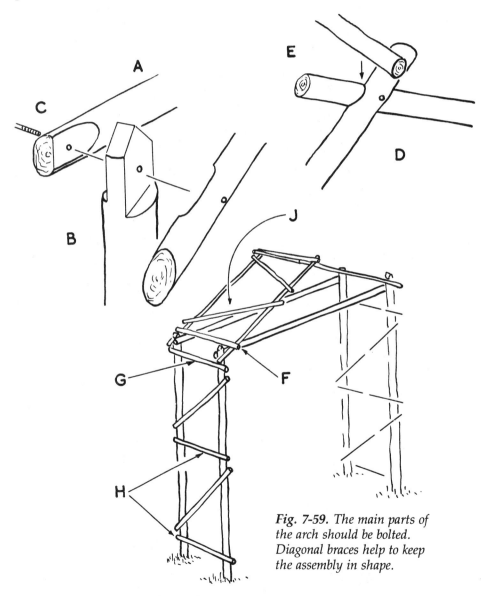

Fig. 7-59. The main parts of the arch should be bolted. Diagonal braces help to keep the assembly in shape.

Lay a pair of posts flat on the ground with their tops square to each other, and put a pair of rafters over them so as to mark the angle the posts' tops are to be cut. The exact angles are not important, but rafters at 25 degrees to 35 degrees to horizontal will be about right. From this trial assembly, you can mark the lengths of the rafters.

Cut the back of the top of each post with a notch to take the end of the crossbar, which will be flattened to fit (FIG. 7-59A). Cut a notch at the front. It will not matter if the cut is square across, but it will look better if it is about the angle of the rafter (FIG. 7-59B). Do not cut away the posts too much; there should be about half thickness left at the center. The tops of the posts can be pointed for appearance and to shed rain water.

Mark the positions of the posts on the ground. Besides being the correct distance apart, check that they are square by measuring diagonals. Erect the posts while checking that tops are level.

Make the crossbars, with flats at the ends. Drill them and the posts for bolts (FIG. 7-59C). Put the bolts in with their ends extending outward.

Make the rafters. At the tops, notch each pair into each other (FIG. 7-59D) and bolt through. Check that the distance between bolt holes will be the same each side, and then drill and bolt to the posts.

The two assemblies have to be linked with short pieces. Put the first at the apex, resting in the V of the rafters (FIG. 7-59E), and nail it in place. This should steady the assembly.

Put more pieces on the rafters above the posts' joints (FIG. 7-59F). Check that the assembly has not gone out of square by seeing that these pieces are the same length. There could be two more pieces put across just below the crossbar joints (FIG. 7-59G).

What other pieces are put across depend on the the pattern of climbing plants you hope to arrange. There could be another piece across level near the ground and one halfway, at each side, and then diagonals between them (FIG. 7-59H). Some of these could be merely nailed on without preparation, but the nailed joints are better if the ends of the pieces are flattened slightly where they contact the posts. Of course, the pieces brace the whole assembly, but only a few are needed for stiffening and the main concern is to provide places for climbers to grip.

Put a few more crosspieces on the rafters (FIG. 7-59J) and diagonals if you prefer. To get the plants to provide a good coverage at the top, closer supports are needed than on the vertical sides.

If the posts have a good grip in the ground, the whole arch should be very firm and rigid. If necessary, diagonal struts could be taken out near the base.

Arbor

If you make a pergola structure with a seat, it becomes an arbor. Foliage grows over it and around it and makes it a shelter. The foliage might be quite dense, except at the front, or it might just form a roof. Roses particularly are associated with an arbor, but you can use any type of climbing plant. You could build a pergola and place a seat under it, but it is better to build the seat in. As this is a permanent structure and since it is exposed to all kinds of weather, you must make the seat of wood. Any softening must be with portable cushions. This fact does not mean the seat cannot be at a comfortable angle, for use without cushions on occasions.

The arbor shown in FIG. 7-60 has inverted V legs supporting a flat top similar to a pergola. At each end, a strut parallel with a leg slopes up to give additional support to the top. This strut sets the angle of the seat back which has vertical slats. You can make the bottom of the seat solid or slatted. The legs go into the ground and crosspieces prevent them from sinking too far. The suggested sizes (FIG. 7-61A) are for an arbor 6 feet high and about 7 feet long, but you can alter these to suit your needs or available space.

You can use softwood treated with preservative or a more durable hardwood. Remember that once you erect the arbor and foliage is growing over it, you cannot do much to treat or repair it. Its original construction must be strong enough to have an expected life of many years. Bolts ought to be galvanized to minimize rust. Any glue should be a waterproof type, and screws should be plated or made of a noncorrosive metal. The main parts are 2 inch × 3 inch or a 4-inch section.

Fig. 7-60. Make an arbor like a pergola so foliage can form a roof over a seat.

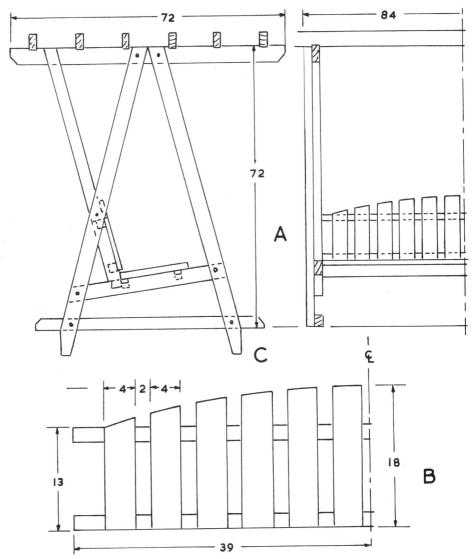

Fig. 7-61. *Sizes of the arbor.*

Start by setting out an end. If you want to set tools, the angles are 15 degrees. From the ground line, draw a centerline square to it, then 72 inches up, mark the apex of a triangle with a 39-inch spread at the base (FIG. 7-62A). Draw the top across (FIG. 7-62B), and mark the widths of the wood. Draw the seat support across the legs (FIG. 7-62C). The seat top is symmetrical about the centerline of this seat support, and the strut slopes up from the back of it, parallel with the front leg (FIG. 7-62D). This layout gives you all the shapes and sizes you need to start construction.

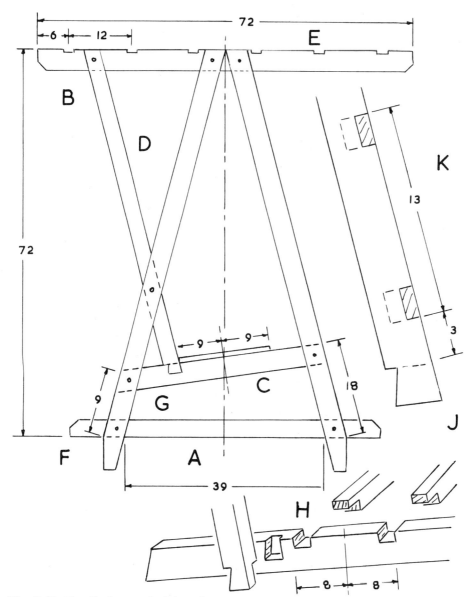

Fig. 7-62. Detail of one end of the arbor.

Notch the tops to take the beams (FIG. 7-62E). Let the legs meet on the beam, and drill through for bolts. Spread the bottoms and secure them with the ground strips (FIG. 7-62F). On this framework, mark where the seat bearers come. Put these pieces across and add the long struts (FIG. 7-62G), marking where they cross and where you want to drill for bolts or where you want to cut joints.

On the seat bearers, mark and cut the notches for the lengthwise seat supports not more than 1½ inches deep (FIG. 7-62H). The strut joins by halving. This

Materials List for Arbor

4 legs	2 × 4 × 84
2 struts	2 × 3 × 70
2 tops	2 × 4 × 74
2 bottoms	2 × 3 × 66
2 seat supports	2 × 4 × 48
6 beams	2 × 4 × 120
4 seat rails	2 × 2 × 84
2 seat dividers	2 × 2 × 20
12 seat slats	1 × 4 × 20
2 seat boards	1 × 6 × 84 or slats
4 platform strips	1 × 4 × 74
6 platform supports	2 × 2 × 22

halving is best cut with a dovetail shape (FIG. 7-62J). Cut the notches to take the lengthwise back supports (FIG. 7-62K). At the top, halve the strut into the top piece. Assemble the pair of ends, with bolts where parts overlap and glue and screws at the joints.

The seat back has vertical slats with a curve cut on their top edge (FIG. 7-61B). You might prefer some other shape. Make the two 2-inch-square rails, notching ends to fit the notches in the struts. Have the back slats too long at first. Fit them temporarily to the rails, then bend a batten over them and draw a curve on their tops. Remove the slats to cut their curved tops, and round all exposed edges. Glue and screw them in place.

Make the seat supports to the same length as the back supports. Put pieces between them—if you divide the length into three, that should be sufficient (FIG. 7-63A). The seat top could be solid and made up of any boards of convenient width (FIG. 7-63B), or you could use slats with gaps between them (FIG. 7-63C). In any case, round the front and top edges. Glue and screw the seat parts together.

Glue and screw the seat rails into the end assemblies. With the aid of the top beams, the seat rails provide lengthwise rigidity to the structure. Check squareness, both upright and front-to-back. Because of handling problems due to weight, it probably will be advisable to erect the arbor in position before fitting the beams. The legs are shown with short points to push into the ground in FIG. 7-61C. If this design does not suit your situation, you could set the legs in concrete, or you might want to bury flat boards under the legs in loose soil. If the ground is not level, you might have to sink the boards by different amounts. Check with a level on the bottom crosspieces and on the seat or on a board between the bottom parts.

Make the beams all identical. They should overhang by 12 inches or more on the ends (FIG. 7-63D). Bevel the undersides of the ends. Drill down through for a 1/2-inch steel rod to be driven in to act as a dowel at each crossing (FIG. 7-63E). To prevent the entry of water and the start of rot and rust, you could drive the rod below the surface and fill the hole with a wooden plug or mastic, or nail a thin piece of wood above it.

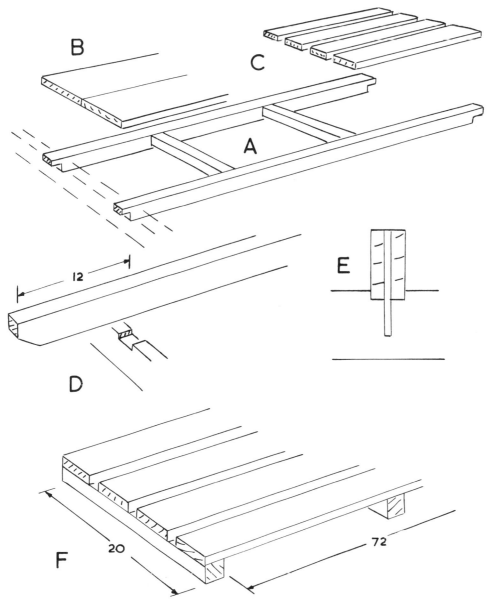

Fig. 7-63. Construction of parts of the arbor.

So plants will grow and engulf the arbor, there should be as much soil area around the base as possible, but you might wish to lay a concrete slab in front of the seat, to provide a clean, dry area for the feet. More in keeping with the arbor would be a platform of slats on crosspieces (FIG. 7-63F). Make it as a unit, so you can lift it occasionally.

If you paint or treat with preservative after you have erected the arbor, do it long before plants start to climb, so solvents will evaporate before the shoots come into contact with the structure. As plants climb, you might have to encourage them to go where you want by tying them to nails or by providing temporary strips of wood across the uprights. Ideally, you should have the arbor in position well before the start of the growing season, then you can watch progress, although it will be a few years before the foliage densely covers the roof and walls of your arbor.

Rustic Pergola

Natural poles make good combination with climbing flowering plants such as roses. The round rods, whether left with bark on or peeled, often look better than sawn and planed wood in support arrangements. They can be used without the same precision. If there are irregularities or dffferences in spacings, it is not as important as with wood cut to regular sections. You can use up pieces of poles that do not always match, and it is possible to use hammer and nail joints with success. These advantages are apparent if you make a round climbing support.

Such a pergola could be any size from about 4 feet in diameter and upward. It should usually be high enough at the eaves to walk in, and the spacing of uprights will have to suit the roses or other plants—18 inches is about right. The example shown in FIG. 7-64 is circular, about 6 feet across, and has a conical, open roof. Diagonal pieces brace the uprights and provide something for the climbers to cling to.

The uprights are straight poles with about a 3-inch maximum diameter. Similar poles can be used for the roof, but other parts can be pieces anywhere between a 1-inch and a 3-inch diameter. All of the construction is nailed. With the interconnected parts supporting each other, this is probably strong enough but, if you prefer, some joints could be cut.

Mark out the circular base plan. Use a strip of wood with a spike as center and a stick scratching against the end as it is pulled around. Alternatively, use a string that is tethered to a center spike and with another at the required radius scratch the circle (FIG. 7-65A).

On this circle, mark where the opening is to be. The gap can be 18 inches to 24 inches wide. Mark the positions of the other posts at about 18-inch intervals around the circle (FIG. 7-65B). Exact, even spacing is not important, but get the gaps about the same.

Drive the poles into the ground. There is no need to sink them to the depth they would have to be if they are to stand unaided, but get them upright and reasonably firm. Put temporary strips between them near the top (FIG. 7-65C) to hold the circle in shape.

Decide on the height you want the tops of the poles. Nail strips around at that level, with their ends overlapping (FIG. 7-65D), and then cut off surplus wood

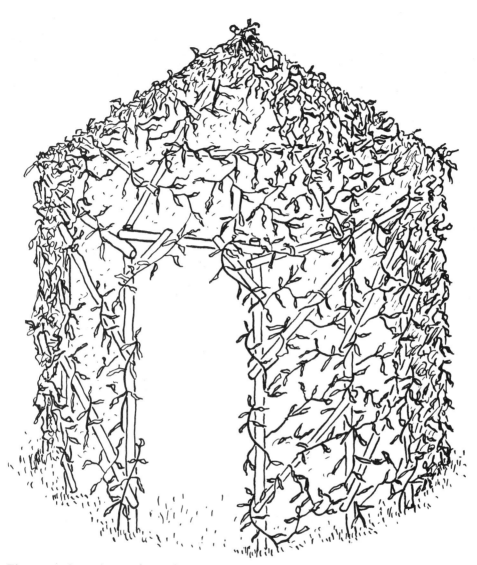

Fig. 7-64. *A rustic pergola can become completely covered with a climbing plant.*

above these joints. The assembly should now be rigid enough for the temporary strips to be removed.

Put light diagonal struts at the top of the opening (FIG. 7-65E), and go around adding diagonals to the sides (FIG. 7-65F). How many and how close depends on what you will be planting, but there should be no need to have strips closer than about 18 inches.

Choose two opposite uprights on which to mount a main truss. Pivot two poles together with a bolt, and lift it into position so that it takes a pleasing angle (somewhere between 25 degrees and 45 degrees to horizontal). Then nail or bolt

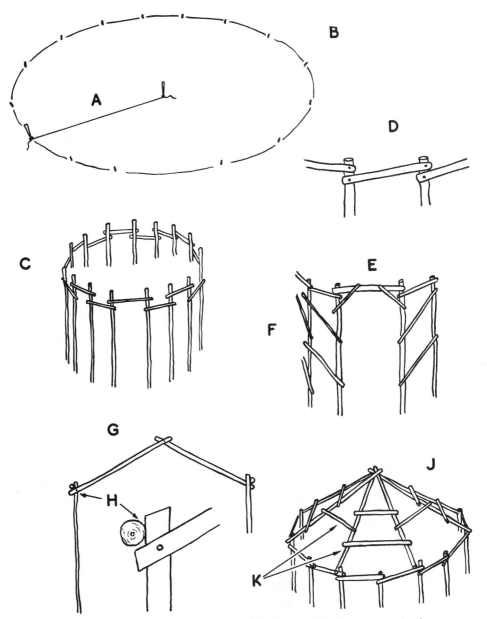

Fig. 7-65. *The pergola is set out as a circle, and then it is built up around poles.*

it to the posts. At the apex (FIG. 7-65G) and at the eaves (FIG. 7-65H), the ends can project slightly. Check that the assembly is put together with the rafters the same length.

Take other poles up the apex. There is no need to do this from every upright, but if there are about six, that should be ample. On a small-diameter pergola, four may be enough. Attach to the upright poles in the same way as the main truss, but at the apex, nail to the parts of the main truss (FIG. 7-65J), or carry one or two ends over them.

Unless the structure is very large, one or two strips between rafters should be enough for training flowers (FIG. 7-65K).

Remove raggedness at the ends. Cut off projections that might be knocked by a passing person. The wood could be treated with preservative, but it would be satisfactory if left in its natural state.

Tall Gate

If a fence is high and intended to provide privacy or act as a windbreak, any gate in it also ought to be high. This means having tall gateposts with a greater risk of the gate fitting badly later if they move only slightly. A move is more likely at the greater height unless the posts can be restrained. Fortunately, it is possible to put a piece across above head height so that the posts are braced to each other and held parallel (FIG. 7-66). This depends on the fence height, but if you can take the posts to 6 feet, 6 inches or more you can make a rigid gateway. The ranch-style piece across could have shallow notches to fit over the posts. Something more than nails will be resisting movement.

Fig. 7-66. A tall gate in a high fence is best with a piece over the opening.

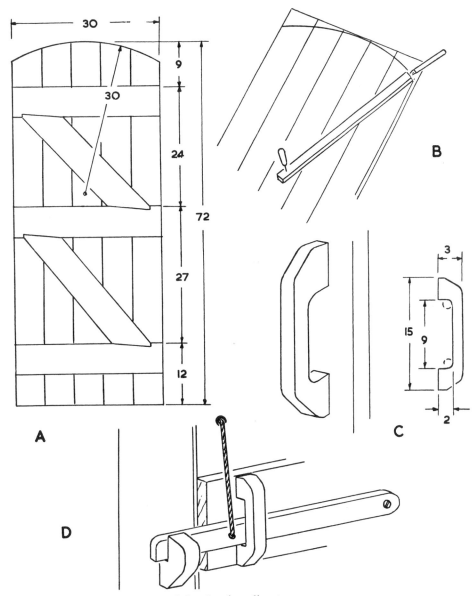

Fig. 7-67. Suggested sizes and details of a tall gate.

Materials List for Tall Gate

5 uprights	72 × 6	× 1
2 crosspieces	30 × 6	× 1
2 diagonals	34 × 6	× 1
2 handles	15 × 3	× 1¹/₄
1 latch	15 × 1¹/₂	× ³/₄
Latches from	12 × 2	× 1¹/₄

The top is shown cut to a curve, but it could be made straight across with a capping if you prefer. The three crosspieces (ledgers) are necessary, but the middle one is better not exactly midway between the other two. If it is central, an optical illusion makes it look lower. (You might decide that does not matter.) You cannot reach over to a fastener so the latch or lock has to be workable from either side.

Set out the door and assemble the outside boards with the crosspieces each held with single screws. Have this square, and position the diagonals so that you can mark their ends and the notches. Because of the different spacings, the diagonals will be at different angles. If you want to keep the slopes the same, you can position one and arrange the other so it is at the same angle, letting its ends come as they will on the crosspieces.

The curve of the top is best left for marking and cutting until after the door is assembled, but you can make the ends approximately to shape. This is particularly appropriate if you want to use up short boards at the outsides.

Assemble the door with all the boards equally spaced. Planed wood will leave gaps up to 1/4 inch between edges.

Improvise a compass with a strip of wood, an awl, and a pencil (FIG. 7-67B). The curve drawn is 30-inch radius, but you can vary this if a flatter or greater curve would look better for your gate. Cut the top, and take off any sharpness of the edges.

Fit a hinge central on each crosspiece—T hinges 12 inches long would be a good choice. Hang the gate temporarily with one screw in each hinge and check its action. Position a stop to let the gate shut with the ledgers level with the post surface.

You could use purchased metal handles on each side of the gate and a latch of the type that allows opening from either side. If it is an outside fence, you might want to fit a lock or use bolts on the inside. Alternatively, you can make handles and a latch. Even if the gate is made of softwood, the handles and latches should be close-grained hardwood for strength and resistance to wear.

The handles are about 1 1/4 inch thick. Mark out (FIG. 7-67C) and drill the corners of the openings, and cut the shape. Make sure the parts come against the door and are kept flat, but all the other edges and corners should be thoroughly rounded. Fit the handles at suitable heights by screwing through the door into them. Stagger them slightly so you can drive screws from both sides.

The latch is a strip of wood loosely pivoted on a screw, with washers under the head and between it and the door. Heavy hardwood about 1 1/2 inches wide, 3/4 inches thick, and 15 inches long would be about right. Within reason, length is an advantage. This drops into a notched block on the post (FIG. 7-67D). The block is made like part of a handle. The bottom of the notch comes opposite the latch strip when it is level. Give its front a rounded slope so the strip will slide into it and drop in when the gate is shut.

On the door, there is a retaining piece over the latch strip. Get its size from the latch temporarily assembled. The bottom edge of the opening should come below the strip when it rests in the bottom of the block on the post. The top edge of the opening should allow the strip to lift clear of the notch. For raising the latch from the other side, use a cord through a hole in the strip and a loosely fitting hole in the door.

Counterbore the hole in the strip so the knot can pull in. Have a loop or large knot in the other end of the cord so it can be gripped and will not pull back through the hole in the door.

Mortised Fence

Instead of nailing rails to the surface of posts, they can be let into mortises. It is not easy to cut mortises in posts that have been erected. The method is better suited to positions where the posts can be prepared in advance and erected to the correct height in holes that allow them to be adjusted with packing stones or other means before tamping tight. The method can be used with natural wood or sawn boards. Cleft poles make good rails for this type of fence (FIG. 7-68).

Round rails, probably no more than 3 inches in diameter, could be used with posts 5 inches in diameter or square. Poles could be cleft along their centers and the fence built with all the flat surfaces to one side. If the fence is to withstand cows or horses pushing against it, the cleft poles could be up to 6 inches in diameter (particularly for the top rails). If you want a natural, rural look to the garden fence, you can use rather lighter posts and rails to get the same effect. The poles do not have to be straight, and a fence of this sort with rails giving a slightly uneven appearance will look right if it separates the cultivated garden from a background of trees and bushes that have been left to nature.

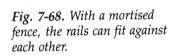

Fig. 7-68. With a mortised fence, the rails can fit against each other.

If flat boards are used, they can be planed and painted in the same way as a nailed fence, or they can be left as sawn and treated with preservative for a more natural appearance. Strength in the joints comes from having the posts fairly thick in relation to the rails; this is particularly important if you are using flat boards, and less important (although still valuable) with round or cleft rails in a fence where the haphazard appearance of extending rail ends does not matter and might even be considered a feature.

For a fence with round or split rails, assemble the materials for the rails. These will determine the spacing of posts. Allow for overlaps at the joints. Short rails and more frequent posts will have the best resistance to sideways pressures. If it is only a garden fence where the loads will not be much, you can have the poles any reasonable length. Depending on the type of wood, bark can be removed or left on; it will not affect construction.

The posts are best left longer than you need them eventually and with sufficient length to go into the ground. Point them if they are to be driven, or leave them square if they will be set in dug holes. If the ground where the fence will be is uneven and you want the rails to be horizontal, work to the highest level and make the posts longer for the lower parts.

The ends of split rails have to be reduced to a rectangular section (FIG. 7-69A). What this size will be depends on the wood, but you have to compromise between width and depth. A thickness about $1^1/2$ inches and depth of $2^1/2$ inches might be possible and is the proportion at which to aim. Do not reduce the ends too much, but the reduced size should extend for about the thickness of a post. Experiment with your poles or with offcuts to get a size that will suit your stock of rails. Precision is not important, but try to keep close to the size on which you settle. Reduce round rails from both sides (FIG. 7-69B). Tapering can be done with a saw, ax, or drawknife.

In the posts, the mortises should suit the thickness you are making the rails and be rather deeper than them. If the rails are $20^1/2$ inches deep, the mortises could be $30^1/2$ inches (FIG. 7-69C). They need not be chopped square and are best made by drilling several holes and removing the waste with a chisel (FIG. 7-69D). Roughness and unevenness inside a mortise will not matter. Prepare posts in groups so mortise spacings match (FIG. 7-69E).

When you erect the fence, work along it by positioning posts loosely in their holes so you can move them a little. Add rails from one end, and tighten the posts in the ground after their rails are fixed. At each post, the rails should be tapered to fit each other (FIG. 7-69F) so when they are forced tight they press against the top and bottom of the mortise. Make the edge tapers as you go so that each one can allow for slight variations of the previous one. You might have to make some length adjustments. The ends that extend through could be left (FIG. 7-69G) or cut off at the post (FIG. 7-69H). If the ends are to be left, try to avoid tapering to a feather edge. It is better to leave $1/2$ inch or so.

In a natural fence, there should be no need to do any more, but if joints shrink and loosen, you can nail through the mortise.

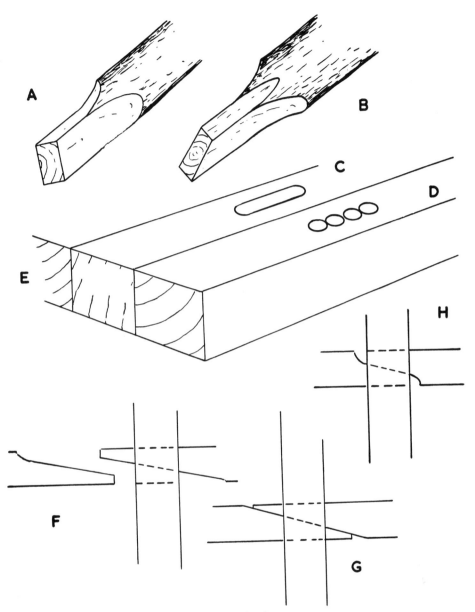

Fig. 7-69. Shape rail ends to fit the mortises in the posts.

If flat boards are to be used for rails, the method of assembly is very similar. Their thickness will settle the width of the mortises. If the depth of a rail is no more than the thickness of the post, there is no need to reduce it (FIG. 7-70A). If it is deeper, there will have to be a shoulder at one or both edges (FIG. 7-70B).

The mortises can still be made by drilling (and left with rounded ends and the rails eased a little with a chisel), or you can chop the ends square (FIG. 7-70C).

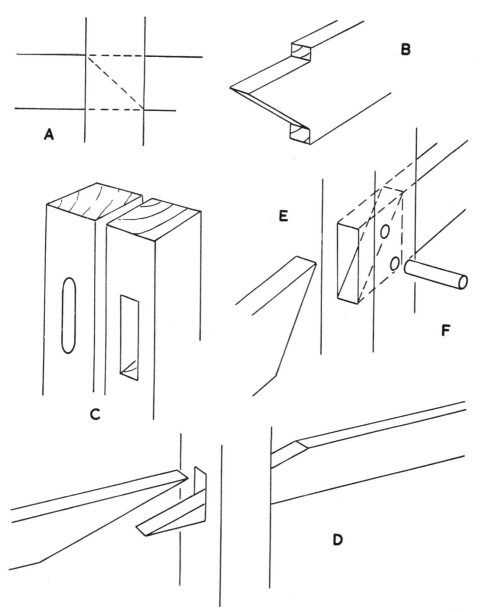

Fig. 7-70. Flat rails should fit together in the mortises.

The rails can have their ends cut to go through in a very similar way to the natural poles (FIG. 7-70D), or they can be angled to fit each other within the thickness (FIG. 7-70E). The second method is neater, but the joints will have to be secured with dowels (FIG. 7-70F).

It is unlikely that posts will be erected with the precision of spacing that you would expect in cabinetry. Differences of an inch or so do not matter, but this means that rails should be cut after the posts are loosely positioned, particularly if you will be making shoulders on them. Measure the distances between posts at ground level, and use this as the distance between them where the rails will be.

In both methods of construction, get the fence erected with all posts still too long. When you are satisfied that it is as you want it, cut the tops off the posts, either at an angle or to a point.

Slatted Plant Stand

Pot plants require frequent watering, and considerable water will land on the shelves. Therefore, it is a good idea to have gaps in the shelves for water to run through. These gaps are made by arranging a series of strips that have to be thicker than the board you would otherwise use, to resist warping unevenly. The use of strips or slats makes the building of shelves of any width easier. If the stand is to take larger plants in tubs or other big containers, you can make stepped supports to any required size.

The plant stand shown in FIG. 7-71 has three wide-slatted shelves that are clear of each other, when viewed from above, so foliage on any level can extend

Fig. 7-71. A slatted plant stand will drain water away. The arrangement allows for high growth.

Materials List for Slatted Plant Stand

4 legs	36 × 2 × 2
2 legs	24 × 2 × 2
Rails from four pieces	36 × 2 × 2
2 struts	15 × 2 × 2
15 slats	36 × 2 × 2
2 struts	48 × 2 × 2

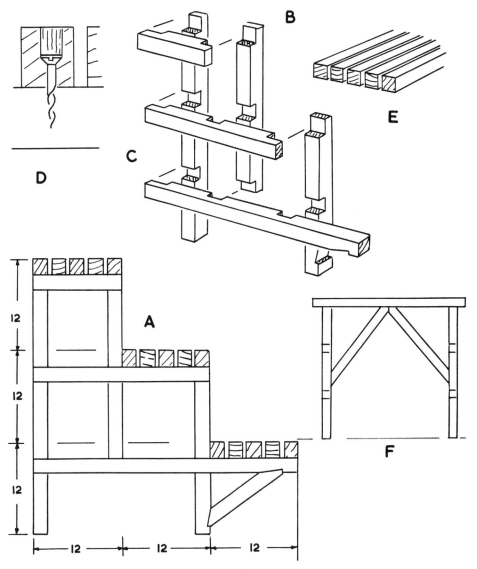

Fig. 7-72. *The parts of the slatted plant stand are halved together.*

upwards without hindrance. The construction suggested has the lower front shelf supported by diagonal struts. The weight of the assembly, plus any pots on the other shelves, should prevent any risk of tipping, but if you place very heavy loads on the lowest shelf, it could be given vertical legs at the front.

Get all the wood first. The whole assembly is intended to be made of 2-inch-×-2-inch stock. Check the actual dimensions of the wood you have, and then set out and cut the joints to suit.

You can make the parts without setting out an end full size (FIG. 7-72A), but you might find it helpful to do so. Heights are to the tops of shelves.

As far as possible, mark out all pieces in the same direction together so that the spacing of joints will match and the assembled ends will stand square. Mark the joints on all uprights (FIG. 7-72B). Put the wood for the rails together and mark their joints. Gauge the depths of the joints from the same surface of all pieces, and then cut the joints. For the diagonal struts, cut the notches in the way used for shelf brackets.

Assemble one end. Waterproof glue and a central screw in each joint should be sufficient. Check squareness, and use the first end as a pattern for making the other one to match. Cut all slats to the same length, and remove any raggedness from the ends.

Attach the slats with long screws or nails. A neat way that uses shorter screws is to counterbore the holes (FIG. 7-72D). Drill holes deep enough to suit the screws, then plug them with dowels after driving the screws.

Arrange the slats evenly spaced (FIG. 7-72E), and let them overhang the end frames by about 2 inches. To keep the assembly in shape while making up the shelves, fit a slat at the back of the top and another at the front of the bottom shelf. Measure diagonals to check squareness, then add the other slats without disturbing the shape.

The assembly might be rigid enough, but if the stand is to be loaded heavily, you should add some bracing. This bracing might come at the back and is most simply arranged with two struts (FIG. 7-72F) between the rear legs and the top rear slat. Although you can notch in the ends of the struts, it should be sufficient to nail or screw them in place.

Bird Feeding Table

Birds prefer to feed in a position where they are free from predators. A high place is safer than feeding on the ground. If you want to watch the birds you attract, it will also be advisable to arrange a feeder about eye level. A central post and a table with a good overhang will make it impossible for cats and squirrels to get at the birds.

This feeding table (FIG. 7-73) should blend in with other things in the yard or garden so it looks attractive. It has a reasonable area for food, with a roofed central area and a swinging perch. Some birds chase away other birds while feeding.

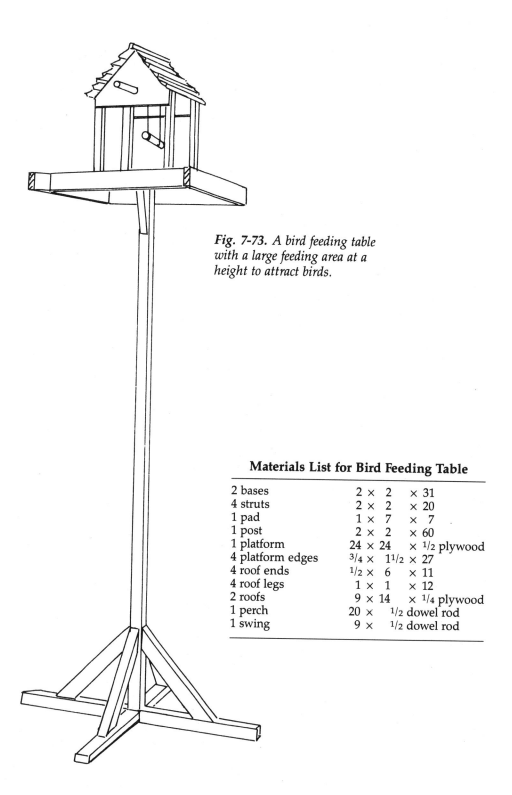

Fig. 7-73. A bird feeding table with a large feeding area at a height to attract birds.

Materials List for Bird Feeding Table

2 bases	2 ×	2	× 31	
4 struts	2 ×	2	× 20	
1 pad	1 ×	7	× 7	
1 post	2 ×	2	× 60	
1 platform	24 ×	24	× 1/2 plywood	
4 platform edges	3/4 ×	11/2	× 27	
4 roof ends	1/2 ×	6	× 11	
4 roof legs	1 ×	1	× 12	
2 roofs	9 ×	14	× 1/4 plywood	
1 perch	20 ×	1/2 dowel rod		
1 swing	9 ×	1/2 dowel rod		

The roofed part will let some smaller birds feed there, while larger birds keep to the outer edges. Many birds scatter food, and this table is given a rim to prevent some of it being pushed over the edge. At the corners of the rim there are extensions with holes that can be used to hang food, such as nuts, in nets.

Paint and preservative hold their smell for a very long time and birds find this objectionable, so it is better to choose a wood which is reasonably durable without treatment. As it weathers, it will blend better into its background than if it had been painted.

This is not the sort of woodworking that calls for elaborate cut joints. Many parts can be merely nailed together. Perhaps the wood won't need to be planed, except that some wood bought as sawn is of irregular section, so parts might not fit very well if you do not plane the surfaces.

The feeding table is shown on a base (FIG. 7-74A). On a hard surface this might be adequate. Weights could be put on the ends of the base. On a suitable surface, the feet could be drilled and spikes driven through. In soft ground you need not bother with the base, but could point the post and drive it in. Elsewhere it might be better to concrete the bottom of the post.

Make the main platform (FIG. 7-74B) from a square of exterior or marine plywood. The border is shown with extensions in turn, so all parts are the same. Drill and round the ends (FIG. 7-74C). Nail through the plywood into the border.

Mark the position of the post centrally underneath the platform. This will be held by four 6-inch metal shelf brackets (FIG. 7-74D). You could make a temporary assembly to locate screw holes, then remove the post and brackets until final assembly.

Make the ends of the covered part with a slope of about 30 degrees (FIG. 7-75A). Nail them to four uprights. Drill for a 1/2-inch dowel rod that will extend to form end perches and support the swinging perch inside (FIG. 7-75 B). The roof could be two pieces of plywood (FIG. 7-75C), or you could use overlapping strips of wood to give a clapboard effect. You might even put a few strips across and thatch the roof.

Locate the four uprights on the platform and drill through so screws can be driven upwards. For the sake of appearance, get the four posts upright.

The main parts of the base are two pieces crossing (FIG. 7-75D). Notch them together so they will stand level. If you are doubtful about the surface they will stand on, put square blocks under the ends to form feet.

The post fits into a square or octagonal block over the crossing pieces. It could have a square cut out to take the full size of the end post, but it will be better if the post is given a tenon made by reducing it 1/4 inch all around, then the block is cut out to fit (FIG. 7-75E).

The post is held upright by four struts (FIG. 7-74E). They are drawn at 45 degrees, but they could be more upright. It would help in maintaining accuracy if you draw two lines square to each other and in them draw a strut. If you cut all four struts to this drawing, accurate assembly should be easy.

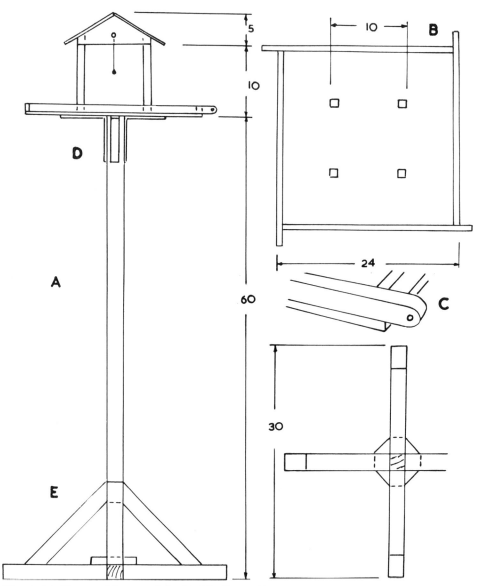

Fig. 7-74. Sizes and layout of the bird feeding table.

Join the post to its base and add the struts, nailing through the tapered ends. Check squareness. You might want to drive nails first only partly into opposite sides of the post, then check that the post appears upright when you stand it before driving the nails fully. Do the same the other way and, you should finish with a satisfactory, upright bird feeding table.

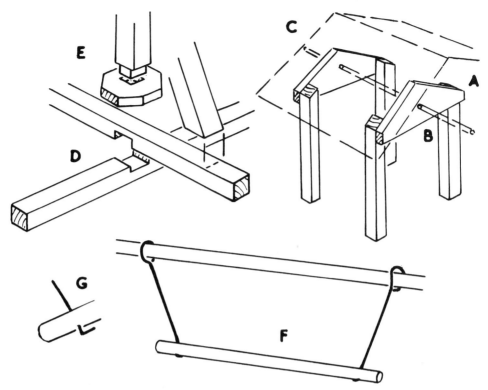

Fig. 7-75. Details of the house (A – C), feed (D,E), and swing (F,G).

Join on the top assembly with its brackets. The swinging perch is a piece of dowel rod (FIG. 7-75). Use wire—preferably copper or other noncorrosive type—loosely around the main perch, and with the other ends taken through holes in the swinging perch and turned over (FIG. 7-75G).

Garden Hose Hanger

A rubber or plastic garden hose is usually a considerable length and it should be looked after. If it does not have its own reel, it should be stored in a way that keeps it free from kinks and tight twists, and in such a way that it is in coils that can be run out without the hose tangling. It is less of a problem if the coils are kept fairly large. Many reels and other storage arrangements tend to curl the hose tighter than it wants to go, so it is difficult to pull it reasonably straight when you want to use it.

A rack on a wall or fence allows you to make a coil of large diameter so the hose is not distorted. This rack (FIG. 7-76), consisting of three horns on a board, is designed to suit coils about 36 inches across (FIG. 7-77A). You do not have to loop up the hose with precision—anything within 12 inches or so will do—but 36

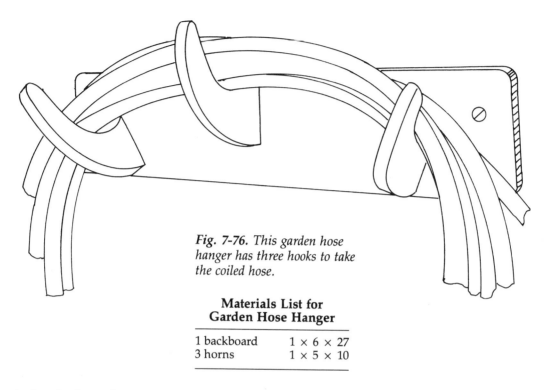

Fig. 7-76. This garden hose hanger has three hooks to take the coiled hose.

**Materials List for
Garden Hose Hanger**

1 backboard	1 × 6 × 27
3 horns	1 × 5 × 10

inches is about the size loops you naturally form when coiling the hose in front of you.

The rack could be made of softwood, preferably treated with preservative. A durable hardwood would be better, particularly if there is a risk of knocking and damaging the horns. How good a finish you give the rack depends on your needs. You could screw the parts together and leave the horns without rounding them. This would support a hose just as well, but good joints and a better finish would be more satisfying. The instructions assume the horns will be tenoned to the backboard.

The three horns are the same. For strength, they should be cut a full 1 inch thick and could be slightly thicker, although the projecting part will be thinned and rounded. Draw the shape on one (FIG. 7-77B), preferably with the grain in the direction of the arrow. Cut this out and use it to mark the shape of the other two, or make a hardboard template and use it to mark all three.

Mark out the backboard with the positions of the horns. The two outer horns are at 60 degrees (FIG. 7-77C). Mark the shapes of the tenons on the horns and the shapes of the mortises on the backboard. Square tenons with a 1/2-inch gap between them should be satisfactory. The section is the central one (FIG. 7-77D). Arrange the others at the marked angles, near the bottom edge of the board.

Well round the extended part of each horn, reducing the thickness slightly towards the rounded points. There is no need to produce a sanded finish for outdoor use.

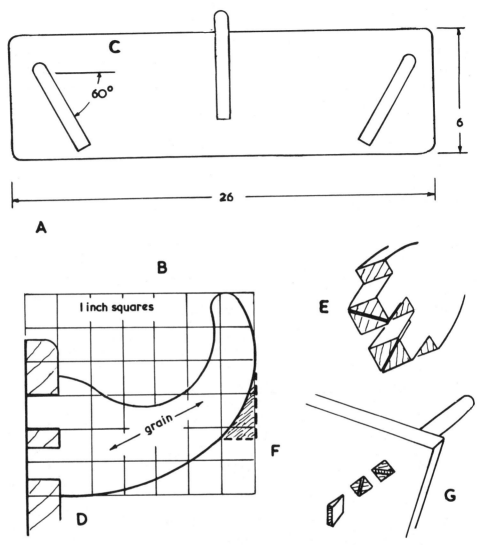

Fig. 7-77. The hooks have their tenons wedged in the back board.

Cut the tenons and mortises. The tenons might be slightly too long for planing level later. Saw diagonally across the tenons for about three-fourths of their depth (FIG. 7-77E).

Finish the outline of the backboard. Round its corners and edges. Drill for fixing screws or bolts.

Glue the tenons in the mortises. If you want to pull the joints tight with clamps, it helps to leave a projection on each horn (FIG. 7-77F) for the clamp to squeeze against, then it can be cut off and the wood rounded after assembly.

At the back, drive glued wedges into the tenons (FIG. 7-77G). When the glue has set, cut them off and plane the tenons level.

Hanging Plant Holder

Hanging plant or flower holders are broadly divided into those that actually have soil contained in them and those that are containers for potted plants. Both can be in various sizes, but this one is intended to hold a pot of moderate size such as might hang in a porch, either alone or as a series of similar ones, to give a color-

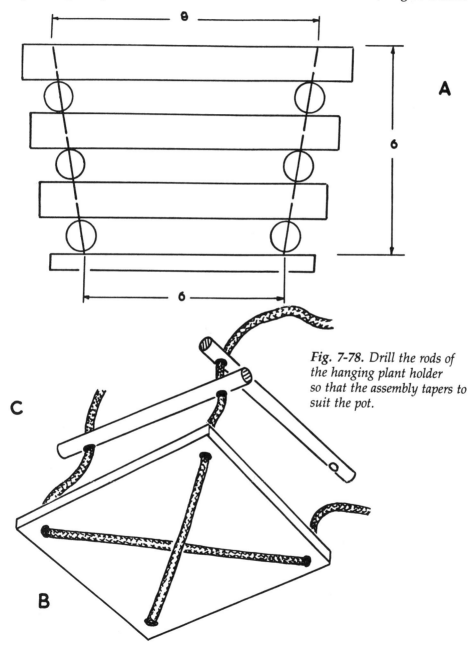

Fig. 7-78. Drill the rods of the hanging plant holder so that the assembly tapers to suit the pot.

**Materials List for
Rod-Hanging Plant Holder**

1 base	8 × 8 × ¹/₂ plywood
Rods from	240 inches of 1-inch dowel rod

ful display of potted flowers. An advantage is that you can use the same holders for other flowers, with minimum trouble, when the first ones are finished. Such a hanging holder also can be taken indoors for further use when the outside weather becomes unsuitable.

The base of the holder is a piece of plywood. The sides are made of wood rod, which is conveniently cut from dowel rod, although you can use old broom handles or similar things. Thread the parts on rope.

The guiding shape is the truncated cone that passes through the base and the rods (FIG. 7-78A). Measure the diameters of the rods, and set out the shape to allow for the chosen number of these thicknesses. This shape gives you the location of the centers of the holes in each layer of rods. Allow the rods to extend about 1 inch outside the holes.

You can cut the ends squarely across and sand away any raggedness. If you have a lathe, you can bevel or round the ends.

Although you would have to drill close-fitting holes at an angle, there is no need for this if you drill the holes large enough to be a very easy fit on the rope. Drill the holes in the rods and the base, and then lightly countersink above and below to reduce the risk of chafe on the rope.

You can use almost any rope, but synthetic fibers will stand up to the weather better than natural fibers. Quite light cord would be strong enough, but for appearance, it is better to use rope of ³/₁₆-inch or ¹/₄-inch diameter. It does not matter if it is plaited or three-strand construction.

Cut double lengths to cross underneath the base (FIG. 7-78B), and then thread on the parts (FIG. 7-78C). Tie a knot in each rope close above the top rods to prevent movement of the parts, and then continue up to tie all four parts together. How far you go depends on the situation where the plant holder is to hang. Long ropes look better and are easier to arrange among foliage (if there is space to have them).

Plant Pot Container

Flowers and plants in pots need something more than the plain pot to complement the foliage. If they have been grown in the pots, however, it might be unwise to disturb them by transplanting into boxes. A wooden container for the plant in its pot can stand on a deck or patio, and a number of similar containers will enhance your outlook over the yard. When one plant has passed its prime, you can exchange it for another in the box without digging up one and replacing it with another.

The container shown in FIG. 7-79 is intended for the more enthusiastic wood-worker who favors traditional construction. A container described later in this chapter provides a similar effect with simpler methods. If the container is to be well made, it is worthwhile starting with a good hardwood that can be finished by varnishing. You can use softwood and paint it to match other work in the garden or yard.

The choice of plywood will affect other parts. Groove the legs centrally for the plywood (FIG. 7-80A). A depth of $3/8$ inch should be sufficient. The grooves do not need to extend below the bottom rail position, but with most methods of grooving, it is easier to cut right through. The part below is not very obvious in the finished container. Groove the rails in the same way (FIG. 7-80B).

Materials List for Plant Pot Container

4 legs	16	× 2	× 2	
8 rails	12	× 2	× 1	
4 tops	14	× 3	× 1	
4 panels	$12^1/2$	× $11^1/2$	× $1/2$	plywood
1 bottom	11	× 11	× $1/2$	plywood

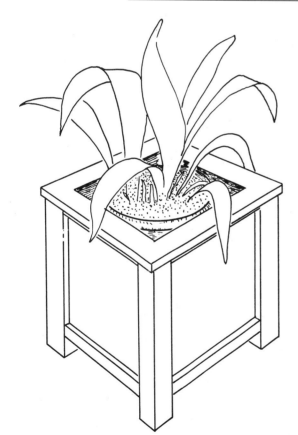

Fig. 7-79. You can make a plant-pot container with plywood panels in solid wood.

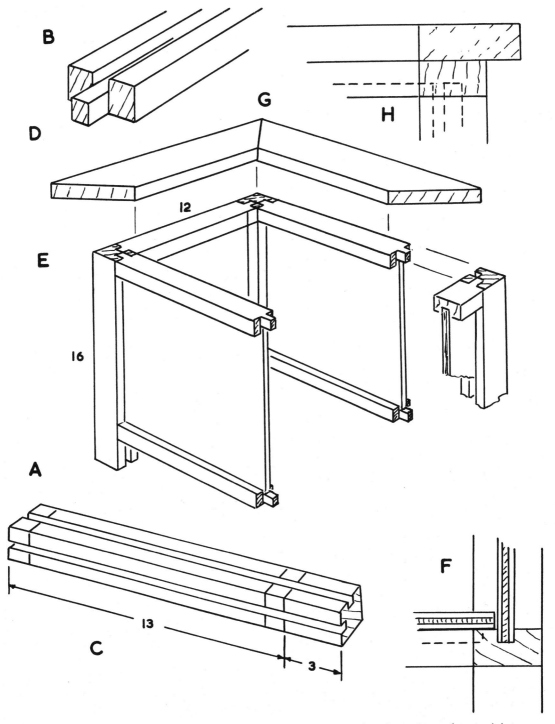

Fig. 7-80. The suggested construction uses grooves for the plywood and mortise-and-tenon joints.

Mark out the legs (FIG. 7-80C). Cut tenons on the ends of all rails (FIG. 7-80D). The tenons should be long enough to just meet in the legs (FIG. 7-80E); deepen the slots to make mortises accordingly. Be careful to mark all legs and all rails together, so that sizes are the same. Otherwise, you will not be able to assemble the container squarely.

The bottom is a piece of plywood resting inside the side plywood panels on the bottom rails (FIG. 7-80F). Cut this to size before completing assembly: You will not be able to fit it in after you join all four sides.

Assemble two opposite sides. Waterproof glue alone should be sufficient, particularly if you clamp the assemblies until the glue sets. Drive thin nails from inside into the tenons if you prefer. Check that they are square, without twisting, and that they match each other.

Assemble the parts the other way and include the bottom. That will keep the assembly square (as viewed from the top). Check squareness the vertical way, and stand the container on a flat surface, with a weight on top if necessary, so that the legs stand without wobbling.

The top (FIG. 7-80G) has its inner edges level with the insides of the legs and rails (FIG. 7-80H). Miter the corners and fit the parts with glue and nails or screws.

Tool Box

In many situations, you can keep garden tools and equipment in a garage or in a shed large enough to walk into and use for potting, putting seeds in trays, and similar things. If you only want to store hand tools and some of the other equipment you tend to accumulate for gardening, it might be better to make a box or locker. If the garden or yard is extensive, you will be glad to have such a box at some point distant from the main storage area.

You can make the box with solid wood described in the next project. The boards you use could have square edges, but if you are able to get tongue-and-groove boards, they will make a weatherproof box. Check what stock sizes of boards are available, and scheme the overall sizes to make the best use of them without wasting much. If you have tongue-and-groove boards, you must allow for cutting tongue or groove off some boards that come at edges. Measure the longest tools you will want to store. Some long handles might fit in diagonally if you want to keep the length to the minimum.

As shown in FIG. 7-81, the lid slopes slightly to shed rain, but it also comes at a height that makes it suitable for a seat. When open, it is held just past upright by ropes.

The pair of ends are the key pieces that settle several other sizes. Frame the ends with strips, but leave gaps at the corners for the lengthwise pieces (FIG. 7-82A). If you are using square-edged boards, bring the edges tightly together as you assemble. If they are made of normally seasoned wood, they will expand a little outdoors and become even tighter. With tongue-and-groove wood, it is better to not force the edges very tight.

Fig. 7-81. *A large tool box will store tools near where you use them and you can use it as a seat.*

Materials List for Tool Box

8 end frames	24 × 2 × 1
8 end boards	24 × 6 × 1
4 lengthwise strips	60 × 2 × 1
7 lengthwise boards	60 × 6 × 1
10 bottom boards	24 × 6 × 1
4 or 5 lid boards	63 × 6 × 1
2 lid cleats	24 × 6 × 1
2 bottom cleats	26 × 2 × 2
2 T hinges to suit	

Join the ends with the four lengthwise strips (FIG. 7-82B), and make sure outer surfaces come level. Nails into end grain at the corners will be sufficient at this stage because the boards fitted next will secure the corner joints. Check squareness by measuring diagonals.

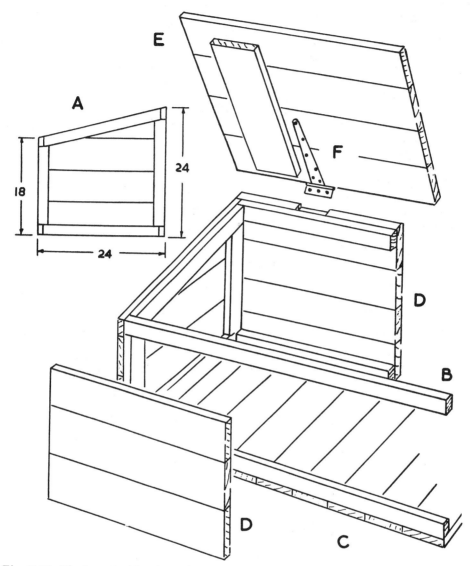

Fig. 7-82. The large tool box is made with boards on framing.

Nail on the bottom. This pattern is shown with boards across the narrow way. You could use long boards, but by using short pieces, there is less risk of the bottom warping and the assembly will be slightly stronger (FIG. 7-82C). With the bottom boards on, the assembly should keep its shape. Check squareness further as you fit the other boards.

Nail on the front and back boards (FIG. 7-82D). If the box is very long and there might be a risk of the boards warping later, fit one or more uprights intermediately. These boards should overlap the bottom.

The lid comes level at the back, but it should overlap the ends and the front by about 1 inch. Cut the boards to suit, and join them with pieces across (FIG. 7-82E). It might be sufficient to put a piece near each end, but for extra strength, particularly with square-edged boards, you could have another piece at the middle.

Large T hinges are recommended (FIG. 7-82F). Preferably, the hinges should reach halfway across the lid. They can go on the surface of the lid, but let the other part in enough for the lid to shut with only a small gap along the back. Put screw eyes in the lid and ends for supporting ropes (FIG. 7-81).

You can screw strips of leather or plastic with loops under the lid to take small tools.

If the box will stand on concrete or be supported on stones, you can leave the bottom unaltered. To keep it away from earth and the risk of rot, fit cleats across at the ends and perhaps intermediately.

Finish the wood with paint or preservative. There could be a handle and a hasp and staple for a lock.

Garden Tool Rack

Many of us keep garden tools in a corner of the garage or spread them in several places. The tools can suffer or get in the way as a result, and we do not always know where to find them. It helps to store the tools on racks, but there might not be enough wall space for all of them. A free-standing rack can hold the hand tools and small equipment all together and protected. If it is on wheels, it can be pushed out of the way when not in use and pulled out to an accessible position when needed.

This rack (FIG. 7-83) is about 48 inches high and wide, with places for long and short tools of various sorts. At the bottom is a roomy container to hold the ends of the long tools and accommodate all the small things that a gardener accumulates. The feet are spread wide enough to provide stability, and they can be fitted with industrial-type, rubber-tired casters for mobility. The suggested sizes (FIG. 7-84H) should suit most needs, but if you adjust the sizes, be sure not to make the rack too small. Start with a few extra spaces for the tools that will, almost inevitably, be acquired.

Materials List for Garden Tool Rack

2 posts	$2 \times 2 \times 46$
2 feet	$2 \times 2 \times 18$
4 rails	$2 \times 2 \times 48$
1 rail	$1 \times 6 \times 48$
2 box sides	$3/4 \times 6 \times 48$
1 box bottom	$14 \times 44 \times 1/2$ plywood
2 box ends	$12 \times 14 \times 1/2$ plywood

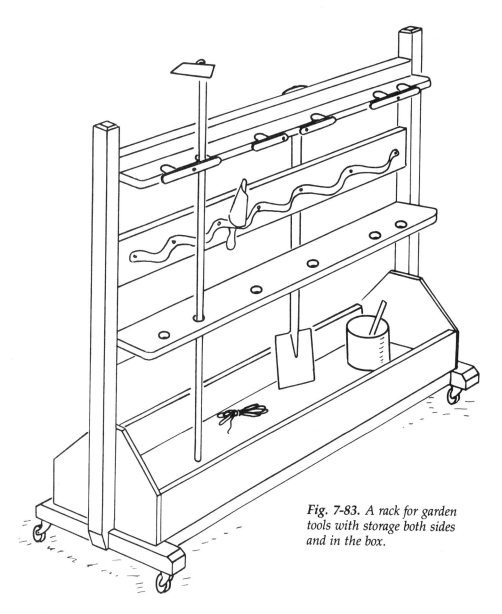

Fig. 7-83. A rack for garden tools with storage both sides and in the box.

Construction can be with softwood, except for the hardwood turnbuttons. The box will probably get wet, so any plywood should be exterior- or marine-grade.

Mark out the posts (FIG. 7-84A) with the positions of the other parts. Test the longest hoe or similar tool that will fit into holes. In use you will have to lift it clear of the lower shelf. Be sure there is enough headroom to allow this in your storeroom or garage.

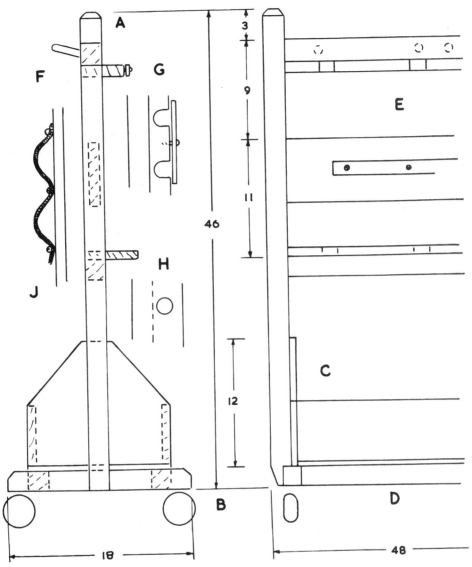

Fig. 7-84. Sizes of the garden tool rack.

Make the two feet (FIG. 7-84B). Cut the joints between the posts and the feet (FIG. 7-85A). The notches are shallow, as the top surfaces of the feet have to extend under the box.

Make the box first (FIG. 7-84C), because it controls the sizes of some other parts. Its base is 14 inches wide, and the ends extend 12 inches up the posts to serve as stiffening brackets. Nail or screw the base and ends to the solid wood sides. An overall box length of 44 inches should be satisfactory.

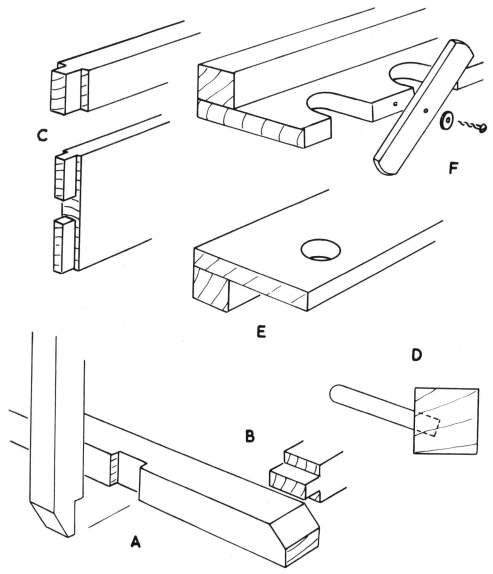

Fig. 7-85. Details of the garden tool rack parts.

Make the two bottom rails (FIG. 7-84D). Their ends could be doweled to the feet or joined with stub tenons (FIG. 7-85B). Let the outside edges of the rails come under the outside edges of the box.

Make the two 2-inch-square rails and the one flat one (FIG. 7-84E) using the box as a guide to length. Joints to the posts could be dowels or stub tenons (FIG. 7-85C).

The top rail (FIG. 7-84F) can have pegs for hanging tools. For spades and similar things with loop handles, there can be single pegs or two spaced close together. For T-shaped handles fit pairs of pegs. Make them 1/2-inch or 3/4-inch dowels, tilted upwards (FIG. 7-85D), so tools will not fall off when the rack is moved.

Under the top rail and projection the other way, make a shelf pierced with slots (FIG. 7-84G). The slots are to take tools with long parallel handles. Slots made by drilling 11/2-inch holes and sawing into them, should give ample clearance. Make the holes quite close to the shelf edge. Spacing should suit your tools. Where the working ends will not interfere with each other, they can be quite close, but if a certain tool has a broad top, you must arange wider spacing.

The lower shelf is on top of its rail and is wider than the top one (FIG. 7-84H). Drill 11/2-inch holes in positions to match those in the top shelf (FIG. 7-85E).

Shape the tops of the posts. Take off any sharp edges on all parts. Round the outer corners of the shelves.

Glue and nail or screw the shelves to their rails. Join all the lengthwise parts to the posts. Screw in the box at the same time as fitting the bottom rails.

To retain the tools in the slotted shelf, make turnbuttons. Where the slots are close, one turnbutton can go over two slots (FIG. 7-84G). If the slots are more widely spaced, make a turnbutton for each slot. A fiber washer between a turnbutton and the shelf edge can provide friction if the turnbutton tends to drop out of position.

For small tools there can be loops along both sides of the wide board (FIG. 7-84J). Webbing 1 inch wide is suitable. Fasten the loops with screws through large washers. Arrange loops of different sizes to accommodate various tools.

A few drainage holes in the bottom of the box will reduce the risk of water being trapped. Although the rack could be used without treatment, it will look better if it is painted.

Screw on casters if the rack is to be mobile.

Kneeler/Tool Carrier

No one needs to be uncomfortable while gardening. For anyone with difficulty in kneeling, close work on such things as flower borders becomes impossible without some aid. The combined tool carrier and kneeler shown in FIG. 7-86 is intended to give padded comfort under the knees, handles high enough to lean on when getting up and down, and boxes at the ends to carry hand tools, seed packets, string, and other small items.

The base and boxes could be light softwood, but the handles are better made of hardwood. The base and the upholstered board could be plywood. Exact sizes are not crucial, but for comfort, do not reduce the gap for the knees between the handles.

Fig. 7-86. This kneeler has an upholstered center and boxes at the ends to carry small tools and other equipment.

Materials List for Kneeler/Tool Carrier

1 base	24 ×	8 × 1/2
2 handles	11 ×	8 × 1
2 box ends	8 ×	4 × 1/2
4 box sides	4 ×	4 × 1/2
1 pad	15 ×	8 × 1/2
1 piece foam	15 ×	8 × 2
1 piece covering material	21 ×	13

You can alter the boxes and give them compartments for specific tools. Also, you can nail or screw the whole assembly together, but you also could use dovetails or other appropriate joints at the corners. Even if you nail other parts, it would be stronger to tenon the handles into the base (as suggested).

Set out the base (FIG. 7-87A) first because that controls many other sizes. Then cut the wood for the handles (FIG. 7-87B). If you are to nail or screw this through the base, cut the bottom square across. For mortise-and-tenon joints, mark out the parts and cut them (FIG. 7-87C). When you assemble, drive wedges into saw cuts in the tenons (FIG. 7-87D) to supplement glue.

Cut the hand holes (FIG. 7-87E) by drilling the ends and sawing between. Round the tops and take off all sharp edges where the hands will grip.

Make the box parts (FIG. 7-87F). Join the handles to the base, and check that they are square across and stand upright. Assemble the box parts to them and to the base.

The base of the upholstered pad should be a piece of solid wood or plywood. Screw it through the base, so that you can remove it if it ever needs attention.

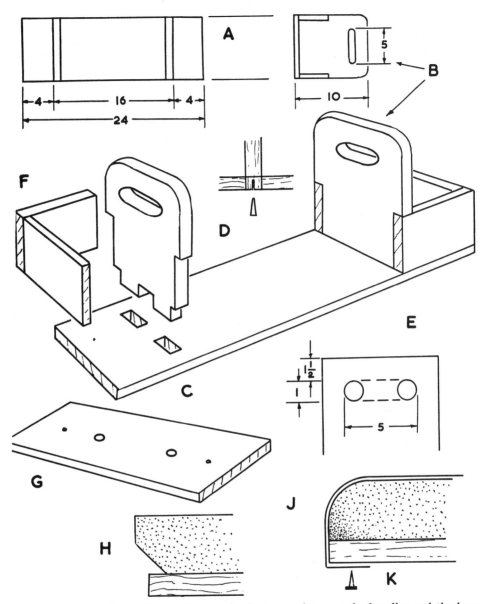

Fig. 7-87. *Strength is given to the kneeler by tenons between the handles and the base (A−G). Use foam for the upholstery (H−K).*

The padding is a piece of plastic or rubber foam about 2 inches thick. Use plastic-coated fabric that will be unaffected by dampness for the cover. Cut the pad wood for an easy fit between the handles. Allow for the thickness of the covering material. Drill two 1/2-inch holes in the base and pad to let air in and out as the foam compresses and expands. Also, drill for two holes for screws (FIG. 7-87G).

Cut the foam slightly oversize to allow for compressing. A thin-bladed knife, kept wet, will cut most foam. Bevel around the underside to about half thickness. This bevel allows the edge to be pulled to a neat curve by the covering material (FIG. 7-87J).

Use tacks (FIG. 7-87K): Position one near the center of each edge, then work out to the corners. A spacing of 1½ inches probably will be about right. Experiment with tensions of the material to get a good appearance on top, then cut off surplus material underneath, and screw the pad in place.

If you are to paint the equipment, remove the pad until you are finished.

Wheelbarrow

A traditional wheelbarrow is the sort of equipment that is almost essential in a yard or garden—from the tiny backyard to property of several acres—even if you have other means of transporting things about. With its single wheel, it will go almost anywhere.

The early wheelbarrow was a very heavy assembly of wood. You can buy light metal alternatives, but they would be difficult to make with the usual home-craftsman equipment. You can make a barrow with a framed plywood box on a light wood framework.

The important part is the wheel and its axle (FIG. 7-89C). It should be a free-running wheel with a 12-inch overall diameter. Many types are possible, and you might be able to buy or recycle something suitable. A tread breadth of about 3 inches will prevent the wheel from sinking into the soil too much, and it will have a hub broad enough to withstand the rocking loads that might sometimes be imposed. A wheel with a solid rubber tire is ideal. There could be an iron rim. You could make a solid wooden wheel with several thicknesses laid across each other and glued and screwed together. However, get the wheel and an axle at least 10 inches long before planning the other parts.

Materials List for Wheelbarrow

1 bottom	20 × 20	× ½ plywood	
1 front	20 × 14	× ½ plywood	
1 back	24 × 9	× ½ plywood	
2 sides	33 × 17	× ½ plywood	
6 framing	25 × 2	× 1	
6 framing	16 × 2	× 1	
2 cappings	33 × 1½	× ¾	
2 cappings	25 × 1½	× ¾	
2 handles	56 × 2	× 2	
1 bracing	20 × 2	× 2	
1 bracing	14 × 2	× 2	
2 axle blocks	9 × 2	× 2	
2 legs	18 × 2	× 2	
8 struts	14 × 1	× 3/16 steel	

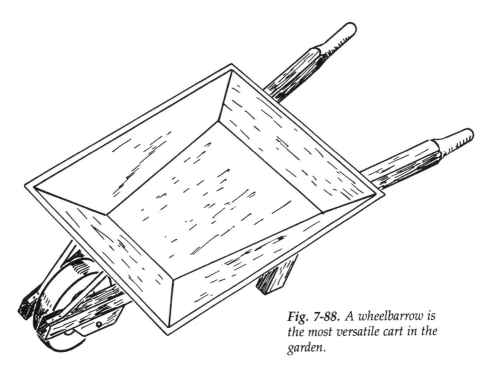

Fig. 7-88. A wheelbarrow is the most versatile cart in the garden.

Flare the box in all directions. This procedure is complicated by the tapered supporting handles, while the rim should be rectangular or nearly so (FIG. 7-88). This design results in outlines of box parts that are odd shapes and different angles. One way of getting over this problem is to make the bottom with parallel sides and have the box sides upright, but that removes some of the advantages of the traditional shape. It is not difficult to make a box with a flare all round (FIG. 7-89), if you work in steps. This shape allows the contents to be tipped forward or sideways without difficulty.

Figure 7-89 shows sizes that will give a reasonable proportion for a light wheelbarrow that should suit the average home garden. Deepen the box if most of your loads are bulky rather than heavy, and increase all sizes if you want to deal with really heavy loads. The drawing is based on a 12-inch wheel.

Start with the box; it is made of 1/2-inch plywood. Work from centerlines to get the bottom and ends symmetrical. Cut the bottom plywood to size (FIG. 7-90A). Frame it around with 1-inch-thick wood, 2 inches wide, against the plywood. Use nails and waterproof glue. At the ends, bevel at 60 degrees (FIG. 7-90B). Leave the sides square, but keep the nails far enough back from the edge to allow for some beveling there later.

Cut the plywood front (FIG. 7-90C) and back (FIG. 7-90D). Frame them around in the same way. The top edges will finish square. The bottom edges should match the box bottom (FIG. 7-89A). Leave the sides square, but allow for them being beveled later.

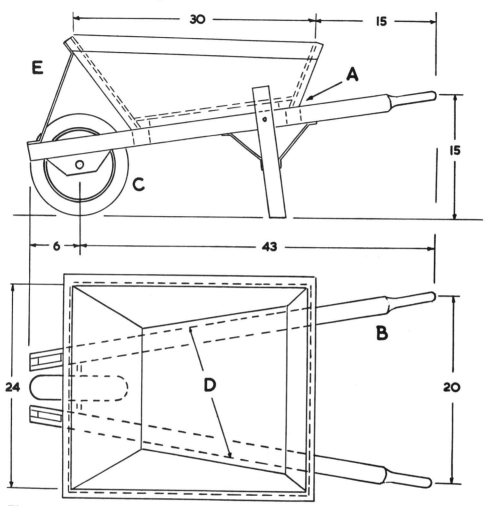

Fig. 7-89. Suggested sizes for a wheelbarrow with a framed plywood body.

Join the ends to the bottom temporarily with one screw near each corner. Hold a piece of plywood for one side against this assembly and mark its outline. Check that the other side matches. Cut both pieces of plywood. If you hold a side against the other parts, you can see by their edges what bevels you need. Plane the bevels. When you have a satisfactory fit, join all the box parts with glue and screws. Plain nails might not be strong enough, but you can use annular ring nails.

There is no need to frame outside the side panels because they are stiffened where they join the other parts. Put a strip along the top edge (FIG. 7-90E). There should be a capping all round to protect the plywood edges (FIG. 7-90F). The bottom plywood will be stiff enough as it is, but if you want to reinforce it, there can be another strip across, under its center.

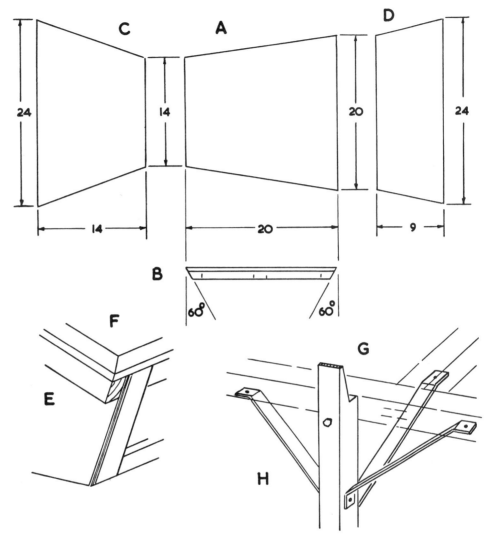

Fig. 7-90. *Sizes of panels (A–D) and constructional details (E–H).*

Make the two handles (FIGS. 7-89B and 7-91A). Reduce the ends to comfortable round grips; a 1¹/₈-inch diameter is a suitable size. At the other end, thicken with blocks glued and screwed on to take the axle that will be about 1 inch below the handle strip (FIG. 7-91B).

For very light work, the handles should get enough steadiness from being attached to the box, but it is advisable to give them their own cross bracing. These are 2-inch-square pieces between the handles and under the ends of the box. You can lay out their lengths and angles by using the box. Invert the box and put the handles in position on it. They should come less than 1 inch in from the sides of the box bottom (FIG. 7-89D).

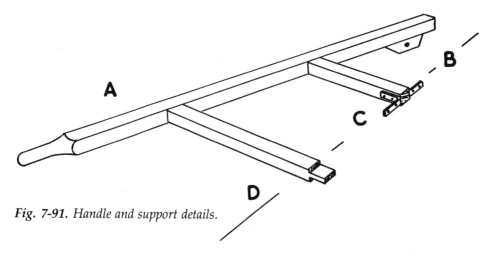

Fig. 7-91. Handle and support details.

The pieces across could fit between the handle parts and be held with brackets (FIG. 7-91C), but this is a place where mortise-and-tenon joints are preferable (FIG. 7-91D). If you want to give a traditional appearance, let the tenons project so you can shape their ends.

If the axle is a rod through, you can assemble the underframe to the box now and leave it until later. If the axle is part of the hub assembly, drill to suit and fit the wheel now. Attach the box with screws down through the stiffening framing into the handles.

Bolt the legs to the handles and extend them up the sides (FIG. 7-90G). Bolting alone will not resist the many loads liable to come on the legs. They should have struts along the handles and to the cross bracing (FIG. 7-91H). Cold strip steel about 1 inch wide and $3/16$ inch thick is easy to bend in a vise, and it should be strong enough.

Similar struts can be put between the ends of the wood on each side of the wheel and the top front framing (FIG. 7-89E), but that is not so important. Check the stiffness of the front wood assembly.

Trimming the bottoms of the legs to length can be left until you have assembled everything. Then cut them to get the barrow to the angle you want and to get the handles to a comfortable height.

Finish the wheelbarrow with paint. If you have made all the box joints with waterproof glue, it should be capable of carrying water or any liquid mixtures.

Garden Trolley

A lightweight means of carrying tools, transporting plants, or gathering weeds is useful in a flower garden or a small vegetable plot where you cannot justify a larger barrow or cart. The trolley shown in FIG. 7-92 has a pair of wheels and two handles. It has space for long and short tools, and there is a bin where you could fit a plastic bag for trash or plants, or where young trees would stand inside. If

Fig. 7-92. A garden trolley will transport tools, plants, and other equipment.

Materials List for Garden Trolley

Middle panel

1 piece	25 × 17 × 1/4 or 1/2 plywood
2 pieces	25 × 2 × 1
2 pieces	14 × 2 × 1

Bottom

1 bottom	21 × 17 × 1/4 or 1/2 plywood
2 pieces	21 × 2 × 1
2 pieces	16 × 2 × 1

Front

1 piece	28 × 17 × 1/4 or 1/2 plywood
2 pieces	26 × 2 × 1
1 piece	16 × 2 × 1
2 sides	27 × 17 × 1/4 or 1/2 plywood
2 handles	36 × 2 × 1
2 legs	31 × 2 × 1
1 back	17 × 9 × 1/4 or 1/2 plywood
3 backs	17 × 2 × 1
2 wheels 8-inch diameter with 25-inch axle	

necessary, you can tilt the whole trolley forward to release the contents, but it usually stands firm on the wheels and two legs.

The construction is almost entirely of 1/4-inch or 1/2-inch plywood on wood 2 inches wide and 1 inch thick. The sizes suggested in FIG. 7-93 are based on wheels

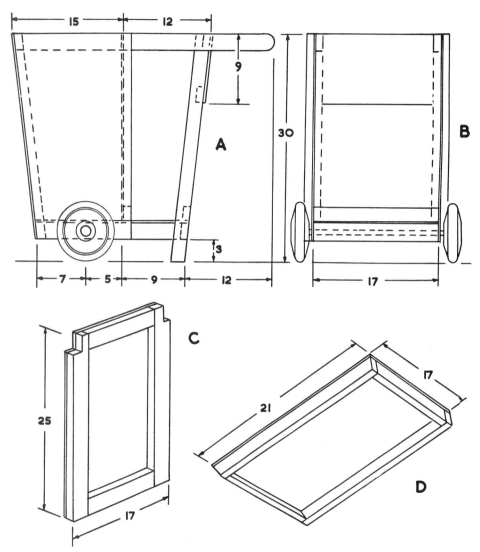

Fig. 7-93. Make the trolley of framed plywood.

about 8 inches in diameter and of the type that fit on a ³/₈-inch or ¹/₂-inch rod axle, are retained by washers and cotter pins. You should obtain the wheels and axle first in case sizes have to be modified to suit them. If you use glue between the plywood panels and the strips of wood, that will provide considerable strength. You only need to nail or screw corners or other joints. Use dowels or mortise-and-tenon joints between some parts, but glue, nails, and screws should be sufficient.

Set out the outline of the side view (FIG. 7-93A) to get the angles of the ends. The center panel is upright and the ends are sloping outward. In the other direction (FIG. 7-93B), the sides are parallel and the width might have to be modified to suit the axle, if you cannot use a plain rod.

The basic part, around which the others fit, is the center panel (FIG. 7-93C). Glue and nail the strips to it and cut out the corners for the handles to pass through.

Next comes the bottom (FIG. 7-93D). This panel is the same width as the center panel. The ends slope. Attach the panel to the bottom, with the plywood forward (FIG. 7-94A). Screws as well as glue are advisable.

Make the handles (FIG. 7-94B) and use them parallel with the bottom to check the height of the front panel. Make and frame that panel (FIG. 7-94C). Glue and nail it to the bottom, and glue and screw the handles to both panels.

Make the plywood sides (FIG. 7-94D), and glue and nail them to the other parts to complete the bin.

Drill through for the axle and temporarily put the wheels in position. This positioning will allow you to make and fit the legs (FIG. 7-94E).

Put a strip across the bottom (FIG. 7-94F) to prevent tools from slipping off. At the top between the handles and legs, stiffen a piece of plywood to fit inside the legs. After painting the wood, put a strap in loops across this to hold small tools (FIG. 7-94G).

Thoroughly paint the wood. Fit the axle and wheels. Put large washers inside the wheels to prevent wear by rubbing on the plywood.

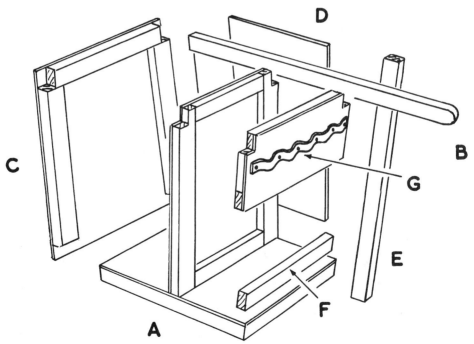

Fig. 7-94. The trolley parts assemble over the base. Loops will hold small tools.

Deck Stairway

Stairs are often needed between a deck and the ground or with another level of deck or the house. They have to be planned so steps taken are the same all the way from ground level to the deck level. Having a higher or lower step at an end could cause the user to falter and have an accident. It is usual for the *rise* of stairs to be no more than 8 inches. If you measure the total height between surfaces, you can divide that into the nearest rise under 8 inches. The amount one step projects ahead of the one above is its *run* (FIG. 7-95A), and this is best if it is more

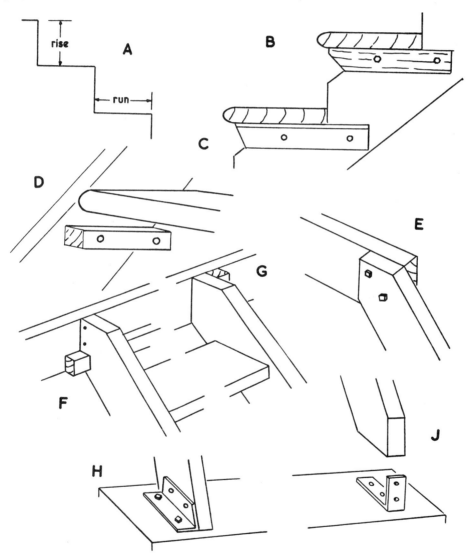

Fig. 7-95. Stairs to a deck must be planned so steps are the same throughout.

than the rise. Shallower rises usually have wider runs. With a rise of 8 inches, the run might be 9 inches. If the rise is only 7 inches, the run would be better 10 inches or 11 inches.

Obviously you have to adapt to the available space. You cannot do anything about the total height, but you could make one more or less rise. Adjust the spread of the stair to fit within the available space. Most stairways are a compromise, but for ease of use, aim at the suggested relation between rise and run. The angle of a stairway is flatter than 45 degrees to horizontal, and you must allow for that. (It should extend more than it rises.)

The two side supports are called *stringers*, and they can support the treads in several ways. Because of the stringer angle in relation to the tread widths, they have to be fairly wide—usually 2 inches thick and 10 inches or 12 inches wide.

Treads are best as wide as the run, or a little more, but some stairways have the rear edge of each tread slightly forward of the nose of the one above. Stair widths are usually between 24 inches and 36 inches, and can have treads 2 inches thick.

It is possible to partially notch treads into stringers and support them with wood cleats securely bolted on (FIG. 7-95B). There could be steel angle instead of wood cleats (FIG. 7-95C). Notching treads into dadoes, as is often done on indoor stairways, is not recommended for exterior work. If the treads are to come wholly within the stringers, they are better on bolted cleats (FIG. 7-95D).

At the top, the stringers must be secured to the decking. If there are joists at convenient spacings, they can be bolted through (FIG. 7-95E). The stringers could be notched over ledgers and toe-nailed, (FIG. 7-95F) but there would be less obstruction to feet with cleats outside (FIG. 7-95G).

If the foot of the stairway is at ground level, it should be a concrete pad to avoid rot. The stringers could have cleats or steel angle outside, with anchor bolts set in the concrete (FIG. 7-95H). Another way to take any thrust uses stout strip iron bolted down with the wood stringers fitted into the bends (FIG. 7-95J).

A stairway could go off the deck squarely at any point. Usually the deck boards are carried out on extended joists (FIG. 7-96A). If the boards are met end-on, cut them back over a piece added inside and fit a cover strip (FIG. 7-96B).

It might be more convenient to have the stairs alongside the deck. In that case, the joists have to be extended to take boards to form a landing (FIG. 7-96C). In most constructions, this can be allowed to cantilever from the deck—providing the extension is no more than 30 inches—but there will have to be another post at the corner.

Less commonly, the stairway top can be set back into the deck. If the cutout is much, there are problems of support, and railings will have to be arranged around the top for safety.

A stairway of just a few treads can be safe without a hand rail, but in most cases there have to be railings or bannisters. Construction can be the same as for the deck and still give a uniform and attractive appearance.

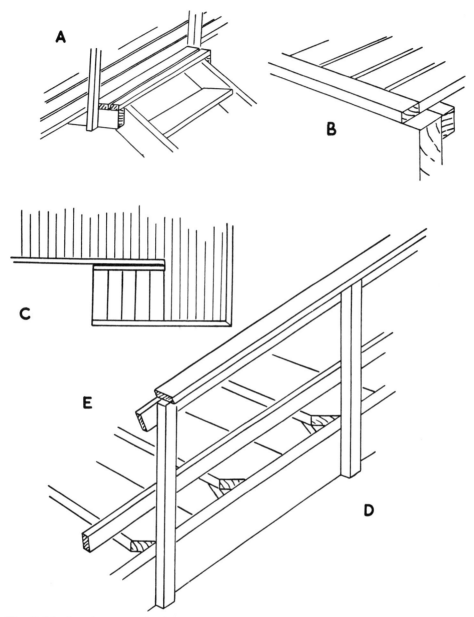

Fig. 7-96. *A stairway can lead squarely or parallel to a deck. Rails should be provided.*

Bolt the rail posts to the outsides of the stringer (FIG. 7-96D). Attach rails to them in the same way as around the deck (FIG. 7-96E). Maintain a similar height above the treads so that anyone using the stairway and the edge of the deck will not have to change the height of their grip.

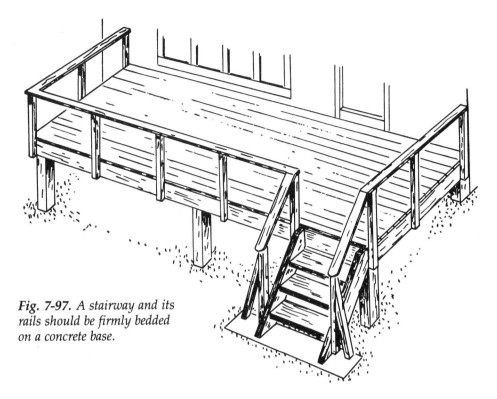

Fig. 7-97. A stairway and its rails should be firmly bedded on a concrete base.

How close you arrange the posts depends on your needs. Posts opposite every tread will give a balluster effect, but placing them at every second or third step—with a rail parallel with the stringer lower down—will provide ample protection.

Attach the foot of the stairs to a concrete base (FIG. 7-97).

Log Seat with Back

Any stool or bench without a back can only provide limited comfort. If anyone wants to sit for long, a backrest is needed. There are ways of fitting backs to log seats, but most of them involve prepared wood. It is possible to make a simple, one-man, half-log seat into a chair with a back that still keeps the rustic appearance and will fit in with a wild garden background (FIG. 7-98). There might not be the comfort of a shaped or upholstered chair, but it is a step up from a simple flat seat.

Make a seat from half a log, with three legs. Allow for 12 inches to 15 inches at the two-leg end forward of where the back will come. The single leg hole must come far enough behind the back for the short grain not to be a source of weakness. That means a flat top 12 inches to 15 inches wide and probably 20 inches or more long. Round the front corners.

Fig. 7-98. A three-leg stool is made more comfortable by the addition of a back.

Prepare the seat parts, but do not fit the legs until after the back has been fitted The back is split from a log. It need not be as wide as the seat. Have it longer than needed until after making the joint.

Thin the bottom of the back to about 1¹/₂ inches (FIG. 7-99A) and on that, mark the width of tenon (FIG. 7-99B). The sides should be parallel, but it does not matter if there is a slight taper in thickness.

Mark the mortise in the seat. The back should fit about 15 degrees to upright (FIG. 7-99C). Cut through the forward edge of the mortise to that angle, with enough waste to allow for working with the drill and chisel, but leave some waste wood at the rear edge of the mortise to trim later.

Cut the rear edge of the mortise progressively so you can try in the tenon. Get as close a fit as you can, but if it is not perfect, the back will drive in and take care of slight inaccuracies. The tenon should go through and project slightly (FIG. 7-99D).

Round the top edge of the back to a curve you like (FIG. 7-99E). The rounded back can be thinned toward the top if the full curve looks too bulky.

It should be sufficient to drive the back in. If it ever loosens, you can drive it farther.

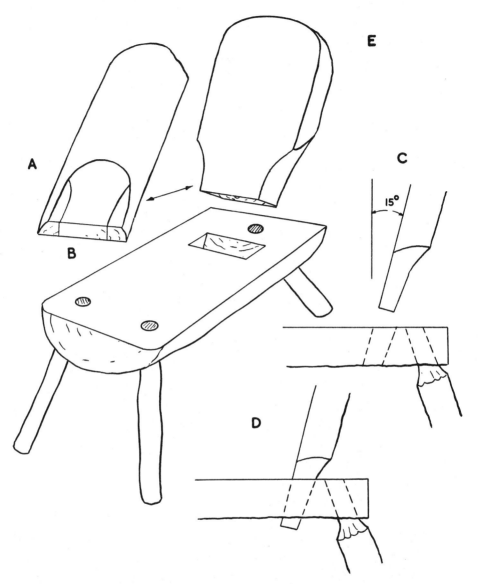

Fig. 7-99. The back is a split log cut to fit into a slot in the seat.

Yard Chair

This strong chair (FIG. 7-100) should be suitable for leaving outdoors for at least part of the year. It could be used on a lawn, beside a path, on the patio, or on a deck.

It is large enough to take cushions, although its shaping offers reasonable comfort unpadded. The slatted seat is curved, and the back slopes. There is nowhere for rain to be trapped, and the wood is easy to wash and dry. The finest chair would be made of hardwood that is durable and resistant to exposure, but

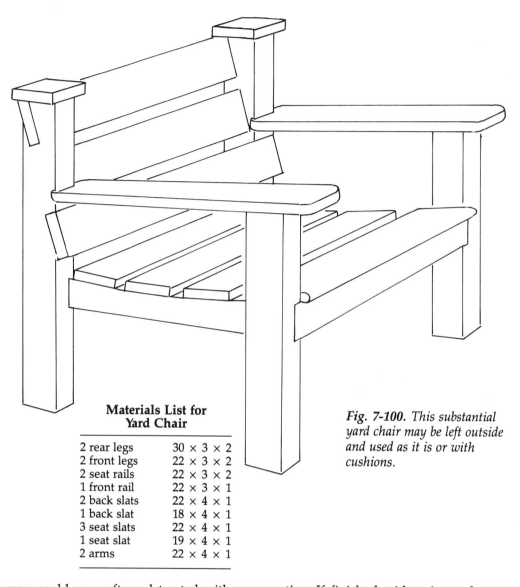

Materials List for Yard Chair

2 rear legs	30 × 3 × 2
2 front legs	22 × 3 × 2
2 seat rails	22 × 3 × 2
1 front rail	22 × 3 × 1
2 back slats	22 × 4 × 1
1 back slat	18 × 4 × 1
3 seat slats	22 × 4 × 1
1 seat slat	19 × 4 × 1
2 arms	22 × 4 × 1

Fig. 7-100. This substantial yard chair may be left outside and used as it is or with cushions.

you could use softwood treated with preservative. If finished with paint and touched up at any subsequent bare patches, a softwood chair should have a long life.

Most parts are either 2 inches × 3 inches or 1-inch-×-4-inch section. Waterproof glue should be used in the joints as well as screws. Steel screws should be zinc-plated or galvanized, but it might be better to use bronze or brass screws. Use bolts instead of screws through the main joints.

The chair stands on a square with 2l-inch sides and is 28 inches high (FIG. 7-101A). It will be a help if you set out the side view of the seat rail (FIG. 7-101B) and the back (FIG. 7-101C) full-size.

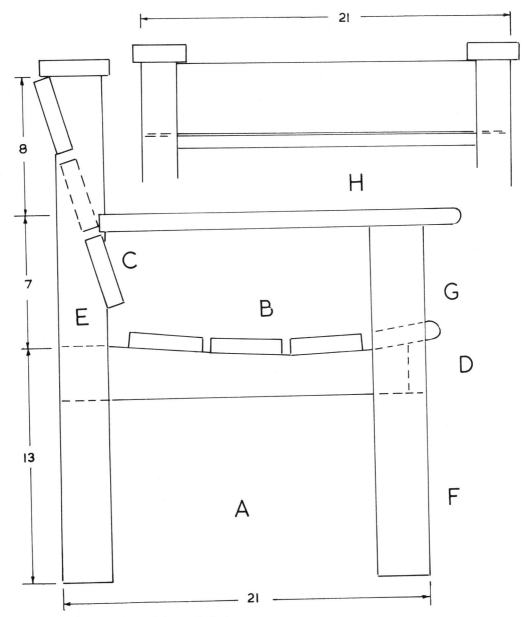

Fig. 7-101. *Main sizes of the yard chair.*

The curve of the seat rail should drop about 1 inch at the center. Continue the curve over the front rail (FIG. 7-101D), and mark on the spacing of the seat slats.

On the upper part of each leg, the three back slats are arranged to slope across the 3-inch face (FIG. 7-101E). Top and bottom slats go through notches (FIGS. 7-102A and B). The center rail is cut short and will be doweled in place (FIG. 7-102C).

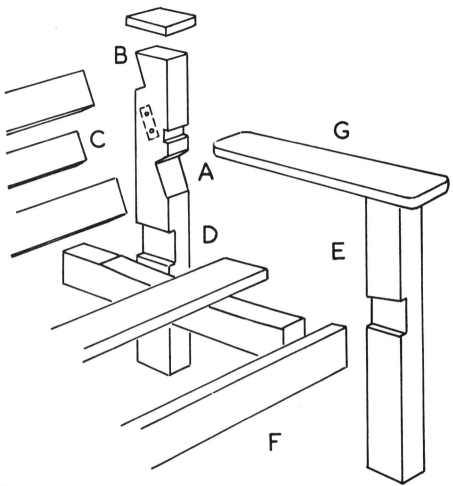

Fig. 7-102. How the parts of the yard chair fit together.

Prepare the wood for the rear legs. Mark and cut the notches for the top and bottom back slats, and mark where the middle slat will come. Mark and cut notches 1/2 inch deep for the seat rails (FIG. 7-102D) and the arms.

Make the two seat rails. Cut back 1 inch at the front for the front rail.

Mark out the pair of front legs (FIGS. 7-101F and 102E). The bottom of the seat rail notches must be level with the notches on the rear legs, but the top edges should follow the curve in the seat rail.

The top of each front leg could be tenoned or doweled into the arms, but it might be sufficient to use nails or screws. Prepare the wood for the joint you prefer.

Cut the front rail (FIG. 7-102F) to fit in the leg notches ahead of the side seat rails. Bevel the top edge to match the curve in the side rails.

Cut the center back slat to length. Check that when this is between the rear legs and the front rail is in its notches, the chair sides will be parallel. Drill the back slat and legs for dowels.

Assemble the chair sides with waterproof glue and screws or bolts through. See that the legs are square to the undersides of the seat rails and that opposite parts match.

Dowel and glue the center back slat in place, and screw the front rail into its notches. Check that the parts are square and that the chair stands upright when put on a flat surface and viewed from several directions.

Screw and glue on the other two back slats. They might be cut too long and trimmed to the legs afterwards.

Fit the seat slats in the same way. Cut the front one to fit between the legs, and round its projecting front edge (FIG. 7-101G). Space the others evenly. They could be allowed to project and have rounded ends, if you wish, but they are shown cut level with the seat rails.

The arms (FIGS. 7-101H and 102G) fit into notches in the rear legs and on top of the front legs, so they are parallel with the ground. Round the edges and all corners of the arms; fit them in place. Besides glue in the notches, you can drive screws diagonally upwards into each joint.

Take sharpness off all exposed edges and corners. If the wood has not already been treated, soak it with preservative. When this has dried, finish the wood with a paint compatible with the preservative. If you have used a durable hardwood, it might be left untreated or be rubbed with oil.

Park Bench

Although much garden seating is crude and simple compared with chairs used indoors, there is a place for better-made furniture. In a formal garden or on a well-equipped deck or patio, something that is not of a very high standard of construction will be rather obvious and not suited to its surroundings. Sometimes a seat is made to commemorate some event. It could be a special anniversary, a particular happening, or even the moving to a new address. Somewhere on the seat would be carved or painted, or a plaque would be added giving details. In that case, the seat should be worthy of its importance.

A seat for an important situation should be made of good wood, with cut joints rather than screws or nails, and the total effect should be pleasing and functional. Seats of this type are often seen in public parks and gardens. There is a similarity about their designs due to necessary comfort and appearance requirements. The seat shown in FIG. 7-103 is a basic form, and possible variations are described. The material should be seasoned hardwood planed all around and free from large knots, particularly in the lengthwise parts. An overall length of 60 inches will accommodate three sitters, but other lengths are possible, down to a single seat. Two single seats might commemorate a wedding anniversary or

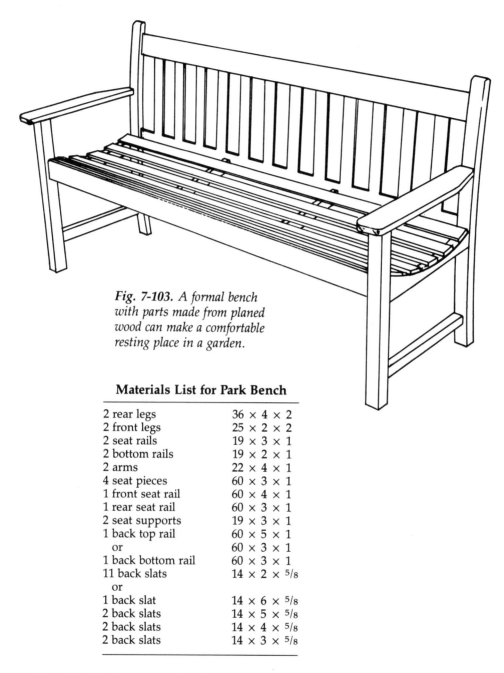

Fig. 7-103. A formal bench with parts made from planed wood can make a comfortable resting place in a garden.

Materials List for Park Bench

2 rear legs	$36 \times 4 \times 2$
2 front legs	$25 \times 2 \times 2$
2 seat rails	$19 \times 3 \times 1$
2 bottom rails	$19 \times 2 \times 1$
2 arms	$22 \times 4 \times 1$
4 seat pieces	$60 \times 3 \times 1$
1 front seat rail	$60 \times 4 \times 1$
1 rear seat rail	$60 \times 3 \times 1$
2 seat supports	$19 \times 3 \times 1$
1 back top rail	$60 \times 5 \times 1$
or	$60 \times 3 \times 1$
1 back bottom rail	$60 \times 3 \times 1$
11 back slats	$14 \times 2 \times 5/8$
or	
1 back slat	$14 \times 6 \times 5/8$
2 back slats	$14 \times 5 \times 5/8$
2 back slats	$14 \times 4 \times 5/8$
2 back slats	$14 \times 3 \times 5/8$

another "double" occasion, but there is more wood and work than required for making a two-person bench. On the other hand, independent chairs allow you to locate them throughout the yard or garden.

The bench has a hollowed seat and a tilted back that is decorated with vertical slats. Except for the bend in the rear legs, shaping of the arms and possible shaping of the top back rail, nearly all the parts are straight. The wood can be machine-planed, but on the visible surfaces the plane marks should be removed by sanding or hand planing if the bench is to be given a clear or untreated finish.

A full-size layout of the end view will be useful, but it is not essential because most information is shown on the drawing. The back legs and seat supports can be laid out on the wood (FIG. 7-104A). Notice the positions of rails and other lengthwise parts in relation to the ends (FIG. 7-104B).

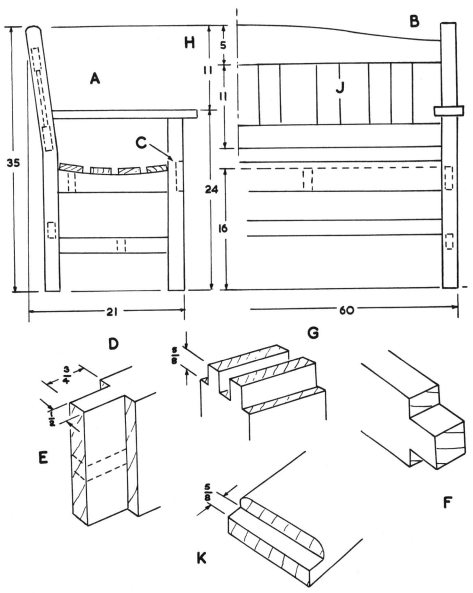

Fig. 7-104. These sizes make a good looking bench. Structural parts should be tenoned.

Mark out the rear legs (FIG. 7-105A). The bend comes above the seat level. Do not make this a sharp angle; curve between the straight sections, particularly toward the rear. Mark on the positions of all joints so that this leg layout can be used as a guide when marking other parts. Cut the legs to shape, but leave some excess length at both ends to be trimmed off after joints have been cut.

Mark out the front legs (FIG. 7-102B) with joint positions matching those on the rear legs. The front seat rail will have its upper edge level with the tops of the seat pieces (FIG. 7-104C). Measure the actual wood being used for the seat to get

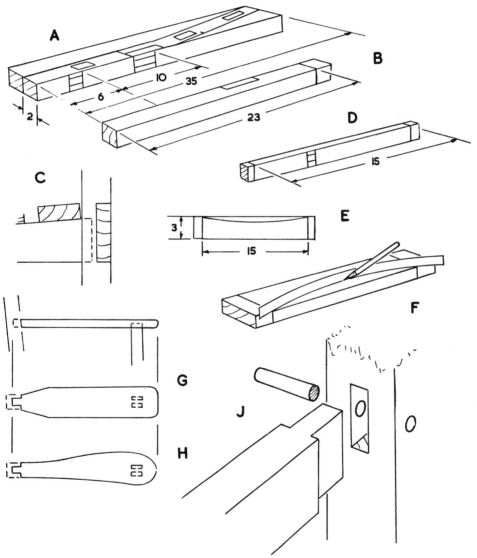

Fig. 7-105. Make the individual parts first. Mark and cut tenoned joints so they can be pegged.

the height of the top of the rail. At the tops of the legs, mark where the underside of the arm will come, and leave more than enough above that for making and cutting the tenons later.

The bottom end rail (FIG. 7-105D) is a simple piece with tenons at its ends and a mortise position slightly forward of halfway for a lengthwise rail (FIG. 7-106A).

Make the seat rails the same length between shoulders as the bottom rails. The amount of hallow in the top is not crucial, but a drop of 3/4 inch at the center

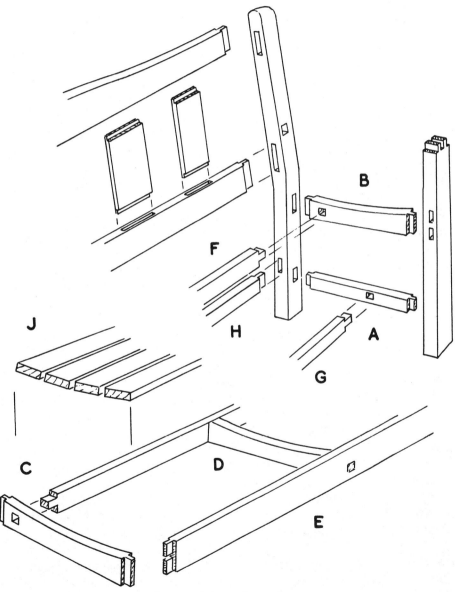

Fig. 7-106. *All parts except the seat slats are tenoned.*

will be satisfactory (FIGS. 7-105E and 106B). This can be drawn by penciling around a sprung lath (FIG. 7-105F). A rear rail (FIG. 7-106C) goes under the back seat piece and will have two seat supports (FIG. 7-106D) evenly spaced and attached to it and the front seat rail. Mark the curves on these now, so all parts have matching shapes, but do not cut them to length yet.

Make the pair of arms. They could be simple, mainly parallel, pieces (FIG. 7-105G) or have shaped outlines (FIG. 7-105H). In any case, round the top and front edges well. Leave more than enough for cutting the tenons at the back, and mark where the front legs will join.

All of the end parts can be joined with stub tenons. It should be sufficient for them to enter mortises about 3/4 inch, with a tenon thickness of 1/2 inch on wood of the sizes specified in FIG. 7-104D. For the parts of 2-inch or less depth, leave the tenons as cut, but for 3-inch pieces, divide the tenons (FIG. 7-104E) if you prefer. Where the rear seat and bottom rails join, allow for narrower tenons going right through (FIG. 7-104F).

At the arms, the tenon into the rear legs will be the same as elsewhere, except the shoulders should slope to match the leg angle. At the front legs, the tenons cannot penetrate very far into the arms, and it is better to make them double (FIG. 7-104G) to give a greater glue area.

Assemble the ends now and cut mortises for the lengthwise parts later, but keep in mind that it is easier to cut joints in separate pieces of wood. Determine the sizes of lengthwise parts, and cut mortises in the legs and end rails now, even if you do not make the matching tenons yet.

Assemble the pair of ends. Use clamps to draw the joints tight. Check squareness and that the opposite ends match and are without twist. For extra security of joints, drill for dowels across them; one 1/4-inch dowel in each joint should be sufficient (FIG. 7-105).

Mark out the front seat rail (FIG. 7-106E), and use it as a guide to lengths between shoulders when making other lengthwise parts. Mark on it the positions of seat supports, and round its top edges. On a 60-inch length, two evenly spaced supports will be enough. Allow for the supports having narrow tenons right through—or stub tenons if you do not want end grain to show at the front.

Make the rear seat rail (FIG. 7-106F). This will be slightly longer than the front seat rail because it goes between end rails and not legs. Mark the bottom rail (FIG. 7-106G); it will be the same length. Both have narrow tenons at the ends.

Mark the positions of the seat supports on the two long rails. Cut these to fit, and glue the joints. Check squareness; the accuracy of this assembly affects squareness of the complete bench.

The bottom rail between the rear legs is a simple piece (FIG. 7-106H) that is the same length between shoulders as the front seat rail. The two back rails should also be this length. Figure 5-26 shows two parallel pieces, but if you want to carve, paint, or attach a plaque to the bench, the center of the top rail is the place for this commemoration. The top rail is drawn with a curved top to provide this space (FIG. 7-104H). The ends are the same depth as straight rails would be.

Therefore, the joints to the rear legs are the same. Make the two back rails to the shape you want. Ends are tenoned to suit the mortises in the legs.

The back could have a pattern of similar, parallel, upright slats (as shown in FIG. 7-103). If the top rail is curved up at the center, this could be complemented by having a wide center slat, and then reducing the widths of the others toward the ends (FIG. 7-104J). This would provide enough space on the center one for an inscription in place of, or in addition to, any on the top rail.

As the slats are not very thick, they can have barefaced tenons on their ends (FIG. 7-104K). The front edges can be rounded. Make the slats and cut the joints. Assemble the slats to the rails while again checking squareness that will affect the finished bench.

All the lengthwise parts can now be joined to the ends. The seat and back assemblies should pull the bench square. Have it standing on a flat surface so that there is no risk of twist. Draw the joints tight and put dowels across most of them.

The seat pieces (FIG. 7-106) should have their upper edges rounded and their ends extending a short distance over the end rails (where they also can be rounded). Mark where the crossings come, and drill for two screws in each piece at each place. Brass screws could finish on the surface, or you can counterbore and plug them.

The bench could be finished by painting, but if a good hardwood has been used it would look better if the grain is visible. If it is a durable wood that will withstand exposure unprotected, leave it to weather to a natural shade. Otherwise, use a clear varnish. This does not have to be a high gloss, but several coats of semiglossy varnish can be effective. Marine varnish will have the longest life.

Swinging Seat

A swinging seat or glider for two people makes a pleasant place to relax. It can be hung from a porch or it could have its own supports for use anywhere in the garden or yard. There are several ways of making such a seat, and many sizes are possible. The seat shown in FIG. 7-107 is shaped to provide comfort as it is, but it could be improved with cushions. The size is intended to suit two persons with plenty of space. A bigger seat could be made in the same way, but if it is made much longer, the sections of the lengthwise wood should be increased.

Materials List for Swinging Seat

2 seat rails	$30 \times 6 \times 1^{1/2}$
2 uprights	$27 \times 4 \times 1^{1/2}$
2 support blocks	$4 \times 4 \times 1^{1/2}$
2 arms	$33 \times 4 \times 1^{1/2}$
1 hanging strip	$72 \times 4 \times 1^{1/2}$
1 bottom strip	$60 \times 4 \times 2$
7 seat slats	$64 \times 2 \times 1^{1/2}$
4 back slats	$64 \times 2 \times 1^{1/2}$

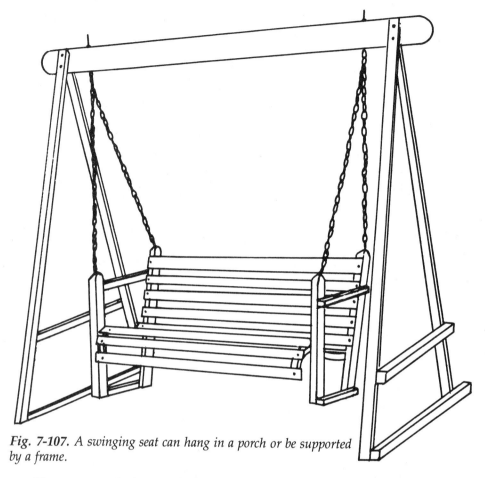

Fig. 7-107. A swinging seat can hang in a porch or be supported by a frame.

The ropes or chains attach to a strip that goes the length of the back and to reinforced front uprights. The support needs to be fairly high to give a more comfortable swinging action than could be possible with short ropes.

All the parts can be made of softwood, but a durable hardwood, such as oak, would be better suited to exposure. If the suggested canopy is made, it will protect the wood from severe weather as well as shield the users from sunlight and showers.

The key assembly that settles the sizes of many other parts is the end (FIG. 7-108A). Draw this full size. How much slope to give the uprights is not crucial, but about 10 degrees is suitable. The curve of the seat can be drawn freehand. Let it dip about 1 inch from the top of the wood and curve down to vertical at the front (FIG. 7-108B). Allow for the 2-inch seat slats being spaced about 1 1/2 inches apart. Use a similar spacing at the back; it can be taken to a different height if you prefer. Curve the tops of the uprights (FIG. 7-108C).

Make the end parts, and check that the opposite assemblies will be a matching pair. Although it would be possible merely to lap the parts and glue and screw

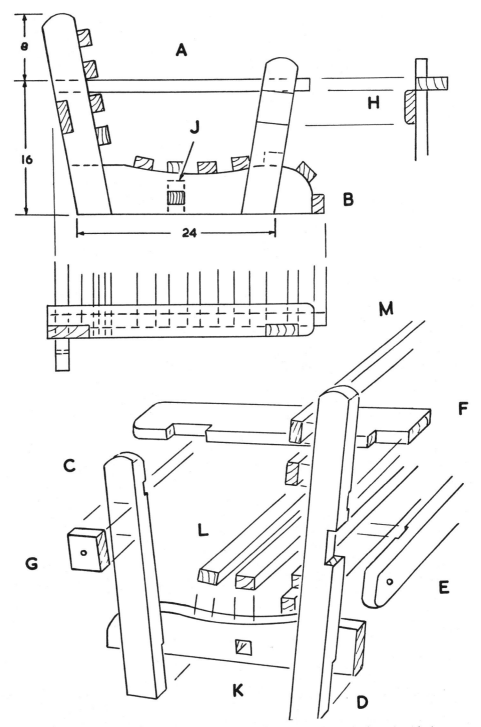

Fig. 7-108. *The seat is built as a unit, with strong parts where the hanging chains come.*

them, notches help in locating the joints and preventing later movement. Keep the notches in the uprights quite shallow (FIG. 7-108D)—1/4 inch will be enough. Where the back hanging strip fits, the shallow notch will be in that and enough must be cut from the rear upright for the rear faces to come level (FIG. 7-108E).

Make the arms to fit into the uprights and come level at the outside (FIG. 7-108F). Round the front corners of the arms and all edges that will be exposed. Take the sharpness off the tops of the uprights.

Assemble the pair of ends. The arms can be glued and screwed. The seat rails are better held with bolts through. Two 1/2-inch-diameter bolts at each crossing should be sufficient.

The front ropes attach to an eyebolt in each end, where the front upright is strengthened with a block outside (FIG. 7-108G), below arm level (FIG. 7-108H). Its exposed edges can be rounded. The eyebolt should go through with large washers at each side of the wood to spread the pressure.

Although the seat and back slats provide considerable stiffness lengthwise, strength in that direction is mainly provided by the back hanging strip and another underneath between the seat rails. The one underneath should be tenoned into the seat rails (FIG. 7-108K). Make this before the other lengthwise parts, and use it to hold the ends while getting their lengths.

Let the back hanging rail extend up to 6 inches beyond the seat ends. Drill the extension for the hanging ropes or shackles for chains. Round the ends. Assemble these two lengthwise pieces to the ends. Check that they fit squarely and that the ends will be upright.

Make the seat slats to fit on the seat rails, either level with them or extending a short distance (FIG. 7-108L). Make the back slats in a similar way (FIG. 7-108M). Round all the slats' outer edges before screwing them into place. It is helpful to use a piece of scrap wood of the correct width to keep regular spacings. Uneven spacing can appear very obvious when the seat is unoccupied. An extended seat might require an intermediate support for the seat slats, but providing they are strong enough, slight springiness is an advantage.

Modern synthetic rope is very strong and most kinds will stand up to exposure without suffering. The seat could be hung with rope about 1/2 inch in diameter (knotted or spliced at the ends). Alternatively, there could be chains that would require shackles to the eyebolts and either large shackles or eyebolts through the rear hanging strip for smaller shackles. Finish the wood with paint or preservative.

Swinging Seat Support

If the swinging seat is to be located in the garden or yard, either in a permanent position or as a freestanding structure, there has to be a support that is high enough to allow a gentle swinging action, wide enough for the seat to move without touching the supports, and with a sufficient base to keep the assembly free from tipping. If the support is to be moveable, the base should be wide enough back to front to resist tipping with the most energetic swinging. That means feet should be about as long as the support is high. If the base is to be bolted or staked down, it need not project much more than the spread of the legs.

The support is for a swing seat like the one just described (FIG. 7-107). The height suits the seat, and its length should be sufficient to have the legs about 24 inches further apart than the overall length of the seat. As with the seat, the sup-

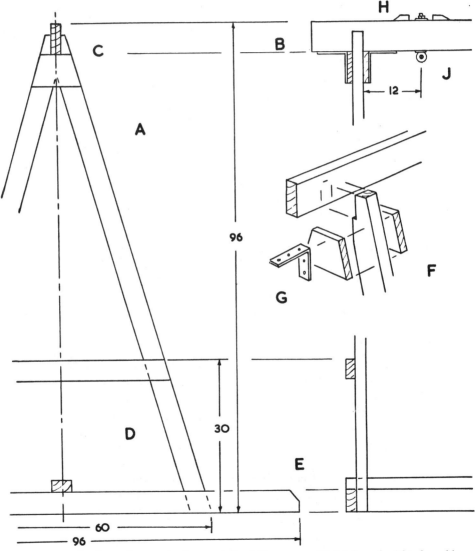

Fig. 7-109. The frame for a swinging seat should be reasonably high and with a broad base for stability and a satisfactory action.

2 legs	102 × 4 × 2
2 feet	96 × 4 × 2
2 rails	48 × 4 × 2
1 beam	108 × 6 × 2
4 gussets	12 × 6 × 1
1 stiffener	100 × 4 × 2
4 steel brackets with 6-inch legs	

port could be made of softwood protected with preservative, but it would be better made of a durable hardwood. Details that follow are for a support without a canopy. If a canopy is to be fitted now or later, there are some slight modifications that should be allowed for during construction.

Set out the main lines of an end view (FIG. 7-109A) to get the lengths of the legs and the angles to cut the parts. A half view at one side of the centerline will tell you all you need.

The wood for the beam and the legs should be chosen for straightness of grain and the absence of flaws. The beam (FIG. 7-109B) is a plain piece, extending far enough to cover the brackets.

At the tops, cut the legs to fit around the beam and against each other (FIG. 7-109C). Mark where the rail and foot come on each piece, but don't cut the bottom until the foot is attached (FIG. 7-109E).

Prepare the feet (FIG. 7-109E) and mark where their legs come. Bevel the ends.

Bring the top of each pair of legs together and join them with gussets, cut with their grain running across (FIG. 7-109F). Arrange the width of the slot so that it will be a tight fit on the beam. Glue and screw the gussets (although there could also be bolts through) clear of where the brackets will come.

Bolt the legs to the feet and the rails to the legs. Cut off any surplus wood, and take off any sharp edges or corners.

Add the beam and the bottom stiffener with the legs on edge. Screw and bolt the beam between the tops of the legs, and use steel brackets underneath to provide stiffness (FIG. 7-109G). When you fit the stiffener to the feet, compare distances at tops and bottoms of the legs and check squareness by measuring diagonals. A bolt through each foot will be better than screws. Bring the assembly upright and check stability and squareness.

The seat ropes could be taken around the beam, possibly located with small blocks of wood to act as cleats to prevent the turns sliding along (FIG. 7-109H). If chain is used, there should be eyebolts through the beam to take shackles (FIG. 7-109J). Locate them to suit the width of the seat. If they are wider apart, they will help to restrict lengthwise movement of the seat. Finish the wood with paint or preservative.

Plain Bench with Backrest

A seat without a backrest might be a welcome sight when you need a brief rest, but if you want to sit for long you need support for your back. There are various degrees of complication in seats with backrests, but the example shown in FIG. 7-110 is simple in appearance and construction. In addition, it can offer reasonable comfort to tired bodies.

Most of the construction is with screws, but the lengthwise stiffening rail has mortise-and-tenon joints at the ends. The material is planed wood, which can be a softwood finished with paint, or a durable hardwood left untreated. Sizes can be varied, but a top 14 inches wide is suggested as a comfortable height for sitting. The rear support is at a height and angle that should suit most users. How long to make the bench will have to be decided in relation to the available space and what wood you have, but a length of 6 feet will suit three people or even four for a short time.

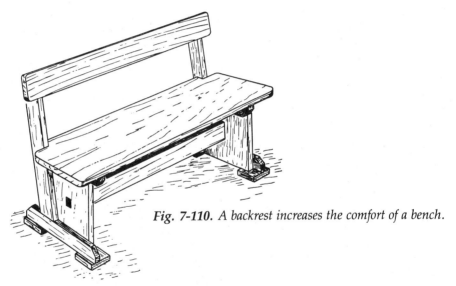

Fig. 7-110. A backrest increases the comfort of a bench.

Materials List for
Plain Bench with Backrest

2 legs	$15 \times 12 \times 1^{1}/_{4}$
2 seat supports	$14 \times 2 \times 1^{1}/_{4}$
2 feet	$18 \times 3 \times 1^{1}/_{4}$
4 pads	$4 \times 4 \times 1^{1}/_{4}$
2 backrest supports	$30 \times 3 \times 1^{1}/_{4}$
1 seat	$72 \times 14 \times 1^{1}/_{4}$
1 backrest	$72 \times 6 \times 1^{1}/_{4}$
1 rail	$70 \times 5 \times 1^{1}/_{4}$

Sort the available wood and relate it to an end view, which will control most sizes (FIG. 7-111A). Make a full-size drawing. Have the seat at a comfortable height and locate the backrest in relation to it. A slope of about 10 degrees from vertical will give a suitable angle for comfort and for attaching to the ends without reducing the useful width of the seat (FIG. 7-111B). To allow for the need for resistance against tipping back, draw the feet farther back than forward of the end (FIG. 7-111C).

The ends could be tenoned into the seat supports and the feet, but they are shown overlapped and glued and screwed. Make the pair of ends carefully squared, and mark where the rail will come (FIG. 7-111D).

Make the rail and cut tenons at its ends. They are the full thickness of the wood, but cut down to shoulders. If the tenons are a little more than half the total width of the rail, that will be right. Cut the mortises and tenons, but do not assemble these parts yet.

Glue and screw on crossbars on the upper surfaces at the tops of the legs (FIG. 7-111E), extending forward to support the seat.

Make the feet (FIG. 7-111F) and attach them to the outsides of the bottoms of the legs, then put pads under the feet (FIG. 7-111G). Make the pads wide enough to extend outward a little and come under the thickness of the legs. Check that the two legs match as a pair.

Make the backrest supports (FIG. 7-111H). Let the bottom of the support come close against its foot. At the top, cut away to let the backrest strip fit in. Round the top corners, and take off the sharpness of all exposed parts. Glue and screw to the legs while checking that the two ends match.

Fit the rail to the legs. Put saw cuts across the ends of the tenons before assembly. Glue in the tenons and spread them with wedges. When the glue has set, level the tenon ends with the leg surfaces.

Make the seat (FIG. 7-111J). If you have to join boards to make up the width, they could be plain glued edges, tongued and grooved, or having cleats across underneath. At the ends, allow the seat to project a short distance past the backrest supports around which they are notched (FIG. 7-111K). Round the extending corners and the front edge. Fit the seat by screwing into the supports and the tops of the legs. This will look best if the screws are counterbored and covered with wood plugs. Assemble on a flat surface, and check that the seat will stand without wobbling.

Make the backrest (FIG. 7-111L). Let its ends extend the same amount as the seat. Round the corners and well round the front edges. Join to the supports with counterbored screws, in the same way as on the seat.

There will probably be no need to sand the seat, but make sure there is no roughness left before painting or applying other finish.

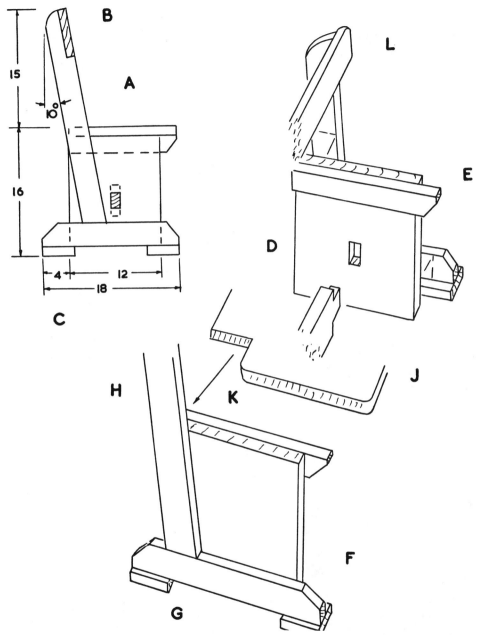

Fig. 7-111. *The backrest is at a slight angle. Most joints are nailed, but the bottom rail is better tenoned.*

Double Garden Seat

A combination of two chairs and a table and shelf gives two users places beside them for refreshments, things they are using, and storage below. The whole thing is a unit that can have a permanent place or be mounted on wheels or casters for moving about.

The two chairs are very similar to individual seats, but each has only two legs on the ground. If all eight legs reached the ground, there might be difficulty in leveling them. To give rigidity to the structure, the seat rail at the back and the lower rail at the front are deep and go through from end to end. The seats are shown flat with slats, but you could hollow them. The table and shelf are shown as made of exterior-grade plywood, but they could also be slats.

Much of the construction can be doweled, but the design is shown with mortise-and-tenon joints where appropriate and simple notches or screwed joints elsewhere. The general appearance (FIG. 7-112) shows that it is easiest to understand if you consider the unit as two chairs with some parts extended to provide the links.

In the front view (FIG. 7-113A), the bottom rail goes across, and the seat rails and the table rails fit between the legs. The shelf rests on the long bottom rail. The important view for sizes is one end (FIG. 7-113B). To help in your marking out, make a full size copy of this end. There is no shaping; you can work from measurements only. The back view (FIG. 7-114) shows the seat rail going across in one piece, but there is another rail to support the tabletop and a lighter lower rail

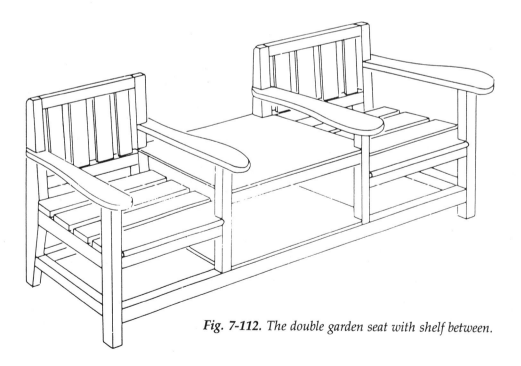

Fig. 7-112. The double garden seat with shelf between.

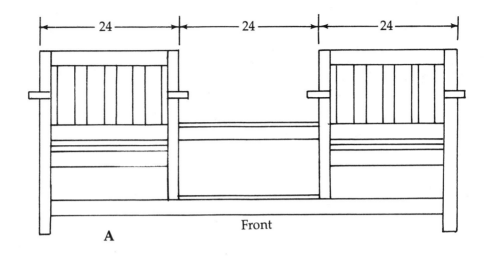

Front

A

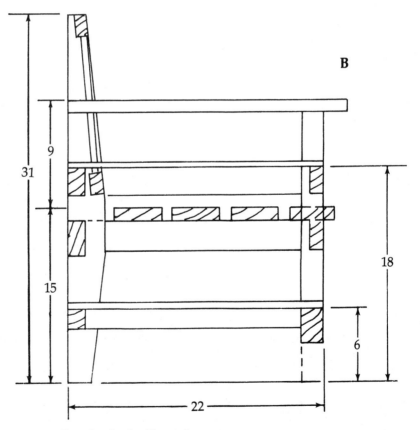

B

Fig. 7-113. Sizes for the double garden seat.

Materials List for Double Garden Seat

Legs			
2 rear	3	× 32 ×	2
2 rear	3	× 28 ×	2
2 front	2	× 25 ×	2
2 front	2	× 21 ×	2
Long rails			
1 seat	3	× 72 ×	2
1 front	3	× 72 ×	2
1 rear	2	× 72 ×	2
Chair parts			
6 rails	2¹/₂	× 24 ×	2
4 rails	2	× 22 ×	2
4 back rails	2	× 24 ×	1
8 back slats	3	× 15 ×	1/2
4 arms	4	× 25 ×	1
8 seat slats	4	× 25 ×	1
Table and shelf			
6 rails	2	× 24 ×	2
2 trays	23	× 26 ×	1/2 plywood

back

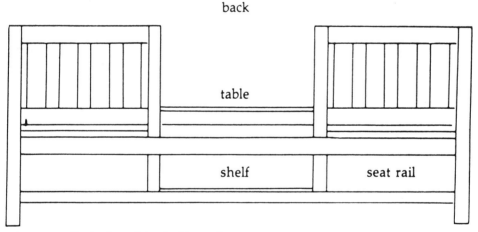

table

shelf   seat rail

Fig. 7-114. Back view of the double garden seat.

going across to take the shelf and inner legs. In both views, the chair backs are shown as vertical slats between horizontal pieces. The chair arms are level with the insides of the legs and extend outside the seats.

Mark out the back legs (FIG. 7-115A). The inner ones are similar, but stop at the bottom rail with stub tenons (FIG. 7-115B). The front outer legs reach the floor (FIG. 7-115C), but the inner ones join the long rail with stub tenons (FIG. 7-115D). The tapers on the back legs start above and below the scat slats and rails. The long seat rail notches into the legs, but you should cut more from the legs than

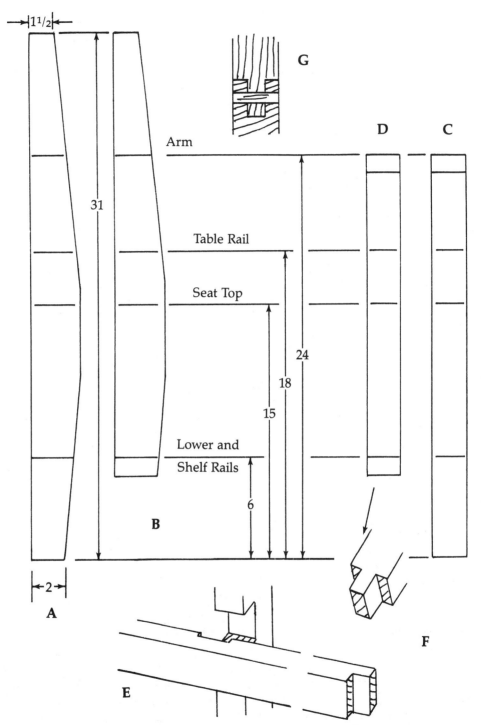

Fig. 7-115. *The upright parts and some joints of the double garden seat.*

the rail so you do not weaken the rail (FIG. 7-115E). Tenon the ends of the rail into the outer legs (FIG. 7-115F).

You can also tenon the long front rail into the outer legs, but at the inner legs make the stub mortises and tenons no more than 1 inch deep. During assembly, you can put a dowel through each joint (FIG. 7-115G).

Other rails that come within the individual seat construction are mortised and tenoned into the legs in the usual way (FIG. 7-116A). All surfaces finish flush, but at the seat level, add small cleats to support the ends of the front seat slats (FIG. 7-116B). You must cut the lower side rails at an angle where they join the tapered rear legs.

Join the horizontal chair back rails to the legs with bareface tenons (FIG. 7-116C) or dowels. The slats also can have barefaced tenons into the rails. Space them so the gaps between them are the same as the gaps next to the legs for a uniform appearance. Round the edges of the rails and slats before assembly.

The arms are 4 inches maximum width, but you can taper or curve them, as you prefer (FIG. 7-116D). The best joint at the front is a stub tenon or a pair of them (FIG. 7-116E). Use foxtail wedging if you think that is necessary. At the rear legs, the arms can notch to the legs to take the load, and then be screwed from outside (FIG. 7-116F).

To support the shelf, there are two long rails running through. You can tenon rails back-to-front into the long rails a short distance from the legs (FIG. 7-117A). That method will be stronger than cutting the joint into the leg where there is already a joint between a leg and a long rail. You need not cut the shelf until you assemble the framework. Then you can make a close fit of it. Glue and screw it downward into the rails. It is probably satisfactory as a plain surface that is easily wiped off. You can put strips around with gaps for removing dirt (FIG. 7-117B).

The tabletop has rails tenoned into the chair legs (FIG. 7-117C). You could tenon rails the other way into the legs as well, but it is convenient to arrange them similarly to those under the shelf into the front and back rails (FIG. 7-117D). Make the tabletop of plywood and fit it like the shelf. Strips at the sides prevent things from falling into the chairs (FIG. 7-117E). A similar strip at the back will stop things from falling there, but you can leave the front open or use partial strips, leaving a gap for cleaning.

Unlike for most chairs, do not make the end assemblies first. Instead get the front and back assemblies together as far as they will go. Use the lengthwise pieces to unite the uprights, check for squareness, and try one assembly over the other. Pull the joints tight, and put dowels through tenons for extra strength. The back assemblies of rails and slats should hold the parts squarely.

Next join in the rails that go back to front. Start with the lower rails and work up through the seat and table rails. When they are tight, bring in the arms. If you need to make any adjustment, that is most easily done at the arms. Assemble on a level surface and check squareness of the assembly without table, shelf, and seat slats. The plywood table and shelf should go in squarely and lock the assembly to shape. Make the seat slats in the usual way, with rounded top edges and

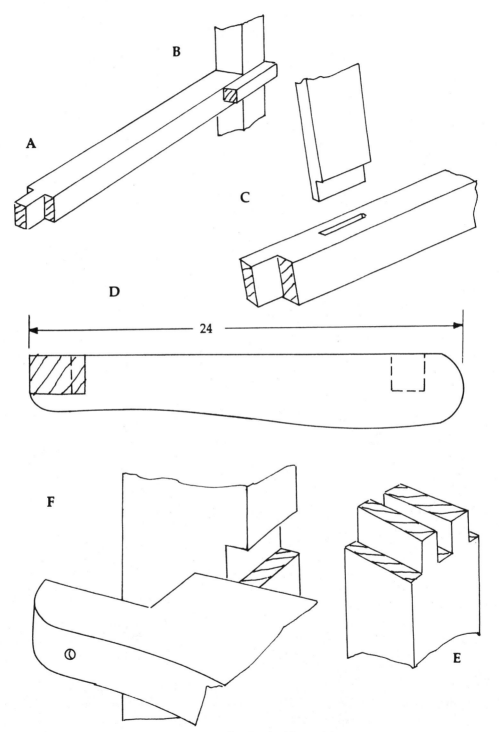

Fig. 7-116. Rail assembly and an arm for the double garden seat.

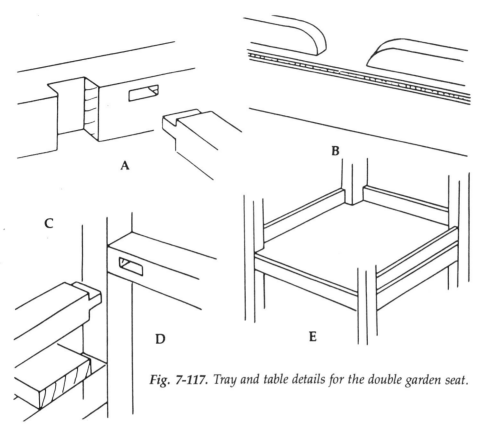

Fig. 7-117. Tray and table details for the double garden seat.

screws downward into their supports. Let the front slats project slightly and well round its outer edges.

If you want to use wheels, choose casters with wheels about 3 inches in diameter on the stem fittings intended to push into holes in the legs. Be careful of making the seats too high. You will need to shorten the lower parts of the legs, if you are using wheels, to keep the seats about 15 inches from the ground. If you are using cushions, allow for their thickness. It is the compressed thickness that counts and that is not usually very much.

If you paint the seat, you can give it the same color all over, or you could make it distinctive by painting seat slats, the tabletop, and the shelf a different color than the rest of the woodwork.

Some modifications are possible. You could have shelves at table level extending outside the chairs. Build in supporting rails between the back and front legs, and make wooden brackets to come under the plywood shelves (which will serve as additional table space).

You can enclose the space between the tabletop and the shelf to make a compartment for game materials or for anything that needs protection from animals. You can make the sides and back of plywood and make a pair of doors to meet at the center. You could hinge doors at the bottom to drop as a flap.

8

Tools and Workshop

When you possess tools for woodwork or metalwork, you can make things for your home, but with those tools you can also make other tools for use in your shop, about the house, or in the garden or yard. Besides actual tools, there are many gadgets and appliances you can make for use in the shop and elsewhere that will enable you to do better, more accurate, or quicker work.

The resourceful craftsman can find many things to make that will add to and improve his tool kit or shop. You can get a lot of satisfaction out of making things on your own bench or in your shop, that will spend most of their time there when finished.

The projects included in this chapter are only a few selected from many books, including most from *The Woodworker's Shop*, where you can find a host of other ideas for tools and equipment to make.

To utilize the full potential of shop ideas, you need to do a little metalworking. A few woodworkers think there is something mysterious about metalworking, but all woodworkers should possess a few metalworking tools. To make a tool that combines wood and metal there should be no more difficulty in making the metal parts than in working wood.

Simple Garden Tools

Several very simple tools might not be available through a manufacturer, yet the craftsman/gardener can make them to aid his hobby. Some of these tools are appropriate to use with window boxes, hanging plant holders, and other small gardening situations where tools of standard size would be too bulky. Sometimes

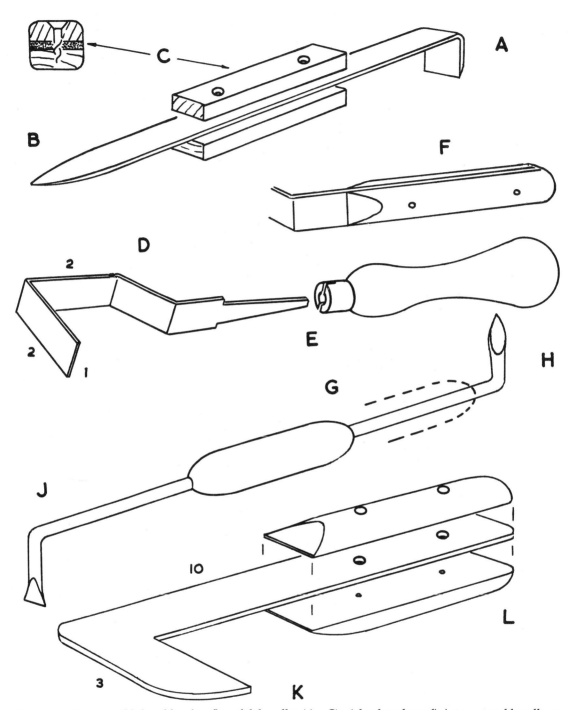

Fig. 8-1. *The reversible hand hoe has flat, slab handles (A – C). A hook tool can fit into a round handle or have slabs (D – F). The paving stone hook has a wooden handle (G – J). A paving stone knife can have a slab handle (K, L).*

Materials List for Simple Garden Tools

Reversible hand hoe

1 blade	10 × 3/4 × 1/8 mild or tool steel
2 slabs	5 × 3/4 × 3/8 wood

Hook tool

1 blade	10 × 1 × 1/16 mild or tool steel
1 handle:	either 2 wood slabs 5 × 1 × 3/8 or a file handle

Paving stone hook

1 rod	15 × 1/4 diameter tool steel
1 handle	5 × 3/4 diameter wood

Paving stone knife

1 blade	10 × 3 × 1/8 tool steel
2 slabs	5 × 1 × 3/8 wood

toylike tools are offered for the purpose, but it would be better to have substantial tools within the limitations. You might alter and develop the tools to suit your needs.

Reversible Hand Hoe You can make a reversible hand hoe from a strip of mild steel that is 3/4 × 1/8 inch and about 10 inches long. Bend one end to make the hoe and file its edge thin (FIG. 8-1A). You can leave the other end square as a little Dutch hoe or file it to a rounded point (FIG. 8-1B). You can make a handle by binding with electrician's tape, but it would be better if you fit two wooden slabs (FIG. 8-1C) about 4 inches long. Drill the top slab and the steel to clear two screws, and then drill undersized holes for the screw threads in the lower slab. Partly shape the slabs before assembly.

Hook Tool In its smallest size, a hook tool acts as a hoe or cultivator. It has about a 2-inch cut when flat or a 1-inch cut when on edge for use in confined spaces. You can make it larger for more general use. For the small version, use steel 1-×-1/16-inch section. Bend to shape (FIG. 8-1D) and file the cutting edges thin. The example is shown with a tang to fit into a file handle (FIG. 8-1E), but you could make it with a wooden slab handle (FIG. 8-1F).

Paving Stone Hook When you form a path with stone slabs, whether squared blocks or natural shapes as crazy paving, weeds will grow in the gaps. You can remove these weeds with the paving stone hook. It should reach into even the narrowest crevices. The hooks are on a strip of 1/4-inch-diameter steel about 15 inches long. Tool steel is advisable if the double hook is to have a long life. The handle is a piece of 3/4-inch wood dowel rod, 5 inches long, and drilled to fit the rod (FIG. 8-1G).

Bend one end and forge and file it to a thin blade (FIG. 8-1H) in line with the rod. Slide on the handle up to that end while you bend and forge the other end to a chisel section (FIG. 8-1J). If you use tool steel, harden and temper the cutters to blue or purple. Slide the handle out of the way as you heat-treat each end. Smear the center of the rod with epoxy glue to secure the handle.

Paving Stone Knife A hook might not be substantial enough for weeds in large cracks. The knife shown in FIG. 8-1K is more capable of standing up to hacking and chopping to greater depths. The blade is cut from sheet tool steel (1/8 inch thick should be satisfactory), and it is shown with a slab handle (FIG. 8-1L). There is no need to thin the edge because it is not intended to cut in line, but its tip works more like a chisel or tiny hoe. It is the temper at the point that is crucial. Harden the end, and then temper by heating near the angle so that the oxide colors spread slowly to the point, which you should quench when purple.

Trowel

One advantage of making your own trowels is that you can choose your own sizes instead of accepting what the manufacturers provide. You also can make several trowels of different sizes for less than the cost of one manufactured tool. If you are going to use the tool only for small plants or seedlings in a box or greenhouse, make it smaller and more slender. For dealing with heavier work in the garden, make the tool larger.

The method of construction suggested includes a tang on the tool to fit into a handle. The handle could be a plain piece of wood, but it is better to have a turned handle with a ferrule to resist any tendency to split. The handle can be any length.

For one-handed use when working with your hand close to the ground, the handle need be no more than 6 inches long. If you prefer not to bend as much , the handle could be 18 inches or longer. For use in a standing position, you could have a handle 48 inches or longer. In any case, a ferrule at the end is advisable. With longer handles, there is a greater inclination to apply more leverage, and that puts a strain on the joint.

The trowel is shown with a blade of moderate curve (FIG. 8-2A). Besides giving a useful shape, the curve provides stiffness.

Cut the blade with a slightly tapered outline (FIG. 8-2B). At the narrow end, the metal can be semicircular or taken to a slight point (as drawn). Do not make a slender point that would be weak and soon bend or wear away.

Curve the blade over an iron rod, extending from the side of a vise, or over the beak of an anvil. The rod should be a smaller diameter than the curve of the blade (FIG. 8-2C). It should be possible to bend the blade by a combination of pressure and hammering; you can hammer one side while you hold the other side with pliers or tongs. Carry the curve along the blade, as close as possible to the point, to ensure stiffness there. It should be possible to shape the blade without heating.

Materials List for Trowel

All mild steel

1 blade	7 × 4 × 16 gauge
1 shaft	10 × 3/8 diameter
1 or 2	3/16 rivets

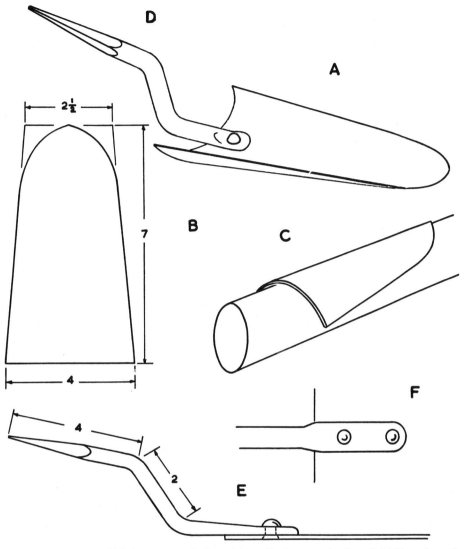

Fig. 8-2. *The trowel blade is cut and shaped (A – C). Its tang is riveted (E, F) and can be brazed.*

If you are making the shaft without the use of heat, flatten the end that will be attached to the blade by hammering and filing. Use a vise to make the double bend. You can hammer over the rod, or you can lever it to shape with a tube slipped over it. Cut off to length, and file the square tang to go into the handle (FIG. 8-2D).

If you are using heat, flatten the end that will take the rivet, by hammering to about half thickness. Then hammer the double bend over an anvil or iron block. Cut off the rod, and hammer the square-pointed tang end.

Drill the shaft and blade for the rivet; a $1/2$- or $3/16$-inch diameter will be suitable. Countersink the hole in the blade underneath (FIG. 8-2E).

File or scrape the meeting surfaces bright, and then rivet the parts together.

Braze or hard-solder the joint. If you do not have facilities for this or for welding, you could flatten the rod far enough to allow two rivets in line (FIG. 8-2F). Allow for raised heads on the rivets underneath. This procedure gives more strength than countersinking heads in thin metal.

Do not paint the working part of the blade. The tool looks best if you paint the shaft and the blade to just ahead of the joint.

Weeder

A small weeder is useful for lifting individual weeds among flowers and plants, and particularly for removing weeds in a lawn, with the minimum disturbance to the surrounding grass. A tool with a forked end will get around deep roots and pull them without breaking off the tops. The tools described here are basically strips of flat mild steel, but some variations are suggested.

For most purposes, you can make a weeder from strip mild steel with a section about $1^1/4 \times {}^3/16$ inch. For more delicate work in window boxes and hanging baskets, you can make the tool of light material. For larger weeds in a more extensive garden, you can make it larger. For many purposes, the tool need not be longer than 12 inches. If you want to use it without stooping too much, you can make a tool 24 inches long.

For the simplest weeder, (FIG. 8-3A), drill a $1/4$-inch hole for the bottom of the fork slot (FIG. 8-3B). Next, draw two lines from this hole, and saw and file to shape. File the ends to rounded points.

At the other end, cut two hardwood slabs about 5 inches long for the handle (FIG. 8-3C). Drill one of them and the steel with clearance holes for two screws. Mark through on the other slab, and drill undersized holes for the threaded parts of the screws. You can shape the slabs before assembly or after screwing them together. The wood is shown with simple bevels, but you can make the handle fully rounded. For extra security, use epoxy glue between the wood and the metal.

By levering or hammering in a vise, bend the blade a short distance behind the cut end. Paint the steel, and either paint or varnish the handle.

If a round handle is preferred (FIG. 8-3D), saw and file that end of the steel to make a tang (FIG. 8-3E). Drill so this tang will drive into the wooden handle, but also cut a slot across the ferrule so the broad part will fit in (FIG. 8-3F). Round any parts of the metal extending outside the ferrule.

You can obtain increased leverage by putting a tube across the main part (FIG. 8-3G). If it extends outside the width of the blade, you will have an increased bearing surface on the surrounding soil or grass. A tube about $1^1/4$ inches in diameter and 3 inches long should be suitable. Attach it by welding or brazing, or

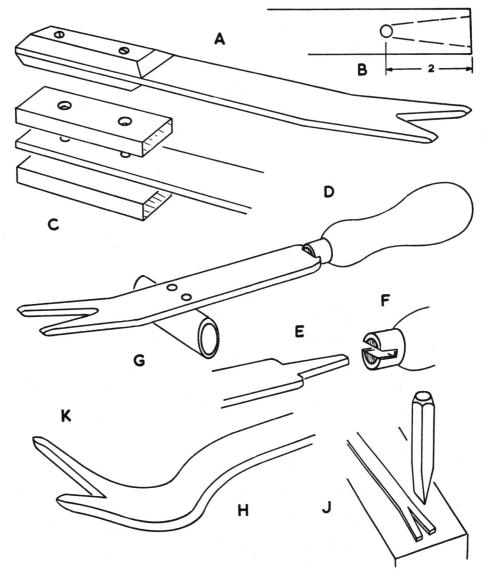

Fig. 8-3. *The weeder made from flat strip steel can have a slab or round handle.*

you could screw through or use rivets—with the inside heads supported on an iron rod—while you form the outside heads.

Another way of increasing leverage, although it does not spread the bearing surface like a tube, is to put a double bend in the blade (FIG. 8-3H). This double bend can be done in a vise, by hammering one way and moving to the second position to hammer the other way. The bends do not have to be sharp and should be left rounded.

You can make the forked end wider than the shaft part if the iron is split instead of sawn to shape. Have an anvil or an iron block ready to work on. Use a chisel and a heavy hammer. It helps if you make the fork on the end of a long piece. This way, you can hold it without getting your hand hot. Then cut the piece to length afterward. Heat the end to redness in a fire or with a propane torch and split it centrally with the chisel (FIG. 8-3J). You can start with a central saw cut if you prefer. Because you have not removed any metal, the jaws will open to give a greater spread (FIG. 8-3K).

A mud scraper is a strip of metal, like a weeder without its forked end, thinned a little to make a scraping edge.

Push-Pull Hoe

The normal Dutch hoe only cuts off weeds or stirs the surface of the soil on the push stroke. If it is given a cutting edge on the back, it will work in the reverse direction as well. This double edge could be an advantage when dealing with awkward weeds or those close to a wall.

Arrange the blade so that its edges are presented to the soil at the correct angle (both ways) without altering the angle at which you hold the handle. While the push-pull hoe is shaped to suit most users, you can alter the angles of the cutting edges and the handle for very tall or short users. The blade is best made of tool steel because it retains its sharp edges longer than mild steel (even when not hardened and tempered). The shafts are mild steel.

Mark out and cut the rectangular piece for the blade (FIG. 8-4A). Sharpen the cutting edges, but avoid making very thin, knifelike edges that would soon blunt. It is better to make the angles fairly steep and leave a slight thickness along the edges.

Bend the blade along the marked bend lines. The amount of bend need not be much, but if the center is about 1/4 inch above the edges (FIG. 8-4B), that should be sufficient. If you will be dealing with a very sandy soil, leave the blade flat or give it only slight bevels.

Forge palms on the ends of the two rods that will form the shafts, and bend them at about 30 degrees (FIG. 8-4C).

Bend the pair of rods inward so they meet. Cut them off so the parallel parts are about 2 inches long.

Grind or file the meeting surfaces (FIG. 8-4D) so they make a tapered tang to go into the handle (FIG. 8-4E). Put rivets loosely in the holes so you can check that the two parts of the shaft make a pair and the tang will be central.

Materials List for a Push-Pull Hoe

1 blade	4 × 3 × 16 gauge tool steel
2 shafts	10 × 3/8 diameter mild steel
2 rivets to suit	
1 wood handle	48 × 1 1/8 with tube ferrule

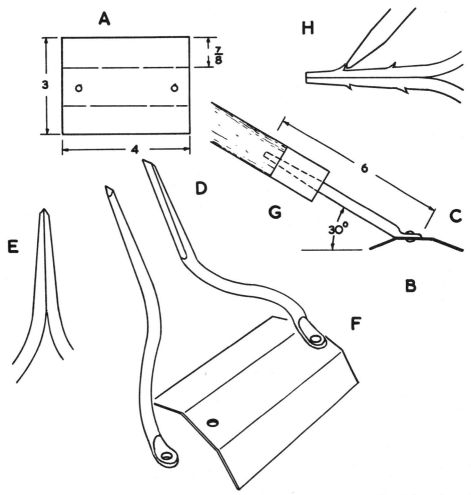

Fig. 8-4. The blade of the push-pull hoe has a double shaft riveted and brazed to it (A – G). Its tang end can have teeth cut in it to resist pulling out of the handle.

Scrape or file the meeting surfaces, and then rivet the shafts to the blade (FIG. 8-4F). Clamp the tang ends together while brazing the shafts to the blade.

If you are to harden and temper the blade, do this now.

Prepare the wooden handle with a tube ferrule at least 1¹/₂ inches long (FIG. 8-4G).

Drill for the tang, and drive the parts together. There will probably be enough friction in the joint to resist pulling apart in use, but if you want to make sure, put a nail through a hole in the ferrule and tang as a rivet. Alternatively, you could raise a few teeth in the tang parts with a cold chisel (FIG. 8-4H) before assembly.

Paint the metal, except for the bent parts of the blade, and varnish the wooden handle.

Marking Gauge

You might already have a marking gauge in your woodworking tool kit, but an extra one is always useful. If a gauge is set to a size you will need again, a second one allows you to mark another width without having to reset the first. This reduces the risk of error. If you do not have even one marking gauge, it is a tool you can make, that should be as efficient as anything you might buy.

Purchased marking gauges use a screw to lock the stock to the stem. Although there are ways of arranging screw adjustments, most of us do not have the facilities for making them, so this marking gauge (FIG. 8-5) uses a wedge, which is a good traditional means of locking.

Use a close-grained hardwood. Some of the best traditional marking gauges were made of rosewood, but you are unlikely to find that. The tool looks good if the wedge is a different color hardwood. The stem is usually made square, but it could be made of 3/4-inch hardwood dowel rod, which would simplify fitting because you only have to drill a hole in the stock. However, a round stem might turn in use unless wedged very tightly.

Prepare the wood for the stock and stem (FIG. 8-6A). Both can be left over-length until they have been fitted to each other. The stem is shown 7 inches long, which should be adequate for most settings and long enough to give a good grip.

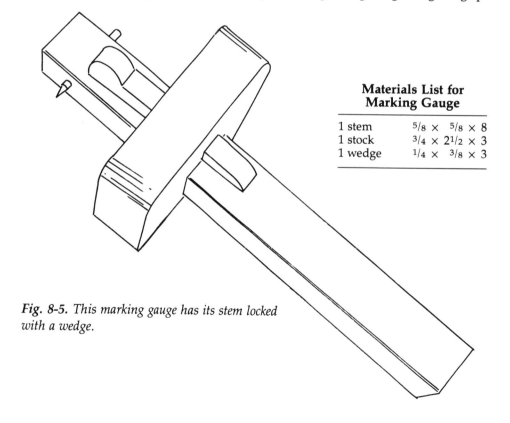

Materials List for Marking Gauge

1 stem	$5/8 \times 5/8 \times 8$
1 stock	$3/4 \times 2^{1}/2 \times 3$
1 wedge	$1/4 \times 3/8 \times 3$

Fig. 8-5. This marking gauge has its stem locked with a wedge.

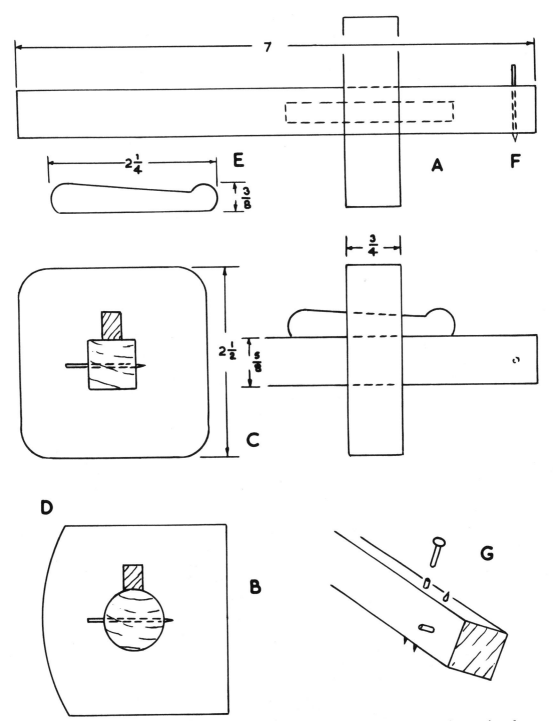

Fig. 8-6. Sizes for a marking gauge with square or round stem and alternative shapes of stock.

Mark a square hole through the middle of the stock. Do this on both sides, so you can cut the hole both ways and avoid the risk of the surface grain breaking out. Drill away most of the waste, and cut the hole to shape. It should slide on the stem with minimum slackness, although some stiffness at first is acceptable. If a round stem is to be used, drill the stock for it (FIG. 8-6B).

The stock can be trimmed square and its corners rounded (FIG. 8-6C). Another shape is shown (FIG. 8-6D) with a curve to fit the hand. If the mortise gauge addition is to be used, it will be better to make the stock square.

Make the wedge (FIG. 8-6E). It is 1/4 inch thick. Both ends are the same height. The exact taper is unimportant. The knob at the low end prevents the wedge from being pushed out of the stock, except when the stem has been removed.

Mark both sides of the stock for the slot for the wedge. At first, mark the low side to the wedge depth close to the knob and the other side to the depth 3/4 inch from that. Try the assembly and the action of the wedge. When at the low position the stem should slide freely, but when you push or knock in the wedge the assembly should lock tightly and squarely. If you have a round stem, the bottom of the wedge could be flat, but it will grip better if it is hollowed to match the rod used for the stem.

The marking pin (FIG. 8-6F) should be a drive fit in a hole in the stem. Ideally, it is a piece of tool steel wire under 1/16 inch in diameter, with a sharpened point. In practice, a nail (which is made of the softer mild steel) will have a very long life and can be sharpened with a file.

If you mark out mortise-and-tenon joints frequently there are almost certainly some widths you use for many of them. Quite often these are 1/4 and 3/8 inch. It is possible to add markpins for stock widths to your marking gauge. Make them by driving in fine nails at the correct distances apart on, the faces square to the main marking pin (FIG. 8-6G). Cut each nail off about 1/8 inch above the wood, and file a point on it. Try marking with the gauge. The widths between the marks can be adjusted to exactly what you want by filing the sides of the points. Make sure the points extend the same amounts.

The pins for marking mortises are shown at the same end of the stem as the main pin. You could put them at the other end and have up to four different widths, but if you do that, you will not be able to take the gauge apart, except by removing the main pin and sliding the stock off that way. There is another advantage in having all the pins at one end. You can then use the other end as a pencil gauge by setting the end of the stem at the correct distance from the stock and holding a pencil against it as it is pushed or pulled along the wood.

Varnish or hard polish would be inappropriate for this tool, but a rub with wax will improve appearance and lubricate the parts for adjusting when they move against the wood being marked.

Panel Gauge

The ordinary marking gauge works fine for scratching lines a short distance from the edge, but if you try to use it for distances approaching 6 inches, it begins to wobble and becomes inaccurate. It is no use making a longer arm if you need to mark fines parallel to an edge but at a greater distance. With the regular use of wider panels, the larger panel gauge is worth having.

A panel gauge works in the same way as the smaller marking gauge, but is bigger and with a steadier bearing on the edge of the wood being marked. The arm length can be what you wish, but a reach of 30 inches is reasonable.

A panel gauge is an interesting project to make, and you will be more satisfied with the tool if you use a good hardwood and finish it by polishing. Some shaping of the stock is shown in FIG. 8-7, but if you do not have a scroll or jigsaw, a plainer outline would not affect the efficiency of the gauge. The end of the arm has a point to scratch a fine in the same way as a marking gauge, but if you turn the arm over so the plain side is against the panel, you can hold a pencil against the end. In any case, the use of the panel gauge is a two-handed operation. One hand presses the rabbet of the stock tight on the wood edge, and the other hand presses down on the marking end of the arm.

This panel gauge has a choice of two ways of locking the arm in the stock. There could be a wedge (FIG. 8-8A) or a screw (FIG. 8-8B).

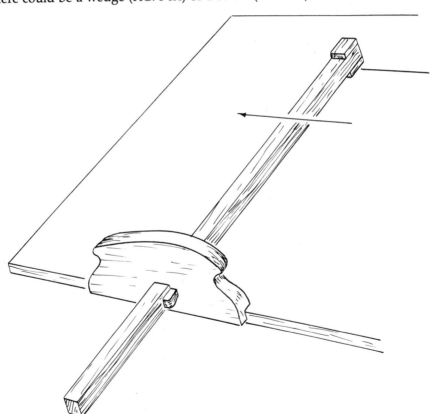

Fig. 8-7. A panel gauge will draw lines parallel with an edge a much greater distance than an ordinary marking gauge.

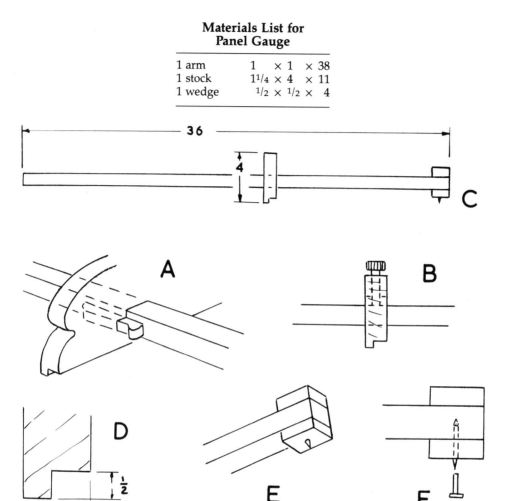

**Materials List for
Panel Gauge**

1 arm	1	× 1	× 38
1 stock	$1^{1}/_{4}$ × 4	× 11	
1 wedge	$^{1}/_{2}$ × $^{1}/_{2}$	× 4	

Fig. 8-8. Size and arrangement of the panel gauge.

Make the arm straight and square. Leave thickening the end (FIG. 8-8C) until the stock has been made, as the thickness has to be the same as the height of the hole above the rabbet.

Cut the rabbet on the stock (FIG. 8-8D). If necessary, sand inside the rabbet so it will slide smoothly. It is advisable to mark the hole for the arm on both sides and cut it from both sides to make edges clean and the hole square. Try the arm through and check its squareness.

If you want to fit a wedge, make it first (FIG. 8-9A). Use it as a guide when cutting the slot for it in the stock. When drawn back to the thinner part, the wedge should be clear of the arm, but if you press it in, it should tighten when there is some of the thicker end still projecting (FIG. 8-9B).

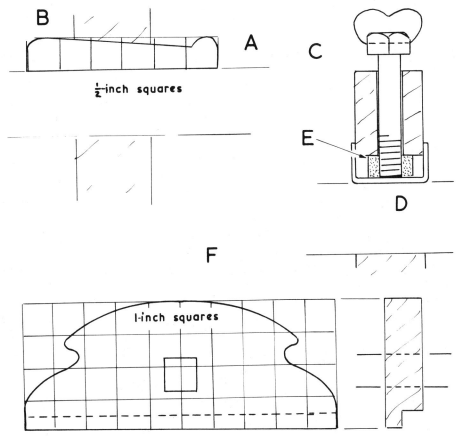

Fig. 8-9. Sizes of panel gauge parts.

For screw locking, choose a screw about $3/8$ inch in diameter, preferably with a wing or knurled head. If you have to use one with a square or hexagonal head and wish to avoid the use of a wrench, you can solder a piece of sheet metal into a sawn slot (FIG. 8-9C). A brass screw will look better than a steel one. Drill a clearance hole through the stock for the screw.

At the hole, cut back for a sheet metal pressure plate. Make this high enough to hide the nut (FIG. 8-9D). Cut away for a nut, preferably a square one, close enough for the wood to prevent it turning (FIG. 8-9E). For extra security, use epoxy adhesive. If you have the facilities, you could make a metal block to fit the recess, with a suitable hole tapped for the end of the screw.

Shape the outline of the stock (FIG. 8-9F). Well round all the upper edges to provide a comfortable grip. At the end of the arm, glue blocks on the top and bottom of the end (FIG. 8-8E).

A simple way of making the scratch point is to drive in a nail, then cut it off and file a point (FIG. 8-8F). If you prefer to use a hard steel point, drill undersize and press it in.

Wedged Bar Clamp

Clamps with a long reach are expensive. You probably do not have enough for pulling large framing parts together or for securing several glued boards to make up a width.

You could improvise the clamp in FIG. 8-10 for a particular job, or you could make one that is ready for any occasion. For a one-off bar clamp, screw on the stops to suit the job (FIG. 8-10A). Allow for packings against the work to spread pressure and prevent damaged edges. One block is cut at the same angle as the wedge, unless you will be using folding wedges.

For this or any other long clamp, use a bar deep enough to resist bending under pressure. A shallow bending bar will allow the parts being clamped to also bend.

A bar clamp that can be adjusted has one fixed block to take the wedges and another that can be located at many positions along the bar (FIG. 8-10B). Make the blocks as deep as anything you expect to clamp. For general purposes, blocks $1^1/2$ inches deep on a bar, preferably hardwood, and $1^1/2 \times 3$ inches and 36 inches long would be adaptable to many applications.

Glue and screw the fixed block at one end. Make the other block long enough to resist tilting. Make cheeks with plywood, and put a piece to spread the pressure across these parts (FIG. 8-10C). To allow for the limit of wedge movement of only about 1 inch, drill holes in the bar at 1-inch intervals. To suit the suggested sizes, they could be holes for a $1/2$-inch dowel rod. The peg could be just a piece of rod, or you could turn a wood or metal peg.

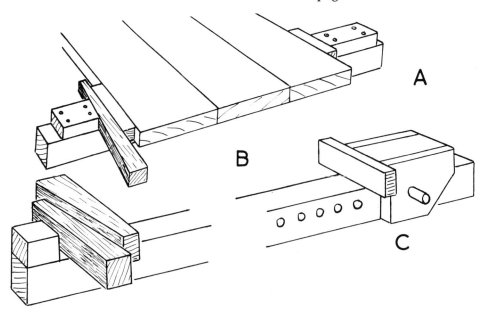

Fig. 8-10. A wedge can be used in a fixed bar clamp (A). A pair of wedges and a movable head can form an adjustable bar clamp (B,C).

Double Bar Clamp

The bar clamp shown in FIG. 8-10 will suit many purposes and is the type to use when assembling a frame when there are parts projecting. When you want to join several boards edgewise to make up a width, there is the problem with this or a metal screwed bar clamp. The assembly will bow under pressure, and you have to use weights or other means to keep the assembly flat.

If there are bars above and below the assembled boards, the tendency to bow is minimized and the double bars themselves prevent movement.

The double bar clamp in FIG. 8-11 can be closed onto the work or packings put under the top bar so there is no risk of boards moving in their thickness.

The bars are not subject to bending loads under pressure, so they can be lighter, say 1-×-2-inch strips, 36 inches long. Make the wedges as thin as the thinnest boards you expect to clamp or have a supply of wedges of different thicknesses.

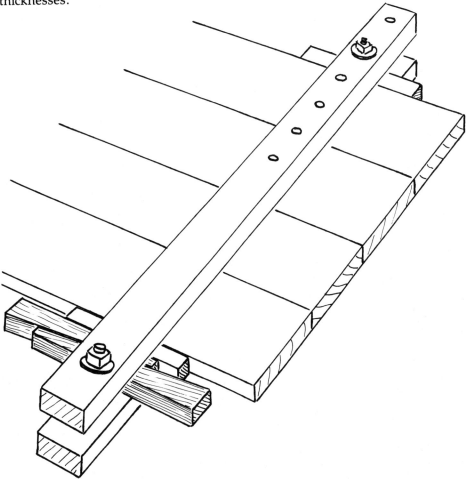

Fig. 8-11. A double bar clamp with wedges is suitable for a greater width.

Bolts can be 3/8 inch in diameter. The clamp is shown with one bolt in a single hole and the other in alternative positions, but you could arrange a series of holes at each end. If the rows of holes are staggered in relation to each other, you will get a greater choice of settings. Suppose the holes at each end are 2 inches apart. If you make the distance between the end holes of each group an odd distance, say 11 inches, you get a choice of overall settings in 1-inch steps.

If you use this clamp tight across glued boards, put paper between the bars and the wood to prevent the clamp from becoming glued in place. Varnishing the bars will also reduce the risk of glue adhering to them.

Round Square

The name seems a contradiction, but can you think of a better one? If you draw a chord across the circumference of a circle and bisect it, the bisecting line will go through the center of the circle or point towards it. If you do this in two places, the bisecting lines will cross at the center (FIG. 8-12A). A combination square might have a center head, which uses this geometric fact to provide a means of finding the center of a round object (FIG. 8-12B). The square head rests against the edge of the round object, and the edge of the blade bisects the points of contact, which are the ends of a chord. If you use the tool in two or more positions and draw along the blade edge, you will locate the center. That is fine for centering, but in several branches of woodwork the need is to draw lines square to quite large curved edges, not to find the center of the circle. This might apply to ellipses and other curves that are not parts of circles. For that purpose there is a round square of different pattern, which uses the same geometric principle. The tool could be made in any size, but this one is of moderate size (FIG. 8-12C) and can be made of plywood and short pieces of dowel rod (FIG. 8-12D). Solid wood could be used, but hardwood plywood is satisfactory. Softwood plywood, such as Douglas fir, would not be strong enough to maintain a good blade edge for long.

Start making the tool by drawing what will be the edge of the blade, then draw a line square to it with the centers for the dowel holes marked equidistant from it (FIG. 8-13A). This is where accuracy is needed—other parts are just outlines, which would not matter if you altered their shape. The design shown allows you to drill a 1-inch hole at the root of the blade (FIG. 8-13B), which is a help in cutting it accurately. Draw the curves of the other parts of the outline (FIG. 8-13C).

Before cutting the outline, drill the two dowel holes, preferably using a drill press or a guide on the drill so that the holes are square to the surface. Drill the hole at the root of the blade, and cut the blade edge into it. Cut the rest of the shape. Trim the blade edge straight and square across. Do not round it, but round all the external edges for comfort in handling.

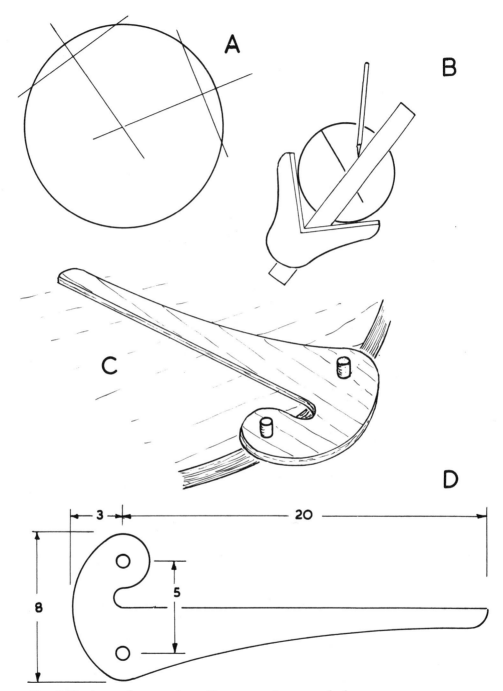

Fig. 8-12. A round square draws lines square to a curved edge.

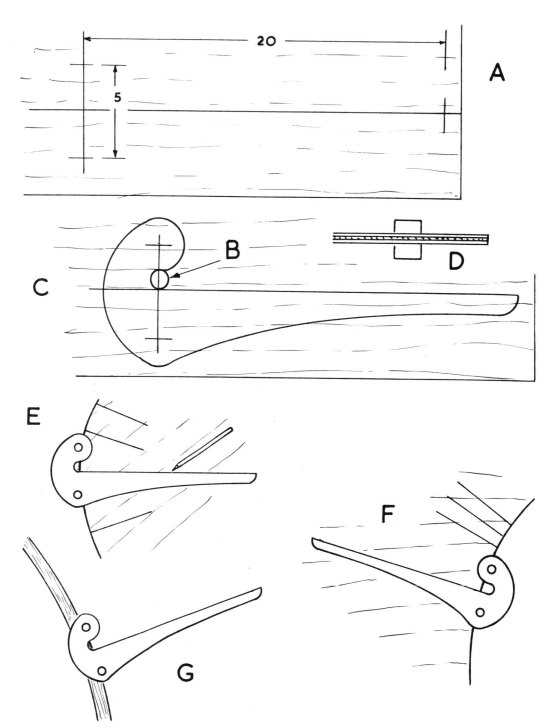

Fig. 8-13. Setting out and using a round square.

Glue in the ⅝-inch dowels so they project both sides and the tool can be used either way—a ½-inch projection (FIG. 8-13D) should be enough. Trim the dowels square across, although if you have a lathe, you might want to curve their ends. If any excess glue is squeezed out, remove it because blobs of glue in the angle will affect the accuracy of the square.

You will use this tool mostly on convex edges (FIG. 8-13E), but it is equal suitable for concave ones (FIG. 8-13F). You can reverse it against a rim of either type (FIG. 8-13G). It will also find the center of a round object, but not if the diameter is less than the distance between the dowels.

Bowl Depth Gauge

When turning the inside of a bowl or a similar hollow article, you have to check depths of cut, so you do not cut so far that you weaken the bowl or stop before you have gone as deep as you want. One way is to put a straightedge across the

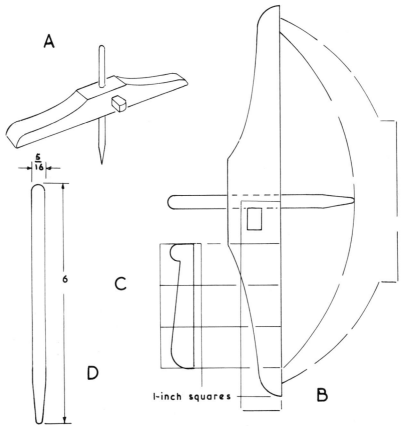

Fig. 8-14. This wide depth gauge helps you check the depth of a bowl being turned.

Materials List for
Bowl Depth Gauge

1 stock	1	×	$1^{1}/_{4}$	×	12
1 wedge	$^{3}/_{8}$	×	$^{5}/_{8}$	×	4
1 probe	6	×	$^{5}/_{8}$ diameter		

rim and measure from it with a rule, but you have to stop the lathe and use two hands to do that. Store-bought depth gauges only have short stocks and are intended for engineering measurements. What is needed is a gauge with a long stock, which can be set and held to the work while it is rotating, if you wish.

This depth gauge has a stock long enough to bridge your largest bowl and a probe held to it with a wedge (FIG. 8-14A). Use close-grained hardwood for stock and wedge. The probe could be turned from hardwood dowel rod.

Mark out the stock (FIG. 8-14B) and drill for the probe before doing any shaping. If you are doubtful about being able to drill through squarely from one side, drill part way from both sides.

Make the wedge (FIG. 8-14C). With that as a guide, cut the groove for it through the stock until the wedge is clear of the probe hole when pushed back but still closes on the probe when about three-quarters of the way in. Turn the probe with a slight taper to a rounded end (FIG. 8-14D).

When you are satisfied with the action, cut the shaped part of the stock, and well round those parts. A waxed finish is appropriate for this tool.

Folding Steps

Because in most shops and at many jobs there are places too high to be reached while standing on the ground, step ladders of moderate height are always worth having. Low, folding steps are useful also as alternative trestles, and they make

Fig. 8-15. Folding steps at trestle height can be used to climb on or to support work.

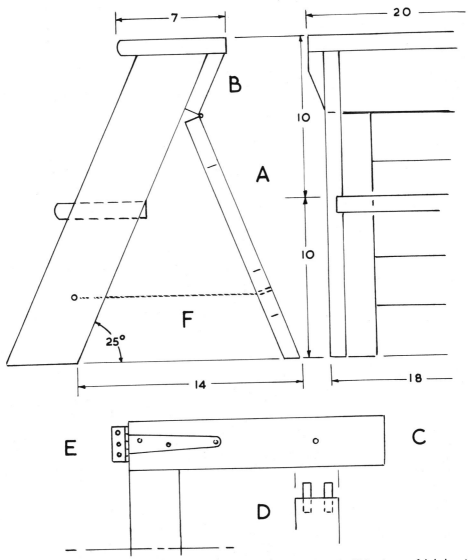

Fig. 8-16. *Suggested sizes for the folding steps and the method of hinging and joining the legs.*

Materials List for Folding Steps

2 sides	1 × 4 × 25
1 step	1 × 6 × 19
1 top	1 × 7 × 22
1 back	1 × 5 × 22
2 legs	1 × 3 × 18
2 rails	1 × 3 × 15

suitable seats when working at a bench. The folding steps in FIG. 8-15 are intended to have the same overall height as trestle. With the two, you can support a full sheet of plywood or other large piece of wood parallel with the floor and at a convenient height for sawing or doing other work.

The two levels are 10-inch steps. It is always wise to make any ladder or steps with exactly the same spacing all the way to avoid stumbling due to different heights. If you make the steps to other heights, keep to an even spacing.

The steps can be made from softwood, all 1 inch thick. The joints shown are 1/2-inch hardwood dowels, but mortise-and-tenon joints could be used.

The steps are shown sloping at a 25-degree angle. The rear legs close level with the bottoms of the main sides and are held in the open position with rope (FIG. 8-16A). The sides are parallel. Be careful when making the parts not to let the bottoms come closer than the tops. An error the other way does not matter.

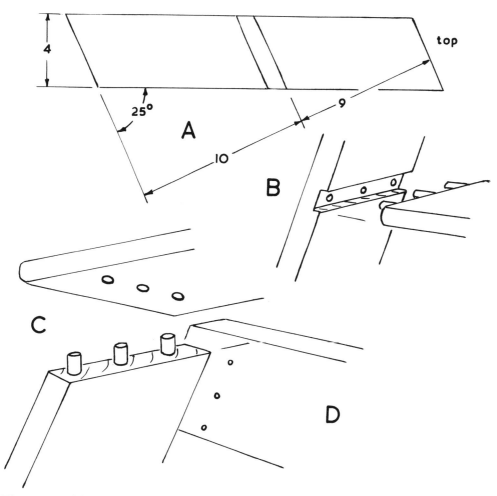

Fig. 8-17. Folding step side details and how the parts are joined.

Cut a pair of sides (FIG. 8-17A). Cut dadoes about one-third the thickness of the wood (FIG. 8-17B).

Round the forward edge of the step. Prepare its ends with dowels to go through the sides. Round the forward edge of the top in the same way and prepare dowel joints into the sides (FIG. 8-17C). In both cases the dowels go through, so you can drill from outside into both parts of each joint.

Make the back (FIGS. 8-16B and 8-17D) with its top beveled to match the sides. This could be doweled, but it is more satisfactory to screw it to the sides and drive a few screws downwards into it from the top. Glue together all the parts made so far. Make the lengths of the rear legs (FIG. 8-16C) to fill the space between the back and the bottoms of the sides but with the ends beveled the other way to rest on the floor. Assemble the legs with rails doweled on (FIG. 8-18D). Join the legs to the back with T hinges (FIG. 8-16E).

Drill the legs centrally opposite the lower rails for rope and put holes in the centers of the sides at the same level. Knot rope through these holes with its length adjusted to keep the treads level when the steps are pulled open (FIG. 8-16F).

Take-Down Frame

Separate trestles will take care of many needs, and a pair will support large work, but they have to be positioned and can move in use. If they can be linked together, you have a much more rigid support under the work, and you know that neither end will move at just the wrong time during a crucial operation. In most shops, there is insufficient space for such an arrangement to be permanently assembled, especially when it is only needed for occasional use.

The take-down frame in FIG. 8-18 consists of two end frames and two pairs of lengthwise braces to bolt on when you need the frame. With the sizes suggested (FIG. 8-19A), the assembly will hold a full-size plywood sheet. It is at a suitable height for working on large pieces of wood and, with stout boards on top, for standing on to reach ceilings or other high places. When disassembled, the braces fold and all parts take up only a few inches against a wall or under a bench.

All parts can be softwood, but hardwood tops will be more durable. Construction is shown with mortise-and-tenon joints, but you could use dowels.

Mark out the four legs (FIG. 8-19B). Leave a little extra length at the tops until after the frames have been assembled. Make the rails (FIG. 8-19C), and cut and fit

Materials List for Take-Down Frame

4 legs	2 × 2 × 24
4 rails	2 × 3 × 21
2 tops	1 × 4 × 25
4 braces	1 × 2 × 66

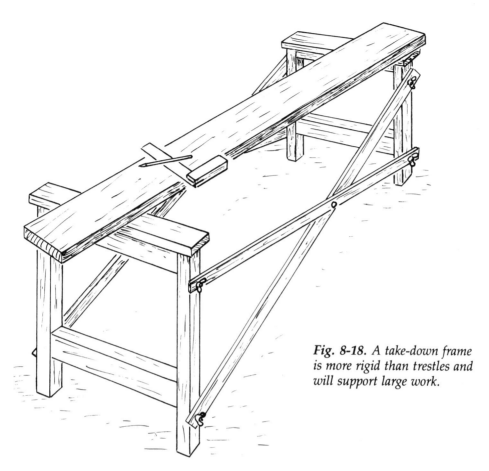

Fig. 8-18. *A take-down frame is more rigid than trestles and will support large work.*

the joints. See that opposite frames match and are without twist. Level the tops of the legs, then add the fat tops, which can have dowels through or be screwed on. The tops overhang about 1 inch all around and can have rounded edges and corners.

Fit the legs with permanently fixed projecting screws to take the braces. There are two possible ways of doing this. You could use 3/8-inch hanger screws (FIG. 8-19D), if these can be obtained with sufficient projection. The alternative is to use 3/8-inch carriage or coach bolts (FIG. 8-19E). The square neck will lock the bolt in the wood and prevent turning.

You can make the braces to lengths to suit your needs, but making them 60 inches between end holes will give an overall length about the same (FIG. 8-19F). Do not cut the ends too close to the holes, or the short end grain might break out. Pivot each pair of braces together at their centers. Because it is unlikely that you will want to separate them, use carriage bolts with locknuts.

Use large washers for the end bolts to reduce wear on the wood, and wing nuts (FIG. 8-19G) or knurled nuts (FIG. 8-19H). You could use plain nuts, but the other types let you avoid having to find a wrench.

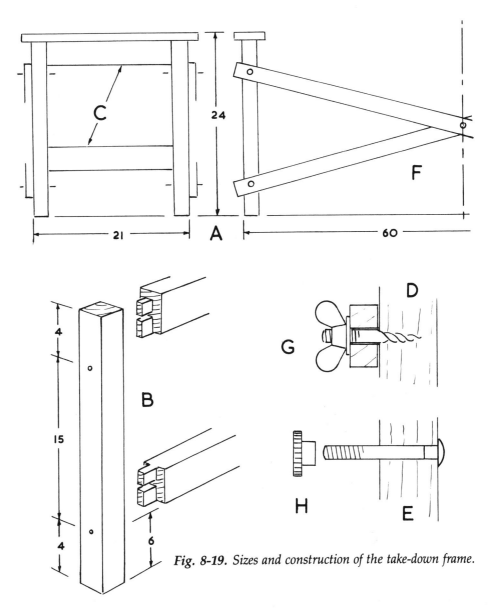

Fig. 8-19. Sizes and construction of the take-down frame.

Work Support

The supporting surfaces built into machines are necessarily small. You might push 10 feet of wood through a jointer, but its table length might be under 3 feet. You might have to cut shapes on a band saw when its table is not much over 12 inches square, yet your plywood is 4 feet across. In a large shop, you might be able to rig benches or other surface to support the excess area, but in the usual small home shop there is no room for permanent extensions to machines when they are only required intermittently.

Materials List for Work Support

1 top	48 × 24 × $\frac{1}{4}$ or $\frac{1}{2}$ plywood
2 top sides	50 × 2 × 1
2 top ends	26 × 2 × 1
4 legs	54 × 2 × 1
2 blocks	15 × 2 × 1
1 crossbar	20 × 5 × 1
2 leg braces	24 × 18 × $\frac{1}{4}$ or $\frac{1}{2}$ plywood

In some cases, you can improvise, but to do good work there has to be adequate support for excess length or area while you machine a particular part. Fortunately, the support does not have to do much more than keep the wood in position, because there is no real working load on it. This means that for many operations the supporting arrangement can be light and folding.

This work support (FIG. 8-20) provides an area 24 × 48 inches at machine height, but when not needed, it folds to 24 × 56 inches and about 6 inches thick. It can be made adjustable in height so that it can be used for more than one machine. The example (FIG. 8-21) is shown able to be at 30 inches or 40 inches above the floor, which might suit the table saw or jointer, then the usually higher

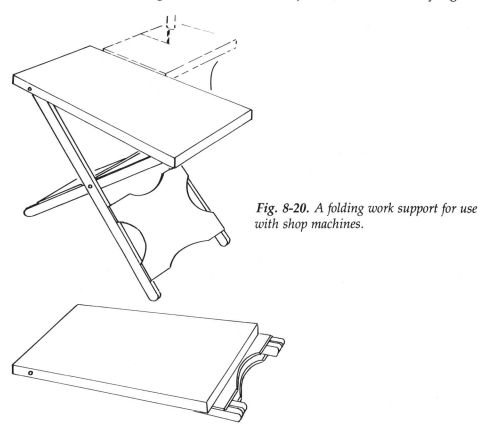

Fig. 8-20. A folding work support for use with shop machines.

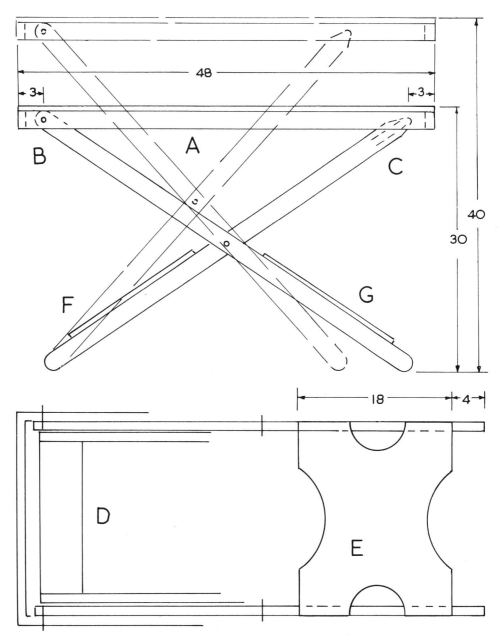

Fig. 8-21. Sizes for the folding work support, with adjustment for two heights.

table of a band saw. Make it to set at any required height and at more than two heights, if you wish. Besides its use in the shop, the work support can be taken elsewhere for use as a spare table indoors or outdoors.

If you design your own table, there are some points to watch. To keep the top level at any height, the lengths of the legs above the pivot point should be the same, and those below should also match each other. It makes the arrangement simpler if all four of these sizes are the same (FIG. 8-22A). It would be possible to make the legs short enough to fold inside the top, but then the unit, particularly in the high position, could be rather unstable due to the feet being closer together.

The suggested top is a piece cut across a standard sheet of plywood and framed round (FIG. 8-22B). The legs pivot inside one end; then there are notched pieces at the other end to provide adjustment. Stiffness in the legs is provided by plywood braces.

Hardwood is advisable for the legs, but the top framing could be softwood. Pivot bolts are 1/4 inch, or 5/16 inch with countersunk heads, washers, and some form of locking nuts.

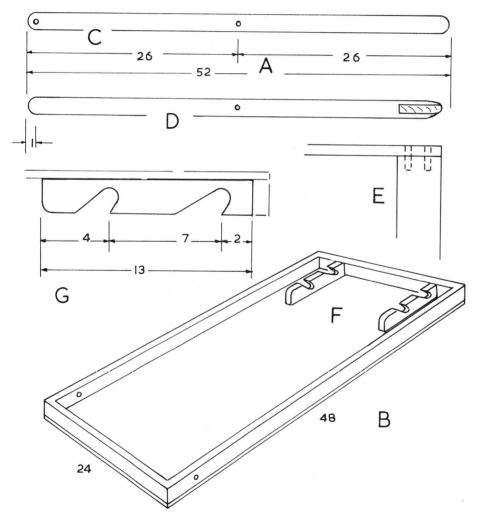

Fig. 8-22. *Sizes of the legs and layout of the underside of the folding work support.*

Cut the top plywood to size and frame it round like a box (FIG. 8-21A). The corners could be screwed or you could use finger joints or dovetails. Drill the sides for the pivot screws (FIG. 8-21B). Make the two outer legs (FIG. 8-22C). Drill for pivot screws at the upper ends, and countersink the holes on the inner surface to clear the other legs when folded.

The inner legs are almost the same (FIG. 8-22D), but at their upper end they have a crossbar with a rounded edge (FIGS. 8-21C and D). This crossbar can be joined to the legs with dowels (FIG. 8-22E). Its length must allow the folded legs to fit easily inside the outer ones. So the work support will keep its top parallel to the floor at any height adjustment, the center of the curve on the crossbar should be at the same distance from the pivot as the hole at the top of the other leg. Slight errors are unlikely to make enough difference to matter.

Stiffen both pairs of legs below the central pivot with plywood braces (FIG. 8-21E). These come on what will be the upper surfaces of the legs (FIGS. 8-21F and G), where they will not interfere with folding. The plywood could be cut with straight edges, but it is shown with cutout edges for the sake of appearance.

For the adjustments suggested, there are two notched blocks at the end of the top (FIG. 8-22F), positioned so they come inside the inner legs and engage with the crossbar. They do not have to come tightly against the legs, but do not leave excessive clearance.

The blocks shown (FIG. 8-22G) adjust the top to 30 inches and 40 inches above the floor, but it is unlikely your needs will be for those heights exactly. For other heights, pivot the legs together and to the top on temporary bolts, and experiment with positions of the crossbar that will give the heights you want. Notch the blocks to suit. Screw and glue the blocks in place.

Make a trial assembly, and try the folding and erecting the action. You might have to ease the tops of the legs to give clearance.

Separate the parts as far as possible, and take the sharpness off edges. You might choose to leave the work support untreated, but paint or varnish will prevent dirt absorption. It will help foster smooth operation if you put thin washers between moving parts, as well as under nuts.

Table Extensions

The band saw in most small shops is not large enough to stand on the floor, but it has to stand on a low bench to get it to working height. Its saw table might be less than 18 inches square, yet the work you do on it can be considerably bigger. At the maximum, you might want to manipulate an entire 48-×-96-inch sheet of plywood to cut a curved end. To do that, you need at least one helper or some good supports.

The outfeed roller for the table saw can be used, if it is the right height or can be adapted. You could clamp temporary supports to your trestles, but for satisfactory holding of large pieces where curves have to be cut, it is better to have flat surfaces than just local support.

Plywood Support

You can make a light folding support to take large work overhanging the band saw table—from 1/2-inch plywood and a piece of 2-×-4-inch wood (FIG. 8-23A). As drawn in FIG. 8-23B, this provides an area about 5 × 24 inches at the same level as the saw table, which should be enough to steady large overhanging work while being cut. When out of use, the support folds flat. A piece of rope controls the

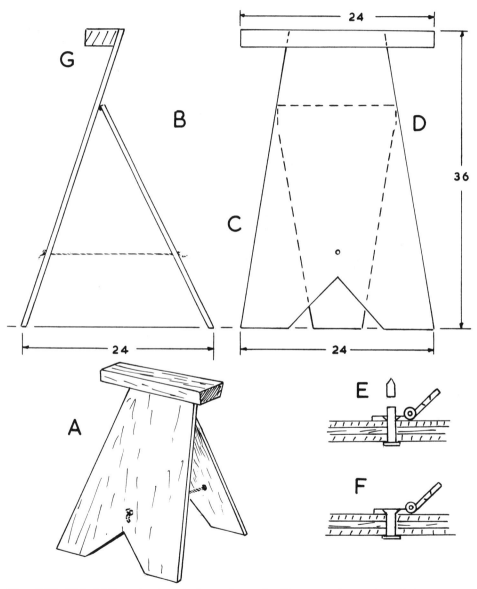

Fig. 8-23. This folding stand made from plywood will support large pieces being cut on a band saw.

spread of the legs. You can alter the height by varying the length of knotted rope, making the support adaptable to supporting work on other machines.

The vertical size will have to be made to suit the height of table on your band saw, but other sizes can be left as shown. The three feet are 6 inches wide. This arrangement will stand firm better than four feet if there is slight unevenness in the floor.

Taper the main leg from 24 to 12 inches, with a notch to form the feet (FIG. 8-23C). Mark across 9 inches down where the top of the short leg will come. Make the top of the short leg to this width, tapering to a 6-inch foot (FIG. 8-23D). Adjust the length of this leg so that the top of the other leg will be centered when the legs are spread 24 inches.

Hinge the legs together. Two 3-inch hinges should be satisfactory, but 1/2-inch plywood does not provide sufficient thickness for screws to grip securely. Instead, you can rivet the hinges, using nails. Soft metal nails are easiest to use—copper is ideal. Drive the nails through undersized holes in the wood. Cut off with enough projecting to make a head in the countersink of the hinge (FIG. 8-23E). Support the nailheads on an iron block and spread the nail end into the countersink of the hinge (FIG. 8-23F).

Put the rope through matching centered holes, and adjust its length between knots so that the top edge of the stand is level with your band saw table. Check the angle needed to give a horizontal top to the bearing surface, and plane the top piece to match (FIG. 8-23G). Nail or screw it on to complete the support.

Folding Extension Table

If your band saw is mounted on a low bench, you should be able to make an extension tabletop to support shaped work while you are manipulating it to make a curved cut. It can clamp onto the bench top. You will have to adapt the arrangements suggested to suit your bench and saw, but the drawing is for an extension table that has a bench edge approximately under the saw table with enough area for two C clamps (FIG. 8-24A). The top then comes level with the saw table. When out of use, it hinges against the upright, and there is a folding leg that reduces in length to fold against the other parts. If the bench is suitable, you might be able to arrange the extension to fit to the back or side of the machine, according to needs.

The key part is the upright (FIGS. 8-24B and 8-24C). Its height should lift the extension tabletop level with the saw table, and its width can be the same as the saw table. Use 1/2-inch plywood, with a 1-×-2-inch strip across the top. At the bottom, arrange two pieces of 2-×-3-inch wood to extend enough to take clamps but with a gap at the center to clear the leg when folded (FIG. 8-24D).

The top is shown 24 inches long, but if your bench and table heights are very different, check that the top you make can fold over the upright (FIG. 8-24E). Where the the top pivots on the upright, rivet through the hinges, as described for the plywood support. Put a strip of 1-×-2-inch wood across the further end of the table for stiffness and to extend a lot when the table is folded.

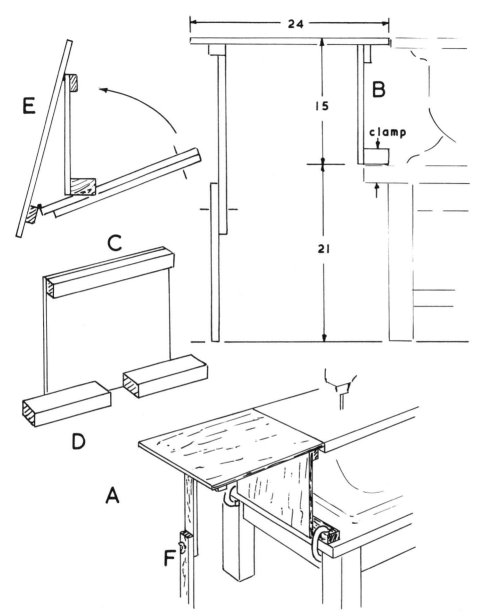

Fig. 8-24. An extension table for a band saw can be made to fold.

Hinge the top part to the center of the strip across the end of the table. Join the two parts with a V4-inch bolt with a wing nut and two washers. This should provide enough friction to keep the leg upright, but you could make holes for two bolts and take one out when you fold the leg. The extension table is intended to serve as a steady and is not meant to take heavy loads, so the folding leg should be strong enough.

Try the assembly in position and see that the parts will fold onto each other. If the action is satisfactory, round all exposed edges and corners, then paint or varnish, if you wish.

Nest of Drawers

For very small items there are compact metal and plastic blocks of drawers that are worth having because they take up less space than anything you make of the same capacity in wood. For greater capacities, you might prefer to make wood containers. These are best arranged as drawers, either fitted into vacant floor space, mounted on a table, or fixed to a wall. The design in FIG. 8-25 is offered as a suggestion to show a method of construction, and you will have to vary the size and layout to suit your needs. Drawers could be fitted with divisions or made to take containers of standard sizes.

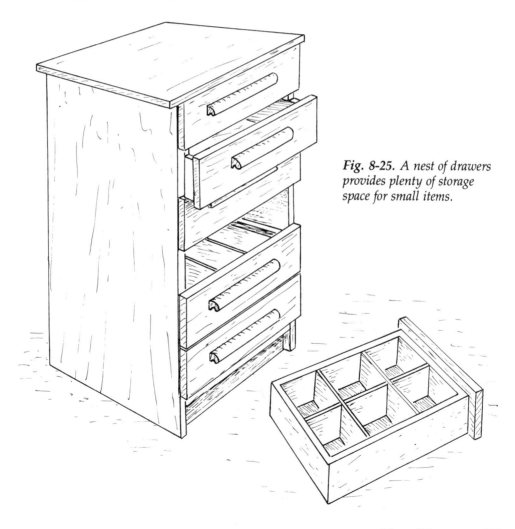

Fig. 8-25. *A nest of drawers provides plenty of storage space for small items.*

As shown (FIG. 8-25A), all drawers are the same size. This allows you to prepare wood to standard sizes and set up any jointing operations all at the same time. You could have drawers of different depths, preferably with the larger ones towards the bottom, for appearance and stability.

It would be possible to use metal or plastic drawer slides, but they need greater clearance at the sides, and drawer fronts would have to overhang more. Some parts could be made of plywood, which has the advantage of being unlikely to warp or twist, but properly seasoned hardwoods or softwoods should be satisfactory. To minimize wear after long use, the drawer sides and their guides are best made of hardwood. Construction of the case is suggested with dado joints with the plywood back let into rabbets. The drawers might be dovetailed, but they could have rabbeted fronts and dadoed backs. This con-

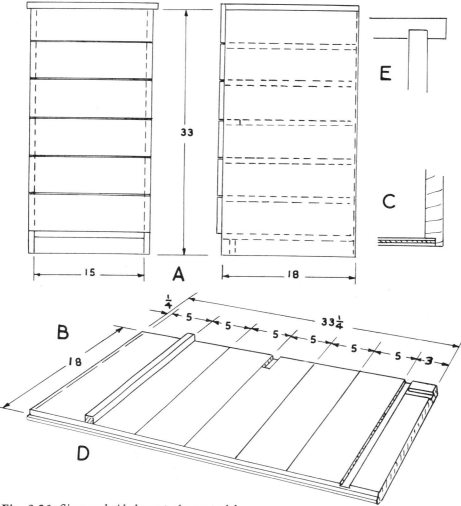

Fig. 8-26. *Sizes and side layout of a nest of drawers.*

struction is suitable for quantity production with a table saw and router. Drawer bottoms should go into grooves.

Start by setting out the two sides, which can be 1/2-inch or thicker plywood, or solid wood 5/8 inch thick with pieces glued together to make up the width (FIG. 8-26B). Rabbet the rear edges to take the plywood back (FIG. 8-26C). Allow for 1/4 inch of a side going into a dado at the top. Cut dadoes for the bottom and a plinth under it. Any distorting of the sides would affect the movement of

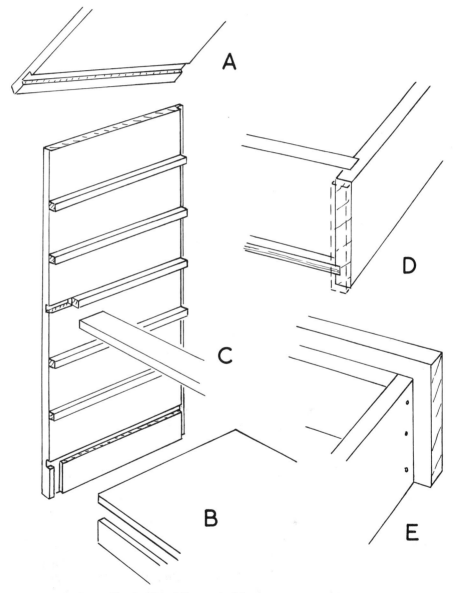

Fig. 8-27. Assembly details of the nest of drawers.

Materials List for Nest of Drawers

2 case sides	$5/8 \times 18$	$\times 34$	
1 case top	$5/8 \times 18$	$\times 18$	
1 case bottom	$5/8 \times 18$	$\times 18$	
1 case plinth	$5/8 \times 2^3/8$	$\times 18$	
1 case back	16×34	$\times 1/4$ plywood	
10 drawer guides	$5/8 \times 5/8$	$\times 18$	
12 drawer sides	$1/2 \times 4^3/8$	$\times 16$	
6 drawer backs	$1/2 \times 4$	$\times 16$	
6 drawer fronts	$5/8 \times 4^3/8$	$\times 16$	
6 false fronts	$5/8 \times 5$	$\times 18$	
6 drawer bottoms	15×18	$\times 1/4$ plywood	

drawers. The back will limit warping, but at the front, cut a dado for a rail at the midposition to prevent movement there. Mark the positions of the drawer guides, and glue and pin on these strips (FIG. 8-26D).

Make the case top (FIG. 8-27A) to fit over the sides (FIG. 8-26E). Make the bottom and plinth (FIG. 8-27B) and the middle rail (FIG. 8-27C) to fit into their dadoes in the sides. Have the back ready to fit in, then pin and glue the parts together.

Make the drawers with the sides slightly too long at the back (FIG. 8-27D). Trim them off during assembly so that they stop against the case back when their fronts are fitting level. At the front of each drawer, make a false piece to overlap the case sides and reach almost to the tops of the guides above (FIG. 8-27E). The gaps at the sides of the drawers will be hidden, and there will only be a small gap between the top of one drawer and the bottom of the next. The top drawer front can overlap the top of the case.

Try each drawer in several positions and trim the backs until a drawer closes level at the front. Several types of handle are possible. You could fit store-bought metal or plastic handles or turn a pair of knobs for each drawer.

Bench-End Tool Rack

Some woodworkers arrange a tool rack along the back of the bench. It is convenient to be able to reach for tools standing in slots there, but this is a problem when you are working on wood that is wider than the bench top. There can be a surprising number of occasions when you need a clear, level surface all over the bench. If there are tool handles projecting above the level, you have to remove them every time you need to spread things across the back of the bench. It might be better to arrange tool racks at one or both ends of the bench below the working level.

A bench-end rack is the perfect place for the tools you regularly want. You can reach for them and know they are ready to use. Much depends on the type of work you do, but you will almost certainly want to have a hammer, mallet, saw, plane, chisels, and basic marking tools such as rule, square, knife, and pencil. You might include an electric drill or another portable power tool.

The size and details of a rack at the end of a bench will depend on available space and access, but in most circumstances you can attach it to the legs and probably to one or more rails. If there is not much overhang to the bench, you might have to fit the rack between the legs, but the rack will be wider, and therefore more accommodating, if you can put it on the surfaces the legs and rails.

The suggested rack in FIG. 8-28 is intended to go on the outsides of the legs and might overlap one rail. Sizes are suggested (FIG. 8-29A) as a guide to construction, but they will have to be adjusted to suit your bench and storage needs. As shown, tools such as saws, hammers, mallets, and other long items go through holes in the top and rest on the bottom shelf. Some other things, like chisels and screwdrivers, go through holes and are supported by their handles.

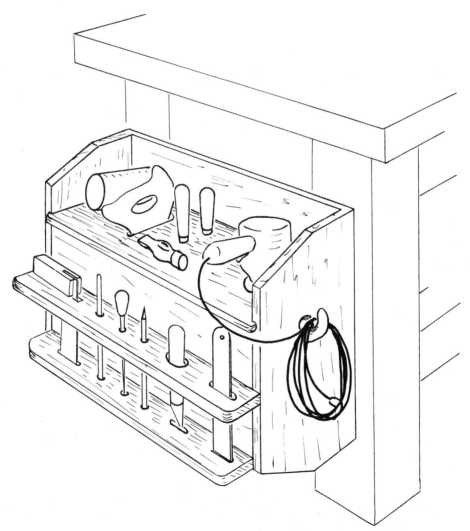

Fig. 8-28. A rack on the end of a bench keeps tools where you can reach them.

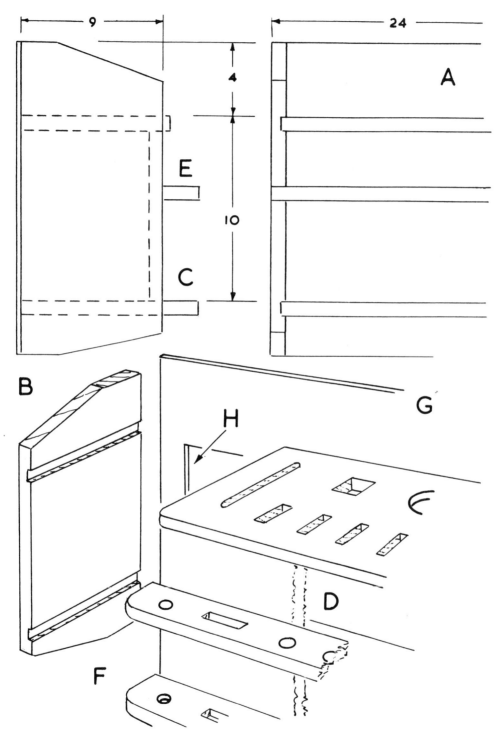

Fig. 8-29. Details of a rack for the end of a bench.

Materials List for
Bench-End Tool Rack

2 ends	$3/4 \times$	9	$\times$ 18	
1 shelf	$3/4 \times$	$9^{1}/4 \times$	25	
1 shelf	$3/4 \times$	11	$\times$ 25	
1 front	$3/4 \times$	$9^{1}/4 \times$	24	
1 rack	$3/4 \times$	2	$\times$ 25	
1 back	17 $\times$	25	$\times$ $1/4$ plywood	

Smaller tools fit in supports across the front. You can put spring clips or hooks on the ends for other tools.

Construction is with solid wood finished $3/4$ inch thick. Plywood could be used. Joints can be screwed or doweled, but dadoes are shown for the shelves.

Make the pair of ends (FIG. 8-29B), grooved to take the shelves. Arrange the shelf lengths to make the rack long enough to go across the bench legs. If you want to hang tools on a loop of cable on the end of the rack that will be at the front of the bench, set it back enough to keep whatever goes there away from the line of the front of the bench. Project the top shelf about $1/4$ inch, but project the bottom shelf 2 inches (FIG. 8-29C) to form the bottom part of the front rack.

Set out and pierce the top shelf to suit the tools that have to fit there. Allow ample clearance and round the edges so tools slip in and out easily. Leave the bottom shelf plain, unless you want to include a tool with a very long handle that has to go through.

Make a front to fit between the other parts (FIG. 8-29D) and screw the upper part of the front rack to it (FIG. 8-29E). Pierce this to suit the tools to be fitted, and make matching hollows in the bottom shelf for those tools that go through and rest on it (FIG. 8-29F). Assemble all these parts with glue and screws or dowels. The front should hold the assembly square, but test it against the bench end. You can make a plywood back but if you make that solid, you will seal the inside of the rack; then if you drop anything through a slot, you cannot retrieve it. To give access for this emergency, cut away the middle of the plywood (FIG. 8-29H) to allow access from the back. Try all the tools in position before fitting the back and screwing to the bench legs and rail. A paint or varnish finish will keep the rack clean. A light color on the top surface will make it easy to see when putting tools away if the rack is in shadow.

Bench-Top Supports

If you put a thin piece of wood in the vise and its ends overhang, it will sag under pressure. If you are planing or doing other work on the top edge, it will not finish true after pressure is released. To prevent this happening, the wood has to be supported under its lower edge for its full length. The obvious place to provide this support is the top of the bench. The problem then is to hold the thin wood upright. You have a choice of methods of holding the wood, all of which depend on a wedging action in a block on the bench.

The first support works in the same way as the apron wedge just described. A block with a V cut takes the work and a wedge and attaches to the bench with two dowels that can be pulled out of their bench holes when not required (FIG. 8-30A). If you regularly work on wood of quite a small section, you might make a support perhaps 1/2 inch thick, but for the more usual sizes in general wood-working, such as 1/2-×-3-inch section, the block could be 2 inches thick. A reasonable length is an advantage because it increases the amount of support. A suggested outline is shown (FIG. 8-31A).

As with the apron wedge, make the wedge from the piece you cut out.

Dowels should be hardwood because they have to take a heavy shearing load in use. Drill through the block and the bench top at the same time to align the holes. Glue the dowels in the block. Ease the holes in the bench so that you can lift the block away. An alternative to drilling squarely is to angle the drill in the direction of thrust in use (FIG. 8-30B) to let the planing action tighten the block on the bench.

The wedged block holds thin wood on edge securely, but you have to tap in the wedge and then loosen it on each occasion. Many pieces can be held in a slightly different block without a wedge. If you have to work on a large number of similar pieces, being able to dispense with a wedge will save time.

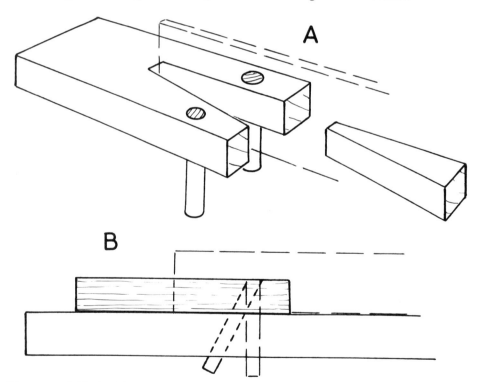

Fig. 8-30. A block with a V cut and dowels into the bench can support wood on edge.

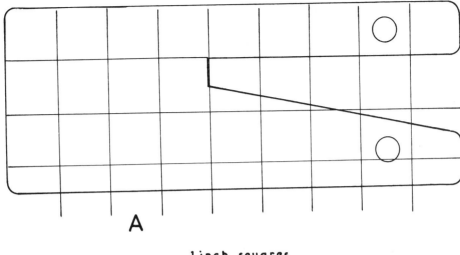

A

B

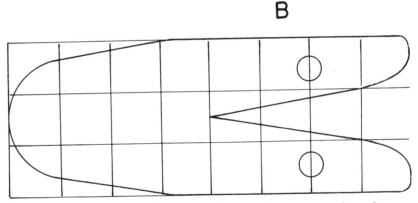

Fig. 8-31. Long blocks with narrow Vs are suitable for holding thin wood on edge.

This block has an acute V opening that is symmetrical to the lengthwise direction of the bench (FIG. 8-31B). Make the block with dowels in the same way as the previous support. The first support is better with very thin wood because it gives sides steadiness, but the second type is good for anything upwards of about 3/8 inch thick, where there is some inherent stiffness.

You will probably find yourself using this block for thicker wood, which might otherwise be worked against the ordinary bench top. Anything up to the width of the opening of the V can be held so it does not move about.

The third support is ingenious, but not so easy to make successfully. Because of the loads put on comparatively thin parts, it has to be made from a tough hardwood. The action of forcing wood into the support causes a grip, which increases as the thrust gets greater.

There are two sides pivoting on dowels arranged vertically into the bench top. At the further ends, the sides have fingers that interleave. When a piece of wood is pushed between the sides, the fingers are forced apart and the thickened near ends press against the sides of the wood. As a result of these combined actions, any wood within the capacity of the support will be locked vertically on the bench allowing its upper edge to be planed. The capacity of the support depends on the spacing of the pivots, but in this example (FIG. 8-32), with the pivots at $2^{1}/_{2}$-inch centers, wood from nil up to 1 inch thick can be held.

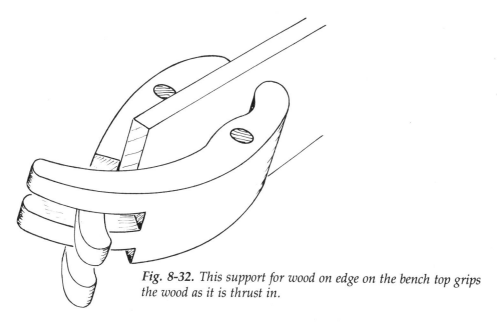

Fig. 8-32. This support for wood on edge on the bench top grips the wood as it is thrust in.

The pivots are $^{3}/_{4}$-inch hardwood dowel rods that are glued in the support sides but push-fit in holes in the bench top so they can be removed. Because of the risk of splitting during construction if shaping is done first, drill holes for the dowels while the wood is in squared blocks.

The parts are drawn 2 inches thick, with two fingers on each side. This is the minimum to be effective. You could make the pieces thicker with more fingers or have thinner fingers in the same thickness. Much depends on the strength and density of the wood chosen.

Mark the shape of two identical pieces (FIG. 8-33A). Drill for the dowels. This must be done square to the faces, using a drill press, if possible. Cut the outlines and smooth them, keeping square to the top and bottom faces.

Mark and cut the end fingers (FIG. 8-33B). Trim and smooth the meeting surfaces to slide in each other without excessive play. Glue in dowels with enough projecting to go through the bench top and project up to 1 inch.

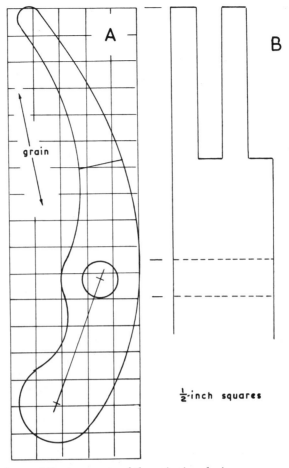

Fig. 8-33. The shape of the two parts of the gripping device.

You might want to drill holes in scrap wood and test for action before drilling the bench top. If you have worked to the sizes given, and the pivot holes are 2¹/₂-inch centers, the jaws should close to grip the thinnest wood while the fingers still have a good overlap. With thicker wood, the finger overlap will increase. Be careful to drill the bench top squarely.

9

Toys and Puzzles

Toys and activity equipment for children can provide much of the output of your shop, particularly if you are a weekend woodworker with a family. Most toys do not need the precision of furniture construction, but it is important that anything for the use of young people should be strong and free from rough edges or the risk of splitting.

The toys and games or puzzles included in this chapter have been selected from many books, with the greatest number from *101 One-Weekend Toy Projects*. The projects have been selected for ease of construction and proven appeal to children. Remember that there is usually no need for the meticulous regard for detail that might appeal to an adult. A child expects a toy to be functional and in a form he can recognize, then his imagination will provide details.

Bead Puzzle

It might not take a weekend to make one of these puzzles, but it could take you most of the weekend solving it, if you do not read the instructions. However, it is the type of project that lends itself to quantity production. You could make a series of puzzles almost as quickly as one, so you could produce a number to mystify your child's friends, or they should sell well. The puzzle (FIG. 9-1A) consists of a piece of wood with cord knotted through two holes and passed through a central hole too small for beads on the loops to pass through. The object is to move one bead across so there are two on one loop (FIG. 9-1B), then move it back again.

The beads could be bought wood or plastic ones 3/4 inch in diameter (FIG. 9-1C). They could be drilled pieces of dowel rod (FIG. 9-1D), or you could cut

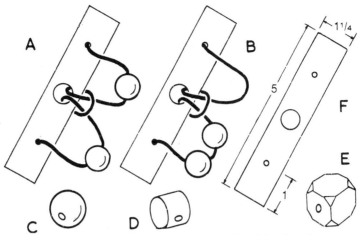

Fig. 9-1. In this bead puzzle, one bead has to be moved to join the other.

square stock and take the corners off (FIG. 9-1E). The wood strip (FIG. 9-1F) can be 1/4 inch thick. Make the central hole too small to pass the beads through and the other holes to suit the cord, which can be almost any type under 1/2 inch diameter. Loop it as shown, and knot the ends behind the small holes. The central knot is called a *lark's head*.

If you want to solve the puzzle yourself, stop here. If not, read on:

Slacken the lark's head enough to pull through the bead to be moved with part of the loop it is on (FIG. 9-2A). Push all the turns from the back through the center hole to the front, then pass the bead along the cord through the loops (FIG. 9-2B,C). Pull those loops back through the hole. Slacken the lark's head and pass the bead through the bottom of it (FIG. 9-2D) to join the other bead. To return the bead, perform the same actions in the opposite direction.

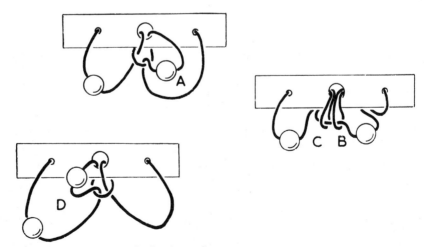

Fig. 9-2. Steps in solving the bead puzzle.

Mosaic Puzzle

Putting together a mosaic pattern is more difficult than doing a jigsaw puzzle. It should be within the scope of a child of about 8 years and up, and this could keep him or her busy for a long time. The object is to get a number of pieces together in a pattern, with colors as well as shapes symmetrical and with no two pieces of the same color adjoining. This puzzle (FIG. 9-3) is assembled in a frame,

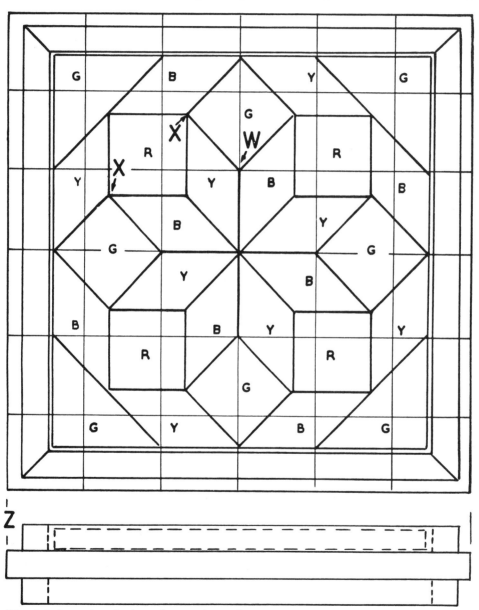

Fig. 9-3. Layout and colors of a mosaic puzzle.

1 base	$9 \times 9 \times 3/8$ plywood
8 frames	$3/8 \times 3/8 \times 9$
Squares from	$1/4 \times 1^1/2 \times 14$
Diamonds from	$1/4 \times 1^1/2 \times 36$
Triangles from	$1/4 \times 1^1/2 \times 12$

arranged with two stages of difficulty. The pattern is outlined on one side, without the colors indicated. This gives a beginner a starting formation, and he or she only has to get the colors correct. The other side is blank, so the design has to be worked out and the colors arranged.

There are eight square pieces, sixteen diamond shaped, and three triangles. The key size is the length of the side of a square. If this is $1^1/2$ inches, the overall size of the frame will be 9 inches. With 1-inch squares it will be 6 inches. Each side of a diamond must be the same length as the side of a square. The long side of each triangle should be twice this.

If you set out a background pattern of six squares of the chosen size each way on a piece of plywood, start by marking four diagonal squares where they meet the grid (FIG. 9-3W). The extremities of these diagonal squares are the outsides of the puzzle. Draw in those lines. Four more squares touch the first four (FIG. 9-3X). With these positioned, draw in the diamonds. The triangles complete the layout.

You can cut the shapes by hand, although a table saw will allow you to make them uniform. Sand the edges and lightly round them. Suggested colors are indicated (R = red, G = green, B = blue, Y = yellow).

The frame base (FIG. 9-3Z) is a square of plywood with frame strips slightly thicker than the wood used for the mosaic. Allow enough clearance for easy handling of the pieces. Draw the pattern on one side. The frame could be white or varnished.

Jigsaw Clock

A clock dial is a mystery to a child, but as he learns numbers it begins to make sense. To help in learning the first numbers and the layout of a clock dial, it is useful to make a jigsaw puzzle of it (FIG. 9-4). For a young child, the parts should not be too small. This puzzle has a framed base 11 inches across, with a central part carrying the hands, so the twelve pieces with the numbers are about $2^1/2$ inches $\times$ 4 inches (FIG. 9-4A).

All of the jigsaw clock could be made in $3/8$-inch or $1/2$-inch plywood, preferably hardwood. In any case, take off sharp edges and corners and sand thoroughly so there is no risk of splintering.

Laying out starts with drawing a hexagon around a circle (FIG. 9-4B). Divide it across into 6 and divide those sectors again to make 12, so they are 30 degrees apart. The numbers will come on these lines. Further lines are needed midway between these sector lines (FIG. 9-4C) for the cuts, so they are at 15 degrees. You

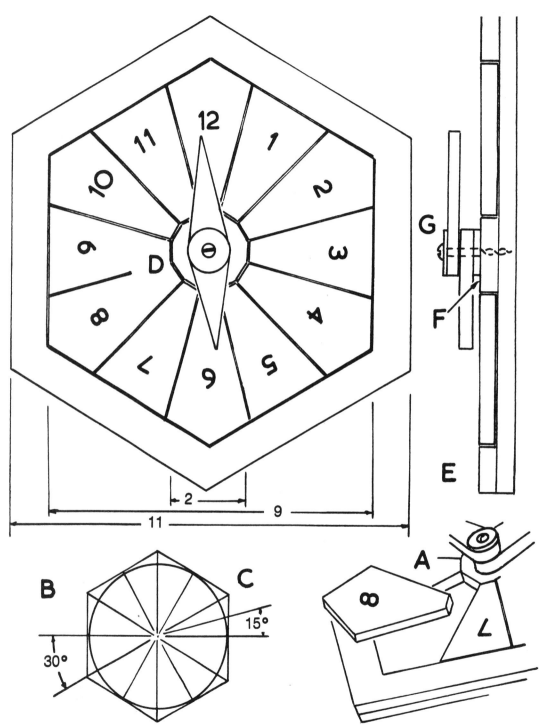

Fig. 9-4. The numbered sections of this clock face have to be put together correctly as a jigsaw puzzle.

Materials List for Jigsaw Clock

2 bases	$11 \times 13 \times 1/2$
Other parts from	$11 \times 22 \times 1/2$

will find it best to do the setting out full size on paper or scrap plywood. For the central block, draw a circle and mark 12 edges on it (FIG. 9-4D).

Cut the base to shape and mount the rim on it (FIG. 9-4E). The rim can be one piece with the inside cut away, or you could miter strips. Mount the block at the center (FIG. 9-4F).

Cut twelve loose pieces. Although you have the setting out as a guide, there might be minor variations, so trim and fit as you go.

The two hands need metal washers below and above. Make the hands with inner ends to match the washers. Mount them on a roundhead screw (FIG. 9-4G), then take apart for painting.

The sectors that make the dial could be a lighter color than the other parts. The hands should be a contrasting color. Mark the numbers prominently. Adjust the hands so they will stay where put, but are not too difficult to move.

Ring Clown

Rings to stack in a particular sequence make a good early learning toy. If they are just rings, they might not arouse much interest after the first experiments. This set of rings assembles into a clown who will not look right if the rings are put together incorrectly (FIG. 9-5).

The project is intended to be made mostly on a lathe, although, you could get very similar results by careful handwork. The central column is a piece of hardwood dowel rod. The rings could be softwood or close-grained hardwood.

You need to settle two diameters first. Young hands have to slip the rings over the column without difficulty, so drill a hole that is a very easy fit over the dowel rod. For $3/4$-inch dowel rod, this might be $7/8$ inch in diameter. For the base you must be able to drill a close fit on the dowel rod.

Saw the discs slightly oversize from 1-inch wood. At the center of the base, drill to fit the dowel rod. At the centers of the others, drill $7/8$-inch holes.

Turn a piece of scrap wood as a spindle. Give it a slight taper so a disc can be pushed on (FIG. 9-5A). Turn each disc to size on this, round its upper edges, and sand it thoroughly before removing. Keep the disc diameters in equal steps (FIG. 9-5B) to maintain a regular taper.

Materials List for Ring Clown

Discs from	$1 \times 5 \times 20$
1 head	$2 \times 2 \times 4$
1 column	$8 \times 3/4$ diameter

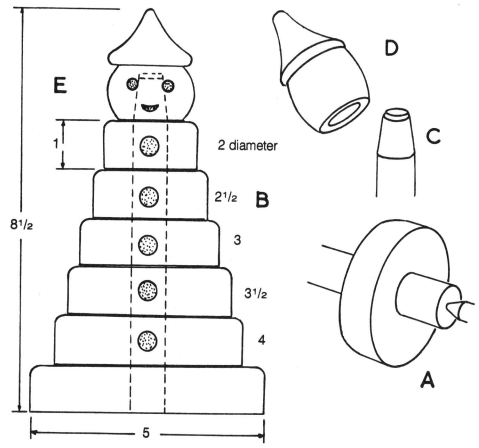

Fig. 9-5. *The parts of this clown are in the form of rings to be sorted and fitted on a rod.*

When you have made all the loose discs, turn down the spindle to take the base, and turn that.

Mount the dowel rod in the lathe and turn a slight taper on what will be the top (FIG. 9-5C). It does not matter if the dowel rod is too long at this stage. Its length can be adjusted when you fit it into the base.

Mount the block that will make the head in the lathe, and drill for the column. Use a chisel to taper the hole to make a push fit on the end of the column.

Turn a piece of scrap wood to plug that hole so you can support the work with the tailstock while you turn the outside (FIG. 9-5D).

Try the parts together. Push the dowel rod through the base until there is the right degree of fit on the discs. There should be some play between the discs when the head is pushed tight on the top of the column (FIG. 9-5E).

Paint the wood in bright colors. A dot on each disc can represent a button. Put eyes and mouth on the head. The child can then arrange the buttons and face in line, as well as put the rings in the correct order. With the head being a push fit, it will be possible for the toy to be carried about without it falling apart.

Humpty Dumpty

This toy (FIG. 9-6A) is a simple assembly exercise for a young child; when he has assembled Humpty Dumpty, he can press or hit a lever and Humpty Dumpty has a great fall. The pieces are then ready to be reassembled. The four parts of the figure stand on a box containing the lever.

You can turn the egg-shaped figure in one piece on a lathe, then separate the parts with a saw. Other parts are flat pieces of wood nailed together. Figure 9-7 shows the separated pieces.

Turn the figure; then, use a fine saw to separate the pieces on the hat and collar lines (FIG. 9-6B). Mark the centers of the ends of the pieces.

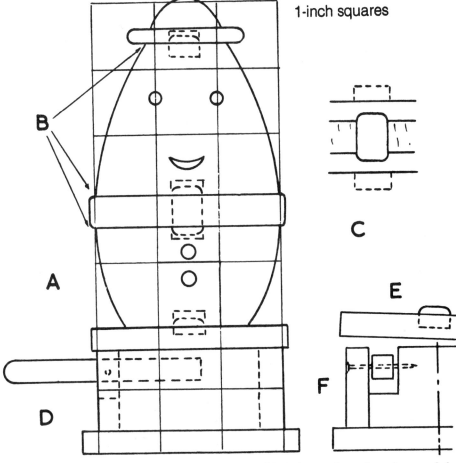

1-inch squares

Fig. 9-6. Humpty Dumpty is in parts to be assembled; then, when a lever is moved, he falls into pieces.

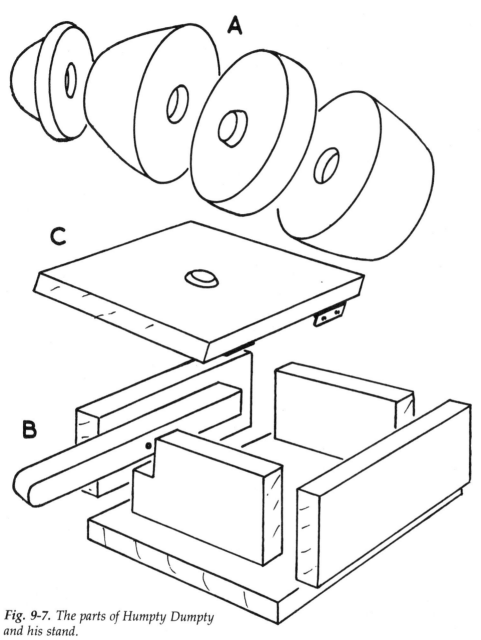

Fig. 9-7. The parts of Humpty Dumpty and his stand.

Materials List for Humpty Dumpty

1 block	$3^1/_2 \times 3^1/_2 \times 7$
4 box sides	$^3/_8 \times 1^1/_4 \times 4$
1 box bottom	$^3/_8 \times 4 \quad \times 4$
1 box top	$^3/_8 \times 4 \quad \times 4$

There are small locating pieces at each center, which can be made from 1/2-inch dowel rods. Drill right through the collar and fit a dowel with rounded ends extending about 1/8 inch on each side. Drill into the mating pieces to take these ends (FIGS. 9-6C and 9-7A). There are similar joints at the top and bottom. Arrange loose fits, as the joints are for locating only and not securing.

Make the lever (FIGS. 9-6D and 9-7B), with a rounded outer end.

Join the four sides of the box, with a notch in one to take the lever. Cut away enough to allow easy movement.

The top and bottom of the box overlap a little. Nail on the bottom. Fit a locating dowel to the center of the top (FIGS. 9-6E and 9-7C). Hinge the top at the side away from the lever.

Pivot the lever on a nail (FIG. 9-6F), and try the action of the toy. Paint it brightly, with some detail on the front.

Noah's Ark Toy Box

A child might not be very inclined to put his toys away in an ordinary box, but if the box is disguised as something else, toy storage becomes more attractive. This box is in the form of a Noah's Ark and is on rollers, so it can be moved about (FIG. 9-8A). The roof opens in two parts to give access. The end decks can be used to put toys on during play.

Box parts are stiffened plywood. The rollers and ends are solid wood. Plywood or hardwood provide that boat shape at the bottom.

Start with the box sides (FIG. 9-9A). They extend far enough to enclose the rollers and take the end blocks (FIG. 9-9B,C).

Make the bottom and ends to fit between the sides (FIG. 9-8B). Bevel the tops of the sides to match the slope of the roof. Assemble these parts with glue and fine nails, reinforced with strips inside (FIG. 9-9D).

The rollers are 2 1/2 inches in diameter with a hole through to revolve on a 3/8-inch dowel rod. Turn them with rounded ends so they will not damage carpets. A roller should project 1/2 inch below the ark and have a 1/2-inch clearance between it, the box, and the end block. Mark and drill holes in the sides to allow

Materials List for Noah's Ark Toy Box

2 sides	15	× 30	× 1/2 plywood
2 ends	12	× 16	× 1/2 plywood
1 bottom	12	× 21	× 1/2 plywood
2 roofs	7	× 23	× 1/2 plywood
2 end blocks	2 1/2 × 8		× 13
2 rollers	2 1/2 ×	2 1/2 × 12	
2 axles	13	×	3/8 diameter
2 decks	10	× 13	× 1/2 plywood
2 sides	3	× 30	× 1/4 or 1/8 plywood or hardboard
4 ends	4	× 9	× 1/4 or 1/8 plywood or hardboard

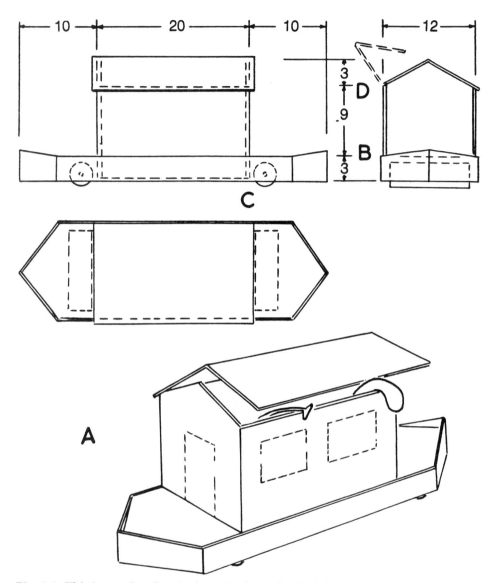

Fig. 9-8. *This is a toy box disguised as a Noah's Ark. The lid swings back, and the ark can be moved on rollers.*

for this (FIGS. 9-8C and E). Notch the end blocks (FIG. 9-9F,G), and round the box side extensions.

Make a plywood top over each end (FIG. 9-9H). Fit the rollers on their waxed dowels, and assemble the ends.

Make plywood or hardboard boat sides (FIG. 9-9J) and ends (FIG. 9-9K), which can rise at the points to 1/2 inch above the deck.

The roof parts meet along the ridge and overhang 1/2 inch at the ends. The

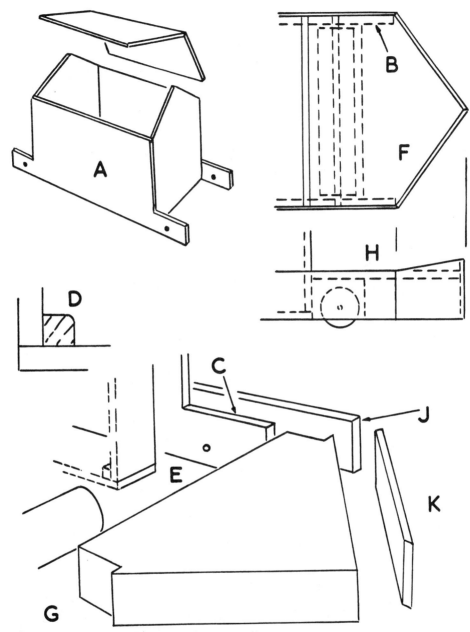

Fig. 9-9. *Construction of the Noah's Ark toy box.*

rear edge, which is hinged (FIG. 9-8D), should be level with the wall, but the front overhangs to provide a grip for lifting. Hinge the parts along the ridge and to the wall.

It would be unwise to cut windows and doors in the box, but you might improve appearance by painting them on when you paint all over.

Doll's Folding Chair

A doll's folding chair is a highchair that a girl can use to seat her doll at table height, but it can be folded so the bottom part forms a table in front of the seat when she wants to play with the doll nearer floor level (FIG. 9-10). The chair base is 15 inches square, and the chair would normally occupy that area and a height of 35 inches. But you can take the assembly apart when the child has grown out of playing with dolls and you want to keep the chair for another child. If you take off the hinges and unscrew the seat, the upper part of the cone will go inside the lower part and the seat will go inside that, reducing the package to a cube of about 15-inch sides.

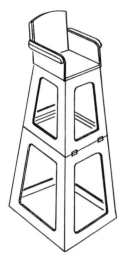 

Fig. 9-10. This doll's chair can be used as a high chair or folded, so the base forms a table in front of a lower chair.

Materials List for Doll's Folding Chair

4 panels	15 × 16 × 1/2 plywood
4 panels	11 × 12 × 1/2 plywood
1 tabletop	15 × 15 × 1/2 plywood
12 strips	3/4 × 3/4 × 16
12 strips	3/4 × 3/4 × 12
4 seat framing	3/4 × 3/4 × 10
Seat plywood from cutout panels	

Construction is with 1/2-inch or thinner plywood and softwood strips 3/4 inch square. Parts can be glued and held with fine nails. Although the shape is conical, and this affects angles, the amount is so slight that you can work with square sections. If you want to be precise, corner angles are under 92 degrees.

Set out a side view of the support (FIG. 9-11A), allowing for the thickness of plywood the other way. Make two sides to this pattern, with a cut across where shown. Lighten the panels by cutting the centers out 2 inches in all round. Frame these parts all round with 3/4-inch strips.

Make the panels in the other direction. Clean the internal cutout edges all around.

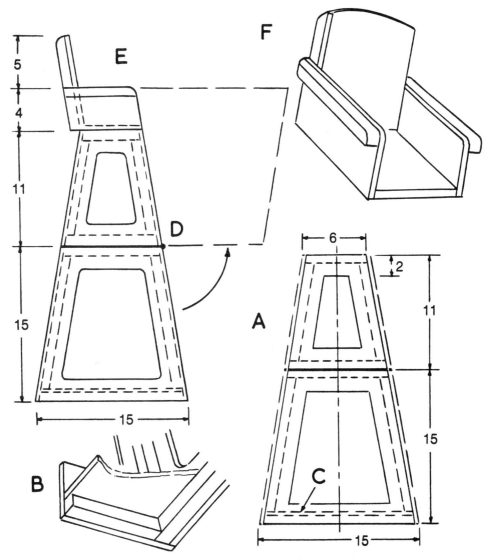

Fig. 9-11. Sizes and details of the parts of the doll's folding chair.

Join the parts to make the square shapes. As you do this, include a piece of plywood inside the bottom (FIG. 9-11 B,C). This forms the tabletop when the chair is folded. Frame inside all parts.

Hinge the parts together (FIG. 9-11D). Two 2-inch hinges should be satisfactory. Fold the bottom up against the top part to give you the angle for the seat. The front and back of the seat follow the angle of the conical base/table (FIG. 9-11E).

Make the seat (FIG. 9-11F) with a base as wide as the support and extending 1½ inches at the back. Cut the sides 4 inches high to fit each side of the base.

Make the back with stiffening uprights, and nail the sides to this and all parts to the base. Join the seat to its support with a few screws, so it can be removed.

Finish with paint, although if you and the young owner want it to look more like existing furniture, you could stain and varnish the wood.

Pole Tennis

Pole tennis is a game with a satisfying demand on children's energy. Two players can compete, or one can get fun out of hitting the ball both ways. A ball is tethered by a cord to the top of a pole (FIG. 9-12A) and can be hit around it. Two players hit opposite ways, and each scores a point when his opponent misses. Ordinary tennis racquets can be used, but for children it might be better to use table tennis paddles.

There can be a considerable load on the pole, so it has to be driven firmly into the ground. A pole in a single length could be used, but if it is in two parts it is more compact for storage or transport. A way is shown for driving the lower part into the ground, without damage to it, before adding the top piece.

The wood for the pole should be straight-grained and stiff. The pivot piece for the top should be close-grained hardwood. A tube, preferably brass, is needed for the joint. This has to slide closely on the poles, so getting matching sizes is a first priority. The best poles are between 1 inch and $1^1/4$ inches in diameter.

Prepare the pivot piece (FIG. 9-12B) with a stout long screw (#12 gauge would be suitable) and a piece of brass tube to fit closely over it. Drill the $7/8$-inch-square wood for the tube and for the cord (about $1/4$-inch diameter). Round the extending ends.

Cut the two poles to length (FIG. 9-12C) and point the bottom one. Fit a $1/2$-inch dowel with a tapered end into the top part, and make a hole to take it in the lower part (FIG. 9-12D). This registers the parts, but a 9-inch tube slides from the top part over the joint and rests against a screw (FIG. 9-12F).

If the joint is not a very close fit and there might be a risk of it separating, drill both ends of the tube for a screw into each part of the pole. Of course, then you need to use a screwdriver when you wish to take the pole apart.

For hammering the bottom part into the ground without damaging its top, make a pad with a dowel to fit the hole (FIG. 9-12G). Use this to take the blows of the hammer. It can be bigger and need not be round.

Materials List for Pole Tennis

2 poles	38 × $1^1/4$ diameter
1 pivot piece	$7/8$ × $7/8$ × 5
2 bats	8 × 11 × $1/4$ plywood
4 bat handles	1 × 1 × 12
1 brass tube	9 to fit poles
1 brass tube	1 to fit screw

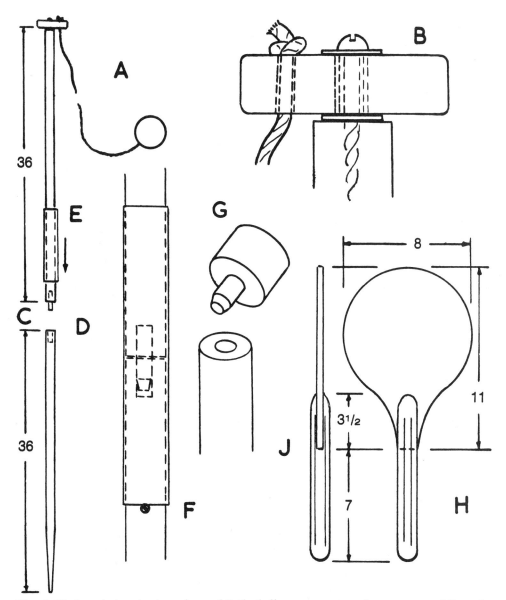

Fig. 9-12. In pole tennis, two players hit the ball on a rope opposite ways around the pole.

Use a hard rubber ball. A large needle or bodkin will be needed to get the rope through it. Knot securely there and through the pivot piece. Have the rope long enough for the ball to be a few inches above the ground when at rest.

Grease around the screw when you first assemble it through the tube into the top of the pole.

A bat has a plywood blade let into a solid wood handle (FIG. 9-12H). Use hardwood 1/4-inch plywood, as this is stronger and directs a better blow to the ball than thicker softwood plywood. Cut so a broad part extends into the handle for strength in the joint.

For comfort and a good grip, the handle should be as thick as a child can hold. A hexagonal section is better than round and this should be at least 1 inch across the flats.

Round the ends of the handles. Cut a close-fitting slot on a blade (FIG. 9-12). Taper over this and glue the joint. If you have to use screws as well, keep them thin.

Paint the pole parts. Leave the bats untreated, but sand them well.

Walker Truck

A child who is still hesitant about walking will appreciate something to hold on to that he can push around. If it is a box on wheels, he can load other toys into it or use it for their storage (FIG. 9-13).

Because this is a toy that the child will outgrow, there is no need for an elaborate construction. The assembly is kept low and the handle comes within the wheel area, so there is little risk of the truck being pulled over.

The main body is a box with the sides extended. Nailed joints could be used, but dadoes are shown. Mark the sides together (FIG. 9-14A). The ends are plain

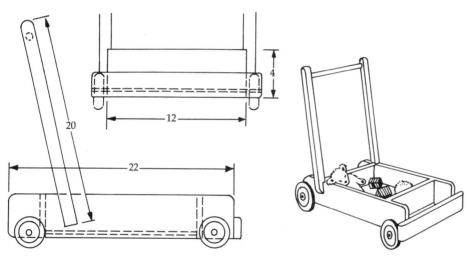

Fig. 9-13. *A walker truck provides mobile storage for a young child who is just learning to walk.*

Materials List for a Walker Truck

2 sides	4 × 22	× 1/2
2 ends	4 × 11 1/4	× 1/2
1 bottom	11 × 16	× 1/4 plywood
2 handle sides	1 × 20	× 1
1 handle	5/8 × 13	× dowel rod

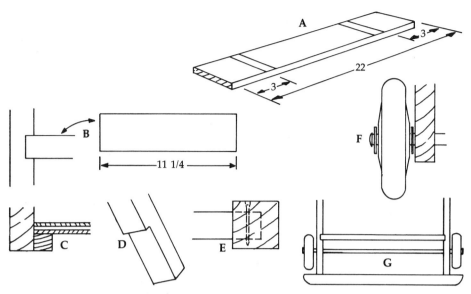

Fig. 9-14. *Details of the walker truck, its handle and its wheels: (A) marked sides; (B) ends; (C) bottom; (D) notched handles; (E) drilled tops; (F) riveted rod; (G) fender.*

pieces to fit between them (FIG. 9-14B). Although the bottom could be nailed on, it is better to put it inside on supporting strips (FIG. 9-14C). Round the corners of the extending sides, and take the sharpness off all edges.

Slope the handle sides, but arrange their tops so the handle is above the rear axle position. Notch the handles over the box sides, but do not cut out so much as to weaken them (FIG. 9-14D). Drill the tops for a piece of dowel rod, which can have a thin nail driven across to supplement glue (FIG. 9-14E).

How the wheels and axles are arranged depends on available equipment. In the arrangement shown, there are 3-inch-diameter wheels with rubber tires on iron rod axles that suit the wheels, probably 1/4 inch in diameter. The axles go through the sides, then there are washers on each side of each wheel. The end of the rod is lightly riveted to prevent the wheel from coming off (FIG. 9-14F).

The front end of the truck could be hazardous to furniture that it is pushed against, so a strip of wood across the front, just wide enough to overlap the wheels to act as a fender would help (FIG. 9-14G). It might be sufficient to round its edges, or you can add some rubber padding.

If the truck will be used outdoors, paint the axles and wheels as well as the woodwork. A few holes in the bottom will let rainwater run out, although they would not be appreciated if the young operator wanted to transport sand.

Tip Truck

This pull-along tip truck will carry a load securely, but by moving a lever at the side it will shoot its load of sand or anything else out of the back (FIG. 9-15A). It

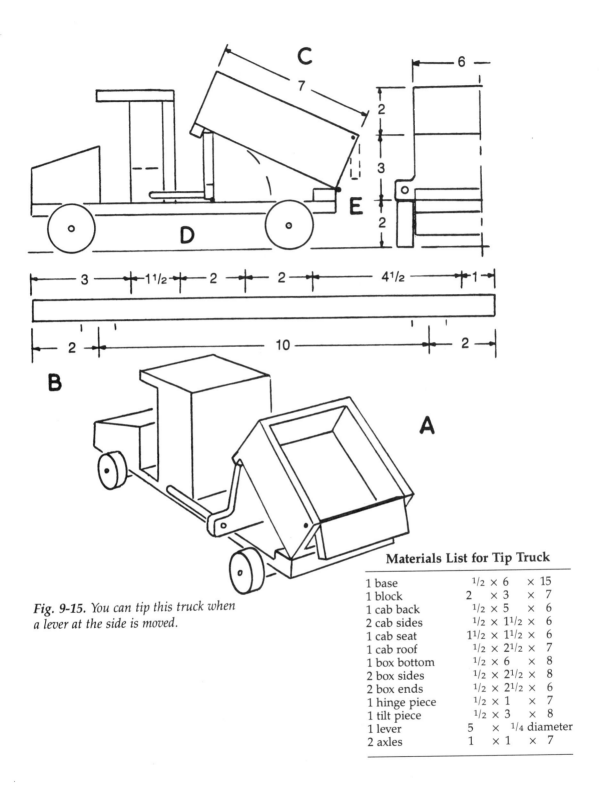

Fig. 9-15. *You can tip this truck when a lever at the side is moved.*

Materials List for Tip Truck

1 base	$1/2$	× 6	× 15
1 block	2	× 3	× 7
1 cab back	$1/2$	× 5	× 6
2 cab sides	$1/2$	× $1^1/2$	× 6
1 cab seat	$1^1/2$	× $1^1/2$	× 6
1 cab roof	$1/2$	× $2^1/2$	× 7
1 box bottom	$1/2$	× 6	× 8
2 box sides	$1/2$	× $2^1/2$	× 8
2 box ends	$1/2$	× $2^1/2$	× 6
1 hinge piece	$1/2$	× 1	× 7
1 tilt piece	$1/2$	× 3	× 8
1 lever	5	×	$1/4$ diameter
2 axles	1	× 1	× 7

could be used in a sand pit or indoors with small blocks. The size allows a small doll to be the driver.

Most parts are 1/2 inch thick. They could be plywood, but are better made of solid wood. You can use up scraps of almost any wood.

Construction is with glue and nails. There is no need for cut joints between any parts. Wheels are 2 inches in diameter and might be made or bought. If you buy wheels and they are bigger than 2 inches, alter the axle blocks so the tops of the wheels come level with the top of the base.

Make the base and mark the positions of the other parts on it; (FIG. 9-15B) that will set their sizes as well as positions.

The front end is made up of simple pieces (FIG. 9-16A). Finished widths should be level with the edge of the base. Make the tipping part as an open-ended box (FIGS. 9-15C and 9-16B). Put a square strip under its front end (FIG. 9-16C) and a piece the same thickness across the end of the base (FIG. 9-16D).

The tilting piece should have its grain across and a 1-inch extension to take the 1/4-inch dowel rod lever (FIGS. 9-15D and 9-16E).

The box could be left open, or there can be a back fitted in and pivoted on two nails at the top (FIG. 9-15E). Make it loose enough to swing open when the load is tilted.

Put axle pieces across, and mount the wheels with washers on roundhead screws.

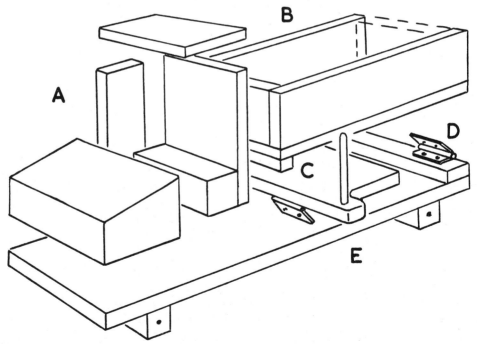

Fig. 9-16. The arrangement of parts of the tipping truck.

Hinges about 1 inch are suitable. Position the tilting piece so the operating lever is nearly horizontal when the piece bears against the stop block on the box.

Finish with bright paint. The young owner's name could go on the side.

Pull-Along Ducks

The youngest toddler enjoys something to pull along, preferably of a pattern which he can recognize, if only from a picture. These ducks on wheels (FIG. 9-17) can be painted brightly and pulled with a cord. There could be just one duck, or you could make a mother duck and as many ducklings as you like to follow her.

The duck bodies may be ¹/₂-inch or thicker plywood. The wings are 4-inch plywood or solid wood. The bases are solid wood ¹/₂ inch or thicker, and the wheels are 2 inches in diameter.

Decide on the size you want. If you treat the squares as 1 inch, the duck body is about 5 inches × 8 inches (FIG. 9-18). This is a suitable size for a single toy or for the mother duck, if there will be others. The ducklings could be the same shape, but based on ¹/₂-inch squares.

Jigsaw or fret saw the bodies to shape. Cut out the wings and glue them on. Smooth all edges before assembly.

Make the bases. They should be wide enough for stability—3 inches would be satisfactory. Attach the body to its base with two screws from below.

The wheels might be colored plastic, but plain wooden ones would be satisfactory. Emphasis should be on the bird, and plain wheels would not detract from it.

Fig. 9-17. You can arrange a mother duck and her ducklings as a pull-along toy.

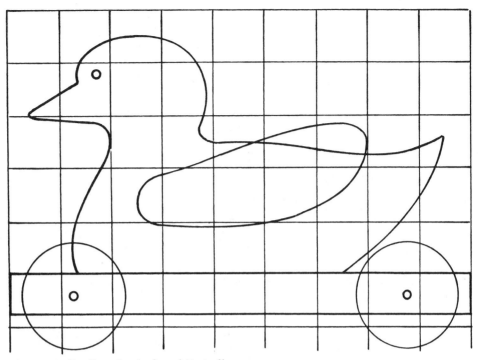

Fig. 9-18. Outline of a duck and its trolley.

Mount the wheels on screws with washers on each side of a wheel.

Put a stout screw eye in the front to take the towing cord. If you want to link several ducks, put screw eyes in each part. Then force one open to link with the other and squeeze it closed again, if you want the linkage to be permanent. If the young user will be able to hook and unhook them himself, use a screw hook instead of one eye at each joint.

Much of the appeal of bird toys is in the colors. The base can be blue for water. There should be a yellow beak and black eyes, with the rest of the bird white, gray, or brown.

Lumber Wagon

Something that can be pulled about, which carries a load that can be used in various ways, will appeal to a toddler. This lumber wagon (FIG. 9-19) carries six boards which could be used alone or with building bricks to make houses and forts or bridges for other wheeled toys to cross. When the job is finished, the boards can be loaded up and towed elsewhere.

The wagon is shown with a handle which steers the front wheels. Alternatively, the extension could be made with a hole instead of a slot so it could be hooked onto another wheeled toy, such as a truck. The sizes drawn (FIG. 9-20A) are based on 2-inch wheels, which you may turn yourself or buy, but get the

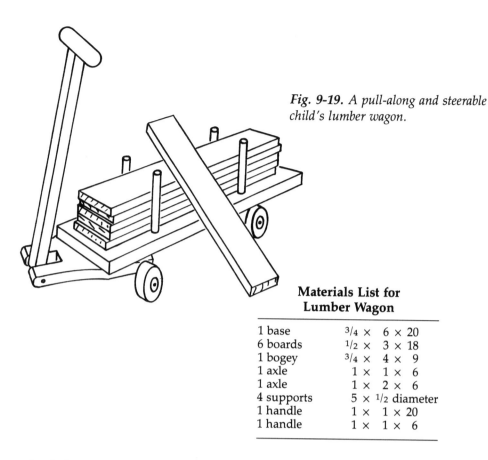

Fig. 9-19. A pull-along and steerable child's lumber wagon.

Materials List for Lumber Wagon

1 base	$^3/_4 \times$	6	$\times$	20
6 boards	$^1/_2 \times$	3	$\times$	18
1 bogey	$^3/_4 \times$	4	$\times$	9
1 axle	$1 \times$	1	$\times$	6
1 axle	$1 \times$	2	$\times$	6
4 supports	$5 \times$	$^1/_2$	diameter	
1 handle	$1 \times$	1	$\times$	20
1 handle	$1 \times$	1	$\times$	6

wheels first in case you have to make any adjustments to size to suit different wheels. It would be advisable to make the wagon of hardwood, but the boards could be softwood.

Make the base (FIGS. 9-20B and 9-21A) and drill it for $^1/_2$-inch dowel rods.

The wheels have to clear the underside of the base by about $^1/_2$ inch, and their centers must be at the same height.

Make the bogey piece (FIGS. 9-20C and 9-21B) with a 1-inch slot for the handle.

Put a block underneath it (FIG. 9-21C) and another block at the other end of the base (FIG. 9-21D), with their wheel pivot centers at the same distance below the base.

Fit the rear block to the base, and drill for a bolt or screw to form the pivot for the bogey.

The dowel lumber supports should have their tops rounded, if possible, or sharpness should be taken off. Make the boards to fit reasonably tight between them (FIG. 9-21E) so they do not slip when being towed.

The handle (FIG. 9-20DD) is a square strip with a T piece at the top. The best way of joining this is with a mortise-and-tenon joint (FIG. 9-21F). Join the handle with a bolt or screw through the bogey piece. Make sure it clears the corners of

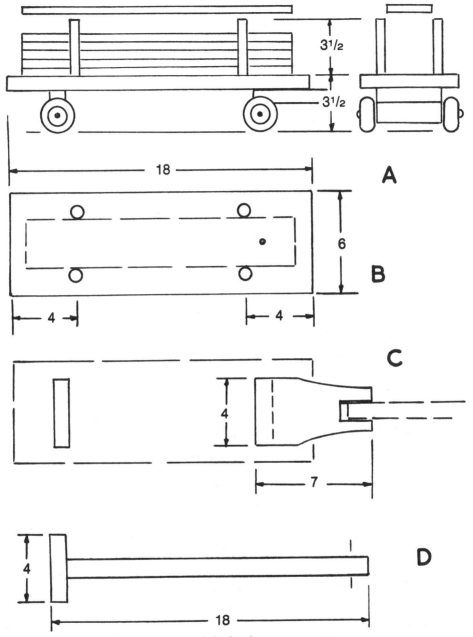

Fig. 9-20. Suggested sizes for parts of the lumber wagon.

the base when pulled around.

Mount the wheels on screws with washers each side.

Paint all the wagon parts, but leave the load of boards plain. Round their corners and edges so there are no rough edges that might scratch small hands.

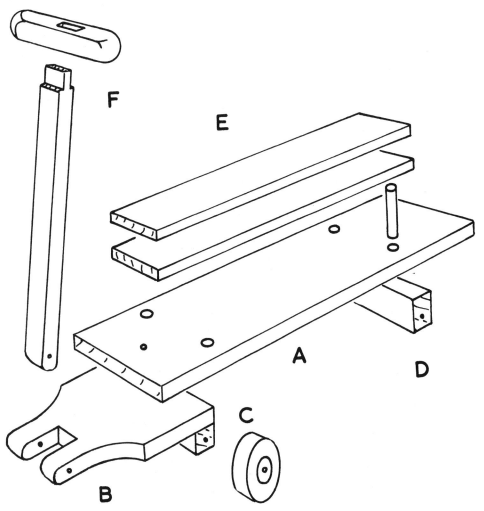

Fig. 9-21. Arrangement of the parts of the lumber wagon.

Doll Baby Carriage

A girl playing with a doll might wish to wheel it about in its own baby carriage and be able to adjust bedding, raise and lower a hood, and generally behave as mother would with a child. This baby carriage (FIG. 9-22) is intended for a toddler and might be suitable for her for a few years. It could also be used as a walking aid for a beginner. The body of the carriage is 12 inches × 24 inches. The handle is 27 inches above the floor, if 6-inch wheels are fitted. Try these sizes in relation to your child. Allow for growing, but you might wish to modify some of the sizes.

Materials List for Doll Baby Carriage

2 sides	10 × 26	× 1/2 plywood
2 chassis	9 × 22	× 1/2 plywood
2 ends	10 × 12	× 1/2 plywood
1 base	12 × 22	× 1/2 plywood
4 ends	3/4 × 11/4 × 10	
2 ends	1 × 1 × 10	
2 hood sides	15 × 15	× 1/2 plywood
2 hood strips	1/2 × 1 × 14	
1 hood cover	15 × 15	× 1/8 hardboard or plywood
2 handle sides	5/8 × 11/4 × 24	
1 handle	14 × 3/4 diameter	

Fig. 9-22. This doll baby carriage is all-wood construction.

Main parts, including the hood, are made from 1/2-inch plywood. The chassis sides fit between the body sides and under its base. The handles and hood come outside the body. The parts that are seen in side view are the important ones, and they should be made first.

The three views of the baby carriage show the general layout. The side view (FIG. 9-23A) should be used as a reference for sizes of the main parts. The plan

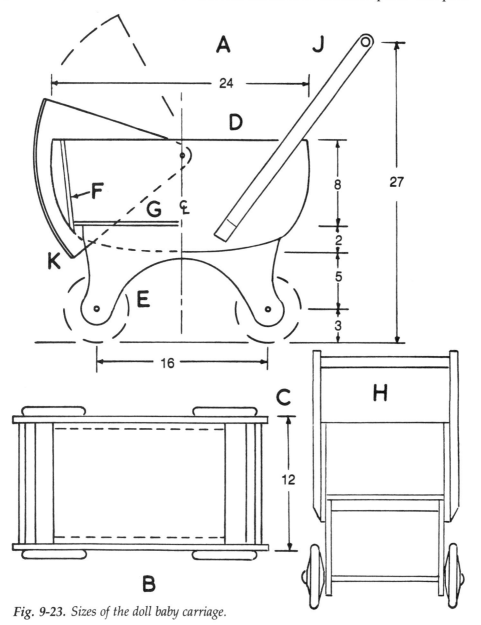

Fig. 9-23. Sizes of the doll baby carriage.

view (FIG. 9-23B) is without the handle and hood. The end view is a section (FIG. 9-23C) and shows the chassis parts and base of the carriage between the sides. For the outline of the shaped parts, refer to FIG. 9-24. Except for the hood and handle, the carriage is symmetrical about the centerline.

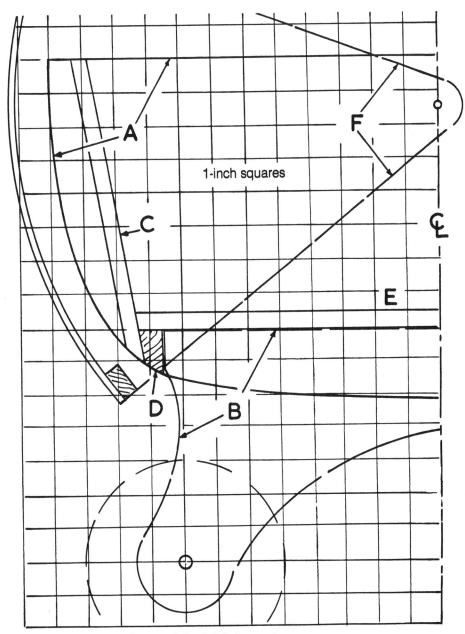

Fig. 9-24. Shapes of parts of the doll baby carriage.

Mark out and cut the two body sides (FIGS. 9-23D and 9-24A). Mark on them the positions of the other parts.

Make the two chassis sides (FIGS. 9-23E and 9-24B). Note that the top edges come against the body base and between the strips on the plywood ends.

At the ends of the sides, add the pieces that will support the ends (FIG. 9-25A). Their inner edges follow the line of the plywood end, and the outer edges are shaped to match the side plywood.

Cut the plywood ends (FIGS. 9-23F and 9-24C) with their bottom edges shaped to match the curve of the body sides.

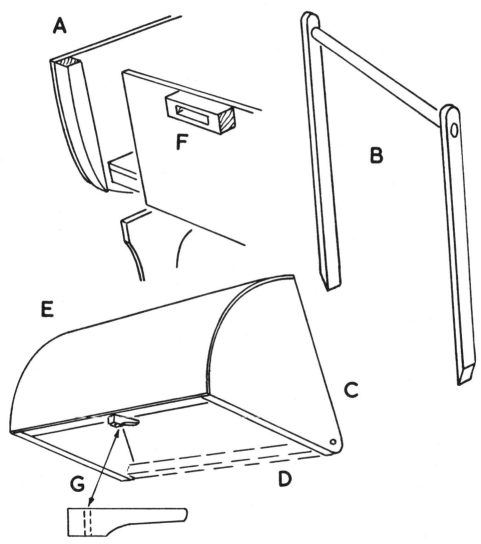

Fig. 9-25. Construction of parts of the doll baby carriage.

Put pieces across to support the base (FIG. 9-24D), also shaped to the curve of the sides. Fit the ends between the sides with glue and fine nails. Fit the chassis sides by screwing from inside to the body sides. They should come up to the base line and fit between the strips across the ends.

Make the base (FIGS. 9-23G and 9-24E) to fit closely. Glue and pin it in place. Make sure that the whole assembly is square, and check for twist by sighting across the top edges.

It should be satisfactory to leave the top edges of the body with the piles exposed, if you round and sand them well before painting. The alternative would be to put on solid wood lips before assembly. Round and smooth all edges and corners.

The handle is made with two flat sides and a piece of dowel rod across the top (FIGS. 9-23H,J and 9-25B). The exact location is not important and might be found by experimenting. It will be stronger to take the dowel rod right through the sides. Attach the handle sides to the body sides with glue and screws from the inside.

The hood sides (FIGS. 9-23K and 9-25C) are sections of a circle pivoted on screws on the centerline of the body sides. In the lowered position, the hood rests against the chassis sides with the top only a little way above the body edge. When raised, the hood edge is not quite upright, but it covers nearly half of the carriage.

Cut the two hood sides (FIG. 9-24F). Drill for pivot screws. Make two pieces to go between the ends of the curve. Glue and nail them there. At the same time, put a strip of scrap wood between the pivot corners with temporary screws to hold it (FIG. 9-25D).

Make a piece of hardboard or 1/2-inch plywood to bend around the curve (FIG. 9-25E). Plywood will bend easier if its outer grain is crosswise. Moistening will help bending if the material will not go around dry.

Use glue and screws into the strips and pins into the edges of the plywood sectors. Start at one end. Pull around gradually, preferably with help, to hold while you screw and nail. You might need clamps on the strips as well, until the glue has set.

To keep the hood in the up position there is a grooved block and a turnbutton. Make the block to go centrally on the carriage end (FIG. 9-25F). Remove the temporary piece from the hood and pivot it temporarily on two awls or screws. This will allow you to check the shape and length of a turnbutton to engage with the groove in the block. Make the turnbutton (FIG. 9-25G), and fit it with a screw and washer under the edge of the hood. Try the action of the hood in up and down positions; then, remove it for painting.

Wheels with tires will probably be intended for 3/8-inch-diameter steel axles, which you might buy at the same time. You might have to check on the method of fitting particular wheels. If there is no other arrangement, you will have to mount the wheels with washers inside and outside; then, drill across for a cotter pin to secure each wheel. Let the steel axles be tight in the wood chassis sides, as they do not have to rotate.

Paint all over, using several colors, if you wish. A light cream color inside is appropriate. The outside could be darker, with the hood a different shade from the rest of the carriage.

The hood could pivot on bolts taken right through or on stout wood screws. Put washers under the heads and between the wood parts.

Go-Kart

The go-kart, a steerable box on wheels in which to ride and be pushed or free-wheel down slopes, is often improvised by children, sometimes with unfortunate results. You can make a better go-kart which is strong and probably more satisfying to the child; moreover, the risks are reduced. This go-kart (FIG. 9-26) has a box seat safely mounted. Steering is by feet and a rope. There are guards to

Fig. 9-26. Steer this go-kart by the feet or push with a handle and steer with a bridle.

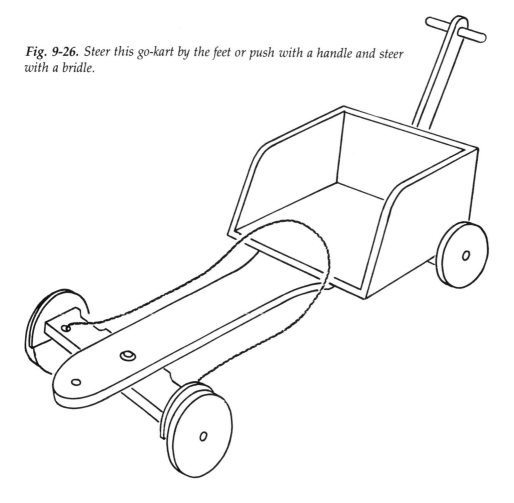

Materials List for Go-Kart

1 lengthwise piece	1 ×	7	× 40
2 axles	1 ×	4	× 17
4 axle blocks	1$1/2$ ×	1$1/2$ ×	6
2 wheel guards	6 ×	9	× $1/2$ plywood
1 handle	$3/4$ ×	1$1/2$ ×	38
1 handle	9 ×	$3/4$ diameter	
1 seat bottom	$3/4$ ×	12	× 16
2 seat sides	$3/4$ ×	9	× 14
1 seat back	$3/4$ ×	9	× 16

keep the feet away from the wheels, and there is a provision at the back for a handle, which a helper can use to control a young user. An average size is suggested (FIG. 9-27A), but you might want to check the leg length of the intended user. You can allow for growing by providing several holes for the pivot bolt, which can be moved along without having much effect on the kart.

Softwood should be satisfactory. Parts of the box seat could be plywood. Choose a reasonably straight-grained board, free from knots or other flaws, for the lengthwise piece. Sizes are based on 6-inch wheels with $3/8$-inch holes. Other sizes can be adapted easily, but much smaller wheels are not advised.

Make the length piece (FIG. 9-27B). Reduce its forward part to 5 inches wide. This can be carried forward to take a hole for a towing rope. If you want a rear handle, allow enough length for that. Round the reduced part, which might come into contact with bare legs.

There could be steel rod axles right across, but the use of carriage bolts is shown (FIG. 9-27C). This gives a smoother and safer outside projection than if an axle goes through and is drilled for cotter pins. Choose carriage bolts long enough to go through a wheel and a block about 3 inches long (FIG. 9-27D).

Make the steering axle support (FIG. 9-27E) notched for the feet and with holes for the steering rope. At the ends, put plywood guards (FIG. 9-27F,G) to stand 1 inch outside the wheel circumference.

Drill the two parts for a $1/2$-inch pivot bolt. The wood parts can bear against each other, but when you assemble, put large washers under the nut and bolt head. Use a locking nut.

The rear axle support is made in the same way, but there are no wheel guards. Screw it to the lengthwise piece and put packings on each side under the box seat (FIG. 9-27H).

Have the box bottom with its grain across, probably making up the wood width with several pieces. The grain of the box back and sides should be horizontal. You can make up the box (FIG. 9-27) with a variety of joints. The rear corners might receive considerable strain sometimes, so they should be strong. Dovetails would be ideal, but screwing should be satisfactory. Put sheet metal straps around near the top corners. Screw the bottom up into the other parts. Round all exposed edges. Screw through the bottom securely into the lower parts.

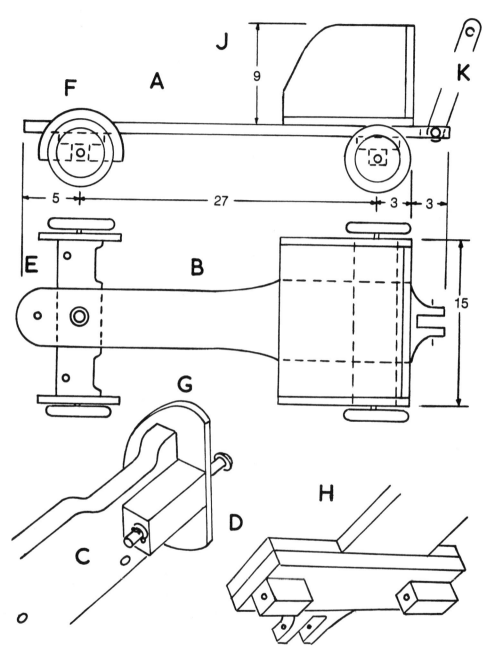

Fig. 9-27. *Sizes of the parts of a go-kart.*

The rear handle could be a strip 36 inches long with a dowel across the top (FIG. 9-27K). The 1/4-inch pivot bolt could have a wing nut so the handle can be removed easily when not required.

Folding Playhouse

You can make the simplest small playhouse entirely from 1/2-inch plywood panels, hinging them together so the house is portable. The house shown in FIG. 9-28 has a roof that lifts off and ends that are hinged centrally (FIG. 9-29A), so it is possible to fold the parts into a bundle which is under 5 inches thick. The greatest packed length is 48 inches, and the greatest packed width is 38 inches.

Sizes are arranged so you can cut them economically from 48-inch-×-96-inch plywood sheets (FIG. 9-29B). As shown, there are openings for window and door. You could hinge on a plywood door and fit plastic sheet to the window, although for the age child this is intended for, simple openings should be satisfactory.

Be careful to square all parts, or they will not fit and fold properly. Make four end pieces (FIG. 9-30A). With these sizes, the roof will slope at about 30 degrees. Make the back and front to match each other and as high as the eaves on the ends (FIG. 9-30B). Cut the door and window openings in the front. Remove sharpness from all edges and round the door and window edges thoroughly.

Fig. 9-28. You can make a basic folding playhouse from plywood sheets.

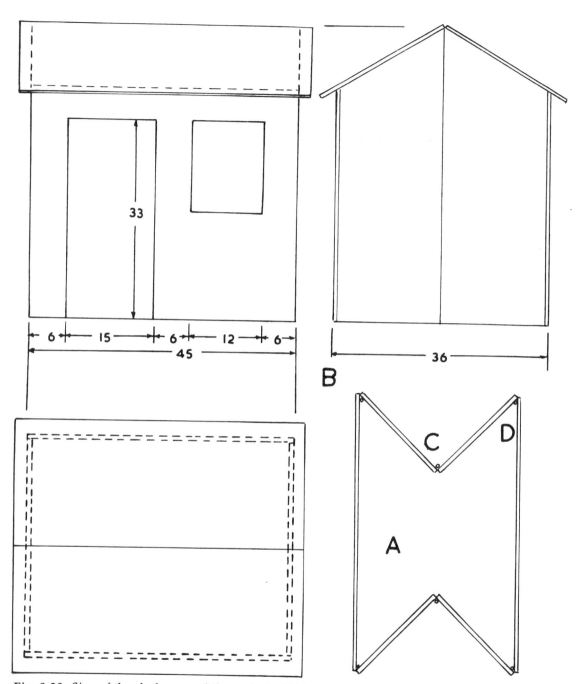

Fig. 9-29. Sizes of the playhouse and the method of folding the walls.

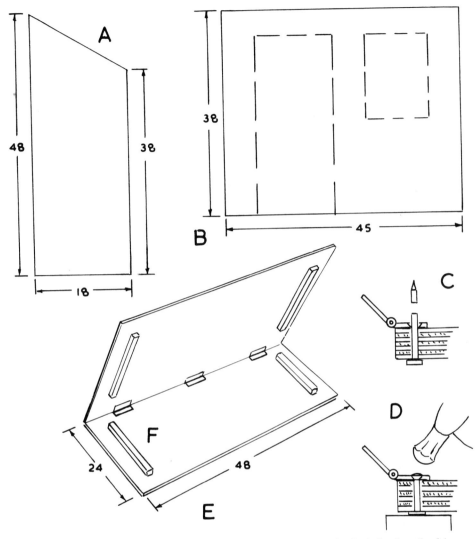

Fig. 9-30. Sizes of the folding playhouse parts and the method of riveting the hinges.

Materials List for Folding Playhouse

4 ends	18 × 48 × ½ plywood
1 front	38 × 45 × ½ plywood
1 back	38 × 45 × ½ plywood
2 roofs	24 × 48 × ½ plywood
4 roof strips	1 × 1 × 21

It should be sufficient to put three 2-inch hinges on each joint. So the parts will fold against each other, the hinges at the centers of the ends come outside (FIG. 9-28C), and those between the ends and the back and front are inside (FIG. 9-29D).

Screws probably will not hold adequately in 1/2-inch plywood. Although it might be possible to use small nuts and bolts, the neatest way of fixing the hinges is by riveting. The riveting avoids projections which could scratch young hands. You can make suitable rivets with soft-metal nails—copper is particularly suitable. Drill slightly undersize for each nail, and drive it through from the other side. Cut off the nail end to leave sufficient length to hammer into the counter-sunk hole in the hinge (FIG. 9-30C). Support the nail head on an iron block, and work around the projecting end so as to spread it gradually, preferably using a light ball-peen hammer. Try to fill the countersink (FIG. 9-30D), filing off any excess. Adjust the amount the hinge knuckle projects so the ends will open flat and the corners finish close when square to each other.

The two roof sections (FIG. 9-30E) will overlap the walls by a small amount. Hinge them together and locate them on the assembled walls so the overhangs are even. Mark the positions of the ends under the roof. Glue and nail strips to fit inside the ends (FIG. 9-30F). Their lower ends should come against the front and back, but the upper ends can be cut back about 2 inches. The roof then will hold the walls in shape. This procedure might be all you need to do, but if the child is able to push the roof, you could fit hooks and eyes outside, under the roof at the ends.

Finish the house in bright colors, with the outside walls a different color from the roof and the inside walls a lighter color. You could edge the openings with a darker color.

If you fit a door, it might be a piece of plywood hinged outside. Put a strip across a top corner inside to act as a stop. A wooden turnbutton outside will allow the child to "lock" the door when leaving the house.

Dollhouse

A dollhouse will keep a young child occupied for hours. One problem might be its size in relation to other things in the room when it is not in use. Sometimes the dollhouse is made too small, and all its furnishings have to be very tiny and fragile if it is to scale, or the dollhouse is too big to be in proportion and looks wrong. The dollhouse in FIG. 9-31 is designed to be in reasonable proportions while avoiding too great an overall size. The house is 24 inches square on a base 28 inches square, and the height is about 18 inches (FIG. 9-32A). The scale is one-twelfth, or 1 inch to 1 foot, which is a common scale for modelmaking. This means that a bed can be 7 inches × 5 inches and a table is 3 inches high, if made true to scale. There are four rooms scaled 12 feet square, which gives scope for good furniture layouts.

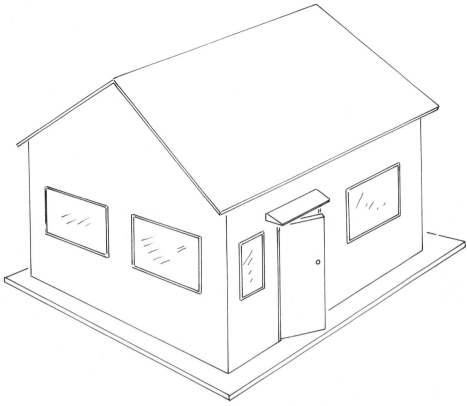

Fig. 9-31. *This dollhouse is lightweight and a convenient size.*

Materials List for Dollhouse

3 walls	18 × 24 × 1/2 plywood
3 walls	10 × 24 × 1/2 plywood
2 roofs	16 × 26 × 1/2 plywood
1 base	23 × 23 × 1/2 plywood
1 base	28 × 28 × 1/2 plywood

The method of construction is simple, using 1/2-inch plywood, with three pieces about the same size one way (FIG. 9-32) and three the other way (FIG. 9-32C). They notch together. Differences come in the window and door arrangements you choose, but overall sizes match. The roof is in two parts (FIG. 9-32D), hinged together at the ridge. The roof can turn back to give part access or be lifted off for complete access to the interior.

Make the three pieces reach the ridge. Notch them to suit the plywood thickness (FIG. 9-32E) to half the depth of the walls. Cut 1/2 inch off the bottom of the one that will be at the center (FIG. 9-32F).

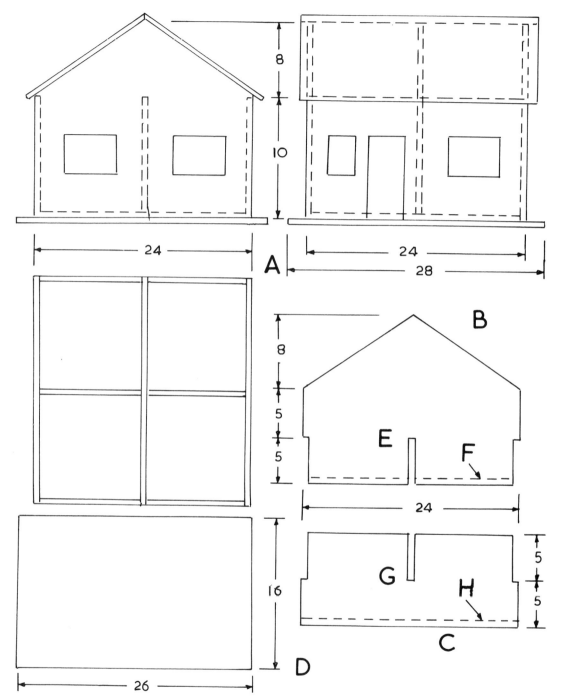

Fig. 9-32. Sizes of the dollhouse and its main parts.

Cut the three other pieces and notch them to match the first (FIG. 9-32G). Cut 1/2 inch off the bottom of the one that will be at the center (FIG. 9-32H).

Try the parts together, then cut window and door openings (FIG. 9-33A). There should be two outside doors, about 7 inches × 3½ inches, and other doors between rooms. The young owner will enjoy looking in, so provide plenty

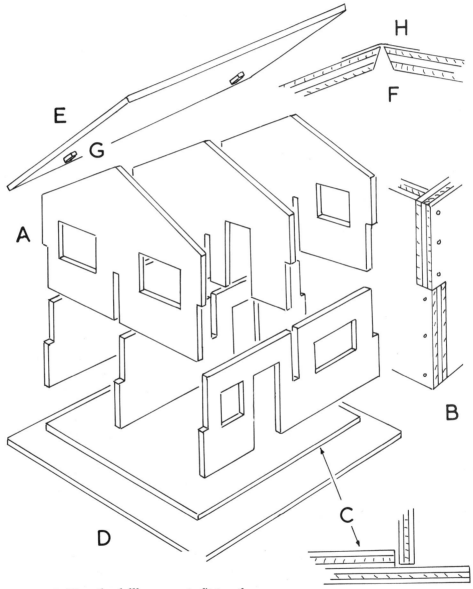

Fig. 9-33. How the dollhouse parts fit together.

of window openings in the outside walls, but leave some space for built-in furniture and pictures.

Join these parts with glue in all joints, and also drive fine nails both ways at the corners (FIG. 9-33B).

Make the upper part of the base (FIG. 9-33C) to fit easily within the outer walls. The lower part of the base (FIG. 9-33D) is shown extending 2 inches all around, but you could make a wider patio or cut the extended width to very little, if you wish.

Make the parts of the roof (FIG. 9-33E), and miter where they meet on the ridge (FIG. 9-33F). Put two small blocks on each piece to fit inside the end walls to locate the roof (FIG. 9-33G) when it is in place.

Join the roof parts with cloth or tape glued on to form a hinge (FIG. 9-33H) so it will be possible to lift one side without the other or fold the parts back when you remove them.

This completes the basic construction, but there is much more you will probably want to do to satisfy the young homeowner. Doors might be pieces of plywood, with small hinges and nails as handles. Details will have to be supplied by painting. Windows could be covered with flexible clear plastic, using fine strips as frames. It is possible to buy windows and many other dollhouse fittings to this scale. You might also be able to get wallpaper or adhesive paper to simulate roof tiles and brickwork or siding. Otherwise, you will have to paint in appropriate colors. You might wish to paint in plenty of fine detail to satisfy your own wishes or to impress other adults, but a child is concerned with practicalities and only needs basic facilities. Her imagination will fill gaps.

Children's Store

Make-believe selling groceries or other goods—or even genuine cookies or drinks—will entertain and occupy children for a long time. This store folds flat and is just about small enough to set up indoors, although it would be better in the yard. When assembled, there is a large opening with a counter at the front and shelves at the back for stock. A door at one or both ends allows entry. The sides fold, so back and front come close together for storage. The roof lifts off and is hinged along the ridge. When assembled, the roof fits over the other parts and, with the shelves, will keep the store in shape.

Construction is with 1/4-inch plywood on a framing of 1-inch square strips for most parts. The shelves and counter can be of solid wood. The bottom is open to the ground, but you could make a plywood floor to fit inside.

The general appearance is plain (FIG. 9-34), but you can decorate the store with painted signs, ornamental figures and anything you or the children fancy. An area could be left with a matte black surface for the storekeeper to chalk on details of special offers. The sizes suggested (FIG. 9-35A) will probably be acceptable, but check your available space and the heights of the children. Construction could be the same with the widely different sizes.

Fig. 9-34. This folding children's store allows make-believe buying and selling of various goods.

Materials List for Children's Store

1 front	48 × 60 × ¼ plywood
1 back	48 × 60 × ¼ plywood
4 sides	15 × 48 × ¼ plywood
2 roofs	34 × 36 × ¼ plywood
18 framing strips	1 × 1 × 50
9 framing strips	1 × 1 × 16
2 framing strips	1 × 1 × 26
8 roof strips	1 × 2 × 36
3 shelves	¾ × 6 × 48
1 counter	1 × 12 × 45
2 counter brackets	1 × 8 × 8

Mark out and cut the front (FIGS. 9-35 and 9-36A), then cut the opening. Make the back the same, but without the opening. Stiffen all edges of both pieces with strips glued and nailed on.

Make the four side panels (FIGS. 9-35C and 9-36B). Cut out the doorway (FIG. 9-36), and put a strip above it when you frame the panel. Put shelf supports on the back pair of panels (FIG. 9-36D).

Hinge the side panels to each other with the hinges outside (FIG. 9-35E). Check the folding action.

Make the shelves. Notch them around the corner framing, and make them a tight fit against the panels so they keep the assembly square.

Make the counter to fit over the edge of the front opening. Notch it so it can be pressed into place (FIG. 9-35F). (It has to be taken out for storage.) Hinge two brackets underneath (FIG. 9-35G).

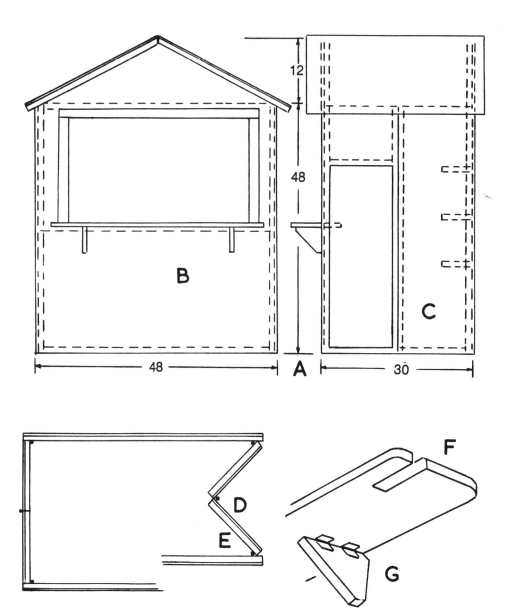

Fig. 9-35. Suggested sizes for the store and the method of folding.

Cut the roof panels so they overhang all round by the width of their 1-inch-×-2-inch framing, with a reasonable clearance for easy fitting (FIG. 9-36E). Miter where they meet at the ridge for hinging inside (FIG. 9-36F). The roof will be kept in place by its own weight.

Check folding actions, then paint all over.

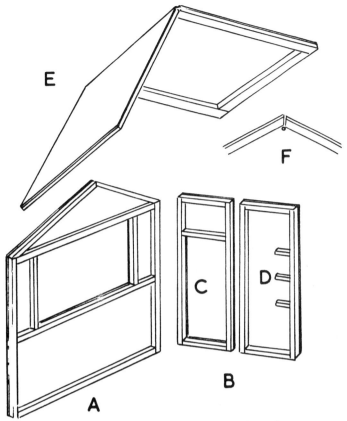

Fig. 9-36. *How the main parts of the children's store are framed.*

Rocking Duck

The various rocking toys that a child can ride on are divided broadly into those where he sits astride, and those where he has a chairlike seat. For a first rocking toy the child will probably prefer a seat and a handle to steady himself.

Many of these toys are based on a horse, but this rocker with a seat is based on a duck (FIG. 9-37). It is difficult to tip, and the rocking motion is fairly mild, to suit the younger user.

Some parts are made of ³/₄-inch plywood. Other parts can be plywood or solid wood. The seat could be upholstered, but it is shown plain. The main duck outline is the basic part; this is fitted between two footboards, which are mounted on the rockers. Projections below the central part act as stops to prevent the toy turning over endways.

Cut the central part (FIGS. 9-38A and 9-39A). Besides the duck outline, the lower part has level ends and projections below the footboard line (FIG. 9-38B).

Fig. 9-37. On this rocking duck the child sits on a seat and uses a handle, instead of sitting astride, as on a horse.

Materials List for Rocking Duck

1 main part	18 × 34	× 3/4 plywood
2 crests	8 × 12	× 3/8 plywood
1 handle	12 ×	3/4 diameter
2 footboards	3/4 × 7 1/2	× 34
2 rockers	1 × 4	× 34
2 strips	1 × 1	× 34
2 ends	1 × 2	× 18
2 seat supports	3/4 × 10	× 10
1 seat	10 × 10	× 3/4
1 seat back	10 × 10	× 3/4

At each side of the duck's head are extra pieces to form its crest (FIGS. 9-38C and 9-39B). These add to appearance, but they also give extra thickness for strength in the handle joint. Glue them on. Round all edges about the head and drill for the handle.

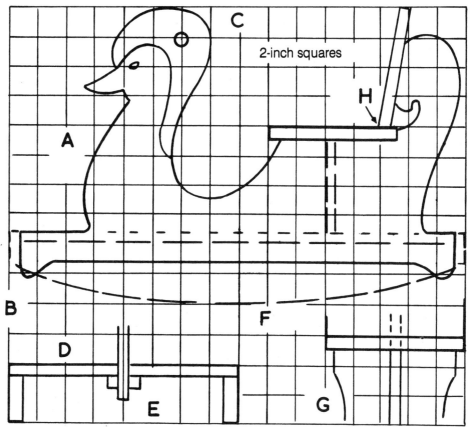

Fig. 9-38. Shapes of the parts of the rocking duck.

The two footboards (FIGS. 9-38D and 9-39C) are straight pieces. Join them to the centerpiece with square strips underneath (FIGS. 9-38E and 9-39D).

Cut the two rockers (FIGS. 9-38F and 9-39E). Screw them under the footboards, with strips across all parts at the ends (FIG. 9-39F). Check that the rockers and the duck parts are upright.

Make two supports for the seat (FIGS. 9-38G and 9-39G). Glue and screw them in place.

The seat parts (FIG. 9-39H) should be round on all exposed edges. The back fits on top of the seat (FIG. 9-38H). Glue and screw them to the supports and the center part.

The handle (FIG. 9-39J) is dowel rod with rounded ends, glued in place.

The young user will probably be glad to get on the rocking duck as it is; however, it should be painted. The duck itself might be white, with a darker color crest and eyes painted on. The other parts could be brighter, such as red or green. Nonslip plastic pieces could be glued to the footboards, and the seat could be padded.

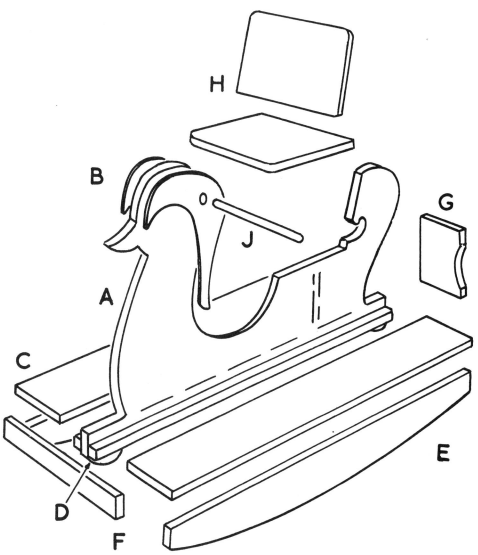

Fig. 9-39. *How the parts of the rocking duck are arranged.*

Indoor Rocker

If two children share a rocker, they can get plenty of enjoyment out of it. This rocker (FIG. 9-40) is designed primarily for indoor use, but it could be used in the yard or on a patio. It is intended for children up to about 5 years. The amount of movement is enough to provide satisfaction, but not enough to be dangerous. Stops at the ends limit movement.

Most parts are made from 1/2-inch plywood. Other 1-inch wood could be hard or soft. Construction is with glue and nails or screws.

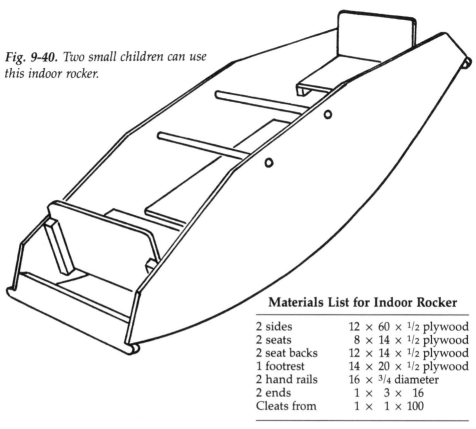

Fig. 9-40. Two small children can use this indoor rocker.

Materials List for Indoor Rocker

2 sides	12 × 60 × 1/2 plywood
2 seats	8 × 14 × 1/2 plywood
2 seat backs	12 × 14 × 1/2 plywood
1 footrest	14 × 20 × 1/2 plywood
2 hand rails	16 × 3/4 diameter
2 ends	1 × 3 × 16
Cleats from	1 × 1 × 100

Start by laying out the pair of sides (FIG. 9-41A). For the radius, make a temporary compass with an awl for center and a radius of 72 inches to the end where you use a pencil (FIG. 9-41B). Adjust the board, so the compass swings to the edge and the same distance at each end, before actually marking the curve.

With the curve marked, draw the outline of the top (FIG. 9-41C). The ends slope along the line of radius, so they point to the center used to draw the curve.

On the sides, mark the positions of the seats and footrest (FIG. 9-41D). Fit 1-inch-square cleats in positions to support the plywood parts.

Make the seats, their backs, and the footrest, all 14 inches long. Drill for the 3/4-inch dowel rod handles.

Fit all crosswise plywood parts in position, and glue the handles in their holes (FIG. 9-41E). The assembly should now be rigid, but before the glue sets, sight across the curves and tops to check that there is no twist.

Cut pieces to go between the ends (FIG. 9-41F) to provide stops, which will project 1 inch below the curved bottom edge and might project a little at the sides. Fit these in position.

Round all projecting corners, and take the sharpness off the top and all edges where a child might grasp.

Finish with bright paint. The sides could be decorated with decals.

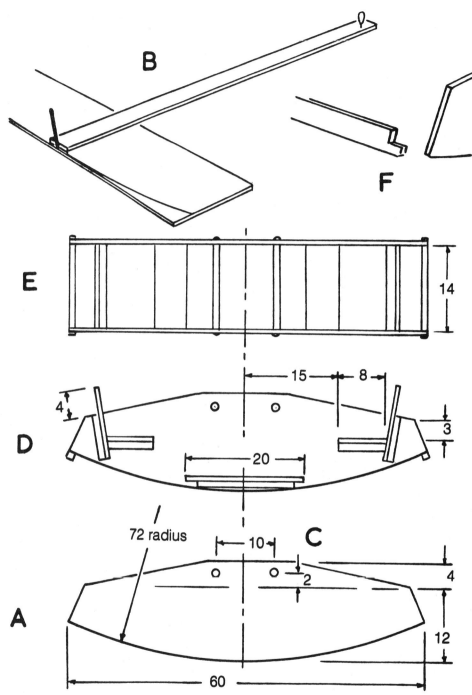

B

F

E

14

15   8

D   4   3

20

72 radius   10   **C**

A   2   4

12

60

Fig. 9-41. Marking out and laying out parts of the indoor rocker.

Step Stool

A step stool allows a child to take two moderate steps up; it permits a toddler to see what mother is doing or to reach a table or worktop without assistance. Moreover, it can be sat on with different heights to suit leg lengths. It also has play possibilities; a child can set out items on the shelves in his play store or the shelves can be somewhere to put books or ornaments when playing house. The whole thing turned on its face can serve as a broad stool or a small table. This step stool (FIG. 9-42)should be stable in use and will allow its young user to climb 10 inches in two steps.

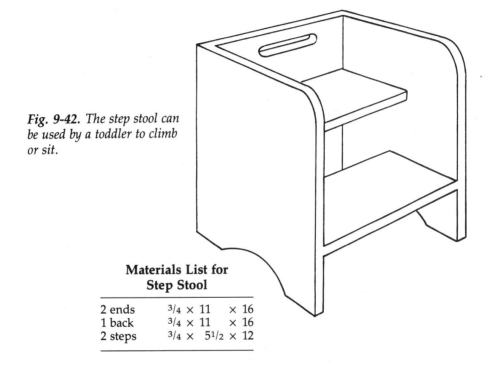

Fig. 9-42. The step stool can be used by a toddler to climb or sit.

**Materials List for
Step Stool**

2 ends	$^{3}/_{4} \times 11$	$\times 16$
1 back	$^{3}/_{4} \times 11$	$\times 16$
2 steps	$^{3}/_{4} \times 5^{1}/_{2}$	$\times 12$

The step stool is designed to be made from softwood bought as 1-inch-×-12-inch section, which in its planed condition will be nearer $^{3}/_{4}$ inch $\times 11^{1}/_{2}$ inches. Sizes can be adapted to suit your needs.

Start by marking out the pair of ends with the outlines and positions of steps and back (FIG. 9-43A). There are several possible ways of arranging construction, depending on your skill and equipment. It would be possible, but unwise, to merely nail or screw through the ends into the steps. Loads on the steps, particularly if used by adults, would soon break or split the joints. Plenty of dowels through the ends should be satisfactory (FIG. 9-43B).

Put cleats across under the steps, glued and screwed to the ends (FIG. 9-43C).

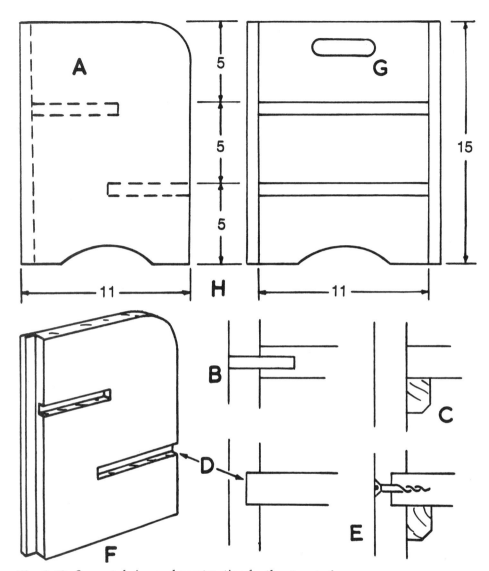

Fig. 9-43. Suggested sizes and construction for the step stool.

For added strength, cut dadoes in the ends (FIG. 9-43D). This is easy with a suitable cutter in a router, but otherwise it means careful work with a saw and chisel. The steps could have rounded fronts with a matching end on each upper dado, avoiding the need for work with a chisel after using a router. Screws through the ends supplement the dadoes. For maximum strength use cleats underneath instead (FIG. 9-43E).

The back could be put between the ends and screwed through, or it would be neater and stronger to cut rabbets in the ends (FIG. 9-43F). The top dadoes would then blend into the rabbets.

Make the back with its grain upright. Cut the hand hole (about 4 inches × 1 inch) by drilling two end holes and sawing away the waste (FIG. 9-43G). Well round the edges of the hand hole. Round what will be exposed edges in the finished assembly.

It is important that the step stool should stand without wobbling on most surfaces. With straight bottom edges it will only stand firm on an absolutely flat floor. There will be less risk of rocking if you cut curves to leave feet at the corners (FIG. 9-43H).

Smooth all surfaces and drill most of the screw holes while the wood is flat; then, assemble with glue and screws. The back and steps should pull the assembly square, but check overall squareness before the glue sets. Test on a level surface. You will be able to correct stability by planing bottom edges, if necessary.

Seal the wood with lacquer or varnish to prevent it from absorbing dirt, but a young user might prefer to have the wood painted brightly, possibly with fairy tale or other decals on the ends and back.

10

Children's Furniture

It is not always easy to define children's furniture. Some of it is suitable for adult use as well. Some is scaled down from normal furniture. It is in seating and the heights of working surfaces that most differences come. There is also the need of a parent to keep toys and all the materials needed for and by a child within bounds.

The furniture described in this chapter has been extracted from many books, although most projects as might be expected, come from *Designing and Building Children's Furniture*. There are some items which are equally suitable for adult use, either as described or increased in size, so even if you are not immediately concerned with the needs of children, you might get worthwhile ideas from some of the following projects.

Low Chair

This chair is intended to give a small child a safe seat in comfort with a tray big enough to provide a play area for toys. The size should suit a child from the time the child is first able to sit up. The footrest is located to suit the smallest child's legs, but when the child gets bigger, it can be removed so his feet will reach the ground. The chair outline is part of a square cone, so the spread of the feet on the floor is larger than the top, and the whole thing should stand firm no matter how active the young user may be.

At a later stage, with tray and footrest removed, the chair can be used by a child alongside a table. When no longer required as a seat, the back can be removed and a top added so the leg assembly then becomes part of a small table.

The design shown in FIG. 10-1 includes some simple upholstery—foam padding and a plastic covering that can be wiped clean. You can also make cushions with tapes so the padding can be removed for cleaning. So the cushions will not move, drill holes to take the tapes through the edges of the seat rails and back.

Although the chair framework slopes both ways, there are no complicated compound angles to cut. Make the two side assemblies first and join them with the crosswise parts. Although some of the wood has to be beveled, those parts that are not square all have the same bevels. One setting of an adjustable bevel will mark and test these surfaces.

Start by drawing the side view full size (FIG. 10-1A). The edges should slope inward 2 inches in the height of 20 inches. This should be the same in the other direction also (FIG. 10-1B). This angle is the one to which the adjustable bevel is set.

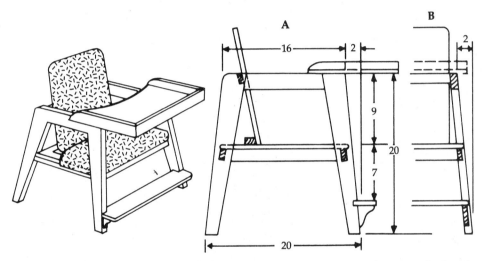

Fig. 10-1. A low chair gives a small child a safe seat. The footrest can be removed when he gets older: (A) side view; (B) opposite direction.

Materials List for a Low Chair

4 legs	3	× 22 × 1
2 top rails	2	× 12 × 1
6 rails	1½	× 20 × ¾
1 seat	20	× 20 × ½ plywood
1 back	15	× 10 × ½ plywood
1 tray	12	× 20 × ½ plywood
1 tray frame	1	× 20 × ½
2 tray frames	1	× 12 × ½
1 footrest	3	× 20 × ½ plywood
2 brackets	3	× 3 × ¾
1 tabletop (optional)	22	× 22 × ¾

The legs should taper from 3 inches to 1½ inches. Check that they match, and mark them out together from your full-size drawing. Then join the top rails to them with dowels (FIG. 10-2A). Leave some excess length on the tops of the legs to trim level after assembly.

The seat rails are better joined with mortise-and-tenon joints (FIG. 10-2B), although they can also be doweled. Assemble the two sides over your full-size drawing and check them against each other. See that they are kept flat while the glue is setting. The joints in the other directions can be prepared after the sides are completed.

In the other direction, the assembly is set to shape by the two rails under the seat and the one behind the back. Cut their ends to the standard bevel. (The lengths are indicated in the full-size drawing.) The two seat rails can be kept level with the inner faces of the legs and joined with barefaced tenons (FIG. 10-2C) or dowels (FIG. 10-2D).

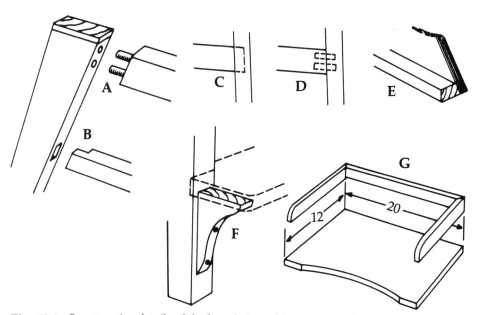

Fig. 10-2. Construction details of the low chair and its tray: (A) dowels; (B) mortise and tenon joints; (C) barefaced tenons; (D) dowels; (E) back rests on strip of wood; (F) supports; (G) framed plywood.

In this sort of joint, dowels are always fitted in line with the wood, although its end is cut at an angle. Never drill at right angles to the sloping face. The rail behind the back can be tenoned or doweled. Plane the top edges of all these rails to the standard bevel before assembly.

Next, notch the piece of plywood that forms the seat around the legs. To ensure squareness of the chair, this should be prepared and fitted at the same time as the crosswise rails, to which it is attached with glue and nails. The plywood edges overlap the rails and should be rounded. If the chair will eventually be converted into a table, the seat can remain as a shelf so it can be fastened down permanently.

The back is a piece of plywood with its top corners and edges rounded, cut to fit between the sides. At the bottom it rests against a strip of wood on the seat (FIG. 10-2E). You can put screws into the rail and the attachment to the seat so the back can be removed later for a table conversion.

The footrest is a piece of plywood notched around the legs. It does not have to bear much load, so there is no need to stiffen it. The supports underneath could be small metal shelf brackets, but wood supports are shown in FIG. 10-2F. Shape the outline so two screws can be driven into each leg, so that it is possible to remove the footrest. Leave only small holes to fill with stopping, and sand level after the parts are no longer needed.

The tray is based on a piece of plywood, framed around (FIG. 10-2G). At the side toward the child, hollow the edge slightly and thoroughly around it. The sides of the framing should taper down to the plywood and be rounded. Then join the tray to the sides with two screws into their tops. If you wish to be able to remove the tray occasionally for cleaning the chair, place a bolt at each side through the top rails, with a nut underneath. In any case, do not use glue, as the tray as well as the footrest will be removed when the child gets bigger and wants to sit at a table.

A painted finish might be best for a young child, but if the chair will be converted to a table later, it would look better if you give the leg assemblies and seat a finish to match the furniture that will be around the table. This will probably be stained, varnished, or lacquered. The footrest, tray, and back can still be brightly painted to attract the child. The tray surface can be decorated with a decal or painted design. Apply the chosen finish at this stage, even if the chair is to be upholstered.

The back is easier to upholster before it is fitted into the chair, although it can be done in position. It is best to make a trial assembly, then withdraw the screws and do the upholstering on the loose piece of wood. The bottom screws can be driven from the plywood into the supporting strip of wood, as they will not be covered by upholstery, but at the rail the screws should be from the solid wood into the plywood, otherwise their heads will be covered. The seat has to be upholstered in position.

Padding can be plastic or rubber foam, not more than $1^1/2$ inches thick. Fit a piece of vinyl or other plastic-coated fabric over the padding. Do not use a woven, porous fabric covering because it will collect dirt and be difficult to dry if it gets wet.

Most foams are soft enough to pull down at the edges, but if a piece is not, do not cut its top surface. Bevel its lower surface by cutting with a sharp, thin-bladed knife. This will allow the padding to pull to a curve with a smooth surface towards the covering (FIG. 10-3A). Trim the foam so it is slightly bigger than the area to be covered so that the covering will pull it into a neat fit.

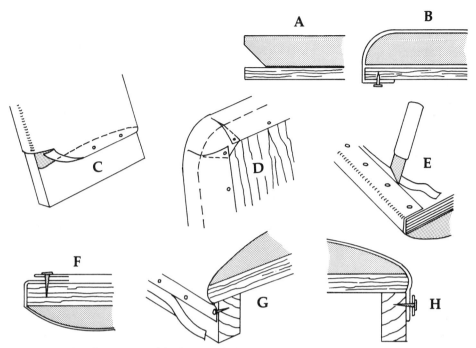

Fig. 10-3. The chair seat and back are upholstered with foam: (A) covering; (B) tacks are driven in; (C) tack front surface; (D) folding; (E) trim fabric; (F) tack more fabric; (G) drive tacks into rails; (H) covering material.

Attach the covering with tacks. On the back, the pull should be just enough to hold the padding. Drive the tacks a short distance in from the edge (FIG. 10-3B). At the bottom, turn under the covering and fit with a few tacks on the front surface of the plywood (FIG. 10-3C). At the top curved corners there will have to be some folding. Two folds at each corner will probably be enough (FIG. 10-3D).

Keep the tacks at an even distance from the edge, then trim the fabric inside them (FIG. 10-3E). For the neatest finish, use another piece of the same fabric, cut to go over the tacks and turn under, with more tacks holding it in place (FIG. 10-3F).

Notch the padding for the seat at the front corners to fit around the legs, but do not cut away very much since the covering will compress the foam. At the back it can be taken close to the plywood below the rear upholstery.

There is no space for tacking under the seat, unless the covering also goes below the rails, so drive tacks into the sides of the rails (FIG. 10-3G). At the rear edge there should be sufficient tension on the turned-in edge to compress the padding, without putting any tacks across the width of the seat. At the front corners, cut the covering diagonally across, leaving plenty of material so tension across the corners will tuck the covering over the filling and pull it down around the wood.

Trim the covering below the tacks. A decorative strip in tape form, called *gimp*, can be tacked over the cut edge, but a parallel strip of the covering material also makes a neat finish (FIG. 10-3H).

When the time comes to convert the chair to a table, remove the tray and back as well as the footrest (if it has not already been removed). Lever away the tacks holding the upholstery. A broad screwdriver is useful for this. Once a few tacks have been removed, it is usually possible to grip the covering material and jerk this away to remove the remaining tacks.

Holes can be filled with stopping, and surfaces might need a fresh coat of varnish or other finish. If the seat (which is now to become a shelf) has been left with a poor surface, cover it with laminated plastic.

The top can be round, octagonal, or square (FIG. 10-4A). It can be slightly bigger than the area outlined by the feet, but not more than a few inches, or the table would be unstable.

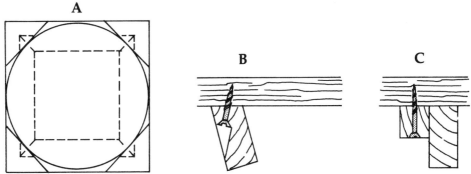

Fig. 10-4. The framework of the low chair can be made into a small table when it is no longer needed for a child: (A) top; (B) pocket screws; (C) screws through framework.

Construction could be in any of the ways described for other tables. Plywood or particleboard could be edged. Assembly will be simplest if the underside is level. Unless the chair has suffered misuse and is now unsteady, the absence of a front rail will not matter. If stiffening is necessary, screw a crossbar to the tops of the front legs. Attach the top with pocket screws upward from the insides of the side rails and from the outside of the sloping back rail (FIG. 10-4B). Another way is to fix square strips around the insides of the framework and drive screws up through them (FIG. 10-4C).

Child's Chair

A toddler can use a chair scaled down to his or her size that will stand up to rough treatment. The chair might be treated as a toy as much as a piece of furniture. The chair in FIG. 10-5 is intended to serve as a strong play seat, not as a permanent piece of living room furniture. It has arms to prevent the child falling

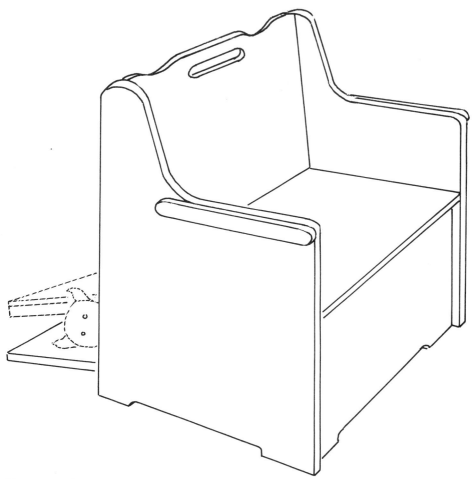

Fig. 10-5. *The child's chair has storage under the seat and a door at the back.*

sideways, and the back, which is high enough to provide support, has a hand hole for lifting. Underneath the seat is a compartment with a door at the back, which should add interest for the young user.

Construction is with 1/2-inch plywood and solid wood square strips, all glued and pinned. There is no need to cut joints between parts of the framing, all of which is hidden. Paint in a bright color would be the best finish, and you could decorate further with decals. For the smallest child, you might wish to attach cushions, which could be discarded when he gets bigger. The sizes suggested in FIG. 10-6A should suit most children.

The pair of sides are the key parts (FIG. 10-6B). Mark out their outlines, then draw on the positions of the other plywood parts. The front is set back 1/2 inch. The door at the back finishes level. Use the plywood positions to locate the strips (FIG. 10-6C).

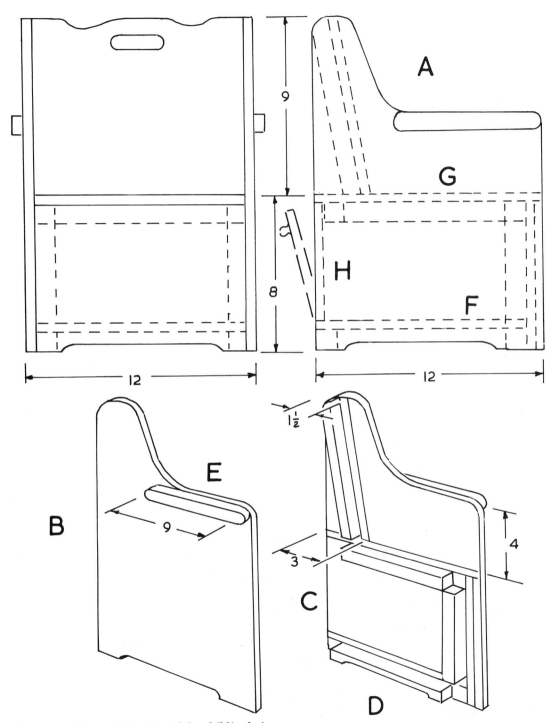

Fig. 10-6. *Sizes and framing of the child's chair.*

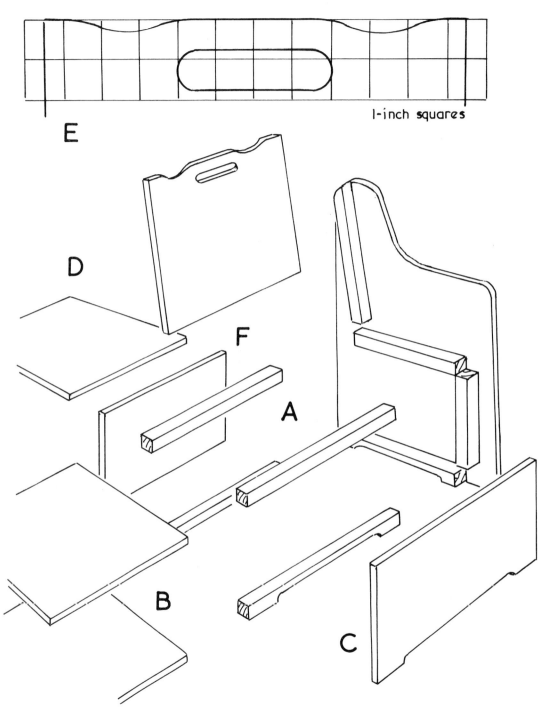

E

1-inch squares

D

F

A

B

C

Fig. 10-7. Shapes and layout of the child's chair.

Materials List for Child's Chair

2 sides	12	× 18 × 1/2	plywood
1 seat	12	× 12 × 1/2	plywood
1 bottom	12	× 12 × 1/2	plywood
1 front	8	× 12 × 1/2	plywood
1 back	10	× 12 × 1/2	plywood
1 door	7	× 12 × 1/2	plywood
2 arms	1 1/2	× 10 × 1/2	plywood
6 frames	7/8	× 7/8 × 9	
8 frames	7/8	× 7/8 × 12	

Cut away the plywood and the strips at the bottom on all four sides (FIG. 10-6D) to about half the strip thickness, so the chair only stands on its corners and is less likely to wobble on an uneven floor.

Thicken the arms (FIG. 10-6E). Well round the thickening piece and all the edges of the upper part of the chair.

Cut four crosswise strips (FIG. 10-7A) and have the bottom ready (FIGS. 10-6F and 10-7B). The bottom comes inside the front. Join the bottom and its strips to the sides.

Fit the front (FIG. 10-7C) and its strips, then the seat (FIGS. 10-6G and 10-7D), which extends the full width of the sides. Round the front edge.

Cut the back to fit in place with its lower edge beveled. Shape the top (FIG. 10-7E) and round the edge and the hole. Fit the back in place. The chair should now be rigid and able to stand level and without twist.

The door (FIGS. 10-6H and 10-7F) hinges on the bottom and closes against the upper strip. Two 1 1/2-inch hinges on the surface would be satisfactory. Fit a knob or handle near the top edge. Use a spring or magnetic catch.

Make sure there are no sharp edges or corners, then paint all over. There could be rubber pads or feet under the corners to protect carpets.

Nursing Chair

For a mother who has to deal with all the requirements of a young baby, most normal chairs are not as convenient as they could be. What is needed is a firm seat, rather lower than normal and without arms or other obstructions. This chair might not be strictly a type of children's furniture, but it is for a child's benefit as well as for the comfort of his or her mother. It might have later uses for a child to sit or kneel on when an adult chair is still too high.

This chair has a seat of normal size, arranged a few inches lower than usual, with firm legs to make it as steady as possible.

The seat and back are upholstered but not enough to impair steadiness when dealing with a baby, as a heavily upholstered seat might. A drawer is provided under the seat, to hold the many small items that a nursing mother needs. As shown, it is intended for right hand use, but it could be made to open at the left.

It could also be made double-ended, with a handle at each side, so it would slide either way. However, there is then the problem of keeping it in place, (which could be done with spring or ball catches). This would also reduce the chair strength slightly, although not enough to matter if joints are made well.

Although the chair is low and the legs are short, rails run between the back and front legs. Most strain on a chair comes in a front-to-back direction. If solid top rails were used at both sides and the drawer omitted, there would be enough stiffness without lower rails, but providing a drawer opening at one side reduces this stiffening effect and the lower rails compensate for it.

The entire structure of the chair could be doweled or mortise-and-tenoned. The sizes in the material list are for doweling, and the lengths of some parts should be increased if tenons are to be used. The only places where tenons are preferable to dowels in any case are the ends of the bottom rails. Material lengths allow for this.

Because the back legs are the only shaped parts, there is no need for a full-size drawing of the chair. Mark out the two legs together (FIG. 10-8A). The tapers start from above and below the seat rail level. Front tapers are straight. At the back, shape the wood to a curve between the upper and lower slopes, but do not make the wood there narrower than 2 1/2 inches.

With the outlines cut, mark on the positions of the seat rails and the lower rails on these legs and the front legs (FIG. 10-8B). Overall seat rail depths are the same at both sides, but at the drawer opening side, there are two narrow rails instead of the one deep one at the other side (FIG. 10-8C). Leave the tops of the front legs a little too long until after joints have been prepared.

Mark on the two back legs where the back rails will come. Their front edges should be level with the sloping fronts of the legs (FIG. 10-9A). Crosswise seat rails have their inner surfaces level with the leg surfaces so they can act as drawer guides (FIG. 10-9B). The bottom rails are better arranged centrally at the legs (FIG. 10-9C). Leave their marking out until other parts are prepared and their lengths and angles can be checked.

The seat fits into rabbets in the rails, 1/4 inch deep and 1/2 inch from the edge (FIG. 10-9D). The corners of the front legs are cut to match (FIG. 10-9E). To ensure accuracy, only partly cut away the leg tops and leave final trimming of these corner recesses until after the chair is assembled.

Temporarily clamp one side rail in position between the front and rear legs. Mark where the lower rail comes on the legs, if this has not already been done. From this mark the length and angles of the shoulders on the wood for the rail (FIG. 10-10A). Allow a further 3/4 inch at each end for tenons. Cut these mortise-and-tenon joints for both sides of the chair.

Rabbet the two back rails in a way similar to the seat rails. The ends should have three 3/8-inch dowels. The top rail should be wider to allow for curving the top edge. Also round the tops of the back legs.

Locate the dowels to miss the rabbet (FIG. 10-10B); then mark and drill the back legs before assembling the chair sides (FIG. 10-9F). First assemble the side

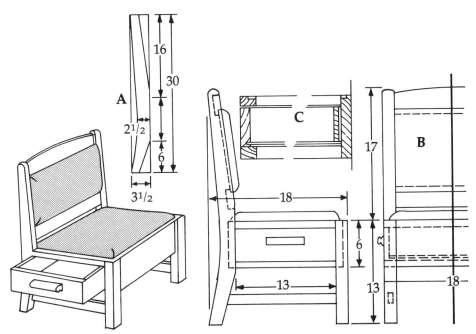

Fig. 10-8. *This low chair is intended for a mother dealing with a young baby. It has storage space in a drawer beneath the seat: (A) marked two legs; (B) marked rails; (C) two narrower rails.*

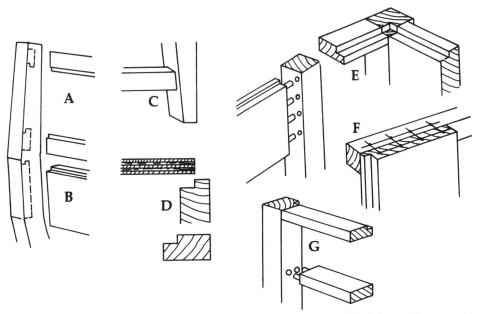

Fig. 10-9. *Chair parts are doweled together: (A) front edges of back legs; (B) crosswise seat rails; (C) bottom rails; (D) seat fits into rabbets; (E) corners of front legs; (F) marked back legs; (G) matching parts.*

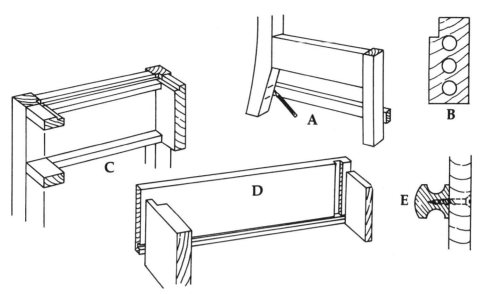

Fig. 10-10. Both sides of the chair get mortise-and-tenon joints..

Materials List for a Nursing Chair

2 rear legs	$3^{1/2} \times 30 \times 1^{1/2}$
2 front legs	$1^{1/2} \times 13 \times 1^{1/2}$
2 cross rails	$6 \times 15 \times 1$
1 side rail	$6 \times 15 \times 1$
2 drawer rails	$1^{1/2} \times 15 \times 1$
2 bottom rails	$1^{1/2} \times 18 \times {}^{3/4}$
1 back rail	$3 \times 15 \times 1$
1 back rail	$2 \times 15 \times 1$
4 drawer runners	${}^{3/4} \times 15 \times {}^{3/4}$
1 seat	$17 \times 17 \times {}^{1/2}$ plywood
1 back	$12 \times 17 \times {}^{1/2}$ plywood
2 back strips	${}^{1/2} \times 12 \times {}^{1/2}$
1 drawer front	$4 \times 14 \times 1$
2 drawer sides	$4 \times 16 \times {}^{5/8}$
1 drawer back	$3^{1/2} \times 14 \times {}^{5/8}$
1 drawer bottom	$14 \times 16 \times {}^{1/4}$ plywood

that has a solid seat rail. Assemble the other side over it to get both parts matching (FIG. 10-9G). Use a large try square to check that the front legs are upright in relation to the seat line.

Let the glue set, then clean off any surplus, and make sure none has gotten into the dowel holes that make the joints the other way. If possible, stagger the dowels in the two directions so the holes do not cut into each other, but if the dowel holes one way cut into the dowels the other way slightly, it does not matter.

Assemble the two sides to each other with the crosswise back and seat rails. Pull the parts together with bar clamps. Check squareness by standing the chair on a flat surface while measuring diagonals across the seat position and across the back. Squareness of the seat part is particularly important if the drawer is to run smoothly.

Fit strips above and below the drawer position at back and front, making them wide enough for the drawer to run on and kick against (FIG. 10-10C).

Cut the drawer front to match the opening. Cut the wood for the drawer sides to slide easily between the runners and the kickers. Groove these parts to take the plywood bottom. The drawer could be made with dovetails for the best traditional construction, but a simpler way is to rabbet the front for the sides that are screwed in. The back fits above the bottom groove in a dado which is also screwed (FIG. 10-10D).

Leave the drawer sides a little too long, so they can be trimmed to stop against the solid side rail when the front of the drawer is level with the rails at the other side. A metal or plastic handle could be used, but a wooden one screwed from the back is shown (FIG. 10-10E).

The seat is a piece of plywood that drops into the rabbets and is notched around the rear legs (FIG. 10-11A). You could drill a pattern of holes into it to allow air in and out as the seat filling expands and contracts when in use. The plywood should be a fairly tight fit after it has been upholstered so its first size should allow for the covering material that will wrap over the edges.

Covering can be over rubber or plastic foam. Keep the tacks far enough from the edge to be clear of the rabbets (FIG. 10-11B). Although the front corner fits into a right angle, take the sharpness off the plywood so it will not wear through the covering material. There is no need to cover the cut edges underneath with another piece of material.

The backboard is also a piece of plywood that fits between the sides and into the rabbets in the rails (FIG. 10-11C). Cut it to a size that allows a tight fit after the

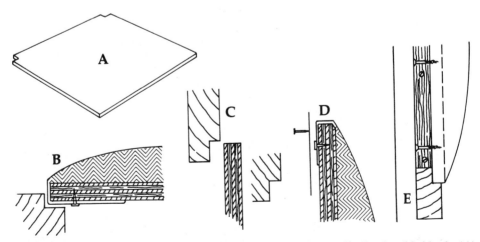

Fig. 10-11. *The nursing chair has a lift-out upholstered seat and a fitted padded back: (A) seat; (B) tack; (C) backboard; (D) thin nails; (E) square strips of wood.*

upholstery covering material has been wrapped around. Although the seat can be lifted out, the upholstered back is fixed in place.

Cover the plywood in the same way as the seat. The rear surface will be visible, though, so put more covering material on the back. If thin nails are used instead of tacks, they can come within the rabbets or under the fixing strips and be hidden (FIG. 10-11D).

Cut two square strips of wood to fit between the back rails. Screw them to the backboard and then to the legs after the board has been pressed into position (FIG. 10-11E). If reupholstery ever becomes necessary, they allow the back panel to be removed.

The woodwork should be painted, varnished, or polished before the upholstered parts are added, but remember to treat the strips that will attach the backboard in the same way. It will probably be best to make a trial assembly, then dismantle for wood finishing. The inner parts of drawers are usually left untreated.

Tilt Box

A young child is more likely to put things away in a box with an opening at the top than he is to use drawers or open a door. This unit should appeal to him because besides being a box with a lid at the center, there are tilt bins at the sides which he can draw out to put things in. Then they drop back under their own weight (FIGS. 10-12 and 10-13). It is a simple enough mechanism for the child to appreciate, as there are no knobs to turn nor levers to operate.

Construction is almost entirely in 1/2-inch plywood. With good quality plywood it will probably be sufficient to glue edges and join them with thin screws. If it is a type of plywood that tends to split when screws are driven edgewise, you can fit strips of wood around the angles in the box section to provide enough stiffening for the whole unit.

The main body is made with two spacers fitted between the sides and attached to a bottom, with all of these parts simple rectangles (FIG. 10-14A). There

Fig. 10-12. A box with a central compartment and tilting end boxes may be finished brightly to please the child or given a finish to match other furniture.

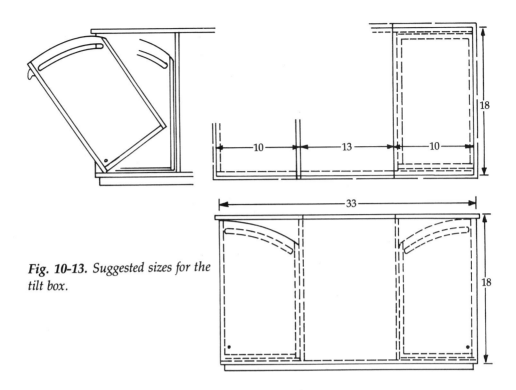

Fig. 10-13. *Suggested sizes for the tilt box.*

Materials List for a Tilt Box

2 sides	18 × 33 × $\frac{1}{2}$ plywood
2 dividers	17 × 18 × $\frac{1}{2}$ plywood
1 bottom	18 × 33 × $\frac{1}{2}$ plywood
2 plinths	1 × 32 × 1
2 plinths	1 × 17 × 1
1 top	13 × 20 × $\frac{1}{2}$ plywood
2 tops	11 × 20 × $\frac{1}{2}$ plywood
2 top bearers	$\frac{1}{2}$ × 18 × $\frac{1}{2}$
4 bin sides	9 × 16 × $\frac{1}{2}$ plywood
2 bin fronts	16 × 17 × $\frac{1}{2}$ plywood
2 bin backs	14 × 17 × $\frac{1}{2}$ plywood
2 bin bottoms	9 × 17 × $\frac{1}{2}$ plywood
2 handles	1 × 6 × $1\frac{1}{4}$

should be a strip across the top of each spacer to take the lifting lid (FIG. 10-14B) and similar pieces go around the other internal angles if necessary (FIG. 10-14C).

Make the plinth below the bottom out of 1-inch-square strips, mitered at the corners, and attach them by screwing down through the box bottom (FIG. 10-14D).

Each bin pivots on two screws or bolts. It's a good idea to make a full-size drawing of one end of the box and a bin to get the shape of the bin sides (FIG. 10-15A). Locate the center on which the bin will pivot, and draw a curve for the top edge using the pivot point as the center for compass. The stop that limits the

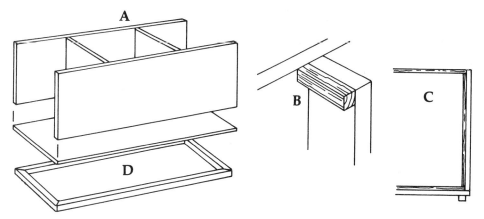

Fig. 10-14. The tilt box has a simple main assembly: (A) main body; (B) strip across the top; (C) strips at internal angles; (D) box bottom.

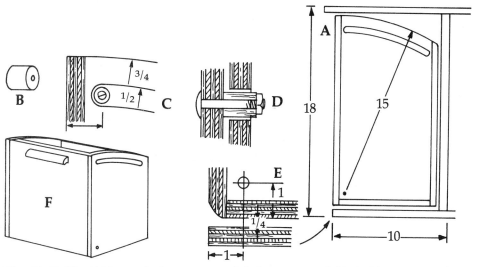

Fig. 10-15. The tilt boxes pivot on screws and their movement is limited by a stop working in a shaped slot; (A) bin sides; (B) dowel rod stop; (C) curves for slot; (D) small bolt and nut; (E) rounded bottom corner; (F) bin sides.

movement of the bin is a piece of dowel rod drilled to take a fixing screw (FIG. 10-15B). Mark where this is to come, and draw further curves for the slot (FIG. 10-15C). It might be sufficient to use wood screws, but a small bolt and nut would be better able to stand up to frequent use (FIG. 10-15D).

At the bottom there will have to be about 1/4-inch clearance and the bottom corner of the front of the bin should be rounded slightly (FIG. 10-15E). Mark the position of the pivot and stop on one actual side. Make one bin side and try its action with awls pushed through these points.

If the trial assembly functions satisfactorily, make the other bin sides and the parts to fit between them (FIG. 10-15F). Drill through for $3/16$-inch bolts at the pivot and stop positions. Make wooden handles or fit metal or plastic drawer pulls near the tops of the bins. Assemble to check the correct action, then disassemble for painting.

The top is in three parts. If you want the grain to show through the final finish, cut these parts from one piece so the grain matches. Then fasten down the two end sections permanently. The central piece fits between them. It could have a frame on the underside to fit in the opening so it can be lifted away completely, but it will probably be better to hinge it at one side, or put hinges on the surface between it and one end section so it will swing flat on to the end. If it is hinged at one side, use a strut or a cord to stop it from swinging past upright.

The top should overhang a small amount all around. Allow a little for final trimming, then assemble the three parts of the top together and trim the edges to match. They could be molded, but it should be sufficient to round the corners and take the sharpness off the edges.

This piece of furniture is probably best finished by painting in bright colors for a young child to use. However, it is the sort of thing that might have uses for other items besides toys when the child gets older, so a matching furniture finish might be more appropriate, although the first bright colors could be painted over later with something less boisterous.

Chest

This chest is a storage box that might have uses for keeping together the toys of a young child, but it is intended to be more suitable for an older boy or girl (FIGS. 10-16 and 10-17). Boy or Girl Scouts would find the box very convenient for storing the ropes and other equipment needed for their many activities. It would also be handy for packing some of the equipment needed for camping, or for a treehouse or a den in the yard. It can easily be brought into the home for storage. The chest also would be useful for tools, fishing gear, and other outdoor activity items. The top is a suitable height for a makeshift seat. It might also be used as a table by children sitting on the ground.

The main parts are plywood, but instead of being framed on the inside in the more common way, all of the framing is outside and can be regarded as a design feature. This makes for a very simple method of construction. You can use fitted joints in some places, but a nailed construction will be satisfactory. With all framing outside, the interior remains smooth. Without any fittings or projections, the inside of the box could be used like the old-time blanket chest for storing clothing, bed linen, and the like. A child might want to fill the chest with dolls' clothing and other soft items. Also, a sliding tray is shown that can be lifted out for those little children's treasures that might get lost amongst the bigger things. The end handles allow two children to drag or carry their chest.

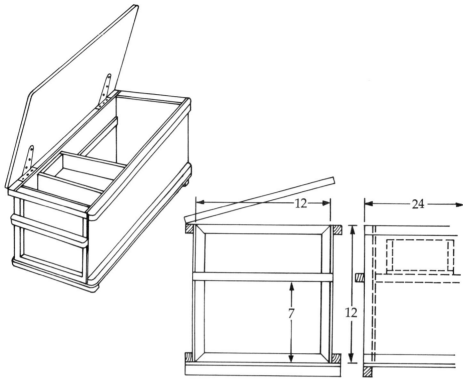

Fig. 10-16. *This storage box is made mainly of framed plywood and is fitted with 2 sliding trays and lifting handles.*

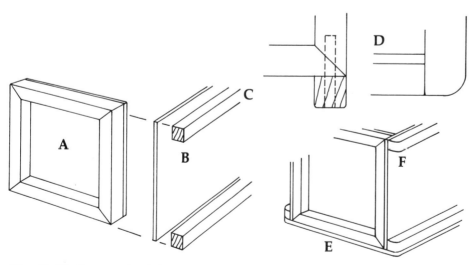

Fig. 10-17. *Constructional details of the box. Stiffened sides are fitted to framed plywood ends: (A) ends; (B) sides; (C) stiffening pieces; (D) end pieces; (E) bottom plywood; (F) rounded corners.*

Materials List for a Chest

2 ends	$12 \times 12 \times 1/4$ plywood
8 end frames	$3/4 \times 12 \times 3/4$
2 sides	$12 \times 24 \times 1/4$ plywood
4 side frames	$3/4 \times 3/4$
1 bottom	$14 \times 26 \times 1/4$ plywood
2 feet	$3/4 \times 14 \times 3/4$
1 lid	$14 \times 26 \times 1/2$ plywood
2 handles	$3/4 \times 14 \times 3/4$
2 runners	$3/4 \times 24 \times 3/8$
2 box sides	$3 \times 12 \times 1/2$
2 box ends	$3 \times 6 \times 1/2$
1 box bottom	$6 \times 12 \times 1/4$ plywood

Sizes can be schemed to cut from an available plywood panel, but the sizes shown (FIG. 10-16) are based on end panels 12 inches square and side panels 12 × 24 inches. All of the external framing is $3/4$-inch-square strips. The box plywood shown is $1/4$ inch thick, but if thinner plywood is available, the chest could be lightened by using it. The lid is a single unframed piece of $1/2$-inch plywood. It would be unwise to reduce this, as anything less might distort it.

Start by making the two ends (FIG. 10-17A). Miter the corners and glue and nail the strips through plywood. Cut the two plywood sides to the same depth as the ends (FIG. 10-17B) and attach their stiffening pieces in the same way (FIG. 10-17C), keeping nails away from the end overlaps. The stiffening pieces might be left on too long for trimming after assembly.

Glue and nail the plywood sides to the ends. The best joints at the corners are made with $1/4$-inch dowels, which should be long enough to go through the miters into the top and bottom end pieces (FIG. 10-17D). Nail and glue on the bottom plywood (FIG. 10-17E). Trim the stiffening pieces and round their corners (FIG. 10-17F), except at the top rear corners where the lid will be fitted.

The bottom is raised off the ground with strips across the ends. A simple way of attaching them would be to locate them far enough in from the ends for nails to be driven downward from inside (FIG. 10-18A), but the completed box (FIG. 10-18) is shown with them level at the ends. They can be fastened there with screws driven upward and deeply countersunk or counterbored and plugged (FIG. 10-18B). Then round the corners to match the other parts.

The tray is a nailed box (FIG. 10-18C), although the corners could be made with dovetails or other joints. Do not make the box too narrow, as a very narrow box might pull askew and be difficult to slide. A plain box might be easy for an adult to grasp and lift out, but for a child, include finger holes for lifting (FIG. 10-18D). The runners need not be very thick—one of the $1/4$-inch strips cut down the center will make both.

One type of handle that would appeal to a child might be a rope loop through a drilled block of wood at each end (FIG. 10-18E). Or there could be a strip of wood across, either screwed or doweled at the ends (FIG. 10-18F). Round the parts that will be held and locate any type of handle above the center of the end.

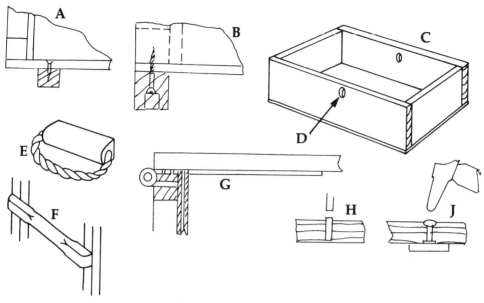

Fig. 10-18. Feet, tray, and handles are fitted to the box. The hinges may be riveted to the lid for extra security: (A) bottom; (B) counterbored and plugged; (C) tray; (D) finger holes; (E) rope loop; (F) strip of wood; (G) lid clearance; (H) countersinks; (J) cross peen hammer.

The lid is a piece of plywood that matches the outline of the top of the box. To get a close fit, leave it too big and trim the ends and front after the back edge has been hinged.

You could use ordinary hinges let into the box edge and lid, but T or strap hinges provide a stronger fastening to the wide, thin lid. The long arm goes on the surface of the lid, but the other part should be let into the box edge enough to allow the lid to close with only slight clearance (FIG. 10-18G).

Screws might hold well enough in the plywood, but a more secure way of fastening is to rivet the hinges. This can be done with stout nails of about the same size as the holes in the hinge, put through drilled holes in the plywood and cut off so enough projects to hammer into the countersinks of the hinges (FIG. 10-18H). Support the nailhead on an iron block and use a ball- or cross-peen hammer to spread the cut end (FIG. 10-18J).

Play Bench and Cupboard

If a toddler does not have some sort of center to serve as a base, toys might end up all over the house. This unit is intended to serve as a table or bench with maximum storage for toys underneath (FIG. 10-19). It could be made any size, but as shown (FIG. 10-20), the top is nearly at normal table height. If this is too much at first, the child might use a low stand on stool; then, the bench will still suit him or her later on.

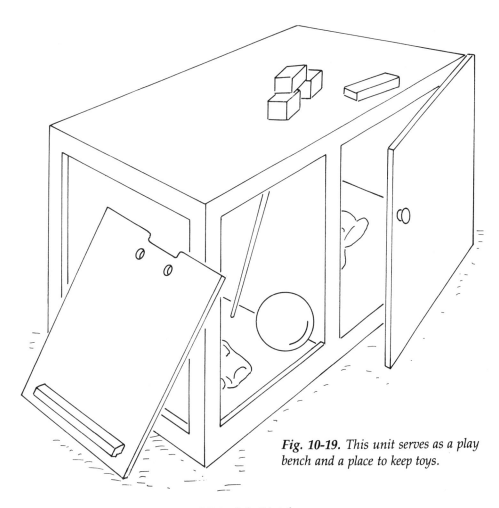

Fig. 10-19. *This unit serves as a play bench and a place to keep toys.*

**Materials List for
Play Bench and Cupboard**

2 panels	36 × 24 ×	1/2 plywood
3 panels	24 × 24 ×	1/2 plywood
1 back	36 × 27 ×	1/2 plywood
2 doors	27 × 18 ×	1/2 plywood
4 strips	38 × 2 × 1	
18 strips	25 × 2 × 1	
1 door stop	18 × 3/4 × 3/4	
1 door stop	17 × 2 × 13/4	

The accommodation is shown divided into two, with one hinged door and one that will lift out. You could fit both of the same type if you wish. The lift-out door gives clear access to the inside, while the loose door might have play uses.

Construction is of plywood framed with 1-×-2-inch softwood strips, with the parts glued and joined together. The panels can be joined with nails or screws. If

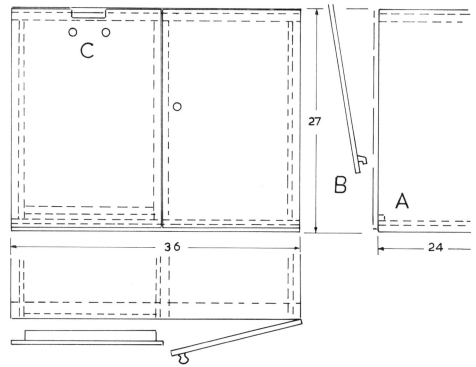

Fig. 10-20. Suggested sizes for the play bench and cupboard.

more children will follow on as the first child grows out of using the bench, it might be regarded as permanent. If not, move it for a further useful life into a storeroom or workshop. Otherwise, if the sections have been screwed together, they could be disassembled to be used in some other construction.

Softwood plywood ½ inch thick is suitable, but if you use hardwood plywood it could be thinner. A painted finish will probably appeal most to a child, so it does not matter if you mix the plywood and solid wood types.

The unit is made from two sizes of framed panels. There are two (FIG. 10-21A) for top and bottom and three for the upright parts (FIG. 10-21B)

Glue and nail strips to the panels for top and bottom. The intermediate cross-piece (FIG. 10-21C) could be at the center or elsewhere if you want the compartments to be different sizes.

Make the square panels to match the width of the long panels.

Assemble these parts with the plywood upwards on top and bottom. Have the framing outwards on the end panels; the intermediate one is better with the plywood side towards the compartment with the lift-out door.

Nail or screw plywood on the back; this will hold the assembly square, ready for leveling edges.

For the lift-out put a ¾-inch-square strip across the bottom of the opening (FIGS. 10-20A and 10-21D).

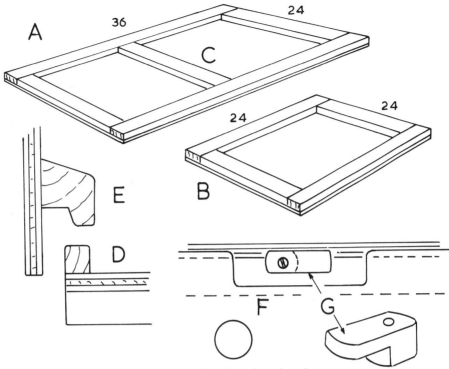

Fig. 10-21. *Details of parts of the play bench and cupboard.*

Cut the plywood lift-out door to a size that will come within $1/4$ inch of the top and bottom of the bench. Its width can reach the outer edge and halfway over the intermediate upright.

Make a notched strip to fit easily between the sides of the door opening and over the strip across at the bottom (FIGS. 10-20B and 10-21E). It has to slip over when the door is tilted, so slope the inside of the rabbet. Make this solid, or join two strips.

Cut away 4 inches long and 1 inch deep at the center of the top of this door. Round the corners and drill two, 1-inch finger holes below it (FIGS. 10-20C and 10-21F). Round all corners and edges.

Attach the strip across the bottom of the door at a height that will bring the top edge of the door to about $1/4$ inch below the top surface of the bench when closed.

Make a turnbutton (FIG. 10-21G), and position it so it can be turned both ways without obstruction. This would be better made of hardwood than softwood. Use a washer on a roundhead screw.

Make the other door to fit over the remaining space. Hinge it to the outer bench end; add a spring or magnetic catch, and a knob or handle.

If either door is not rigid enough, frame it inside with strips kept far enough in from the edges to go inside the openings.

Finish the bench with paint. A light color inside will make it easier to see what is kept there. The top might be covered with Formica. Brighten the outside with decals.

Combined Unit

Although separate items of furniture allow various arrangements in a room and it is possible to move one piece elsewhere without affecting other things, there are places where one piece of furniture combining several functions might be preferred. This applies where space is small, as a combined unit will normally take up less than several units of the same total capacity.

It is also a good idea when a child is expected to restrict his activities and toys or hobby material to a particular place. If the storage space is all in one piece of furniture, there can be no doubt where things have to be put.

The design shown (FIGS. 10-22 and 10-23) is just a suggestion. There are many possible variations. The sizes given should bring everything within the reach of a child aged about 8 years or older.

There is a main body and a front divided down the center so there are three drawers at one side and a door at the other. Both halves could have doors or there could be drawers in both halves or long drawers across the width. The top of the chest is intended to be a work surface, but at the back there is a bookshelf unit that is screwed on and could be removed. The unit is shown with one high shelf so there could be large books below it or space for large toys or construction kits.

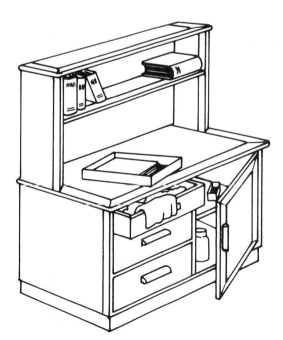

Fig. 10-22. A combined unit gets the functions of many separate pieces of furniture into a small space and gives a child a center for his play and hobbies.

Materials List for a Combined Unit

2 ends	18	× 25 ×	3/4 plywood
2 ends	2	× 25 ×	3/4
1 divider	18	× 25 ×	3/4 plywood
1 divider	2	× 25 ×	3/4
1 chest top	19	× 30 ×	3/4 plywood
1 chest top	2	× 32 ×	3/4
1 chest top	2	× 20 ×	3/4
1 bottom	18	× 30 ×	3/4 plywood
1 bottom	2	× 30 ×	3/4
2 top frames	2	× 30 ×	3/4
2 top frames	1	× 19 ×	3/4
4 drawer dividers	2	× 14 ×	3/4
4 drawer dividers	1	× 19 ×	3/4
1 shelf	14	× 19 ×	3/4 plywood
2 shelf battens	1 1/2	× 14 ×	3/4
2 plinths	3	× 28 ×	3/4
2 plinths	3	× 19 ×	3/4
1 door	14	× 23 ×	3/4 plywood
2 doors	2	× 15 ×	3/4
2 doors	2	× 24 ×	3/4
1 drawer front	9 1/4	× 14 ×	3/4
1 drawer front	7 1/4	× 14 ×	3/4
1 drawer front	5 1/2	× 14 ×	3/4
1 drawer back	8 1/2	× 14 ×	1/2
1 drawer back	6 1/2	× 14 ×	1/2
1 drawer back	4 3/4	× 14 ×	1/2
2 drawer sides	9 1/4	× 19 ×	1/2
2 drawer sides	7 1/4	× 19 ×	1/2
2 drawer sides	5 1/2	× 19 ×	1/2
3 drawer bottoms	14	× 19 ×	1/4 plywood
4 handles from 1	1	× 24 ×	1 1/4
2 bookcase sides	6	× 20 ×	3/4 plywood
2 bookcase sides	2	× 20 ×	3/4
1 bookcase top	7	× 30 ×	3/4 plywood
1 bookcase top	2	× 30 ×	3/4
2 bookcase tops	2	× 8 ×	3/4
1 shelf	7	× 30 ×	3/4 plywood
1 shelf	2	× 30 ×	3/4
Bookcase joint from 1		3/4 × 44 ×	3/4

Closer shelves could be fitted and the back might be extended upwards with more shelves—to room height, if desired. Consider how the furniture will be moved, but if the bookcase part can be taken off, it should be possible to move the parts through any doorway and around bends in staircases.

All of the major construction is intended to be in 3/4-inch plywood, with exposed edges lipped with solid wood. Plow a groove in the plywood and make a tongue in a piece of solid wood to fit in it (FIG. 10-24A). If the solid wood is made slightly too thick, it can be planed to match after gluing. Miter any corners that are exposed (FIG. 10-24B).

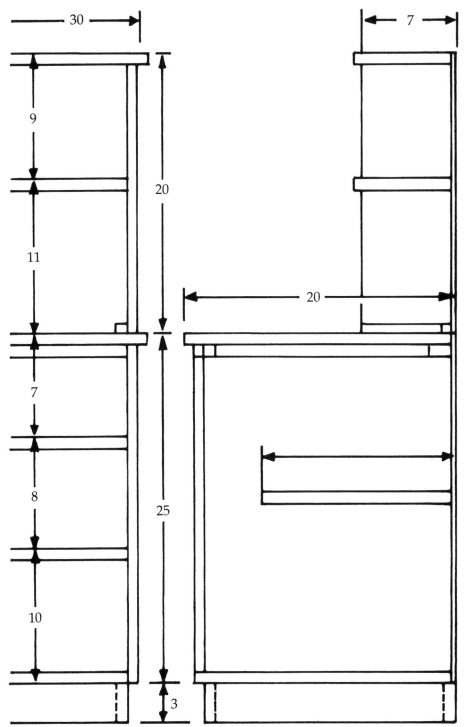

Fig. 10-23. *Suggested sizes for the combined unit.*

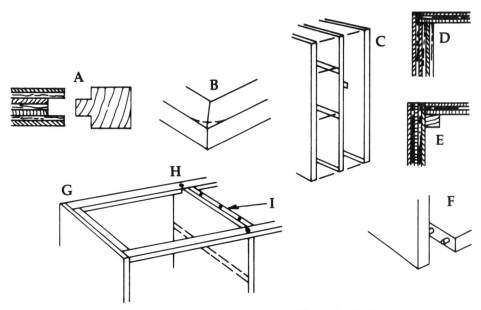

Fig. 10-24. Plywood parts should be edged with solid wood. Similar parts should be marked together. They are linked with dowels and framing: (A) plowed groove; (B) mitered corners; (C) chest divider; (D) rabbeted back edges of the ends; (E) inside strips; (F) bottom; (G) solid wood frame; (H) divider; (I) chest top.

The lipping could be treated as a decorative feature by making it in a wood that contrasts with the plywood. A dark rim to light-colored plywood looks attractive and is complementary to the otherwise rather severe lines of the design.

Prepare the pieces of plywood that have to be lipped first. The top of the bookcase and the top of the chest should be lipped at fronts and ends. All other parts that show their edges to the front—including the bookshelf, the chest bottom, and its division as well as its ends—should be lipped on those edges.

The rail under the top, the drawer dividers, and other narrow parts can be solid wood. The door and drawer fronts would look attractive lipped all around, especially if the furniture is expected to have long use and is given a clear finish.

For a painted finish, make the whole piece of furniture with the plywood edges uncovered. If care is taken to avoid tearing out the edges and they are sanded, a few coats of paint will disguise the exposed plys.

Plywood does not take well to many of the usual joints for solid wood, so it is better to use screws with their heads sunk by counterboring, then plugged in many of the main joints. There are, however, some places where dowels are more appropriate.

The chest divider and the two ends can be marked out together to get overall sizes and spacings correct (FIG. 10-24C).Cut the divider to length and mark one side of one for the drawer dividers and the other side for the shelf. The back edges of the ends should be rabbeted (FIG. 10-24D), but if there is a risk of the plywood breaking out, there can be strips inside for the plywood chest back (FIG. 10-24E).

The bottom goes right across and fits between the ends, either with screws or dowels (FIG. 10-24F). Under the top there is a solid wood frame of the same size, with its corners doweled and its ends screwed to the chest ends (FIG. 10-24G). The divider is screwed upward through the bottom and downward through the top frame (FIG. 10-24H) with a strip across it on the side away from the drawers for screwing upward into the chest top (FIG. 10-24J).

The drawer dividers are made up as frames, similar to the top frame, but fitting between the end and the chest divider (FIG. 10-25A). Be careful that corners are square, the runner parts are screwed at right angles to the front, and spaces between them are parallel (FIG. 10-25B). If a shelf is to be provided, it can rest on bearers, so it can be removed (FIG. 10-25C). The door can be hinged at either side, but unless there is a special reason for doing otherwise, it is most convenient to have its handle near the center of the chest.

The back is a piece of thin plywood. Although the bookcase part will hide its edge if taken over the chest top, it is probably better to rabbet the top, so the back plywood will not show if the chest is ever used without the bookcase (FIG. 10-25D).

The plinth comes level with the back, but is set in about $3/4$ inch at ends and front (FIG. 10-25E). Back corners can lap, but the front corners should be mitered.

All four corners can be strengthened with blocks glued inside. Attach the plinth with screws upward through blocks inside (FIG. 10-25F).

The drawers can be made in any of the ways already described. If their fronts are solid wood, dovetails will be the best joints. Otherwise a screwed lap joint

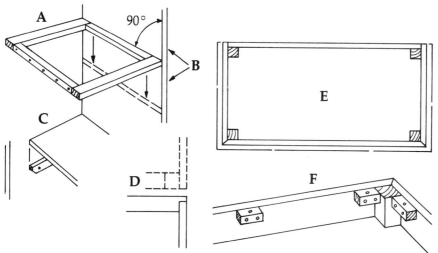

Fig. 10-25. *Assemble parts squarely. Fit the plinth with screwed blocks: (A) Dividers; (B) parallel spaces; (C) shelf; (D) edge; (E) plinth; (F) inside blocks.*

can be used. Fit stops to the front drawer rails. Choose or make drawer and door handles that match.

Next, make the two ends of the bookcase. Like the ends of the chest they should have rabbets for the back (FIG. 10-26A). The top could also be rabbeted, but as it is above the line of sight, it would not matter if the back plywood went over it (FIG. 10-26B). The top projects at the ends and front and it can be attached to the sides with screws or dowels (FIG. 10-26C). There could be, shallow dados through only one or two plys to give a positive location (FIG. 10-26D), but there would still have to be dowels or screws.

For the shelf joints, I suggest you make dadoes to resist the downward load, along with dowels or screws (FIG. 10-26E). If the front of the shelf projects the same amount as the top it can cover the dado ends (FIG. 10-26F). At the bottom of the bookcase arrange strips around the inside of the ends and back for screwing into the chest top. (FIG. 10-26G).

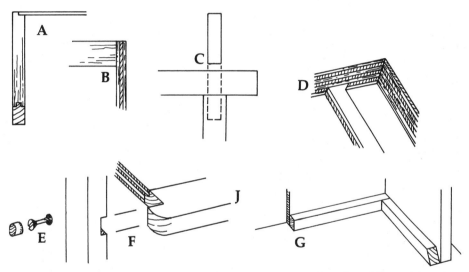

Fig. 10-26. *The bookcase is made independently and joined to the cabinet with strips of wood: (A) ends; (B) top; (C) top attachment; (D) shallow dadoes; (E) shelf joints; (F) dado ends covered; (G) strips.*

This completes the basic construction, but there are some possible modifications. For instance, there could be intermediate uprights in the bookcase to prevent partial rows of books from falling over (FIG. 10-27A). One or more drawers could be slung below the shelf for small items. The drawer can run on hooked pieces which are hidden by an overlapping front (FIG. 10-27B).

In addition, there could be racks at the back of the lower part of the bookcase for tools, paintbrushes, and similar things. One rack could go the whole width and be pierced with holes and slots (FIG. 10-27C). If it is attached by screwing through the back, it can be removed if alterations are needed.

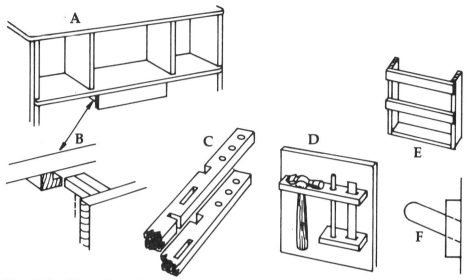

Fig. 10-27. The unit can be modified by adding partitions, a drawer and racks for tools: (A) uprights; (B) drawer; (C) pierced rack; (D) fitted rack; (E) another rack; (F) upward dowel rod.

The inside of the door can be another place for racks. Tools could have their fitted rack (FIG. 10-27D) or spring clips can be used. Another type of rack would hold flat papers, like sheet music or thin booklets (FIG. 10-27E). Coiled cord or loops of ribbon could hang from pegs. These could be pieces of dowel rod angled upward (FIG. 10-27F). Screw hooks would be better driven into a batten than directly into the door because then anything hanging would be kept clear of the door.

It is also possible to fit racks at one or both ends of the chest. There could be a rack for magazines and other flat papers. Its front might be a piece of plywood or several strips of wood (FIG. 10-28A). Another end fitting could be a towel rail made with a thick dowel rod supported in holes in blocks screwed to the chest (FIG. 10-28B). Such a rack could be doubled with lighter dowel rods into staggered holes (FIG. 10-28C).

A board for drawing or modeling could be stored on battens so it rests like a lid inside one of the drawers (FIG. 10-28D). A sliding tray or pencil rack, as de-scribed for some desks, could be fitted inside a drawer. A rack for a drawing board could go on one end.

In any place where something is to hang or fit into racks, it is a good idea to either draw the outline of it or paint its shape in a different color, so it is possible to see when the thing is not in place and the pattern there shows the child which way it has to be replaced.

There could be a mirror fitted inside the back of the bookcase, particularly for a girl making clothes for herself or her dolls.

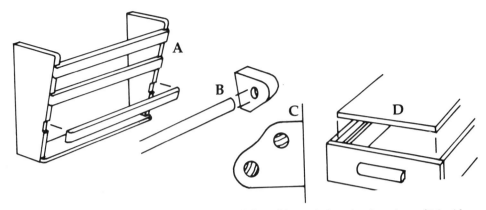

Fig. 10-28. Racks can be fitted to the ends of the cabinet. A drawing board can fit inside a drawer: (A) front; (B) dowel rod; (C) staggered holes; (D) drawing board.

Bookrack

A young child should not be expected to deal with loose bookends and he or she might not have enough books to justify a proper bookcase, but a definite place for books is helpful, both for the sake of tidiness and training in putting things away.

This rack tray is intended for a rather small number of books of the larger-page size common for children. Proportions can be altered to suit the thicker and smaller books that come later.

The bottom is a board about 12 inches longer than the thickness of the books to be accommodated. It could be raised on thin strips (FIG. 10-29A), which will give a steadier base on an uneven surface than if the whole bottom was bearing on the table. The book supports are shown rectangular with rounded corners, but they can be cut to animal designs or other outlines, providing there is enough area left to bear against the books. Notch the back into the supports (FIG. 10-29B). Then check its length against the marked positions on the base and nail or screw the parts together.

The rack would be functional as it is, but the attraction to a child would be enhanced by some decorative figures at the ends. The choice of these is almost

Materials List for
a Bookrack

Suggested sizes:

1 bottom	$8 \times 20 \times 5/8$
2 supports	$8 \times 8 \times 5/8$
1 back	$2 \times 10 \times 5/8$
2 feet	$2 \times 8 \times 5/8$
2 figures, as required	

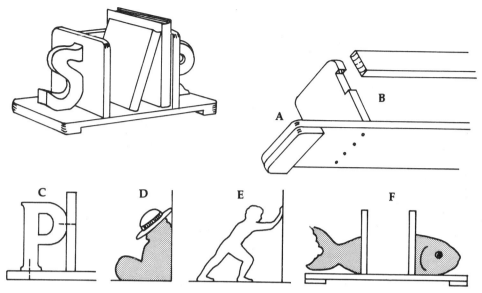

Fig. 10-29. *A bookrack can be made to hold first books and decorated with initials or other cutouts; (A) bottom is raised; (B) back is notched; (C) cutout letters; (D) cutout book character; (E) cutout figures; (F) cutout animals.*

limitless. One way to personalize the rack is to use the child's own initials, but some letters are better than others for this. Cut the letters from thick wood and attach them with screws through flattened parts (FIG. 10-29C). Other possibilities are cutouts of the child's favorite characters or something from a picture in a book (FIG. 10-29D). Whatever you choose must be made so that the flattened parts are at right angles to each other, so as to bear against the two surfaces.

Besides improving appearance, the figures serve to hold the ends upright. If figures can be made to show they are doing this (FIG. 10-29E), that will appeal to the child also. Another treatment that might amuse the child would be an arrangement where the animal or other figure appears to go through the books (FIG. 10-29F).

For a young child the rack could be finished in bright colors. As the figures will usually be in a contrasting color to the rest of the wood, first make a trial assembly, then remove the figures for painting and not replace them until all paint is dry.

Play Corner

If available space for a child's activities is limited, it is a good idea to make as much use as possible of the corner of a room. This unit has a surface at a suitable height for activities while standing (FIGS. 10-30 and 10-31). Underneath is storage space that can be open shelves, but is better enclosed with a door. There is also a tilting bin opening towards the end.

Fig. 10-30. *A unit built into a corner can combine storage with a bench top and chalk and bulletin boards.*

Materials List for a Play Corner

1 back	30	×	42	×	1/4	plywood
1 extension back	15	×	42	×	1/4	plywood
1 upright	5	×	42	×	5/8	
1 top shelf	5	×	17	×	5/8	
1 book shelf	5	×	15	×	5/8	
1 top	15	×	30	×	1/2	plywood
1 bottom	15	×	30	×	1/2	plywood
1 front	10	×	22	×	1/2	plywood
1 divider	15	×	22	×	1/2	plywood
1 door	15	×	22	×	1/2	plywood
1 door stop	3/4	×	22	×	3/4	
1 shelf	15	×	22	×	1/2	plywood
2 chalkboard frames	2	×	25	×	1/2	
2 chalkboard frames	2	×	18	×	1/2	
2 plinths	1 1/4	×	30	×	1 1/4	
2 plinths	1 1/4	×	15	×	1 1/4	
2 handles	1	×	7	×	1 1/4	
1 bin front	14	×	22	×	1/2	plywood
2 bin sides	10	×	22	×	1/2	plywood
1 bin back	14	×	20	×	1/2	plywood
1 bin bottom	10	×	14	×	1/2	plywood
1 back bin stiffener	3	×	22	×	1/2	

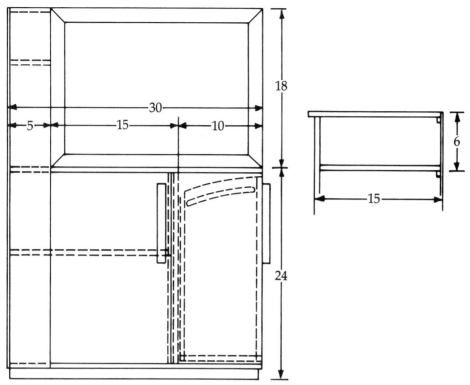

Fig. 10-31. *Suggested sizes for a play corner.*

The part of the unit in the corner extends upward with two shelves that could hold books or toys. The space below them might be used as a sort of bulletin board where the child can put his own decorations and change them around. At the back there is a framed chalkboard. This allows plenty of room for drawing and prevents damage to the wall. The whole unit could be free-standing, but a few screws into the wall would aid rigidity and prevent the child from moving the unit.

Most of the parts can be made out of plywood. For a painted finish that would hide the plys, there would be no need for lipping the edges that show. The material list does not allow for lipping, but for a clear finish, use lipped edges. Similarly, the back plywood is fitted over the edges without rabbets, but for a quality finish, you have to use some more advanced joints.

Particleboard can be used for some parts. Whatever material you use for the top, you could cover it with laminated plastic to give an attractive appearance and an easily cleaned surface.

Unlike most furniture construction, this piece is best started with the back sheet of plywood. Except for the plinth, it reaches the edges all around. Mark on it where everything else will come and it will serve as a full-size drawing for the other parts (FIG. 10-32A). If the bottom and the edge that will come in the room

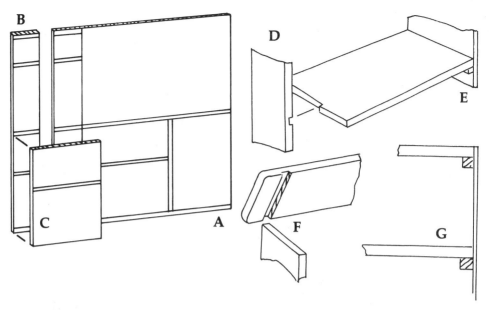

Fig. 10-32. *Check that heights match. Most parts are notched or nailed: (A) back plywood sheet; (B) front upright; (C) divider; (D) rectangular top; (E) nailed strip of wood; (F) notches upright; (G) battens.*

corner are made at right angles to each other, a little surplus can be left on the other edges for planing to size after assembly.

Mark the board that will make the front upright from the back plywood (FIG. 10-32B), and from this, mark out the divider (FIG. 10-32C). The top is a plain rectangle, except the joint to the upright ought to be a dado for strength (FIG. 10-32D). At the back it will be nailed through the plywood and supported by a strip of wood as far as the divider (FIG. 10-32E). The bottom is made in a similar way, but you can notch it around the upright without cutting that away.

At the top of the upright, the covering shelf could overhang a short distance and the upright be notched into it (FIG. 10-32F). However, a simple nailed joint would do for a less important piece of furniture. The other shelf could fit into a dado or be supported on a batten. At the back, join both shelves to the plywood with batten (FIG. 10-32G) that come against the chalkboard frame.

For the chalkboard, paint the back plywood with nongloss black or gray paint and frame around. Make the framing out of strips that have rounded edges and fit directly to the surface (FIG. 10-33A). Miter the corners. It is best to first make a trial assembly, then remove the framing for painting and leave its permanent fitting until you put the whole unit together.

The shelf will be supported on battens and its front kept far enough back to give clearance for the door. Do not notch it into the upright as this would bring its edge too far forward. Although you can attach the shelf to its battens, it might be preferable to keep it loose so it can be removed for cleaning.

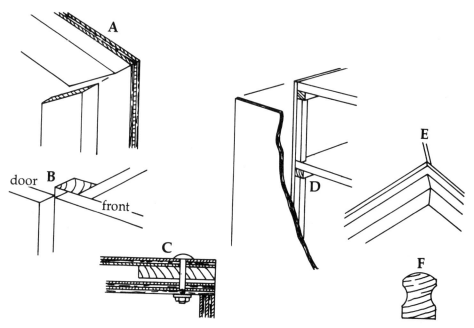

Fig. 10-33. *Door and front close level. Plywood parts are framed. Back, plinth and handle are nailed or screwed on: (A) rounded strips; (B) front overlaps divider; (C) stiffened plywood; (D) horizontal parts meet; (E) plinth (F) handle.*

The front over the bin compartment overlaps the divider (FIG. 10-33B), going partly on to a strip of wood that reinforces the joint and acts as a door stop. A similar strip could be put at the back of the divider if there is a risk of nails going through the back directly into the divider and splitting it.

The thick plywood front will be stiff enough at the bin opening without further treatment, but at the back the 1/4-inch plywood should be stiffened with solid wood wide enough to give a good overlap on the pivot and stop positions (FIG. 10-33C).

With all of the parts prepared, attach the battens and strengthening pieces that are needed at the back. Put another piece of thin plywood behind the end extension. Where the plywood overlaps the upright, nail directly, but where it meets the back plywood, put strips along the edge of the back between where the various horizontal parts come (FIG. 10-33D).

Next, assemble the top, bottom, and shelves between the back and the upright. Put in the divider and the front. With the back plywood squared, there should be little risk of the assembly being out of square, but check diagonals across the front in case there is any tendency to twist.

The door is a piece of plywood to match the front. Hinge it to the upright. Fit a catch inside, either to the shelf or to the door stop. The plinth is solid wood, mitered and attached under the bottom (FIG. 10-33E) in a way similar to earlier parts.

The operation of the bin and its construction are similar to the one already described. Measure the actual assembly and mark out a bin side. Cut this out and locate the position of the pivot point. Use this as the center for drawing the curves of the top and the slot. Try this side in position to check its clearance when it is swung. If this is satisfactory, make the other side and other parts to assemble the bin.

Upright handles are shown in FIG. 10-31. These should be the same on the door, and the bin and can be made to section (FIG. 10-33F) in a long length. Screw from inside.

Bed Tray

If the child is ill and has to eat in bed and you want to avoid spilled food and drink, there has to be something rigid on which to put things. This tray or table stands on legs far enough apart to straddle the legs of anyone in bed and rest on the comparatively steady mattress (FIG. 10-34). The size is sufficient to allow leg movement without tipping the table, and the same item could be used by an adult.

The legs of the table fold inward so the folded thickness is less than 3 inches for storage. The tray can be carried with the legs folded and opened when it is put in position on the bed. If the sizes are altered, they must be arranged so there is space for both sets of legs to fold inward without interfering with each other. The distance between the legs must be slightly more than double the leg length.

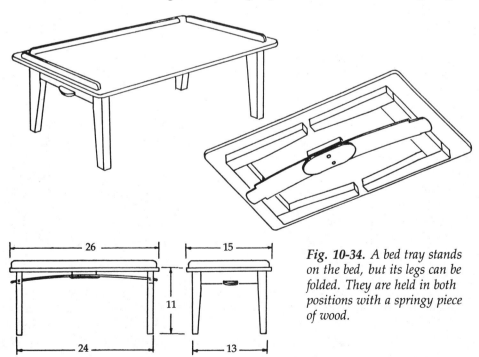

Fig. 10-34. A bed tray stands on the bed, but its legs can be folded. They are held in both positions with a springy piece of wood.

It will help visualize sizes if you draw one corner full-size (FIG. 10-35A). The legs should be set in 1 inch from the ends and sides of the top. The lips around the tray should come midway between the leg tops and the edge of the tray.

Join the legs at each end with a crossbar (FIG. 10-35B). The only joints to make are between these parts. You could use two dowels in each joint, but cut mortise-and-tenon joints would be better (FIG. 10-35C). Mark out the legs together and taper them to 1 inch square at their bottoms. Leave some waste wood at the top until the joints have been made.

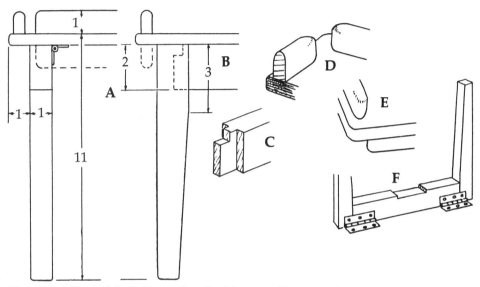

Fig. 10-35. *Sizes of the bed tray. Details of frame and legs: (A) drawn corner; (B) crossbar joins legs; (C) mortise-and-tenon joints; (D) corner connections; (E) lip piece; (F) leg assemblies.*

Carefully square the joints during assembly and check that the tops of the assemblies are both straight and with right angles between the faces, as the accuracy of the top edge controls the leg attitude when open.

The top is a piece of 1/2-inch plywood. Round its corners and angles. There could be a frame all around the top with mitered corners. It could have a long side open toward the user. In the arrangement shown, the frame is made of three lips on top. They do not meet at the corners. This allows easier cleaning (FIG. 10-35D). The long side without a lip will probably be stiff enough as it is, but there could be another lip piece put underneath (FIG. 10-35E). All of the lips should be well rounded. Fix them with glue and screws through the plywood.

The leg assemblies have hinges on the inside (FIG. 10-35F). They could be piano hinges taken across the full width or a pair of shorter hinges at each end. Do not let them in. The legs will swing clear as they are folded. Arrange the hinges so the tops of the legs bear against the tray when they are upright.

Materials List for a Bed Tray

1 top	15	×	26	×	$1/2$ plywood
4 legs	$1^{1/2}$	×	11	×	$3/4$
2 crossbars	2	×	12	×	$3/4$
2 lips	1	×	25	×	$1/2$
2 lips	1	×	14	×	$1/2$
1 spring	3	×	26	×	$1/4$
1 packing	3	×	6	×	$1/2$
1 stiffener	3	×	6	×	$1/4$

Locking the legs in position is done with a springy piece of wood. The amount of spring needed is not excessive and there are several hardwoods that could be used, but something with known springy characteristics, like ash, would be best. The thickness might have to be adjusted by trial thinning of the wood to give an easier action, but $1/4$ inch should be satisfactory.

The spring piece is fitted under the tray on a packing (FIG. 10-36A). There are two screws across its center, but to spread the load on them and prevent cracking there, put a stiffener under the screw heads. This is elliptical and thinned toward the ends (FIG. 10-36B). It should be satisfactory if it is the same length as the packing, but if the spring is not stiff enough, a longer stiffener can be used. Have the spring too long at first.

Cut notches in the centers of the crossbar, $1/2$ inch narrower than the spring and $1/4$ inch deep at first (FIG. 10-36C). Temporarily assemble the table. One screw in each hinge will do. Flex the spring in position and mark where it will have to be shouldered to drop into the notches. Cut these shoulders (FIG. 10-36D), and trim and round the projecting ends (FIG. 10-36E). Note how much the notches in the crossbars should be trimmed for the spring to drop in neatly. Taper the bottoms of the notches to suit (FIG. 10-36F).

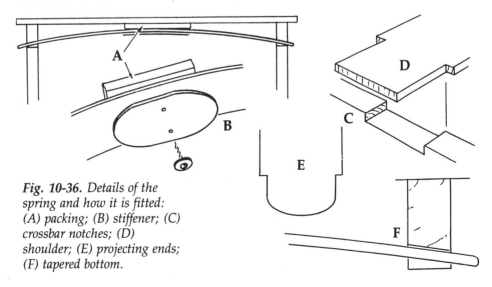

Fig. 10-36. Details of the spring and how it is fitted: (A) packing; (B) stiffener; (C) crossbar notches; (D) shoulder; (E) projecting ends; (F) tapered bottom.

Take the sharpness off any projecting edges or angles. The spring has to be lifted from each notch to allow the legs to fold, but it should then close onto them and prevent them from swinging away from the tray.

A painted finish is probably best, although the spring could be given a clear varnish treatment. There could be a picture on the surface of the tray for a young child, but it would probably be better to allow for the use of a cloth or place mat. An alternative to paint is to use plywood veneered on the surface and hardwood for the lips. A clear finish would make a more attractive piece of furniture for an older child.

Bunk Beds

If two children are to sleep in the same room it is convenient to have two identical beds that can be used independently or stacked one over the other to give double-decker sleeping accommodations (FIGS. 10-37 and 10-38). It is then possible to use both beds on the floor where there is plenty of space, or to have them in different rooms.

For convenience in getting into the upper bed there is a ladder. A safety guard can be fitted at the head end of it, assuming the other side of the stacked beds are against a wall. If not, there should be guardrails on both sides.

One bed fits onto the other with pegs or dowels projecting upward to engage with holes. Obviously the two beds must match or they cannot be joined. If the

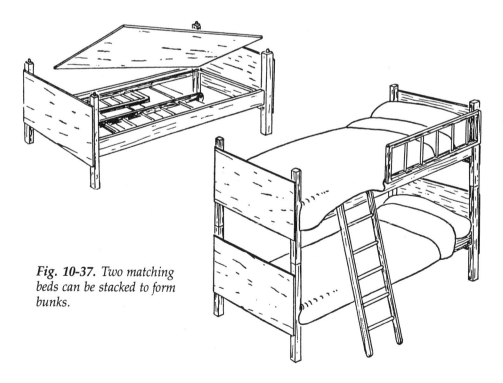

Fig. 10-37. Two matching beds can be stacked to form bunks.

Materials List for Bunk Beds

8 legs	$1^3/4 \times 34 \times 1^3/4$
8 rails	$1^3/4 \times 37 \times 1^3/4$
4 panels	$22 \times 38 \times {}^1/4$ plywood
4 sides	$5 \times 75 \times 1$
4 mattress supports	$1 \times 75 \times 1$
4 mattress supports	$1 \times 36 \times 1$
2 mattress supports	$36 \times 75 \times {}^1/2$ plywood
2 ladder sides	$1^1/2 \times 60 \times 1$
5 ladder sides	$1^1/2 \times 12$ dowel rods
8 pegs	${}^3/4 \times 3$ dowel rods
1 ladder top	$1 \times 14 \times {}^1/2$
2 safety guards	$1^1/2 \times 36 \times 1^1/2$
2 safety guards	$1^1/2 \times 13 \times 1^1/2$
5 safety guards	${}^1/2 \times 12$ dowel rods

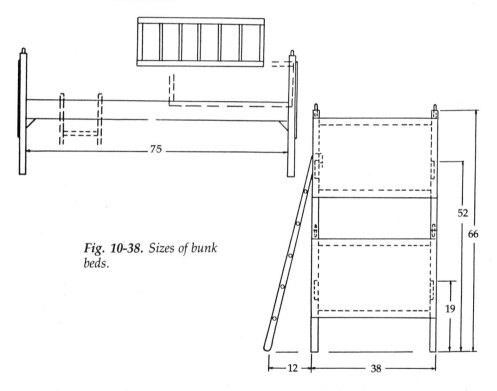

Fig. 10-38. *Sizes of bunk beds.*

safety guard is made to fit only one bed, that should be the upper one and it need not have pegs at the top of its legs.

To make sure the beds will match, mark all similar parts for both beds at the same time and assemble the two beds in matching stages, rather than completing one before the other.

Sizes are intended for mattresses of standard length and 36-inch widths (FIG. 10-38), but the two mattresses should be obtained first and measured before marking out wood. There should be enough clearance for bed-making, but make sure the mattresses are not too loose or there will be a risk of a restless sleeper twisting the mattress in relation to the bed.

All four end frames are made in the same manner. Join the legs by rails and put plywood panels on the surface. Make all eight legs first (FIG. 10-39A). Note that the tops of the legs or posts stand above the top rails and the lower rails are below the level of the bed sides. The rails could be joined to the legs with single $3/4$-inch dowels, but tenons would be stronger (FIG. 10-39B).

Drill the tops and bottoms of the legs for hardwood dowels—$3/4$ inch in diameter should be satisfactory. For the sake of appearance, you can taper the squares to round. Draw a circle, then chisel and sand the shapes (FIG. 10-39C). The dowels should go about $1^1/2$ inches into each leg and the projecting top should be rounded to ease assembly (FIG. 10-39D). If a lathe is available, you can give the end a slight taper as well (FIG. 10-39E).

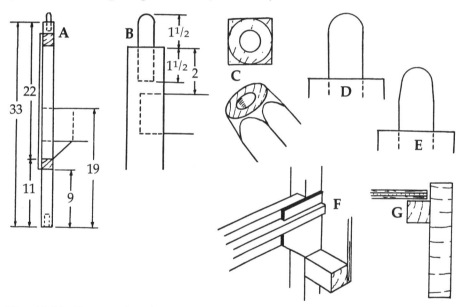

Fig. 10-39. *Construction of bunk beds and the arrangement of dowels for joining them: (A) legs; (B) tenons; (C) sand shapes; (D) rounded projecting top; (E) tapered end; (F) plywood gussets; (G) inside strips.*

The bed sides should have their inner surfaces level with the inner edges of the legs. You can dowel or tenon into the legs and then place plywood gussets on the inner surfaces to provide extra bracing (FIG. 10-39F). Glue and screw the gussets after attaching the bed sides to the legs.

It would be possible to use rubber webbing, but to keep the beds light for lifting, you can drill the plywood mattress supports with a pattern of holes and support them on strips inside the sides and ends (FIG. 10-39G). The plywood need not be fastened down.

Attach the end plywood panels to the bed ends with glue and nails, the nails punching below the surface and then covering them with stopping. Round all exposed edges. When the two beds are stacked, they should hold together safely without further fastening, but if you want additional security, you could add fasteners of the hook-and-screw-eye-type joining one leg to the other at each corner.

The ladder is intended to slope (FIG. 10-38) and hook over the side of the upper bed. Its length is best determined by putting the wood for one side against the stacked beds and marking the top edge when the slope is satisfactory.

The hook over the top is made with plywood cheeks and a crossbar inside (FIG. 10-40A). This does not have to make a tight fit over the bed side. It can be loose enough to be lined with cloth. The bottoms of the ladder sides should be rounded.

Divide the distance from the bed edge to the ground equally. The child should step the same distance at the top and bottom as he does between the rungs. Spaces of about 9 inches should be satisfactory (FIG. 10-40B). The rungs can be 3/4-inch dowel rods taken right through the sides. For the strongest construction make saw cuts across the ends before assembly and drive in glued wedges across the grain (FIG. 10-40C).

The safety guard is made with its corners doweled or tenoned and dowel rods set into holes (FIG. 10-40D). The simplest way to attach the safety rod securely is to use bolts and butterfly nuts, two through the bed side and one through the post (FIG. 10-40E).

When the two beds are to be used independently, it is possible to arrange storage for the ladder and guard under the mattress support of the lower bed. Storage under the upper bed would limit headroom in the lower bed when the two are fitted together.

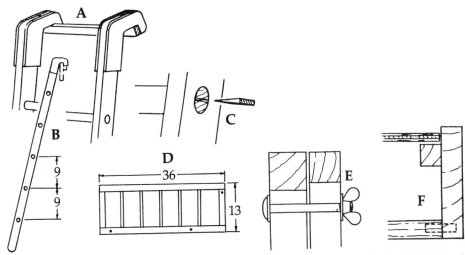

Fig. 10-40. *A ladder hooks over the top bed and a guardrail can be bolted to it: (A) hook; (B) 9 inch spaces; (C) glued wedges; (D) safety guard; (E) butterfly nut; (F) doweled rails.*

For this storage space, the mattress support must be left loose so it can be lifted out. Three rails are equally spaced in the length of the bed and fitted across between the sides. They can be doweled or tenoned when the bed is assembled (FIG. 10-40F). There will then be space for both items to be put away out of sight.

Child's Bed

When a child has grown big enough to move from a cot or crib to a proper bed, you have the problem of deciding if the bed is to be a scaled-down type or a full-size one which can be converted to adult use later on. A small bed might be the choice if there are more children following on and several years of use are anticipated. Otherwise, it might be better to have a bed long enough for later adult use.

This bed (FIG. 10-41) is designed around an internally sprung or foam mattress 36 × 78 inches. Adapt the sizes to suit whatever mattress is available. Two guards are shown to prevent a child from falling out. If the bed is to go alongside a wall, you might only need one guard. When the bed moves on to become a more adult place of rest you can remove the guards. The bed is a few inches lower than a normal adult bed. This might not matter for later adult use, but you could raise the legs on blocks, or use casters to raise the bed about 2 inches.

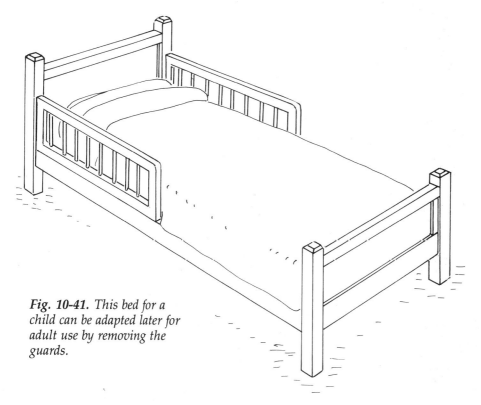

Fig. 10-41. This bed for a child can be adapted later for adult use by removing the guards.

Materials List for Child's Bed

2 legs	29 ×	2	× 2
2 legs	22 ×	2	× 2
2 rails	38 ×	2	× 2
2 rails	38 ×	4	× 2
1 panel	36 ×	13	× 1/4 or 1/2 plywood
1 panel	36 ×	8	× 1/4 or 1/2 plywood
2 bed frames	82 ×	4	× 1
2 bed frames	40 ×	4	× 1
2 bed frames	82 ×	2	× 1
2 bed frames	40 ×	2	× 1
1 bed panel	80 ×	36	× 1/2 plywood
4 guard strips	32 ×	11/2 × 1	
4 guard strips	12 ×	11/2 × 1	
10 spindles	11 ×	1/2 diameter	
6 spindles	13 ×	1/2 diameter	

The bed is deliberately plain. A child might want to stick pictures to it, paint on it, or use chalks. He or she might also treat it fairly roughly. If you keep it plain, it will stand up to hard knocks and the child's attempts at decoration, but eventually you can bring the woodwork back into presentable condition with a coat of paint. You could use hardwood and give it a clear finish, but softwood with paint might be better for a child. The panels are plywood.

The mattress fits into a frame over a piece of plywood. The head and foot are separate assemblies, so the parts can be taken through doorways or up stairs and assembled with bolts. The mattress and the plywood it rests on are also transported loose. With the mattress fitting inside its frame, there is less risk of a fidgeting child pushing all of his or her bedding over the side.

Get your mattress first, because it controls the sizes of the woodwork. They are not always exactly the size specified, so you can modify the frame to fit the actual mattress.

Make the mattress frame first (FIG. 10-42A). It is an open box with 4-inch-deep sides. Corners could be screwed, or you might use dovetails; however, finger joints screwed both ways are effective. The frame should be an easy fit around the mattress.

Put 2-inch strips (FIG. 10-42B) around the inside of the frame for the plywood to rest on.

The plywood base (FIG. 10-42C) might be a single sheet fitting in loosely, or you can use two or three pieces across. If the plywood is not very stiff, put strips across under where these pieces meet.

Air has to move in and out of the mattress if it is to function most comfortably. Put a few widely spaced, 1-inch holes in the plywood (FIG. 10-42D). Arranging them about 18 inches apart should be adequate.

The head (FIG. 10-42E) and foot (FIG. 10-42F) are made in the same way. Both have framed plywood panels, which need only be 1/4 inch thick, but you could use any plywood up to 1/2 inch. It has to fit in grooves, which might be cut right

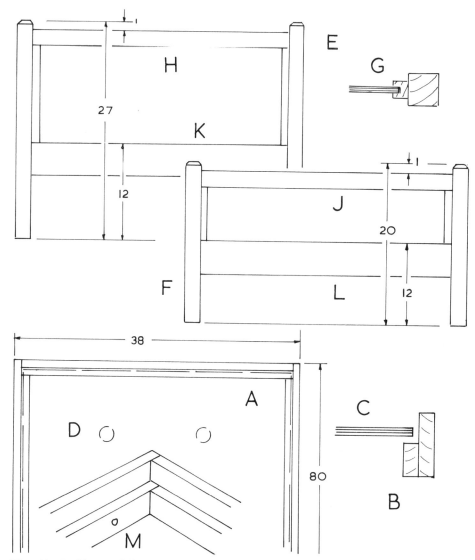

Fig. 10-42. *Sizes and details of the child's bed.*

through on the parts for the top and bottom frame. If you have a suitable router or other cutter to make a groove just for the required distance in each leg, the plywood panel can go into that. If your equipment is only suitable for cutting a groove the full length of a piece, separate grooved fillets at the legs are suggested (FIG. 10-42G).

Groove all the wood for the top and bottom tails and the fillets. The plywood should make a fairly close fit. Grooves 1/2 inch deep are suitable.

Mark all four legs with the positions of the other parts. Take care that the 4-inch strips, which will come opposite the bed frame, are exactly the same height from the floor. Chamfer the tops of the legs or decorate them in any way you wish.

Make the top square rails (FIGS. 10-42H and 10-42J) and the bottom rails (FIGS. 10-42H and 10-42L). They might be tenoned into the legs, or use 3/8- or 1/2-inch dowels, three in each joint.

Attach the fillets to the legs to come between the rails. Cut the plywood to size. Be careful that it does not reach the bottoms of the grooves, or you could have difficulty in pulling the joints tight.

Assemble both end frames. The plywood should ensure squareness, but check that the ends match.

For assembly of the bed, allow for four 3/8-inch coach bolts through the ends into the bed frame with the outer holes within a few inches of each corner (FIG. 10-42M). Place the heads outside and put large washers under the nuts inside.

After a trial assembly, separate the parts, and sand off any roughness or edges liable to splinter; then finish with paint. There is no need for any treatment on the plywood under the mattress or the inside of the bed frame.

The guards (FIG. 10-43) are added to the bed after it has been assembled in position. The guards are fairly light sections; it might be better to use the stronger hardwood frames and dowels, even if the rest of the bed is softwood.

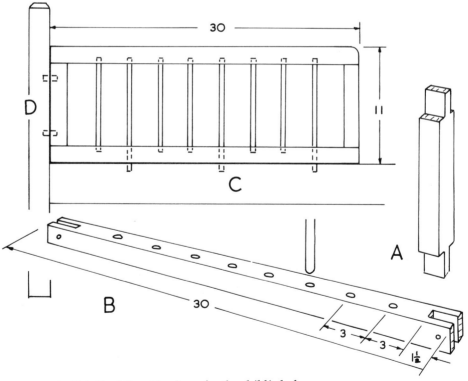

Fig. 10-43. Details of the side pieces for the child's bed.

Because of the slim sections, bridle joints make a stronger bed (FIG. 10-43A) than doweling the corners.

Spindle spacing must be close enough to prevent a child getting its head through and 1/2-inch dowels at 3-inch centers are shown (FIG. 10-43B). Drill for dowels going about 1/2 inch into each piece except that three dowels in the bottom edge of a guard go through into the bed side (FIG. 10-43C).

Fit two dowels into each upright that comes against a rear leg (FIG. 10-43D).

Assemble the two guards squarely, with projecting dowels in position. Round the outer corners and exposed edges. Corner joints can be strengthened with dowels across, if you think it necessary. You might paint or apply a clear finish before attaching to the bed. Even if the bed parts are painted, hardwood guards with a clear finish will look good.

Drill holes in the bed sides and rear legs for the guard dowels. Slacken the bolts holding the head to the bed frame; then, first glue the dowels into the bed sides and glue the dowels into the legs as you retighten the bolts. If you expect to have to disassemble the bed occasionally, leave the dowels into the legs dry.

Headboard

Although much can be done with bedside tables and racks, it is often better to include various items in a combined assembly forming the head of the bed (FIG. 10-44). If all a child should need is within reach, he has less reasons for getting out of bed, and if these things are on fixed furniture there is no risk of them being pushed about or knocked over.

In a small room, a headboard unit can take the place of several items of furniture and economize on space. A headboard can also make an attractive feature along a wall.

The headboard can be attached to the bed itself, it can be attached to the wall so the bed can be moved away from it, or it can be attached to both bed and wall, usually in a temporary manner so the parts can be moved for cleaning. Only the lighter structures are suitable for attaching to the bed. If the unit has depth, possibly enough to contain a bookrack, it might not be steady enough to stand unaided, so it must be attached to the wall. Built-in side tables or cabinets can also give the wider base needed by a deeper unit for steadiness without fastenings.

The simplest headboard is made like the headboard on the bed just described, but extended at the side enough to take shelves. That arrangement should not be made too big or the load on the screws into the bed frame will be too much. Instead, provide struts behind the board and let them extend down the legs (FIG. 10-44A). In the example, the board is a piece of plywood extended on both sides, so there can be a shelf to serve as a table on one side and racks for books at the other side (FIG. 10-44B). The sizes suit a 36-inch bed. The height might have to be adjusted according to the thickness of the mattress and bedding.

The backboard is a piece of 1/2-inch plywood supported by two struts that extend down the bed legs (FIG. 10-45A). Taper the ends of the struts and round

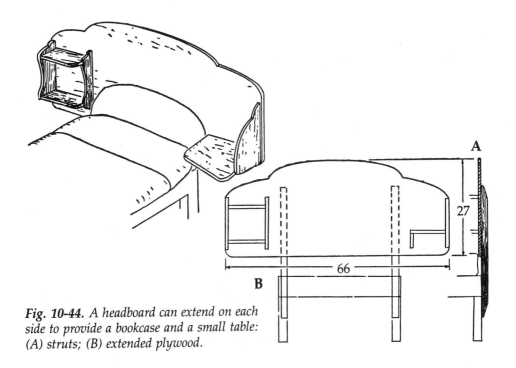

Fig. 10-44. A headboard can extend on each side to provide a bookcase and a small table: (A) struts; (B) extended plywood.

Materials List for a Headboard

1 back	27	× 66 × $^1/_2$ plywood
2 struts	$1^1/_2$ × 36 × $1^1/_2$	
1 table	15	× 15 × $^1/_2$ plywood
1 table bracket	5	× 12 × $^1/_2$ plywood
1 table bracket	12	× 13 × $^1/_2$ plywood
2 bookshelves	5	× 15 × $^1/_2$ plywood
1 bookshelf	5	× 15 × $^1/_2$ plywood
1 bookshelf upright	3	× 13 × $^1/_2$ plywood

their exposed edges as they might be pushed against or be rubbed along the wall when you are moving the bed. You might want to glue strips of foam rubber or plastic along them to avoid marking wall coverings.

Shape the top of the back with stepped curves that are carried into the brackets as well. A suggested curve for the top edges is shown in FIG. 10-46A. You can make a half paper template. Turn it over to get the back symmetrical. Round the bottom corners. For most beds it will be sufficient to cut the bottom edge straight across, but in some cases, it will be necessary to cut away the center of the bottom edge so the two wings hang lower.

The parts attached to the back are plywood as shown, but they could be particleboard with a plastic facing. If possible, make the joints to supports with dado joints. If the material you choose is unsuitable for cutting in this way, put strips

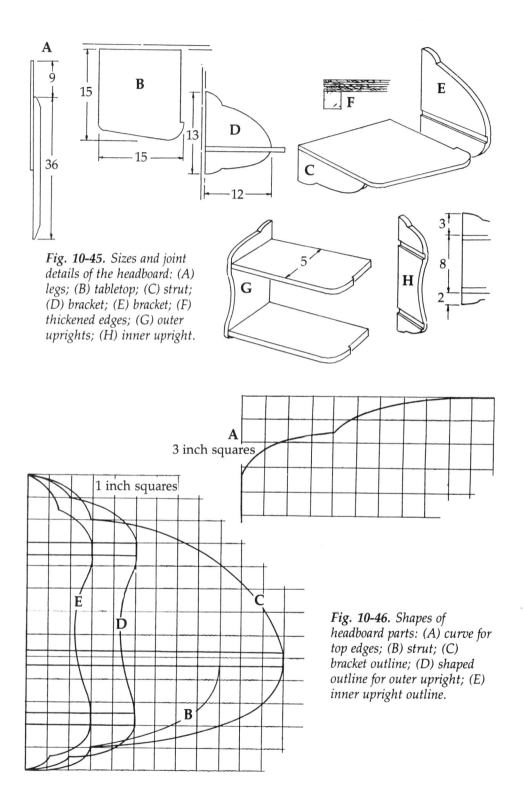

Fig. 10-45. *Sizes and joint details of the headboard: (A) legs; (B) tabletop; (C) strut; (D) bracket; (E) bracket; (F) thickened edges; (G) outer uprights; (H) inner upright.*

Fig. 10-46. *Shapes of headboard parts: (A) curve for top edges; (B) strut; (C) bracket outline; (D) shaped outline for outer upright; (E) inner upright outline.*

under the shelves, screwed both ways. The sizes for bookcase and table will give reasonable proportions, but they can be adapted to suit a particular situation.

If the bed is in a corner and the extension can only be at one side, bookshelves could be arranged above the table. Too great an extension of the table should be avoided because of the method of supporting it. A larger table would need supports to the floor.

The tabletop should taper toward the bed (FIG. 10-45B). Put a strut underneath the edge toward the bed (FIGS. 10-45C and 10-46B). At the outer edge the bracket should extend above and below the table (FIGS. 10-45D and 10-45E) with a matching outline (FIG. 10-46C). If the table is notched around it, cut a dado groove right across. If you use 1/2-inch plywood, this might not give a very secure hold for screws driven through the back, so thicken edges with strips where they will not show (FIG. 10-45F).

The bookrack has shelves of the same width, but the supports are a different width to give a tapered effect toward the bed so books are easily removed. Cut the outer upright (FIG. 10-45G) with stopped dado joints for the shelves since they are the same width. You should also give the outer a shaped outline (FIG. 10-46D). Cut the dados through the inner upright (FIG. 10-45H), and notch the shelves upright around in a way similar to the table bracket. Cut it to a matching outline (FIG. 10-46E). Thicken under the shelves so that screws can be taken through the back (FIG. 10-46F). You will have to drive screws directly into plywood in some parts of both fitments, but the main load will rest on the reinforced parts.

Folding Crib

A crib is an important item for a year or two of a child's life, then it might not be needed again for some time. It is helpful if it can be taken down or folded for storage. Being able to fold it is also useful if you want to take it with you on an overnight visit.

A crib, whether it folds or not, must be stable. A boisterous child must not be able to rock it over. He should not be able to get out. There should be no risk of him getting hurt. There must be no gaps he can get his head through. Any access arrangements have to be secure against investigating hands from inside.

Although the crib might not have long-term use, it should look good and blend with other furniture. To keep it light and of good appearance, it should be made of hardwood and given a good finish.

Sizes depend on the mattress. A common size is 24 inches by 48 inches. The mattress should be obtained first so variations of size can be allowed for. This crib (FIG. 10-47) is designed around a mattress of that size. One or both sides of the crib can be swung down for easy access. The mattress frame holds the crib in shape. When it is lifted out, the two ends fold inwards to bring the sides towards each other. Although height and length remain the same, the closed thickness is no more than 6 inches. There is no fear of inadvertent folding when the crib is in use.

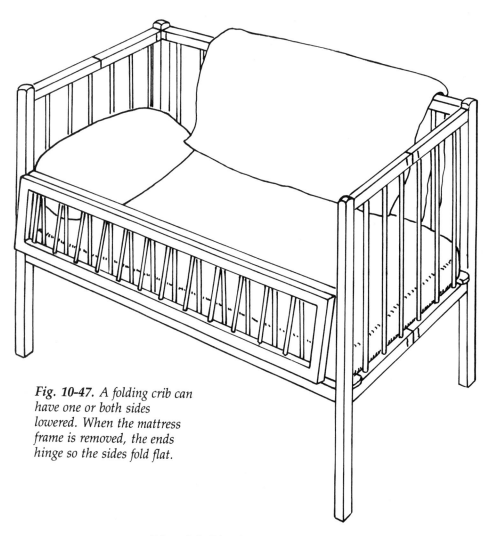

Fig. 10-47. A folding crib can have one or both sides lowered. When the mattress frame is removed, the ends hinge so the sides fold flat.

Materials List for Folding Crib

4 legs	$1^{1}/_{4}$ ×	$1^{1}/_{4}$ ×	36	
4 rails	$1^{1}/_{4}$ ×	$1^{1}/_{4}$ ×	50	
4 rails	$1^{1}/_{4}$ ×	$1^{1}/_{4}$ ×	24	
2 opening frames	$1^{1}/_{4}$ ×	$1^{1}/_{4}$ ×	14	
2 opening frames	$1^{1}/_{4}$ ×	$1^{1}/_{4}$ ×	48	
2 mattress frames	1 ×	2 ×	51	
2 mattress frames	1 ×	2 ×	24	
1 mattress base	24 ×	48 ×	$^{1}/_{8}$ or $^{1}/_{4}$	
		hardboard or plywood		
34 spindles	24 ×	$^{1}/_{2}$ dowel rods		

Most parts are made from square strips, with the upright spindles made from dowel rods. To ensure satisfactory construction, make sure all the wood sections are the same before you start.

Check that sizes suit your mattress (FIG. 10-48A). It is the inside measurement between the legs (FIG. 10-48B) that is important. The mattress frame (FIG. 10-48C) fits between the sides and its ends extend through the ends of the crib.

Mark out the four legs. If only one side is to swing open, the front legs (FIG. 10-49A) will not have top mortises. They will be joined with rails lower down. If the other side is to open, it is made the same otherwise the rails will come at top and bottom (FIG. 10-49B).

At the same time, mark out the ends of the opening frame (FIG. 10-49C).

The lengthwise rails (FIG. 10-48D) are all the same. At the ends arrange stub tenons into the legs (FIG. 10-49D). Mark all the rails together for the spindle holes, which can be at 4-inch centers. If making the crib to other sizes, do not exceed this spacing between spindles because of the risk of a child getting his head through. Use a stop on the drill press to get all holes the same depth—$5/8$ inch deep is suitable.

Cut mortises in the legs and round the leg tops (FIG. 10-49E). Join the rails to the legs with spindles between them. Check that the opposite sides match, are square, and without twist.

Make the opening frame an easy fit between its legs. Use simple tenons at the top (FIG. 10-49D), but haunch them at the bottom (FIG. 10-49F). Space the spindles to match those in the fixed part.

The two end frames are in two parts so they will fold (FIG. 10-48E), but they should be made the full width and cut apart after the spindles have been glued in. Mark the rails for six spindles equally spaced (FIG. 10-48F). To keep the rails the same distance apart as those in the unopening side, use two pieces of scrap wood as spacers while gluing in the spindles (FIG. 10-48G). Cut the rails at their centers and mark the meeting ends to avoid confusion during assembly.

Fit the hinges inside and out on the ends (FIG. 10-48E) and test the folding action. At the back, hinge to the long rail. At the front, hinge to the leg.

Make the mattress frame (FIG. 10-48C) with its sides long enough to pass through the crib ends. Make the ends of the mattress frame to hold the sides far enough apart to slip inside the legs at the corners. Join the frame parts with stub tenons (FIG. 10-49G). Round the projecting ends.

Cover the mattress frame with a wire mesh or thin plywood or hardboard. If the base is made in this way, drill ventilating holes in it (FIG. 10-49H)—1-inch holes spaced 6 inches apart should be satisfactory. Nail or screw the base to the frame.

Hinge the opening frame to the rail below it. If necessary, notch to clear the hinges on the folding ends. At its ends the opening frame can be held up with bolts on the outside (FIG. 10-49J).

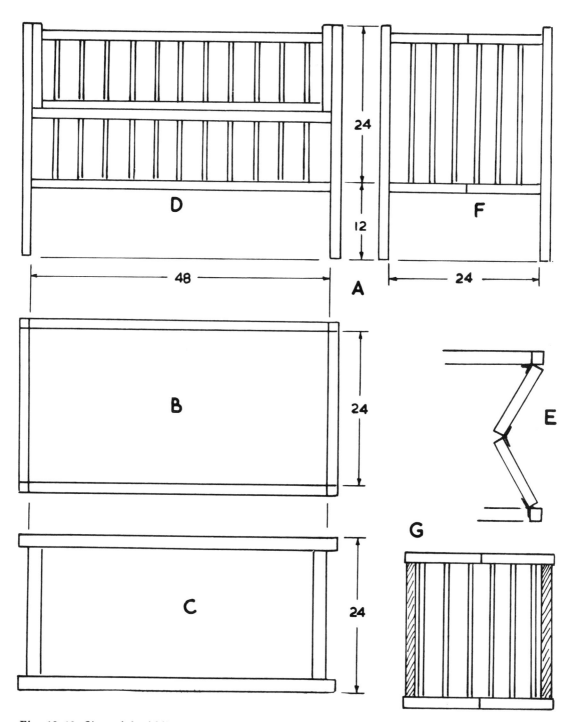

Fig. 10-48. Sizes of the folding crib parts.

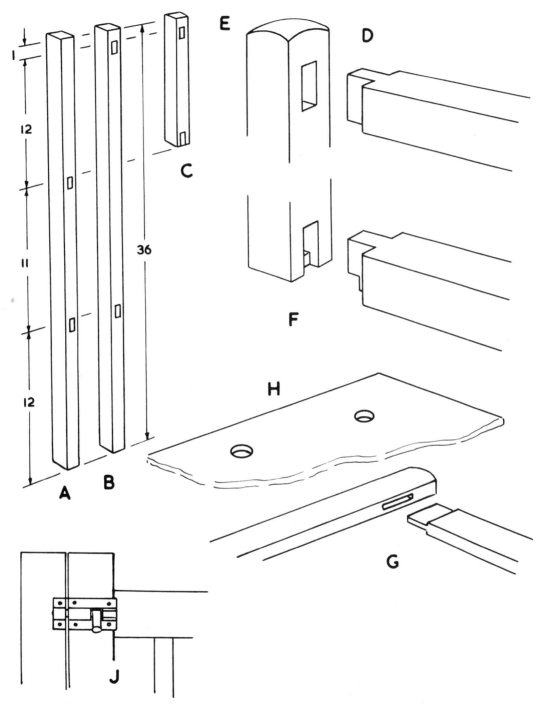

Fig. 10-49. Leg sizes and construction details of the folding crib.

Sand all parts. Take off all sharp edges and corners. The screws to the hinges should fit level and not be roughened by a slipping screwdriver. Pay particular attention to the hinges joining the ends to the inside of the legs because they will be within reach of prying hands. If necessary, file off the edges and corners of these hinges.

Take-Down Cradle

Because a small cradle is often not needed for a very long time, any simple assembly that can be reduced to a few flat pieces when not required has attractions. When it will no longer be needed, it can be taken completely apart to yield wood for other uses.

There are two plywood ends, two ladder-like sides, and a lift-out bottom piece of plywood. Assembly is with eight screws. When in use the cradle is rigid and cannot fold or collapse (FIG. 10-50).

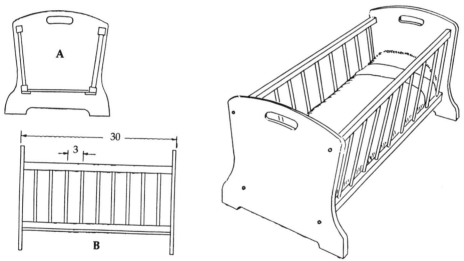

Fig. 10-50. A simple cradle with plywood ends can be screwed together so it can be taken apart when no longer needed: (A) end; (B) side.

In the illustration two are shown. The ends can be made so the cradle can be rocked, or their bottoms can be arranged so that it will stand level. Except for the variations in the bottoms, the cradles are made the same way.

Draw the end full size (FIGS. 10-51A or 10-51B). The rocking version is wider than the other, which is cut away to let the cradle stand on four feet. Hand holes can be provided for lifting. They can be hearts or the more usual cutout shape of about 5 × 1½ inches curved to match the shaped top (FIG. 10-50A). Round all external edges and inside the hand holes.

The two sides are made from square lengthwise strips. Mark these pieces together for rungs at 3-inch intervals (FIG. 10-50B). Make sure the lengths are

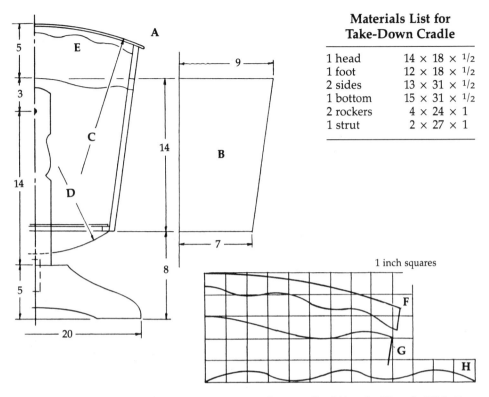

Materials List for Take-Down Cradle

1 head	14 × 18 × 1/2
1 foot	12 × 18 × 1/2
2 sides	13 × 31 × 1/2
1 bottom	15 × 31 × 1/2
2 rockers	4 × 24 × 1
1 strut	2 × 27 × 1

Fig. 10-51. *Sizes and sections of two ways to make a cradle: (A) end; (B) end; (C) bottom strips; (D) supporting strips; (E) dowel rod; (F) cup washers; (G) bottom.*

exactly the same and the rung holes are of uniform depth. Cut all the pieces of dowel rod to length. If you are marking by hand, a simple jig or stop will suffice to set the length cut.

Except for rounding the edge the top strips should be left square. The bottom strips have to be beveled (FIG. 10-51C). The angle can be found from the shape of an end, but if it is planed on a jointer, the angle is 7 degrees. Attach strips to support the bottom (FIG. 10-51D). They can finish level with the rail or have a rounded projection.

Assemble the sides. See that the rungs finish square to the rails.

If you do not expect that the cradle will have to be disassembled, the side can be doweled or screwed permanently to the ends. For disassembly it should be possible to screw and unscrew several times without the screw thread becoming worn.

There are special nut-and-bolt assemblies where one part is let into the wood to engage with the bolt, but in this case it should be possible to use wood screws. They have to go into end grain, so provide additional bite to prevent the screws from pulling out after several assemblies. This is done by putting pieces of dowel rod through the ends (FIG. 10-51E) so the screw engages across its grain.

Position the two sides on one end and pencil around the rails. Locate the screw holes through both ends centrally in each of these places. So the screws do not deface the wood when being driven and withdrawn several times, use screws with round heads over washers. Another way is to support flat head screws with cup washers (FIG. 10-51F).

The bottom is a piece of thin plywood or hardboard cut to rest in the assembled cradle (FIG. 10-51G and 10-51H). Drill a pattern ventilating holes in it. There is no need to fasten it down.

Swinging Cradle

The alternative to rocking a cradle on the floor is to hang it so it can swing. This cradle (FIG. 10-52) hangs from supports that can be disassembled when not required or when it must be transported. Hardwood is advisable. The spindles are dowel rods. The sizes suggested (FIG. 10-53A) should suit most needs. If they are altered, make the feet broader than the cradle, which should hang low below its pivot but swing clear of the bar on the supports.

The cradle itself is made with two frames with the hanging uprights, as well as dowels, connecting them. Draw the main lines of an end view (FIG. 10-53B), with the top frame 20 inches and the bottom frame 16 inches across, to obtain the angles at the sides.

Shape the top ends (FIG. 10-54A) and make two sides (FIG. 10-54B). Cut open mortise-and-tenon, or bridle, joints at the corners but tilt the sides at the angle shown on your drawing. Cut the bottom parts (FIG. 10-54C) with similar corner joints and the sides tilted. The cradle bottom could be plywood nailed underneath, but the sides might be grooved to take thin wood slats (FIG. 10-54D).

Mark top and bottom sides together for drilling to take $1/2$-inch dowel rods at $2^{1}/2$-inch intervals. At the ends, allow for the rods filling the space in a similar way (FIG. 10-53C).

Make the two hanging uprights (FIGS. 10-53D and 10-54E). Notch them and the frame ends for accurate location. The notches need not be more than $1/8$ inch deep.

Materials List for Swinging Cradle

2 top ends	$1^{1}/4$	$\times 3$	$\times 22$
2 lower ends	$1^{1}/4$	$\times 1^{1}/4$	$\times 18$
4 sides	$1^{1}/4$	$\times 1^{1}/4$	$\times 40$
38 spindles	17	$\times$ $1/2$ diameter	
9 bottom slats	$1/4$	$\times 4$	$\times 17$
2 hanging uprights	1	$\times 2$	$\times 24$
2 feet	$1^{1}/4$	$\times 4$	$\times 26$
2 posts	$1^{1}/4$	$\times 4$	$\times 32$
1 bar	$1^{1}/4$	$\times 4$	$\times 45$
3 pegs	1	$\times 1$	$\times 6$

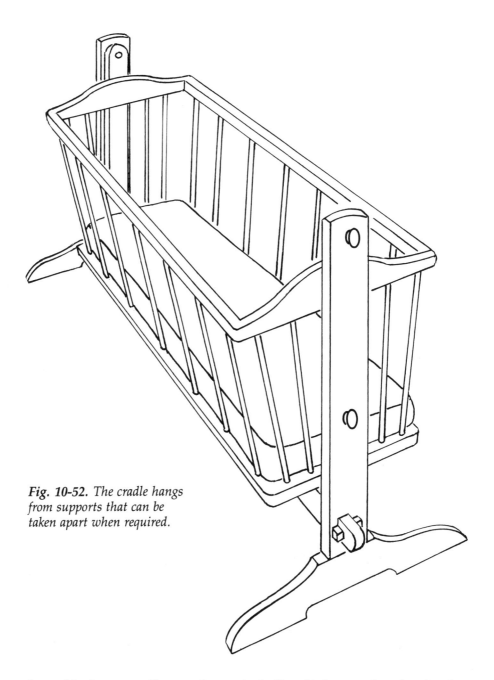

Fig. 10-52. *The cradle hangs from supports that can be taken apart when required.*

Assemble the top and bottom frames including the bottom slats. Let the glue set, then level the joints and round the edges.

Join the frames with the dowel rods and hanging uprights. Check that the assembly is square and symmetrical.

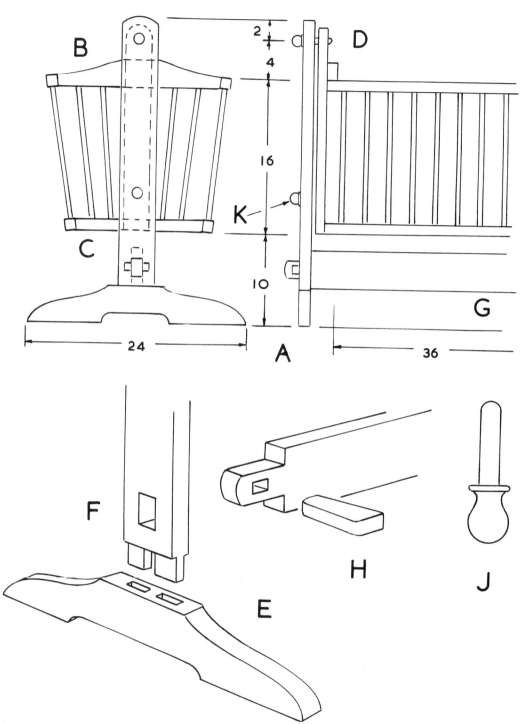

Fig. 10-53. Sizes and support joint details for the swinging cradle.

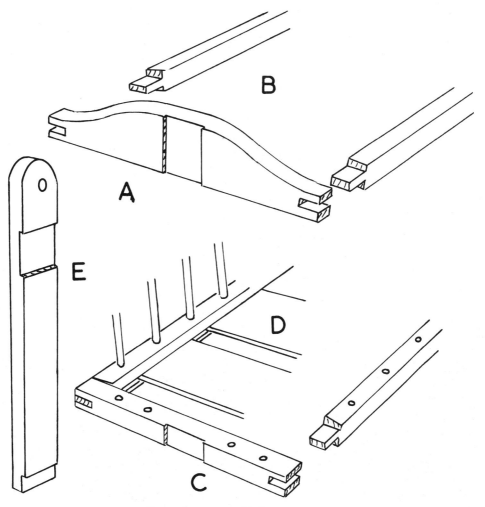

Fig. 10-54. *How the cradle parts are assembled.*

Mark out the feet (FIG. 10-53E), but leave shaping until after the joints to the posts have been cut (FIG. 10-53F). Make the bar with a length between the shoulders that will allow about 1/8-inch clearance between each post and hanging upright. Cut mortise-and-tenon joints to go through far enough to take a wedge (FIG. 10-53H).

The pivots could be pieces of 1/2-inch dowel rod, but it will be better to turn pivots with knobs (FIG. 10-53J) so they can be more easily withdrawn. When you assemble, it is worthwhile putting a fiber or fabric washer on each pivot between the wood parts.

So the cradle can be locked when it is not required to swing, you can drill a hole into both parts at one end for another peg (FIG. 10-53K), which need go only partly into the inner piece.

11

Lathework

The projects described in this chapter include parts to be turned on a lathe, either entirely or for the greater part, and they could not be made without a lathe. Because of this they should appeal to the enthusiastic wood turner and might encourage others to become interested in the fascinating work which becomes possible when you have the use of a lathe. The instructions for the last project tell you how to make a simple lathe based on an electric drill.

Some projects described elsewhere in this book include parts to be turned on a lathe, but in many cases they are only minor parts of the whole object and it is possible to substitute pieces made by other means if you do not have the use of a lathe. Some projects described in other sections which will be of interest to a turning enthusiast include:

In chapter 3—Spindle chair, Shaker rocking chair, firehouse armchair.

In chapter 6—spindle-supported shelves.

Dresser or Desk Set

There is usually a need for a great many containers of various sorts on a dresser or anywhere used as a dressing table, and all of these can he made by a wood-turner. Many similar items, although for different uses, can be used on a desk. Some of them can also be used by an artist, by anyone enjoying a hobby involving many small things, or by a cook in the kitchen. The items described here are particularly related to a dresser, but the alternative uses will be apparent.

Although you might attempt to use uniform design characteristics for the sake of a balanced appearance to the set, this is not quite so important as you might think, as the fact that everything is round may give enough similarity to make the whole collection look a set. It also helps to use the same wood throughout or stain different woods to match. For articles made of more than one part, use contrasting woods. For instance, a ring stand could have a light-colored stem, while the lower part retained a balanced visual appearance by being made of the same wood as other items.

A good close-grained hardwood with interesting grain markings would be a good choice. None of the items are large, so you might be able to find pieces of rarer woods, which are unavailable in larger sizes.

A selection of articles is shown (FIG. 11-1). You do not have to make everything at one time, but you can build up the set at intervals. However, if you are using an uncommon wood, make sure you have enough for all parts.

Fig. 11-1. Turned items for use on a dresser or desk.

Materials List for
Dresser or Desk Set

Tray

1 piece	5	× 5	× 1¹/₄

Tray/ring stand

1 piece	5	× 5	× 1¹/₄
1 piece	4	×	³/₄ diameter

Ring stand

1 piece	3	× 3	× ⁷/₈
1 piece	4	×	³/₄ diameter

Bracelet stand

1 piece	5	× 5	× 1¹/₄
1 piece	6	×	³/₄ diameter
2 pieces	3	×	¹/₂ diameter

Necklace stand

1 piece	5	× 5	× 1¹/₄
1 piece	5	×	³/₄ diameter
2 pieces	3	×	¹/₂ diameter

Ashtray

1 piece	6	× 6	× 1

Upright container

1 piece	4¹/₂ × 4¹/₂ × 1		
1 piece	6	× 3¹/₂ diameter	

The most general need is for one or more small bowls (FIG. 11-2A). You might want to make a pair at the same time. Whatever the outside shape, make the inside to a smooth curve flared outwards (FIG. 11-2B), so you can use your fingers to scoop anything out over the side. You should be able to turn a bowl on a screw center or a small faceplate. Cloth on the finished bowl will hide the hole.

A ring stand can be made to match the basic bowl. Turn it in the same way, but leave a projection at the center (FIG. 11-2C). The size of the projection depends on the stem. Rings do not have to fit tightly, so a taper from about ¹/₂ inch to ¹/₄ inch should be satisfactory. Turn the stem with a dowel to fit a hole in the bowl projection. Blend the curves of the two parts into each other (FIG. 11-2D), or turn a bead where they join (FIG. 11-2E), which will hide any slight differences in size.

The bowl below gives the ring stand a second use, but if you only need a stand for rings, fit the stem to a base (FIG. 11-3A). If you turn the whole thing in one piece, that means cutting away a lot of wood to waste. It might be better to turn the base on a screw center and the stem between centers. You could produce a pair of his-and-her ring stands.

Further developments of this design are stands for bracelets and necklaces. For hanging bracelets, the stem must be taken up to an enlarged top, into which two or three pegs are doweled (FIG. 11-3B). All of this has to be fairly slender, so it looks graceful, but the loads are light. Holes for the pegs will run into each other

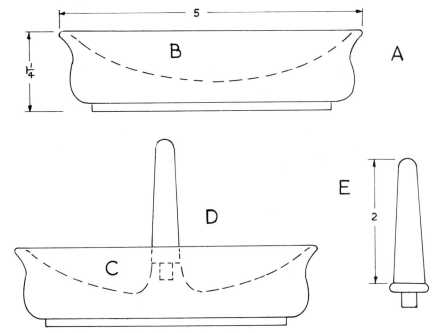

Fig. 11-2. *Sizes for a small bowl and a ring stand.*

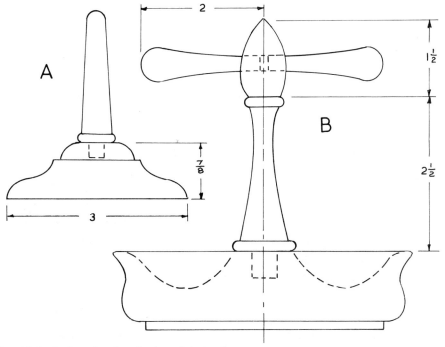

Fig. 11-3. *A ring stand and a bracelet stand.*

and need care in drilling, but when the parts are glued there will be ample mutual strength. The stem could be continued so rings can be held as well as bracelets.

A stand to hang necklaces would have to be higher than the one for bracelets. You could combine the two (FIG. 11-4). Arrange the two or three pegs at each level so they are in alternate positions. You could continue the stem to hold rings, but that would make the stand rather high. In any case, with the extra height you need the stability of a heavy base, so you could make the bowl a larger diameter, or it could be turned thicker under a shallower inside.

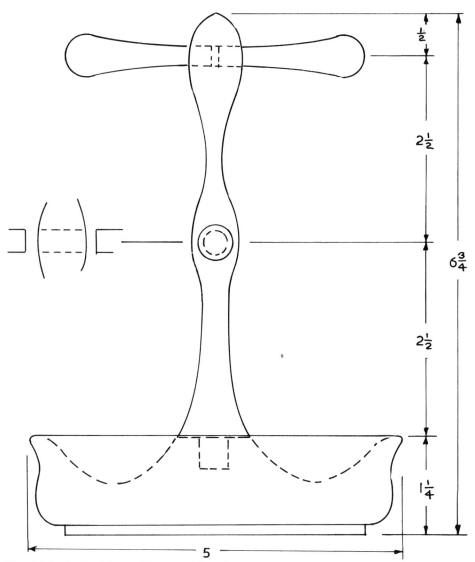

Fig. 11-4. A stand for necklaces and bracelets.

If the user of the dresser or desk is a smoker, there will have to be an ashtray. A wooden bowl would soon be disfigured by charring, so the actual tray should be metal. A simple pressed sheet-metal ashtray would be suitable for mounting on a wood base to match other articles. The size of wood will depend on the metal tray you use, but one about 5 inches across should do. It will usually have two or three grooves pressed in the flat rim (FIG. 11-5A).

The base can be a turned block with a hollow to match the tray, but there is no need for an exact fit, and the block is shown turned deeper (FIG. 11-5B). Turn the block so its outer edge curves close to the metal tray size. Use a gouge or round file to make the hollows in the wood to take the shaped tray (FIG. 11-5C). Glue the tray to the block with epoxy adhesive.

You will want one or more upright containers to hold long things, such as brushes and files on a dresser or pens on a desk. A pair of these containers will be decorative, whether you have enough things to fill them or not.

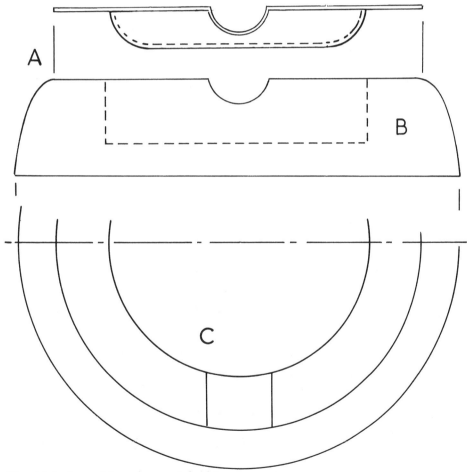

Fig. 11-5. A wood base for a metal ashtray.

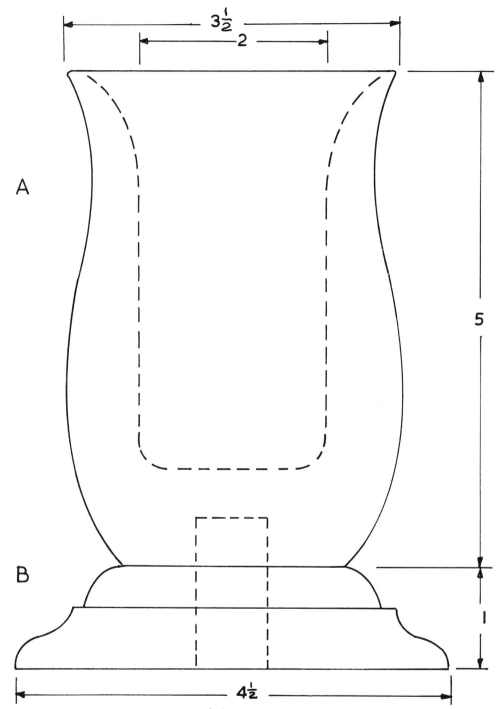

Fig. 11-6. An upright container made in two parts.

In this design (FIG. 11-6) the main container has its grain upright (FIG. 11-6A), the base can be turned with its grain across (FIG. 11-6B), and these parts are joined with a separate dowel (FIG. 11-6C). The outline of the main part matches the bowls and the base matches the ring holder.

The inside can be turned to any section, but the parallel form with a flared top gives plenty of capacity.

All of these parts should be given a finish that will withstand handling and should match in appearance. You might need to stain before polishing.

In most cases the set will be used on a polished surface. You could plug any holes and sand level, then leave the surface unpolished, but it would be better to glue on discs of felt or other cloth to reduce slipping and prevent marking the dresser or desk top.

Candlesticks

Over the centuries, some of the most attractive products of the lathe have been candlesticks in a multitude of different forms. Wood does not often endure for long periods, but there are brass candlesticks in churches and cathedrals that show their origin a great many years ago as they were cast from wooden originals. In many cases, the wooden candlestick would have been just as servicable, if not as durable, as the brass version made from it. These candlesticks provide examples of design which would still be worth following.

Candles are no longer an essential of life, but candlesticks are still sought after for their decorative value and for use as table centers on special occasions. The fashion for ornamental candles has brought a revival of interest in things to hold them, and this is an opportunity for the turner.

When planning a candlestick design, it should be related to its use. If it is only expected to be decorative in itself with possibly an occasional use with a plain candle, the design is self-contained. If a very ornate candle is to be used with it, the woodwork should be supplementary to the candle, so the total effect would benefit by having the woodwork fairly plain.

In its simplest form, the central column is turned with the socket in the same piece of wood (FIG. 11-7A). The hole in the end should suit the chosen size of the candle. It will be between $3/4$ inch and 1 inch for standard candles, but to check on locally available candles before starting work.

Make a plug to represent the end of the candle. Let this be a little longer than the socket to be drilled and retain its center hollow (FIG. 11-7B). Rough-turn the piece of wood that is to form the column; then, drill the hole for the candle using a drill in a tailstock chuck (FIG. 11-7C). Push the plug into this hole and do the rest of the turning with the plug in place (FIG. 11-7D).

Further turning is straightforward. Drill a hole in a piece of scrap wood and use this to check the dowel end of the column, either directly or by using it as a guide to caliper setting. Turn the base to match on a faceplate.

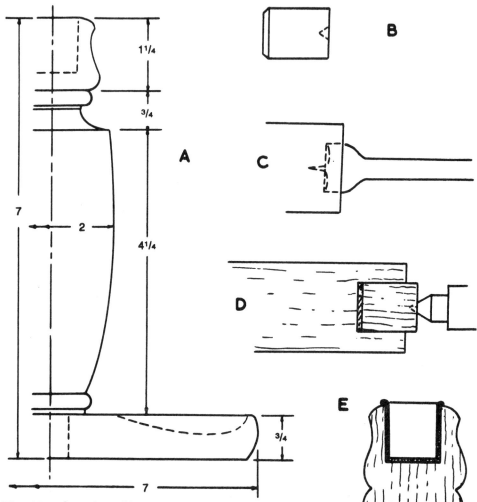

Fig. 11-7. Steps in making a wooden candlestick.

Metal candle sockets can be bought to fit in the top of the column (FIG. 11-7E). If one of these is used, that will settle the size hole to drill. A metal socket makes a neat mount for the candle, but check first that it matches available candles.

There are many developments on this basic candlestick. If serious use is intended, there should be a drip ring to catch candle grease. This improves the appearance of the candlestick in any case, even if candles will rarely be lit. A good way to include this is to let the actual candleholder and the drip ring fit over a dowel end on the column (FIG. 11-8A). Both parts are drilled to a size to suit the candle, and the top of the column turned to fit.

The candleholder has its grain lengthwise. If a self-centering chuck is available, the blank can be held in this to drill through. Otherwise, an overlength piece can be made cylindrical between centers, then drilled from the tailstock

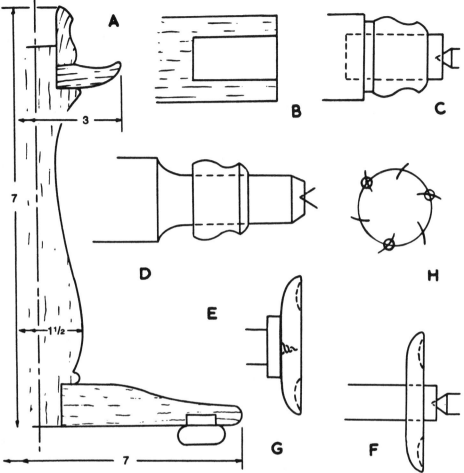

Fig. 11-8. Details of a candlestick with feet and a drip ring.

(FIG. 11-8B). The outside can be finished with plug in the hole (FIG. 11-8C). Alternatively, the blank can be mounted on a mandrel (FIG. 11-8D).

If the drip ring is not very large, it might also have its grain parallel with the hole, but for most sizes, it will have to be turned from a disc with its grain across. It might be possible to turn it on a screw center so the flat part can come on the underside (FIG. 11-8E). The hole is drilled after turning has been completed. The screw hole will center the drill accurately. This could leave too large an area of flat for some purposes. It might be better then to do all of the turning with the ring mounted on a mandrel (FIG. 11-8F).

A flat surface on the bottom might be satisfactory since most candlesticks stand on level surfaces. Cover the bottom with cloth or one of the self-adhesive cloth-like plastics. Alternatively, turn the bottom hollow so it rests on the rim. A way of ensuring that the candlestick stands level, whatever the surface, is to arrange the weight to be taken on three feet, which will rest without wobbling no matter how uneven the surface. The feet can be turned with dowels to fit into holes in the base (FIG. 11-8G). To get an even-pitch circle, draw a circle of the desired size and step off the radius around it. As the radius goes exactly six times, the dowel holes are at alternate points (FIG. 11-8H).

Steps in making the candlestick (FIG. 11-9) include turning the base while the wood is mounted on a pad on the faceplate (FIG. 11-10). The pedestal is turned with a dowel to suit the candleholder at the tailstock end and a dowel to fit the base at the other end (FIG. 11-11). Arbors are used to mount the candleholder (FIG. 11-12) and drip ring (FIG. 11-13) for turning.

A candlestick does not have to be tall. For the best display of decorative candles that are individually made, it is better for the holder to be little more than a block of wood with a hole in it (FIG. 11-14A). Anyone with a lathe will want to do

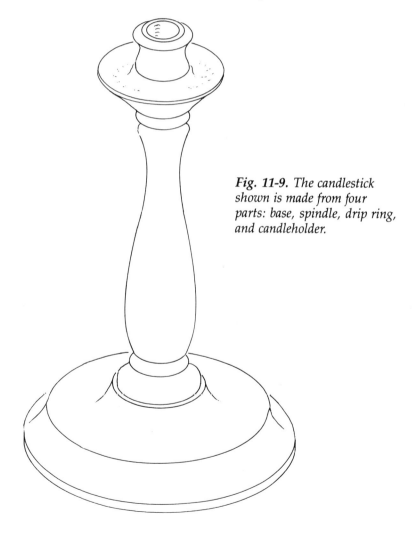

Fig. 11-9. The candlestick shown is made from four parts: base, spindle, drip ring, and candleholder.

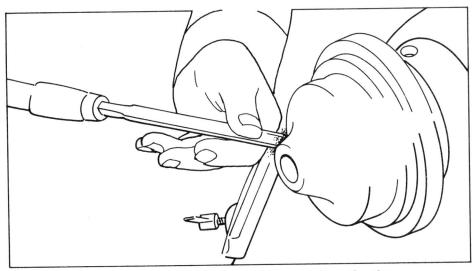

Fig. 11-10. Turning the candlestick base mounted on a pad on a faceplate.

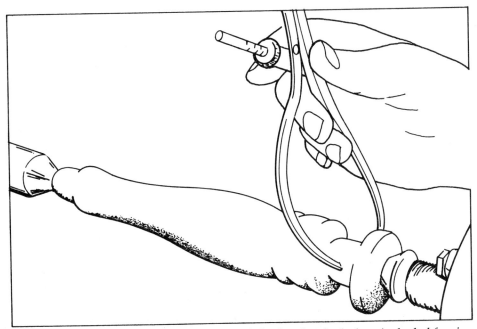

Fig. 11-11. The pedestal has been turned, and the dowel to fit the base is checked for size.

something more than just have a plain block, but excessive turning detail should be avoided. The finished work should have a broad base if the candle is very large (FIG. 11-14B). Blocks could be built up with different colored woods.

This is an opportunity to use up scrap wood too small to be built into anything large. In some cases it might be advisable to join two pieces so the actual

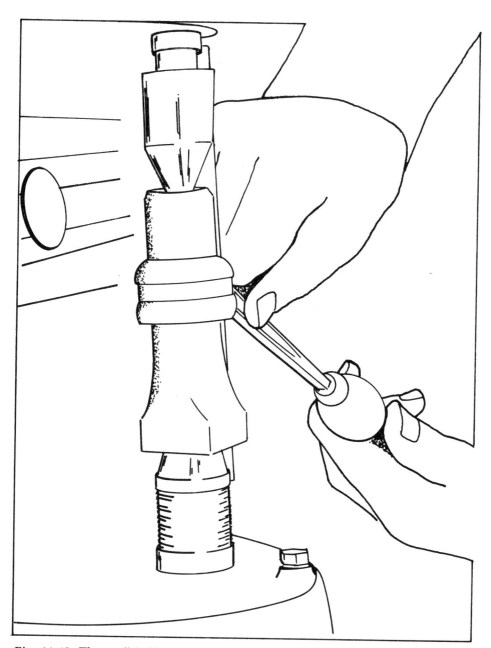

Fig. 11-12. The candleholder is made from a drilled block mounted on an arbor.

holder is mounted on another piece which forms the base (FIG. 11-14C). This could be developed further and the base turned up like a bowl to hold small items and look like the candlestick that people used to carry about the home before the days of electricity. To complete the illusion, there could be a handle let

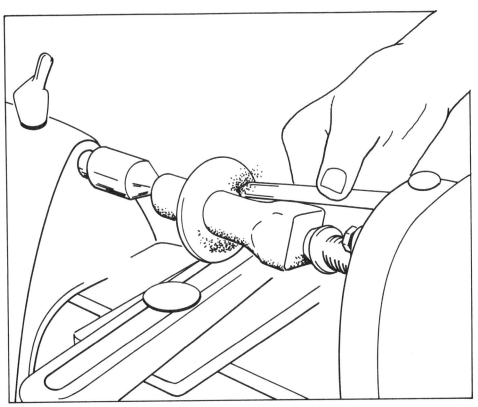

***Fig. 11-13.** The drip ring on an arbor has to be turned on both sides.*

into the rim (FIG. 11-14D). Another treatment would be a turned handle doweled into the base (FIG. 11-14E).

Single block stands can be used to suit the small candles used as Christmas decorations, but bottoms should be broad and heavy (FIG. 11-14F). A lit candle of any size could be a fire hazard if knocked over.

Mallets

Mallets, or wooden-headed hammers, are used for a surprising number of crafts, games and activities. All can be made on a lathe, and many of them are small enough to be turned on the smallest machine. Although the basic design of a head on a shaft will be the same, there are subtle differences. For instance, what you make for a chairperson controling a meeting is very different from what is needed by a craftsman beating metal or another carving wood.

There has to be weight in the head for a mallet to be effective. This is usually a combination of size and the density of the wood. Use close-grained wood as hard as possible, and therefore dense and heavy. Hardest is *lignum vitie*, but it is costly, and turning it is almost like turning metal. Box might be a good choice.

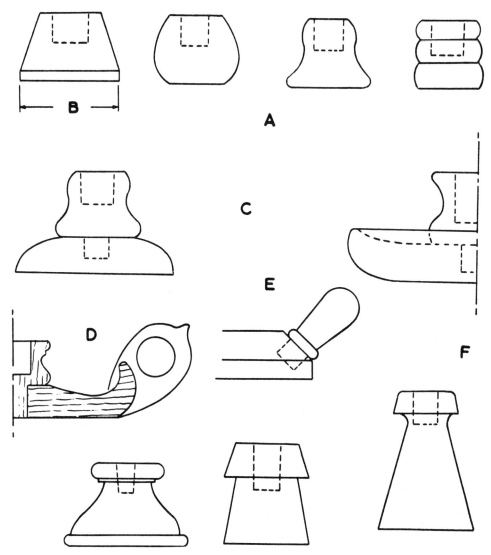

Fig. 11-14. Some examples of small candlesticks.

Many satisfactory mallets have beech heads, but it would be unwise to use anything softer than that if the mallet is for serious use. If it is a gavel or other mallet that does not have to be little more than decorative, any attractive wood can be used.

If the shaft or handle will be subject to much heavy use, it needs to be springy to absorb shock and resist breaking. Ash and hickory are by far the best for this purpose and should be used for any mallet that will get much heavy use. The shock transmitted to your hand is then very much less than with a more rigid wood. Whatever wood you use for a handle, its grain lines should run the full length and there should be no flaws. Knots would obviously weaken the shaft, but *shakes*, too, (lengthwise cracks) are best avoided.

Mallets vary in size from dainty little ones, for some light craftwork, up to a section of tree trunk on a two-handed shaft for setting paving stones. They all provide you with interesting challenges.

The head of a basic mallet (FIG. 11-15A) is a simple cylinder. Bevel or round the ends (FIG. 11-15B) to reduce or delay breaking out of the grain after prolonged use. It helps to cut a line or groove around the center (FIG. 11-15C) to locate the shaft hole. Such a plain mallet might be used for general purposes, such as driving light stakes or pegs, and it is the type favored for sheet metalwork.

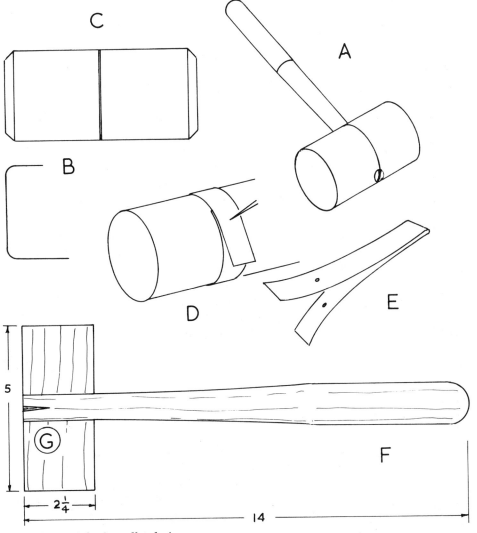

Fig. 11-15. A basic mallet design.

The hole might be 3/4 inch or 7/8 inch. Keep it straight if you drill from both sides. If there is a dividing head on your lathe, you can locate the opposite centers easily. Otherwise, a simple way is with a strip of paper. Wrap it round and push a pin or spike through the overlap (FIG. 11-15D) at the position of the hole at one side. Open the strip and fold it so the pin holes meet (FIG. 11-15F). The fold marks halfway, so put the strip back around the mallet head and mark where the fold comes for the other center.

Turn the handle (FIG. 11-15F) a tight fit in the head hole; then give it a gradual taper towards the grip. Experiment with holding a cylindrical strip of wood. You will probably find that no more than 1 1/8 inches in diameter is about right to hold. To allow for different hands, the handle end could have a slight taper away from the end. Round the extreme tip.

Put a saw cut across the end of the shaft that will go in the hole. When you assemble, have this across the grain of the head and drive in a wedge (FIG. 11-15G) then cut the end level. Traditional mallets were assembled without glue, but you could put glue through the hole and on the wedge.

If the head loosens in use, hold the shaft without any support under the head, and hit its end. What is called a *moment of inertia* will cause the head to move further onto the shaft and the taper will provide a new grip. Rewedge and trim the end.

A plain parallel cylindrical head suits most purposes. There are advantages in giving the head ends a slight doming (FIG. 11-16A). This concentrates a hit at the center. It reduces wear around the circumference, where splits or splintering might occur. However, do not dome excessively, or a slightly misdirected blow can glance off.

If you want something different from a plain cylinder, remember that any cutting away of wood lightens the head, and you do not want much of that. A slight barrel shape (FIG. 11-16B) might be more pleasing. Cut a few lines around any section if you want to give it individuality.

If the head hole at the wedge side can be opened to a slight taper, the wedge will expand the shaft into it (FIG. 11-16C) and the security will be greater. Turning the taper in the lathe would be an awkward chucking problem. It is the taper at the end grain which matters, and you could cut that with a gouge or round file.

Instead of long taper on the shaft, arrange a shoulder or knuckle a few inches from the head (FIG. 11-16D). This allows for a slender neck (FIG. 11-16E) to give spring where it is needed. The amount of slimming has to be a compromise between maximum springiness and the thickness needed to resist breaking.

Your hand needs a length of at least 5 inches to settle into a comfortable position on the handle. You might be able to hold a plain handle without slipping, but most will welcome an improved grip. It might be sufficient to cut lines around a plain handle (FIG. 11-16F).

Enlarging the end is always a good idea (FIG. 11-16G) to stop your hand from slipping off. One of the best ways of ensuring a good grip is to give the handle an

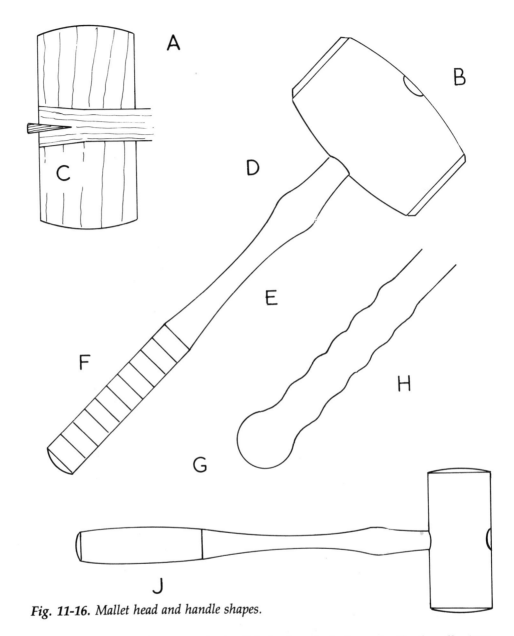

Fig. 11-16. *Mallet head and handle shapes.*

undulating shape (FIG. 11-16H). A slightly barreled shape to the handle (FIG. 11-16J) actually conforms better to your hand, but it does not prevent slipping off and is best kept for mallets intended for lighter uses.

Sheet-metal workers use a plain mallet in several sizes, as just described, and might refer to it as a *tinman's mallet*. They also use a *bossing mallet* (from "embossing") for hollowing work. This has a pear-shaped head (FIG. 11-17A) and can be

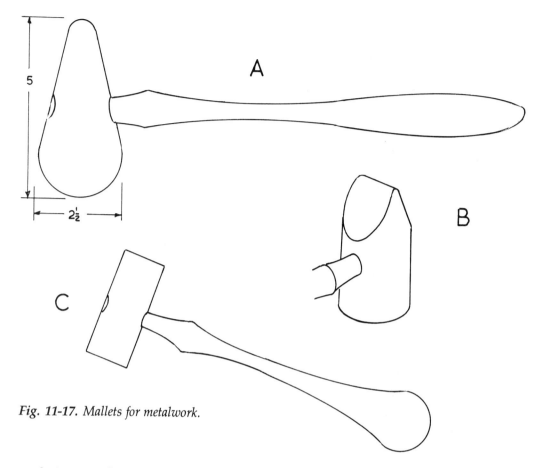

Fig. 11-17. Mallets for metalwork.

made in several sizes besides that shown. As far as possible, the ends of the heads should be hemispherical.

Another sheet-metal worker's mallet can be domed or flat at one side, but the other side is something like the cross-pane of a carpenter's hammer (FIG. 11-17B). Well round the cross part. You could make more than one of these mallets with the straight edge rounded to different curves, possibly 3/8 inch and 3/4 inch in diameter.

A sheet-metal worker often uses a mallet for long periods, so spring in the shaft is important to reduce strain on the hand.

One form of light sheet-metal work is called *repoussé*. Mallets and hammers have to deliver large numbers of fairly light blows, with the handle loosely held and moving something like a ball-and-socket joint in the palm of the hand. The head can be small, but the shaft is slender, leading to a ball-shaped handle (FIG. 11-17C), smoothed to pivot in your palm.

The mallet favored by most woodcarvers takes a different form. Its head is cylindrical lengthwise. Plenty of weight is needed, but the handle is short. The head and the handle can be turned from one piece of wood, which might be a satisfactory method for a thin and light mallet. However, this would involve turning much wood to waste in making a large size, so a separate handle is better. This allows you to use a dense hardwood for the head and a cheaper wood for the handle.

A typical carver's mallet of average size is shown (FIG. 11-18A). Turn the head with the grain in the direction of the handle, which can be taken right through and wedged in the usual way, but it is suggested the hole only goes about halfway, then the handle is tightened with a concealed wedge (FIG. 11-18B). Prepare a short, thick wedge, then apply glue to all parts and drive them together so the wedge hits the end of the hole and expands the cut handle end.

A chairperson's gavel is a mallet which is more a symbol of office than a practical tool, although its owner might bang it hard on the table during a noisy meeting. It gives the turner scope for some decorative work. A gavel need not be big. If it has to be carried between meetings, a head 2 inches long and a handle 6 inches long allows stowing in a case or pocket. You might be able to use rare or decorative wood. A few suggested designs are shown (FIG. 11-19A). The shaft can go through the head, but it should be satisfactory glued into a hole taken in about three-quarters of the thickness.

There is scope for mixing woods. Besides using a different wood for handle and head, you could laminate contrasting woods in one part. Put differing woods on a dowel of another color, and (FIG. 11-19B) turn this into an interesting head. Do the same on the grip end of the handle; turn it down for pieces of differing woods to slide and be glued on before being shaped (FIG. 11-19C).

The chairperson might not be seated at a table he or she can hit, because of a

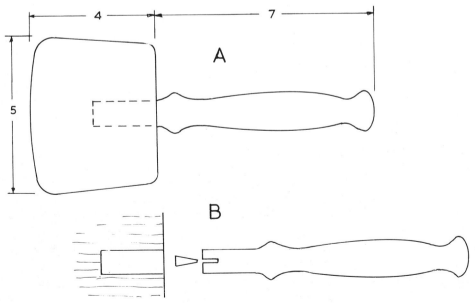

Fig. 11-18. Details of a carver's mallet.

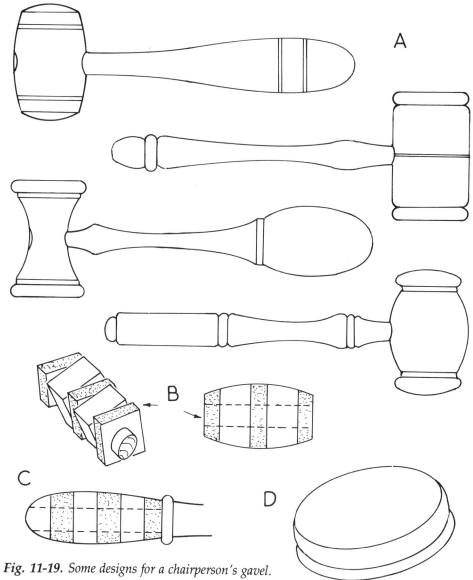

Fig. 11-19. *Some designs for a chairperson's gavel.*

cloth covering or fear of damaging the finish, so you can make an anvil (FIG. 11-19D). Use wood at least as hard as the mallet head and glue cloth underneath to prevent slipping.

Large, two-handed mallets, or *mauls*, can be made in the same way as the smaller plain mallets. One large type, which is not necessarily massive, is a croquet mallet. For a serious game, standard sizes are needed. Make a single one as a replacement, but if you want a set, make at least four.

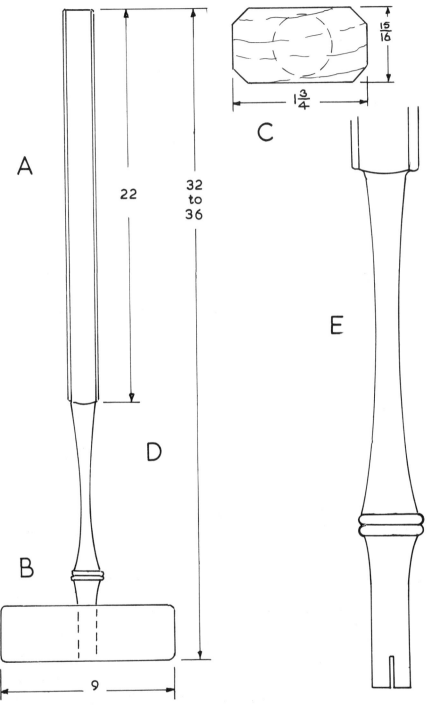

A

B

C

$\frac{15}{16}$

$1\frac{3}{4}$

22

32
to
36

D

E

9

Fig. 11-20. Sizes and shapes of a croquet mallet.

A croquet mallet follows the usual construction, with the shaft through the head and wedged. The head should be heavy, so if lignum vitie is unobtainable you might use ebony or hard maple. The handle could be ash or hickory. For backyard or indoor croquet, turn the handles for the full length, and reduce the mallet size. The measurements shown suit the expert game (FIG. 11-20A).

Turn the head as a cylinder with flat ends and rounding to reduce splintering (FIG. 11-20B). Drill a 7/8-inch hole across the center. Note that the diameter should be between 2 1/2 inches and 2 3/4 inches.

The overall length of the mallet should be between 32 inches and 36 inches. For two-thirds of its length, it has a grip which is not turned. Its section should be rectangular with the corners removed (FIG. 11-20C). Below this, it is turned in a very similar way to other mallets (FIG. 11-20D). The handle part is finished thinner than the knuckle, so start with wood 1 1/2 inches thick and plane down the handle after the lower part has been turned. Make the end of the shaft to fit in the head hole; then broaden to the knuckle, which could be beaded. From this, sweep back to the unturned part, reducing to a minimum of 5/8 inch in diameter to provide spring (FIG. 11-20E).

When you join the handle to the head, the long way of the handle section should be exactly in line with the mallet head. In the finished mallet, the octagonal handle has to be bound all over with cord or strip leather and the exposed wood should be varnished.

Floor Lamp Standard

A stand to support a lamp that could be 60 inches from the floor would be too long to turn in one piece in most lathes. In any case, it is better made in parts. This brings the pieces of wood down to a length that will fit between lathe centers. It also means greater economy, as you do not have to turn away large amounts of waste if the same piece included thick and thin parts. It also allows easier drilling of a hole the entire length to take wires. Most drills intended for long drilling from the tailstock can cope with depths of about 12 inches, so by drilling from opposite ends you can deal with 24-inch sections. Keeping these hole lengths reasonably short is desirable because a drill can wander out of true if taken too deep.

Joints between parts are not difficult to arrange because a turned dowel or tenon on one piece can fit a hole in the next piece. With both parts of the joint cut on the lathe, the sections should automatically finish in line. Beads at the joints disguise the meeting lines.

A tall lamp standard needs a broad and heavy base to resist knocking over. This project (FIG. 11-21) has a base turned, so plenty of wood is left to provide weight; then the piece next above it is also heavy. Stability is increased further with three extending legs. The rest of the column is in two parts, so there is nothing longer than 23 inches to turn.

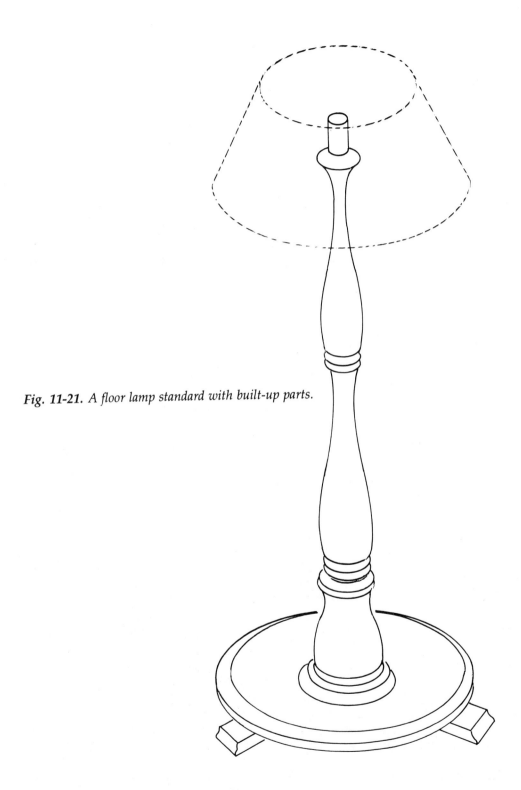

Fig. 11-21. A floor lamp standard with built-up parts.

A ³/₈-inch hole the entire length should be ample to pass wires. Dowels and their holes can be 1 inch in diameter and 1¹/₄ inch deep (FIG. 11-22A). The dowels are upward, except at the bottom (FIG. 11-22B). The extreme top is shown cylindrical (FIG. 11-22C), but you will have to make this to suit your chosen lamp and shade fitting.

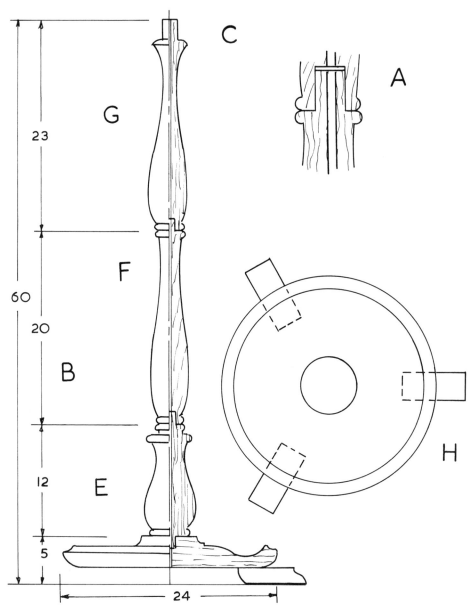

Fig. 11-22. Sizes and sections of the floor lamp standard.

1 base	$24 \times 24 \times 3^1/2$
3 feet	$8 \times 3 \times 1^1/2$
1 section	16×6 diameter
2 sections	24×4 diameter

Settle on a standard width for beads—$^3/8$ inch would be suitable. Beads of adjoining parts should have matching diameters. The bulbous shapes of the three upright sections should complement each other, with the lower thicker parts proportionately bulkier, which gives a more balanced aesthetic appearance than if the proportion were the other way around.

The base is shown 24 inches in diameter (FIG. 11-22D) and $3^1/2$ inches deep at the center. Its shaping gives a lighter appearance, but there is actually plenty of bulk to provide weight. Drill the dowel and wire holes through the center. Mark the positions of the three feet underneath.

The bottom section of the pillar (FIG. 11-22E) has dowels at both ends (FIG. 11-23B), but it will be advisable to do most of the other turning before reducing them to size, in case the ends become too weak. The top beads on this piece have a gap between. Make the top bead $3^1/4$ inches in diameter to match another on the next section. The other bead may be $4^1/2$ inches in diameter. Drill the wire hole and make the dowels to fit a test hole in a piece of scrap wood.

The middle section (FIG. 11-22) has a hole at the bottom and its own dowel at the top (FIG. 11-23C). The beads at both ends can be $3^1/2$ inches in diameter. Drill the wire hole from both ends.

Turn the top section (FIG. 11-22G) with a hole and bead to match the section below. Prepare the top to suit your lamp fitting. There is a flare below that (FIG. 11-23D) and shaping it might be a little slimmer than the pattern below, for the sake of appearance. Drill the wire hole from both ends.

The feet (FIGS. 11-22H and 11-23E) are flat and 3 inches wide. Shape the outer end and round the inner end. Glue and screw below the base.

As you assemble the parts, thread the electric wires into each section or put in a plain wire that can be used to pull the others through. Otherwise, you might have difficulty in pushing wire through the whole length, and there might be a risk of the hole becoming blocked with glue at the joints.

Join the top two sections first and check their straightness on the bench. Add the third section and again check straightness. Join this assembly to the base, while that is on a level surface. View from several directions to see that the lamp standard is upright.

Stain and varnish or polish the lamp standard after completion; consider dealing with each part in the lathe. It is possible to get a good finish with a friction polish, such as wax of shellac, while the wood is rotating.

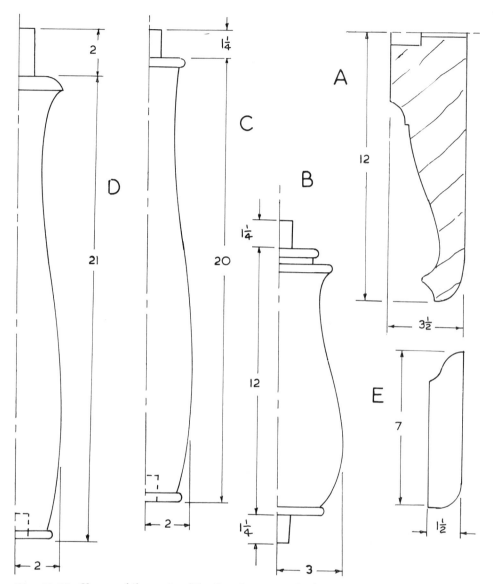

Fig. 11-23. Shapes of the parts of the floor lamp standard.

Rush-Pattern Stool

A traditional method of seating stools and chairs used rushes twisted into a rope as work progressed. The resulting pattern was in a form tapering downwards from the corners to the center to provide an attractive and comfortable seat. The finished top design (FIG. 11-24) hides its method of construction, and the work of early craftsmen was probably regarded as a trade secret. In fact, the method of making such a seat top is surprisingly simple.

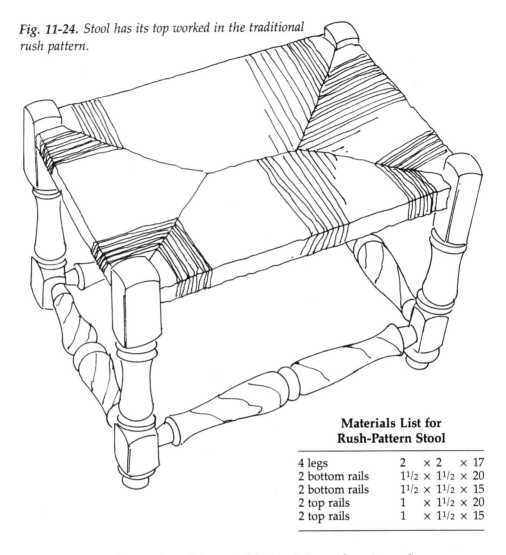

Fig. 11-24. Stool has its top worked in the traditional rush pattern.

Materials List for Rush-Pattern Stool

4 legs	2	×	2	×	17
2 bottom rails	1¹/₂	×	1¹/₂	×	20
2 bottom rails	1¹/₂	×	1¹/₂	×	15
2 top rails	1	×	1¹/₂	×	20
2 top rails	1	×	1¹/₂	×	15

Twisting rushes might still be possible, but it is much easier and more convenient to use prepared cords. Very fine line is not advisable, but any natural or synthetic cord up to a ¹/₄ inch diameter can be used. The nearest in appearance to the traditional rushes is seagrass. It is in a form of rope sold by craft shops in its natural brown/green color or dyed in a few bright colors.

The stool frame shown (FIG. 11-25) has turned legs and lower rails. A design that does not need the use of a lathe is also suggested.

It would be unwise to use softwood because it might not provide sufficient strength in the joints. Any furniture hardwood can be used and finished as you wish. It is advisable to do any staining and at least the first coat of polish or varnish before working the top. Apply only a finishing coat later to reduce the risk of marking the seat with finishing materials.

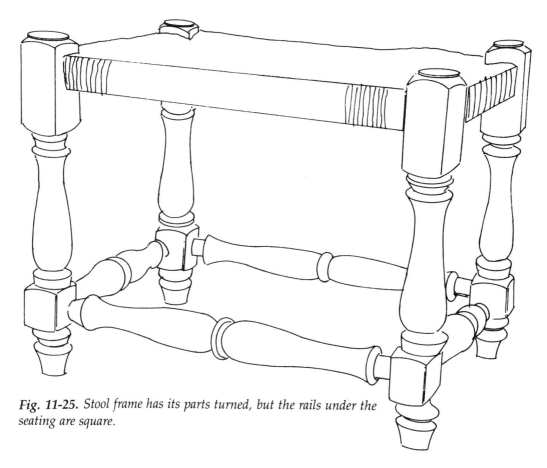

Fig. 11-25. *Stool frame has its parts turned, but the rails under the seating are square.*

The suggested size (FIG. 11-26) makes a comfortable occasional seat or foot-stool. It might be altered to a square or to a different size, but any variations will not affect the working of the top. Wood sections could be reduced slightly for a lighter stool, but a fairly substantial appearance of the framework goes with this type of top.

The wood for the legs should be carefully squared, although much of it will be turned away. Allow extra length at the tops for driving at the headstock. The tail center could go directly into the bottom of the leg. Center the wood by drawing diagonals so the square section runs true in the lathe.

It helps to mark the limits of the square parts before mounting the wood in the lathe. Use a narrow strip of wood to mark the positions of the parts of the turning. You can hold it alongside your work as a guide to where to cut. After turning one leg you can use it as a pattern as you turn others. You can use your own ideas for a leg pattern, but the suggested design (FIG. 11-27A) is a suitable match for the rails and seat.

Turn the parts between the squares, then the foot end. Round the corners of the squares. Get that part satisfactory before dealing with the top. At that end,

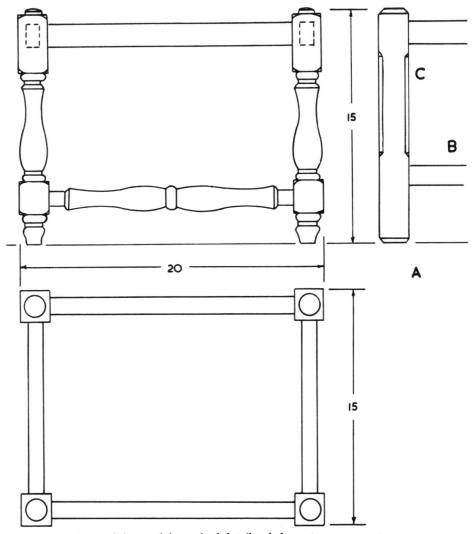

Fig. 11-26. Sizes of the stool frame had details of alternate square parts.

reduce the wood enough to turn a shallow button. Slightly dome the button and turn it down as far as possible before parting off. Because the buttons are prominent in the completed stool, do any hand sanding necessary to get a good shape and surface.

The shape of the long rails is shown (FIG. 11-27B). The short rails are similar, with the ends and central bead, but with the long curves shortened.

At the end of the rails, turn the wood parallel or with a very slight taper to fit the holes that will be drilled in the legs. Use the drill ($7/8$ inch is suitable) to make a hole in a thin scrap piece of wood for testing the rail ends.

The top rails are 1 inch by $1^1/2$ inches, with tenons $1/2$ inch thick (FIG. 11-27C).

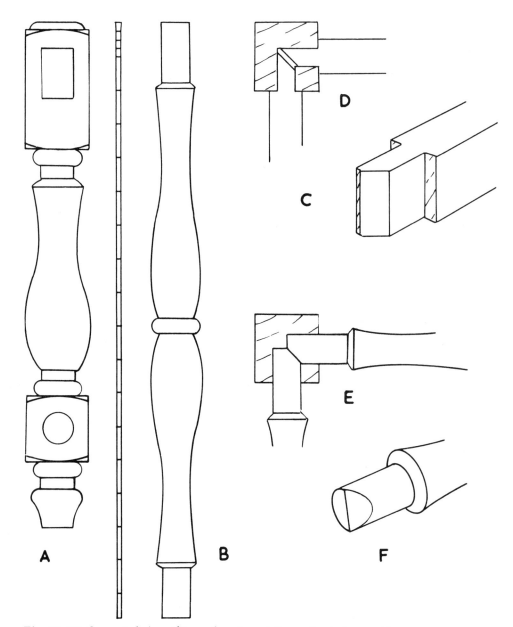

Fig. 11-27. *Suggested sizes of turned parts and the method of assembly.*

Round the edges that will come under the seating cord. Mark and cut the mortises in the legs deep enough to meet, then miter the ends of the tenons (FIG. 11-27D).

The holes for the lower rails need not go quite as deep (FIG. 11-27E). The rail ends should be partially mitered (FIG. 11-27F).

Assemble the two long sides first. Clamp the top rail joints tight. Their shoulders will set the size, but you can move the bottom rail joints in or out to get the assembly square. The joints can be locked while the glue is still soft with pins or fine nails driven through them from inside the legs. See that opposite sides match. Add the rails the other way and leave the framework on a flat surface while the glue sets.

Do any preliminary finishing before working the top. The top rails will be completely hidden; there is no need for stain or polish on them.

To make a stool without a lathe, the square legs can be beveled top and bottom (FIG. 11-26A). The bottom rails can be square and can be a little higher than in a turned stool frame (FIG. 11-26B). The legs could be left plain, although wagon beveling will improve appearance (FIG. 11-26C).

Seating

Make a few scrap wood shuttles for winding the cord, rope, or seagrass (FIG. 3-7A). A wooden needle and a pointed rod, also on that drawing, are not essential. They can be used towards the end of the pattern, if you have them.

Load several shuttles with cord. The amount on each does not matter. Nearly all joins will be hidden inside the pattern.

Knot one end of cord and tack it to the inside of a rail (FIG. 11-28A). From there take the cord over the next rail close to the leg, underneath and back over and under the first rail (FIG. 11-28B). That is the entire action that has to be mastered. Most further work is just repetition.

From the first corner, go to the rails at the next leg and do the same. Pull as tight as possible with every action you take. When you come around to the corner where you started, make the next wraps close alongside the first, and so on (FIG. 11-28C).

This will build up a pattern of turns developing from each corner, with the same design above and below. Check tension and squareness. Keep the turns pushed tight towards the legs so the rails do not show between turns. Check frequently that the lines of cord are square at each corner, and that the lines of the pattern on top point squarely towards the opposite sides.

The cords going from corner to corner will be hidden when the seat has been completed. Any joins should be made along them (FIG. 11-28D) with weaver's knots (FIG. 3-7E,F,G).

There is little scope for variations in the pattern, but you can include other colors. They could be worked in anywhere and look best near the corners (FIG. 11-28E). Arrange the colored cords as you wish. Make sure you have the same full arrangement showing on top at each corner, with knots where you change color in the lines between corners.

Continue until the short rails are filled. Press the turns tight along the rails so you get in as many as possible on the short rails. Insufficient turns here will lead to gaps near the center of the seat.

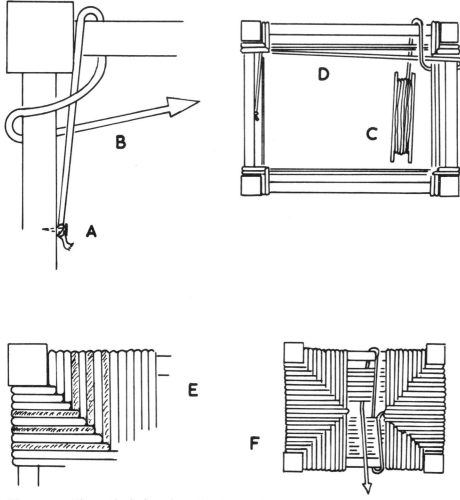

Fig. 11-28. The method of working the stool seat.

Change to going over and under in a figure-eight manner on the long rails (FIG. 11-28F). As with the previous wrapping, pull every turn tight as it is made, and press the turns tight together on the rails. Use a pointed stick to push them close at the crossing. If you have to make any joins in this part, have the knots underneath. Leave the ends a few inches long so they can be turned in and buried.

Get in as many figure-eight turns as possible (FIG. 11-29). You will not be able to use a shuttle, but the loose cord must be passed through. A wood needle is useful. Finally, gaps to pass the end will have to be forced open with a pointed stick to allow the maximum number of turns to be passed.

Take the last turn under and tack through it into the rail. Cut off with a few inches to bury inside.

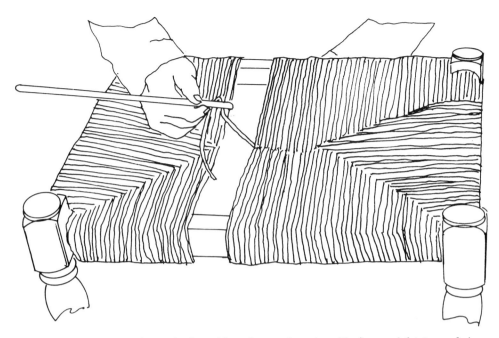

Fig. 11-29. Nearing the end of working the stool seat, with figure-eight turns being taken. The lengthwise parts that will be hidden may be seen in the space.

Lazy Susan Bowls

You might enjoy turning bowls, but there is a limit to the demand for simple bowls, and you could reach a stage where you are looking for further developments on the same theme on which to exercise your skill. This project is a large bowl or tray into which three other bowls fit. You could leave it at that, but this design goes on to include a base and a ball-bearing turntable, so that the large bowl and its contents can be revolved (FIG. 11-30). The three smaller bowls can be lifted out. The complete project might have many uses, particularly for offering a selection of fruit, nuts, and other foods.

Three inner bowls are chosen for geometric reasons; they can be made to fit against each other and the large bowl with the minimum waste space (FIG. 11-31A). If you fit four bowls, they will be smaller and there will be a larger gap in

Materials List for
Lazy Susan Bowls

1 bowl	14 × 14 × 2½
1 base	14 × 14 × 1
3 bowls	6 × 6 × 2¼

Fig. 11-30. Three bowls contained in another which is on a revolving base.

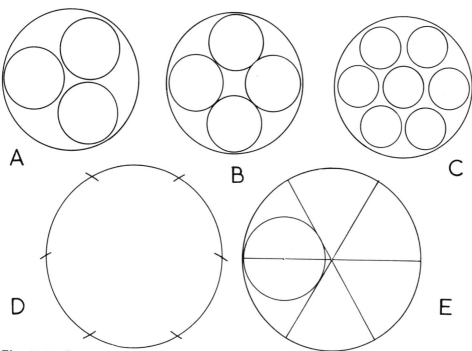

Fig. 11-31. Layout possibilities for the lazy Susan bowls.

the middle (FIG. 11-31B). This might be a good arrangement if you want to have a lifting handle at the center. The next geometric step where small bowls can be arranged to touch each other and fit closely, is seven (FIG. 11-31C), but that would result in rather tiny bowls, unless you made the whole assembly quite large.

For the project shown (FIG. 11-32A) sizes might be dictated by the wood available and the maximum circle you can turn on your lathe. When you know the size, draw the intended inside circle and step off the radius around the circumference (FIG. 11-31D). Join these six points. The size of a small bowl will be a circle drawn on one line to touch the adjoining lines and the large circle (FIG. 11-31E). In the project as drawn, the circle inside the large bowl is 12 inches in diameter, and a small bowl is 5³/₄ inches in diameter. Allow a little clearance. Turn the large bowl, and check its inside diameter before setting out and deciding on the size of the small bowls.

Select a good hardwood. The small bowls could be a different color wood

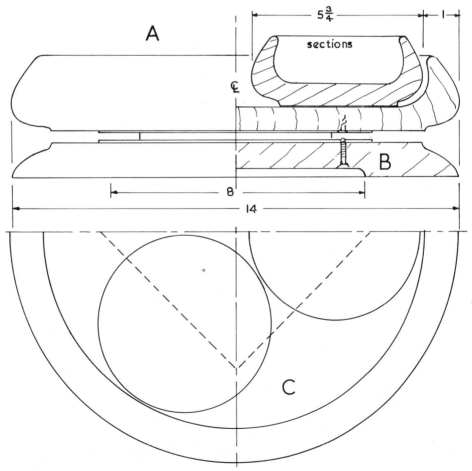

Fig. 11-32. Suggested sizes for the lazy Susan bowls.

from the large bowl and its base. If you have to glue pieces to make up width for the large parts, they could alternate in different colors.

It is possible to get several sizes of lazy Susan bearings. As an example, a 6-inch one is used. This is on a square plate with a diagonal of 8¼ inches, so you must turn the meeting parts of bowl and base more than this. Thickness of the bearing is about ¼ inch. The method of fitting is with four wood screws into the bottom of the bowl and small bolts or self-tapping screws through the base (FIG. 11-32B). Recess the base to allow for the bolts; this helps the base to stand firmly in its rim. Get the lazy Susan bearing before turning the wood in case you have to modify sizes.

The large bowl has a flat bottom, which you can screw to a faceplate. Turn it to 14 inches in diameter. The rim is 2½ inches thick. Hollow and shape to the suggested section (FIG. 11-33A) to give an inside diameter of 12 inches. The curve has to clear the small bowls. Keep the bottom flat across, so the small bowls will stand level.

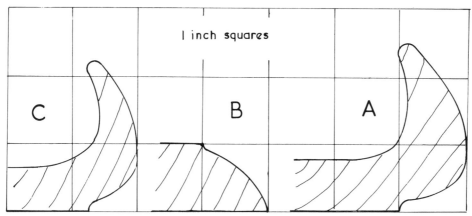

Fig. 11-33. Edge sections for bowl and base parts.

You can turn the base with its upper surface against the faceplate. Turn the outside to shape (FIG. 11-33B). The top diameter should match the bowl bottom. Turn a recess in the lower side to clear the holes needed for the lazy Susan bearing.

Check the circle sizes for the three bowls to fit inside (FIG. 11-32C) .Turn three matching bowls to a section to fit inside the large bowl (FIG. 11-33C).

Mark the hole positions for the bearing, being careful to arrange it central. Drill through the base for the bolts or self-tapping screws; then use wood screws into the bowl before driving the bolts up through the base. Check the action, then withdraw the bolts so you can get at all parts for staining and polishing. Cloth under the base rim will prevent slipping on a polished tabletop.

Egg Timers

There is a fascination about a sand-glass egg timer, although logically it is out-dated. Construction depends on the size of the glass part, so this should be obtained first. The reversible turned case of the first example has small parts, so this could be a project to use scraps of attractive wood, and it could be made on the smallest lathe. Many variations are possible, but the usual egg timer (or hour glass in a larger size) has disc ends and three turned pillars (FIG. 11-34). The two end pieces grip the glass, and the pillars are spaced to give a small clearance to the glass part (FIG. 11-35A).

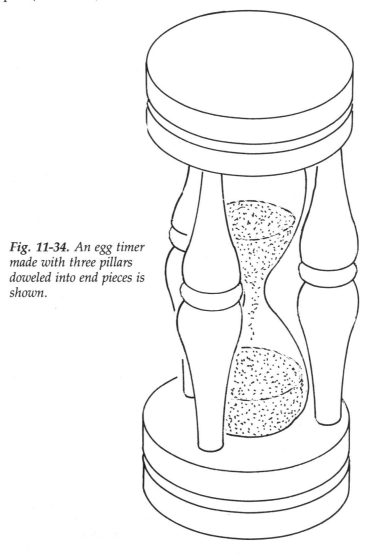

Fig. 11-34. An egg timer made with three pillars doweled into end pieces is shown.

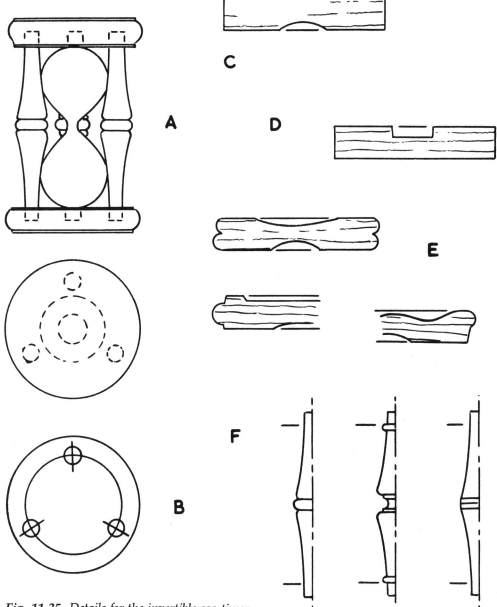

Fig. 11-35. Details for the invertible egg timer.

Draw a circle on a piece of paper or card of the greatest size of the glass. Outside this, draw a pitch circle for the pillar positions. Step the radius around this and mark alternate places as holes for the ends of the pillars. Draw another circle outside this as the actual size of an end disc (FIG. 11-35B). Use this drawing as a guide to size when turning the wooden parts.

There can be a shaped hollow in each disc for the glass (FIG. 11-35C) or a shallow hole will do (FIG. 11-35D). Because the timer has to stand on either end, these should be basically flat, although there can be a turned design (FIG. 11-35E).

The pillars look best if their thicker parts are near the center, opposite the narrow part of the glass. The ends can taper to dowels or be shouldered (FIG. 11-35F). If there is a taper without a shoulder, it is possible to have the holes a little too deep and adjust the distance between the discs as you glue so as to firmly hold the glass part. However, be careful that all pillars finish with the same length exposed when glued and that the timer stands upright. Shouldering the pillars automatically gets the discs parallel, but does not allow adjustment. A disc of card can be put at an end of the glass if slack has to be taken up.

It is advisable to polish or varnish the wooden parts before assembling with the glass; otherwise, it is difficult to get a satisfactory finish without marking the glass.

Tubular Egg Timer

This type of egg timer has the glass enclosed, and the whole thing must be turned over to make the sand run the other way. Sizes will depend on the available glass, but the one shown suits a parallel glass about 3 inches long and 5/8 inch in diameter (FIG. 11-36A). Get your glass first and settle the wood sizes around it (FIG. 11-36B). Any wood can be used, but more care will be needed turning softwoods than the preferable hardwoods.

There are two possible ways of making the egg timer. A tube to fit around the glass could form one part, then separate ends glued on after the glass has been inserted. It is probably better to make the tube and one end as a single piece of wood; then turn the other end separately.

With this type of assembly, it is always wiser to drill the hole first. Make it an easy fit on the glass, but not so loose that it moves about. There should not be any need to glue or pack the glass. Drilling could be done in the lathe or on a drill press. Freehand drilling with an electric drill is not advised, because the hole produced might not finish truly in line with the wood. Have the piece of wood long enough to allow some waste at the headstock end (FIG. 11-36C).

Turn a plug to support the wood at the tailstock end (FIG. 11-36D). With this arrangement, you can turn the main part to size. Before you part off, check the fit of the glass inside and turn the other end so when the loose part is fitted, it will just touch the end of the glass and hold it.

To avoid having a hole showing in the separate piece, drill a shallow hole for the recess first. Do this so it can be pushed onto a plug of scrap wood mounted on a screw center or in a chuck.

The pair of cutaways in the tubular part should be made with a fine-toothed fretsaw or coping saw. Doing this will keep cleaning up with a file or an abrasive to a minimum. The amount removed should be enough for the state of the sand to be seen, but there is no need to cut far towards the ends of the glass tube. If

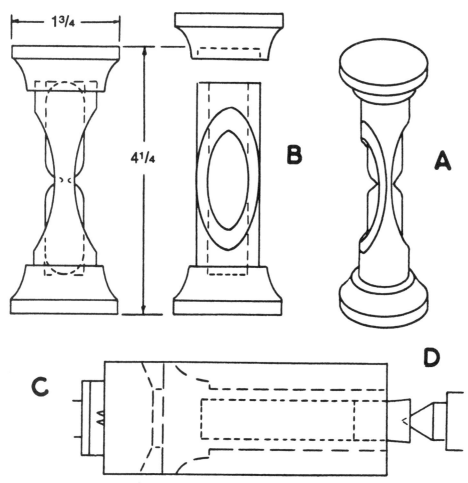

Fig. 11-36. A tubular invertible egg timer.

you want to stain or polish the wood, that is best done before you finally fit the glass and glue on the end. To prevent the timer from slipping on a smooth surface, glue a disc of cloth on each end.

Rotating Egg Timer

This egg timer uses a sand glass of the cylindrical type, which is sometimes mounted by its gripped center on a backboard or fitted between two end pieces joined by pillars. In this timer. the glass is mounted on a disc that can be rotated on a pillar projecting from a steady base (FIG. 11-37). The design suits a waisted sand glass about 3¹/₂ inches in diameter, with a timing of 3 to 4 minutes (FIG. 11-38). The disc should be made of close-grained hardwood in order to reduce the risk of the thin section breaking. The other parts can be anything you wish.

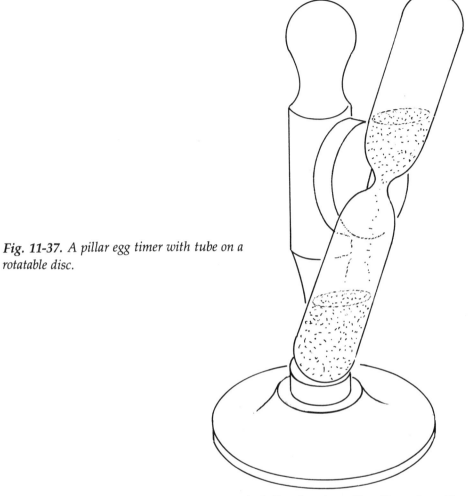

Fig. 11-37. A pillar egg timer with tube on a rotatable disc.

Turn the base on a screw center, and drill it for the pillar. Turn the pillar between centers. A basic design is shown, but you can elaborate the pattern if you wish. Leave sufficient parallel section where the disc attaches, however. The dowel at the bottom need not go right through the base.

The disc could be made with its grain across or through. If you want to make several egg timers, it would be easier to turn them along a cylinder with the one end faced and cut off ready for the same to be done to the next. Drill centrally for a slim screw ⁵/₈ or ³/₄ inch long.

Groove across the front of the disc. It need not be an exact match to the sand glass, but get it fairly close. Use a file or gouge. The glass will be fixed with epoxy glue, which has some gap-filling properties. Countersink lightly for the screw head in the groove. Drill an undersize hole for the screw to thread in the post. Flatten around that hole if you wish.

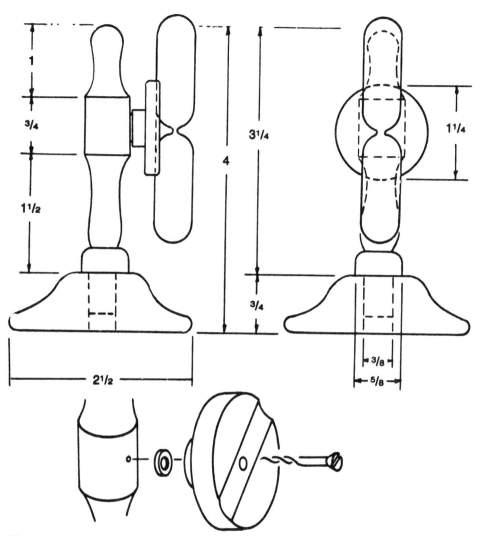

Fig. 11-38. Details for the rotatable egg timer.

Glue the post to the base, then varnish or polish all of the wood, but leave the groove in the disc bare so that it will absorb glue. Put a washer on the screw between the wood parts and adjust the screw so the disc will turn easily—but not so freely that it might rotate when you do not wish it to rotate. Put a few spots of epoxy glue between the glass and the grooved disc. Leave the assembly on its side with a light weight over it until the glue has set.

Drill as a Lathe

It is tempting to consider using a portable electric drill as the power head for a lathe, particularly if you do not have the use of a lathe and the idea of being able to produce turned work appeals to you. It is possible, but you have to accept some limitations. Do not expect to turn metal—the bearings of most drills do not run with the precision required. You might file or polish a rod held in the chuck, but that is about as far as work in metal goes.

Wood turning of quite good quality is possible, providing you limit your work to such things as spindles, tool handles, and other things of small diameter that can be held between centers. The largest work of this type normally feasible is a stool leg. Do not expect to do faceplate or screw-center work without the support of a tail center. This still leaves a lot of interesting and valuable work that can be done on a lathe in which the drive comes from a portable electric drill. Be careful not to overload the drill motor by trying to take heavy cuts off very hard wood of large diameter. Plane the corners off square wood before mounting it, so you do not have to impose the loads of a tool hitting the square corners before the work runs smoothly nearer round. Mounting eccentric wood puts a heavy load on the comparatively small motor, and it might not cope in the way the headstock and motor of a regular lathe could.

If you want to make a lathe to use your portable electric drill, keep its sizes reasonable, then you will not be tempted to load it with oversize work. The lathe in FIG. 11-39 has the centers 2 inches above the bed and $1^1/4$ inches above the tool rest, which lets you turn up to $2^1/2$ inches in diameter. The length is what you wish, but 16 inches between centers might be maximum, which allows stool or chair legs to be made. Hardwood is advisable throughout if you intend to do much turning and expect the lathe to last.

Prepare the two strips for the bed first (FIGS. 11-40A and B). They should be straight-grained to match each other. They will overlap the drill support and a short post at the other end. Measure your drill and allow for a driving center in the chuck when you settle the overall length of these pieces to give you the distance you want between centers.

At the head end of the lathe, there is a supporting block, a peg in the end of the drill (FIG. 11-40A), and a clamping drill (FIG. 11-41A). Allow for the bed pieces to fit in (FIG. 11-41B). Put the bolts in place before assembling as there will not be space to insert them when the beds have been attached.

Make the support at the other end of the drill similar to that on the horizontal stand, but at the increased height and with the block notched to take the bed pieces. Mount the support parts on a short base with dowels. A base the full length of the lathe is not suggested because that would make turning the wing nuts under the bed difficult. At the other end of the bed, make a support to fit between the strips (FIG. 11-40C and D), and join it to its own base with a tenon or dowels. When the lathe is finished, screw the bases down to a bench to keep the assembly firm and minimize vibration, but the bed strips should keep the lathe in shape.

The tool rest consists of a horizontal piece mounted on a slotted strip (FIGS. 11-40E and 11-42A). Make the total height above the bed the same as the centerline of the drill, or very slightly lower. Round the top edge. You might want to adjust

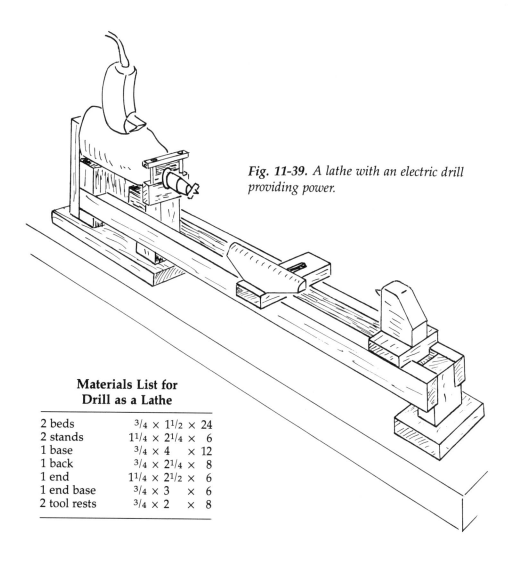

Fig. 11-39. A lathe with an electric drill providing power.

**Materials List for
Drill as a Lathe**

2 beds	$^3/_4 \times 1^1/_2 \times 24$
2 stands	$1^1/_4 \times 2^1/_4 \times 6$
1 base	$^3/_4 \times 4 \times 12$
1 back	$^3/_4 \times 2^1/_4 \times 8$
1 end	$1^1/_4 \times 2^1/_2 \times 6$
1 end base	$^3/_4 \times 3 \times 6$
2 tool rests	$^3/_4 \times 2 \times 8$

the amount of curve when you start using the lathe. Make a slot to clear a $^1/_4$-inch carriage bolt square neck, long enough for the rest to be taken in to the centerline and out to rather more than the largest diameter you expect to turn. There is no adjustment for height or angle, but the whole rest can be swung on its bolt when you wish to conform to shaped work.

The tailstock is simple. Make a block to rest across the bed and notched to slide along it (FIGS. 11-40F and 11-42B). Fit a carriage bolt through its center before adding the block above.

Glue and screw the top block (FIG. 11-40G) from below. The center can be a piece of $^3/_8$-inch-diameter steel rod with a 60-degree point on it. Turn the point if possible, but you might still do good work with a carefully filed center. Fix the center in a hole with epoxy adhesive.

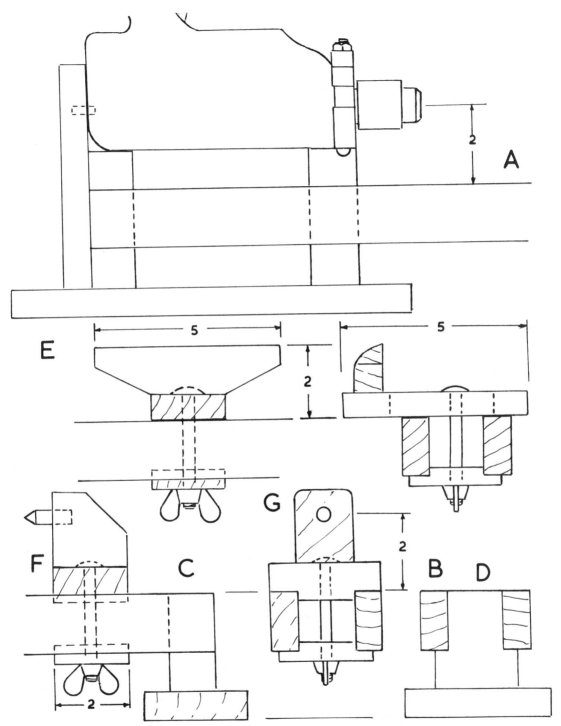

Fig. 11-40. *Details of parts of the lathe.*

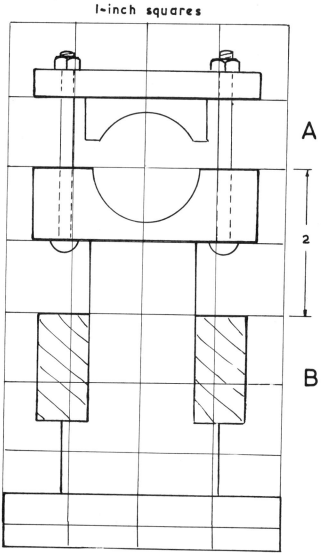

1-inch squares

A

2

B

Fig. 11-41. Sizes for the drill holder on the lathe.

For locking the tool rest and tailstock, make blocks to slide underneath and notch to hold them parallel under the bed (FIG. 11-42C). Use thin washers under the wing nuts.

A driving center might be bought, but you can make one to fit in the drill chuck. Use a piece of steel rod of as large a diameter as the chuck will hold. Make the driving part from steel about $1/16$ inch thick (FIG. 11-42D). Let the central spur project, and file the two side pieces almost to knife edges. Braze or solder this piece into a sawn cut in the end of the bar. Cut the bar so that it goes fully into the chuck, but projects no more than is necessary.

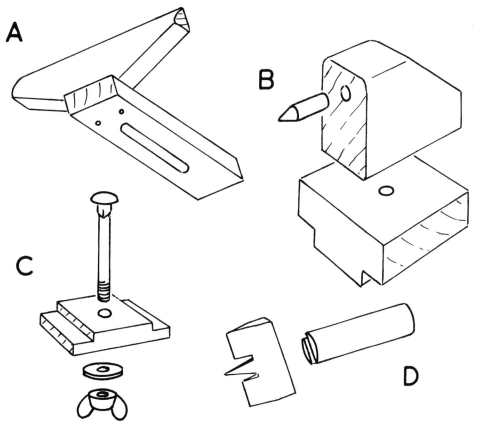

Fig. 11-42. Details of the tool rest and tailstock for the drill table.

Glossary

architrave—Molding around a door or window.

arris—Meeting of two surfaces. A sharp edge.

backflap hinge—One that swings back farther than a normal hinge.

baluster—Vertical pillar supporting a handrail.

bar—Intermediate member in a glazed frame.

barefaced—Not notched, as a barefaced tenon.

bargeboard—Inclined boards on the roof end at the gable of a house.

baseboard—Board around room at the bottom of walls.

batten—Narrow strip of wood.

beam—Horizontal load-carrying structural wood or steel member.

binder—Beam supporting floor joints.

bird's mouth—Angled notch in the end of one piece to fit the corner of the supporting strip.

blind—Not carried through (particularly through holes and mortises).

bolt—Fastener screwed to take a nut.

box—To enclose.

bracket—Support for a horizontal surface from a vertical one.

butt hinge—Common hinge usually fitted to the edge of a door.

button—Small piece of wood turning on a screw to act as a catch.

cant—External splayed angle.

cant rail—Horizontal rail behind vertical boarding.

cantilever—Beam supported at one end.

capping—Cover strip, as at the top of a gate.

carcass—The main structure of a piece of furniture.

casement—Hinged or pivoted sash window.

cast—Twist.

ceiling—Lining in a boat. Top surface of a room.

chase—Groove.

clamp—Device drawing parts together. Strip across a wide board to prevent warping.

clapboard—Overlapping boards outside house or forming a fence.

cleat—Small piece joining parts together.

coach screw—Large wood screw with head for wrench.

cock—Stand above surface.

cogging—One piece notched over another to prevent movement.

coping—See *scribing*.

cottered—Metal wedges used to tighten an iron band around a wood joint.

counterbore—To enlarge the top of a hole to let a screw head go below the surface.

countersink—Conical sinking at the top of a screw hole so the head finishes with the surface.

cramp—See *clamp*.

dado—Groove.

diminishing—Reducing, particularly a door stile.

dog—Metal U-shaped double spike to draw boards together.

donkey—Quick-acting vise for thin material.

dormer—Window in an extension so it is vertical in a sloping roof.

draw—To pull together, as in drawbore or pin.

face marks—Marks applied to show a side and edge to work from.

fascia—Flat board edgewise, as at the edge of a roof.

fastenings (fasteners)—Nails and screws used for joining.

feather—Strip of wood used as tongue. Figure in wood grain.

featheredge—Wood thinned toward one edge.

fillet—Narrow strip of wood used as filling or to support a part.

fillister—Plane for cutting rabbets, with stops for width and depth.

fish—To join end to end with strips each side.

flitch—Log prepared for conversion. Beam made from two pieces bolted together.

flying shore—Temporary support between walls and not attached to the floor.

folding wedges—Two similar wedges used overlapping to apply pressure.

foxtail wedging—Wedges to spread the end of a tenon inside a blind mortise.

framed—Strips joined to form a carcass to be filled or covered with panels.

frank—Exposed. Reversed haunch in mortise and tenon joint.

gauge—Marking tool or means of testing. Definition of size by numbers.

grating—Framework of crossing bars used as a floor.

groove—Any long narrow channel.

gunstock stile—Door stile tapered at the lock rail for wider panel above.

halved—Crossing pieces notched to fit into each other.

handed—Arranged in pairs.

hanging stile—The door stile to which the hinges are fitted.

haunch—A shortened part of a tenon.

heel straps—Metal straps around joints between rafters on tie beams.

hip—Roof with slope at the end as well as the sides.

horn—Extension beyond joint.

housing—Groove to take an end of a board in another. A dado joint.

inserted—Added, as when a tenon is set in the end as well as into a mortise.

jamb—Vertical side of a window or doorway.

jig—Guide for holding or shaping work.

joggle—Double bend. A horn.

jointing—Any joint, but particularly boards glued edge to edge.

joist—Horizontal members, particularly carrying floors or ceilings.

kerf—The slot made by a saw.

key—Wedge. Cotter. Veneer in slot across miter.

king post—Central upright in a roof truss.

knuckle—Pivot of a hinge.

laminate—To make up in layers, particularly in curved work.

lap—Overlap, particularly where part of a piece crosses another in a joint.

lath—Strip of wood of small section.

lipping—Facing an edge with a strip, as with solid wood on a plywood shelf.

locking stile—Door stile opposite to the edge that is hinged.

lock rail—Rail across the door at the same height the lock will be.

louver—Opening with inclined boards across.

mansard roof—Roof with double pitch on both sides.

mason's miter—Mitered molding cut into the solid of one meeting part.

matched boarding—Boards tongued and grooved to each other.

meeting stiles—Door stiles that meet in double doors.

miter—Joint where the meeting angle is divided, as at the corner of a picture frame.

mortise lock—Lock that fits into a mortise in the edge of a door.

mullet—Groove block used for testing the edge of a panel that will have to fit another grooved part.

mullion—Vertical division of a window.

muntin—Vertical division between rails of framing.

nest—To fit together, as with a nest of tables.

newel—Post carrying the handrail to a flight of stairs.

nog—Wood built into wall for attaching to or supporting a shelf.

nosing—Semicircular molding, as at the edge of a step.

pallet—Wood frame for transporting goods. Slip of wood in brickwork for attaching to with nails or screws.

pedestal—Supporting post. Base for a column.

pegging—Dowels or pegs across a joint.

pilaster—Decorative half column fitted on a flat surface. Pier projecting from the wall.

pilot hole—Small hole drilled as guide for larger one.

pin—Fine nail. Rod through knuckle of hinge. Peg.

pintle—Vertical pin on which another part is pivoted.

planted—Attached molding or other part not worked in the solid.

plinth—Base of furniture. Bottom of column. Block at bottom of architrave.

plow—Tool for cutting grooves along grain.

plumb—Upright. Vertical.

purlin—Horizontal beams on rafters under roof covering.

quadrant—Quarter of a circle. Stay for flap or fanlight window.

queen post—Secondary upright in roof truss.

rabbet—Angular sectioned cut, as in the back of a picture frame.

rafter—Sloping member of a roof below its covering.

rail—Horizontal member in framing.

rake—Incline to horizontal.

return—Continuation around corner, particularly a molding.

rim lock—Door lock that attaches to the surface.

riser—Upright part of a stair tread.

rising butt hinge—Door hinge that lifts the door as it opens.

rod—Board with full-size details and used when marking out. Any slender pole. Obsolete measure of length ($5\frac{1}{2}$ yards).

router—Hand or power tool for leveling bottom of recess.

saddle—Seating for shaped part or end of one piece against another.

sash—Window frame that carries glass, and that can be movable.

scribing—Cutting over a molding to give the appearance of a miter.

shingle—Wood tile.

shooting (shuting)—Making an edge straight.

shore—Wood prop. Temporary support.

shuttering—Woodwork in which concrete is formed.

shutting stile—See *lock stile*.

sill—Bottom horizontal member of framing.

skirting—See *baseboard*.

slat—Narrow thin strip. Horizontal rail in chair back.

soffit—Underside of eaves or stairs. Narrow ceiling.

sole—Bottom of plane and many other things.

spindle—Round slender part. Molding machine.

splat—Central upright part in a chair back.

splay—Spread out.

spline—Narrow strip of wood fitted into meeting grooves.

stile—Upright side of door or framing.

stopped—Not carried through, as in a stopped chamfer or rabbet.

stretcher—Lengthwise rail between lower parts of a table or chair.

string—Side support of stairs. Side of ladder.

stub—Shortened, as in a stub tenon.

stud—Vertical parts in hollow wall. Threaded rod. Nail with ornamental head.

tang—End of tool to fit in handle.

template—Shaped pattern to draw around when marking out.

tie beam—Horizontal piece across the feet of the rafters of a roof truss.

tread—Horizontal part of a stair that is stepped on.

treenail—Peg or dowel driven through a joint.

trellis—Crossing strips usually with a single nail at each crossing.

tusk—Projection, particularly a tenon extending through its mortise.

veneer—Thin wood usually glued over a thicker base as decoration.

waling—Horizontal piece tying together vertical boards.

wall plate—Wood along the top of the wall forming base for roof parts.

warping—Hollow and shrinking due to changes in moisture content.

weatherboard—See *clapboard*.

wicket—A small gate set in a larger one.

winder—Radiating step for change of direction in a stair.

winding—Twisting of a board in its length.

Index

R

racks
- bathtub clothes drier, 13-16
- book rack, child-sized, 687-688
- book rack, take-down type, 46-48
- bottle rack with tabletop, 194-198
- clothes-hook bar with mirror, 71-72
- display rack, kitchen projects, 262-265
- drop-arm drying rack, 63-65
- hose hanger, 503-505
- key rack, mirrored, 1-4
- kitchen utensils and tools, 247-252
- magazine rack, carry-all container, 33-36
- magazine rack, television table, 330-333
- magazine rack, with tabletop, 92-95, 184-187
- paper-towel holder with box, 36-38
- tea-towel holder, four-armed, 16-19
- tie rack, 11-13
- tool rack, bench-end mounted, 596-599
- tool rack, garden tools, 513-517
- towel drier, two-armed, 62-63
- trolley cart, wine rack, 281-290
- umbrella stand, 66-69
- wine rack with trolley, 281-290

raised-panel designs, chest, 342-346
refectory tables, 163-169
ring clown, toys and games, 609-611
ring stand, lathe-turned, 718-725
rocking chair, Shaker-style, 129-133
rocking duck, 647-650
rocking toy, 650-652
rolling tilt bin, 82-85
rush-seated turned stool, 744-751
rush-woven seat pattern, 134-135

S

sawbuck tables, 169-171
seating (*see* benches and stools; chairs)
Shaker-style rocking chair, 129-133
shed, 407-412
shelves
- bed headboard type, 386-391
- book shelves, angled shelves, 351-354
- book shelves, staggered depth, wall-mounted, 328-329
- book shelves, stepped level, 354-357
- box, hanging box with shelf, 42-44
- corner-fitted, 337-340
- corner-fitted, turned supports, 95-98
- countertop-type, 266-273
- cupboard, small, wall-mounted, 85-87
- desk/cabinet/bookshelf unit, child-sized, 680-687
- display cabinet, corner-fitted, 88-92
- display rack, kitchen projects, 262-265
- display shelves, 311-315
- divider with tabletop, 361-365
- hall table, wall-mounted, 210-212
- hanging or bedboard, 315-318
- island-type kitchen work center, 256-262
- mirrored shelves, 69-71
- paper-towel holder with box, 36-38
- plant stand, slatted shelf, 497-499
- spindle-supports, 318-321
- "stiffened" shelves, 98-100
- telephone table, wall-mounted, 22-24
- tool rack, 513-517
- trolley cart, barbecue table, 306-310
- trolley cart, folding, 279-281
- trolley cart, wine rack, 281-290
- wall-mounted units, 325-327
- Welsh dresser, 273-278

sofa, upholstered, 152-158
spindle-back chair, 125-129
squares, round measures, 576-579
stairway for deck, 528-531
step stool, 78-82
- child-size, 653-655

steps, folding, 580-583
store building, children's toy, 644-647
studio building, 464-471
summer house, 439-449
sun shelter, 401-407
swinging bench, 543-548
swivel-top table, 181-184

T

tables, 159-239
- basic style, 159-163
- basic style, with drawer and shelf, 290-294
- benches and matching table, 174-178
- bookcase and table, 214-217
- butcher-block top, 233-237
- candle stand, hexagonal, 212-214
- classic, basic-style, 159-163
- coffee table, shelf underneath, 187-191
- coffee table, take-down type, 198-200
- desktop, wall-mounted, 321-325
- divider with tabletop, 361-365
- dresser table, 200-205
- dressing table, corner-fitted, 365-367
- drinks table, bottle rack, 194-198
- drop-leaf, 178-181
- end-of-counter mounted, 294-297
- hall table, wall-mounted, 210-212
- hexagonal table with shelf, 217-221

Other Bestsellers of Related Interest

COUNTRY ELEGANCE: Projects for Woodworkers
—Edward A. Baldwin

Add a cozy country mood to your home with this one-of-a-kind collection of challenging and rewarding project plans that you're sure to like—no matter what your skill level! This book presents step-by-step, illustrated instructions for 29 original country furniture designs for every room in your home. Projects are as practical as they are attractive, and range in difficulty from a small door harp to a deacon's bench and chest combination. 256 pages, illustrated. Book No. 3768, $14.95 paperback, $26.95 hardcover

HOW TO GET MORE MILES PER GALLON IN THE 1990s—Robert Sikorsky

This new edition of a best-seller features a wealth of commonsense tips and techniques for improving gas mileage by as much as 100 percent. Sikorsky details specific gas-saving strategies that will greatly reduce aerodynamic drag and increase engine efficiency. New to this edition is coverage of the latest fuel-conserving automotive equipment, fuel additives, engine treatments, lubricants, and maintenance procedures that can help save energy. 184 pages, 39 illustrations. Book No. 3793, $7.95 paperback, $16.95 hardcover

PRACTICAL HOUSEBUILDING: For Practically Everyone—Frank Jackson;
Illustrations by Spike Hendriksen

This idea-packed guide tackles the subject of housebuilding with humor and candor. You're walked through every area of knuckle-busting, do-it-yourself construction and you'll emerge chuckling but confident, with the same know-how as those who learned the hard way. Step-by-step instructions and over 250 detailed illustrations show you how to design and build your own home. 272 pages, illustrated. Book No. 3808, $14.95 paperback only

THE DRILL PRESS BOOK: Including 80 Jigs and Accessories to Make—R. J. De Cristoforo

The drill press, after the table saw, is the second most important tool in the workshop. In this well-illustrated guide, you'll discover unique ways to develop the tool's potential in over 80 project plans. As De Cristoforo guides you through each application of this versatile tool, you'll benefit from hundreds of hints based on his years of woodworking experience. 304 pages, 406 illustrations. Book No. 3609, $16.95 paperback, $25.95 hardcover

ONE-WEEKEND COUNTRY FURNITURE PROJECTS—Percy W. Blandford

Transform simple materials into beautiful, functional objects with this brand-new selection of original projects to use in and around your home, in an easy, one-weekend format, especially for time-conscious hobbyists. A basic understanding of woodworking techniques is all you need to build an attractive durable piece of furniture in as little as 12 hours. You get nearly 50 original project plans—all requiring only simple hand tools and inexpensive materials—and ample drawings and instructions for every design. 240 pages, 163 illustrations. Book No. 3702, $14.95 paperback, $24.95 hardcover

PUZZLES, BOXES AND TOYS: Creative Scroll Saw Patterns—Percy W. Blandford

In this book, a master craftsman explores the surprisingly diverse uses for the scroll saw. Here you'll find an assortment of project plans—ranging from simple toys and outdoor ornaments to elaborate tables and cabinets—that take advantage of the scroll saw's capability for piercing wood and making intricate cuts. Most plans are suitable for beginners with a basic set of tools, while some are designed to challenge more experienced woodworkers. Each project includes a drawing of the finished piece, patterns, step-by-step assembly instructions, and a materials list. 224 pages, 158 illustrations. Book No. 3706, $12.95 paperback, $19.95 hardcover

BEFORE YOU BUILD: 100 Home-Building Pitfalls to Avoid—Kenneth L. Petrocelly

The author gives you from start to finish with expert advice on the 100 most common problems experienced by homebuilders—problems that can cause delays and budget overruns. Petrocelly shows you how to avoid costly mistakes by taking actions that will prevent problems from occurring. He provides sound advice in the 10 areas he has found most important to homebuilders. 224 pages, 93 illustrations. Book No. 3712, $15.95 paperback, $25.95 hardcover

DECORATIVE FISH CARVING—Rick Beyer

Let a world-champion carver get you started in the hottest new area of wildlife modeling! This is an excellent guide for those just starting out and an inspiration to all woodworkers. Beyer, who has won awards for his wildlife carvings, gives you explicit instructions, from choosing tools and wood to step-by-step directions for carving the fish. 120 pages, 154 illustrations, 8-page color section. Book No. 3568, $14.95 paperback, $22.95 hardcover

RIP-OFF TIP-OFFS: Winning the Auto Repair Game—Robert Sikorsky

Don't get ripped off when you take your car for repairs. This book gives you the ammunition to stop repair scams before they start. Sikorsky exposes popular tactics used by cheats and describes how to ensure a fair deal. If you have been ripped off, he tells you how to complain effectively—both to get your money back and to put the charlatans out of business for good. But most importantly, Sikorsky tells how to avoid getting burned in the first place by learning how your car works and by keeping it in good condition. 140 pages, 29 illustrations. Book No. 3572, $9.95 paperback, $16.95 hardcover

HOW TO PLAN, CONTRACT AND BUILD YOUR OWN HOME—2nd Edition—Richard M. Scutella and Dave Heberle, Illustrated by Jay Marcinowski

In this revised edition, soon-to-be homeowners will find the information they need to plan, contract, and build a home to their specifications. Covering the entire decision-making process, this guide outlines many of the important details you should consider before building a new home. New material includes helpful information on: laundry and utility room design, plumbing, specialty homes, garages, maintenance programs, and burglar-proofing. 414 pages, 320 illustrations. Book No. 3584, $16.95 paperback, $25.95 hardcover

COUNTRY CLASSICS: 25 Early American Projects—Gloria Saberin

If you like to work with wood, you can easily make authentic reproductions of Early American antiques by following the plans in this guide. Each project, selected for its unique charm and simplicity, includes a photo of the finished piece, historical information about the item, materials list, instructions, working plans, and construction tips. A special section of full-color photographs is also included. 184 pages, 198 illustrations, 4 full-color pages. Book No. 3587, $12.95 paperback, $19.95 hardcover

THE WEEKEND MECHANIC'S AUTO BODY REPAIR GUIDE—Robert Grossblatt and Billy Boynton

Dings, dents, bumps, crunches, and crashes have happened to cars since the discovery that they were *not* indestructible. To avoid the typical repair-bill shock to your system, follow this professional advice and do your own body repairs and painting. This is the manual you need to take you from "oh, no!" to the final buff on your undetectable repair. 160 pages, 140 illustrations. Book No. 3497, $13.95 paperback, $23.95 hardcover

THE WOODTURNER'S BIBLE—3rd Edition—Percy W. Blandford

Long considered the most comprehensive guide available on woodturning techniques, this book is an authoritative reference to every aspect of the craft, from choosing a lathe to performing advanced turning techniques. Blandford covers every kind of lathe and turning tool available, then gives step-by-step instructions on tool handling techniques and lathe applications. This expanded edition offers added coverage of turning wood patterns for metal-castings and tips on using high-speed steel tools. 272 pages, 210 illustrations. Book No. 3404, $16.95 paperback, $26.95 hardcover

MARQUETRY & INLAY: 18 Decorative Projects—Alan and Gill Bridgewater

Use up-to-date, easy-to-follow techniques to bring the beauty of an ancient craft into your home. You are guided from drawing the design through the final finish. After an introduction to tools and techniques, the Bridgewaters show you how to give a unique look to furniture, wooden toys and games, jewelry boxes, tiles, and other household items. 176 pages, 136 illustrations, 4 full-color pages. Book No. 3426, $15.95 paperback, $24.95 hardcover

TROUBLESHOOTING AND REPAIRING POWER TOOLS—Homer L. Davidson

Improve the performance and lengthen the life span of your power tools with this comprehensive guide to the care and repair of electric and battery-powered tools. Using clear instructions and work-in-progress photographs, it shows you how to extend the life of everything from cordless screwdrivers to electric mowers through simple cleaning, lubricating, and sharpening procedures. Most of the procedures detailed can be accomplished using common tools, and all can be followed safely and successfully. 256 pages, 311 illustrations. Book No. 3347, $17.95 paperback, $26.95 hardcover

**THE WONDERFUL WORLD OF WHIRLIGIGS &
WIND MACHINES: 15 Projects**
—Alan and Gill Bridgewater

Here are complete instructions for wind-operated sculptures. Projects include: a New England soldier whirligig, a Dutch windmill weathervane, a pecking bird whirligig, and a fisherman windmill. You get working drawings with grids for sizing, detailing, cutting, and painting, plus illustrated step-by-step instructions. You'll develop and test your woodworking skills using a scroll saw, coping saw, hand drill, woodcarving tools, turning chisels, and lathe. 208 pages, 192 illustrations. Book No. 3349, $12.95 paperback, $21.95 hardcover

**DECKS AND PATIOS: Designing and Building
Outdoor Living Spaces**—Edward A. Baldwin

This handsome book will show you step by step how to take advantage of outdoor space. It's a comprehensive guide to designing and building decks and patios that fit the style of your home and the space available. You'll find coverage of a variety of decks, patios, walkways, and stairs. Baldwin helps you design your outdoor project, and then shows you how to accomplish every step from site preparation through finishing and preserving your work to ensure many years of enjoyment. 152 pages, 180 illustrations. Book No. 3326, $16.95 paperback, $26.95 hardcover